ATV HANDBOOK

CHILTON'S

President	Dean F. Morgantini, S.A.E.
Vice President–Finance	Barry L. Beck
Vice President–Sales	Glenn D. Potere
Executive Editor	Kevin M. G. Maher, A.S.E.
Manager–Consumer	Richard Schwartz, A.S.E.
Manager–Professional	George B. Heinrich III, A.S.E., S.A.E.
Manager–Marine/Recreation	James R. Marotta, A.S.E., S.T.S.
Manager–Production	Ben Greisler, S.A.E.
Production Assistant	Melinda Possinger
Project Managers	Will Kessler, A.S.E., S.A.E., Todd W. Stidham, A.S.E., Ron Webb
Schematics Editor	Christopher G. Ritchie, A.S.E.
Author	Christopher Bishop, A.S.E.

CHILTON™ Automotive Books

PUBLISHED BY **W. G. NICHOLS, INC.**

Manufactured in USA
© 1999 W. G. Nichols
1020 Andrew Drive
West Chester, PA 19380
ISBN 0-8019-9123-4
Library of Congress Catalog Card No. 99-072321
1234567890 8765432109

Contents

Contents

SAFETY NOTICE

Proper service and repair procedures are vital to the safe, reliable operation of all motor vehicles, as well as the personal safety of those performing repairs. This manual outlines procedures for servicing and repairing all terrain vehicles using safe, effective methods. The procedures contain many NOTES, CAUTIONS and WARNINGS which should be followed, along with standard procedures, to eliminate the possibility of personal injury or improper service which could damage the vehicle or compromise its safety.

It is important to note that repair procedures and techniques, tools and parts for servicing motor vehicles, as well as the skill and experience of the individual performing the work, vary widely. It is not possible to anticipate all of the conceivable ways or conditions under which vehicles may be serviced, or to provide cautions as to all possible hazards that may result. Standard and accepted safety precautions and equipment should be used when handling toxic or flammable fluids, and safety goggles or other protection should be used during cutting, grinding, chiseling, prying, or any other process that can cause material removal or projectiles.

Some procedures require the use of tools specially designed for a specific task. Before substituting another tool or procedure, you must be completely satisfied that neither your personal safety, nor the performance of the vehicle, will be endangered.

Although information in this manual is based on industry sources and is complete as possible at the time of publication, the possibility exists that some manufacturers made later changes which could not be included here. While striving for total accuracy, Chilton Marine cannot assume responsibility for any errors, changes or omissions that may occur in the compilation of this data.

PART NUMBERS

Part numbers listed in this reference are not recommendations by Chilton Marine or any product brand name. They are references that can be used with interchange manuals and aftermarket supplier catalogs to locate each brand supplier's discrete part number.

SPECIAL TOOLS

Special tools are recommended by the vehicle manufacturer to perform their specific job. Use has been kept to a minimum, but, where absolutely necessary, they are referred to in the text by the part number of the tool manufacturer. These tools can be purchased, under the appropriate part number, from your local dealer or regional distributor, or an equivalent tool can be purchased locally from a tool supplier or parts outlet. Before substituting any tool for the one recommended, read the SAFETY NOTICE at the top of this page.

ACKNOWLEDGMENTS

Chilton Marine expresses appreciation to the following companies who supported the production of this manual by providing information, products and general assistance:

- All Rite Products—Mountain Green, VT
- Arctic Cat—Thief River Falls, MN
- Bell Helmets—Irvine, CA
- Blue Ribbon Coalition—Pocatello, ID
- Deltran Corporation/Battery Tender—Cypress, CA
- Hannum's Honda/Kawasaki—Media, PA
- Honda Power Corporation—Duluth, GA
- Innovative Products Inc.—Mountain Green, VT
- James Lucky Enterprises—Trinity Center, CA
- Kawasaki Motors Enterprises—Irvine, CA
- K&N Engineering Inc.—Riverside, CA
- Load Rite Trailers Inc.—Fairless Hills, PA
- Martin Motorsports—Pottstown, PA
- Olympia Sports Company—Hawthorne, NY
- Polaris—Minneapolis, MN
- Rider Wearhouse/Aerostitch—Duluth, MN
- RPM Products—Central Point, OR
- Suzuki Motor Corporation—Brea, CA
- Sympatex/Sidi—Poway, CA
- The Ramp Master—Essex Junction, VT
- Warn Industries Inc.—Clackamus, OR
- Widder Enterprises—Ojai, CA
- Woodbury Powersports—Woodbury, NJ
- Yamaha Motors USA—Cypress, CA
- Yuasa-Exide—Reading, PA

Chilton Marine also expresses sincere appreciation to the Department of Conservation and Natural Resources, Pennsylvania Bureau of State Parks for their cooperation in the production of this manual.

ALL RIGHTS RESERVED

1

INTRODUCTION

HOW TO USE THIS BOOK

This book is designed to be a handy reference guide to choosing, buying and maintaining your ATV, riding gear and accessories. We strongly believe that regardless of how many or how few years of riding or wrenching experience you may have, there is something new waiting here for you. And, probably more importantly, we feel that information contained in this book should be available to all ATV enthusiasts before they sit on an ATV, or spend money on it.

Since the inception of the first ATV, the idea was simple; FUN. Over the years, the ATV has been adapted to serve a variety of uses, from a farm tractor to a hunting accessory all the way to a fully modified sand drag racer. Manufacturers now offer many types of ATV's, each designed for a purpose. Whether you're into carving up the sand dunes on a tricked-out Yamaha Banshee, or plowing the snow from your driveway with a Honda Foreman, this book will address the basic needs of all ATV enthusiasts.

This book IS NOT at complete repair manual and no attempt has been made to supplant the need for one if you desire to fully rebuild or repair an ATV. Instead, this manual covers all of the topics that a factory service manual (designed for factory trained technicians) and a manufacturer owner's manual (designed more by lawyers these days) will not. This manual will take you through the basics of maintaining an ATV, step-by-step, to help you understand what the factory trained technicians already know by heart. By using the information in this manual, any ATV owner should be able to make better informed decisions about what he or she needs to do to maintain and enjoy his/her ATV.

Keeping all of that in mind, we have divided the book into the following topics:
- HOW TO USE THIS BOOK
- CHOOSING THE RIGHT ATV
- RIDING GEAR
- ENGINE & DRIVETRAIN MAINTENANCE
- CHASSIS MAINTENANCE
- BEFORE YOU RIDE
- ACCESSORIZING YOUR ATV
- CLEANING YOU ATV
- TROUBLESHOOTING YOUR ATV
- STORING YOUR ATV

Even if you never plan on touching a wrench (and if so, we hope that you will change your mind), this book will still help you understand what a technician needs to do in order to maintain your ATV. And, even if you don't perform the maintenance services, we will provide information from accessorizing to detailing, from pre-ride checks to pre-winter storage preparation.

Can You Do It? (and Should You?)

▶ See Figures 1, 2, 3 and 4

If you are not the type who is prone to taking a wrench to something, NEVER FEAR. The procedures in this book cover basic topics at a level virtually anyone will be able to handle. And just the fact that you purchased this book shows your interest in better understanding your ATV.

You may find that maintaining your ATV yourself is preferable in most cases. From a monetary standpoint, it could also be beneficial. The money spent on hauling your ATV to a shop and paying a tech to pull the air cleaner out and service it could buy you gas for a whole weekend's riding. If you don't trust your own mechanical abilities, at the very least you should fully understand what a service technician does for your ride. You may decide that anything other than changing oil and adjusting cables be performed by a technician (and that's your call), but every time you throw a leg over an ATV, you are placing faith in the technician's work and trusting him or her with your well-being, and maybe your life. Understanding what that technician has done for your ATV will allow you to keep an eye on its condition and its adjustments.

Where to Begin

Before spending any money on parts or accessories, and before removing any nuts or bolts, read through the entire procedure or topic. This will give you the overall view of what tools and supplies will be required for work or what questions need to be answered before purchasing gear. So read ahead and plan ahead. Each operation should be approached logically and all procedures thoroughly understood before attempting any work.

Fig. 1 Performing maintenance like a valve adjustment is a lot easier than it looks

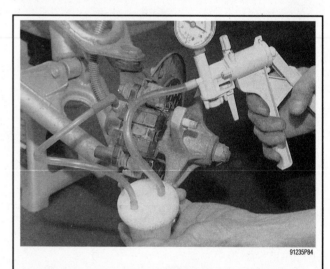

Fig. 2 Some tasks may seem difficult, but can be made easy with the proper tools

Fig. 3 Diagnosing electrical problems is much easier with a meter

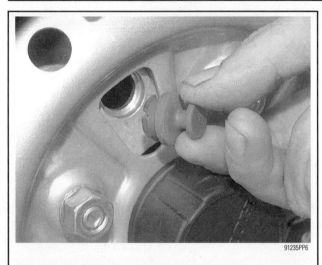

Fig. 4 Some maintenance tasks are as simple as looking through an inspection hole to check for wear

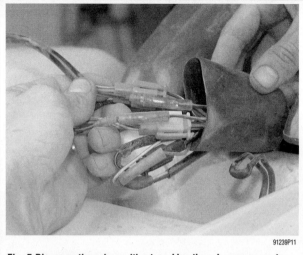

Fig. 5 Disconnecting wires without marking them is a sure way to get yourself in trouble

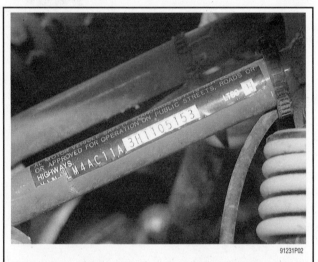

If you have to order parts from a dealer, supplying the parts person with a VIN can be very helpful

Avoiding Trouble

▶ **See Figure 5**

Some procedures in this book may require you to "label and disconnect . . ." a group of lines, hoses or wires. Don't be lulled into thinking you can remember where everything goes — you won't. If you reconnect or install a part incorrectly, things may operate poorly, if at all. If you hook up electrical wiring incorrectly, you may instantly learn a very, very expensive lesson.

A piece of masking tape, for example, placed on a hose and another on its fitting will allow you to assign your own label such as the letter A, or a short name. As long as you remember your own code, the lines can be reconnected by matching letters or names. Do remember that tape will dissolve in gasoline or other fluids. If a component is to be washed or cleaned, use another method of identification. A permanent felt-tipped marker can be very handy for marking metal parts; but remember that fluids such as degreaser or brake cleaner will remove permanent marker. Also, remove any tape or paper labels after assembly.

SAFETY is the most important thing to remember when performing maintenance or repairs. Be sure to read the information on safety in this book.

Maintenance or Repair?

▶ **See Figures 6, 7 and 8**

Proper maintenance is the key to long and trouble-free ATV life, and the work can yield its own rewards. A properly maintained ATV performs better than one that is neglected. As a conscientious owner and rider, set aside a Saturday morning, at least once a month, to perform a thorough check of items which could cause problems. Keep your own personal log to jot down which services you performed, how much the parts cost you, the date, and the exact odometer reading at the time. Keep all receipts for parts purchased, so that they may be referred to in case of related problems or to determine operating expenses. As a do-it-yourselfer, these receipts are the only proof you have that the required maintenance was performed. In the event of a warranty problem, these receipts will be invaluable.

The literature provided with your ATV when it was originally delivered includes the factory recommended maintenance schedule. If you no longer have this literature, replacement copies are usually available from the dealer, or, you can purchase a repair manual through the dealer parts department. For the most part, we will provide average recommended replacement and inspection guide-

Fig. 6 This rusted and stretched chain will have to be replaced because it was not properly maintained

Fig. 7 Changing your oil on a regular basis will help ensure long engine life

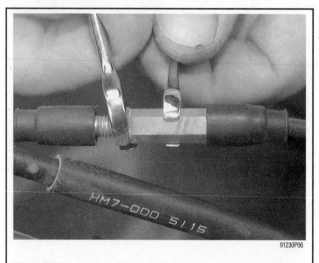

Fig. 8 Cables usually have a means of adjustment to compensate for wear

lines with the information in this book. But, remember that ATV's and manufacturers do vary. Don't take a chance on missing an odd item or replacement interval that is unique to your year or model. Refer to the manufacturer's recommended maintenance charts, whenever possible.

It's necessary to mention the difference between maintenance and repair. Maintenance includes routine inspections, adjustments, and replacement of parts that show signs of normal wear. Maintenance compensates for wear or deterioration. Repair implies that something has broken or is not working. A need for repair is often caused by lack of maintenance. Example: draining and refilling the brake fluid is maintenance recommended by some manufacturers at specific mileage intervals. Failure to do this can allow internal corrosion or damage and impair the operation of the brake system, requiring expensive repairs. While no maintenance program can prevent items from breaking or wearing out, a general rule can be stated: MAINTENANCE IS CHEAPER THAN REPAIR.

Two basic mechanic's rules should be mentioned here. First, whenever the left side of the ATV is referred to, it is meant to specify the your left while sitting in the riding position. Conversely, the right side means your right side while seated. Second, most screws and bolts are removed by turning counterclockwise, and tightened by turning clockwise. An easy way to remember this is: righty, tighty; left loosey. Corny, but effective. And if you are really dense (and we have all been so at one time or another), buy a ratchet that is marked ON and OFF, or mark your own.

Professional Help

♦ **See Figure 9**

You ride ATV's for fun, so maybe you need to see a psychiatrist. Okay, seriously this time. Occasionally, there are some things when working on an ATV that are beyond the capabilities or tools of the average Do-It-Yourselfer (DIYer). This shouldn't include most of the topics of this book, but you will have to be the judge. Some ATVs require special tools or a selection of special parts, even for basic maintenance.

Talk to other riders of the same model and speak with a trusted dealer or repair shop to find if there is a particular system or component on your ATV that is difficult to maintain. For example, although the technique of valve adjustment may be easily understood and even performed by a DIYer, it might require a handy assortment of shims in various sizes and a few hours of disassembly to get to that point. Not having the assortment of shims handy might mean multiple trips back and forth to the parts store, and this might not be worth your time.

You will have to decide for yourself where basic maintenance ends and where professional service should begin. Take your time and do your research first (starting with the information in this book) and then make your own decision. If you really don't feel comfortable with attempting a procedure, DON'T do it. If you've gotten into something that may be over your head, don't panic. Tuck your tail between your legs and call a service technician. Dealer service departments and independent shops will be able to finish a job for you. Your ego may be damaged, but your ride will be properly be restored to its full running order. So, as long as you approach jobs slowly and carefully, you really have nothing to lose and everything to gain by doing it yourself.

Fig. 9 If you are unsure about a complicated repair, get the details from a professional first

Avoiding the Most Common Mistakes

♦ **See Figures 10, 11, 12 and 13**

Pay attention to the instructions provided. There are 3 common mistakes in mechanical work:

1. Incorrect order of assembly, disassembly or adjustment. When taking something apart or putting it together, performing steps in the wrong order usually just costs you extra time; however, it CAN break something. Read the entire procedure before beginning disassembly. Perform everything in the order in which the instructions say you should, even if you can't immediately see a reason for it. When you're taking apart something that is very intricate, you might want to draw a picture of how it looks when assembled at one point in order to make sure you get everything back in its proper position. When making adjustments, perform them in the proper order; often, one adjustment affects another, and you cannot expect satisfactory results unless each adjustment is made only when it cannot be changed by any other.

2. Overtorquing (or undertorquing). While it is more common for overtorquing to cause damage, undertorquing may allow a fastener to vibrate loose

Fig. 10 DON'T DO THIS! Always use the PROPER tool for the job

Fig. 11 Proper use of a torque wrench will prevent warpage and leaks

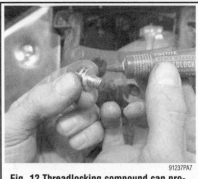

Fig. 12 Threadlocking compound can provide you with peace-of-mind when assembling critical parts

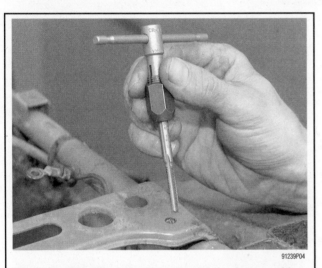

Fig. 13 Overtightnening fasteners may result in breakage, requiring drilling and tapping

causing serious damage. Especially when dealing with aluminum parts, pay attention to torque specifications and utilize a torque wrench in assembly. If a torque figure is not available, remember that if you are using the right tool to perform the job, you will probably not have to strain yourself to get a fastener tight enough. The pitch of most threads is so slight that the tension you put on the wrench will be multiplied many times in actual force on what you are tightening.

A good example of how critical torque is can be seen in the case of aluminum side covers on some engines. The aluminum side covers found on many ATV engines today can be damaged by heating and cooling if not tightened evenly. Failure to use a torque wrench may allow the cover to warp in service, causing leaks.

There are many commercial products available for ensuring that fasteners won't come loose, even if they are not torqued just right (a very common brand is Loctite®). If you're worried about getting something together tight enough to hold, but loose enough to avoid mechanical damage during assembly, one of these products might offer substantial insurance. Before choosing a threadlocking compound, read the label on the package and make sure the product is compatible with the materials, fluids, etc. involved.

3. Crossthreading. This occurs when a part such as a bolt is screwed into a nut or casting at the wrong angle and forced. Crossthreading is more likely to occur if access is difficult. It helps to clean and lubricate fasteners, then to start threading with the part to be installed positioned straight in. Always, start a fastener, etc. with your fingers. If you encounter resistance, unscrew the part and start over again at a different angle until it can be inserted and turned several times without much effort. Keep in mind that some parts may have tapered threads, so that gentle turning will automatically bring the part you're threading to the proper angle, but only if you don't force it or resist a change in angle. Don't put a wrench on the part until it has been tightened a couple of turns by hand. If you suddenly encounter resistance, and the part has not seated fully, don't force it. Pull it back out to make sure it's clean and threading properly.

Always take your time and be patient; once you have some experience, working on your ATV may well become as enjoyable as riding!

Storing Parts

▶ See Figure 14

Above all, we can't emphasize too strongly the necessity of a neat and orderly disassembly. Even if you are an experienced mechanic, parts can get misplaced, misidentified and just plain lost.

Start with an indelible marker, lots of cans and/or boxes and tags. Each time a part is removed, label it and store it safely. "Parts" includes all fasteners (bolts, nuts, screws, and washers). Bolts and nuts may look the same and not be alike. Similar looking bolts may be different lengths or thread pitch. Lockwashers may be required in some places and not in others. Everything should go back exactly from where it came.

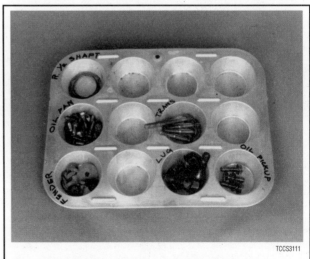

Fig. 14 Don't laugh, but that old muffin baking tray can be very helpful in the garage once its life is over in the kitchen

SAFETY IN ATV SERVICE

It is virtually impossible to anticipate all of the hazards involved with maintenance and service, but care and common sense will prevent most accidents.

The rules of safety for mechanics range from "don't smoke around gasoline," to "use the proper tool(s) for the job." The trick to avoiding injuries is to develop safe work habits and to take every possible precaution. Whenever you are working on your ATV, pay ATTENTION to what you are doing. The more you pay attention to details and what is going on around you, the less likely you will be to hurt yourself or damage your ride.

Do's

▶ **See Figure 15**

• Do keep a fire extinguisher and first aid kit handy.
• Do wear safety glasses or goggles when cutting, drilling, grinding or prying, even if you have 20–20 vision. If you wear glasses for the sake of vision, wear safety goggles over your regular glasses.
• Do shield your eyes whenever you work around the battery. Batteries contain sulfuric acid. In case of contact with the eyes or skin, flush the area with water or a mixture of water and baking soda, then seek immediate medical attention.
• Do use adequate ventilation when working with any chemicals or hazardous materials. Like carbon monoxide, the asbestos dust resulting from some brake lining wear can be hazardous in sufficient quantities.
• Do disconnect the negative battery cable when working on the electrical system. The secondary ignition system contains EXTREMELY HIGH VOLTAGE. In some cases it can even exceed 50,000 volts.
• Do follow manufacturer's directions whenever working with potentially hazardous materials. Most chemicals and fluids are poisonous if taken internally.
• Do properly maintain your tools. Loose hammerheads, mushroomed punches and chisels, frayed or poorly grounded electrical cords, excessively worn screwdrivers, spread wrenches (open end), cracked sockets, slipping ratchets, or faulty droplight sockets can cause accidents.
• Likewise, keep your tools clean; a greasy wrench can slip off a bolt head, ruining the bolt and often harming your knuckles in the process.
• Do use the proper size and type of tool for the job at hand. Do select a wrench or socket that fits the nut or bolt. The wrench or socket should sit straight, not cocked.
• Do, when possible, pull on a wrench handle rather than push on it, and adjust your stance to prevent a fall.
• Do be sure that adjustable wrenches are tightly closed on the nut or bolt and pulled so that the force is on the side of the fixed jaw. Better yet, avoid the use of an adjustable if you have a fixed wrench that will fit.
• Do strike squarely with a hammer; avoid glancing blows. But, we REALLY hope you won't be using a hammer much in basic maintenance.

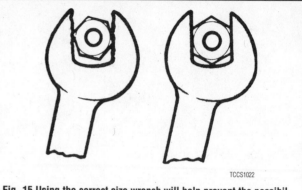

TCCS1022

Fig. 15 Using the correct size wrench will help prevent the possibility of rounding off a nut

Don'ts

• Don't run the engine in a garage or anywhere else without proper ventilation—EVER! Carbon monoxide is poisonous; it takes a long time to leave the human body and you can build up a deadly supply of it in your system by simply breathing in a little every day. You may not realize you are slowly poisoning yourself. Always use power vents, windows, fans and/or open the garage door.
• Don't work around moving parts while wearing loose clothing. Short sleeves are much safer than long, loose sleeves. Hard-toed shoes with neoprene soles protect your toes and give a better grip on slippery surfaces. Jewelry, watches, large belt buckles, or body adornment of any kind is not safe working around any vehicle. Long hair should be tied back under a hat or cap.
• Don't use pockets for toolboxes. A fall or bump can drive a screwdriver deep into your body. Even a rag hanging from your back pocket can wrap around a spinning shaft or rotor.
• Don't smoke when working around gasoline, cleaning solvent or other flammable material.
• Don't smoke when working around the battery. When the battery is being charged, it gives off explosive hydrogen gas. Actually, you shouldn't smoke anyway. Save that cigarette money and trick out your ride!
• Don't use gasoline to wash your hands; there are excellent soaps available. Gasoline contains dangerous additives which can enter the body through a cut or through your pores. Gasoline also removes all the natural oils from the skin so that bone dry hands will suck up oil and grease.
• Don't use screwdrivers for anything other than driving screws! A screwdriver used as an prying tool can snap when you least expect it, causing injuries. At the very least, you'll ruin a good screwdriver.

THE WORK AREA (SETTING UP SHOP)

▶ **See Figure 16**

The size and complexity of your work area will vary with the amount of work you plan to do on your ATV. It is easy (and fun) to get carried away when setting up a shop, but the more time you spend in it, the more you will appreciate the preparation work. What we have described here is all that most people would ever need to maintain an ATV. That doesn't mean you can't maintain your ATV if you don't have a garage, it just means that you might not be as comfortable. Face it, trying to check an adjustment in the rain or worse, prepping for winter storage with snow melting down your back just isn't much fun.

So, if you are lucky enough to set up a shop just to work on your ride, here are some things you'll want to consider.

Floor Space

▶ **See Figure 17**

The average one car garage will give you more than enough workspace, but a decent sized tool shed will also do the trick. A floor plan of 16 X 12 feet (4.8 X

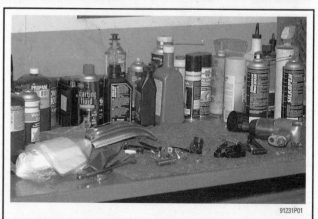

91231P01

Fig. 16 Even a small work area can be helpful when maintaining your ATV

Fig. 17 At our photo studio, adequate floor space is rarely a problem

Fig. 18 Typical homemade wood shelves, crammed with stuff. These shelves are made from spare ¾ x 6 in. pressure treated decking

3.6 meters) is more than sufficient for shelving, workbenches, tool shelves or boxes and parts storage areas. 12 X 16 (4.8 X 3.6) works out to 192 square feet (or about 17 square meters). You may think that this sounds like a lot of room, but when you start building shelves, and constructing work benches almost half of that can be eaten up!

Also, you may wonder why a lot of floor space is needed. There are several reasons, not the least of which is the safety factor. You'll be working around a large, heavy, metal object — your ATV. You don't want to be tripping, falling, crashing into things or hurting yourself, because your ATV takes up a surprising amount of your work space. Accidents can happen! You can easily trip over a misplaced tool.

Most garages have concrete floors. Portable lifts or work stools roll best on a smooth surface. If your garage floor has cracks with raised sections or blocks with deep grooves, you may have a problem if you plan on using either of these. If the wheels hang up on these cracks or grooves while moving an ATV on a workstand, you might be in for an unpleasant surprise.

Storage Areas

SHELVES

♦ See Figures 18, 19 and 20

You can't have enough shelf space. Adequate shelf space means that you don't have to stack anything on the floor, where it would be in the way.

Making shelves isn't tough. You can make your own, buy modular or buy prefab units. The best modular units are those made of interlocking shelves and uprights of ABS plastic. They're lightweight and easy to assemble, and their load-bearing capacity is more than sufficient. Also, they are not subject rust or rot as are metal and wood shelves.

Probably the cheapest and best shelves are ones that you make yourself from one inch shelving with 2 X 4 uprights. You can make them as long, wide and high as you want. For at least the uprights, use pressure treated wood. Its resistance to rot is more than worth the additional cost.

TOOL CHESTS

♦ See Figures 21 and 22

There are many types and sizes of tool chests. Their greatest advantage is that they can hold a lot of tools, securely, in a relatively small area. If you decide that you need one, make sure that you buy one that's big enough and mobile enough for the work area. Remember, you get what you pay for, so purchase a good brand name, and it should last a lifetime.

There are several things to look for in a tool chest, depending on how much you plan on using it, and just how many tools you plan to stuff in it. Check the overall construction. In general, bolted-together chests are stronger than riveted

Fig. 19 Modular plastic shelves, such as these are inexpensive, weatherproof and easy to assemble

Fig. 20 These shelves were made from the frame of old kitchen cabinets

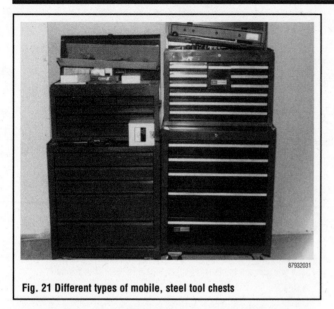

Fig. 21 Different types of mobile, steel tool chests

Fig. 23 Homemade workbenches

Fig. 22 A good tool chest has several drawers, each designed to hold a different type tool

or tabbed, because they are sturdier. Drawers that ride on ball bearings are better than compound slide drawers, because they can hold more and are easier to open/close. Heavy-duty, ball bearing casters are better than bushing type wheels, because they will roll better and last longer. Steel wheels are better than plastic, as they are less prone to damage. Compare different boxes, you'll have to make up your own mind exactly what style is best for you.

WORK BENCHES

▶ **See Figure 23**

As with the shelving, work benches can be either store-bought or home-made. The store-bought workbenches can be steel, precut wood, or even plastic kits. They all work (though heavy duty benches are obviously better suited to heavy parts and related work), and most types should be available at your local building supply stores or through tool catalogs.

Homemade benches, as with the shelves have the advantage of being made-to-fit your workshop. A freestanding workbench is best, as opposed to one attached to an outside wall. The freestanding bench can take more abuse since it doesn't transfer the shock or vibration to wall supports.

A good free-standing workbench should be constructed using 4 X 4 pressure treated wood as legs, 2 X 6 planking as header boards and ¾ inch plywood sheathing as a deck. Diagonal supports can be 2 X 4 studs and it's always help-

ful to construct a full size ¾ inch plywood shelf under the bench. Not only can you use the shelf for storage but also it gives great rigidity to the whole bench structure. Assembling the bench with screws rather than nails takes longer but adds strength and gives you the ability to take the whole thing apart if you ever want to move it.

Lighting

▶ **See Figures 24 and 25**

The importance of adequate lighting can't be over emphasized. Good lighting is not only a convenience but also a safety feature. If you can see what you're working on you're less likely to make mistakes, have a wrench slip or trip over an obstacle. A lot of frustration can be avoided when you can see all the fasteners on which you are working (some of which may be hidden or obscured).

For overhead lighting, at least 2 twin tube fluorescent shop lights should be in place. Most garages are wired with standard light bulbs attached to the wall studs at intervals. Four or five of these lights, at about a 6 foot height combined with the overhead lighting should suffice. However, no matter where the lights are, your body is going to block some of it so a droplight or clip-on type work light is a great idea.

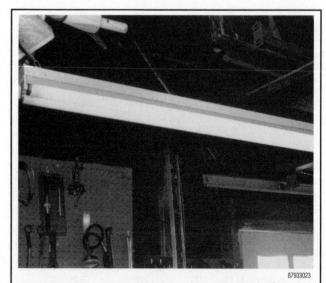

Fig. 24 At least two of this type of twin tube fluorescent light is essential

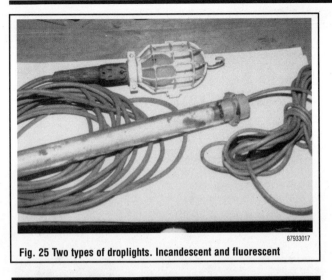

Fig. 25 Two types of droplights. Incandescent and fluorescent

Fig. 26 Three essential pieces of safety equipment. Left to right: ear protectors, safety goggles and respirator

Ventilation

At one time or another, you'll be working with chemicals that may require adequate ventilation. Now, just about all garages have a big car-sized door and all sheds or workshops have a door. In bad weather the door will have to be closed so at least one window that opens is a necessity. An exhaust fan or regular ventilation fan is a great help, especially in hot weather.

Heaters

If you live in an area where the winters are cold, as do many of us, it's nice to have some sort of heat where we work. If your workshop or garage is attached to the house, you'll probably be okay. If your garage or shop is detached, then a space heater of some sort — electric, propane or kerosene — will be necessary. NEVER run a space heater in the presence of flammable vapors! When running a non-electric space heater, always allow for some means of venting the carbon monoxide!

Electrical Requirements

Obviously, your workshop should be wired according to all local codes. As to what type of service you need, that depends on your electrical load. If you have a lot of power equipment and maybe a refrigerator, TV, stereo or whatever, not only do you have a great shop, but your amperage requirements may exceed the capacity of your wiring. If you are at all in doubt, consult your local electrical contractor.

Safety Equipment

▶ See Figure 26

FIRE EXTINGUISHERS

▶ See Figure 27

There are many types of safety equipment. The most important of these is the fire extinguisher. You'll be well off with two 5 lbs. extinguishers rated for oil, chemical and wood.

FIRST AID KITS

Next you'll need a good first aid kit. Any good kit that can be purchased from the local drug store will be fine. It's a good idea, in addition, to have something easily accessible in the event of a minor injury, such as hydrogen peroxide or other antiseptic that can be poured onto or applied to a wound immediately. Remember, your hands will be dirty. Just as you wouldn't want dirt entering your engine when you open the oil filler plug, you certainly don't want bacteria entering a blood stream that has just been opened!

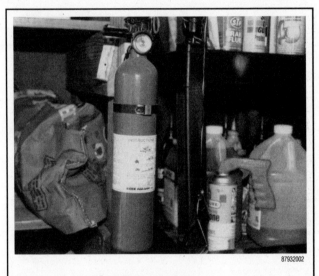

Fig. 27 A good, all-purpose fire extinguisher

WORK GLOVES

▶ See Figure 28

Unless you think scars on your hands are cool, enjoy pain and like wearing bandages, get a good pair of work gloves. Canvas or leather are the best. And yes, we realize that there are some jobs involving small parts that can't be done while wearing work gloves. These jobs are not the ones usually associated with hand injuries.

A good pair of rubber gloves (such as those usually associated with dish washing) or vinyl gloves is also a great idea. There are some liquids such as solvents and penetrants that don't belong on your skin. Avoid burns and rashes. Wear these gloves.

And lastly, an option. If you're tired of being greasy and dirty all the time, go to the drug store and buy a box of disposable latex gloves like medical professionals wear. You can handle greasy parts, perform small tasks, wash parts, etc. all without getting dirty! These gloves take a surprising amount of abuse without tearing and aren't expensive. Note however, that it has been reported that some people are allergic to the latex or the powder used inside some gloves, so pay attention to what you buy.

WORK BOOTS

It's up to you, but I think that a good, comfortable pair of steel-toed work boots is a sensible idea. Primarily because heavy parts or tools get dropped

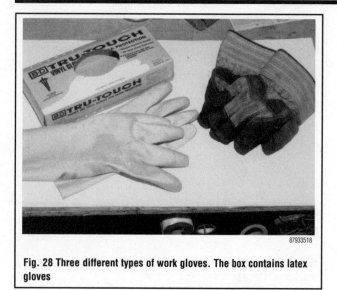

Fig. 28 Three different types of work gloves. The box contains latex gloves

sooner or later. A heavy piece of metal can do significant damage to a sneaker-clad foot.

Good work boots also provide better support, — you're going to be on your feet a lot — are oil-resistant, and they keep your feet warm and dry.

To keep the boots protected, get a spray can of silicone-based water repellent and spray the boots when new, and then periodically thereafter.

EYE PROTECTION

▶ **See Figure 29**

Don't begin any job without a good pair of work goggles or impact resistant glasses! When doing any kind of work, it's all too easy to avoid eye injury through this simple precaution. And don't just buy eye protection and leave it on the shelf. Wear it all the time! Things have a habit of breaking, chipping, splashing, spraying, splintering and flying around. And, for some reason, your eye is always in the way!

If you wear vision correcting glasses as a matter of routine, get a pair made with polycarbonate lenses. These lenses are impact resistant and are available at any optometrist.

EAR PROTECTION

Often overlooked is hearing protection. Power equipment is noisy! Loud noises damage your ears. It's as simple as that!

Fig. 29 It is always a good idea to wear safety goggles when working, since letters and words can fly right off the screen at random

The simplest and cheapest form of ear protection is a pair of noise-reducing ear plugs. Cheap insurance for your ears. And, they may even come with their own, cute little carrying case.

More substantial, more protection and more money is a good pair of noise reducing earmuffs. They protect from all but the loudest sounds. Hopefully those are sounds that you'll never encounter since they're usually associated with disasters.

WORK CLOTHES

Everyone has "work clothes." Usually this consists of old jeans and a shirt that has seen better days. That's fine. In addition, a denim work apron is a nice accessory. It's rugged, can hold some spare bolts, and you don't feel bad wiping your hands or tools on it. That's what it's for.

If you're so inclined, shop aprons are a cheap and easy way to protect your clothes. They're rugged and can be put on quickly for quick tasks.

When working in cold weather, a one-piece, thermal work outfit is invaluable. Most are rated to below zero (Fahrenheit) temperatures and are ruggedly constructed.

Chemicals

There is a whole range of chemicals that you'll find handy for maintenance work. The most common types are, lubricants, penetrants and sealers. Keep these handy, on some convenient shelf. There are also many chemicals that are used for detailing or cleaning, but these are covered elsewhere.

When a particular chemical is not being used, keep it capped, upright and in a safe place. These substances may be flammable, may be irritants or might even be caustic and should always be stored properly, used properly and handled with care. Always read and follow all label directions and be sure to wear hand and eye protection!

LUBRICANTS & PENETRANTS

▶ **See Figure 30**

In this category, a well-prepared shop should have:
• A full complement of fluids for your ATV (engine oil, transmission or drive oil, brake fluid, etc.)
• Anti-seize
• Lithium grease
• Chassis lube
• Assembly lube
• Silicone grease
• Silicone spray
• Penetrating oil

Anti-seize is used to coat certain fasteners prior to installation. This can be especially helpful when two dissimilar metals are in contact (to help prevent

Fig. 30 A variety of penetrants and lubricants is a staple of any DIYer's garage

corrosion that might lock the fastener in place). This is a good practice on a lot of different fasteners, BUT, NOT on any fastener which might vibrate loose causing a problem. If anti-seize is used on a fastener, it should be checked periodically for proper tightness.

Lithium grease, chassis lube, silicone grease or a synthetic brake caliper grease can all be used pretty much interchangeably. All can be used for coating rust-prone fasteners and for facilitating the assembly of parts that are a tight fit. Silicone and synthetic greases are the most versatile.

➡**Silicone dielectric grease is a non-conductor that is often used to coat the terminals of wiring connectors before fastening them. It may sound odd to coat metal portions of a terminal with something that won't conduct electricity, but here is it how it works. When the connector is fastened the metal-to-metal contact between the terminals will displace the grease (allowing the circuit to be completed). The grease that is displaced will then coat the non-contacted surface and the cavity around the terminals, SEALING them from atmospheric moisture that could cause corrosion.**

Silicone spray is a good lubricant for hard-to-reach places and parts that shouldn't be gooped up with grease.

Penetrating oil may turn out to be one of your best friends when taking something apart that has corroded fasteners. Not only can they make a job easier, they can really help to avoid broken and stripped fasteners. The most familiar penetrating oils are Liquid Wrench® and WD-40®. A newer penetrant, PB Blaster® also works well. These products have hundreds of uses. For your purposes, they are vital!

Before disassembling any part (especially on an exhaust system), check the fasteners. If any appear rusted, soak them thoroughly with the penetrant and let them stand while you do something else. This simple act can save you hours of tedious work trying to extract a broken bolt or stud.

SEALANTS

♦ See Figure 31

Sealants are an indispensable part for certain tasks on ATV's, especially if you are trying to avoid leaks. The purpose of sealants is to establish a leak-proof bond between or around assembled parts. Most sealers are used in conjunction with gaskets, but some are used instead of conventional gasket material.

The most common sealers are the non-hardening types such as Permatex®No.2 or its equivalents. These sealers are applied to the mating surfaces of each part to be joined, then a gasket is put in place and the parts are assembled.

➡**A sometimes overlooked use for sealants like RTV is on the threads of vibration prone fasteners.**

One very helpful type of non-hardening sealer is the "high tack" type. This type is a very sticky material that holds the gasket in place while the parts are being assembled. This stuff is really a good idea when you don't have enough hands or fingers to keep everything where it should be.

The stand-alone sealers are the Room Temperature Vulcanizing (RTV) silicone gasket makers. On some engines, this material is used instead of a gasket. In those instances, a gasket may not be available or, because of the shape of the

Fig. 31 Sealants are essential for preventing leaks

mating surfaces, a gasket shouldn't be used. This stuff, when used in conjunction with a conventional gasket, produces the surest bonds.

RTV does have its limitations though. When using this material, you will have a time limit. It starts to set-up within 15 minutes or so, so you have to assemble the parts without delay. In addition, when squeezing the material out of the tube, don't drop any glops into the engine. The stuff will form and set and travel around the oil gallery, possibly plugging up a passage. Also, most types are not fuel-proof. Check the tube for all cautions.

CLEANERS

♦ See Figures 32, 33 and 34

You'll have two types of cleaners to deal with: parts cleaners and hand cleaners. The parts cleaners are for the parts; the hand cleaners are for you.

There are many good, non-flammable, biodegradable parts cleaners on the market. These cleaning agents are safe for you, the parts and the environment. Therefore, there is no reason to use flammable, caustic or toxic substances to clean your parts or tools.

As far as hand cleaners go, the waterless types are the best. They have always been efficient at cleaning, but leave a pretty smelly odor. Recently though, just about all of them have eliminated the odor and added stuff that actually smells good. Make sure that you pick one that contains lanolin or some other moisture-replenishing additive. Cleaners not only remove grease and oil but also skin oil.

One other note: most women know this already but most men don't. Use a hand lotion when you're all cleaned up. It's okay. Real men DO use hand lotion! Believe it or not, using hand lotion **before** your hands are dirty will actually make them easier to clean when you're finished with a dirty job. Lotion seals your hands, and keeps dirt and grease from sticking to your skin.

Fig. 32 Three types of cleaners. Some are caustic; some are not. Always read and follow label instructions

Fig. 33 This is one type of hand cleaner that not only works well but smells pretty good too

Fig. 34 The best thing to clean up all types of spills is "kitty litter"

SHOP TOWELS

▶ **See Figure 35**

One of the most important elements in doing shop work is a good supply of shop towels. Standard household paper towels just don't cut it! Most auto parts stores sell packs of shop towels, usually 50-100 in a pack. They are relatively cheap and can be washed over and over. Some manufacturers now produce a heavy paper towel, just for shop use, and these are often just as good as the cloth types (although they are obviously disposable and might not be considered as environmentally friendly. Not that washing oil soaked rags would be considered "environmentally sound" either . . .). Ideally, you may want to keep both types handy.

One of the best shop towels known to science, is the old-fashioned cloth diaper. They're highly absorbent and rugged, but, in these days of disposable diapers, are hard to find.

Fig. 35 A pack of shop towels

TOOLS

▶ **See Figures 36, 37 and 38**

Tools; this subject could require a completely separate book. Again, the first thing you will need to ask yourself, is just HOW involved do you plan to get. Most ATV's come with a small tool kit for unexpected trailside repairs. And, with some kits, you could reasonably perform all required maintenance using only the kit. But, that is probably more the exception than the rule and if you are serious about your ATV maintenance you will want to gather a quality set of tools to make the job easier, and more enjoyable. BESIDES, TOOLS ARE FUN!!!

Almost every do-it-yourselfer loves to accumulate tools. Though most find a way to perform jobs with only a few common tools, they tend to buy more over time, as money allows. So gathering the tools necessary for maintenance does not have to be an expensive, overnight proposition.

When buying tools, the saying "You get what you pay for" is absolutely true! Don't go cheap! Any hand tool that you buy should be drop forged and/or chrome vanadium. These two qualities tell you that the tool is strong enough for the job. With any tool, power or not, go with a name that you've heard of before, or, that is recommended buy your local professional retailer. Let's go over a list of tools that you'll need.

Most of the world uses the metric system. However, some American-built ATV's and aftermarket accessories use standard fasteners. So, accumulate your tools accordingly. Any good DIYer should have a decent set of both U.S. and metric measure tools.

Don't be confused by terminology. Most advertising refers to "SAE and metric", or "standard and metric." Both are misnomers. The Society of Automotive

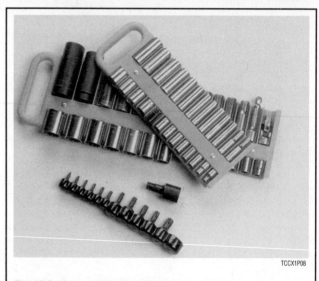

Fig. 37 Socket holders, especially the magnetic type, are handy items to keep tools in order

Fig. 36 The well-stocked garage pegboard. Pegboards can store most tools and other equipment for ease of access. Besides, they're cool looking

Fig. 38 A good set of handy storage cabinets for fasteners and small parts makes any job easier

Engineers (SAE) did not invent the English system of measurement; the English did. The SAE likes metrics just fine. Both English (U.S.) and metric measurements are SAE approved. Also, the current "standard" measurement IS metric. So, if it's not metric, it's U.S. measurement.

Hand Tools

SOCKET SETS

▶ **See Figures 39, 40, 41 and 42**

Socket sets are the most basic, necessary hand tools for ATV repair and maintenance work. For our purposes, socket sets basically come in three drive sizes: ¼ inch, ⅜ inch and ½ inch. Drive size refers to the size of the drive lug on the ratchet, breaker bar or speed handle.

You'll need a good ½ inch set since this size drive lug assures that you won't break a ratchet or socket on large or heavy fasteners. Also, torque wrenches with a torque scale high enough for larger fasteners (such as axle nuts) are usually ½ inch drive. The socket set that you'll need should range in sizes from ⁷⁄₁₆ inch through 1 inch for standard fasteners, and a 6mm through 19mm for metric fasteners.

A ⅜ inch set is very handy to have since it allows you to get into tight places that the larger drive ratchets can't. Also, this size set gives you a range of smaller sockets that are still strong enough for heavy duty work.

¼ inch drive sets can be VERY handy in tight places, though they usually duplicate functions of the ⅜ inch set.

As for the sockets themselves, they come in standard and deep lengths as well as standard and thin walled, in either 6 or 12 point.

Standard length sockets are good for just about all jobs, however, some stud-head bolts, hard-to-reach bolts, nuts on long studs, etc., require the deep sockets.

Thin-walled sockets are not too common and aren't usually needed in most work. They are exactly what you think, sockets made with a thinner wall to fit into tighter places. They don't have the wall strength of a standard socket, of course, but their usefulness in a tight spot can make them worth it.

6 and 12 points. This refers to how many sides are in the socket itself. Each has advantages. The 6 point socket is stronger and less prone to slipping which would strip a bolt head or nut. 12 point sockets are more common, usually less expensive and can operate better in tight places where the ratchet handle can't swing far.

Most manufacturers use recessed hex-head fasteners to retain many of the engine and chassis parts from engine covers to caliper pins. These fasteners require a socket with a hex shaped driver or a large sturdy hex key. To help prevent torn knuckles, we would recommend that you stick to the sockets on any tight fastener and leave the hex keys for lighter applications. Hex driver sockets are available individually or in sets just like conventional sockets. Any complete tool set should include hex driver sockets.

More and more, manufacturers are using Torx® head fasteners, which were

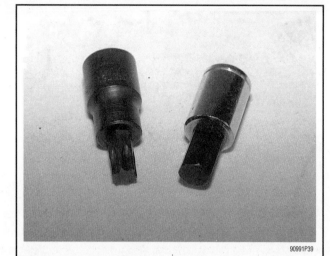

90991P39

Fig. 40 Two common drivers for ATV service: Left, a Torx® drive socket; right, a hex drive socket

90991P38

Fig. 41 A swivel (U-joint) adapter, and two types of drive adapters

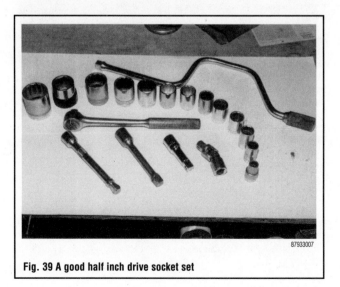

87933007

Fig. 39 A good half inch drive socket set

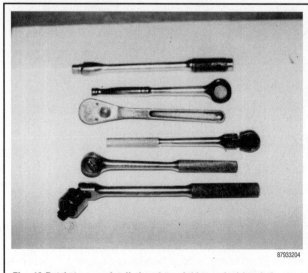

87933204

Fig. 42 Ratchets come in all sizes from rigid to swivel-headed

once known as tamper resistant fasteners (because many people did not have tools with the necessary odd driver shape). They are still used where the manufacturer would prefer only knowledgeable technicians or advanced Do-It-Yourselfers (DIYers) be working.

There are currently three different types of Torx® fasteners; internal, external and a new tamper resistant. The internal fasteners require a star-shaped driver. The external fasteners require a star-shaped socket. And, the new tamper resistant fasteners use a star-shaped driver with a small hole drilled through the center. The most common are the internal Torx® fasteners, but you might find any of them on your particular ATV.

Torque Wrenches

▶ **See Figure 43**

In most applications, a torque wrench can be used to assure proper installation of a fastener. Torque wrenches come in various designs and most supply stores will carry a variety to suit your needs. A torque wrench should be used any time you have a specific torque value for a fastener. A torque wrench can also be used if you are following the general guidelines in the charts accompanying the fastener information in this section. Keep in mind that because there is no worldwide standardization of fasteners, the charts are a general guideline and should be used with caution. Again, the general rule of "if you are using the right tool for the job, you should not have to strain to tighten a fastener" applies here.

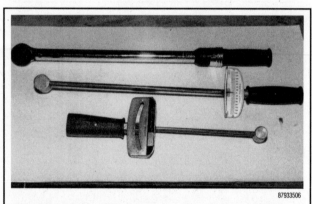

Fig. 43 Three types of torque wrenches. Top to bottom: a ½ inch drive clicker type, a ½ inch drive beam type and a ⅜ inch drive beam type that reads in inch lbs.

BEAM TYPE

▶ **See Figure 44**

The beam type torque wrench is one of the most popular types. It consists of a pointer attached to the head that runs the length of the flexible beam (shaft) to a scale located near the handle. As the wrench is pulled, the beam bends and the pointer indicates the torque using the scale.

CLICK (BREAKAWAY) TYPE

▶ **See Figure 45**

Another popular torque wrench design is the click type. To use the click type wrench you pre-adjust it to a torque setting. Once the torque is reached, the wrench has a reflex signaling feature that causes a momentary breakaway of the torque wrench body, sending an impulse to the operator's hand.

PIVOT HEAD TYPE

▶ **See Figure 46**

Some torque wrenches (usually of the click type) may be equipped with a pivot head that can allow it to be used in areas of limited access. BUT, it must be used properly. To hold a pivot head wrench, grasp the handle lightly, and as you pull on the handle, it should be floated on the pivot point. If the handle comes in contact with the yoke extension during the process of pulling, there is a very good chance the torque readings will be

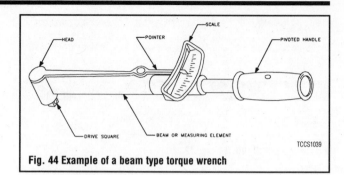

Fig. 44 Example of a beam type torque wrench

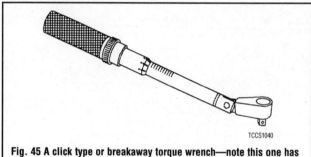

Fig. 45 A click type or breakaway torque wrench—note this one has a pivoting head

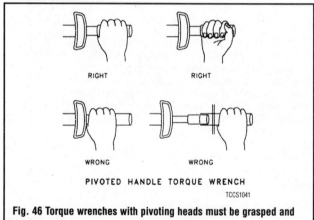

Fig. 46 Torque wrenches with pivoting heads must be grasped and used properly to prevent an incorrect reading

inaccurate because this could alter the wrench loading point. The design of the handle is usually such as to make it inconvenient to deliberately misuse the wrench.

➡ **It should be mentioned that the use of any U-joint, wobble or extension would have an effect on the torque readings, no matter what type of wrench you are using. For the most accurate readings, install the socket directly on the wrench driver. If necessary, straight extensions (which hold a socket directly under the wrench driver) will have the least effect on the torque reading. Avoid any extension that alters the length of the wrench from the handle to the head/driving point (such as a crow's foot). U-joint or wobble extensions can greatly affect the readings; avoid their use at all times.**

RIGID CASE (DIRECT READING)

▶ **See Figure 47**

A rigid case or direct reading torque wrench is equipped with a dial indicator to show torque values. One advantage of these wrenches is that they can be held at any position on the wrench without affecting accuracy. These wrenches are often preferred because they tend to be compact, easy to read and have a great degree of accuracy.

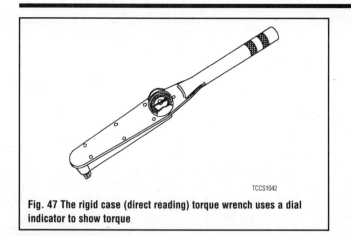

Fig. 47 The rigid case (direct reading) torque wrench uses a dial indicator to show torque

Torque Angle Meters

▶ See Figure 48

Because the frictional characteristics of each fastener or threaded hole will vary, clamp loads which are based strictly on torque will vary as well. In most applications, this variance is not significant enough to cause worry. But, in certain applications, a manufacturer's engineers may determine that more precise clamp loads are necessary (such is the case with many aluminum cylinder heads). In these cases, a torque angle method of installation would be specified. When installing fasteners that are torque angle tightened, a predetermined seating torque and standard torque wrench are usually used first to remove any compliance from the joint. The fastener is then tightened the specified additional portion of a turn measured in degrees. A torque angle gauge (mechanical protractor) is used for these applications. You will probably never have the use for a torque angle meter for most normal maintenance.

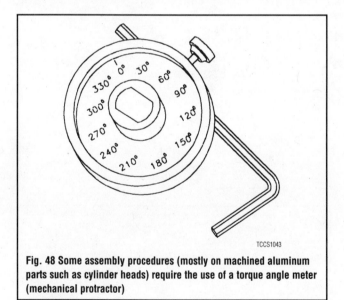

Fig. 48 Some assembly procedures (mostly on machined aluminum parts such as cylinder heads) require the use of a torque angle meter (mechanical protractor)

Breaker Bars

▶ See Figure 49

Breaker bars are long handles with a drive lug. Their main purpose is to provide extra turning force when breaking loose tight bolts or nuts. They come in all drive sizes and lengths. Always wear gloves when using a breaker bar

Speed Handles

▶ See Figure 50

Speed handles are tools with a drive lug and angled turning handle that allow you to quickly remove or install a bolt or nut. They don't, however have much

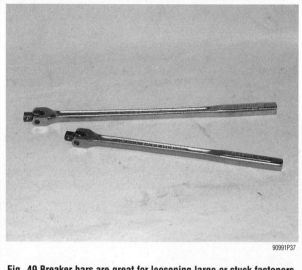

Fig. 49 Breaker bars are great for loosening large or stuck fasteners

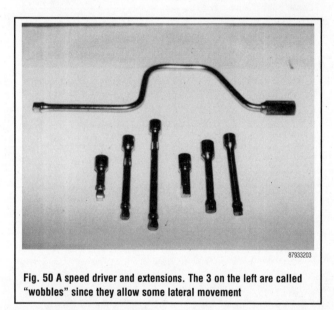

Fig. 50 A speed driver and extensions. The 3 on the left are called "wobbles" since they allow some lateral movement

torque ability. You might consider one when installing a number of similar fasteners such as an engine cover.

WRENCHES

▶ See Figures 51, 52, 53 and 54

Basically, there are 3 kinds of fixed wrenches: open end, box end, and combination.

Open end wrenches have 2-jawed openings at each end of the wrench. These wrenches are able to fit onto just about any nut or bolt. They are extremely versatile but have one major drawback. They can slip on a worn or rounded bolt head or nut, causing bleeding knuckles and a useless fastener.

Box-end wrenches have a 360° circular jaw at each end of the wrench. They come in both 6 and 12 point versions just like sockets and each type has the same advantages and disadvantages as sockets.

Combination wrenches have the best of both. They have a 2-jawed open end and a box end. These wrenches are probably the most versatile.

As for sizes, you'll probably need a range similar to that of the sockets, about ¼ inch through 1 inch for standard fasteners, or 6mm through 19mm for metric fasteners. As for numbers, you'll need 2 of each size, since, in many instances, one wrench holds the nut while the other turns the bolt. On most fasteners, the nut and bolt are the same size.

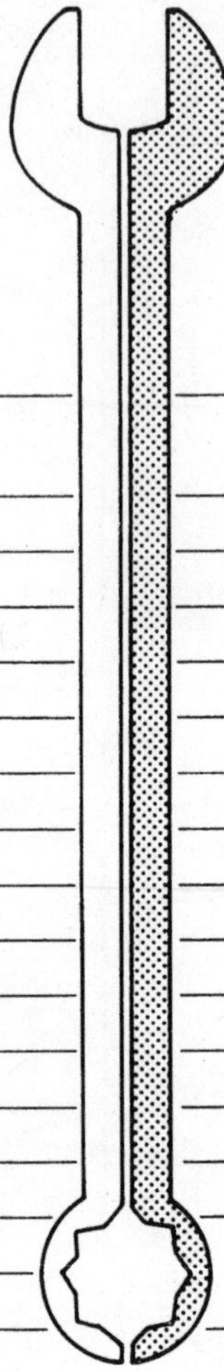

INCHES	DECIMAL		DECIMAL	MILLIMETERS
1/8"	.125		.118	3mm
3/16"	.187		.157	4mm
1/4"	.250		.236	6mm
5/16"	.312		.354	9mm
3/8"	.375		.394	10mm
7/16"	.437		.472	12mm
1/2"	.500		.512	13mm
9/16"	.562		.590	15mm
5/8"	.625		.630	16mm
11/16"	.687		.709	18mm
3/4"	.750		.748	19mm
13/16"	.812		.787	20mm
7/8"	.875		.866	22mm
15/16"	.937		.945	24mm
1"	1.00		.984	25mm

87933106

Fig. 51 Comparison of U.S. measure and metric wrench sizes

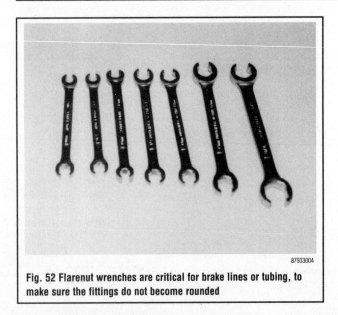

87933004

Fig. 52 Flarenut wrenches are critical for brake lines or tubing, to make sure the fittings do not become rounded

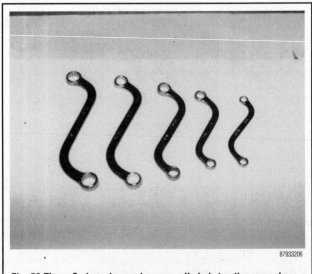

87933206

Fig. 53 These S-shaped wrenches are called obstruction wrenches

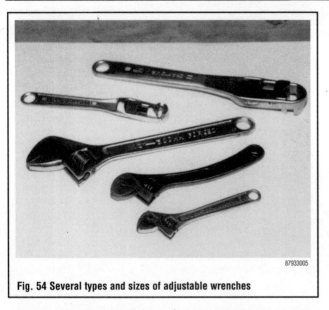

Fig. 54 Several types and sizes of adjustable wrenches

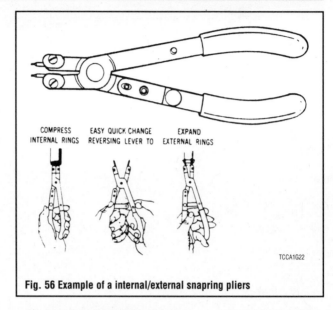

Fig. 56 Example of a internal/external snapring pliers

➡Although you will typically just need the sizes we specified, there are some exceptions. Occasionally you will find an axle nut or swingarm nut which is larger. For these, you will need to buy ONE expensive wrench or a very large adjustable. Or you can always just convince the spouse that we are talking about safety here and buy a whole, expensive, large wrench set.

One extremely valuable type of wrench is the adjustable wrench. An adjustable wrench has a fixed upper jaw and a moveable lower jaw. The lower jaw is moved by turning a threaded drum. The advantage of an adjustable wrench is its ability to be adjusted to just about any size fastener. The main drawback of an adjustable wrench is the lower jaw's tendency to move slightly under heavy pressure. This can cause the wrench to slip if the wrench is not facing the right way. Pulling on an adjustable wrench in the proper direction will cause the jaws to lock in place. Adjustable wrenches come in a large range of sizes, measured by the wrench length.

PLIERS

▶ See Figures 55 and 56

At least 2 pair of standard pliers is an absolute necessity. Pliers are simply mechanical fingers. They are, more than anything, an extension of your hand.

In addition to standard pliers there are the slip-joint, multi-position pliers such as ChannelLock® pliers and locking pliers, such as Vise Grips®.

Slip joint pliers are extremely valuable in grasping oddly sized parts and fasteners. Just make sure that you don't use them instead of a wrench too often since they can easily round off a bolt head or nut.

Locking pliers are usually used for gripping bolts or studs that can't be removed conventionally. You can get locking pliers in square jawed, needle-nosed and pipe-jawed. Pipe jawed have slightly curved jaws for gripping more than just pipes. Locking pliers can rank right up behind duct tape as the handyman's best friend.

SCREWDRIVERS

You can't have too many screwdrivers. They come in 2 basic flavors, either standard or Phillips. Standard blades come in various sizes and thicknesses for all types of slotted fasteners. Phillips screwdrivers come in sizes with number designations from 1 on up, with the lower number designating the smaller size. Screwdrivers can be purchased separately or in sets.

HAMMERS

▶ See Figure 57

You always need a hammer — for just about any kind of work. For most metal work, you need a ball-peen hammer for using drivers and other like tools, a plastic hammer for hitting things safely, and a soft-faced dead-blow hammer

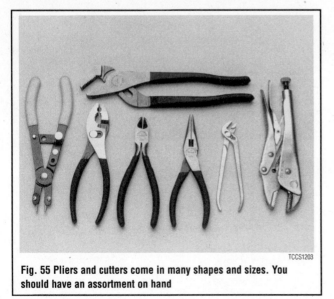

Fig. 55 Pliers and cutters come in many shapes and sizes. You should have an assortment on hand

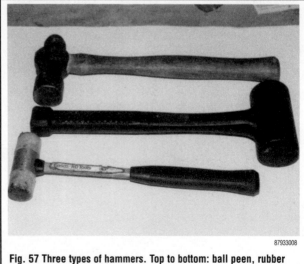

Fig. 57 Three types of hammers. Top to bottom: ball peen, rubber dead-blow, and plastic

for hitting things safely and hard. Hammers are also VERY useful with impact drivers (if you are not fortunate enough to have an air compressor).

OTHER COMMON TOOLS

▶ **See Figures 58 thru 67**

There are a lot of other tools that every workshop will eventually need (though not all for basic maintenance). They include:

- Funnels (for adding fluid)
- Chisels
- Punches
- Files
- Hacksaw
- Bench Vise
- Tap and Die Set
- Flashlight
- Magnetic Bolt Retriever
- Gasket scraper
- Putty Knife
- Screw/Bolt Extractors
- Prybar

Chisel, punches and files are repair tools.

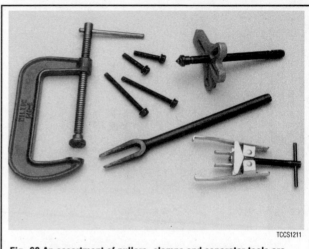

TCCS1211

Fig. 60 An assortment of pullers, clamps and separator tools are also needed for many larger repairs (especially engine and suspension work)

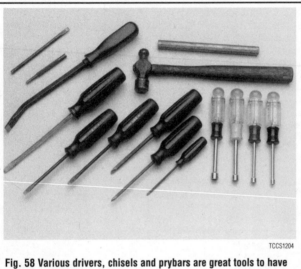

TCCS1204

Fig. 58 Various drivers, chisels and prybars are great tools to have in your box

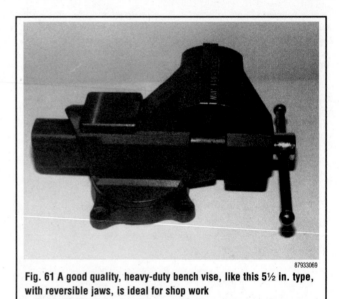

87933069

Fig. 61 A good quality, heavy-duty bench vise, like this 5½ in. type, with reversible jaws, is ideal for shop work

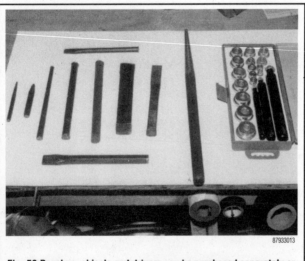

87933013

Fig. 59 Punches, chisels and drivers can be purchased separately or in sets

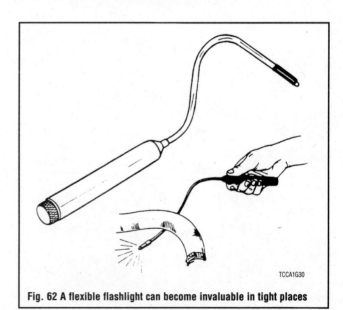

TCCA1G30

Fig. 62 A flexible flashlight can become invaluable in tight places

Chisel, punches and files are repair tools. Their uses will come up periodically.

Hacksaws have just one use—cutting things off. You may wonder why you'd need one for something as simple as maintenance, but you never know. Among other things, guide studs for parts installation can be made from old bolts with their heads cut off.

A large bench vise, of at least 4 inch capacity, is essential. A vise is needed to hold anything being worked on.

A tap and die set might be something you've never needed, but you will eventually. It's a good rule, when everything is apart, to clean-up all threads, on bolts, screws and threaded holes. Also, you'll likely run across a situation in which stripped threads will be encountered. The tap and die set will handle that for you.

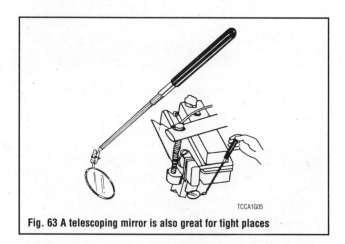

Fig. 63 A telescoping mirror is also great for tight places

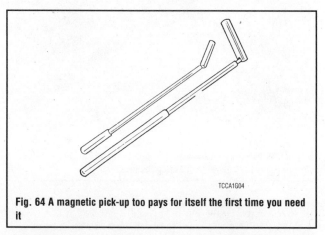

Fig. 64 A magnetic pick-up too pays for itself the first time you need it

Fig. 65 Two good tap and die sets; US measure (left) and metric

Fig. 66 A set of drill bits and a set of screw extractors

Fig. 67 A really handy tool is the nut splitter. When a frozen nut simply won't budge, use one of these

Gasket scrapers are just what you'd think, tools made for scraping old gasket material off of parts. You don't absolutely need one. Old gasket material can be removed with a putty knife or single edge razor blade. However, putty knives may not be sharp enough for some really stubborn gaskets and razor blades have a knack of breaking just when you don't want them to, inevitably slicing the nearest body part! As the old saying goes, "always use the proper tool for the job". If you're going to use a razor to scrape a gasket, be sure to always use a blade holder.

Putty knives really do have a use in an ATV repair shop. Just because you remove all the bolts from a component sealed with a gasket doesn't mean it's going to come off. Most of the time, the gasket and sealer will hold it tightly. Lightly driving a putty knife at various points between the two parts will break the seal without damage to the parts.

A small — 8-10 inches (20–25 centimeters) long — prybar is extremely useful for removing stuck parts. NEVER, NEVER, use a screwdriver as a prybar! Screwdrivers are not meant for prying. Screwdrivers, used for prying, can break, sending the broken shaft flying!

Screw/bolt extractors are used for removing broken bolts or studs that have broke off flush with the surface of the part.

SPECIALTY TOOLS

▶ See Figure 68

Almost every ATV (or motor vehicle) around today requires AT LEAST one special tool to perform certain tasks. In most cases, these tools are specially designed to overcome some unique problem or to fit on some oddly sized component.

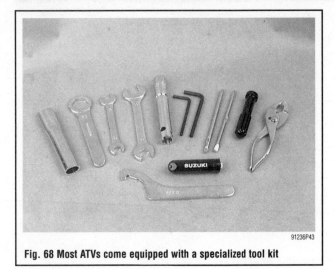

Fig. 68 Most ATVs come equipped with a specialized tool kit

When manufacturers go through the trouble of making a special tool, it is usually necessary to use it to assure that the job will be done right. A special tool might be designed to make a job easier, or it might be used to keep you from damaging or breaking a part.

Don't worry, MOST basic maintenance procedures can either be performed without any special tools OR, because the tools must be used for such basic things, they are commonly available for a reasonable price. It is usually just the low production, highly specialized tools (like a super thin 7-point star-shaped socket capable of 150 ft. lbs. =[203 Nm=] of torque that is used only on the crankshaft nut of the limited production what-dya-callit ATV) that tend to be outrageously expensive and hard to find. Luckily, you will probably never need such a tool.

Special tools can be as inexpensive and simple as an adjustable spanner wrench (which are used on many ATV's to adjust preload on the shocks) or as complicated as an adjustable axle measurement tool. A few common specialty tools are listed here, but check with your dealer or with other riders of your type of ATV for help in determining if there are any special tools for YOUR particular model. There is an added advantage is seeking advice from other riders, chances are they may have already found not only what special tool you will need, but how to get it cheaper.

Air (Tire Pressure) Gauge

♦ See Figures 69, 70 and 71

Ok, maybe this isn't a SPECIALTY tool, but it is more important to an ATV owner than it is to most other people. We all know people who too frequently

Fig. 69 ATV tires use very little air pressure . . .

Fig. 70 . . . and require a special gauge to obtain an accurate reading

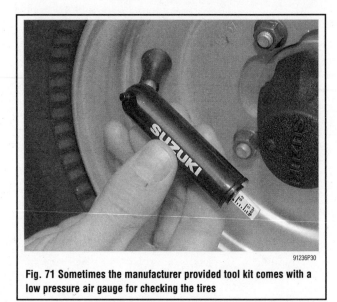

Fig. 71 Sometimes the manufacturer provided tool kit comes with a low pressure air gauge for checking the tires

ignore the air in their car's tires (perhaps someone reading this is even guilty). BUT, on an ATV, your tires are your BEST FRIENDS. Treat them well and check the air very often. Keep an accurate tire gauge handy at all times (especially when you travel long distances).

Pressure gauges come in various styles. The pencil type gauge fits just about all wheels and is small enough to keep with you at all times. We prefer dial gauges around the shop. Most are equipped with an air bleed, which makes setting tire pressures a snap. You start by adding some air to a tire. Then, once the gauge is held onto the air valve, you can use the bleed to lower pressure until the desired setting is reached.

Battery Testers

The best way to test a non-sealed battery is using a hydrometer to check the specific gravity of the acid. Luckily, these are usually very inexpensive and are available at most part stores. Just be careful because the larger ones available at many automotive stores are usually designed for larger, automotive batteries and may require more acid than you will be able to draw from the battery cell. Smaller testers (usually a short, squeeze bulb type) will require less acid and should work on most ATV batteries.

Electronic testers are available (and are often necessary to tell if a sealed battery is usable) but these are usually more than most DIYer's are willing to spend. Luckily, many auto part stores have them on hand and are willing to test your battery for you.

Battery Chargers

▶ **See Figure 72**

If you are a weekend warrior and don't ride every day (or at least every week), then you will most likely want to buy a battery charger to keep your battery fresh. There are many types available, from low amperage trickle chargers to electronically controlled battery maintenance tools which monitor the battery voltage to prevent over or undercharging. This last type is especially useful if you store your ATV for any length of time (such as during the severe winter months found in many Northern climates).

Even if you use your ATV on a regular basis, you will eventually need a battery charger. Remember that most batteries are shipped dry and in a partial charged state. Before a new battery can be put into service it must be filled AND properly charged. Failure to properly charge a battery (which was shipped dry) before it is put into service will prevent it from ever reaching a fully charged state.

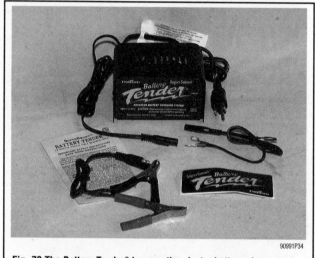

90991P34

Fig. 72 The Battery Tender® is more than just a battery charger, when left connected, it keeps your battery fully charged

Carburetor Synchronization Tool

▶ **See Figure 73**

If your ATV has more than one carburetor (rare), then you'll eventually find a need for a carburetor synchronization tool. Most carb sync tools take the form of

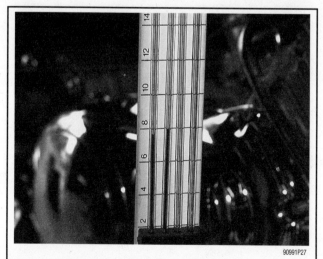

90991P27

Fig. 73 This carburetor sync tool (the mercury tube-type) can be used on ATVs with two or more cylinders

vacuum gauges (either mercury tube types or the traditional calibrated dial-type). They are connected to vacuum ports on the individual carburetors or intake manifolds in order to measure the amount of vacuum present at each. By adjusting the carburetor balance screw(s) while watching the sync tool, you can make sure each carburetor runs its cylinder(s) at the same speed as the others.

Chain Breaker/Link Pin Tool

▶ **See Figures 74, 75, 76 and 77**

If your ATV uses a chain final drive, you are probably going to want to buy a chain service tool set. These kits usually consist of a combination, chain breaker, chain link removal and link installation tool. Essentially the tools are usually high strength, threaded presses or c-clamps with the appropriate adapters to enable you to perform the necessary chain service.

➡ **If your OE and replacement chains use master links, then you can USUALLY get away without this tool, but it still makes master link installation A LOT easier on many models.**

Chain Cleaner/Oiler Tool

This is another tool that although it is not absolutely necessary, it can be VERY handy for riders whose ATV's use a chain final drive. There are various

91235P60

Fig. 74 A chain breaker grabs the outside of the link . . .

91235P61

Fig. 75 . . . then presses the link pin through . . .

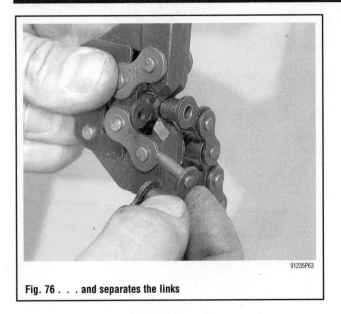

Fig. 76 . . . and separates the links

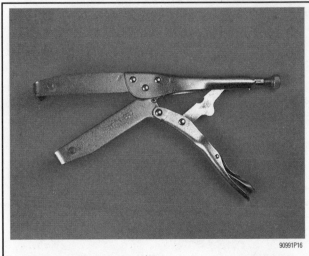

Fig. 78 This clutch basket tool is like a pair of locking pliers that met a spanner wrench . . .

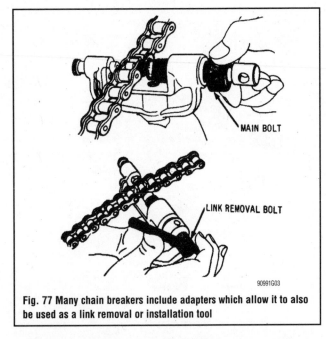

Fig. 77 Many chain breakers include adapters which allow it to also be used as a link removal or installation tool

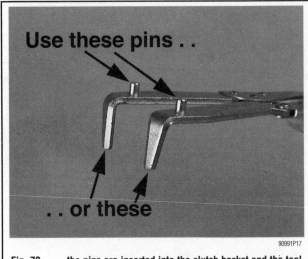

Fig. 79 . . . the pins are inserted into the clutch basket and the tool is held to keep the basket from turning

types available, but many are designed to scrub the chain using a stiff bristled brush, while encasing a few links of the chain at a time to give a mess free spray area for chain oiling.

Clutch Basket Tool

▶ See Figures 78 and 79

Mutli-disc clutch removal (not a basic maintenance item, but they do wear out) will usually require some sort of tool to hold the clutch basket assembly while the fasteners are removed. For many ATV's, the tool is similar to a spanner in that it is a pinned adjustable wrench which keeps the basket from turning. A different type of tool is more like an automotive lockplate tool (the reverse of a puller) that compresses and holds the disks.

ATV Jack/Lift

▶ See Figures 80, 81, 82 and 83

Most of the time, you may never have a need for one of these, but wouldn't it be nice to stand or sit comfortably while changing a bent axle? Of course, price is always a factor here. Good Ol' fashion plastic milk crates work just fine for supporting the rear end of your ride while you change wheels.

Fig. 80 Automotive jack stands can also be used to support your ATV, but won't provide a good work height

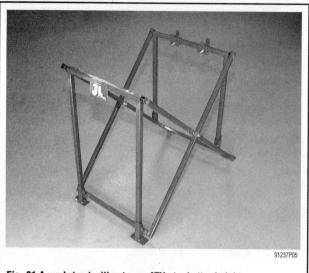

Fig. 81 A workstand will put your ATV at a better height . . .

91237P05

Fig. 82 . . . making maintenance and repair much easier

91237P08

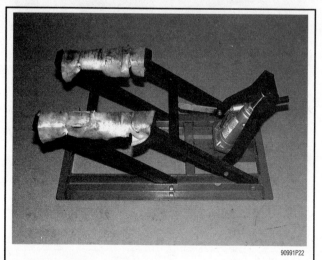

Fig. 83 There are many types of lifts on the market for home use (this is a very basic one)

90991P22

Now most people are not going to be able to justify the cost of a pneumatic platform lift (like the ones you see in your local shop's workbay). But, the good news is that because so many people find the need for these, a lot of companies have come up with RELATIVELY inexpensive jacks that will serve the purpose sufficiently.

When purchasing a lift/workstand, look for one with handy features such as heavy-duty casters (which allow it to be easily rolled around the work area) AND one with some form of protective rubber on the lift points (to help protect the frame). It is also good for the ends of the lift arms to contain raised stops which will prevent the ATV from sliding off the end while you are working on it. The model pictured did not have protective pads (so we added some foam using wire ties . . . not the best solution, but it works).

The important thing to keep in mind with a lift is to make sure that the ATV is well balanced and stable on the lift. A pair of automotive jack stands can be used to provide additional stability to your ATV while it is on the stand (if it is a low type). And of course, the usual safety precautions must be observed to keep your ATV from falling over and getting damaged, or worse, injuring you.

Lift Precautions

• Thoroughly read the lift manufacturer's instructions before attempting use, and be sure to follow them closely when you do.

• Whenever possible secure the ATV, either using ratcheting tie-down straps across the frame and around the lift (once it's raised and in position), or by using automotive jack stands under various frame points (or other large metal parts which are directly bolted to the frame).

• Use extra caution when levering or hammering on a part (not that you want to be hammering your ride much, but a rubber mallet can work wonders now and again).

• Do not sit on your ATV when it is on a lift. The extra weight could cause the lift to give, or shift the center of gravity, causing both you and your ride to come crashing down (causing massive amounts of damage and grief).

• Be careful not to bump into the ATV when it is on the lift to make sure you don't tip it over (also causing massive amounts of damage and grief).

Spanner Wrench

♦ See Figure 84

A spanner is different than a normal wrench in that it typically uses 2 or more tabs that are placed within a slot and used to turn the shock sleeve. As mentioned earlier, a spanner wrench is required to adjust the shock pre-load on many ATV's. There are various types and sizes of spanners available, so make sure the one you are about to buy fits your shocks. Check the tool kit before purchasing one, because they are often (but not always) included in the tool kit that comes with your ATV.

91236P35

Fig. 84 A spanner wrench is required to adjust the preload on ATV shocks

Measuring Tools

Eventually, you are going to have to measure something whether it is the thickness of a brake pad/rotor or the amount of play in a chain or drive belt. To do this, you will need at least a few precision tools in addition to the special tools mentioned earlier.

MICROMETERS & CALIPERS

Micrometers and calipers are devices used to make extremely precise measurements. The simple truth is that you really won't have the need for many of these items just for simple maintenance. You will probably want to have at least one precision tool such as an outside caliper to measure rotors or brake pads, but that should be sufficient to most basic maintenance procedures.

Should you decide on becoming more involved in ATV mechanics, such as with repair or rebuilding, then these tools will become very important. The success of any rebuild is dependent, to a great extent on the ability to check the size and fit of components as specified by the manufacturer. These measurements are made in thousandths and ten-thousandths of an inch.

Outside Micrometers

▶ See Figure 85

Outside micrometers can be used to check the thickness parts such as the brake rotors. They are also used during many rebuild and repair procedures to measure the diameter of components such as the pistons from a caliper or wheel cylinder. The most common type of micrometer reads in 1/1000 of an inch. Micrometers that use a vernier scale can estimate to 1/10 of an inch.

A micrometer is an instrument made up of a precisely machined spindle which is rotated in a fixed nut, opening and closing the distance between the end of the spindle and a fixed anvil.

To make a measurement, you back off the spindle until you can place the piece to be measured between the spindle and anvil. You then rotate the spindle until the part is contacted by both the spindle and anvil. The measurement is then found by reading the gradations in the handle of the micrometer.

Here's the hard part. we'll try to explain how to read a micrometer. The spindle is threaded. Most micrometers use a thread pitch of 40 threads per inch. One complete revolution of the spindle moves the spindle toward or away from the anvil 0.025 in. (¼₀ in.).

The fixed part of the handle (called, the sleeve) is marked with 40 gradations per inch of handle length, so each line is 0.025 in. apart. Okay so far?

Every 4th line is marked with a number. The first long line marked 1 represents 0.100 in., the second is 0.200 in., and so on.

The part of the handle that turns is called the thimble. The beveled end of the thimble is marked with gradations, each of which corresponds to 0.001 in. and, usually, every 5th line is numbered.

Turn the thimble until the 0 lines up with the 0 on the sleeve. Now, rotate the thimble one complete revolution and look at the sleeve. You'll see that one complete thimble revolution moved the thimble 0.025 in. down the sleeve.

To read the micrometer, multiply the number of gradations exposed on the sleeve by 0.025 and add that to the number of thousandths indicated by the thimble line that is lined up with the horizontal line on the sleeve. So, if you've measured a part and there are 6 vertical gradations exposed on the sleeve and the 7th gradation on the thimble is lined up with the horizontal line on the sleeve, the thickness of the part is 0.157 in. (6 x 0.025 = 0.150 . Add to that 0.007 representing the 7 lines on the thimble and you get 0.157). See?

If you didn't understand that, try the instructions that come with the micrometer or ask someone that knows, to show you how to work it. Also, if you didn't understand . . . don't worry. We said you probably won't ever need this for basic maintenance.

Inside Micrometers

Inside micrometers are used to measure the distance between two parallel surfaces. For example, in engine rebuilding work, the inside mike measures cylinder bore wear and taper. Inside mikes are graduated the same way as outside mikes and are read the same way as well.

Remember that an inside mike must be absolutely perpendicular to the work being measured. When you measure with an inside mike, rock the mike gently from side to side and tip it back and forth slightly so that you span the widest part of the bore. Just to be on the safe side, take several readings. It takes a certain amount of experience to work any mike with confidence.

Metric Micrometers

Metric micrometers are read in the same way as inch micrometers, except that the measurements are in millimeters. Each line on the main scale equals 1 mm. Each fifth line is stamped 5, 10, 15, and so on. Each line on the thimble scale equals 0.01 mm. It will take a little practice, but if you can read an inch mike, you can read a metric mike.

Inside and Outside Calipers

▶ See Figure 86

Inside and outside calipers are useful devices to have if you need to measure something quickly and precise measurement is not necessary. Simply take the reading and then hold the calipers on an accurate steel rule.

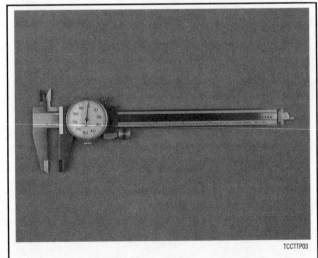

TCCTTP03

Fig. 86 Outside calipers are fast and easy ways to measure pads or rotors

DIAL INDICATORS

A dial indicator is a gauge that utilizes a dial face and a needle to register measurements. There is a movable contact arm on the dial indicator. When the

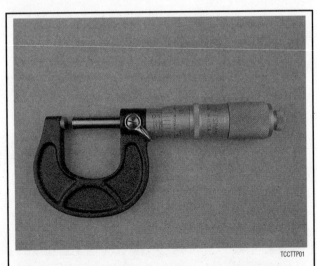

TCCTTP01

Fig. 85 Outside micrometers can be used to measure bake components including rotors, pads and pistons

arms moves, the needle rotates on the dial. Dial indicators are calibrated to show readings in thousandths of an inch and typically, are used to measure end-play and runout on various parts of an ATV. As for maintenance, they may be used to check the end-play on the wheels, and they can also be used to check for warpage (runout) on the brake rotors.

Dial indicators are quite easy to use, although they are relatively expensive. A variety of mounting devices are available so that the indicator can be used in a number of situations. Make certain that the contact arm is always parallel to the movement of the work being measured.

TELESCOPING GAUGES

A telescope gauge is used during rebuilding procedures (NOT usually basic maintenance) to measure the inside of bores. It can take the place of an inside mike for some of these jobs. Simply insert the gauge in the hole to be measured and lock the plungers after they have contacted the walls. Remove the tool and measure across the plungers with an outside micrometer.

DEPTH GAUGES

▶ **See Figure 87**

A depth gauge can be inserted into a bore or other small hole to determine exactly how deep it is. The most common use on maintenance items would be to check the depth of a rivet head (on riveted style brake pads) or to check tire depth. Some outside calipers contain a built-in depth gauge so money can be saved by just buying one tool.

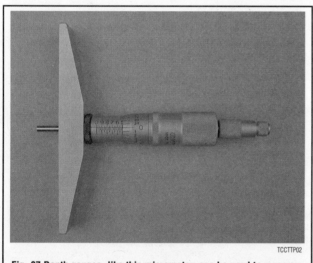

Fig. 87 Depth gauges, like this micrometer, can be used to measure the amount of pad or shoe remaining above a rivet

Electric Power Tools

▶ **See Figures 88 and 89**

Power tools are most often associated with woodworking. However, there are a few which are very helpful in maintenance and repair.

The most common and most useful power tool is the bench grinder. If you get serious about maintenance and repair, then you will eventually want a grinder with a grinding stone on one side and a wire brush wheel on the other. The brush wheel is indispensable for cleaning parts and the stone can be used to remove rough surfaces and for reshaping, where necessary.

Almost as useful as the bench grinder is the drill. Drills can come in very handy when a stripped or broken fastener is encountered.

Power ratchets and impact wrenches can come in very handy. Power ratchets can save a lot of time and muscle when removing and installing long bolts or nuts on long studs, especially where there is little room to swing a manual ratchet. Impact wrenches can be invaluable especially with frozen bolts, screws

Fig. 88 Three types of common power tools. Left to right: a hand-held grinder, drill and impact wrench

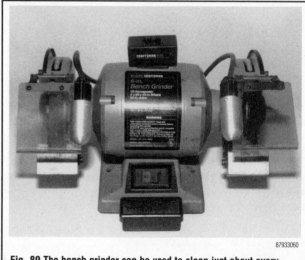

Fig. 89 The bench grinder can be used to clean just about everything

with partially damaged heads or on spinning shafts, when it is difficult or impossible to hold the shaft. Let's be real for a second: will you actually need them for maintenance? probably not. But, when you finally do need them one day, BOY WILL YOU BE GLAD YOU HAD EM'.

➡**One last thought before you buy any electric tools. If you plan on buying an air compressor (and there are many reasons why you should at least think about it), then you might save money on tools by purchasing air tools instead of electric. Shop around and compare prices to your needs, then make your decision.**

Air Tools and Compressors

▶ **See Figures 90 and 91**

Air-powered tools are usually not necessary for simple maintenance procedures. They are, however, useful for speeding up many jobs and for general clean-up of parts. If you don't have air tools, and you want them, be prepared for an initial outlay of a money.

The first thing you need is a compressor. Compressors are available in electrically driven and gas engine driven models. As long as you have electricity, you don't need a gas engine driven type.

The common shop-type air compressor is a pump mounted on a tank. The pump compresses air and forces it into the tank where it is stored until you need it. The compressor automatically turns the pump on when the air pressure in the tank falls below a certain preset level.

There are all kinds of air powered tools, including ratchets, impact wrenches, saws, drills, sprayers, nailers, scrapers, riveters, grinders and sanders. In general, air powered tools are usually cheaper than their electric counterparts (but be careful, there are some cheap electric tools available that might not last as long as comparably priced air tools).

When deciding what size compressor unit you need, you'll be driven by two factors: the Pounds per Square Inch (PSI) capacity of the unit and the deliver rate in Cubic Feet per Minute (CFM). For example, most air powered ratchets require 90 psi at 4 to 5 cfm to operate at peak efficiency. Grinders and saws may require up to 7 cfm at 90 psi. So, before buying the compressor unit, decide what types of tools you'll want so that you don't short-change yourself on the compressor purchase.

If you decide that a compressor and air tools isn't for you, you can have the benefit of air pressure rather cheaply. Purchase an air storage tank, available in sizes up to 20 gallons at most retail stores that sell auto products. These storage tanks can safely store air pressure up to 125 psi and come with a high pressure nozzle for cleaning things and an air chuck for filling tires. The tank can be filled using the common tire-type air compressor, or even at the corner gas station (with their tire pressure hose).

Fig. 90 This compressor operates off ordinary house current and provides all the air pressure you'll need

87933062

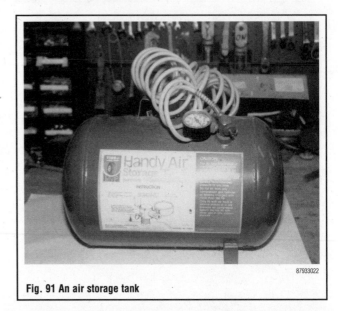

Fig. 91 An air storage tank

87933022

FASTENERS, MEASUREMENTS AND CONVERSIONS

Bolts, Nuts and Other Threaded Retainers

▶ See Figures 92, 93, 94 and 95

Although there are a great variety of fasteners found in the modern ATV, the most commonly used retainer is the threaded fastener (nuts, bolts, screws, studs, etc). Most threaded retainers may be reused, provided that they are not damaged in use or during the repair. Some retainers (such as stretch bolts or torque prevailing nuts) are designed to deform when tightened or in use and should not be reinstalled.

➡ Most ATV's use recessed socket head fasteners which require hex key or Torx® drivers.

Whenever possible, we will note any special retainers which should be replaced during a procedure. But you should always inspect the condition of a retainer when it is removed and you should replace any that show signs of damage. Check all threads for rust or corrosion which can increase the torque necessary to achieve the desired clamp load for which that fastener was originally selected. Additionally, be sure that the driver surface of the fastener has not been compromised by rounding or other damage. In some cases a driver surface may become only partially rounded, allowing the driver to catch in only one direction. In many of these occurrences, a fastener may be installed and tightened, but the driver would not be able to grip and loosen the fastener again. (This could lead to frustration down the line should that component ever need to be disassembled again).

If you must replace a fastener, whether due to design or damage, you must ALWAYS be sure to use the proper replacement. In all cases, a retainer of the same design, material and strength should be used. Markings on the heads of most bolts will help determine the proper strength of the fastener. The same material, thread and pitch must be selected to assure proper installation and safe operation of the vehicle afterwards.

Thread gauges are available to help measure a bolt or stud's thread. Most part or hardware stores keep gauges available to help you select the proper size. In a pinch, you can use another nut or bolt for a thread gauge. If the bolt you are replacing is not too badly damaged, you can select a match by finding another bolt which will thread in its place. If you find a nut which threads properly onto the damaged bolt, then use that nut to help select the replacement bolt. If however, the bolt you are replacing is so badly damaged (broken or drilled out) that its threads cannot be used as a gauge, you might start by looking for another bolt (from the same assembly or a similar location on your ATV) which will thread into the damaged bolt's mounting. If so, the other bolt can be used to select a nut; the nut can then be used to select the replacement bolt.

In all cases, be absolutely sure you have selected the proper replacement. Don't be shy, you can always ask the store clerk for help.

✳✳ WARNING

Be aware that when you find a bolt with damaged threads, you may also find the nut or drilled hole it was threaded into has also been

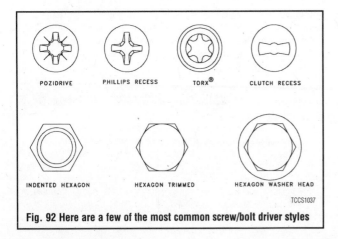

POZIDRIVE PHILLIPS RECESS TORX® CLUTCH RECESS

INDENTED HEXAGON HEXAGON TRIMMED HEXAGON WASHER HEAD

TCCS1037

Fig. 92 Here are a few of the most common screw/bolt driver styles

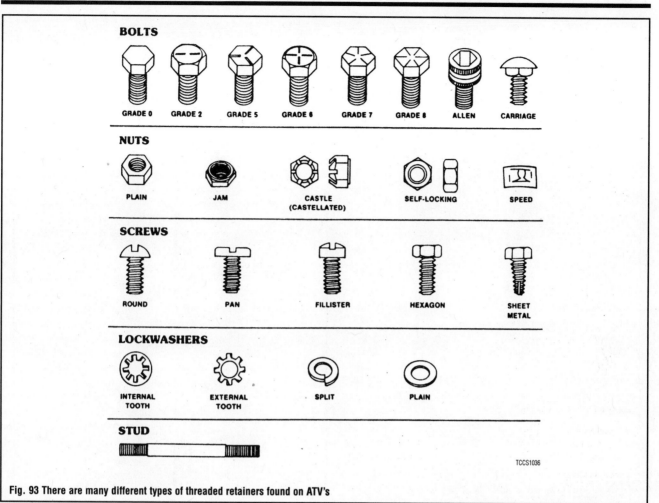

Fig. 93 There are many different types of threaded retainers found on ATV's

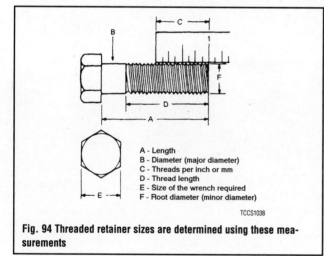

A - Length
B - Diameter (major diameter)
C - Threads per inch or mm
D - Thread length
E - Size of the wrench required
F - Root diameter (minor diameter)

TCCS1038

Fig. 94 Threaded retainer sizes are determined using these measurements

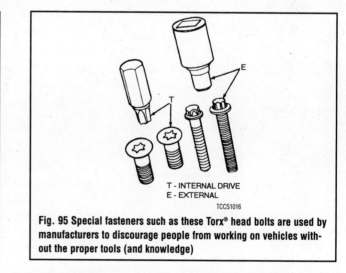

T - INTERNAL DRIVE
E - EXTERNAL

TCCS1016

Fig. 95 Special fasteners such as these Torx® head bolts are used by manufacturers to discourage people from working on vehicles without the proper tools (and knowledge)

damaged. If this is the case, you may have to drill and tap the hole, replace the nut or otherwise repair the threads. NEVER try to force a replacement bolt to fit into the damaged threads.

Torque

▶ See Figures 96 and 97

Torque is defined as the measurement of resistance to turning or rotating. It tends to twist a body about an axis of rotation. A common example of this would be tightening a threaded retainer such as a nut, bolt or screw. Measuring torque is one of the most common ways to help assure that a threaded retainer has been properly fastened.

When tightening a threaded fastener, torque is applied in three distinct areas, the head, the bearing surface and the clamp load. About 50 percent of the measured torque is used in overcoming bearing friction. This is the friction between the bearing surface of the bolt head, screw head or nut face and the base material or washer (the surface on which the fastener is rotating). Approximately 40 percent of the applied torque is used in overcoming thread friction. This leaves only about 10 percent of the applied torque to develop a useful clamp load (the force which holds a joint together). This means that friction can account for as much as 90 percent of the applied torque on a fastener.

	Mark	Class		Mark	Class
Hexagon head bolt	 Bolt head No. 4 — 5 — 6 — 7 — 8 — 9 — 10 — 11 —	4T 5T 6T 7T 8T 9T 10T 11T	Stud bolt	No mark	4T
	 No mark	4T			
Hexagon flange bolt w/ washer hexagon bolt	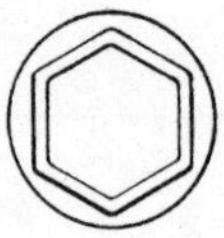 No mark	4T		Grooved	6T
Hexagon head bolt	 Two protruding lines	5T			
Hexagon flange bolt w/ washer hexagon bolt	 Two protruding lines	6T	Welded bolt		
Hexagon head bolt	 Three protruding lines	7T			4T
Hexagon head bolt	 Four protruding lines	8T			

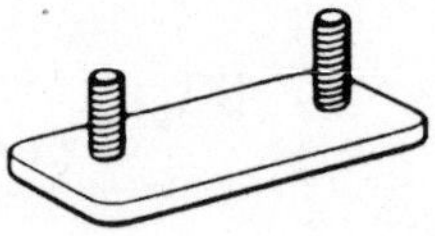

TCCS1240

Fig. 96 Determining bolt strength of metric fasteners—NOTE: this is a typical bolt marking system, but there is no worldwide standard

Class	Diameter mm	Pitch mm	Specified torque					
			Hexagon head bolt			Hexagon flange bolt		
			N·m	kgf·cm	ft·lbf	N·m	kgf·cm	ft·lbf
4T	6	1	5	55	48 in.·lbf	6	60	52 in.·lbf
	8	1.25	12.5	130	9	14	145	10
	10	1.25	26	260	19	29	290	21
	12	1.25	47	480	35	53	540	39
	14	1.5	74	760	55	84	850	61
	16	1.5	115	1,150	83	—	—	—
5T	6	1	6.5	65	56 in.·lbf	7.5	75	65 in.·lbf
	8	1.25	15.5	160	12	17.5	175	13
	10	1.25	32	330	24	36	360	26
	12	1.25	59	600	43	65	670	48
	14	1.5	91	930	67	100	1,050	76
	16	1.5	140	1,400	101	—	—	—
6T	6	1	8	80	69 in.·lbf	9	90	78 in.·lbf
	8	1.25	19	195	14	21	210	15
	10	1.25	39	400	29	44	440	32
	12	1.25	71	730	53	80	810	59
	14	1.5	110	1,100	80	125	1,250	90
	16	1.5	170	1,750	127	—	—	—
7T	6	1	10.5	110	8	12	120	9
	8	1.25	25	260	19	28	290	21
	10	1.25	52	530	38	58	590	43
	12	1.25	95	970	70	105	1,050	76
	14	1.5	145	1,500	108	165	1,700	123
	16	1.5	230	2,300	166	—	—	—
8T	8	1.25	29	300	22	33	330	24
	10	1.25	61	620	45	68	690	50
	12	1.25	110	1,100	80	120	1,250	90
9T	8	1.25	34	340	25	37	380	27
	10	1.25	70	710	51	78	790	57
	12	1.25	125	1,300	94	140	1,450	105
10T	8	1.25	38	390	28	42	430	31
	10	1.25	78	800	58	88	890	64
	12	1.25	140	1,450	105	155	1,600	116
11T	8	1.25	42	430	31	47	480	35
	10	1.25	87	890	64	97	990	72
	12	1.25	155	1,600	116	175	1,800	130

TCCS1241

Fig. 97 Typical bolt torques for metric fasteners—WARNING: use only as a guide

Standard and Metric Measurements

▶ See Figure 98

Specifications are often used to help you determine the condition of various components on your ATV, or to assist you in their installation. Some of the most common measurements include length (in. or cm/mm), torque (ft. lbs., inch lbs. or Nm) and pressure (psi, in. Hg, kPa or mm Hg).

In some cases, that value may not be conveniently measured with what is available in your toolbox. Luckily, many of the measuring devices which are available today will have two scales so Standard or Metric measurements may

easily be taken. If any of the various measuring tools which are available to you do not contain the same scale as listed in your ATV's specifications, use the accompanying conversion factors to determine the proper value.

The conversion factor chart is used by taking the given specification and multiplying it by the necessary conversion factor. For instance, looking at the first line, if you have a measurement in inches such as "free-play should be 2 in." but your ruler reads only in millimeters, multiply 2 in. by the conversion factor of 25.4 to get the metric equivalent of 50.8mm. Likewise, if the specification was given only in a Metric measurement, for example in Newton Meters (Nm), then look at the center column first. If the measurement is 100 Nm, multiply it by the conversion factor of 0.738 to get 73.8 ft. lbs.

CONVERSION FACTORS

LENGTH–DISTANCE

Inches (in.)	x 25.4	= Millimeters (mm)	x .0394	= Inches
Feet (ft.)	x .305	= Meters (m)	x 3.281	= Feet
Miles	x 1.609	= Kilometers (km)	x .0621	= Miles

VOLUME

Cubic Inches (in3)	x 16.387	= Cubic Centimeters	x .061	= in3
IMP Pints (IMP pt.)	x .568	= Liters (L)	x 1.76	= IMP pt.
IMP Quarts (IMP qt.)	x 1.137	= Liters (L)	x .88	= IMP qt.
IMP Gallons (IMP gal.)	x 4.546	= Liters (L)	x .22	= IMP gal.
IMP Quarts (IMP qt.)	x 1.201	= US Quarts (US qt.)	x .833	= IMP qt.
IMP Gallons (IMP gal.)	x 1.201	= US Gallons (US gal.)	x .833	= IMP gal.
Fl. Ounces	x 29.573	= Milliliters	x .034	= Ounces
US Pints (US pt.)	x .473	= Liters (L)	x 2.113	= Pints
US Quarts (US qt.)	x .946	= Liters (L)	x 1.057	= Quarts
US Gallons (US gal.)	x 3.785	= Liters (L)	x .264	= Gallons

MASS–WEIGHT

Ounces (oz.)	x 28.35	= Grams (g)	x .035	= Ounces
Pounds (lb.)	x .454	= Kilograms (kg)	x 2.205	= Pounds

PRESSURE

Pounds Per Sq. In. (psi)	x 6.895	= Kilopascals (kPa)	x .145	= psi
Inches of Mercury (Hg)	x .4912	= psi	x 2.036	= Hg
Inches of Mercury (Hg)	x 3.377	= Kilopascals (kPa)	x .2961	= Hg
Inches of Water (H_2O)	x .07355	= Inches of Mercury	x 13.783	= H_2O
Inches of Water (H_2O)	x .03613	= psi	x 27.684	= H_2O
Inches of Water (H_2O)	x .248	= Kilopascals (kPa)	x 4.026	= H_2O

TORQUE

Pounds–Force Inches (in–lb)	x .113	= Newton Meters (N·m)	x 8.85	= in–lb
Pounds–Force Feet (ft–lb)	x 1.356	= Newton Meters (N·m)	x .738	= ft–lb

VELOCITY

Miles Per Hour (MPH)	x 1.609	= Kilometers Per Hour (KPH)	x .621	= MPH

POWER

Horsepower (Hp)	x .745	= Kilowatts	x 1.34	= Horsepower

FUEL CONSUMPTION*

Miles Per Gallon IMP (MPG)	x .354	= Kilometers Per Liter (Km/L)
Kilometers Per Liter (Km/L)	x 2.352	= IMP MPG
Miles Per Gallon US (MPG)	x .425	= Kilometers Per Liter (Km/L)
Kilometers Per Liter (Km/L)	x 2.352	= US MPG

*It is common to covert from miles per gallon (mpg) to liters/100 kilometers (1/100 km), where mpg (IMP) x 1/100 km = 282 and mpg (US) x 1/100 km = 235.

TEMPERATURE

Degree Fahrenheit (°F)	= (°C x 1.8) + 32
Degree Celsius (°C)	= (°F − 32) x .56

TCCS1044

Fig. 98 Standard and metric conversion factors chart

ENGLISH TO METRIC CONVERSION: MASS (WEIGHT)

Current **mass** measurement is expressed in pounds and ounces (lbs. & ozs.). The metric unit of mass (or weight) is the kilogram (kg). Even although this table does not show conversion of masses (weights) larger than 15 lbs, it is easy to calculate larger units by following the data immediately below.

To convert ounces (oz.) to grams (g): multiply th number of ozs. by 28
To convert grams (g) to ounces (oz.): multiply the number of grams by .035

To convert pounds (lbs.) to kilograms (kg): multiply the number of lbs. by .45
To convert kilograms (kg) to pounds (lbs.): multiply the number of kilograms by 2.2

lbs	kg	lbs	kg	oz	kg	oz	kg
0.1	0.04	0.9	0.41	0.1	0.003	0.9	0.024
0.2	0.09	1	0.4	0.2	0.005	1	0.03
0.3	0.14	2	0.9	0.3	0.008	2	0.06
0.4	0.18	3	1.4	0.4	0.011	3	0.08
0.5	0.23	4	1.8	0.5	0.014	4	0.11
0.6	0.27	5	2.3	0.6	0.017	5	0.14
0.7	0.32	10	4.5	0.7	0.020	10	0.28
0.8	0.36	15	6.8	0.8	0.023	15	0.42

ENGLISH TO METRIC CONVERSION: TEMPERATURE

To convert Fahrenheit (°F) to Celsius (°C): take number of °F and subtract 32; multiply result by 5; divide result by 9

To convert Celsius (°C) to Fahrenheit (°F): take number of °C and multiply by 9; divide result by 5; add 32 to total

Fahrenheit (F)		Celsius (C)		Fahrenheit (F)		Celsius (C)		Fahrenheit (F)		Celsius (C)	
°F	°C	°C	°F	°F	°C	°C	°F	°F	°C	°C	°F
−40	−40	−38	−36.4	80	26.7	18	64.4	215	101.7	80	176
−35	−37.2	−36	−32.8	85	29.4	20	68	220	104.4	85	185
−30	−34.4	−34	−29.2	90	32.2	22	71.6	225	107.2	90	194
−25	−31.7	−32	−25.6	95	35.0	24	75.2	230	110.0	95	202
−20	−28.9	−30	−22	100	37.8	26	78.8	235	112.8	100	212
−15	−26.1	−28	−18.4	105	40.6	28	82.4	240	115.6	105	221
−10	−23.3	−26	−14.8	110	43.3	30	86	245	118.3	110	230
−5	−20.6	−24	−11.2	115	46.1	32	89.6	250	121.1	115	239
0	−17.8	−22	−7.6	120	48.9	34	93.2	255	123.9	120	248
1	−17.2	−20	−4	125	51.7	36	96.8	260	126.6	125	257
2	−16.7	−18	−0.4	130	54.4	38	100.4	265	129.4	130	266
3	−16.1	−16	3.2	135	57.2	40	104	270	132.2	135	275
4	−15.6	−14	6.8	140	60.0	42	107.6	275	135.0	140	284
5	−15.0	−12	10.4	145	62.8	44	112.2	280	137.8	145	293
10	−12.2	−10	14	150	65.6	46	114.8	285	140.6	150	302
15	−9.4	−8	17.6	155	68.3	48	118.4	290	143.3	155	311
20	−6.7	−6	21.2	160	71.1	50	122	295	146.1	160	320
25	−3.9	−4	24.8	165	73.9	52	125.6	300	148.9	165	329
30	−1.1	−2	28.4	170	76.7	54	129.2	305	151.7	170	338
35	1.7	0	32	175	79.4	56	132.8	310	154.4	175	347
40	4.4	2	35.6	180	82.2	58	136.4	315	157.2	180	356
45	7.2	4	39.2	185	85.0	60	140	320	160.0	185	365
50	10.0	6	42.8	190	87.8	62	143.6	325	162.8	190	374
55	12.8	8	46.4	195	90.6	64	147.2	330	165.6	195	383
60	15.6	10	50	200	93.3	66	150.8	335	168.3	200	392
65	18.3	12	53.6	205	96.1	68	154.4	340	171.1	205	401
70	21.1	14	57.2	210	98.9	70	158	345	173.9	210	410
75	23.9	16	60.8	212	100.0	75	167	350	176.7	215	414

TCCS1C01

ENGLISH TO METRIC CONVERSION: LENGTH

To convert inches (ins.) to millimeters (mm): multiply number of inches by 25.4

To convert millimeters (mm) to inches (ins.): multiply number of millimeters by .04

Inches		Decimals	Milli-meters	Inches to millimeters inches	mm	Inches		Decimals	Milli-meters	Inches to millimeters inches	mm
	1/64	0.051625	0.3969	0.0001	0.00254		33/64	0.515625	13.0969	0.6	15.24
	1/32	0.03125	0.7937	0.0002	0.00508	17/32		0.53125	13.4937	0.7	17.78
	3/64	0.046875	1.1906	0.0003	0.00762		35/64	0.546875	13.8906	0.8	20.32
1/16		0.0625	1.5875	0.0004	0.01016	9/16		0.5625	14.2875	0.9	22.86
	5/64	0.078125	1.9844	0.0005	0.01270		37/64	0.578125	14.6844	1	25.4
	3/32	0.09375	2.3812	0.0006	0.01524	19/32		0.59375	15.0812	2	50.8
	7/64	0.109375	2.7781	0.0007	0.01778		39/64	0.609375	15.4781	3	76.2
1/8		0.125	3.1750	0.0008	0.02032	5/8		0.625	15.8750	4	101.6
	9/64	0.140625	3.5719	0.0009	0.02286		41/64	0.640625	16.2719	5	127.0
	5/32	0.15625	3.9687	0.001	0.0254	21/32		0.65625	16.6687	6	152.4
	11/64	0.171875	4.3656	0.002	0.0508		43/64	0.671875	17.0656	7	177.8
3/16		0.1875	4.7625	0.003	0.0762	11/16		0.6875	17.4625	8	203.2
	13/64	0.203125	5.1594	0.004	0.1016		45/64	0.703125	17.8594	9	228.6
	7/32	0.21875	5.5562	0.005	0.1270	23/32		0.71875	18.2562	10	254.0
	15/64	0.234375	5.9531	0.006	0.1524		47/64	0.734375	18.6531	11	279.4
1/4		0.25	6.3500	0.007	0.1778	3/4		0.75	19.0500	12	304.8
	17/64	0.265625	6.7469	0.008	0.2032		49/64	0.765625	19.4469	13	330.2
	9/32	0.28125	7.1437	0.009	0.2286	25/32		0.78125	19.8437	14	355.6
	19/64	0.296875	7.5406	0.01	0.254		51/64	0.796875	20.2406	15	381.0
5/16		0.3125	7.9375	0.02	0.508	13/16		0.8125	20.6375	16	406.4
	21/64	0.328125	8.3344	0.03	0.762		53/64	0.828125	21.0344	17	431.8
	11/32	0.34375	8.7312	0.04	1.016	27/32		0.84375	21.4312	18	457.2
	23/64	0.359375	9.1281	0.05	1.270		55/64	0.859375	21.8281	19	482.6
3/8		0.375	9.5250	0.06	1.524	7/8		0.875	22.2250	20	508.0
	25/64	0.390625	9.9219	0.07	1.778		57/64	0.890625	22.6219	21	533.4
	13/32	0.40625	10.3187	0.08	2.032	29/32		0.90625	23.0187	22	558.8
	27/64	0.421875	10.7156	0.09	2.286		59/64	0.921875	23.4156	23	584.2
7/16		0.4375	11.1125	0.1	2.54	15/16		0.9375	23.8125	24	609.6
	29/64	0.453125	11.5094	0.2	5.08		61/64	0.953125	24.2094	25	635.0
	15/32	0.46875	11.9062	0.3	7.62	31/32		0.96875	24.6062	26	660.4
	31/64	0.484375	12.3031	0.4	10.16		63/64	0.984375	25.0031	27	690.6
1/2		0.5	12.7000	0.5	12.70						

ENGLISH TO METRIC CONVERSION: TORQUE

To convert foot-pounds (ft. lbs.) to Newton-meters: multiply the number of ft. lbs. by 1.3

To convert inch-pounds (in. lbs.) to Newton-meters: multiply the number of in. lbs. by .11

in lbs	N-m	in lbs	N-m	in lbs	N-m	in lbs	N-m	in lbs	N-m
0.1	0.01	1	0.11	10	1.13	19	2.15	28	3.16
0.2	0.02	2	0.23	11	1.24	20	2.26	29	3.28
0.3	0.03	3	0.34	12	1.36	21	2.37	30	3.39
0.4	0.04	4	0.45	13	1.47	22	2.49	31	3.50
0.5	0.06	5	0.56	14	1.58	23	2.60	32	3.62
0.6	0.07	6	0.68	15	1.70	24	2.71	33	3.73
0.7	0.08	7	0.78	16	1.81	25	2.82	34	3.84
0.8	0.09	8	0.90	17	1.92	26	2.94	35	3.95
0.9	0.10	9	1.02	18	2.03	27	3.05	36	4.0

TCCS1C02

ENGLISH TO METRIC CONVERSION: TORQUE

Torque is now expressed as either foot-pounds (ft./lbs.) or inch-pounds (in./lbs.). The metric measurement unit for torque is the Newton-meter (Nm). This unit—the Nm—will be used for all SI metric torque references, both the present ft./lbs. and in./lbs.

ft lbs	N-m	ft lbs	N-m	ft lbs	N-m	ft lbs	N-m
0.1	0.1	33	44.7	74	100.3	115	155.9
0.2	0.3	34	46.1	75	101.7	116	157.3
0.3	0.4	35	47.4	76	103.0	117	158.6
0.4	0.5	36	48.8	77	104.4	118	160.0
0.5	0.7	37	50.7	78	105.8	119	161.3
0.6	0.8	38	51.5	79	107.1	120	162.7
0.7	1.0	39	52.9	80	108.5	121	164.0
0.8	1.1	40	54.2	81	109.8	122	165.4
0.9	1.2	41	55.6	82	111.2	123	166.8
1	1.3	42	56.9	83	112.5	124	168.1
2	2.7	43	58.3	84	113.9	125	169.5
3	4.1	44	59.7	85	115.2	126	170.8
4	5.4	45	61.0	86	116.6	127	172.2
5	6.8	46	62.4	87	118.0	128	173.5
6	8.1	47	63.7	88	119.3	129	174.9
7	9.5	48	65.1	89	120.7	130	176.2
8	10.8	49	66.4	90	122.0	131	177.6
9	12.2	50	67.8	91	123.4	132	179.0
10	13.6	51	69.2	92	124.7	133	180.3
11	14.9	52	70.5	93	126.1	134	181.7
12	16.3	53	71.9	94	127.4	135	183.0
13	17.6	54	73.2	95	128.8	136	184.4
14	18.9	55	74.6	96	130.2	137	185.7
15	20.3	56	75.9	97	131.5	138	187.1
16	21.7	57	77.3	98	132.9	139	188.5
17	23.0	58	78.6	99	134.2	140	189.8
18	24.4	59	80.0	100	135.6	141	191.2
19	25.8	60	81.4	101	136.9	142	192.5
20	27.1	61	82.7	102	138.3	143	193.9
21	28.5	62	84.1	103	139.6	144	195.2
22	29.8	63	85.4	104	141.0	145	196.6
23	31.2	64	86.8	105	142.4	146	198.0
24	32.5	65	88.1	106	143.7	147	199.3
25	33.9	66	89.5	107	145.1	148	200.7
26	35.2	67	90.8	108	146.4	149	202.0
27	36.6	68	92.2	109	147.8	150	203.4
28	38.0	69	93.6	110	149.1	151	204.7
29	39.3	70	94.9	111	150.5	152	206.1
30	40.7	71	96.3	112	151.8	153	207.4
31	42.0	72	97.6	113	153.2	154	208.8
32	43.4	73	99.0	114	154.6	155	210.2

TCCS1C03

ENGLISH TO METRIC CONVERSION: FORCE

Force is presently measured in pounds (lbs.). This type of measurement is used to measure spring pressure, specifically how many pounds it takes to compress a spring. Our present force unit (the pound) will be replaced in SI metric measurements by the Newton (N). This term will eventually see use in specifications for electric motor brush spring pressures, valve spring pressures, etc.

To convert pounds (lbs.) to Newton (N): multiply the number of lbs. by 4.45

lbs	N	lbs	N	lbs	N	oz	N
0.01	0.04	21	93.4	59	262.4	1	0.3
0.02	0.09	22	97.9	60	266.9	2	0.6
0.03	0.13	23	102.3	61	271.3	3	0.8
0.04	0.18	24	106.8	62	275.8	4	1.1
0.05	0.22	25	111.2	63	280.2	5	1.4
0.06	0.27	26	115.6	64	284.6	6	1.7
0.07	0.31	27	120.1	65	289.1	7	2.0
0.08	0.36	28	124.6	66	293.6	8	2.2
0.09	0.40	29	129.0	67	298.0	9	2.5
0.1	0.4	30	133.4	68	302.5	10	2.8
0.2	0.9	31	137.9	69	306.9	11	3.1
0.3	1.3	32	142.3	70	311.4	12	3.3
0.4	1.8	33	146.8	71	315.8	13	3.6
0.5	2.2	34	151.2	72	320.3	14	3.9
0.6	2.7	35	155.7	73	324.7	15	4.2
0.7	3.1	36	160.1	74	329.2	16	4.4
0.8	3.6	37	164.6	75	333.6	17	4.7
0.9	4.0	38	169.0	76	338.1	18	5.0
1	4.4	39	173.5	77	342.5	19	5.3
2	8.9	40	177.9	78	347.0	20	5.6
3	13.4	41	182.4	79	351.4	21	5.8
4	17.8	42	186.8	80	355.9	22	6.1
5	22.2	43	191.3	81	360.3	23	6.4
6	26.7	44	195.7	82	364.8	24	6.7
7	31.1	45	200.2	83	369.2	25	7.0
8	35.6	46	204.6	84	373.6	26	7.2
9	40.0	47	209.1	85	378.1	27	7.5
10	44.5	48	213.5	86	382.6	28	7.8
11	48.9	49	218.0	87	387.0	29	8.1
12	53.4	50	224.4	88	391.4	30	8.3
13	57.8	51	226.9	89	395.9	31	8.6
14	62.3	52	231.3	90	400.3	32	8.9
15	66.7	53	235.8	91	404.8	33	9.2
16	71.2	54	240.2	92	409.2	34	9.4
17	75.6	55	244.6	93	413.7	35	9.7
18	80.1	56	249.1	94	418.1	36	10.0
19	84.5	57	253.6	95	422.6	37	10.3
20	89.0	58	258.0	96	427.0	38	10.6

ENGLISH TO METRIC CONVERSION: LIQUID CAPACITY

Liquid or fluid capacity is presently expressed as pints, quarts or gallons, or a combination of all of these. In the metric system the liter (l) will become the basic unit. Fractions of a liter would be expressed as deciliters, centiliters, or most frequently (and commonly) as milliliters.

To convert pints (pts.) to liters (l): multiply the number of pints by .47
To convert liters (l) to pints (pts.): multiply the number of liters by 2.1
To convert quarts (qts.) to liters (l): multiply the number of quarts by .95

To convert liters (l) to quarts (qts.): multiply the number of liters by 1.06
To convert gallons (gals.) to liters (l): multiply the number of gallons by 3.8
To convert liters (l) to gallons (gals.): multiply the number of liters by .26

gals	liters	qts	liters	pts	liters
0.1	0.38	0.1	0.10	0.1	0.05
0.2	0.76	0.2	0.19	0.2	0.10
0.3	1.1	0.3	0.28	0.3	0.14
0.4	1.5	0.4	0.38	0.4	0.19
0.5	1.9	0.5	0.47	0.5	0.24
0.6	2.3	0.6	0.57	0.6	0.28
0.7	2.6	0.7	0.66	0.7	0.33
0.8	3.0	0.8	0.76	0.8	0.38
0.9	3.4	0.9	0.85	0.9	0.43
1	3.8	1	1.0	1	0.5
2	7.6	2	1.9	2	1.0
3	11.4	3	2.8	3	1.4
4	15.1	4	3.8	4	1.9
5	18.9	5	4.7	5	2.4
6	22.7	6	5.7	6	2.8
7	26.5	7	6.6	7	3.3
8	30.3	8	7.6	8	3.8
9	34.1	9	8.5	9	4.3
10	37.8	10	9.5	10	4.7
11	41.6	11	10.4	11	5.2
12	45.4	12	11.4	12	5.7
13	49.2	13	12.3	13	6.2
14	53.0	14	13.2	14	6.6
15	56.8	15	14.2	15	7.1
16	60.6	16	15.1	16	7.6
17	64.3	17	16.1	17	8.0
18	68.1	18	17.0	18	8.5
19	71.9	19	18.0	19	9.0
20	75.7	20	18.9	20	9.5
21	79.5	21	19.9	21	9.9
22	83.2	22	20.8	22	10.4
23	87.0	23	21.8	23	10.9
24	90.8	24	22.7	24	11.4
25	94.6	25	23.6	25	11.8
26	98.4	26	24.6	26	12.3
27	102.2	27	25.5	27	12.8
28	106.0	28	26.5	28	13.2
29	110.0	29	27.4	29	13.7
30	113.5	30	28.4	30	14.2

TCCS1C05

ENGLISH TO METRIC CONVERSION: PRESSURE

The basic unit of pressure measurement used today is expressed as pounds per square inch (psi). The metric unit for psi will be the kilopascal (kPa). This will apply to either fluid pressure or air pressure, and will be frequently seen in tire pressure readings, oil pressure specifications, fuel pump pressure, etc.

To convert pounds per square inch (psi) to kilopascals (kPa): multiply the number of psi by 6.89

Psi	kPa	Psi	kPa	Psi	kPa	Psi	kPa
0.1	0.7	37	255.1	82	565.4	127	875.6
0.2	1.4	38	262.0	83	572.3	128	882.5
0.3	2.1	39	268.9	84	579.2	129	889.4
0.4	2.8	40	275.8	85	586.0	130	896.3
0.5	3.4	41	282.7	86	592.9	131	903.2
0.6	4.1	42	289.6	87	599.8	132	910.1
0.7	4.8	43	296.5	88	606.7	133	917.0
0.8	5.5	44	303.4	89	613.6	134	923.9
0.9	6.2	45	310.3	90	620.5	135	930.8
1	6.9	46	317.2	91	627.4	136	937.7
2	13.8	47	324.0	92	634.3	137	944.6
3	20.7	48	331.0	93	641.2	138	951.5
4	27.6	49	337.8	94	648.1	139	958.4
5	34.5	50	344.7	95	655.0	140	965.2
6	41.4	51	351.6	96	661.9	141	972.2
7	48.3	52	358.5	97	668.8	142	979.0
8	55.2	53	365.4	98	675.7	143	985.9
9	62.1	54	372.3	99	682.6	144	992.8
10	69.0	55	379.2	100	689.5	145	999.7
11	75.8	56	386.1	101	696.4	146	1006.6
12	82.7	57	393.0	102	703.3	147	1013.5
13	89.6	58	399.9	103	710.2	148	1020.4
14	96.5	59	406.8	104	717.0	149	1027.3
15	103.4	60	413.7	105	723.9	150	1034.2
16	110.3	61	420.6	106	730.8	151	1041.1
17	117.2	62	427.5	107	737.7	152	1048.0
18	124.1	63	434.4	108	744.6	153	1054.9
19	131.0	64	441.3	109	751.5	154	1061.8
20	137.9	65	448.2	110	758.4	155	1068.7
21	144.8	66	455.0	111	765.3	156	1075.6
22	151.7	67	461.9	112	772.2	157	1082.5
23	158.6	68	468.8	113	779.1	158	1089.4
24	165.5	69	475.7	114	786.0	159	1096.3
25	172.4	70	482.6	115	792.9	160	1103.2
26	179.3	71	489.5	116	799.8	161	1110.0
27	186.2	72	496.4	117	806.7	162	1116.9
28	193.0	73	503.3	118	813.6	163	1123.8
29	200.0	74	510.2	119	820.5	164	1130.7
30	206.8	75	517.1	120	827.4	165	1137.6
31	213.7	76	524.0	121	834.3	166	1144.5
32	220.6	77	530.9	122	841.2	167	1151.4
33	227.5	78	537.8	123	848.0	168	1158.3
34	234.4	79	544.7	124	854.9	169	1165.2
35	241.3	80	551.6	125	861.8	170	1172.1
36	248.2	81	558.5	126	868.7	171	1179.0

TCCS1C06

ENGLISH TO METRIC CONVERSION: PRESSURE

The basic unit of pressure measurement used today is expressed as pounds per square inch (psi). The metric unit for psi will be the kilopascal (kPa). This will apply to either fluid pressure or air pressure, and will be frequently seen in tire pressure readings, oil pressure specifications, fuel pump pressure, etc.

To convert pounds per square inch (psi) to kilopascals (kPa): multiply the number of psi by 6.89

Psi	kPa	Psi	kPa	Psi	kPa	Psi	kPa
172	1185.9	216	1489.3	260	1792.6	304	2096.0
173	1192.8	217	1496.2	261	1799.5	305	2102.9
174	1199.7	218	1503.1	262	1806.4	306	2109.8
175	1206.6	219	1510.0	263	1813.3	307	2116.7
176	1213.5	220	1516.8	264	1820.2	308	2123.6
177	1220.4	221	1523.7	265	1827.1	309	2130.5
178	1227.3	222	1530.6	266	1834.0	310	2137.4
179	1234.2	223	1537.5	267	1840.9	311	2144.3
180	1241.0	224	1544.4	268	1847.8	312	2151.2
181	1247.9	225	1551.3	269	1854.7	313	2158.1
182	1254.8	226	1558.2	270	1861.6	314	2164.9
183	1261.7	227	1565.1	271	1868.5	315	2171.8
184	1268.6	228	1572.0	272	1875.4	316	2178.7
185	1275.5	229	1578.9	273	1882.3	317	2185.6
186	1282.4	230	1585.8	274	1889.2	318	2192.5
187	1289.3	231	1592.7	275	1896.1	319	2199.4
188	1296.2	232	1599.6	276	1903.0	320	2206.3
189	1303.1	233	1606.5	277	1909.8	321	2213.2
190	1310.0	234	1613.4	278	1916.7	322	2220.1
191	1316.9	235	1620.3	279	1923.6	323	2227.0
192	1323.8	236	1627.2	280	1930.5	324	2233.9
193	1330.7	237	1634.1	281	1937.4	325	2240.8
194	1337.6	238	1641.0	282	1944.3	326	2247.7
195	1344.5	239	1647.8	283	1951.2	327	2254.6
196	1351.4	240	1654.7	284	1958.1	328	2261.5
197	1358.3	241	1661.6	285	1965.0	329	2268.4
198	1365.2	242	1668.5	286	1971.9	330	2275.3
199	1372.0	243	1675.4	287	1978.8	331	2282.2
200	1378.9	244	1682.3	288	1985.7	332	2289.1
201	1385.8	245	1689.2	289	1992.6	333	2295.9
202	1392.7	246	1696.1	290	1999.5	334	2302.8
203	1399.6	247	1703.0	291	2006.4	335	2309.7
204	1406.5	248	1709.9	292	2013.3	336	2316.6
205	1413.4	249	1716.8	293	2020.2	337	2323.5
206	1420.3	250	1723.7	294	2027.1	338	2330.4
207	1427.2	251	1730.6	295	2034.0	339	2337.3
208	1434.1	252	1737.5	296	2040.8	240	2344.2
209	1441.0	253	1744.4	297	2047.7	341	2351.1
210	1447.9	254	1751.3	298	2054.6	342	2358.0
211	1454.8	255	1758.2	299	2061.5	343	2364.9
212	1461.7	256	1765.1	300	2068.4	344	2371.8
213	1468.7	257	1772.0	301	2075.3	345	2378.7
214	1475.5	258	1778.8	302	2082.2	346	2385.6
215	1482.4	259	1785.7	303	2089.1	347	2392.5

TCCS1C07

Service Record

Date/Mileage	Service	Next Due

90991G01

Service Record

Date/Mileage	Service	Next Due

90991G01

Service Record

Date/Mileage	Service	Next Due

90991G01

2

BUYING
YOUR ATV

CHOOSING THE RIGHT ATV

♦ **See Figures 1, 2 and 3**

Volumes of material have been written on the best way to go about purchasing a house or a car. But much less is available to someone who is shopping for an ATV, which could be one of the next most expensive purchases you might make. If you shop for a car or truck, there are many questions you must ask yourself, such as "How will I use this vehicle" and "How much money do I have to spend?" These are valid questions, which also must be asked when you are looking at ATVs. The popularity of ATVs has grown tremendously and manufacturers have begun producing ATVs for specific purposes. This increases your options, and will allow you to find an ATV that suits your specific needs.

Nothing is more frustrating than shelling out your hard-earned money for an ATV, and finding out it is not even close to what you wanted. Hopefully, this book will help you avoid this problem by discussing your options as a potential ATV owner. Also, aftermarket manufacturers have products available to further customize your ATV to suit your needs. With such a large aftermarket of parts and accessories, most people end up customizing their ATV is some form or another, whether its for looks or for comfort or function.

The diversity of today's ATVs have allowed them to become more specialized, allowing superior performance for their designed use. The numerous features and options that each manufacturer includes can be of great benefit to you. Usually,

Fig. 3 The Honda Fourtrax 300 can serve double-duty as a workhorse and weekend warrior

you'll have to make a compromise somewhere on a potential ATV to get the features that you desire. Try to look ahead to the future when making these decisions. Will your ATV be the one that you wanted a couple of years from now? Is the overall design and /or features of your ATV going to benefit you, or leave you disappointed with its performance? Ask yourself as many questions as you can possibly stand, and then consider all the possibilities. Weigh out your options very carefully. You might have to look around a little more than you want to, but you'll be glad to have the ATV of your dreams when everything is over. Otherwise, you may spend all of our hard earned money on an ATV that some salesman convinced you to buy, and find out later that it's not even close to what you wanted. NEVER let someone tell you what YOU want or need. Gather as much information as possible about an ATV that interests you, so you can make an educated decision and decide if its really the ATV that you really want.

Purpose

♦ **See Figures 4 thru 17**

ATVs can be roughly grouped in three categories (Utility, Trail/Sport and High-Performance) but there is a lot of crossover between categories. Simply put, most ATVs are designed with one or more intended uses in mind. It is not

Fig. 1 Sport riders will appreciate the Honda Fourtrax 400EX for its light weight and powerful engine

Fig. 2 The Wolverine is a "sport-utility" model from Yamaha

Fig. 4 The Kawasaki Bayou 220 is a light weight, low cost ATV with many features from the larger Kawasaki ATVs

important to decide whether an ATV's use defines its style or if its style defines its use. Just recognize that some ATVs are designed to do a particular job better than others and one or more types may best suit your needs.

The first question you have to ask before buying an ATV is simple—What do you intend to use it for? ATVs can be anything from weekend toys, to a hunting accessory or farm tool. The non-riding public often doesn't realize the variety of ATVs which are available. Manufacturers have been responding to customer demands and providing "crossover" models that provide elements from both camps.

Once you've decided on the purpose of your ATV, (or justified to your spouse why you NEED one) your choices may dwindle to a few particular models. The main thing to consider when deciding on a particular model or type is its PRIMARY use. If you want to go hunting on your ATV, a four-wheel drive type should be on your list. A two-wheel drive Yamaha Banshee might not make a good hunting machine. The high-strung two-stroke engine doesn't perform well at slow speeds, and the fuel economy isn't as good as a four-stroke. However, even a big four-wheel drive utility ATV can serve as a fun-to-ride weekend trail blazer AND a hunting accessory or farm tool.

If your primary interests are fast trailriding and occasional competition, a two or four-stroke sport model might be up your alley. Sport models usually don't come equipped with cargo racks or electric starters, in an effort to cut down on weight. Other characteristics may include a close-ratio transmission, heavy-duty disc brakes and long-stroke suspension travel.

Fig. 7 The Mojave 250 from Kawasaki offers serious high-performance with its liquid cooled, four valve, dual overhead cam engine

Fig. 5 Cargo racks combined with long-travel suspension make the Kawasaki Lakota 300 the "sport-utility" of ATVs

Fig. 8 The Arctic Cat 400 4x4 makes a great workhorse, with 1,050 lbs. of towing capacity and liquid cooling

Fig. 6 The Polaris DIESEL 4x4 can share fuel with your tractor—The ultimate workhorse!

Fig. 9 Junior riders can join in on the fun with Suzuki's pint-sized Quadsport 80

91232P27

Fig. 10 For the up-and-coming ATV youngster, the Yamaha Badger is an excellent choice for learning the basics of ATV riding

91232P23

Fig. 13 The long-running Warrior from Yamaha comes with a close-ratio six speed transmission and a torquey 350 cc four-stroke engine

91232P46

Fig. 11 The ultra-heavy duty Big Boss 6x6 from Polaris has tandem rear axles for 800 lbs. of carrying capacity

91232P24

Fig. 14 With its screaming twin cylinder two-stroke engine, the Yamaha Banshee is the quintessential high performance ATV

91232P45

Fig. 12 The oil injection system on the two-stroke Trail Blazer from Polaris allows worry-free refueling

91232P31

Fig. 15 The Fourtrax 300EX from Honda offers sporty features for a lower price

Fig. 16 The two-wheel drive, two-stroke Xpress 300 from Polaris puts the "sport" in sport-utility ATVs

Fig. 17 The Polaris Sport 400 has Scrambler features without the four-wheel drive system

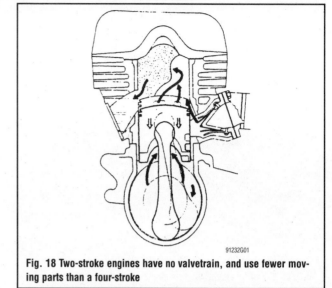

Fig. 18 Two-stroke engines have no valvetrain, and use fewer moving parts than a four-stroke

Fig. 19 Two-stroke engines are simple, and are easily rebuildable

Engine

The choice is 50/50 here, since most ATVs come with either four-stroke or two-stroke engines. Deciding on an engine type directly reflects the primary purpose of your potential ATV, as described earlier.

TWO-STROKE

▶ See Figures 18 thru 23

If you seek high performance, this engine excels. The two-stroke engine can produce substantial power for its size and weight; and everyone who is interested in speed knows about weight. Why is a two-stroke so much smaller and lighter than a four-stroke? Well, there is no valvetrain. Camshafts, valves and pushrods can really add weight to an engine. A two-stroke engine doesn't use valves to control the air and fuel mixture entering and exiting the engine. There are holes, called ports, cut into the cylinder which allow for entry and exit of the fuel mixture. The two-stroke engine also fires on every second stroke of the piston, which is the primary reason why so much more power is produced than a four-stroke.

Since two-stroke engines discharge approximately one fourth of their fuel unburned, they have come under close scrutiny by environmentalists. Personal watercraft and small outboard two-stroke engines are the current whipping post,

Fig. 20 Some two-stroke ATVs have an oil injection system. This consists of a oil tank . . .

91234P27

Fig. 21 . . . and a pump, which is usually mounted on the engine

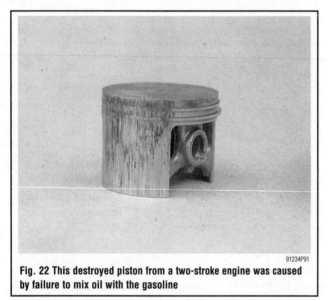

91234P91

Fig. 22 This destroyed piston from a two-stroke engine was caused by failure to mix oil with the gasoline

91232P41

Fig. 23 The Polaris Trail Boss 250 is a great buy for entry-level riders

while two-stroke motorcycles and ATVs are not far behind. California has tightened its grip on two-strokes, and certain new models of ATVs and motorcycles cannot be sold by manufacturers within the state. Check out your state regulations about the use of two-stroke engines BEFORE you buy an ATV equipped with a two-stroke engine.

Let's discuss the advantages and disadvantages of the two-stroke engine. This will help in the decision-making process. We've already pointed out the advantage of the weight and power of the two-stroke engine. From a convenience and maintenance standpoint, there are some things to consider.

Because of the design of the two-stroke engine, lubrication of the piston and cylinder walls must be delivered by the fuel passing through the engine. Since gasoline doesn't make a good lubricant, oil must be added to the fuel and air mixture. The trick here is to add just enough oil to the fuel to provide lubrication. If too much oil is added to the fuel, the spark plug can become "fouled" because of the excessive oil within the combustion chamber. If there is not enough oil present with the air/fuel mixture, the piston can "seize" within the cylinder. What usually happens in this case is the piston and cylinder become scored and scratched, from lack of lubrication. In extreme cases, the piston will turn to liquid and eventually disintegrate within the cylinder.

Most two-stroke engines require that the fuel and oil be mixed before being poured into the fuel tank. This is known as "pre-mixing" the fuel. This can become a real hassle. You must be certain that the ratio is correct. Too little oil in the fuel could cause the piston to seize to the cylinder, causing major engine damage and completely ruining your weekend. Some two-stroke ATVs have an oil injection system that automatically mixes the proper amount of oil with the fuel as it enters the engine. If the particular model you are considering is a two-stroke, this system could be greatly beneficial, because pre-mixing the fuel with oil is not required. If you own more than one ATV, or are riding with friends that own four-stroke ATVs, having to pre-mix fuel can be a real hassle because you can't share fuel. A fuel container dedicated to your two-stroke will be required.

Another point to consider, is that a two-stroke engine doesn't lend itself to constant low speed operation. Operating the engine at low speeds will cause the engine to "load up" and foul the spark plugs. This is caused by excess quantities of fuel and oil which accumulate in the combustion chamber. Usually a couple of quick snaps of the throttle will keep things cleaned out.

On a final note, the inherent noise level of a two-stroke engine should be taken into consideration. Two-strokes are usually fairly noisy machines. However, most two-stroke ATVs have mufflers built to suppress engine noise to an acceptable level. This aspect could be particularly important if you are considering an ATV for hunting use. Of course purchasing a two-stroke ATV does not mean you are excluded from hunting activities, but you might have a hard time coming home with something, and also severely annoy fellow hunters by chasing off game spooked by noise. Treading lightly is an important factor when hunting, and excessive noise could make things dismal.

FOUR-STROKE

▶ **See Figures 24, 25 and 26**

The four-stroke engine, with its somewhat more complex mechanicals, operates just like an automobile engine. The fuel economy is better than a two-stroke, and mixing the fuel isn't required. Possibly the only drawback of the four-stroke engine is the weight-to-horsepower ratio.

As a workhorse, the four-stroke engine shines. Four-strokes are inherently torqey, regardless of displacement. This characteristic makes towing and hauling a strong point of the four-stroke. Also, if you plan to ride in areas with a lot of steep hills, rocks or tight, twisty trails, a four-stroke would be a prime candidate.

From a maintenance standpoint, a four-stroke might require slightly more maintenance than a two-stroke. The valve lash must be kept in adjustment for maximum engine performance. Also, the camshaft drive chain needs to be periodically adjusted on some engines. Adjustment intervals vary from one manufacturer to another, and some manufacturers equip their four-stroke engines with automatic cam chain adjusters. However. this periodic maintenance in no way designates a four-stroke as a "high maintenance" engine. Four-stroke engines are typically very reliable and will provide many years of service before a major overhaul is required, making them an excellent choice for most ATVs.

One final thing to consider when deciding between a two-stroke and a four-stroke is fuel economy. A two-stroke engine is an inherently inefficient engine, even though more power is produced per cubic centimeter than a four-stroke. Because of the inefficient (put powerful) operation of the two-stroke, significant amounts of raw fuel exit directly through the exhaust system. A two-stroke will consume more fuel than a four stroke, no matter how you look at it. This will limit your overall range of your ATV, unless a larger fuel tank is fitted.

Driveline

Now that you've decided upon an engine type, let's consider the choices of drivelines available. Fortunately, the last few years have brought forth some technological advances to the ATV industry. Push-button transmissions, reverse, four-wheel drive, and automatic transmissions have been adapted to ATVs. All of these advances in ATVs allow for more diversity and convince for you, the consumer.

Keep in mind that some manufacturers may offer certain configurations of a particular driveline set-up that might require a compromise in your selection. For example, an ATV equipped with an automatic transmission might be available only with four-wheel drive, or even yet, might be available only with a two-stroke engine. If this is the case, weigh your choices carefully.

TWO-WHEEL DRIVE

▶ **See Figures 27, 28, 29, 30 and 31**

The majority of ATVs manufactured today are two-wheel drive. For most ATV users, a two-wheel drive ATV will perform quite adequately. With the vast selection of tires available, ATVs can tackle mud and sand with ease. A two-wheel

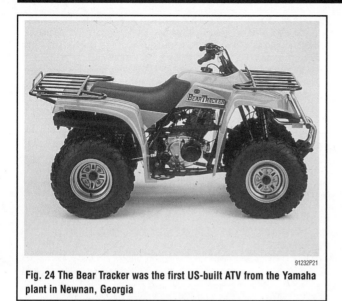

Fig. 24 The Bear Tracker was the first US-built ATV from the Yamaha plant in Newnan, Georgia

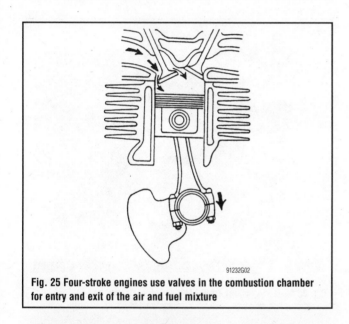

Fig. 25 Four-stroke engines use valves in the combustion chamber for entry and exit of the air and fuel mixture

Fig. 26 Although heavier, four-strokes provide better gas mileage and low end torque

Fig. 27 The Arctic Cat 400 2x4 has all of the features and advantages of the 4x4 with the exception of four-wheel drive

Fig. 28 The Yamaha Big Bear comes in a 2x4 version for those who prefer the simplicity and lighter weight of two-wheel drive

Fig. 29 The Arctic Cat 300 2x4 has a 220 watt alternator to operate power tools and accessories while on the job

Fig. 30 Kawasaki has also made two-wheel drive versions of the Prairie 400

Fig. 31 The Bayou 300 from Kawasaki has a dual mode differential which can be locked in position to provide extra traction

drive ATV will provide good traction in all but the most demanding conditions. Also, two-wheel drive is most definitely an advantage for racing and high-performance, due to its light weight and simplicity.

Because of the fact that the engine drives only the rear wheels, a two-wheel drive ATV will be easy to maintain, since the drivetrain is relatively simple. Usually all that is required is cleaning and lubricating the chain, or if its equipped with shaft drive, periodically changing the gear oil.

FOUR-WHEEL DRIVE

▶ See Figures 32 thru 53

For heavy-duty farm and utility use, a four-wheel drive ATV is a real workhorse. Nothing beats the grip of all four wheels turning together to get through really rough terrain. Also, some four-wheel drive ATVs come equipped with a dual range transmission, which is an advantage when hauling or towing heavy loads or traversing a heavily boulder-strewn trail. If you plan on using your ATV in the wintertime to plow snow from driveways and roads, four-wheel drive is almost essential.

From a maintenance standpoint, a four-wheel drive might require more a little more tending to, due to a more complex driveline. Usually all that is required is periodically changing the gear oil in the front and rear axles. However, keep in mind that since all four wheels are driven (instead of just the rear two, as on a

Fig. 32 Most four-wheel drive ATVs are shaft driven

Fig. 33 The Big Daddy of Arctic Cats, the 500 4x4. The 500 features 7.2 inches of suspension travel and 31 ft. lbs. of torque

Fig. 34 The Polaris Xplorer 300 4x4 has 8.5 inches of rear suspension travel to smooth out the trail

Fig. 37 With a three range, five speed transmission and fan-assisted liquid cooling, the Arctic Cat 300 4x4 is well suited for slow speeds

Fig. 35 The Fourtrax Foreman ES 4x4 from Honda features push-button electric shifting

Fig. 38 Polaris' Scrambler 500 4x4 proves that four-wheel drive, automatic transmissions, and sport can mix

Fig. 36 The longitudinally mounted engine in the Honda Fourtrax Foreman S 4x4 improves driveline efficiency

Fig. 39 With 8.8 inches of suspension and a 400cc two-stroke engine, the Scrambler 400 4x4 is a serious contender in the sport market

91232P48

Fig. 40 The Suzuki LT-F500F Quadrunner 4x4 comes equipped with heavy-duty cast aluminum wheels and Quad link rear suspension

91232P34

Fig. 43 The Foretrax 300 from Honda is also available in a 4x4 version

91232P49

Fig. 41 Suzuki's LT-F300F King Quad 4x4 gets the job done with over 35 gear combinations for pulling power

91232P08

Fig. 44 The Kawasaki Prairie 300 4x4 features a dual-range automatic transmission and a limited-slip front differential

91232P50

Fig. 42 The LT-F250F Quadrunner 4x4 from Suzuki offers King Quad features with a smaller engine

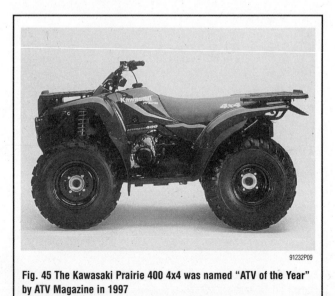

91232P09

Fig. 45 The Kawasaki Prairie 400 4x4 was named "ATV of the Year" by ATV Magazine in 1997

Fig. 46 The Kawasaki Bayou 300 4x4 features a dual automatic clutch and shaft drive

Fig. 49 The Sportsman 335 4x4 from Polaris features independent rear suspension and thumb-activated four-wheel drive

Fig. 47 Completely revamped in 1999, the four-wheel drive Kodiak from Yamaha has long been the cornerstone of their utility lineup

Fig. 50 The Big Bear 4x4 also comes in a specially equipped "Hunter Edition" with camouflage accessories

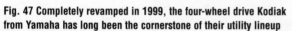

Fig. 48 The Yamaha Big Bear 4x4 mixes components from the Wolverine model to put a little sport into this utility ATV

Fig. 51 The Timberwolf 4x4, from Yamaha, comes equipped with MacPherson Strut type suspension and shaft drive

Fig. 52 Polaris uses independent rear suspension for a smooth ride on the Sportsman 500 4x4

Fig. 54 Shaft drive is fully enclosed, and lessens required maintenance

Fig. 53 The composite racks on the Xplorer 400 4x4 from Polaris help to cut down on weight

Fig. 55 The Honda Recon, made in the U.S.A.!

standard ATV) there are twice the amount of mechanicals included in the driveline. So when it's time for a major overhaul, it may cost as much twice the amount of money for repairs.

Another aspect of the four-wheel drive ATV to consider is the overall weight of the vehicle. A four-wheel drive ATV will weigh considerably more than a two-drive, due to the mechanically complex driveline. This is a small price one must pay though, for excellent traction on most any surface.

SHAFT DRIVE

♦ **See Figures 54, 55, 56 and 57**

Shaft drive on an ATV is similar to the layout of a rear-wheel drive automobile, with a driveshaft propelling the axle(s) via ring and pinion gear. Since shaft drive is fully enclosed to provide adequate lubrication to the gears, frequent maintenance is not required, as with chain drive. Keeping the oil level correct, and periodically changing the oil is usually all that is necessary to maintain a shaft drive system.

If you plan to ride in wet and muddy conditions frequently, you should seriously consider shaft drive. Since shaft drive is fully sealed system, you can be buried up to your gas tank in mud, and be at ease. Because deep inside the shaft drive casing, the drive gears are faithfully spinning in clean gear oil, and not through the mud as with a chain drive.

Fig. 56 Shaft drive lowers the required maintenance on the Magnum 500 4x4 from Polaris

Fig. 57 With front and rear shaft drive, the Kawasaki Bayou 400 4x4 is well-suited for wet-weather use

Fig. 58 Chain drive is simple and lightweight, but requires frequent maintenance

The drawbacks of shaft drive are the advantages of chain drive. A shaft drive equipped ATV will be slightly heavier than a chain drive, because of the drive-shaft enclosure and the weight of the ring and pinion gears. The additional weight is nominal, and easily can be justified by the ease of maintenance. Also, keep in mind that with a shaft drive system, changing the overall gearing usually isn't possible. This is usually something that most ATV riders don't bother with, except those who are interested in any kind of racing. On a final note, most shaft drive ATVs have a characteristic "jacking" effect under hard acceleration. This is caused by a combination of the geometry of the rear swing axle and the twisting motion of the driveshaft. Some riders find this a particularly irritating trait, and stick to the old tried and true chain drive. Test ride a shaft drive ATV for yourself and decide if this is something that bothers you. Overall, shaft drive is beneficial to most utility and general trailriding, for its low maintenance and fully enclosed gear case.

CHAIN DRIVE

▶ **See Figures 58, 59 and 60**

The simplicity and accessibility of chain drive makes it a top choice for sport/racing type ATVs. With chain drive, the ability to change final drive gearing is relatively simple. This is especially important for racing, because each track is different. For example, if you normally ride your ATV on tight, twisty trails, a reduction in overall gearing would be of benefit, since all of the gears are "lower" than they would be with a stock set of sprockets. This would allow you to travel at a lower speed, while keeping the engine in its proper operating range. If you plan on riding primarily on sand dunes, raising the overall gearing slightly might be of benefit, allowing better use of the lower gears. Of course, keep in mind that changing sprockets may require a shorter or longer chain. In addition of being a relatively simple style of final drive, chain drive is much lighter than shaft drive, which is also of importance to the performance-minded.

Since chain drive is not enclosed (there are exceptions) like shaft drive, dirt, mud and sand are free to cling to a freshly oiled chain. Frequent maintenance is required to keep the chain from wearing out the chain as well as the sprockets. Dirt is a chain's biggest enemy. Keeping the chain in proper adjustment and oiling it frequently will provide a long service life for a chain and sprockets. If you plan on riding in muddy or wet areas frequently, or just want to avoid the maintenance of a chain drive, then consider shaft drive. Chains and mud don't make a good combination. If you are interested in high performance, light weight, and simplicity, chain drive will be a benefit.

MANUAL TRANSMISSION

Just like an automobile with a manual transmission, an ATV with a manual transmission requires operating the clutch and a gear selector lever. A significant amount of ATVs have manual transmissions, anywhere from four to six speeds, as well as reverse. If you drive a car or truck with a manual transmission, riding an ATV with a manual transmission will be almost second nature.

Fig. 59 Failure to maintain a chain drive will result in accelerated sprocket and chain wear

Fig. 60 The light weight chain drive Yamaha Blaster is an excellent entry level sport model

One advantage of a manual transmission is the ability to select any gear at any given time for a situation. You shift when you want to, which adds to the riding experience.

From a maintenance standpoint, an ATV equipped with a manual transmission usually only requires periodic oil changing and keeping the clutch properly adjusted. For reliability and versatility, the manual transmission is a reliable, proven design.

AUTOMATIC TRANSMISSION

▶ **See Figures 61, 62 and 63**

The choice between manual and automatic transmissions was very limited during the early years of ATV production, until Polaris combined the clutch and transmission with a special belt and pulley system called the Polaris Variable Transmission (PVT) which allows the engine to operate at its peak power range at all speeds. Some ATVs have a "semi-automatic" transmission, which is actually a self-activating clutch. Shifting from one gear to another is still required, but without having to operate a clutch. These features are great for convenience and ease of riding, greatly benefiting utility/farm users who frequently are getting "off and on" their ATVs. From another angle, an automatic transmission or clutch may appeal to you simply because it takes less effort to ride.

Fig. 61 Polaris automatic transmissions use a large drive belt with variable pulleys

Fig. 62 The Prairie 300 from Kawasaki features a Continuously Variable Transmission (CVT) that completely eliminate shifting

Fig. 63 The Yamaha Breeze, with its fully automatic transmission, is an excellent entry-level model

If an automatic transmission or automatic clutch equipped ATV sounds appealing to you, try to talk to someone who owns one and ask them how they feel about its performance. Ultimately, getting to ride an ATV equipped with a transmission of your liking will give the best impression. You may find you prefer the feel of shifting for yourself, or like just like the "gas and go" ability of a fully automatic model.

FURTHER DECISIONS

▶ **See Figures 64 thru 70**

Manufacturers are constantly meeting the consumer demands of the ATV market and offering more models and options. This ultimately will allow you find an ATV to specifically suit YOUR purpose. Various little features and gadgets can be useful, and even fun, but can complicate and weigh down your ATV, as well as jack up the price tag. Items like push-button starting, reverse, and automatic locking hubs may or may not be of interest to you. Decide if it's worth your money to have these features, and if you really need them for your purpose. Investigate these features for yourself and decide on their usefulness and practicality. Every manufacturer has their own method of activating certain features; some are easy, and some a bit cumbersome. Some manufacturers practically make you jump through a hoop just to get into reverse gear. For those who need to use reverse on a regular basis, consider the method required to engage

Fig. 64 ATVs equipped with odometers make maintenance intervals easier, since you can keep track of mileage

Fig. 65 Auxiliary starters are a nice feature which can pull you out of trouble if the battery dies

Fig. 68 Some ATVs have rubber engine mounts to cut down on vibration

Fig. 66 Some ATVs come with MacPherson strut suspension . . .

Fig. 69 With a dual-range transmission The two-wheel drive LT-F250 Quadrunner is a solid and reliable utility ATV from Suzuki

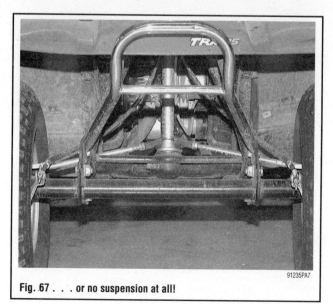

Fig. 67 . . . or no suspension at all!

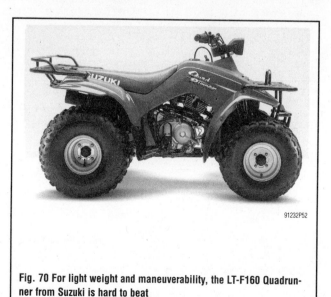

Fig. 70 For light weight and maneuverability, the LT-F160 Quadrunner from Suzuki is hard to beat

reverse gear. decide for yourself what seems easiest to YOU. Keep referring back to the primary question: "how am I going to use this ATV?" You'll easily be able to eliminate a lot of choices and features with this question. Keep in mind, though, that you might have to sacrifice certain features and options to get to get the model you really want. Unfortunately, because ATVs are becoming more specialized, there are few or none that will do everything. Weigh out everything carefully, and make an educated decision. Don't let a salesman talk you into something you don't really need or want. After all you're the one spending the money, right?

BREAK-IN

The biggest problem with breaking in a new ATV or engine is that, well, everyone has their own opinion. And everyone claims to back it up. Maybe some people even have some data to back it up. This is another one of those items that you are really going to have to decide for yourself. But, there are a few important things to consider.

Warranty

The first, and most important thing to consider when deciding how to break-in an ATV is the manufacturer's warranty. The bottom line is that the manufacturer has spent a lot of money on engineering and it was probably those engineers who recommended the break-in conditions for their ATV. Also, a manufacturer has a lot in stake in the way of reputation, so they would never steer you wrong, or WOULD THEY?

We would also have to assume that a manufacturer is also driven by factors including costs. They would typically recommend something that will not affect their bottom line (meaning will not cost them anything). But most manufacturer's only offer a base warranty of 12 months. Consider the fact that the vast majority of ATV riders do NOT place mileage on their machines that would be anywhere close to the 10,000–15,000 mile (16,000–24,000 km) per year average of the automobile driver. That would mean that by the time a machine has 10,000 miles on it, it is usually out of warranty. Many reputable engine builders would tell you that an engine really isn't broken-in until is has at least 10k miles (16k km) on the clock.

So what are you to do? You don't really think that we are going to recommend you ignore your manufacturer's recommendations for break-in, DO YOU? Of course not, you might void the warranty. If you plan on utilizing that warranty, it is extremely important that you follow the recommendations, ESPECIALLY when it comes fluid changes (which are never a bad idea whether you believe the ATV needs it or not).

The same would be true for an engine rebuild. If the rebuilder provides a warranty, then you should follow their instructions. At least most rebuilders have a much more personal stake in the performance of your PARTICULAR ATV than a major manufacturer.

Popular Theories

When asked about engine break-in, most people (including manufacturers) will probably fall in one of two camps. Most will caution you to "baby" the machine. Don't go too fast. Don't turn too sharp. Don't jam on the brakes. Don't race the engine. The minority camp is to "beat the living daylight out of it" or break it in the way you plan to use it.

Our experience is that most people fall somewhere in between. The people who want to beat the ATV in, tend to ease up and come in somewhere this side of actual abuse. The people who want to baby it usually break down and get on the throttle a little. It's really hard to resist nailing it just once and find out what your new baby can really do.

We tend to fall in the "realistic use" category. Remember that both extremes can have detrimental affects. I would like to tell you a story involving motorcycle engines (which are in many ways similar to ATV engines). I once saw a very authoritative article from a European motorcycle magazine that performed an experiment. They took multiple models of the same manufacturer and broke them into 2 groups. One group had the living daylight run out of them, while the other followed the manufacturer's recommended babying period almost to a "t". Well, after some significant miles they put them all to the dyno, and guess what. The hard used and thoroughly abused models scored a few percent higher in horsepower on a dynamometer than the babied machines. Of course, I never saw a LONG term test and I don't know how reliable the machines were 20 or 50 thousand miles later.

So what should you do? We feel you should follow the manufacturer's instructions, within reason. Don't beat the machine, but don't over baby it either. Most manufacturer's say that you should VARY the engine speed and this is probably the single most important point. Also, make sure the engine is fully warmed before taking any liberties with the throttle. Even after break-in, goosing the throttle on a cold engine is just plain a BAD idea.

Typical Recommendations

For the first 10–12 hours of operation:
- Keep the engine speed below ½ of total rpm before redline, but vary the speed. Varying the engine speed is an important aspect of proper engine break-in.
- Do not operate the engine at a constant low speed
- Avoid full throttle operation
- Allow the engine to warm-up fully every-time you ride
- NO hard starts
- NO hard stops

Then, at whatever interval the manufacturer recommends, begin regular service and maintenance with a complete fluid change, inspection and adjustment routine. Be aware than many manufacturers will recommend that a complete break-in inspection be performed at a short interval after delivery. This is because that is the amount of time and distance necessary for all of the new parts to wear in and seat, meaning that adjustments should be performed to make certain everything is operating properly. Keeping your ATV serviced at the dealership will avoid any problems with warranty claims if any problems arise.

Break-In of Other Components

BRAKES

New brake pads (or shoes) need an adjustment period where they are scrubbed in to provide optimal service. Any time your brakes are replaced, you should avoid HARD stops for the first few rides. Obviously if you need them in an emergency, USE THEM. Just remember that before they are fully worn-in, it is possible that they might not stop you as well, so ride accordingly, using extra caution.

3

RIDING GEAR

RIDING GEAR

♦ **See Figure 1**

This section is designed to help you choose the proper riding gear for riding your ATV. The goal here is familiarize you with what options are available when it comes to buying protective gear and with what features you should look for in that gear. We have chosen examples of gear from some of the industries known leaders (and in some cases from lesser known, but just as high quality manufacturers), and we would like to thank the manufacturers again for their help with the production of this section. That is not to say the brands pictured here are your only options. However, it is to say that they are VERY GOOD examples of high quality gear that is available and, as such, are excellent standards for comparison with the gear you look at when deciding on a purchase.

When it comes to riding ATVs, there is one inescapable fact regarding protective gear (and other forms of clothing)— What you are wearing when you get on your ATV is what you will be wearing when you get off! There's just no way around it, this is going to be true regardless of whether you PLANNED on getting off at a particular time or not.

When it comes to selecting riding gear, the type of gear you choose should depend as much on your feelings of risk assessment as it will on what type of riding you intend to do (trail riding, hunting, racing . . .). Some people would NEVER consider getting on an ATV without full protective gear from helmet to boot, while others think nothing of climbing onto their ATV wearing nothing more than a T-shirt and jeans. And time after time, a whole lot of people ride without protective clothing and nothing bad happens. So why the big deal?

Well, it is a lot like playing the lottery. If you don't play that number the day it comes up, then you lose. If you don't wear your protective gear the day you have a mishap, then you lose. The difference being that when you lose the lottery you probably won't need two ER attendants to hold you down while a nurse scrubs gravel, dirt and sand out of your open wounds using a stiff-bristle brush. (It would also probably be interesting to hear the statistics on winning the lottery versus the possibility of having some sort of ATV related accident). Don't play the lottery. Whenever you ride, wear appropriate safety gear.

Fig. 1 Regardless of your type of riding, protective gear should always be worn to prevent injury

Buying The Right Gear

CHOOSE SOMETHING THAT YOU LIKE

Probably the single MOST important factor in buying the right gear is to pick items that you like. If you buy a high quality item that is comfortable and versatile, then you are far more likely to WEAR IT. If you hate the look or the fit (or if you think that you look like a complete dork in a piece of gear), then you are probably going to want to leave it at home. And as we already said, the gear doesn't do you ANY GOOD if you are not wearing it when you need it.

CHOOSE GEAR TO MATCH YOUR RIDING

♦ **See Figures 2 and 3**

The second consideration when buying gear is to ask yourself "how do you ride?" If your ATV never leaves the garage unless it is warm outside and the ground is dry, then you probably don't need gear that is very warm or completely waterproof. But, if you plan on using your ATV during hunting season, riding in the winter months, then chances are good that you will have to deal with at least some rain and varying temperatures. The gear you choose for more varied or extreme riding conditions is going to have to do a whole lot more than gear purchased only for summer riding.

But, this is not to say that gear can't be versatile enough to use for both. And if your wallet doesn't allow for separate warm, cool and cold riding gear, then you would be wise to select items which can be used in different conditions. Besides, even if you plan on NEVER going riding unless the weather is perfect, there is one thing you can count on—the weather can always change. Even in the desert, it gets cool as the sun sets. Yes, it does actually rain in Southern California (sometimes). And if your riding takes you up in altitude, there can be snow on the top of some mountains even when it is warm and sunny down by the sea.

Fig. 2 These two guys are ready for some serious trail action

Fig. 3 The weekend rider can still have fun in less specialized apparel

CHOOSE QUALITY GEAR

The last and probably most difficult part of choosing the right gear is making sure that what you have selected is high quality. There are a couple of ways to do this, but they all come down to gathering information about the product. You can never have too much information about something before you buy it.

Look At Name Brands

Now we are not going to say that a certain piece of riding gear is high quality just because a company puts its name brand on it. But, a company that has been around for a long time and that has a good reputation must be doing something right. And you probably want to buy something from a company that has a reputation SPECIFICALLY in the off-road industry, not just that has a good reputation for clothing. A boot maker that makes a lot of outdoor gear might make excellent products, but if they don't have the experience in what makes a riding boot different from their other products, they might not make a boot that is any good for riding ATVs.

Talk to other ATV enthusiasts and see what brands they have come to trust. If everyone has something good to say about a company, they have probably done something to deserve the praise. Read magazine articles and reviews of gear before deciding to buy something. If you can't find a review on that particular item, look for similar items by the same company and look at how the reviewers feel about that company's products. Often, if someone writes a review for a product that is out of line (good or bad) with what they have come to expect from a manufacturer, they will often tell you that in the review. ". . . Although much of the gear we have tested from this company has left us less than dazzled, their new blab blab blab helmet was a real departure from the past and seems to represent a great value . . ."

Look At Attention To Detail

▶ See Figure 4

A company that has taken great care on the finish of their product has probably put that quality throughout the gear. A helmet with a poor paint finish or a jacket with seams that are tearing is usually not made of the best materials or workmanship and you would be wise to steer clear of it.

On the other side of the coin, a jacket that has many different features such as a removable lining, vents for cooling, handy pockets with large zipper pulls, etc. Obviously has had a lot of thought put into its design and will likely be well made using durable materials.

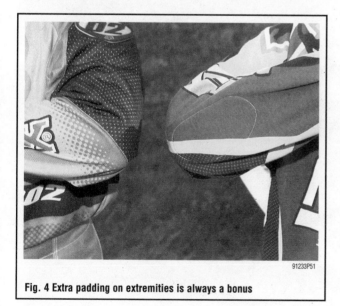

91233P51

Fig. 4 Extra padding on extremities is always a bonus

Look At The Price

We are not going to say that an inexpensive item is no good. Nor are we going to tell you that by spending a whole wad of cash that you are guaranteed to get a high quality item. But it is hard to get away from the old fact that you tend to get what you pay for. Most high quality gear will carry a price tag that is higher than their lower quality equivalents.

Remember that many companies (even those with very good reputations) have high and low line items. If you are working on a budget, one of their low line items might offer you a chance to get a relatively high quality piece of gear, but that is probably missing some of the more convenient or versatile features of their more expensive counterparts.

A few other things to consider here. One, that good quality gear is normally going to last a long time (especially if it is cared for properly) so that a few dollars invested now may last a LONG TIME. Two, that because gear can be very durable you may be able to find it cheaper used (if you don't mind used clothing). People change and might grow out of a decent piece of gear (especially items like riding pants or other snug fitting clothing).

✳✳ WARNING

One warning here. Some types of gear designed as crash protection use impact absorbent materials (usually some form of foam or hard plastic). These materials lose some of their effectiveness as they age and they are usually designed to do their job only ONCE. If a piece of gear that relies upon this material is exceptionally old or appears to have been dropped or to have been down (meaning it has kissed the ground in use) before, then steer clear of it. Especially when it comes to helmets, a good drop from the seat of your ATV or from your kitchen counter may significantly reduce its ability to absorb an impact in the future.

Money is a tough issue when it comes to safety. We really can't tell you what to do here, but remember that gear is designed to PROTECT the user. It's your **butt**, it's your **head**, they're your **fingers** . . . . well you probably get the picture here. There are a lot of things we would consider saving money on, but don't save money if it is going to cost you protection. Think hard about this. A new exhaust system, or a new helmet? (if you're smart, you'll buy a helmet first).

CHOOSE SOMETHING THAT FITS PROPERLY

Fit is important in off-road gear for two reasons. The first is simply comfort. If a helmet is too tight, if a jacket restricts movement, or a pair of gloves are so big that they don't allow for proper control of the ATV, you will be unhappy at best or unsafe at worst. The second reason comes back to safety, which is the basis for protective gear in the first place. A helmet that is too loose may fly right off of your head during an accident. A jacket that is too big might ride up and expose skin during a crash.

Another thing you should keep in mind with ATV riding gear is that it is designed to fit a certain way and this may not agree with what you have been taught is proper fitting for fashion or other applications. For instance, the sleeves of a riding jacket tend to be a little longer than most other jackets. The reason is that you don't want them to ride up too far past the wrist when your arms are bent in a proper riding position. Pants and gloves are also made this way. Make sure you consider the unique way riding gear is used before you decide for sure if an item fits or not.

91233P25

Modeling ATV riding gear is really hard work

Helmets

The human brain is arguably the most important part of the body. The human brain is also the only organ almost completely encased in bone. Is this a coincidence? Definitely not. If the brain is damaged, the rest of the body cannot function properly. Even with this built-in protection, a moderate impact to the head can cause major brain damage. Brain damage can cause memory loss, mental retardation, paralysis, even death.

With that said, if you're not wearing a helmet when you fall off your ATV and you smack your head on a gigantic boulder, you're gonna get pretty hurt. There's no way around it. I know, I know, "I'm a really good rider, and I never crash. Besides, helmets don't do any good anyway." BULL. Even the best race car drivers in the world occasionally crash. You can never predict when an accident will happen. Being well-prepared for mishaps is essential when riding an ATV, and wearing a helmet will significantly reduce your chances of sustaining a dangerous blow to the head. The old saying "Be prepared for the worst, and expect the best" is well applied in this situation.

Wearing a helmet while riding an ATV can be compared to an automobile carrying a spare tire. A motorist never plans on having to change a flat tire, but always carries a spare tire and jack if a flat were to occur. A foolish driver might remove his spare, feeling that he has good tires, and carrying a spare is just hauling around extra weight and taking up space. But, WHEN he gets a flat tire, he's out of luck. The same can be said for wearing a helmet. A smart rider will always wear a helmet, never planning on crashing, but protecting his head just in case something does happen. This is where things become more extreme. Instead of just being stranded on the side of the trail, the bare-headed rider who never planned on crashing but suddenly lost control of his ATV, and may get hauled off in a medic helicopter due to major head trauma.

Most people with the means to buy an ATV are big boys and girls, and are simply going to have to make decisions for ourselves. It's a fact that if you are wearing a helmet during an accident and you hit your head on something (a rock, a tree, etc.) The chances are strong that the helmet will significantly reduce the trauma of that impact on your head.

Now seriously, do you really think riding your ATV without a helmet on is worth risking brain damage or death? Buy a good helmet and wear it whenever you ride.

WHAT IS A HELMET?

▶ **See Figures 5 and 6**

The primary purpose and function of a helmet is to reduce the shock of an impact from your head. It is NOT a panacea for all mishaps, but a simple tool that, if used effectively, may REDUCE (not eliminate) the risk to your head during an accident. Helmet technology has advanced significantly in the last 15 years, and engineers have developed excellent ways of isolating impacts to the head with helmets. Not to mention that helmets are significantly more light weight and more comfortable than ever before.

Generally speaking, a helmet consists of a rigid head covering and a retention system of flexible straps. The rigid covering portion of the helmet has 2 parts, the stiff outer shell and the crushable liner. The job of the outer shell is to protect by spreading a concentrated impact on its surface across a larger area of the liner (and eventually the user's head). The liner does its job by absorbing impact energy as it compresses. In this way less of the impact energy is conducted directly to your skull.

The helmet retention system is vitally important because the helmet isn't going to do as much good if it comes off of your head or moves out of place during an accident. So the job of the retention system is exactly as it sounds, to keep the helmet in place during a fall or an accident.

HOW TO SELECT A HELMET

So how do you select a helmet? Remember the 4 basics mentioned at the beginning of this section:
1. Choose something you like.
2. Choose something that fits your riding.
3. Choose something that is high quality.

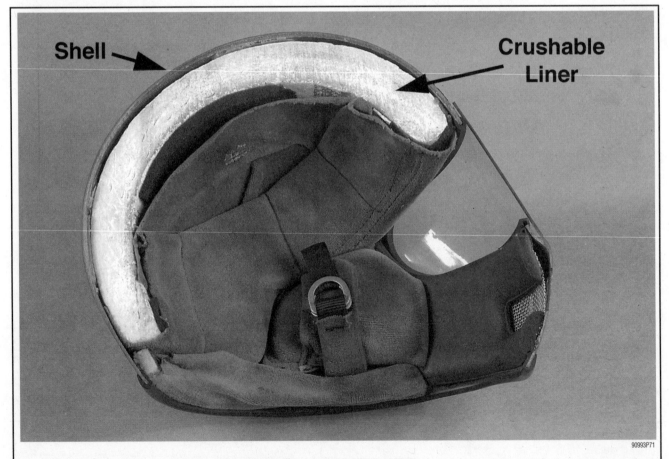

90993P71

Fig. 5 This helmet has been cut away to reveal the crushable liner found under the hard shell

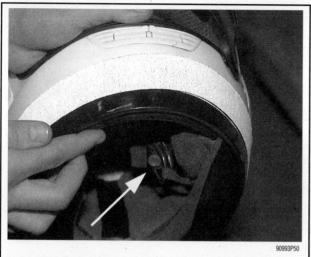

90993P50

Fig. 6 The helmet chin strap is VERY important, since the helmet won't do any good if it comes off in an accident

4. Choose something that fits properly.

But, in order for a helmet to do its job properly there is one additional VERY IMPORTANT requirement:

5. Choose something that has never been damaged or mistreated (READ THIS: Don't buy it used).

Choose a Helmet You Like

OK, this one's easy. Choose something that is styled to your tastes. If you think of yourself as boy racer, then you are probably going to be happier with a helmet that contains replica graphics of your favorite racer. On the other hand, you might be happier with a simple single color helmet.

If you are really worried about style, then you may also want to take into consideration what type (and color) of jacket or ATV you will be buying also. A neutral color helmet will coordinate with a lot more atvs than a repli-racer model. Heaven knows you wouldn't want to CLASH, would you ??? Seriously though, if you are always buying and selling atvs, it is a good idea to find a helmet that matches just about anything. A white helmet would fit this description perfectly.

But like we keep saying, it is just important that you feel comfortable with how your helmet looks, because you are FAR more likely to wear it if you like it. Don't buy a pink helmet just because it's cheaper than other colors. You'll never want to wear it around your friends. Unless of course, you're comfortable wearing pink on a regular basis. Certain full face helmets leave you looking like Darth Vader, and others like Dale Earnhardt. If you like Darth Vader or Earnhardt, then you're in luck. The bottom line here is choose something that has a style that you prefer.

When you are choosing a style and color of helmet, remember to answer the important need for visibility. Bright colors help to provide extra visibility during the day. And, when riding in hot weather, a bright color is going to reflect more of the sun's rays then a dark colored helmet to keep your head a little cooler. For this reason, a black helmet isn't recommended.

Choose a Helmet To Match Your Riding (Types of Helmets)

Different riders have different needs. For example, let's face it, if you primarily use your ATV for hunting, A full face helmet might not be the best choice. An open face helmet might be better suited for hunting purposes, since the additional visibility of an open face might be an advantage (of course your field of vision can change from one helmet to another, regardless of helmet style). On the other side of things, a serious sport rider would most definitely opt for the full face helmet. Pick out something that best suits your primary type of riding.

There are essentially 2 types of helmets commonly available to ATV riders. Their names give you some idea of the area and degrees of protection they offer your head (and in some cases face):

- Full face
- Open face (or ¾ helmet)

FULL FACE HELMETS

♦ See Figures 7 thru 12

A full face helmet offers you the most protection in the form of headgear. It is usually defined as a helmet which covers your entire head and that ALSO contains a chin bar. The purpose of the chin bar is to support your face off the ground in the event of a mishap. It should be obvious that in an accident there is a chance your face will slide along (or slam into) the ground, so a chin bar could save some of those precious features you are so proud of (your nose, your chin . . .). One of the wonderful advantages of a full face helmet is its

91233P85

Fig. 7 Full face off-road helmets offer the most protection for your head during an accident, and still allow a clear field of vision

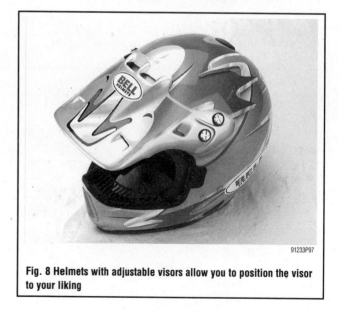

91233P97

Fig. 8 Helmets with adjustable visors allow you to position the visor to your liking

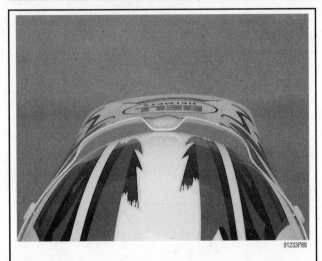

Fig. 9 This helmet has vents in the visor to cut down on turbulence (or lift) at high speed

Fig. 10 Cold weather riders might want to consider a snowmobile helmet

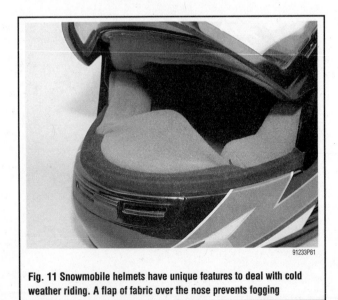

Fig. 11 Snowmobile helmets have unique features to deal with cold weather riding. A flap of fabric over the nose prevents fogging

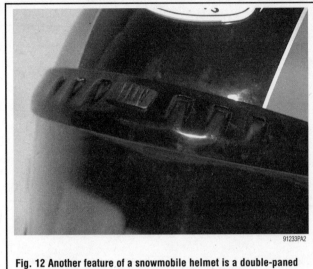

Fig. 12 Another feature of a snowmobile helmet is a double-paned lens with vents, which also helps cut down on fogging

ability to protect your whole head (face included) from not only accidents, but from the elements. These helmets provide good protection from wind noise, from cold weather riding, riding in heavy rain and even (if the helmet is well ventilated) decent protection from the sun's rays during warm weather riding.

All of this protection does not come without a cost (like some other forms of protection, the full face helmet sometimes brings the complaint, "it just doesn't feel the same when I wear one." But that isn't necessarily a good excuse to not wear some protection.) The costs of all this safety may include restricted air flow, and a reduction in the sounds you'll be able to hear. Some full face helmets tend to give a feeling of being closed in, with the chin bar in the bottom most portion of one's peripheral vision. If your a claustrophobic type, a full face helmet might give you the creeps.

Now most modern full face helmets have made significant improvements in minimizing their drawbacks One feature that MUST be included in a full face helmet (unless you only plan to ride in sub-freezing temperatures) is adequate ventilation. A good helmet is going to contain a few air inlets and outlets to help keep a flow of forced air through the lining and help cool your head by evaporating sweat. Keeping cool is really important during the summer months.

From these descriptions it should obvious that a full face helmet is probably the gear of choice for riders who are concerned with maximum protection. This should include any riders with a higher risk of going down (sport riders and racer-types) or any rider who feels the need for the best protection they can get. A full face helmet will offer the most complete protection of any type of helmet.

OPEN FACE (¾) HELMETS

▶ See Figures 13, 14 and 15

An open face or ¾ helmet might be considered a compromise. It provides a large area of protection for your head, but because it does not have a chin bar, it does not provide the same protection for your face that a full face helmet can. Open face helmets therefore also do not provide as much protection from wind noise or the elements. So with that said you might ask, "why do people wear them?" It is simple, an open face helmet provides much of the head impact protection of a full face helmet while providing something the full face cannot—protection of your face.

People choose to wear open face helmets for a variety of reasons, all of them having something to do with the lack of a face shield and/or a chin bar. They can provide an enhanced line of vision for non-riding applications (this is not to say that a full face helmet restricts your field of vision for riding, but that the chin bar can make looking at trail maps, looking down at something, looking into your pockets or even your jacket zipper a bit awkward). This enhanced line of vision is probably most significant in simply adding to the experience of being outside, on an ATV. Some people feel that full face helmets make you feel like you are in a cage, and like the less confining freedom that an open face helmet.

There are also open face helmets that have removable/adjustable chin guards. They appear to be a full face helmet, but don't be deceived. These of helmets don't really offer much more protection than a standard open face in the event of a moderate fall. They do however, provide protection from dirt and

Fig. 13 A fine example of an open face helmet

Fig. 14 These closeable vents are nice for keeping a cool head during summer months

Fig. 15 With goggles in place, an open face helmet covers most of your head, with the exception of your mouth and chin

rocks kicked up from the tires of other riders, and keep you from eating dirt. The other main advantage of this type of helmet is that the chin guard can be removed quickly if desired. This type of helmet might be appealing to some of you, but please be aware that these are not to be considered a full face helmet and do not provide as much protection as a full face. However, they do provide more protection than a regular open face helmet, and the option of the removable chin guard might be a good compromise.

Open face helmets allow you to more easily converse with other riders, because they do not muffle your voice. Since they provide less protection from noise, they allow you to hear different sounds that would be muffled by a full face, like other riders approaching on a trail. Again, this is not to say that full face helmets provide a dangerous restriction of sound. In fact, most experts agree that the noise protection of a full face helmet filters out many of the inconsequential engine noises from your ATV, allowing you to hear other things better.

Because open face helmets do not provide as much facial protection from the elements, Riding in rain or snow might be a little painful. But again, this is the sacrifice one must make when choosing an open face helmet. So if you plan to ride a lot during the rainy season or during snowstorms, a full face helmet might be better suited than an open face.

Like full face helmets, a better made open face is going to have features that make it more useful. These features often include things like vents and snap on face shields or sun visors to make them more adaptable to varied weather conditions.

After reading our descriptions of helmets, you might be curious what our choices are when it comes to this important issue of personal protection. The best recommendation is to wear as much safety gear as possible at all times. Some people might think you're paranoid, but it is always better to play it safe and be fully prepared at all times. When it comes to helmets, a full face helmet is always recommended. A full face helmet will almost always offer more protection than an open face. Open face helmets are basic protection, and aren't going to keep you from smashing your face against a tree. If you decide to wear an open face helmet, be aware of the lesser degree of protection that you have.

Choose a Quality Helmet

◗ See Figures 16, 17, 18 and 19

As we stated at the beginning of the section, determining the quality of riding gear is not always a black and white issue, especially when it comes to helmets. Deciding if it is high quality has a lot to do with the materials used in construction and the helmet's design. A good starting point is to avoid anything that is $9.99 and is displayed under a sign saying "for novelty purposes only."

In the U.S., the department of transportation (dot) helps us choose a quality helmet by setting standards of impact protection that helmets must meet in order to be legal for use in areas where a mandatory helmet law is in effect. Helmets which meet these standards are equipped with a dot sticker showing that they meet the requirements and are legal for use. Unfortunately, dot does not test helmets and publish lists of which ones meet the standards. Instead it is up to the each individual helmet's manufacturer to "certify" that their helmets are in compliance (not very reassuring if you are a suspicious type).

There is a non-profit group that tests helmets and certifies them (and whose standards differ from dot, because they look at different factors). The snell memorial foundation, inc. Was incorporated under california law as a non-profit organization in 1957 and exists solely for the purpose of engaging in scientific and educational activities in order to promote safety, well-being and comfort to people engaged in any type of travel or vehicular transportation. The foundation (formed by friends of william "pete" snell, a race car driver who died of massive head injuries received during a racing accident) conducts tests on helmets for various factors. What is comforting about the snell standard is that the helmet manufacturers participate voluntarily by submitting samples for testing (and the foundation also performs random sample testing from stocks intended for retail sales).

The Snell tests are designed to examine a particular helmet's properties which are most critical in providing protection:
• **Impact management** or how well the helmet protects against collisions with large objects.
• **Positional stability** or how well a helmet remains in place on a head when it is properly secured.
• **Retention system strength** or the ability of the helmet chin straps to hold the helmet during an entire accident.
• **Level of protection** or the area of the head that is protected by the helmet.

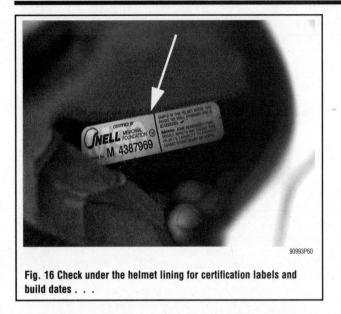

Fig. 16 Check under the helmet lining for certification labels and build dates . . .

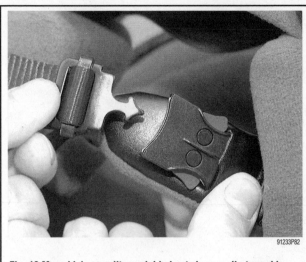

Fig. 18 Many higher-quality model helmets have a clip-type chin strap

Fig. 17 . . . this helmet has a build date stamped on its chin strap—Remember it should be replaced after 5 years

Fig. 19 A SNELL rating is a sign of a quality helmet

Snell tests vary depending on which properties they are checking. One test includes dropping helmets (with a headform installed in the helmet) in a specified manner onto any of three unyielding anvils and then measuring the amount of shock delivered to the headform. Another test involves dropping a metal cone of specified weight, from a specified height onto the helmet and making sure that there is no penetration. Other tests include applying a solvent mix to check resistance to chemical attack from solvents or petrochemicals, testing the permanently attached chin bars of full face helmets, testing the face shields with lead pellets, checking the diameter of ventilation holes, and even checking the peripheral vision allowed by the opening.

This is a lot of testing, and the results are probably a market full of helmets which are significantly safer than if there were no such testing or certifications. But, unfortunately we cannot say that these tests will ASSURE you of a quality helmet every time or that even if you get a quality helmet, that it will protect you from all unforeseen accidents. Remember that we are talking about plastic and Styrofoam here. If you slam your helmeted head into a sharp enough object or even a dull (but immovable) object at a great enough velocity you are not going

to have to worry about helmets ever again (unless you believe in reincarnation). Remember that helmets are great tools, but they have their limits. And, although quality control by most modern helmet manufacturers is exemplary, there does exist the possibility of a bad helmet slipping through.

Also remember that a helmet may be damaged on display or just from aging. The protective capabilities of a helmet diminish over time and many experts recommend a limited shelf life for helmets. At time of publication, the Snell foundation recommends that all helmets be replaced after a maximum of 5 years (or less if the helmet manufacturer has tighter standards).

So how do you try to assure yourself of a quality helmet. Buy a helmet that has BOTH DOT and SNELL stickers showing compliance with both standards. Check the manufacturer helmet labels which should include a production date to be sure it is not excessively old (remember though that you probably won't find a helmet that was produced last week or last month, but keep that 5 year life span in mind). Examine the helmet thoroughly for signs of having been dropped or of other abuse. Look at the helmet shell for evidence of cracks. Check the lining for unusual or irregular depressions showing where it may have been compacted from misuse.

Choose a Helmet That Fits Properly

▶ See Figures 20, 21, 22 and 23

A helmet does not do any good if it comes off during an accident. Therefore, the proper fit of a helmet is just as important as the quality of its construction. A helmet should fit snug, but not tight, since a tight helmet will likely place uncomfortable pressure on your head and may give you a headache. But a helmet should not be too loose, because if it is, it would be much more likely to come off or out of place during an accident.

Any helmet should be snug enough to prevent you from inserting a finger between your forehead and the helmet lining (we are not talking about prying your finger into place, just lightly inserting it). Similarly the padding of a full face helmet should press lightly against your cheeks, but here you are much more likely to be able to insert a finger or two. With the helmet in place, try to rotate it without turning your head. If the helmet turns significantly on your head (especially if it turns enough to interfere with your vision), it is too loose and you should try the next smaller size. Without tightening the chin straps, shake your head briskly from left-to-right a few times. The helmet should follow your head and not come out of place.

➡Remember that the crash protective portion of the helmet lining is made of a compactable material and will give slightly during use, which may make a slightly tight helmet just right or a borderline helmet slightly too loose. Take your time when trying on and selecting the right helmet.

Try out the chin strap retention system. When it has been snugged (in such a way that you can still breath or swallow), make sure it is still comfortable. An awkward retention system is going to discourage you from using it properly and then we are right back to the why bother wearing a helmet thing again because if it is not snugged properly, it may come off during an accident.

The Snell foundation recommends a simple method for checking helmet fit and making sure that you have properly secured it on your head EACH TIME you put it on:

"Position the helmet on your head so that it sits low on your forehead; if you can't see the edge of the brim at the extreme upper range of your vision, the helmet is probably out of place. Adjust the chinstraps so that, when in use, it will hold the helmet firmly in place. This positioning and adjusting should be repeated to obtain the very best result possible. The procedure initially may be time consuming. TAKE THE TIME."

"Try to remove the helmet without undoing the retention system closures. If the helmet comes off or shifts over your eyes, readjust and try again. If no adjustment seems to work, this helmet is not for you; try another."

One more thing to consider when it comes to proper helmet fit. If you wear eyeglasses, even part of the time, be sure to try on a helmet with the eyeglasses that you plan to wear with it. Some helmets are better suited than others for glasses and if you have the wrong combination of eyewear and helmet it may place uncomfortable pressure on your temples (causing a headache) or on the bridge of your nose.

Fig. 21 . . . and tighten the chinstrap snugly. If you can fit more than one finger through the helmet and your chin, it may be too loose

Fig. 22 Next, move your head back and forth. Your head should not move inside the helmet. If things are snug fitting . . .

Fig. 20 To check if a helmet is sized properly, fit it over your head . . .

Fig. 23 . . . try moving your head up and down. The helmet should move with your head. It should be snug, but not tight

Don't Buy A Used Helmet

Now we are probably going to take some heat over this one too, but we don't care how honest the guy looks. "I never wore it, I just bought it and it didn't fit and i've never dropped it . . . Ever . . . Really." Look, it is your HEAD, so why take the risk? Remember that a helmet's ability to protect your head is, generally speaking, a one-time thing and it diminishes over time or with any mistreatment of the helmet. Repeated bumps into doorways and an occasional drop from the tailgate of your truck may be enough to significantly reduce its ability to absorb an impact when you really need it.

If you do decide to buy a used helmet, examine it just like you would a new one. ANY evidence of damage should make you extremely suspicious and cautious.

If you have the luxury of examining a used helmet before purchasing it (or if the price was sooooo low that you decided to risk the money), then return the helmet to the original manufacturer for examination before use. This is true of a helmet you have owned for a while and dropped as well. It is too easy to say, "ohhhhh that drop didn't hurt it" when you really don't know.

HOW TO CARE FOR YOUR HELMET

▶ See Figures 24 and 25

Don't Drop/Bang It

Well, if you read the part on NOT buying a used helmet, you are already aware of the most important form of care for your helmet—DON'T DROP IT. Don't bang it into things, don't let it bounce around in the bed of the truck on the way to go riding. Don't pile things on it in the garage . . . Etc.

Don't Leave It Baking In The Sun

But there are other things you should be aware of when it comes to helmet care. Don't let it sit and bake in the sun every day. This is going to have an effect on the shell and the lining. Occasionally leaving it on the seat of your ATV may do no real harm, but doing it every day, all day is going to have a cumulative effect and weaken its ability to protect you.

Don't Place It On The Handlebars

Placing a helmet over something, so that it is supported by the impact lining, and not on the edges of the hard shell will compact the foam causing a hard

Fig. 24 Placing your helmet on the handlebars will crush and distort the foam liner, lessening the helmet's ability to protect your head

spot which will not crush during an accident. This spot will not only not do its job in an accident, but it can directly transmit the shock from the shell to your skull, which is exactly what it was supposed to prevent. Don't leave your helmet on the ends of the handlebars where the liner can get crushed.

Don't Expose It To Solvents

Have you ever poured gasoline in a Styrofoam cup and watched the cup disappear? Well, the impact resistant material under your helmet's shell is remarkably similar to that cup. Read the ingredients of any cleaner or chemical that you plan to use on your helmet and steer clear of those that may damage the shell or lining.

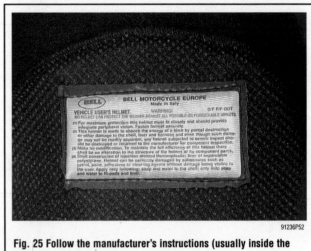

Fig. 25 Follow the manufacturer's instructions (usually inside the helmet) regarding cleaning and examination

Do Clean And Examine It Regularly

Do yourself a favor and clean the lining with a little water and mild soap (your friends will thank you.). Also, give the hard shell the same treatment. Remove bugs and dirt so that you will easily notice any damage that may occur through use. A potentially dangerous crack could be hidden by dirt and mud. If you are really vain (and aren't we all sometimes) polish it with some high quality wax once in a while, it will make it easier to keep clean.

➡Be sure to check with the helmet manufacturer before using any chemicals or detergents on your helmet. Be certain that whatever you use will not harm the shell or protective lining.

Goggles

▶ See Figures 26 thru 31

Most off-road goggles are all basically all the same design, looking very similar to modern ski goggles. They are usually constructed out of flexible plastic, with soft foam around the perimeter of the area that fits to your face. Most all off-road goggles are vented, using thin foam to filter out airborne dust and dirt that can irritate your eyes. Off-road goggles also have adjustable thick elastic straps to compensate for different helmet sizes.

Most goggles also have lenses that can be easily changed, which can be a real advantage. If you're riding on a really sunny day, a tinted lens can be quickly snapped in to cut down on glare. Or if your lens is becoming severely scratched up, a new one can be popped in, saving the cost of buying new goggles. If you ride in a lot of mud, then you know what it's like to scratch up your goggles after just a couple of rides.

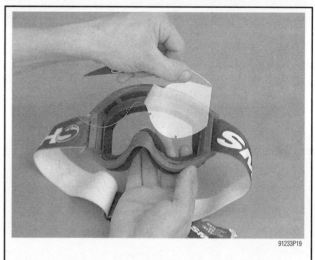

91233P07

Fig. 26 Goggles provide protection for your eyes from dust and fly-ing objects

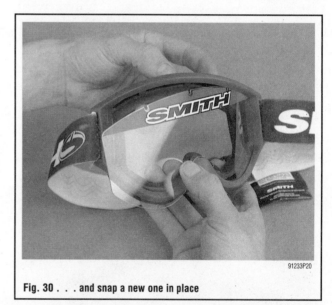

91233P19

Fig. 29 To change a lens, simply separate the frame from the lens . . .

91233P35

Fig. 27 Riding an ATV with just a helmet is okay for your head, but doesn't do much for your eyes . . .

91233P20

Fig. 30 . . . and snap a new one in place

91233P33

Fig. 28 But with goggles, you are fully protected

91233PA1

Fig. 31 If you wear glasses, goggles are not a problem. Most brands are large enough to fit over glasses

❈❈ CAUTION

Using sunglasses in place of goggles is really dangerous. Sunglasses do not provide the protection that goggles give. A piece of dirt or a rock can easily knock sunglasses right off your face. Sunglasses also will not shield your eyes from airborne dust and dirt as goggles do. Protecting your eyes from dirt and debris extremely important when riding an ATV.

HOW TO SELECT GOGGLES

▶ See Figure 32

So how do you select suitable eye wear? Remember the 4 basics mentioned at the beginning of this section:
1. Choose something you like.
2. Choose something that fits your riding.
3. Choose something that is high quality.
4. Choose something that fits properly.

Choose Something You Like

Finding goggles that you like will most likely be pretty easy. The big thing here is finding goggles that fit your face. Finding the right color is important too, just like picking out a helmet. Be sure to find goggles that match your helmet. The main thing here is don't buy goggles that you think look dumb, you are more likely to just bag them and take unnecessary chances if you hate your gear. Make sure to get what you really want, not just what is on sale at the local dealer.

Choose Gear To Match Your Riding

No matter what type of lens your goggles have, you should remember that although you may plan to ride only during the day, light conditions will vary. You could get caught in a storm, you might ride through a cool canyon or dark forest. Even on bright sunny days, you may find that tinted eye wear suddenly has become more of a danger than a benefit, so make sure you always keep some clear eye wear handy too.

Also, remember that your needs will vary based on your type of riding. If you are riding in the forest, a yellow tinted lens might be useful, since they help define the terrain in low-light conditions. Be careful to familiarize yourself with the tint before using it when riding. Some types of tint will actually hide varia-

tions in the terrain on particular surfaces. This could lead to some unexpected problems if you are unaware of the tint's ability of hiding or exaggerating terrain variations. The same can be said for polarized lenses. During really bright, sunny days a polarized lens could be really helpful. But, if the trail suddenly takes a turn into the low-light conditions of the forest canopy, vision might suddenly become impaired.

Choose Quality Gear

▶ See Figures 33 and 34

This one is easy. Look, if you buy cheesy-ass goggles from a five-and-ten, don't expect them to protect your eyes, because they probably won't do a darn thing for you (except make you look dumb). This is the same issue as wearing a helmet: how much is your vision worth? "if you have a five dollar set of eyes, then buy yourself some five dollar goggles." Seriously, spend the money and buy yourself a quality set of goggles. Not only will they do a better job of pro-

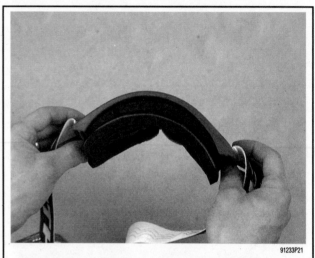

91233P21

Fig. 33 Look for quality foam that surrounds the frame; it protects your eyes from dust and provides a cushion for your face

91233P01

Fig. 32 Off-road goggles are available in many different sizes and styles

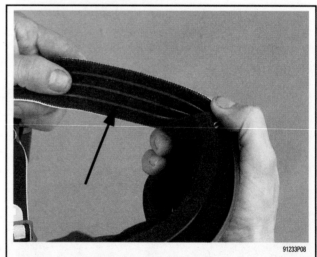

91233P08

Fig. 34 A nice feature of some goggles is a silicone strip on the strap to prevent slippage

tecting your eyes, they will last a lot longer. If you can't see when you're riding, you're liable to really hurt yourself, as well as other riders. So the bottom line is this: don't buy cheap gear! The only thing worse than having an eye doctor or er surgeon dig a pebble out of your eye would be to have the same person dig a piece of plastic instead, because you skimped out on buying real goggles.

Choose Something That Fits Properly

Most goggles made today are available in a ton of different sizes, so you can almost always find something that custom fits to your face. Make sure to try them on BEFORE you buy them, so you can verify a proper fit. When trying them on, check that there aren't any gaps between your face and the foam on the goggles. Dust and dirt can (and will) come up through the gaps and irritate your eyes. If you wear contact lenses, you are already aware of how much of a problem this can be. Also make sure the goggles don't press down on the bridge of your nose. If things feel kind of tight, the goggles may be too small for you. It may not seem that bad when you're trying them on, but after a couple of hours of riding, your nose might be in serious pain, or you might get a headache. Good fitting goggles should almost become unnoticed after some time spent riding. However, make sure the fit is correct BEFORE you buy them. The retailer is not going to let you return your funky, sweaty goggles after you find out they are too big for your face.

After you have found something that fits your face, look at the elastic strap. Does it look like it will last for a while? Is it adjustable? Nothing is worse than a saggy, limp strap that won't even hold your goggles to your face. Make sure that the strap is adjustable so you can position the goggles so they're not too tight on your face. Just like goggles that don't fit right, goggles that are too tight will definitely give you a headache. Adjustability is an important feature when buying a pair of goggles.

Also, be sure to examine the frame. Does it appear to be well constructed, or does it look cheap? Is the foam around the perimeter of high quality? As the old saying goes, "You get what you pay for" really comes into play here. Do yourself a favor, and buy some high quality goggles. Let your friends buy the cheap stuff, and watch how long it lasts. You will most definitely have the last laugh here.

HOW TO CARE FOR YOUR GOGGLES

The first rule is ALWAYS clean your goggles with a soft, damp cloth. You may be able to get away with glass cleaner and paper towels on some surfaces, but a soft damp cloth will never harm your eye wear. If your goggles are really muddy or dirty, immersing them in water to get off the big stuff will help avoid scratching them up. Let them air dry, and then gently wipe them clean with a damp cloth. It may be easier to pop the lens out to clean the inside portion. Just remember, lenses are made of PLASTIC, and plastic always scratches easier than glass will.

Products like Rain-X® Can be FANTASTIC on some lenses, but some lenses are completely destroyed by it. SO, never use a product on your goggles without first testing it on an inconspicuous area. Try it on a small patch of the corner of your goggles. Or better yet, try it out on an old, scratched up lens. This can save your weekend. If you just grab whatever cleaner you have in the back of your seat in your truck and spray down your goggles, you could be in for a really big shock. Certain cleaners attack plastics, so watch out. Play it safe and stick with good old fashioned water if you don't feel comfortable with a particular cleaner you have laying around.

➡**Here's a small tip for keeping your goggles free from dust for a longer period of time. Buy a spray bottle (you'll need a NEW one that doesn't have ANY residue from previous products) and some liquid fabric softener. Pour about 10 percent fabric softener with 90 percent water in the bottle. The mixture may foam up a little, but it will settle down after a while. Be sure to mix it up real good. Next, spray a fine mist on both sides of the lens on your goggles, and let it sit for a minute. Then wipe it off with a soft cloth. The fabric softener that prevents "static cling" on your favorite shirt will also keep airborne dust from sticking to your gog-**

gles. Experiment with different fabric softeners and ratios to find what works best for you.

Here's a final tip to keeping your goggles in good shape over years of use. Don't keep them stretched out over your helmet as if you are wearing them. Eventually, all of the straps on goggles will lose their "snap" from constant use. Keeping your goggles stored on your helmet will only shorten the life of `em. It is always best to keep your goggles in your gear bag, safe from being scratched up.

Boots

What you wear on your feet when riding is topic that is sometimes not given its due by ATV riders. But think about it for a second—most people have lots of specialized footwear for different purposes. Most of us have one pair of shoes for work, another for hiking, a different pair for sports, running or working out. So, why wouldn't you have a special pair of shoes or boots for riding?

A good pair of riding boots will address the specific needs of an ATV rider, including comfort, functionality and protection. Although you can easily ride an ATV in a pair of regular work boots, the fact is that they won't serve the purpose as well as a pair of boots designed specifically for ATV riding. Motocross boots will provide plenty of protection, but the smooth sole will cause you problems if you ride an ATV equipped with floorboards or if you do any light hiking. Some gear manufacturers have addressed the needs of ATV riders and make specialized boots for riding atvs. They are similar to a motocross boot, with the exception of a cleated sole. The cleated sole provides extra traction for floorboard-equipped atvs, and makes walking around in the dirt and mud a little easier.

An important function of your boots is to provide protection against injury. It is particularly important that the boots provide support to help protect the ankle. This will help prevent injuries to your feet and joints if your foot is caught by the pegs, shifter or brake pedal in an accident.

But unlike other gear whose major purpose is crash protection, you will use the most important features of your boots EVERY time you ride.

Past the key features of a good sole and some measure of crash protection, riding boots can offer a list of additional features similar to that of other riding equipment. Boots can offer you waterproofing (or water resistant materials), and walking and riding comfort.

HOW TO SELECT A PAIR OF BOOTS

So how do you select a pair of riding boots? Remember the 4 basics mentioned at the beginning of this section:
1. Choose something you like.
2. Choose something that fits your riding.
3. Choose something that is high quality.
4. Choose something that fits properly.

Choose Something You Like

As usual, the easiest of the qualifications for deciding on a good ATV boot is to chose something that you like. It would be safe to say that most ATV and motorcycle boots look basically the same. So, pick out a color that matches the rest of your gear. Any color but white would do. Why not get a white pair of boots, you ask? Think about it—they're going to get real dirty, real fast. Remember that if you don't like the way your boots look, you probably won't wear them. But, before you go making compromises on style or functionality, look for both in one package.

If you really can't find a boot that genuinely matches both the styling and functionality you want, then you can start thinking about compromises. Think about your personality when making the decision. Some people are simply more concerned about style while some are more concerned about function. If buying a pair of really good boots means that the color isn't exactly what you want, then consider making a compromise. Again, if you really don't like the boots, just don't buy them.

Choose Gear To Match Your Riding

▶ See Figures 35, 36 and 37

If you are primarily interested in trail riding, special boots designed specifically for riding atvs should be on the top of your list. ATV boots typically have a cleated sole, which is a real benefit to most riders. Say you're on a long trail ride, and you find a cool landmark a short hike away. And maybe the trail is a little muddy, too. This is where your cleated soles on your boots really come into play. If you were wearing motocross boots, you would be slipping and sliding all over the place. Off-road boots with a smooth sole are great for motorcycle racers, since they are always putting their feet on the ground during turns. The smooth sole allows their foot to slide in the dirt when taking a turn. But, motocross riders are in a controlled environment, (a track) and don't really need to worry about walking around a campsite, or pushing a buddy's atv out of the mud. But you, the atv rider, need the traction of a cleated sole for these reasons. As previously stated, the cleated sole of a specialized atv boot can also be an advantage to atv riders with floorboards, instead of footpegs. The cleated sole will give a little more traction on the floorboard.

If you're a sand dune rider, don't think for a second that you don't need boots to protect your feet when you ride. If you've ever had the rear tire of your ATV

Fig. 37 Although work boots are sufficient, specialized off-road boots offer unequaled protection and support

Fig. 35 Depending on your primary type of riding, specialized off-road boots may appeal to you . . .

climb up the back of your leg, then you know the importance of boots. Cleated ATV boots might not be necessary, and an off-road motorcycle boot with a smooth sole might work just fine.

Waterproofing is not all that common a feature in off-road boots (though there are models with Gore-Tex® linings). Most boot manufacturer's seem to feel that the Gore-Tex® is overkill, since people have always applied waterproofing oils and treatments to leather boots with great success. However, if you are a hunter, or do a lot of deep woods riding, then seek out a water-resistant boot. A completely waterproof boot specifically designed for ATV riding may be hard to find. If you have already purchased a pair of boots, then consider treating them with leather waterproofing treatment. Your boots won't be waterproof, because of the seams, but they will be water resistant and should work just fine for wet weather riding.

Choose Quality Gear

▶ See Figures 38 and 39

Like with so many things, good riding gear is usually specially designed for off-road riders. Your first place to look for a decent pair of boots is going to be an ATV/motorcycle gear supplier. Look at name brands from companies that make OFF-ROAD gear. It doesn't matter how good a work, hiking or cowboy

Fig. 36 . . . or regular work boots

Fig. 38 Most off-road boots have a special toe patch to prevent a wear spot from shifter use

Fig. 39 Another feature to look for is a reinforced area around the inside of the leg where constant rubbing and contact are frequent

Fig. 41 Better quality boots, like these examples from SIDI® , use a cam-type buckling system to provide a snug fit

Fig. 42 Once the strap is adjusted properly, simply latch it into place

boot a company produces, if it doesn't understand your specific needs, then the boot will not do as good a job as one which was well thought out for off-road ATV/motorcycle use.

Remember to buy boots made of high quality materials with decent workmanship which will provide support and protection in the event of a mishap. Check out the boot's method of "lacing them up". If the outer flap is made of hook-and-loop, make sure it is of high quality. How do you know if it is high quality? If you have to pull really hard to separate the halves, its the good stuff. The boots have cam-type buckles, inspect them closely and make sure they're of good quality. A pair of quality made construction workboots will provide decent protection, but real ATV boots are really the way to go. They're your feet, dude.

Choose Something That Fits Properly

♦ See Figures 40, 41, 42 and 43

Anyone who has broken-in a new pair of boots at some point in their life knows the pain which can be caused by an ill fitting boot. Luckily, when most boots break-in, the materials stretch and the padding settles so the pain goes away. BUT, if the boot is improperly sized, remember that the pain will probably stay with you as long as you wear the boots.

A boot which is too small at the time of purchase may not stretch enough to alleviate the pressure (and subsequent pain) in the months of wear that fol-

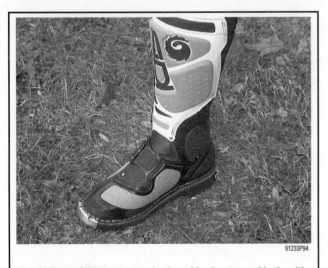

Fig. 40 These SIDI® boots use plastic and leather to provide the ultimate in looks and protection

Fig. 43 A hook and loop fastening system at the top of these SIDI® boots allows for a snug fit, and keeps out excess dirt and debris

lows. A boot which is too large will move around the foot when walking and will likely cause blisters. Ideally, you want a boot which is SNUG (not tight) when you try it on the first time. If you wear special socks (such as thick, sweat-wicking sport socks), then you should be wearing those socks when you try on the boot.

Any ATV rider will eventually spend some time walking in their boots. So it is imperative that you buy a pair of boots which will be comfortable for more than just sitting on an ATV. Make sure your toes are not scrunched up inside your boots when you're standing up straight.

The best riding boots will offer cam-type buckles, laces or hook and loop adjustments to assure proper fit. Remember that a slip-on boot must be loose enough to pull it on and off, and it usually cannot provide the comfort, protection or snug fit that is obtained by adjusting a boot after it is on your foot. This is why it is so important to have buckles and laces.

HOW TO CARE FOR YOUR BOOTS

▶ **See Figure 44**

Almost all ATV riding boots are leather, and as such, the same rules of care apply to your boots as to any other leather garment. Keep them clean and keep them fed with natural oils. Saddle soap is the most traditional method of removing dirt, grime and other mung from your leather boots.

Whenever the boots are exposed to water, from bad weather or from a cleaning, you should immediately coat them with a high quality leather treatment. The water will remove the natural oils which are so important to the leather's well being, allowing the boots to dry-out and crack. Although some cracks in the surface of the leather will happen no matter what, deep cracking will weaken the material and eventually lead to splits (and ruining a good pair of boots).

Fig. 44 Be sure to clean and treat your boots regularly using a quality product made for leather like Lexol®

Gloves

▶ **See Figures 45 and 46**

Everyone owns a pair of gloves, right? And all gloves have one thing in common, whether they are ski gloves, work gloves, or driving gloves—they are all designed to protect your hands. ATV riding gloves are no different, they are designed to protect your hands from everything you might encounter while riding an ATV. And like most types of ATV gear, they should be specially designed to live up to all of the varied tasks a motorcyclist will put to them.

A good pair of riding gloves will first and foremost provide some kind of abrasion protection in the event of a slide or crash. But your gloves will likely

Fig. 45 Specialized riding gloves offer excellent protection and good looks . . .

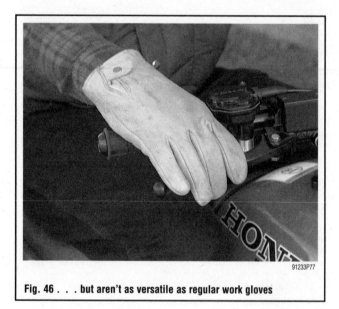

Fig. 46 . . . but aren't as versatile as regular work gloves

do a lot more than that. They will protect your hands from the heat of the engine when you fumble under the gas tank for the reserve petcock, or when you reach around the cylinder head to adjust the idle speed on your carburetor. Your gloves will likely be called upon to help lessen the stinging of rocks or insects which your hands come into contact with while holding the grips cruising down the trail. They will be asked to keep your hands warm on cool nights (or cold winter days) and dry on rainy afternoons.

In many ways, a good pair of gloves will become another one of your best friends on the trail.

HOW TO SELECT A PAIR OF GLOVES

So how do you select a pair of riding gloves? (here we go again . . .) Remember the 4 basics mentioned at the beginning of this section:
1. Choose something you like.
2. Choose something that fits your riding.
3. Choose something that is high quality.
4. Choose something that fits properly.

Choose Something You Like

If you've read the rest of this section then you already should have the hang of this category, but just in case you've missed the other gear we've been describing we'll summarize it again. Don't buy gloves which you think LOOK STUPID, you won't wear them. Seems like common sense right? Well, sometime we need to state the obvious.

The rule is still simple, buy what you like, just make sure it will work for your type of riding. A pair of fingerless, chrome-studded black biker gloves might be something that you like, but let's face it; they won't do squat for protection in a crash. Look at the other topics (make sure the glove also fits your needs, is high quality and just plain FITS).

➡**If much of your riding will be taking place in HOT weather, then a light colored glove will often keep your hands a little more comfortable than a black glove would. Perforated gloves and gloves without full fingers can also provide better comfort for hot weather, but remember they come with the price of less protection should they be called upon for the primary purpose of abrasion protection.**

Choose Gear To Match Your Riding

The neat thing about gloves is that compared to other ATV riding gear, they are inexpensive (meaning you may be able to justify owning more than one pair) and they are relatively compact (meaning you should even be able to carry more than one pair with you on the ride). We all like to save money and it is really convenient to own just one all purpose pair, so you will probably want to look for that first. But remember that most all purpose garments make compromises and when it comes to gloves you have a real option here to get 2 or 3 specialized pairs each of which does one particular thing VERY WELL.

UTILITY

▶ **See Figures 47, 48 and 49**

A utility glove would be best described as a good ol' fashioned pair of rawhide work gloves. For all of the hunters and farmer-utility types, this glove is your best bet. Sturdy, simple and inexpensive, the utility work glove will provide adequate protection, keep your hands warm, and allow for operation of the controls on your ATV without much hassle.

Fig. 47 Utility gloves are great for all-around use, and can also be used for other things besides ATV riding

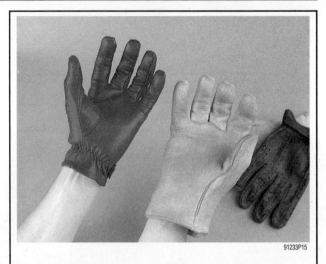

Fig. 48 When using utility gloves for ATV use, consider the thickness of the glove and your ability to operate controls

Fig. 49 Make sure that all of the buttons and switches can be easily used

SPORT

▶ **See Figures 50, 51 and 52**

A sport-type glove for ATV use will look like a motocross glove—flashy, brightly colored, and usually vented to keep hands cool. Sport gloves are light in weight, and have plastic pads sewn on the top of the glove to protect your hand from the **roost** (flying rocks and dirt thrown from the tires of other ATVs) of other riders. These are the most desirable type of gloves for sport-type riders who ride in warm weather. These gloves hold up well if they become wet, and will still protect your hands in the event of an accident. However, your hands will be just as wet as the stream you just rode through, and will become quite cold when the wind starts to howl past them. Unless it is hot outside, this could get pretty uncomfortable.

SUMMER

The challenge of a good summer glove is to provide protection to your hand while keeping your hands from sweating to the point of discomfort. There are

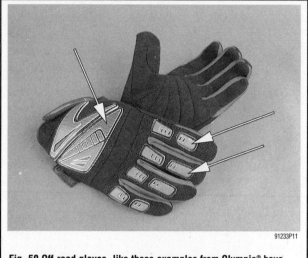

Fig. 50 Off-road gloves, like these examples from Olympia® have plastic pads to protect the top of the hand and fingers

Fig. 51 Another feature of off-road gloves is padding in the palm which is shaped to prevent bunching

Fig. 52 If off-road gloves provide a little too much ventilation in cooler weather, try street riding motorcycle gloves

various methods of achieving this including, bright colors (to reflect heat), lighter leather, breathable materials, and perforated material.

Some lighter materials may also offer waterproofing, especially the non-leather breathable materials (ballistic nylon and Gore-Tex®). A light weight, but waterproof glove can become invaluable on a long trip, should the weather take a turn for the worse. There are few things more miserable than to be prepared with good waterproof rainwear (jackets, pants and boots), and then to have your cold hands, squishing water out from the fingers of your gloves every time to reach for the brake levers.

WINTER

▶ See Figure 53

The first and foremost job of a winter glove is to keep your hands warm. The best winter gloves will have a good layer of insulating material underneath a windproof shell. The shell on many winter gloves is NOT leather, but the better ones will have some sort of leather or ballistic material for the fingers and for the palms (again providing abrasion protection for mishaps).

Many winter gloves will also contain a waterproofing layer (such as Gore-Tex®) which is handy when the cold weather turns wet as well. A medium weight insulated winter glove may be useful for cold summer, spring and fall riding when the weather turns wet. Remember that moisture in the dead of winter usually means snow and that means really, really cold riding weather.

✺✺ WARNING

Be careful about oversized or overstuffed winter gloves. If you can't safely operate the controls of the ATV, then who cares how warm the glove is, it is useless for riding.

Another thing to consider is whether or not the glove is a gauntlet. A gauntlet-styled glove can be worn over the ends of your jacket sleeves (effectively blocking all air flow). A glove which fits over the sleeves like that is great in the winter because it helps seal out the cold air, but it may not be so great in the summer, if you are looking for a cooling air flow. Snowmobile and motorcycle riders have been using these for years. Just be careful when using these gloves, as they are usually thick and bulky, and could hinder your ability to operate the controls of your ATV.

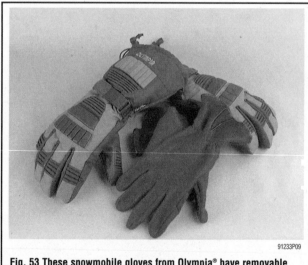

Fig. 53 These snowmobile gloves from Olympia® have removable liners that can also be used separately

GEL

▶ See Figure 54

Glove manufacturers have taken a lesson from mountain bikers and many now offer a variety of gloves with a gel padding in the palm. This can be especially nice on ATVs which vibrate heavily through the handlebars. With these types of gloves comfort can be increased on both high-revving buzzy sport-type

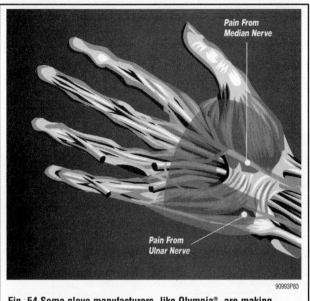

Fig. 54 Some glove manufacturers, like Olympia®, are making gloves with gel inserts to cushion the nerves in your hands and reduce pain or numbing

ATVs which can transmit a high-frequency, numbing vibration to your hands, and some heavy-throbbing, solid-mounted utility-types which can transmit a low-frequency, but equally numbing vibration.

Choose Quality Gear

▶ See Figure 55

Can you ride with a pair of cloth work gloves? Sure, but don't expect them to stay together in a fall. Like most ATV gear, the majority of the best stuff is specially designed for off-road ATV and motorcycle riding. You are going to find the best quality gear from shops or catalogs that cater to serious riders.

Look for products from companies that specialize in off-road riding apparel. Heavy race weight leather or other high quality ballistic materials are good signs that a company is serious about its gear. Fingers which are constructed of mul-

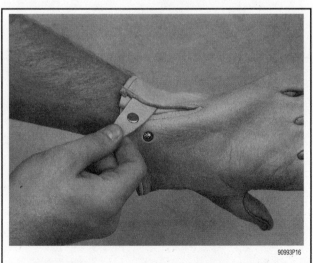

Fig. 55 Snaps, zippers or hook and look adjustments help to seal the glove to your jacket, helping to keep your whole body warm

tiple sections, allowing the hand to curl around the grip without stretching the material will allow for the best fit. Reinforced areas on the palm and the fingers are also good hints that the glove is designed for function and not just fashion.

Choose Something That Fits Properly

▶ See Figure 56

Have you ever tried to pull a zipper or work a throttle in a glove that doesn't fit? If you have too much fabric in the fingers, then you will not be able to grip anything. With gloves that are too big, your hands will be stumbling over the levers, grips and controls of your ATV. On the other side of the coin, a glove that is too small will pull back on your fingers, fighting your grip. A small glove will make it hard and uncomfortable to maintain your grip of the handlebars and other controls.

When trying on a pair of gloves, the tips of the fingers should just touch when you interlock your hands and push down at the base of the fingers. This is a good way to tell if the gloves are the proper size. Another test is to put on a glove, and make a fist, as tight as you can. If the glove feels really tight over the knuckles, it may be too small. Or if the tips of your fingers feel tight, the glove may also be too small for your hand. Try on a few different sizes, and perform these tests on each pair until you find a pair that fits your hands.

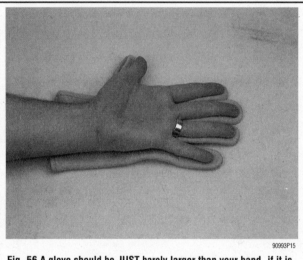

Fig. 56 A glove should be JUST barely larger than your hand, if it is too tight or too loose it will probably make it difficult to work the controls

HOW TO CARE FOR YOUR GLOVES

Most gloves are made with leather, or at least contain a leather shell. As usual, the routine to keep leather healthy involves periodic cleaning and treatment to replenish its natural oils. There are some gloves which use ballistic materials and these should be cared for according to their manufacturer's instructions.

Jackets

Ok, you're thinking, "why do I need a jacket to go riding?" Well, you don't. But, in all but the hottest weather, wearing one is recommended. The protection of a specialized riding jacket is far better than a standard jacket or a jersey. If you're riding in really hot weather, wearing a jersey with pads in the sleeves is recommended. Whatever you do, DON'T wear a short sleeve T-shirt. But the rest of the time, you really should wear a riding jacket. Read on, and find out the benefits and advantages of a specialized off-road riding jacket.

OFF-ROAD JACKET FEATURES

▶ **See Figures 57 thru 67**

When most people think of a jacket, they think of something to protect you from the elements, and that is certainly true of a off-road riding jacket. But riding an ATV places certain demands on your gear that would not be applicable to most other activities. And unfortunately, many people either don't realize or don't believe the need for a riding jacket to do something more. A real off-road riding jacket will to protect you in the case of crash (read that as a riding jacket may be needed to keep your skin on your bones).

A riding jacket will first and foremost offer some protection against abrasion and, if it is truly designed to help minimize the possibility of injury, it will also offer some impact protection. As with helmets, you are going to have to do your own risk assessment here and make a decision with how much of a risk you feel comfortable. Many people don't think twice about riding in a T-shirt or a denim jacket, but unless you have a very minor get-off, neither of these is going to provide significant protection to your upper body.

The best off-road riding jackets will have a combination of these features:
- Abrasion protection
- Impact protection
- A cut to fit your body when riding (and various adjustments or retention systems to keep them in place in the case of a mishap)

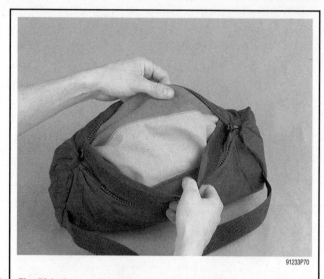
Fig. 59 Let's open the zipper and see what's inside . . .

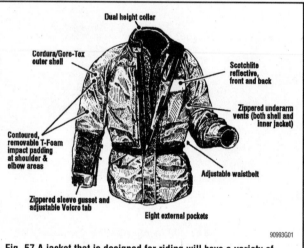
Fig. 57 A jacket that is designed for riding will have a variety of useful features (this example is an off-road motorcycle jacket from Aerostitch® sold by the Riderwearhouse® catalog)

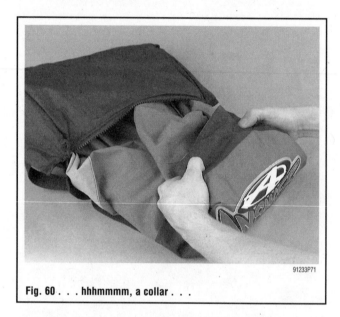
Fig. 60 . . . hhhmmmm, a collar . . .

Fig. 58 What's this? A small fanny pack?

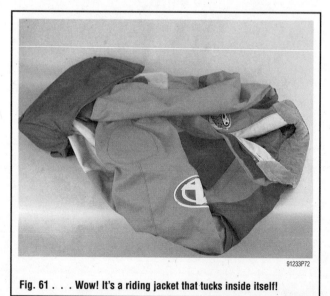
Fig. 61 . . . Wow! It's a riding jacket that tucks inside itself!

Fig. 62 The pocket on the rear of the jacket serves double duty; it turns into a "bag" when the jacket is rolled into itself

Fig. 65 Hook and loop straps on the sleeves are another essential feature of a riding jacket for keeping out cold wind

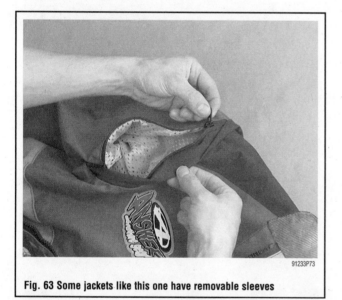

Fig. 63 Some jackets like this one have removable sleeves

Fig. 66 Most jackets can also fit over chest protectors, providing maximum protection

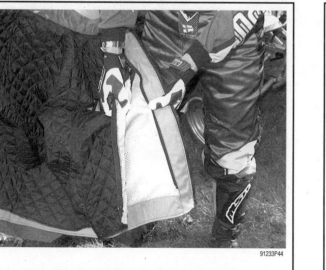

Fig. 64 Removable liners are nice for warm weather riding

Fig. 67 The flap across the shoulders on this jacket provides ventilation

- Ventilation to help keep you cool in hot weather
- A lining to help keep you warm in cold weather
- Pockets to store things (with zippers or snaps to keep from losing them)
- Bright colors and/or reflective material to help keep you visible
- Waterproof or water-resistant layer to help keep you dry in damp or wet weather

Abrasion Protection

▶ See Figure 68

A jacket that is specifically designed for off-road riding will be made of a durable material that has been shown to provide a measure of wear-through protection in case of a crash. The materials that ATV riding jackets are made from won't tear under the severe stress of an accident. A sweatshirt or long-sleeve T-shirt will tear almost instantly in the event of an accident. As soon as the sweatshirt tears through, the flesh on your arms and shoulders will be torn up micro-seconds later. A riding jacket is a "second skin" that will keep rocks and dirt from becoming embedded in your flesh in the event of a fall.

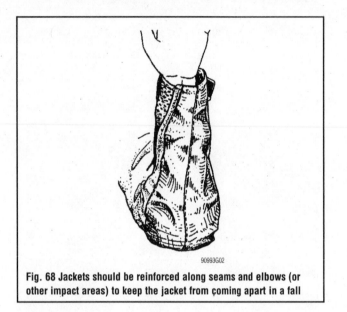

Fig. 68 Jackets should be reinforced along seams and elbows (or other impact areas) to keep the jacket from coming apart in a fall

Impact Protection

▶ See Figures 69, 70, 71 and 72

This important part of a jacket is often overlooked. Even a minor fall can transmit a serious shock to elbows or shoulders. And a good riding jacket should come with some form of padding in these areas to absorb some of the shock for you. A popular feature of many high quality jackets is the inclusion of removable plastic and/or foam body armor that works in a similar way to the crushable lining of a helmet. In the event of an impact, the foam condenses to absorb the shock instead of directly transmitting it to your bones.

A Cut To Fit Your Body When Riding

Take your favorite dress or casual jacket, put it on and then sit on your ATV. Chances are you will notice a few things that make this jacket comfortable the rest of the time, may not make it suitable for riding. For one thing, when you lean forward, even slightly, and grasp the handle bars, the sleeves will probably pull back exposing your arms, and the hem may pull upward, exposing your back. Depending on the material and the collar, it may flap or even whip you in the wind. And there probably aren't any other retention points, such as a cinching system at the waist to seal cold air out and keep it in place in the case of a crash.

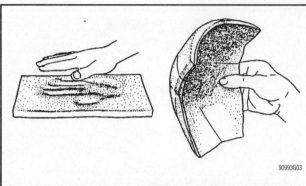

Fig. 69 The better made jackets will have some form of hard plastic and/or crushable foam impact protectors

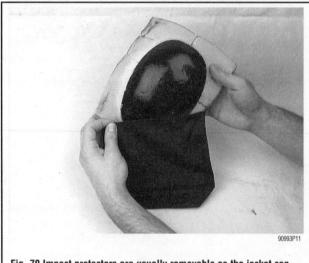

Fig. 70 Impact protectors are usually removable so the jacket can be worn with or without them (and so they can be replaced if necessary)

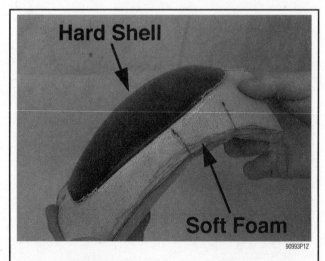

Hard Shell

Soft Foam

Fig. 71 This protector from an Aerostitch® jacket has a hard plastic shell and crushable foam padding

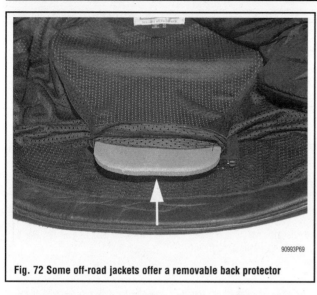

Fig. 72 Some off-road jackets offer a removable back protector

The sleeves of most will be a little long when you are standing around before a ride, but when you climb in the saddle they should fit just right. Sleeves should have a hook and loop tab for adjustment and/or a zipper so it can be sealed to keep the air out on cold days (or nights). Waists should also have some sort of belt or adjustment to seal air.

Ventilation

Any riding jacket will keep you out of direct sunlight on a hot day, and if there is sufficient airflow to allow your sweat to evaporate, it can keep you cool as well. The most popular way to do this is with a series of zippered vents and a mesh or removable liner which will allow air to circulate. Air can enter from unzipped sleeves, or through intake vents (under the arms or on either side of the lapel) and can exit one or more vents across the back.

Linings

▶ See Figure 73

A lining of insulating material is necessary to keep you warm on cold days or nights. A removable lining is even better since it means the jacket can probably also be used in warmer weather. And if you are really going for the gusto, some companies offer detachable sleeves so the jacket can be turned into a vest.

Pockets

▶ See Figure 74

When you travel on an ATV, you learn to pack light. But there are a lot of little things which you like to keep handy, like wallets or lip balm, an oil rag or a trail map. A jacket with a lot of pockets is going to become a convenient trail companion. Of course, the pockets should have zippers or snaps to close them and prevent these precious items from falling out. Put on a glove, and see how easy it is to access the pockets. This is important, since you don't want to have to keep taking off your gloves every time you need something from a pocket on your jacket.

❄❄ CAUTION

Be careful what you decide to put in your pockets. Hard and sharp objects are probably not good ideas in the case of a get-off. Remember that a key, a pair of eyeglasses or that little screwdriver you like to keep handy could be driven into your body in a crash. If you wouldn't like to fall on a particular object, DON'T WEAR IT in one of your jacket pockets.

Fig. 73 Serious riders want a jacket with a lining that can be removed (making the jacket suitable for all weather)—Some jackets include a lining which can be worn separately, as a windbreaker

Fig. 74 Big pockets that are easy to get into are especially important, since a gloved hand will be accessing them

Waterproof Or Water-Resistant

▶ See Figure 75

If you live and ride on the east coast, you will eventually ride through some rain. There is no way around it. Whether it is a damp morning fog in the

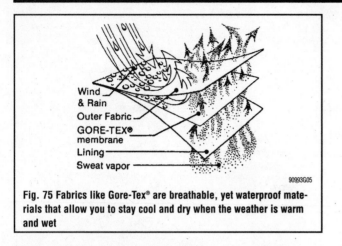

Fig. 75 Fabrics like Gore-Tex® are breathable, yet waterproof materials that allow you to stay cool and dry when the weather is warm and wet

woods, or an all day downpour in Tennessee, a jacket that will help keep you warm and dry is a nice plus, especially if you're a ways from your truck or campsite.

Any decent jacket will protect you from light rain or mist, especially if you keep it well treated. But, there are options today with materials like Gore-Tex® which allow a very high degree of resistance to rain and even all day downpours and still provide plenty of ventilation. For one thing, if your jacket is already waterproof, you will never have to face the decision, "should I turn around and head back to the truck and wait this one out?" You can just keep on riding.

HOW TO SELECT A JACKET

So how do you select a jacket? Remember the 4 basics mentioned at the beginning of this section:
1. Choose something you like.
2. Choose something that fits your riding.
3. Choose something that is high quality.
4. Choose something that fits properly.

Choose Something You Like

First thing's first, you've got to like the look of the jacket you pick so we are not going to tell you to buy a bright purple jacket just to be more visible if you think you look really stupid in it. Go to dealerships and try on some jackets to get a feel for what you want.

BUT, here are some things to keep in mind. If you do a lot of hot weather riding, a dark-colored jacket may not be your best choice. Remember that a lighter color will help to reflect the sun's rays and will keep you cooler in direct sunlight. We've already said a couple of times that a brighter color helps to keep you visible to other riders in low light conditions, so it helps there too.

➡**Keep in mind that in very hot weather and direct sunlight, taking the jacket off will not keep you as cool as you would be under the right jacket. The direct sun will heat your skin, rather than allowing a jacket to reflect some of that heat. The direct sunlight will further warm your skin which will prevent you from fully realizing the benefit of sweat evaporation (and there is that whole sunburn thing to worry about as well). Look at Arabs in the desert—they cover themselves completely with loose fitting, light colored robes. This reflects the sun's rays (and therefore some of its heat) allowing their sweat to evaporate and take body heat with it.**

Choose Gear To Match Your Riding

Hard-core sport riders are probably going to place more emphasis on crash protection (abrasion and impact resistance) than they would on number of pock-

ets. Someone who does a lot of hauling stuff around the farm every day is going to want a jacket that protects them from the elements (keeps them warm, cool or dry).

Obviously, if you live in the desert your needs are going to be a little different than if you live in Maine right? But that still doesn't mean the desert dweller NEVER has to worry about cold weather. You'll have to take an assessment of what your needs and desires are in a jacket, but remember that the more versatile the jacket is, the more likely you are to keep it on all of the time.

Look at the various features we listed earlier and decide which ones are most important to you. Look for a jacket that fills all your needs.

Most off-road riding jackets usually use a breathable and a waterproof or water-resistant material. There are a few major advantages here. The light, breathable materials can be more comfortable to wear than a regular jacket, and will help to keep you cool on hot days, while still offering protection. And, unlike many sealed, nylon or plastic rainsuits, a breathable water-resistant jacket allows your sweat to escape keeping you significantly more comfortable on rainy summer days. These jackets are often easier to clean, as they can often be thrown in the washing machine.

Choose Quality Gear

If the gear is produced or sold by a company that makes its living from off-road riders, and has many of the features that we've described, then the chances are it is high quality. Again, there are no guarantees here, so you should do some sleuthing before you decide to buy. Look at motorcycle and ATV brand name merchandise. Look at the quality and construction (especially the seams). Even a heavyweight riding jacket won't do you much good if the seams are not reinforced to keep it from coming apart in a fall.

Choose Something That Fits Properly

When you try a jacket on, the best thing to do is to climb on your ATV (or a similar model in the dealership showroom) and see how it fits your riding position. Do the sleeves pull back or does the waist ride up excessively? If a sample ATV like yours is not handy, try lifting your hands over your head, the sleeves should not expose too much of your wrists. Make sure that the jacket does not bind in the shoulders, but that it is also snug enough to stay in place in the even of the mishap (again, adjustment tabs or belts are handy for this).

If there is a lining, ask yourself if it will be sufficient for all of your riding needs. And if it won't, make sure there is some room under the jacket for one or more additional layers (might we suggest polar fleece and/or electric garments for cold weather). Just make sure the jacket isn't TOO BIG either, since it may balloon and be impossible to seal the wind out when riding at speed.

HOW TO CARE FOR YOUR JACKET

How you will need to care for your jacket will vary depending on the materials from which it is made. The first thing to do is read the labels or any literature that came with the jacket. The manufacturer will probably give you the best information for the particular materials used in your jacket. The materials that modern riding jackets are made from might have specific cleaning instructions. Be sure to follow the instructions provided to ensure a long life for your jacket.

Kidney Belt

◗ See Figure 76

A kidney belt, or support belt, is basically a large elastic band that is worn around the waist to help support your back and internal organs. Motocross riders have worn them for many years, and ATV riders are quickly discovering their advantages. It is a good idea for all ATV riders to wear a kidney belt to avoid bruising internal organs. If you have ridden an ATV before for any length of time, chances are that you are quite familiar with the "kicked in the stomach" feeling. A kidney belt will help eliminate bruising, and support your lower back.

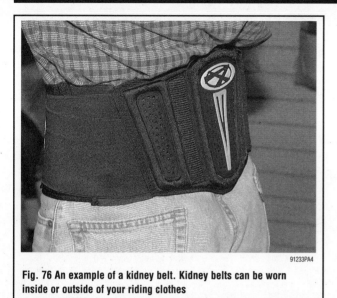

Fig. 76 An example of a kidney belt. Kidney belts can be worn inside or outside of your riding clothes

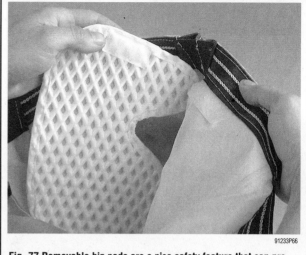

Fig. 77 Removable hip pads are a nice safety feature that can provide a little extra protection in the event of a fall

Choose Something You Like

When you wear a kidney belt, most of it will be covered by your pants, so colors and styles won't matter too much. There are a large variety of belts available, all made from different materials. Some belts use hard foam for support, and others are made with plastic rods woven inside the fabric. Look for something that suits your taste.

Choose Gear To Match Your Riding

When it comes to kidney belts, **every** ATV rider can benefit from wearing one. All types of riding can really shake up your internals, and a kidney belt can help alleviate the symptoms. Riders that spend a lot of time riding on rough, rocky surfaces are going to benefit the most from a kidney belt. Farmers and utility riders might have less need for a kidney belt, since actual riding time can be short.

Choose Quality Gear

When looking for a quality kidney belt, the main thing to look for is high quality hook and loop fasteners. Check the strength when you separate the halves; if it takes considerable effort to pull them apart, then you can be assured of high quality. Anything less will lose its grip after a short time.

Choose Something That Fits Properly

Finding a kidney belt that fits properly shouldn't be a problem, since they are elastic and have hook and loop for adjustment. Most kidney belts are the same width; though some are available in Junior sizes. Also, keep in mind the width of the belt. A thick belt will provide good support, but may feel constrictive in anything but the most upright sitting position. Narrow belts will allow a little more freedom, but may not be as supportive. If you have never worn a kidney belt, ask to try one on and sit on an ATV in the showroom. If the belt feels too restrictive, try a narrower belt until you find one that fits to your liking.

Pants

▶ See Figures 77 and 78

Specialized ATV riding pants offer the same unique features that a riding jacket offer. The position of a rider is taken into consideration, so the possible problems of binding and tightness that you might experience from regular pants

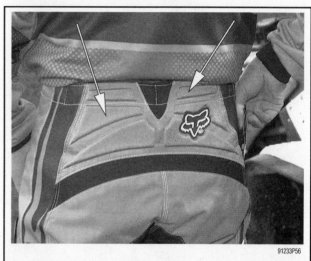

Fig. 78 These pants have sewn-in padding around the back for additional protection and support

are eliminated. There are also knee pads and hip pads that are sewn into the pants to provide crash protection that denim pants do not. Some pants have removable hip and knee pads that are secured by hook and loop, or are held in place by special pockets.

So how do you select a pair of riding pants? Remember the 4 basics mentioned at the beginning of this section:

1. Choose something you like.
2. Choose something that fits your riding.
3. Choose something that is high quality.
4. Choose something that fits properly.

Choose Something You Like

As with all of your other gear, find a pair of pants that appeal to you. Plain and subtle, or loud and colorful, there is something out there for you.

Choose Gear To Match Your Riding

The majority of weekend riders usually wear denim pants. If you are considering a pair of specialized off-road riding pants, chances are you're a sport-type rider. The pants featured here are designed for high-performance riding; but just about any ATV rider can benefit from the extra protection and convenience that riding pants can provide. Knee pads and hip pads sewn into riding pants can greatly reduce injury in the event of an accident.

Most riding pants are made from breathable, water-resistant materials. If you spend any time riding in wet weather, this is something to consider. Another feature to consider in a pair of riding pants is ease of cleaning. If the riding pants are machine washable, they can be tossed into the laundry with your regular clothes.

Choose Quality Gear

▶ **See Figures 79 and 80**

Buying a quality pair of riding pants is just like any other garment. You'll want to look for durable material, heavy-duty stitching, etc. Some pants have

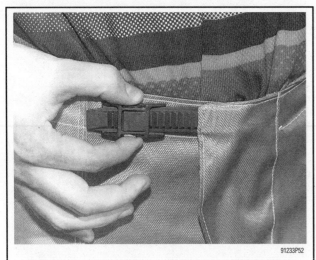

91233P52

Fig. 79 These pants feature a heavy-duty plastic clip instead of buttons. Features of this type mean high quality

91233P53

Fig. 80 High-wearing areas such as the knees should be reinforced

reinforcement panels on the inside of the knees, made from leather-type materials. Also, check to see if the pants have integrated padding, or if the pads are removable. Usually, removable pads allow the pants to be placed into a dryer. (the foam and plastic pads may melt.) Of course there are always exceptions, and there are may be pants without removable pads that can be machine dried.

Choose Something That Fits Properly

ATV riding pants are sized just like regular pants—according to waist size. However, the length of riding pants is usually standard. Riding pants are supposed to be worn inside your boots, (to prevent them from becoming caught on frame rails, chain sprockets, and hot exhaust pipes) so the length is not very important. When trying on a pair of pants, consider the extra space needed for hip pads, a jersey, and a kidney belt. If possible, it is best to trial fit pants while wearing a jersey and kidney belt; this will provide a more accurate fit. Another factor to consider is room for layers (thermal underwear) for winter riding.

HOW TO CARE FOR YOUR PANTS

How you will need to care for your pants will vary depending on the materials from which they are made. The first thing to do is read the labels or garment owner's manual. The manufacturer will probably give you the best information for the particular materials used in your gear, and the required method for safe washing.

The same general advice that we gave for jackets tends to apply to pants of the same material. The lower legs of your pants are usually subjected to a lot more dirt and mud than your jacket. After riding through a mud-strewn field, it is not unlikely to find that you are COMPLETELY FILTHY from the knees down. If your pants are soaked through with mud and dirt, it is best to soak them in water to loosen the dirt from the fibers. Depending on the garment, you may be able to machine wash (and maybe even dry) the pants after they are clean of loose dirt. Remember, always follow the manufacturer instructions regarding cleaning to avoid damaging the pants.

If your pants are made from a water-resistant material, or have been treated with a waterproofing spray like 3M Scotchgard® , constant washing and drying may reduce the ability to resist water.

Chest Protectors

▶ **See Figures 81 and 82**

A chest protector is worn over or under a jacket to provide extra crash protection to your chest, shoulders and back. They are usually made from flexible

91233P47

Fig. 81 An example of a chest protector

Fig. 82 Chest protectors can also be worn under a riding jacket

plastic, and use suspended mesh or foam padding. If you ride in rocky areas, are into sport-type riding, or just looking for additional protection, you should seriously consider a chest protector.

HOW TO SELECT A CHEST PROTECTOR

▶ **See Figure 83**

Chest protectors are offered in many different styles, each for a specific use. A basic chest protector, which is usually a foam or plastic pad worn over the chest, offers minimal protection from flying rocks and debris from other riders. A more elaborate chest protector may include shoulder pads, elbow pads and back pads, providing the ultimate in upper body protection. Some manufacturers offer modular chest protectors, so you can add (or remove) pads to customize a chest protector to your liking.

As with most of the gear within this section, there are four basic guidelines to follow:
1. Choose something you like.
2. Choose something that fits your riding.
3. Choose something that is high quality.
4. Choose something that fits properly.

Choose Something You Like

Some chest protectors can make you feel like a Storm Trooper from a Star Wars movie set. You might feel strange trying one on, but keep in mind that chest protectors are for protection, not looks. As with most off-road gear, a variety of colors are available, so you can match your chest protector with your other gear. You can also wear your chest protector under your riding jacket (make sure it fits under your jacket before you buy it) if you don't care for the color or style. Remember, you're going for maximum protection here, so looks shouldn't be a top priority.

Choose Gear To Match Your Riding

Obviously, if you only use your ATV for working on the farm, a chest protector is a bit excessive. Sport-types and racers are going to benefit the most from a chest protector. In the event of a crash, a chest protector will greatly reduce the chance of injury, especially one equipped with shoulder and elbow pads.

Choose Quality Gear

▶ **See Figures 84, 85 and 86**

When looking at a chest protector, check where the straps attach to the plastic. Higher quality chest protectors will actually rivet or sew the nylon straps right on to the plastic. Look for a well-made connection. Also, look at the padding; how is it attached to the plastic? Is the plastic flexible, but strong, or does it seem to be brittle? As with other apparel, thoroughly inspect the quality of the construction.

Choose Something That Fits Properly

Chest protectors usually don't come in shirt sizes. Typically, there are two sizes—small and large. When trying on a chest protector, sit on an ATV in the showroom and see if the way things fit changes. Move your arms back and forth—does anything bind or constrict your movement? Different brands of chest protectors offer different features, and some might fit you better than others. If possible, try on a few chest protectors; hopefully one will fit you properly and won't constrict your movement.

CHEST PROTECTOR CARE

Most chest protectors are made from plastic, foam, and fabric webbing. Cleaning your chest protectors in most cases is simply a matter of wiping them clean with a soft cloth. If they are covered in mud, hosing them off with fresh water will help to loosen any heavy dirt, to avoid scratching. Be very careful with

Fig. 83 Chest protectors come in different styles and types to fit your needs

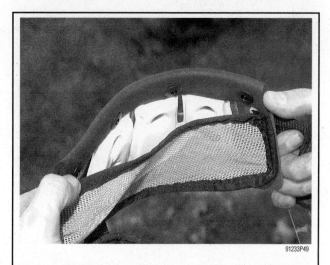

Fig. 84 The shoulder pads on this chest protector use mesh to suspend the outer shell above the shoulder

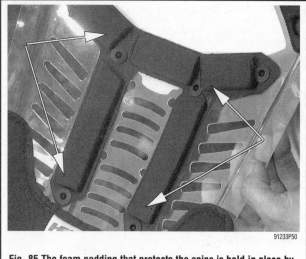

Fig. 85 The foam padding that protects the spine is held in place by plastic clips on this chest protector

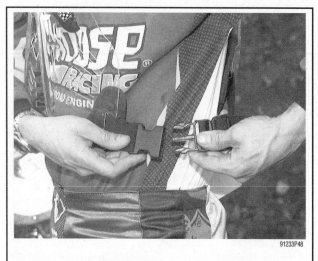

Fig. 86 The plastic buckles on this chest protector make for easy removal

Fig. 87 If your jacket is made from Gore-tex® or other water-resistant material, you may not need a rainsuit

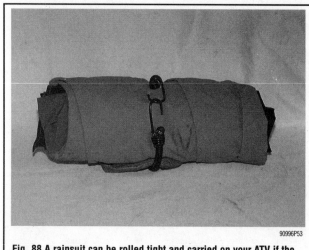

Fig. 88 A rainsuit can be rolled tight and carried on your ATV if the rain becomes severe

chemicals; the plastic or foam can easily be damaged. Light soap and water is always a safe way to clean your chest protectors.

In addition to keeping your chest protector clean, regular inspection of any rivets, webbing, or glued joints is essential. If a worn piece of webbing or broken rivet is found, fix it (or have it fixed) immediately. Your chest protector won't do you any good if it is falling apart. If your chest protector develops any cracks in the plastic, it should be replaced, since it's ability to safeguard you in an accident is greatly diminished.

Rainsuits

♦ **See Figures 87 and 88**

HOW TO SELECT A RAINSUIT

If you spend a lot of time riding your ATV in rainy weather, a rainsuit is just about a requirement. Rainsuits can make wet weather riding a much more bearable experience, and to some of you, even fun. If you're warm and dry inside your rainsuit, and it is pouring rain outside, splashing through water and mud can be a real hoot.

So how do you select gear to protect you from the rain? Remember the 4 basics mentioned at the beginning of this section:

1. Choose something you like.
2. Choose something that fits your riding.
3. Choose something that is high quality.
4. Choose something that fits properly.

Choose Something You Like

As usual, buy what you like, but keep a realistic perspective on things. When you're riding in the rain, its probably because you have to. So, it is safe to say that looks are not near as important as function when buying a rainsuit. Buying a rainsuit you like is probably going to mean buying one that works.

Choose Gear To Match Your Riding

If a lot of your riding takes place in cold, nasty weather, (like when you're hunting for the weekend and the weather turns foul) then you may wish to opt for an insulated rainsuit. But, if your riding may lead to hot, sticky rain showers, then something breathable is going to offer better comfort (just keep in mind that on a hot, sticky summer night, with rain and humidity in the 100% area, then nothing is going to be particularly comfortable, breathable or not).

You'll have to decide between 1-piece and 2-piece suits. We've often heard that 1-piece suits are supposed to be more storm worthy. Something about there not being much of a chance for water getting in between the jacket and pants. But our experience has proven otherwise with a few different suits. Depending on your riding position, a 1-piece suit may allow water to puddle in a bunched crotch area and seep through zippers and seams. Also, the increased difficulty which sometimes comes with pulling these monsters over your gear may stress and tear at seams. Add to this a major downside that they are either ON or OFF. If your own a 1-piece suit, you can never wear only the jacket or pants.

A 2-piece suit is nice because of the versatility. You can wear only the pants or jacket (whether you are riding or not, the jacket can be used as a windbreaker or rain coat). If it rained overnight, you can put only the pants on to deal with the mud spray until the ground dries out. You can also find more creative ways to pack a 2-piece, since each piece folds or rolls into a smaller package than the 1-piece rainsuit. Your only concern with a 2-piece suit should be whether or not it leaks at the waist and, as long as the hem on the jacket is long enough, this should not be an issue. As a matter of fact, if the hem is below your crotch, it may prevent water from pooling and leaking through zippers, a definite advantage over 1-piece suits.

Choose Quality Gear

If the material feels really cheap and the price supports your suspicion, then walk away from it. Chances are, light and cheap rainsuits won't survive their first real day of riding in the rain. Even if a cheap suit makes it through one or two storms, it will probably eventually tear when you take it off (or worse, when you put it on) sometime.

Good signs that a rainsuit will last are those same details we talked about with jackets and pants. Look for a rainsuit with a lining (it doesn't have to be insulated, just a lining which makes is easier to slide the material over damp clothing or boots). Storm flaps which help seal zippers (the better storm flaps are usually equipped with hook and loop fasteners to hold them closed over the zippers) are signs that a rainsuit is really designed to keep you dry. Good suits will have plenty of other handy features such as a variety of pockets, bright colors and or reflective materials and, if you are buying a REALLY good suit, heat resistant panels in the legs (to help prevent it from becoming a melted puddle on your engine).

Choose Something That Fits Properly

They key to a decent rainsuit is that it must be big enough to fit over your normal riding gear, yet still be small enough to prevent excessive flapping or tearing. If a large rainsuit balloons up too badly, it will give more places for water to find its way in. If it is too oversized you may find yourself tripping over it.

HOW TO CARE FOR YOUR RAINSUIT

Whenever you wear a rainsuit the first thing you want to do when you get home is to hang it up in the shower or the garage and let it dry. Even if most of it seems dry already, don't just roll it up and stuff it in a bag, you will be surprised just how bad it can smell when you unroll it at a later date and find it was still damp when you put it away.

If you are completely covered in mud, take a moment to rinse the suit off with a hose or even in the shower. If you like, you don't have to take it off to rinse it (remember it is designed to keep you dry). Try to avoid wiping the dirt off it once it is dry because you risk scratching or tearing it.

If the suit is made from Gore-Tex® or some other breathable material, follow the manufacturer's instructions regarding cleaning. Suits like this will vary from the type which can be placed in the washing machine to ones which must be carefully hand rinsed.

Electric Garments/Cold Weather Gear

◆ See Figures 89 and 90

If you put your ATV away during winters because you live in a part of the country where the weather gets cold and uninviting, then there may be a way to lengthen your riding season. As a matter of fact, barring snow and ice, we've found that even here in cold Pennsylvania, we can get away without storing our ATVs for the winter, largely thanks to owning the right gear.

The key to cold weather riding is proper riding gear. A good full face helmet (like a snowmobile or street motorcycle type), a high quality jacket, pants and boots which also cut the wind and insulate you will make a tremendous difference. But even when all of this is combined, you may still find that a weekend ride is tough even with snow melting. The answer then becomes electric garments.

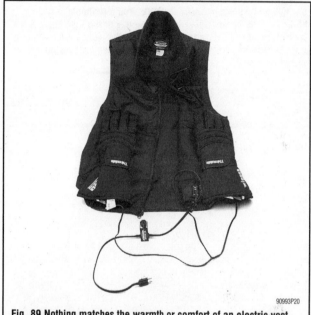

90993P20

Fig. 89 Nothing matches the warmth or comfort of an electric vest and a pair of electric gloves on a cold day—this combination from Widder® shows the gloves, wiring harness with thermostat and vest with heated collar

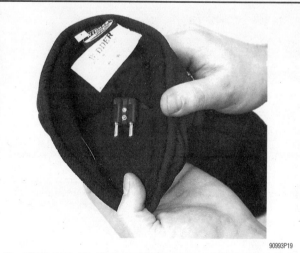

90993P19

Fig. 90 Most electric gloves are attached to your ATV's battery using easy to connect plugs like these banana plugs found on Widder® gear

Widder Enterprises®, supplied us with some equipment for testing when working on this book. By using their electric gloves and vest, you are set for just about any weather (at least any weather that your ATV will start in). The Widder® vest provides the all important warming of your central core which actually makes the rest of your gear feel like it is doing a better job from your jacket to your boots. One very cool (uhhh, make that warm) feature of the vest we tested was a heated collar that brought heat right up to the base of your neck, just below the helmet.

❊❊ CAUTION

One VERY IMPORTANT POINT to make here is that electric components can fail (whether it is the accessory jack, the wiring or the garment itself). Although we have had NO problems with the test gear, the fact is that they COULD stop working with little notice, so DO NOT attempt a long distance ride without enough layers or other gear to keep you warm, JUST IN CASE. You'd probably survive a short trip if the harness shorted out one day or the fuse blew. But, wouldn't it suck to freeze to death deep in the woods or on a mountainside because you accidentally cut the wiring harness on the muffler clamp while checking the rear chain.

HOW TO SELECT COLD WEATHER GEAR

So how do you select an electric garment? Remember the 4 basics mentioned at the beginning of this section:

1. Choose something you like.
2. Choose something that fits your riding.
3. Choose something that is high quality.
4. Choose something that fits properly.

Choose Something You Like

Let's face it, most electric garments are worn under your other riding gear so style is not particularly important here. Unless of course someone is dumb enough to make an electric vest in only one color (hot pink), in which case you probably would think twice about buying it anyway.

Of course electric gloves are a little different since they will probably be seen. Then again, most types that we have seen were not radically styled and would look decent with most riding gear. And it is really hard to escape the fact that even if someone does decide to poke fun at you for how your gear looks, chances are they are freezing their obnoxious asses off anyway, while you are riding along toasty. Ohhhhh, what was that? You want to stop to warm up for a minute?. Nahh let's keep going, I could easily do another couple hours. . . .

Choose Gear To Match Your Riding

There are two things to keep in mind when selecting electric riding apparel, match your needs AND your ATV's alternator output.

ASSESS YOUR NEEDS

▶ **See Figures 91 and 92**

When it comes to your needs, we suggest a conservative approach. Start by riding with your best non-electric gear and see what gets cold. Make sure that you have blocked the wind as effectively as you can. A helmet lining or balaclava will help a lot, and make sure you seal the helmet to your jacket (the BEST method we have found for this is the Aerostitch® wind triangle).

Then, once you have decided that electric garments are the way to go, start with a vest or jacket lining. The act of warming your core will help to keep the rest of your body warmer as blood carries that heat out towards your extremities. If the vest alone does not do the trick, you might want to consider gloves and/or pants. We have found that the vest should be sufficient for most situations, but only if you have high quality gear in the form of pants, boots and gloves (as we described in earlier sections). If your hands are not behind some form of brush guard, these are the next likely to get cold (even with a good regular pair of winter gloves) and many companies, like Widder® offer electric gloves to be used with their vest. This combination can make you feel right at home even in sub-freezing temperatures.

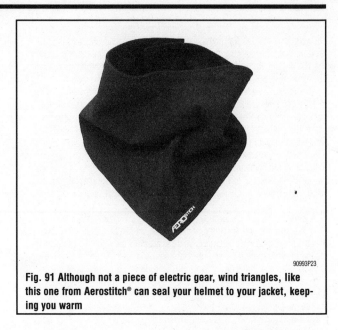

Fig. 91 Although not a piece of electric gear, wind triangles, like this one from Aerostitch® can seal your helmet to your jacket, keeping you warm

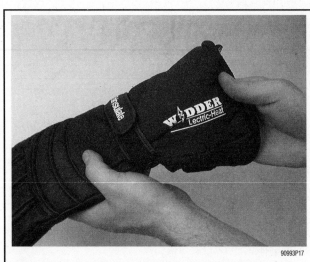

Fig. 92 An electric vest or jacket may be enough, but if not, consider a pair of gloves to keep your hands warm too

ASSESS YOUR ATV'S ABILITY

Your ATV has one, important limiting factor when it comes to electric apparel; the alternator output. The simple fact is that if you add enough accessories, you will eventually start consuming more electricity than your alternator can produce (you may notice the result if your headlight starts to fade once you have turned on all of your toys). The good news is that virtually all modern ATVs have alternators with sufficient capacity to run one or two pieces of electric clothing.

➡**Some older ATVs might have underpowered charging systems. They might have difficulty keeping up with the demand of electric clothing, once the engine RPM drops below a certain point. With these older models, you've got two options; Upgrade the alternator (or lighting coil) with a higher output kit, or, you can just keep the revs up (and watch the headlight, if it goes from dim to bright at a certain point, you know where the revs should be).**

Choose Quality Gear

There aren't that many makers of electric riding apparel. But with that said, even fewer of them have a reputation. Ask around, and look at any articles or reviews you can get your hands on. The company who supplied samples for our testing has an EXCELLENT reputation. We have even had some dealing with their customer service groups (a few years ago, Widder® was kind enough to repair a glove at no charge which was out of their warranty period, but had developed an open in the heater grid . . . impressive).

Like with most gear, if the company has a name it has earned in the ATV and motorcycle industry, that is a good indication of the quality merchandise they sell.

Choose Something That Fits Properly

When it comes to proper fit, most electric garments should fit like their non-heated counterparts. Gloves should not be too big or too small. Pants should fit comfortably over your jeans. The difference is with vests or with jacket linings. Most manufacturer's recommend that the garment be comfortable but snug (to prevent cold air from finding its way between you and the garment). You probably want to leave additional room between the garment and the jacket for other insulation layers, especially if you want to be prepared for the worst, should you unexpectedly be unable to use the electric heater one day.

HOW TO CARE FOR YOUR COLD WEATHER GEAR

▶ **See Figure 93**

Because electric apparel has a few features most of your other riding gear lacks (like wires and heating elements) it is important that you follow the manufacturer's instructions closely. Most garments however can be washed. You should periodically inspect the wiring for breaks in the insulation and take care with when connecting or disconnecting it. Never pull directly on a wire, ALWAYS grasp and pull the wiring connector. A little dielectric grease on the connectors won't do any harm and may help make the connections easier to fasten and unfasten.

Any electric gloves which contain leather shells should be treated, just like normal leather. Clean it carefully and treat it with Lexol® or another appropriate leather treatment to restore the material's natural oils.

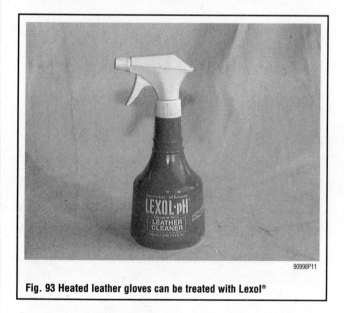

Fig. 93 Heated leather gloves can be treated with Lexol®

INSTALLING AN ACCESSORY OUTLET

▶ **See Figures 94 thru 99**

Some of the later model ATVs already have built in accessory outlets, and for the rest of you, well, you're on your own. One neat feature about installing an accessory jack is that it instantly gives you an easy way to check your battery (using a voltmeter) or to attach a Battery Tender® or other battery maintaining device when you are not riding.

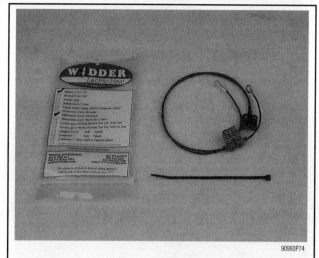

Fig. 94 Most electric garments will come with an adapter that is wired to the battery and becomes your accessory outlet

Fig. 95 To install the outlet, start by accessing the battery and disconnecting the wiring

Before installing the outlet, figure out where it should go in relation to the apparel. Start by putting on all of your riding gear and climbing onto your ATV. Look at where the wiring harness hangs and where it would be most convenient to locate the outlet. It is really nice to be able to plug and unplug the jack from the seated position, but this is not possible on all models and on some you will have to plug in before climbing on board.

Once you have a good idea where you would like the outlet to go, you will have to access your battery for installation. On many models, all that is required to access the battery is to remove the seat. Check your owners manual, as it usually gives you some idea how to get at the battery.

1. Make sure the ignition switch is OFF and remove the key.
2. Locate your ATV's battery and remove any components necessary to access it.
3. Once the battery is accessible, loosen the negative battery cable by turning the retaining bolt counterclockwise. Usually this can be done with a screwdriver, wrench or a socket. The wrench or socket is really the best method to make sure you don't strip the terminal bolt, but it really depends on the amount of access you have.
4. Once the negative cable is disconnected it is always a good idea to wrap some electrical tape around it or put a small plastic baggie over the end

to prevent it from touching the battery again and accidentally completing a circuit.

5. Loosen the bolt and remove the positive battery cable from the battery. Be careful never to short the battery by allowing the wrench or other tool to bridge the gap between the terminals.

6. Place the accessory outlet wiring over the battery terminal bolts, then insert the bolts back through the cables and into the battery. Start with the positive cable. If there is an inline fuse in the accessory outlet wiring, be sure to connect it to the positive battery cable.

7. Secure the positive battery cable to the battery, then secure the negative cable.

8. Use a voltmeter to check for battery voltage across the terminals of the accessory jack. Then use the voltmeter to check voltage directly across the 2 battery terminals. The voltage should be identical or VERY, VERY close. If not,

there is likely a problem with one of the two connections and you should double-check them before proceeding. If there is a significant difference in the voltages, your accessory jack may not work.

9. Once you are sure the connections are good, route the accessory outlet wiring the way you have planned to position the jack. Be sure to keep the wiring away from any moving parts (running it along frame rails and along other chassis wiring is a good idea).

10. Use a few wiring ties to make sure the accessory outlet wiring and jack remain in position.

11. Double-check battery voltage across the jack terminals one last time, then install the seat, as necessary. When installing any remaining plastic pieces, pay close attention that none of the pieces will interfere with or damage the wiring once they are in position.

12. Ride Warm.

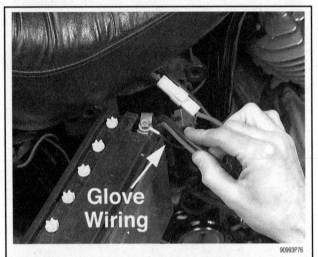

Fig. 96 Place the wiring on the battery cable retaining bolt, but make sure it does not get between the cable and battery (put it on the backside of the cable, closer to the bolt)

Fig. 98 If the battery is removed to install the outlet, be VERY CAREFUL not to pinch the wires as it is reinstalled

Fig. 97 Route the wiring so that it will not be damaged by rubbing on other components in use

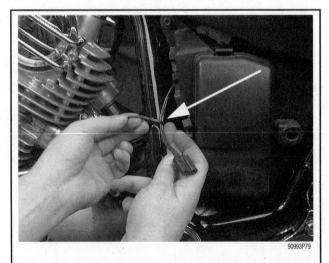

Fig. 99 Once you have finished, use one or more wire ties to hold the outlet securely in place

4

ENGINE AND DRIVETRAIN MAINTENANCE

ENGINE MAINTENANCE

♦ **See Figures 1, 2 and 3**

In this world of throw away appliances and "drive it till it breaks" attitudes, it is easy to see why people often ignore maintenance on things from household oil burners to cars and trucks. But, ignoring to properly maintain your ATV could cost you (or others) greatly.

If you are serious about safety, then you should take a serious interest in the maintenance of your ATV. Learn from the examples of those involved with other machines that are unpleasant to be around when mechanical failures occur. Aircraft mechanics and racing pit crews are two examples of people who take their jobs VERY, VERY seriously. They use checklists and keep log books to be certain that no maintenance procedures are overlooked and that no critical part is used beyond its normal working life. To these people, maintenance is PREVENTATIVE not corrective.

Don't wait until a part stops working to give your ATV attention. Periodic maintenance to the engine, drivetrain and chassis will help to make for a safer riding experience. It doesn't matter if you are racing, trail riding, or just working on a jobsite, knowing that your ATV is in top shape and that it will get the job done safely will allow you to concentrate on the better things, like that big hill ahead or the rocks on the trail.

Fig. 1 From changing spark plugs . . .

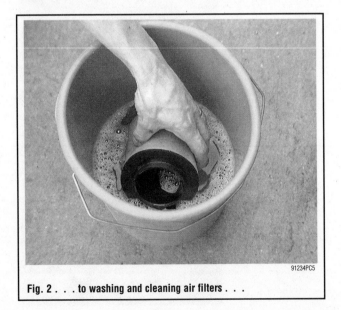

Fig. 2 . . . to washing and cleaning air filters . . .

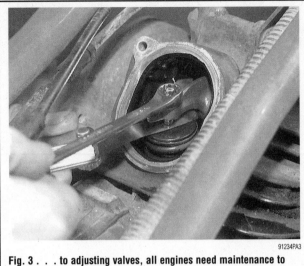

Fig. 3 . . . to adjusting valves, all engines need maintenance to keep them running properly

Before reading any further, be sure that you have a copy of the owner's manual for your particular ATV. Although we will provide information regarding what is common to ATV maintenance, you should always check your owner's manual first. Remember that every ATV is built different, and a manufacturer may have a unique maintenance requirement, that although it is not the norm for the industry, might be very important on your particular model.

For example, manufacturers have different ways of checking the engine oil with a dipstick. Some require unscrewing the dipstick, wiping it clean and screwing it in all the way to obtain a reading. Others simply require wiping the dipstick and sticking it into the opening, without screwing it in at all. If you look at the dipstick on your particular ATV, the difference between the two methods can mean drastically overfilling your engine or running it dangerously low on oil. Your owner's manual will give specifics on these type of requirements.

The topics in this chapter cover most of the powertrain maintenance procedures common to ATVs built today. But, not all ATVs will contain all systems. For instance, if you have an air cooled engine, then you do not have Glycol coolant to check or replace periodically (your engine uses air and oil for cooling purposes, NOT coolant). Another example is that ATVs use various means of final drive, either a chain, or a driveshaft, or a belt, and your ATV will usually only have one of these (there are exceptions). Identify the topics which apply to your ATV by comparing the maintenance chart of your owners manual to the list of items in this (and the next) sections' table of contents.

Make sure that you have a complete checklist of maintenance items for your model, then follow the techniques provided to help assure a long and healthy life for you and your ATV.

A Word About Warranties

If you have a new ATV with a manufacturer's warranty, then it is critically important that you follow ALL OF THE MANUFACTURER'S recommendations regarding care and maintenance. It is also very important that you document everything that you do (or that a mechanic does, if you choose). Keep a log book with receipts, time and dates of services and notes of anything in particular that was noticed during your service. For instance:

June 12th, I performed a 600 mile service. Changed all fluids (receipt attached). I noticed that the drive belt was just out of spec (3/4 in. deflection, overnight cold). So I adjusted it, it's dead center of spec now (7/16 in.). I'll make a note to keep a close eye on that . . .

If you perform your own maintenance on an ATV that is under warranty, this will be the only proof that the required procedures were performed (just in case something goes wrong that the manufacturer is reluctant about fixing for free).

MANUFACTURER'S FLUIDS

♦ See Figure 4

This is a tough one. Ask anyone involved with ATV maintenance and they will probably have an opinion on which fluids are best for your ATV. Some will say to use only specially made oils only for ATVs and motorcycles, while others will swear that normal automotive fluids are fine. Each will probably have a story to back up their position like, "I once knew a guy who used synthetic car oil in his ATV and BAMMM! It blew up! Just like that, I mean he poured it in an' both he and the ATV, well they was vaporized in an instant, like one of them thar ray-guns on TV."

Ok, maybe we are exaggerating a little here. Well, we are going to give you some recommendations. We may even suggest that there are alternatives to the special products sold by ATV and motorcycle manufacturers (in some cases). BUT, again, remember that if your precious baby is under warranty, you have another source of motivation to buy your oil from the dealer.

Manufacturers will have less to complain about if they want to dispute a warranty claim and you can prove that you have used NOTHING but their recommended fluids in your ATV. ALSO, the more often you go in and buy oil from your local dealer (the same guy/gal who would be responsible for convincing the manufacturer's rep to go ahead and pay for a warranty repair), the more likely it is that they are going to know you. And they are going to remember you as one of their valued customers, who is always in their shop every couple of months buying oil, a filter, some gaskets and a new T-shirt (hey you didn't think they made ALL their money from ATV sales and oil did you?).

Once the warranty expires on your ATV, well, then you have a lot more freedom to make your OWN decision on what fluids to use and where to buy them.

Fig. 4 You are never WRONG using a manufacturer's fluid, it is just not always necessary

MANUFACTURER PARTS

♦ See Figure 5

Using manufacturer parts while your ATV is under warranty is just like using manufacturer lubricants. It is always a good idea to stick with what the manufacturer recommends in the owner's manual, should there become any problems with your ATV. Using a factory oil filter would be a much better choice than an aftermarket one, granted it may cost you a few extra bucks. The manufacturer will have little to dispute if you've shown that factory parts and fluids have been used for maintaining your ATV.

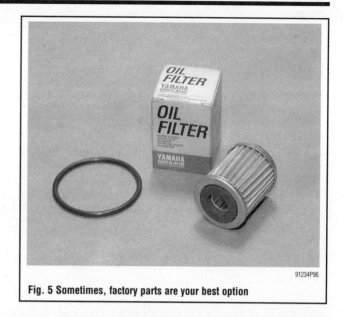

Fig. 5 Sometimes, factory parts are your best option

Fuel Requirements

SELECTING THE PROPER FUEL

♦ See Figure 6

Gasoline is a mixture of hydrocarbons (composed of hydrogen and carbon), produced by refining crude oil. When gasoline burns, these compounds separate into hydrogen and carbon atoms and unite with oxygen atoms. The results obtained from burning gasoline are dependent upon its most important characteristics: octane rating, volatility and density.

Gasoline mixtures and additives will vary slightly from brand-to-brand, but it could also vary from station-to-station too (if a particular station has a problem with moisture or contamination in one or more of its tanks). When deciding on a gasoline, start with the manufacturer's recommended octane rating and try tank fulls from various local stations. Run a few tank fulls of each and settle on the one which gives you the best gas mileage and anti-knock protection. If you get similar results from various brands and stations, then you can likely count of those results from most fill-ups. If one particular gas station or brand seems to give your ATV trouble, avoid it.

➡ **DON'T WASTE YOUR MONEY overbuying gasoline with super-high octane. If your manufacturer doesn't require it, and your ATV runs fine on a lower octane, then go ahead and use the lower octane. For the most part, the quality of the gasoline and the use of additives will be reasonably comparable from one octane to another with a single brand of gas. Always filling-up with Super-Elite-Mega-Premium 115 octane probably will not have any appreciable benefits over the same brand's regular gasoline, unless your engine is seriously high compression (read as extreme aftermarket engine work) or seriously clogged with carbon.**

Octane Rating

Simply put, the octane rating of a gasoline is its ability to resist knock, a detonation or uncontrolled combustion in the cylinder which sounds like a sharp metallic noise. Knock can occur for a variety of reasons, one of which is the incorrect octane rating for the engine in your ATV. To understand why knock occurs, you must understand why knock doesn't occur.

Under normal operating conditions, the firing of the spark plug initiates the burning of the fuel/air mixture in the combustion chamber. Once the plug fires, a wall of flame starts outward from the plug in all directions at once. This flame front moves evenly and rapidly throughout the entire combustion chamber until the entire fuel/air mixture is burned. This even, rapid progress of the burning fuel/air mixture is highly dependent on the octane rating of the gasoline. If the

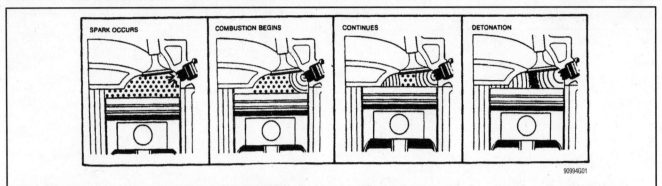

Fig. 6 Using the proper octane fuel will help prevent detonation (a damaging condition which occurs when the anti-knock quality of the fuel used does not meet the engine requirements allowing part of the mixture to combust before the spark plug ignites the rest)

octane rating is too low, the last part of the compressed fuel/air mixture may ignite before the flame front reaches it, in effect creating two areas of combustion within the cylinder. The problem occurs because, while the original combustion is proceeding at a carefully controlled rate, this new combustion is simply a sudden sharp explosion. This abrupt increase in pressure is what creates the knocking sound in the combustion chamber. As far as the piston is concerned, the damage it inflicts is exactly like striking the piston top with a heavy hammer. Knock is very damaging to the engine, since it causes extraordinary wear to bearings, piston crowns, and other vital engine parts. Engines can actually be destroyed through excessive engine knock.

Engine knock can be controlled by using a gas with the proper octane rating. Octane measurements made under laboratory conditions have led to "Research" and "Motor" octane ratings. In general, the research octane number tends to be about 6 to 10 points higher than the motor octane rating (for what is essentially the same gasoline). Since the early seventies, most octane ratings on gas pumps in the U.S. have been the average of the research and motor octane numbers. For instance, if the gasoline had a research octane rating of 100, and a motor octane rating of 90, the octane rating found on the pump would be 95.

Your owner's manual will probably indicate the type and octane of gasoline recommended for use in your ATV. however, octane requirements can vary according to the vehicle and the conditions under which it is operating. If you encounter sustained engine knock, wait until your tank is nearly empty, then try a gasoline with a slightly higher octane rating. Don't overbuy—it's a waste of money to buy gasoline of a higher octane than your engine requires in order to satisfy its antiknock need.

As a new ATV is driven, combustion deposits build up and the octane requirement increases until an equilibrium level is reached. Other factors which can increase the octane an engine requires are higher air or engine temperatures, lower altitudes, lower humidity, a more advanced ignition spark timing, a leaner carburetor setting, sudden acceleration, and frequent stop-and-go driving which increases the build-up of combustion chamber deposits.

Volatility

The volatility of any liquid is its ability to vaporize. A highly volatile gasoline will help a cold engine start easily and run smoothly while it is warming up. However, the use of a highly volatile gasoline in warm weather tends to cause vapor lock, a condition not uncommon for older, carbureted automobiles, but almost never seen in ATVs. The condition occurs when gasoline actually vaporizes before it arrives at the carburetor jet where atomization is supposed to take place. This premature vaporization used to occur in the fuel lines or in a section of the carburetor on automobiles. When use of too highly-volatile fuel leads to vapor lock, the engine becomes starved for fuel and will either lose power or stall. Although refiners used to vary the percentage of volatile components in their gasoline according to season and locality, in order to help prevent this, vapor lock was more likely to occur in the early spring, when some stations may not have received supplies of lower-volatility gasoline.

Luckily, the design of most carbureted ATVs make vapor lock unlikely. Whereas carbureted automobiles used long fuel lines to travel from the fuel tank to the engine (and a large carburetor fuel bowl which sat right on TOP of the engine), the gasoline in most ATVs has a short trip to take from the tank to the float bowl (which is smaller than car's) and to the intake manifold. The gasoline spends less time in the lines and float bowls and they are both likely to be cooler than their counterparts on an automobile.

Density

Density is another property of gasoline which can affect your fuel economy. It indicates how much chemical energy the gasoline contains. Density is generally measured in BTU's per gallon (the BTU, or British Thermal Unit, is a standard unit of energy), and usually varies less than 2% among most gasolines but can vary as much as 4–8%. This indicates that gas mileage could vary by as much as 4–8%, depending on the density of the gasoline you happen to choose.

Oxygenated gasoline has become popular (or necessary) in many areas in order to help reduce emissions. Oxygenated gasoline contains less combustible material than a non-oxygenated counterpart. The result is fewer hydrocarbons per gallon. Oxygenated fuels do not harm your ATV, they do however rob it of some power and some gas mileage.

Additives

Practically as important as octane rating and volatility are the additives that refiners put into their gasolines. The fuel injector cleaners found in nearly every major brand of gasoline today include detergent additives which help clean the tiny passages in the carburetor or fuel injector systems. This helps to ensure consistent fuel/air mixtures necessary for smooth running and good gas mileage. Winter additives include fuel line de-icers to reduce carburetor icing. Other additives are used to help control combustion chamber deposits, gum formation, rust, and wear.

Engine Lubrication

▶ See Figure 7

SELECTING THE PROPER OIL

▶ See Figures 8 and 9

Probably because engine oil is the single most important part of routine engine maintenance (for just about internal combustion engines in the world today), there are probably more myths, misunderstandings and urban legends regarding engine oil, than any other mechanical "thing." What we would like to do here is help demystify engine oil and help you make the best decision for what type of oil to purchase for your ATV.

When it comes to engine oil, there are 3 ways you can help improve your ATV's mileage and insure that it delivers good economy for a longer time: 1) understand the functions of oil in your engine, 2) choose the proper oil for various operating conditions, and 3) change the oil and filter at the proper intervals.

The Functions of Engine Oil

What does oil do in your engine? If you answered "lubricate," you're only partially right. While oil is primarily a lubricant, it also performs a number of other functions which are vital to the life and performance of your engine. In addition to being a lubricant, oil also dissipates heat and makes parts run cooler; it helps reduce engine noise; it combats rust and corrosion of metal surfaces; it acts as a seal for pistons, rings, and cylinder walls; it combines with the oil filter to remove foreign substances from the engine.

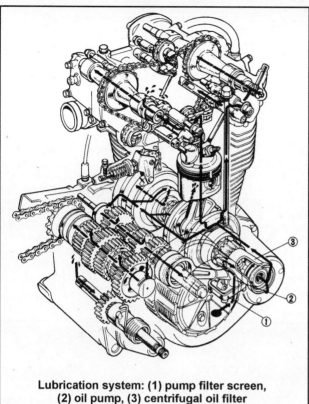

Lubrication system: (1) pump filter screen,
(2) oil pump, (3) centrifugal oil filter

90994G02

Fig. 7 This diagram follows oil paths through a typical unitized (engine and transmission in one case) ATV engine

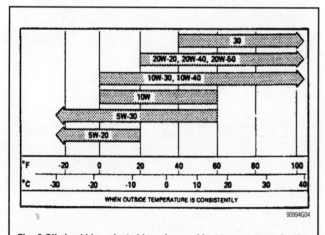

90994G04

Fig. 8 Oil should be selected based on ambient temperatures for the upcoming months—Note this is an example of typical recommendations, refer to your owner's manual to see what your manufacturer recommends

Types Of Engine Oil

Every bottle of engine oil for sale in the U.S. should have a label describing what standards it meets. Engine oil service classifications are designated by the American Petroleum Institute (API), based on the chemical composition of a given type of oil and testing of samples. The ratings include "S" (normal gasoline engine use) and "C" (commercial and fleet) applications. Over the years, the S rating has been supplemented with various letters, each one representing the latest and greatest rating available at the time of its introduction. During recent years these ratings have included SF, SG, SH and most recently (at the time of

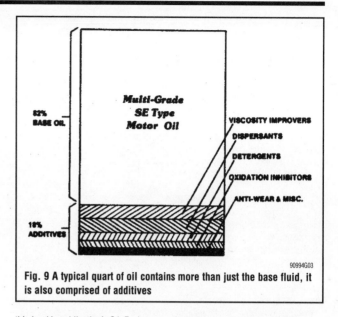

90994G03

Fig. 9 A typical quart of oil contains more than just the base fluid, it is also comprised of additives

this book's publication), SJ. Each successive rating usually meets all of the standards of the previous alpha designation, but also meets some new criteria, meets higher standards and/or contains newer or different additives. Since oil is so important to the life of your engine, you should obviously NEVER use an oil of questionable quality. Oils that are labeled with modern API ratings, including the "energy conserving" donut symbol, have been proven to meet the API quality standards.

OIL VISCOSITY

In addition to meeting the classification of the American Petroleum Institute, your oil should be of a viscosity suitable for the outside temperature in which you'll be riding. Oil must be thin enough to get between the close-tolerance moving parts it must lubricate. Once there, it must be thick enough to separate them with a slippery oil film. If the oil is too thin, it won't separate the parts; if it's too thick, it can't squeeze between them in the first place—either way, excess friction and wear takes place. To complicate matters, cold-morning starts require a thin oil to reduce engine resistance, while high speed driving requires a thick oil which can lubricate vital engine parts at temperatures.

According to the Society of Automotive Engineers' (SAE) viscosity classification system, an oil with a high viscosity number (such as SAE 40 or SAE 50) will be thicker than one with a lower number (SAE 10W). The "W" in 10W indicates that the oil is desirable for use in winter driving, and not stand for "weight". Through the use of special additives, multiple-viscosity oils are available to combine easy starting at cold temperatures with engine protection at high speeds. For example, a 10W40 oil is said to have the viscosity of a 10W oil when the engine is cold and that of a 40 oil when the engine is warm. The use of such an oil will decrease engine resistance and improve your miles per gallon during short trips in which the oil doesn't have a chance to warm up.

Some of the more popular multiple-viscosity oils are 5W30, 10W30, 10W40, 20W-40, 20W-50, and 10W-50. In general, lower weight oils, like 5W-20 or 5W-30 are used for temperatures below 0°F, while medium weight oils like 10W-30 or 10W-40 are used whenever the lowest temperature expected is 0°F., and heavier weight oils like 20W-40 or 20W-50 are recommended whenever the lowest temperature expected is 32°F. However, be certain to consult your owner's manual to determine the proper viscosity range for your ATV and the outside temperature range in which it operates. Air cooled ATVs tend to recommend heavier oils for summer or desert operation (which may bring extreme operating temperatures into play), while water cooled ATVs can usually remain with multi-weight oils because of their more consistent cooling systems.

ADDITIVES

A high-quality engine oil will include a number of chemical compounds known as additives. These are blended in at the refinery and normally fall into the following categories:

Pour Point Depressants help cold starting by making the oil flow more easily at low temperatures. Otherwise, the oil would tend to be a waxy substance just when you need it the most.

Oxidation and Bearing Corrosion Inhibitors help to prevent the formation of gummy deposits which can take place when engine oil oxidizes under high temperatures. In addition, these inhibitors place a protective coating on sensitive bearing metals, which would otherwise be attacked by the chemicals formed by oil oxidation.

Rust and Corrosion Inhibitors protect against water and acids formed by the combustion process. Water is physically separated from the metal parts vulnerable to rust, and corrosive acids are neutralized by alkaline chemicals. The neutralization of combustion acids is an important key to long engine life.

Detergents and Dispersants use teamwork. Detergents clean up the products of normal combustion and oxidation while dispersants keep them suspended until they can be removed by means of the filter or an oil change.

Foam Inhibitors prevent the tiny air bubbles which can be caused by fast-moving engine parts whipping air into the oil. Foam can also occur when the oil level falls too low and the oil pump begins sucking up air instead of oil (like when the kids finish a milkshake). Without foam inhibitors, these tiny air bubbles could cause a loss of lubricating efficiency and cause hydraulic valve lifters to collapse while reducing engine performance and economy significantly.

Viscosity Index Improvers reduce the rate at which an oil thins out when the temperature climbs. These additives are what makes multiple-viscosity oils possible. Without them, a single-weight oil which permitted easy starting on a cold morning might thin out and cause you to lose your engine on a hot afternoon. Using a multiple-viscosity oil cover both bases, allowing the oil to be thin enough to permit cold-weather starting, and provide sufficient lubrication once warmed up.

Friction Modifiers and Extreme Pressure additives are valuable in so-called boundary lubrication, where there is metal-to-metal contact due to the absence or breaking down of the oil film between moving parts. Friction modifiers, or anti-wear agents, deposit protective surface films which reduce the friction and heat of metal-to-metal contact. Extreme pressure additives work by reacting chemically with metal surfaces involved in high pressure contact.

Automotive Oils

Bring this subject up the next time you are bench racing. We dare ya. OK, our lawyers want us to take back that dare, right now.

✳✳ CAUTION

After a really hard ride, DO NOT agitate a fellow rider with whom you have been drinking by bringing up the automotive vs. special ATV oil debate. This can be seriously hazardous to your physical and mental well being. DO NOT ATTEMPT THIS at home or at a campsite. We are serious. Oh and, if you can't walk home, take a cab.

Ask 10 different people and you are almost sure to get as many different opinions on whether or not you can use automotive oils in your ATV. Just picking up our enormous stack of magazines led us to literally dozens of articles mentioning the subject.

Many of the articles punted, saying that you should always follow the manufacturer's recommendations for your ATV. That's a safe position, hard to be wrong with that approach.

Some of the articles mentioned reasons why ATV specific oils might be better. On ATVs where the engine and transmission share the oil, "automotive oils may not stand up to the punishing conditions of transmission gears and wet clutches." Well, that might be true in certain cases.

A few just extolled the virtues of regular oil changes and avoided the issue by recommending that you use a "high quality" oil. Ohhhhhh, go out on a limb won't ya?

Of course time marches on. And, the API has come up with its latest and greatest automotive oil specifications now. A whole new army of "experts" have taken this opportunity to once again denounce automotive oils as not containing enough "special" additives to be used in an ATV. But then again, most name-brand automotive oils are designed to protect a great variety of internal combustion engines from hard working, slower turning pushrod truck motors to high rpm OHC sports cars.

What do we suggest is to talk to other ATV riders (preferably those who ride the same model) and see what they use. Choose a name brand oil which meets the requirements set by your ATV's manufacturer. Of course, probably more important than anything else, use the correct viscosity for the ambient temperature range and change your oil/filter often.

Synthetic Oil

▶ See Figure 10

Synthetic oils are another of those topics which can raise the blood pressure of many who are just "certain" that they have the answer to the world's problems. When synthetics were first marketed, like with so many innovations, people reacted as if this mysterious oil was evil and would surely lead to the downfall of the person who used it (and the engine in which it was used), if not to the complete downfall of our entire civilization.

BUT, take a look around you. Synthetic oils are the first choice of many people who are HARD on their engines. Many racing teams, in all forms of motorsports, rely upon synthetic oils to protect their high dollar, high rpm and high visibility investments. So what is the big deal?

Conventional oils are based on hydrocarbons, but because they are refined, the sizes and shapes of these molecules are highly irregular. Synthetic oils are assembled from different compounds into specifically sized and shaped hydrocarbons. They are completely compatible with conventional oils, but they benefit from having more predictable reactions to severe conditions. In high heat conditions (such as that which can be found in many ATV engines and transmissions), synthetics will resist breaking down better than conventional oils.

Synthetic oils are often more expensive than conventional oils, but if the extra protection they offer is worth it to you (sorta like an insurance policy without the hassle of an agent), then you may want to give them a try.

Fig. 10 A lot of aftermarket oil companies are offering synthetic oils for ATVs and motorcycles

TWO STROKE APPLICATIONS

▶ See Figures 11, 12 and 13

Two-stroke engines are unique in the way that they are lubricated, since the crankcase and transmission are usually completely separated from each other internally. To provide lubrication to the crankcase, oil is added directly into the fuel, and carried into the crankcase with the air and fuel mixture. The reason that a two-stroke engine has to be lubricated in this manner is because of the ports, or holes, that are on the sides of the cylinder wall. If there was engine oil in the crankcase, the oil would escape through the ports (and make quite a mess!).

So, since two-strokes have this unique design, there is no "engine oil" to check or change. The oil you change in a two-stroke engine is actually the transmission oil. Make sure to use the proper oil in the transmission, since the clutch is usually of the "wet" type. A wet clutch is immersed in the same oil that provides lubrication for the transmission gears, and is specially made for this purpose. Certain oils may affect the behavior of the clutch, as well as the shifting of the transmission.

✳✳ CAUTION

It is absolutely imperative that you follow the manufacturer's guidelines regarding the correct mixture ratio of fuel and oil for your two-

Fig. 11 Two-stroke engines use special oil to mix with the fuel

Fig. 12 Oil injection pumps can take some of the hassle out of owning a two-stroke ATV

Fig. 13 This destroyed piston is from a two-stroke engine that did not have the proper ratio of oil mixed into the fuel

stroke engine. Insufficient quantities of oil mixed into the fuel can cause serious engine damage.

Using the manufacturer recommended two-stroke oil while the ATV is under warranty is advisable, just in case problems arise. If a seizure occurs, having proof that factory lubricants were used (and properly mixed into the fuel) will help to avoid any battles with the manufacturer, should you make a warranty claim.

Once your two-stroke ATV is "out of warranty" you can use whatever oil you choose. Since two-stroke engine oils can be vegetable based, petroleum based or synthetic, you have quite a large selection of oils to choose from. If you don't know a lot about different types of two-stroke oils, talk to other owners of two-stroke ATVs and see what they use. You might get a lot of different opinions, but you'll get some ideas on what types and brands of oil are popular.

Different two-stroke oils recommend different mixture ratios that may or may not agree with what the manufacturer of your ATV specifies. A word of caution here—if you feel uncomfortable with the ratio that the oil company recommends, (which, in the case of synthetics, can specify some lofty ratios) try mixing a little on the rich side. You might foul a plug or two, and gum up your expansion chamber, but it is MUCH cheaper to replace a spark plug than a cylinder, piston and rings.

CHECKING YOUR OIL

▶ **See Figure 14**

You should make this procedure a regular part of your life. Get to know your ATV engine, and its appetite for oil. Hopefully a four-stroke does not eat much oil between changes; but it is important that you monitor how much it does use. Any change in appetite means a change in mechanical condition (either it has started to use or lose more oil) and you should take steps to find out why.

Most manufacturer's recommend that you check the engine oil HOT. This means that the engine has been run for some time (at least long enough to bring the oil up to normal operating temperature). BUT, this does NOT mean that you have just finished a long blast at supersonic speeds across the desert (that may be TOO HOT). It also means that the engine has been shut off for a few minutes, giving the oil time to seep back down into the crankcase.

The ATV should be parked on a level surface to make sure that you get a correct reading. Make sure that it is sitting level (side-to-side **and** front-to-back) when you check the oil.

There are basically three methods of checking engine oil on most ATVs:
1. **With a dipstick**
2. **With a sight glass**
3. **With a check plug**

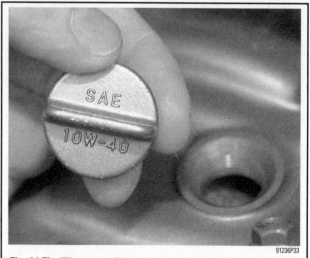

Fig. 14 The filler cap on this engine specifies 10w-40 oil. Follow the manufacturer recommendations regarding oil

With A Dipstick

▶ **See Figures 15, 16, 17 and 18**

1. With the engine warmed to normal operating temperature, park the ATV on a level surface.

2. Remove the dipstick from the engine case. Most ATVs use a threaded dipstick; gently turn the tab counterclockwise until it is free. Then remove it by pulling straight upward.

3. Wipe the dipstick clean using a rag or paper towel (making sure that no debris or lint is left on the dipstick when it is inserted back into the oil).

4. Insert the dipstick back into the crankcase or oil tank. On most threaded dipsticks the level is marked so that the dipstick is inserted into the hole, BUT is not threaded in place. Instead, leave the dipstick sitting on the top of the threads.

5. Remove the dipstick and hold it vertically with the level mark(s) toward the bottom of the dipstick. We know this is contrary to what you have seen every television gas station attendant do. Just trust us here, if you try to hold it horizontally there is a good chance that the oil will flow up the dipstick and give a false high reading (or worse, a false acceptable reading when the level is really low). If however, you follow our advice and hold it vertically the oil will NOT flow up the dipstick (unless it is anti-gravity oil) and you will never be left with too little oil in your ATV.

6. If necessary, add oil (of the proper type and viscosity) to keep the level between the markings.

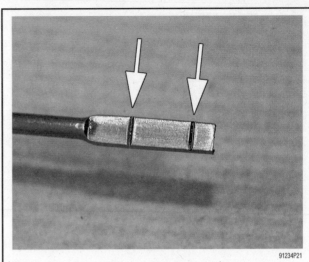
Fig. 17 The oil level should always be between the two marks on the dipstick

Fig. 15 On engines with a dipstick, unscrew the dipstick, wipe it off . . .

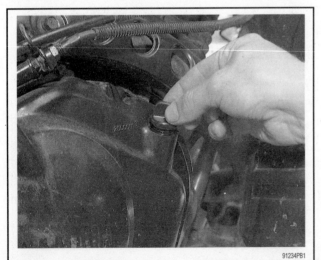
Fig. 16 . . . then (for most engines) insert it into the case, without screwing it back in

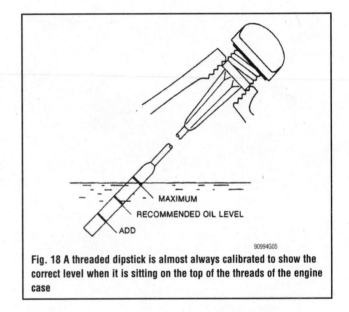
Fig. 18 A threaded dipstick is almost always calibrated to show the correct level when it is sitting on the top of the threads of the engine case

With A Sight Glass

▶ **See Figures 19, 20 and 21**

Virtually ALL ATVs that are equipped with a sight glass are designed to check the oil while completely level. This can easily be accomplished by simply parking the ATV on a level surface.

1. Start the engine and let it warm up for approximately two to three minutes.

2. After the engine is warm, shut it off and let the oil settle to the bottom of the crankcase for about two minutes.

3. Looking through the sight glass, note the oil level. If your ATV has no markings on the glass, proper oil level usually is correct when the oil level is in the middle of the sight glass. Always check your owner's manual for details about the correct way to view the oil level.

➡ **You are usually in good shape as long as some oil is visible through the glass. BUT, be careful since the oil level viewed through the glass can be VERY sensitive to lean. If the ATV is not perfectly level, the oil level will appear incorrect (that includes side-to-side and front-to-back).**

4. If necessary, add oil (of the proper type and viscosity) to keep the level between the markings. Add oil slowly since even a small amount of oil will normally make a difference in the sight glass reading.

5. Do not forget to install the filler hole cap after adding oil to the engine.

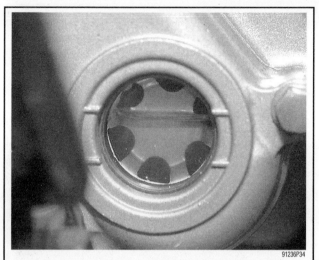

Fig. 19 Just like dipsticks, the oil level in the sight glass should always be maintained between the two lines

Fig. 20 Engines equipped with a sight glass usually have a plug on the top of the engine case for adding oil

Fig. 21 If the oil is low, add fresh oil to the engine to bring up the level

With a Check Plug

1. Start the engine and let it warm up for approximately two to three minutes.

2. After the engine is warm, shut it off and let the oil settle to the bottom of the crankcase for about two minutes.

3. Locate the check plug on the side of the engine case (the check plug is usually noted with an arrow or markings on the side of the engine case).

4. With a rag handy, remove the check plug from the side of the engine. With the ATV on a fully level surface, a small amount of oil should dribble from the hole.

5. If oil does not come out of the hole, the oil level is low, and oil should be added.

6. Leave the check plug out, and add oil through the fill hole in the top of the engine. Add oil (of the proper type and viscosity) slowly; when oil starts to dribble out of the check hole, the oil level is correct.

➡**When adding oil, be careful not to add too much too quickly. If oil begins to pour out of the check hole, do not add any more oil. Wait until the oil slows to a small drip; this indicates a proper oil level.**

7. Install the check plug and tighten it securely. In most cases, you can get away without having to replace the washer on the check plug; however, keep a new one handy should the old washer start to leak.

8. Wipe off the excess oil from the check plug area with a rag or paper towel.

9. Don't forget to install the fill hole cap!

CHANGING YOUR ENGINE OIL AND FILTER

▶ **See Figures 22 thru 40**

This is the most basic, yet most important maintenance procedure that you can do for your ATV. Manufacturers usually differ in their recommendations of how often this should be performed. But your friends here at Chilton are going to simplify it for you.

Change your oil every month or 100 miles, whichever comes first, period! Now we understand that most ATVs aren't equipped with odometers for keeping track of mileage, so you'll have to "guesstimate."

Now that recommendation is probably a little more conservative than most manufacturers today, who tend to give a wide range of service intervals. Also, it is pretty obvious that most ATVs do not come equipped with odometers. So, the "100 miles" turns into an estimation of how many miles you've put on your ATV since the last service. If your ATV is equipped with a speedometer, keeping track of your maintenance will be much easier. The rest of us though, have to guess and follow our instincts, and change your oil when you feel that it is time to do so.

An alternative to eliminating the "guesstimating" between service intervals would be to install an hourmeter onto your ATV. Boats and portable generators typically have an hourmeter to help keep track of maintenance intervals, which ensures a long life for the engine. Basically, an hourmeter is operated by a voltage signal when the engine is in use, and runs like a clock. When the engine is

Fig. 22 Always use a box end wrench or a socket to loosen a drain plug; adjustable wrenches can round off the plug head

Fig. 23 Push inward on the plug while unscrewing it from the engine, then pull it away to release the oil (hopefully not all over your hands)

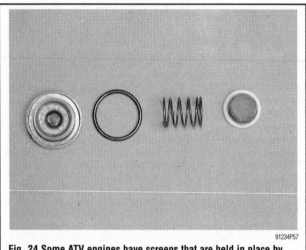

Fig. 24 Some ATV engines have screens that are held in place by the drain plug. Be careful not to lose the components when draining the oil

Fig. 25 Inspect the screen for any debris; clean thoroughly with solvent before installing the screen

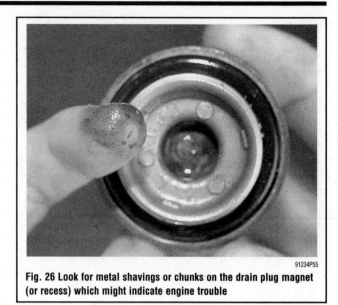

Fig. 26 Look for metal shavings or chunks on the drain plug magnet (or recess) which might indicate engine trouble

turned off, the voltage is cut to the hourmeter, and it simply stops until the next time it is supplied voltage. Mounting an hourmeter to an ATV can really make it easy to adhere to a maintenance schedule. Most hourmeters are small enough to be mounted under the seat or fender, away from trouble, but easily readable.

If you do have an hourmeter installed on your ATV, you might ask, "how many hours of use equal 100 miles?" Now of course we cannot truthfully answer that question for all riders. The easiest way to figure your hours is to estimate your average speed during a ride. For example, if you **average** 10 miles an hour for 5 hours over a weekend, that would be 50 miles. After a couple of rides, you can get a good feel for what is an average speed, and base your hours of operation upon that estimation. From there, you can follow the hourmeter, keeping track of your maintenance intervals.

The bottom line here, is you can **never** change oil too often. If you can afford to change all of your fluids in your ATV after every ride, then hey, have at it. You might spent a lot of money, but your ATV will be in top shape internally. Understand that doing this is rather extreme, but exceeding the service intervals cannot cause any harm in most cases. So, the more you change your oil, the better off your ATV will be.

Notice how we gave a **time** limit along with the mileage. This is one of those "too many people ignore" points we like to make. Mileage is not the only enemy of your oil, so is time. Oil will wear out over time as acids present from combustion attack it. Besides, those acids are one of the items that you want to get OUT of the crankcase (with the used oil) since they will attack the precious metals inside your engine (bearings, etc.).

You see it goes something like this. Oil oxidizes during exposure to air, and this naturally affects its efficiency. Acids get into the oil when the engine is started cold. While the cylinder walls are not yet a normal operating temperature, the acids formed by the combustion process may condense on them and then get into the oil. Unless the lubricant is changed, these acids will slowly destroy the oil's lubricating properties.

Most manufacturers give an oil change interval which is based on **ideal** usage. If your ATV is NOT used under any of the following conditions, you may be able to follow their recommendations:

- Extended periods of high-speed operation
- Extended periods of operation at high ambient temperatures
- Operation in extremely dusty environments
- Infrequent operation (especially during the winter months).
- Extended short hops (such as running out to the barn for a bail of hay)

Usually, one or more of the above conditions apply to all of our riding. Therefore, we stand by our original advice concerning the frequency with which you should change your oil.

Two-stroke Engines

As stated earlier in this section, the very design of a two-stroke engine means that it usually does not use a high-pressure lubrication system like four-stroke engine. Oil is added to the gasoline in order lubricate the ball or roller bearings of the motor and the cylinder walls. Some use a separate oil tank, which should be checked at each gas fill. Others mix the oil with the gasoline during fill-up. Be sure to check your owner's manual to determine the proper amount of oil and how to add it to your particular model.

For this reason, periodic oil and filter changes are normally not necessary or possible on two-stroke engines. If you are looking for information about changing the transmission oil or axle oil, refer to the Driveline Maintenance heading within this section.

Four-stroke Engines

A large majority of ATVs with four-stroke engines are designed in a manner which allows for the transmission and the engine to share the same oil. There are some models that **do** have separations within the engine case and require different oils for the engine and transmission. If you are unsure, contact a dealer to find out which type of set-up you have on your ATV. Using the wrong oil in your engine could possibly result in poor clutch operation and shifting, depending on the design of your engine.

Oil Changing Tips

Before you get started, lets discuss some important pointers and tips regarding changing oil.

DRAINING OIL INTO A PROPER RECEPTACLE

Before you even loosen the drain plug, find a drain pan or something similar that will safely hold the oil that is to be drained. Make absolutely certain that your drain pan is large enough to hold ALL the oil that you are draining. If the drain pan is too small, it could overflow, spilling oil everywhere and making a big mess.

Something else to consider in this situation is the ability to easily pour out the used oil from the pan into a container suitable for transporting the oil to a recycling facility. A basic, round drain pan might be super cheap at the local auto parts store, but will be a pain in the rear to pour oil from without spilling everywhere. A drain pan with a funnel built into the tip will be of great benefit in the long run. Spilling oil all over the place all of the time can get really irritating after a while, and a pan with a built-in funnel will make transferring oil from the drain pan to a transport container much easier.

USING A FUNNEL

Using a funnel when adding fresh oil is necessary on most ATVs. It would be nice if the manufacturers would allow for easy oil filling straight from the container, but hey, this is the real world, and rarely do we get to have our cake and eat it too. The important issue here is to find a funnel that fits inside the fill hole on your ATV engine.

Hardware stores and auto parts stores usually stock a large variety of plastic funnels, each a different size and shape. Make a couple of measurements, head down to the store, and find something that will work on your ATV. Using the wrong style of funnel will only frustrate you and make a mess. Spending a little time to plan ahead and purchase the proper equipment for maintenance tasks will save you a lot of clean up time and aggravation.

REPLACING O-RINGS AND COPPER WASHERS ON DRAIN PLUGS

Ok, we have all done it—changing the oil and installing the drain plug without using a new O-ring or washer. It is hard to teach old dogs new tricks, but break the habit. The extra pennies spent on a new washer or O-ring will keep a big oil spot from forming on the floor of your garage. Yes, you can reuse a washer or O-ring in a pinch, but how often does one change their oil "in a pinch"? If you're at the dealer picking up an oil filter and oil, why not get a new drain plug gasket too? Do yourself (and your garage floor) a big favor and replace the drain plug gasket EVERY time you change your oil.

A leaking drain plug may not seem like a big deal, but a constant dripping over the course of a weekend ride can add up to a significant amount of oil. If you happen to run low on oil to the point of the oil pressure light coming on, kiss your engine goodbye! All because of a little gasket! If you notice the drain plug is leaking, REPLACE THE GASKET! your ATV's engine will thank you.

DON'T OVERTIGHTEN THE DRAIN PLUG !

Since we are on the subject of drain plugs, another word of caution: DON'T overtighten the drain plug!!!! We all think that that extra little tug on the wrench will keep the drain plug from backing out, but in reality, the only thing you're doing is stressing the threads inside of the case. Usually, the drain plug is made of steel, and the case is made of aluminum. (A quick quiz—what's stronger; aluminum or

steel? in this case, steel is stronger) Use a torque wrench when installing the drain plug to confirm the proper torque that the manufacturer specifies for your ATV. If you really want to play it safe, drill a small hole sideways through the head of the bolt and run aircraft safety wire through it, to keep it from backing out. A large amount of racers use safety wire on critical bolts on their ATVs. The only drawback to using safety wire is the fact that you have to cut it and replace it every time you remove the bolt. This is a small price to pay for the satisfaction of knowing that your drain plug isn't going to fall out when you're in the middle of nowhere.

DON'T OVERFILL !

> ### ❊❊ CAUTION
>
> **When you add or change oil, be careful not to overfill the engine Overfilling the engine can in most cases, harm the engine. If there is excessive oil inside the crankcase, the crankshaft will whip the oil into a foamy mess, and will inhibit the lubrication of the bearings and gears. Always add oil in small increments, and re-check the level often to avoid overfilling.**

A WORD ABOUT OIL FILTERS

A quick word about oil filters. Occasionally you hear Joe the ragman talking about how he can save a few bucks by using this spin-on oil filter from a Honda

91234P58

Fig. 27 The oil filter housing will leak a small amount of oil when it is loosened; use a rag or paper towel to help contain any oil

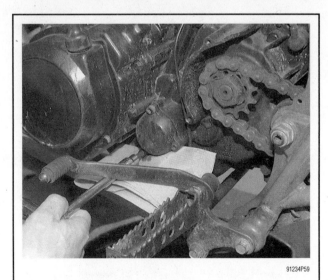

91234P59

Fig. 28 Now the bolts for the oil filter cover can be removed

Fig. 29 Be careful when removing the cover, since spacers or springs may reside behind the cover

Fig. 32 Before installing the new filter, wipe the filter housing clean

Fig. 30 Remove the filter from the engine carefully, since it may have loose debris which may fall off the filter from rough handling

Fig. 33 Be sure to properly position the O-ring or gasket to prevent leaks

Fig. 31 Before you toss the filter, check it for excessive clutch material or metal shavings, which may indicate internal problems

Fig. 34 When installing the filter cover bolts, be sure to tighten them equally to prevent leaks

Civic or something on his ATV. DON'T DO THAT!!!! Always buy the filter that is designed for and sold for your particular model. You cannot tell anything from the outward physical appearance of an oil filter (except by reading the part number) and just because a filter fits does not mean it will do the job properly.

Remember that the oiling systems of each vehicle made today varies somewhat. If an oil filter becomes clogged (offering too much resistance to the oil pump to force oil through the filtering media), your engine will be saved by a pressure bypass valve. This valve is spring-loaded and rated ONLY to open at a certain pressure that could be significantly higher (or lower) than your engine's pump pressure if the **wrong filter** is used.

If a filter with too low a bypass rating is used, then part way through the filter's life that bypass valve may open, preventing it from actually filtering the oil during normal service. But, much worse, if the rating is much higher than your pump, if the filter should clog the valve may NOT open. This would result in starving your bearings of oil and may cause significant engine damage before it is noticed.

LOOKING FOR CLUES IN THE OIL AND FILTER

After all of the old oil has drained from the engine, (or axle), don't be too quick to toss it out. Dip a gloved finger into the oil, and inspect it closely. Does the oil have a "metallic" glow to it? Are there chunks of metal in the oil? Is the oil black, or does it have a milky appearance? Closely inspecting the oil that you've drained can tell a lot about the mechanical parts inside your ATV.

If you clean the drain pan thoroughly before draining the oil, you can look for further problems by carefully draining the drain pan out and inspecting the residue at the bottom. This is where you can find metal and other debris that is too heavy to float in the oil. A small amount of tiny metal flakes, under most circumstances, can be considered acceptable. This would indicate normal wear of the internal parts. Any chunks of metal within the oil might indicate serious problems.

If your ATV is equipped with a cartridge-type oil filter, be sure to thoroughly inspect it in the same manner as the oil. The oil filter will trap any particles or debris that may be circulating around inside the engine, and will allow you to see first hand any problems that may be occurring. The good thing about the oil filter is that it will keep any debris from circulating around inside the engine and causing any harm.

If your ATV has a spin-on type oil filter, you can inspect it by carefully cutting it open with some metal shears. (Be careful when you cut the filter open; the thin metal casing can turn into a razor blade after it is cut open.) Whatever you do, DON'T use a hacksaw to open the filter. It'll be mighty hard to distinguish any contamination in the filter when there are metal shavings all over it! Once you get the casing removed and expose the paper element, inspect the filter for metal shavings, excessive clutch material, dirt, lint, etc. Any of these materials excessively deposited on the oil filter may indicate internal problems.

OIL CHANGING ITEMS

To change the engine oil and filter you'll need the following items:

1. **A good drain pan**—make sure it has a built-in funnel to make pouring out old oil easier.

2. **A funnel**—make sure the funnel fits into the oil hole in the top of the engine case.

3. **A couple of rags**—a couple of drops of oil are bound to go astray here and there.

4. **A wrench or socket that fits the drain plug**—DON'T use a crescent wrench !! A drain plug is too critical of a component to ruin with a wrench that does not properly fit the bolt.

5. **Kitty litter or sawdust**—in case any spills occur, kitty litter can quickly absorb oil and keep it from spreading all over the garage floor.

6. **An oil filter wrench**—if you have a spin-on type filter

7. **A new oil filter**

8. **A new oil filter housing gasket** —if your ATV has an internal cartridge-type filter

9. **Drain plug gasket**—usually a nylon or copper washer, or a rubber O-ring

10. **Oil**—of the proper type and viscosity

OIL CHANGING PROCEDURE

✳✳ CAUTION

The oil will be (1) HOT and (2) toxic. I know a lot of us have poured oil all over ourselves for many years, but the medical profession is seriously frowning on that know. Used engine oil contains a lot of toxins, some of which will be readily absorbed into the skin. Be nice to your body, and buy some disposable plastic gloves. They will definitely protect against the toxins and they will reduce the chance of burning yourself.

1. Before you start loosening drain plugs, make sure your ATV is level. This will ensure that all of the oil will drain out of the crankcase.

2. Set the parking brake, or block the wheels to prevent the ATV from rolling.

3. Start the ATV and let the engine reach normal operating temperature.

4. Shut off the engine after it is warm.

5. Place a drain pan underneath the engine. If the drain plug is set at an angle, position the drain pan so the oil will not overshoot it.

6. Using the proper wrench or socket, carefully loosen the drain plug.

➡ **Don't forget that your engine is HOT, and the exhaust system even hotter. Be careful not to burn yourself.**

7. Once the drain plug is loose, carefully finish unscrewing it by hand while pushing upwards.

8. After the drain plug is completely free of the case threads, quickly pull it away and let the oil drain. Some drain plugs have a small screen behind them secured with a spring. The spring may pop out, or the screen may drop into the oil. Don't panic—if you drop the screen or spring, you can fish the parts out of the drain pan after the oil has drained and cooled.

Fig. 35 On some ATV engines with a spin-on filter, a drain plug is provided to drain the filter before removal.

Fig. 36 In most cases, a filter wrench is required for removal of spin-on filters

Fig. 37 Make sure to lubricate the gasket on the filter before installation

Fig. 38 When installing a spin-on filter, hand-tightening is usually all that is required

Fig. 39 This engine has the oil capacity written on the engine case, near the dipstick. It is important not to overfill the engine with oil

Fig. 40 The last step is to add fresh oil to the engine. Make sure to use a funnel

➡The oil will drain quicker if you remove the fill plug/dipstick on the top of the engine.

9. Now that all of the oil has been drained out of the crankcase, the oil filter can be removed. Cartridge type oil filters are usually located on the side of the engine case behind a cover that is held in place by two or three bolts. When removing the cover, there may be a spring or spacer that holds the filter in position. Don't lose track of the order of any springs and spacers.

10. If your ATV has a spin-on type filter, use an oil filter wrench to remove the oil filter.

11. Discard any gasket or O-rings.

12. Don't discard the filter quite yet, though. Closely examining the filter as described earlier will provide clues to the condition of the internal parts of the engine.

To install:

13. Spin-on filters:

a. Wipe the sealing surface clean.

b. Apply a small amount of fresh oil to the gasket on the filter, and then screw it on to the mounting surface of the engine.

c. Tighten the filter no more than one turn after the gasket touches the sealing surface. This usually translates into "hand tight". Don't overtighten the filter!

➡Although it is not absolutely necessary, it is a good idea to prime spin-on oil filters by filling them ½ way with clean, fresh engine oil before installation. This will shorten the amount of time necessary for the oil pump to build pressure through the lubricating system on the first start-up since it has less area to fill in the filter. If the oil filter sits "face down" on the engine case, then pre-filling the oil filter is out of the question, since the minute you turn it upside down it will pour out of the filter.

14. Cartridge-type filters:

a. Clean out the oil filter housing with a clean, lint free cloth. If necessary, wipe out any sludge or deposits with an appropriate tool.

b. Once the filter housing or sealing surface is clean, install the new filter in the proper direction.

c. Install a new O-ring or gasket onto the filter housing cover.

d. If there are any spacers or springs, install them in the proper order, and place the filter cover onto the

e. When tightening the filter housing bolts, make sure they do not get overtightened. It is a good idea to use a torque wrench in a situation like this; applying equal pressure to the fasteners will facilitate even pressure to the sealing surface of the oil filter cover.

15. Replace the gasket on the drain plug. Don't flake out on this one, people. The cost of a new O-ring or washer is far too cheap to say that you can't afford it.

16. Install the drain plug and tighten it securely. If the drain plug retains a screen and spring, make sure to install them in the proper order.

17. Fill the engine with fresh oil to the proper level.

18. With the engine kill switch in the **off** position, crank the engine over a couple of times to distribute the fresh oil inside the engine.

19. Wait approximately one minute, and check the level of the oil again. If it is low, add oil accordingly.

20. Start the engine. While the engine is running, check for any leaks from the filter housing and the drain plug.

21. Shut the engine **off** and wait for approximately two minutes for the oil to settle in the crankcase.

22. Check that the oil level is correct. If the level is too low, add oil in small increments until it is correct. Be careful not to overfill the engine. If the level of oil in the engine is too high, loosening the drain plug (but not removing it) and allowing oil to escape is the only method of removing oil from the engine.

➡After you change your oil, you'll have to get rid of the old oil. Whatever you do, DON'T dump it into the ground, into the gutter, into the sewer, or your neighbor's yard, no matter now much you hate him. Used oil contains acids and heavy metals, which can contaminate a water supply and cause health problems. Find a local gas station or auto parts store that will let you dispose of used oil properly. This is the only way of legally disposing of used motor oil. Any other method of disposing of used motor oil (like pouring the used oil back into the new oil containers and throwing them in the trash) is considered criminal, and could land you some time in court and a heavy fine if you get caught. But hey, why take the risk? Proper oil disposal helps to clean up the environment.

Air Filters

Virtually all internal combustion engines are equipped with an air filter of some type, to prevent foreign matter from entering into the combustion chamber. The air filter is used to remove fine particles of dirt or debris present in the air which is drawn into the air induction system of an engine. By removing these particles **before** the inducted air flows through the carburetor, the engine and carburetor are protected from unnecessary wear and damage.

A clogged air filter will decrease the efficiency and life of the engine. A clogged air filter starves the engine of air, which will richen the air/fuel mixture. If the filter becomes damaged or torn, it could allow fine particles to enter the engine allowing for rapid wear of delicate parts such as the piston rings, cylinder walls and bearings. Dirt could also clog the tiny passages found in carburetors, causing lean or rich air/fuel mixtures and idle problems.

REMOVAL AND INSPECTION

◆ **See Figures 41 thru 49**

Most manufacturers recommend "cleaning or replacing the air filter when it becomes dirty." Duh . . . ! That's about as obvious as telling someone not to breathe water, or they'll die. Well, in order to find out if your air filter is dirty, you'll need to inspect it regularly. Keep in mind that riding your ATV in excessively dusty (the desert) or muddy conditions require more frequent inspections and cleaning/replacement of the air filter. Remember that a clogged air cleaner will cost you money (in gas) and fun (in performance). A damaged air cleaner could cost you a lot more in engine damage.

No matter what type of air cleaner element your ATV uses one thing is certain— it is mounted in a semi-enclosed housing that has an air inlet tract, and an air outlet tract, which goes to the carburetor. Accessing the filter element will vary slightly from model to model, but on most ATVs, the air filter is accessed by removing the seat. The air filter cover is usually held in place with spring clips or screws.

✳✳ WARNING

Be careful when installing the air filter cover. Many of the backing plates are made of plastic and are easily stripped (requiring a special order part and some downtime). Also, remember that there are usually only 4 or 5 screws holding the air filter cover in place; stripping one or two of the screws may affect the ability to properly mount the cover.

✳✳ WARNING

Never run an ATV engine without the air cleaner installed. Dirt and debris can easily be sucked into an unfiltered carburetor.

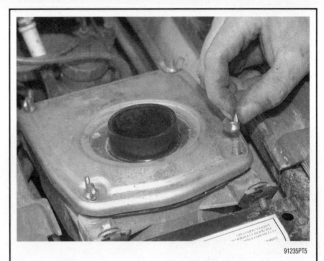
Fig. 41 Accessing the air filter on most ATVs involves removing an air box cover . . .

Fig. 42 . . . But there may be small differences from one model to another . . .

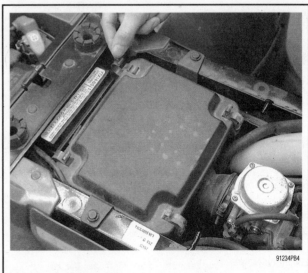
Fig. 43 . . . such as clips . . .

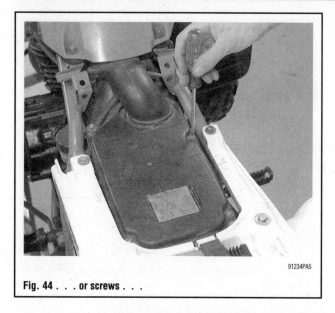

Fig. 44 . . . or screws . . .

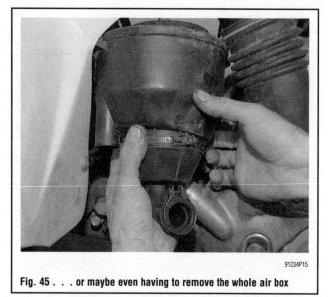

Fig. 45 . . . or maybe even having to remove the whole air box

Fig. 46 Many ATVs have their own unique air boxes. This one has a serviceable cartridge that slips into place

Fig. 47 This ATV has a spring clip that retains the air filter. It is easily removed by pulling the clip out

Fig. 48 Here's an example of a clamp-on type filter. Removal is accomplished by loosening the hose clamp

Fig. 49 Notice the word "UP" written on the washer. This filter is held in place by a single screw at the top of the filter

CLEANING AND REPLACEMENT

▶ See Figures 50, 51, 52 and 53

There are basically 4 types of air cleaners found on ATVs today:
- **Paper**
- **Cotton Gauze**
- **Foam**
- **Metal Mesh**

Paper Elements

▶ See Figure 54

Paper filter elements are usually treated in the same manner as automotive air filters. They are simply installed and checked from time to time. Once their recommended life span has expired or once they appear damaged or excessively dirty, they should just be replaced. Be careful when visually inspecting a paper element since it could be very clogged and not appear too dirty to the eye. The best method of checking most paper elements is to see if a light (from a drop light or flash light) will pass through. Hold the element up and place a light in the center of it, then check if you can see the light through the wall of the element. If the element blocks too much of the light it should be replaced.

If a paper element is not excessively dirty, you can service it by gently tap-

Fig. 52 . . . be sure to fully clean the inside of the air box

Fig. 50 This filter has been severely neglected. never let your air filter get this dirty!

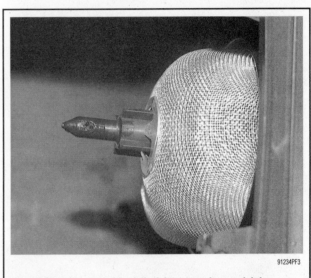

Fig. 53 Also, be sure to check the inlet screen for any debris

Fig. 51 Before installing your freshly cleaned filter . . .

Fig. 54 Paper cartridge-type filters can be simply discarded and replaced with a new unit

ping it on a work surface to dislodge any loose particles, brushing some of the dirt deposits off the outside.

✳✳ WARNING

Contrary to what you may have heard in the past, you should not use compressed air to blow the element clean. Compressed air, even low level of only a few psi (kPa) can damage or tear the element, allowing particles to pass through the gaps.

➡Although MOST paper elements are run dry and cannot be cleaned (other than the way we just outlined), there are some exceptions. There are paper compound elements that can be cleaned by washing in warm water, drying and returning to service. Also, some aftermarket companies have offered a paper-like element which is oiled before use, but this type is rare.

Cotton Gauze

▶ See Figure 55

Used mostly as an aftermarket replacement, this type of filter is noted for excellent filtration ability combined with long life and ease of service. K&N® makes the most widely used and popular versions of these filters, normally consisting of a cotton gauze filter media housed between a metal mesh support.

This type of element MUST be oiled to work properly. It can be removed, inspected, cleaned and re-oiled periodically. Under normal service this type of element can give very long intervals between cleaning and oiling, but as usual, that varies with the environment in which the engine is operated.

➡Consult the filter manufacturer's recommendations for cleaning or re-oiling techniques and intervals.

In general, these elements can be cleaned with warm soap and water or with a appropriate filter element cleaner. Once the element has dried thoroughly (which can take up to 24 hours), oil can be applied to the element. Avoid the notion to cover the element in oil; a small amount is all that is required for the element to filter the air properly. Once the filter element is oiled, let it sit for a while (preferably 24 hours) to allow for the oil to soak in evenly. Any light spots indicate a dry area, and should be touched up with a small amount of oil. Excessive oil in the element will actually restrict air flow, and will drip oil inside the air box.

Fig. 55 A cotton gauze filter (left) with pleats has more surface area than a foam unit (right) allowing for better breathability

Foam Elements

▶ See Figures 56 thru 63

Foam air filter elements are quite popular on many ATVs. They are still in use today and are often used as aftermarket replacements for paper type elements on some types of ATVs. Foam elements are normally oiled before installation, the

oil and foam work together to provide filtering. The foam and oil can capture small bits of foreign matter, while the combination is less restrictive to air than some other styles of filters.

Foam elements also have the advantage of being cleaned using a mild solvent and reused. The combination of high air flow, good filtering ability and long part life has made these filters very popular with high performance applications (or even just mild performance modifications to otherwise almost stock ATVs).

✳✳ CAUTION

DO NOT USE GASOLINE TO CLEAN YOUR AIR FILTER! Gasoline is extremely volatile, and can ignite without warning, causing severe personal injury.

To service an oiled foam element, you should wash it thoroughly in a heavy detergent or mild solvent, letting the filter soak like a sponge. Then, squeeze the element dry. Repeat this until the detergent or solvent being squeezed from the element ceases to carry off dirt.

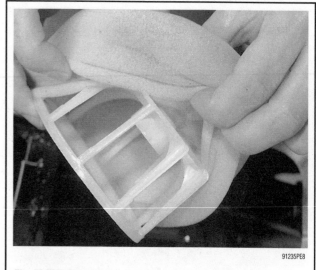

Fig. 56 This foam filter is held in place with a plastic frame

Fig. 57 This is another type of foam filter that has an inner screen. When washing the filter, remove any type of screen or frame to make washing easier

Fig. 58 Using biodegradable degreaser is a safe way to clean an air filter. Experiment with ratios and find what works best for you

✳✳ WARNING

Be sure that you SQUEEZE the solvent from the element and do not wring it out. Twisting the element in a wringing fashion will risk tearing and will likely damage the close-knit pores of the element.

Once the element has been cleaned, soak it the proper type of oil, as recommended by the filter manufacturer. An easy way to distribute the oil onto the foam element is with the use of a plastic bag. Place the foam element in the bag, followed by pouring a little oil into the bag. (Some use standard engine oils, some use gear oils and others use special filter oil). Close off the end of the bag, then squeeze the element to allow for the oil to soak in until it is completely saturated. Once you are done oiling the element in the bag, take it out of the bag, squeeze off the excess and return it to service. You don't need a bag to oil your filter element, it just keeps your hands from getting soaked with oil.

There are also filter oils that are available in a spray; with this method, however, only the outer layer of the foam is saturated with oil. If your ATV doesn't get used in really dusty conditions, using oil spray may be adequate. But for heavy dust and dirt, soaking the foam element in oil is recommended.

Like any other air cleaner, even the reusable foam element will have a limited life span. Be sure to check it carefully for damage, deterioration or tears and replace it when it has become unserviceable.

Fig. 59 After some scrubbing, your air filter should be clean and free of any dirt and filter oil

Fig. 61 After the filter is clean and dry, place it into a plastic bag . . .

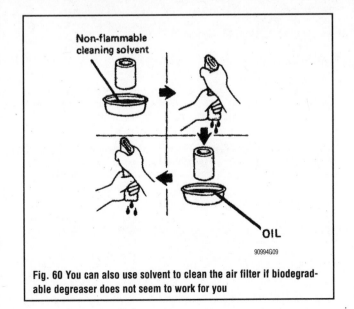

Non-flammable cleaning solvent

OIL

Fig. 60 You can also use solvent to clean the air filter if biodegradable degreaser does not seem to work for you

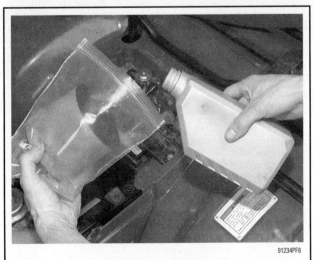

Fig. 62 . . . then pour the filter oil into the bag with the filter, and squeeze the filter until it is evenly soaked with oil

Fig. 63 There are also sprayable filter cleaners and oils available for servicing air filters

Fig. 64 Open air cooling is the most basic form of cooling for an engine

Metal Mesh

▶ See Figure 57

Metal mesh filters are almost always used in conjunction with a foam or cotton gauze air filter. In most cases, the metal mesh is integrated into a metal or plastic frame, and holds the outer filter (foam or gauze) in place. The metal mesh also helps to contain a flame from an engine backfire. The mesh, when coated with oil, attracts dirt particles and keeps them from entering the engine. Mesh filters don't usually provide enough filtration of dirt on their own, so they are most always wrapped with an outer layer of filtration.

☀ WARNING

Don't use a mesh core as the only means of air filtration for the engine. The mesh core of an air filter does not provide adequate air filtration on its own, and may cause engine damage.

Cooling Systems

Since the internal combustion engine produces heat, a means of regulating the temperature must be used to prevent overheating. The two most popular ways of removing excess heat from an engine are with air and water. Both methods have their advantages, depending on the specific application. Let's discuss in detail the three main types of engine cooling systems and the maintenance required for optimum efficiency.

OPEN AIR COOLING

▶ See Figure 64

Open air cooling is popular with small, single cylinder engines because of the simplicity and almost non-existent need for maintenance of any kind. The reason for this is the fact that there are no moving parts to the open air cooling system. The **cooling fins** cast onto the cylinder and cylinder head are responsible for cooling the engine. The purpose for the fins is to increase the surface area of the cylinder and head, which allows the heat to dissipate into the air faster. A cylinder and head without fins will still be cooled by the air passing around them, but not as much as if they were equipped with fins.

In order for the cooling fins to operate properly, ambient air needs to travel over the fins at a moderate speed. This is where one of the drawbacks of open air cooling comes into play. If air is not traveling over the fins and transferring heat fast enough, the efficiency is lost, and the operating temperature of the engine rises. To put this in a practical perspective, if your not moving fast enough on your ATV, it may overheat.

From a maintenance perspective, open air cooling is a no-brainer. The only two things to keep in mind are to keep the cooling fins free of dirt and mud, and most of all, **don't break them off!** If a cooling fin breaks off of the cylinder or

cylinder head, a "hot spot" will develop, possibly causing engine damage. If you do break off a cooling fin, welding may be possible, depending on the type of metal that the cylinder (or cylinder head) is made from.

FORCED AIR COOLING

▶ See Figures 65, 66 and 67

Forced air cooling operates in the same manner as open air cooling, with the addition of a few extra components designed to increase the efficiency of the cooling fins. A blower motor and ductwork enclosing the cylinder head are employed to force air over the fins at a higher rate than open air cooling can provide. This becomes a real advantage while traveling at low speeds, when air flow would normally be low on an open air cooled engine.

Since forced air cooling uses moving parts (a blower), some occasional maintenance may be required to keep things in top running order. Since the blower is essentially an air pump, it sucks air from one area (usually from within the air box) and blows it out of another. Occasionally, debris can get sucked into the blower, and get caught between the cooling fins. It is important to occasionally remove the ductwork and clean the cooling fins and blower impeller of any accumulated dirt and debris.

The major drawback of forced air cooling is the power required from the engine to spin the blower impeller. On a large displacement engine, this is hardly a problem and the horsepower required to spin the blower impeller is minimal. With that said, small displacement two-stroke engines (which make good horsepower, but little torque) may have to sacrifice a small amount of power to keep things cool. Overall, forced air cooling is a relatively inexpensive and reasonably efficient way to cool an ATV engine.

WATER COOLING

Using water to cool an engine is nothing new, since water cooling has been around since the turn of the century, used mainly for automobile engines. Within the last ten years, water cooling ATV engines has become quite popular, and in time, could become the standard within the industry.

➡**The term "water cooled" is slightly misleading because the liquid coolant should never be more than 50 percent water. The balance of the solution should usually be a high-quality ethylene-glycol (or propylene-glycol) solution otherwise known as antifreeze, or coolant.**

Using water, mixed with ethylene-glycol, is the most effective way to cool an internal combustion engine. (unless you want to talk to the guys at NASA, who have probably come up with something better.) The water is circulated through the engine with a water pump (which is usually operated from the crankshaft) to the radiator. Heat from within the engine is transferred to the water, which travels through "jackets" or passages surrounding the cylinder head. The radiator then cools the coolant mixture with the air that flows through hundreds of

Fig. 65 Engines with forced air cooling have ductwork that surrounds the cylinder head

Fig. 66 It is a good idea to periodically remove the ductwork for inspection

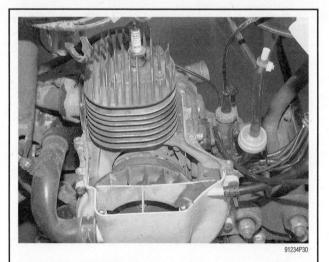

Fig. 67 With the ductwork removed, check for any debris between the cylinder fins and the fan blades

cooling fins on the radiator core. Once the heat is removed from the mixture, it flows back to the engine to pick up another load of heat generated by the engine.

The major components of a water cooling system are:

- **Radiator**
- **Water Pump**
- **Thermostat**
- **Hoses**
- **Coolant**

Water cooling an engine may add performance and reliability, but it also adds complexity, as shown by the list of additional components. It is another system that must be properly maintained in order to keep the engine working properly. One of the most common misunderstandings about cooling systems is that the coolant can be ignored and considered maintenance free. You know, "I can see some in the tank, so it must be fine." Well, WRONG! Coolant must be changed on a regular basis. It is not sufficient to just have the system level full. As coolant ages, it loses its ability to resist boiling and conduct heat. But, more importantly, it also loses its anti-corrosion properties, and will allow the build-up of scale and residue in the cooling system. This build-up will reduce the cooling system's ability to do its job and could eventually render the system useless. To prevent this oxidation of the aluminum cooling passages you should replace your engine coolant AT LEAST once every two years.

Checking Your Coolant

▶ See Figures 68 thru 74

You should check the coolant level in your ATV as frequently as you check the level of your oil. It can be just as important to the life of your engine. If the level begins to drop suddenly (and you don't see any leaks), then IMMEDIATELY check your oil to see if it is being diluted by the coolant. If so, you must perform a major repair quickly, before the engine is ruined by the diluted oil.

But, most of the time you will probably notice that the coolant level remains the same. Then it is just a matter of keeping an eye on it and replacing it every 2 years.

Most water cooled ATVs use a coolant reservoir so the level can be checked without removing the radiator or pressure cap. The reservoirs are typically marked with LOW and FULL or COLD and HOT markings. Usually, manufacturers suggest that the coolant level should be checked with the ATV on a level surface and with the engine at normal operating temperature. BUT, there are always some exceptions, so check your owners manual to be sure.

If you experience a coolant related problem, like boiling over and pouring out the overflow tube, for example, check the specific gravity of the coolant using a hydrometer. These should be readily available at most automotive stores. Make sure that the hydrometer is small enough to obtain a sufficient cooling sample; some of the larger ones found in automotive stores may require more coolant than you can obtain from your ATV's cooling system. The hydrometer can help you determine if the mixture of coolant and water is incorrect, or if the coolant is

Fig. 68 On some ATVs, the radiator cap and expansion tank access is hidden beneath a cover on the front fender

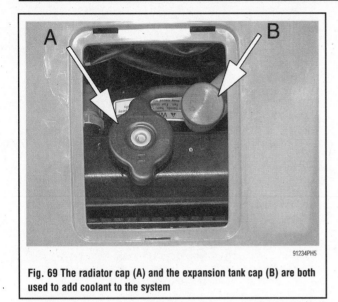

Fig. 69 The radiator cap (A) and the expansion tank cap (B) are both used to add coolant to the system

Fig. 72 Some ATV and motorcycles have specialized cooling systems that may require special coolant with additives for aluminum radiators

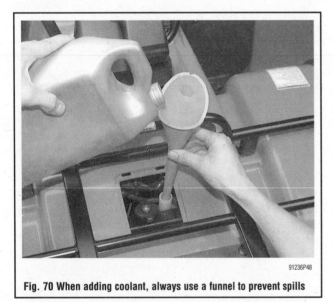

Fig. 70 When adding coolant, always use a funnel to prevent spills

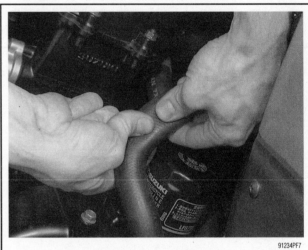

Fig. 73 Check coolant hoses for pliability by feeling for hardness or excessive sponginess

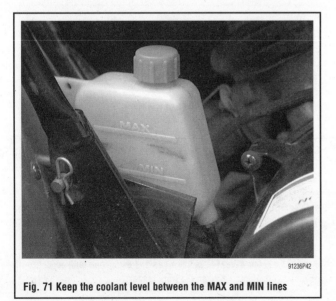

Fig. 71 Keep the coolant level between the MAX and MIN lines

Fig. 74 Although getting to your ATV's cooling system may not be easy, it is important to check hoses and connections regularly

old and has lost its heat transferring abilities. Of course, if you are unsure just how OLD the coolant in your ATV is, then you should replace it immediately and see if the problem goes away.

➡ **You should always use distilled water in the cooling system since the minerals and chemicals that are usually present in tap or drinking water may contribute to internal system corrosion. And that is exactly what you are trying to avoid by changing the coolant in the first place.**

Whenever you check your coolant, take a few minutes to inspect the condition of your coolant hoses as well. With the engine cool, run your hands along the hoses looking for damp or soft spots which indicate a weakening hose that could be getting ready to burst. Excessively hard or cracking hoses should also be replaced. Check the clamps at the ends to be sure the hoses are secure on the fittings. Clamps should be snug, but not over-tight (which might cause the ends of the hose to crack and split). Replace any hose that seems suspect, you wouldn't want it to burst on the trail and leave you stranded.

Flushing And Filling The System

We'll say it again. AT LEAST, once every 2 years be sure to completely drain, flush and refill your cooling system with a high-quality antifreeze/coolant and distilled water.

DRAINING THE COOLING SYSTEM

▶ **See Figure 75**

1. Place the ATV on a level surface, with the engine **cold**.

❄ CAUTION

Never open, service or drain the radiator or cooling system when hot; serious burns can occur from the steam and hot coolant. Also, when draining engine coolant, keep in mind that cats and dogs are attracted to ethylene glycol antifreeze and could drink any that is left in an uncovered container or in puddles on the ground. This will prove fatal in sufficient quantities. Always drain coolant into a sealable container. Coolant should be reused unless it is contaminated or is several years old.

2. If necessary for access, remove the sidecovers or any other plastic.
3. Position a catch pan and drain the engine cooling system:

   a. Remove the system pressure cap to de-pressurize the system. It usually looks just like a radiator cap, but on ATVs it isn't always mounted on the radiator.

   b. Most ATVs have a water pump drain screw and sealing washer. If equipped, remove the screw and allow the system to drain.

   c. In addition to draining the water pump housing, loosen the clamp on the lower radiator hose and disconnect it from the radiator. This will allow the engine and radiator to both drain.

Fig. 75 The water pump on this ATV has a drain plug to allow for complete drainage of the cooling system

91234PH2

d. Disconnect the radiator overflow hose from the reservoir tank and siphon the fluid from the tank. If necessary, the tank can be completely removed, rinsed and re-installed.

4. Once the cooling system is empty you have 3 choices. (1) Flush the system by removing the thermostat and using a garden hose. (2) Flush the system using warm water and by running the engine to open the thermostat. (3) Just refill the system. It's your choice, but we've listed them in descending order from best to least best.

FLUSHING BY REMOVING THE THERMOSTAT

1. Drain the cooling system.

❄ CAUTION

Ethylene-glycol antifreeze is highly toxic. It is also cool and green. Some children might think it looks a lot like a soft drink so KEEP IT AWAY FROM THEM. Also, it has a sweet taste and smell which can attract animals, and in sufficient quantity it could kill them, so protect your kids AND your pets from coolant.

2. Locate and remove the thermostat. On some models it is conveniently located directly under the system pressure cap, but on others you will have to unbolt and remove the housing. Pay attention to the direction of the thermostat is situated.

3. If you did not remove the lower radiator hose in order to drain the system, disconnect it from the radiator now.

4. Close the rest of the system by reinstalling the pressure cap.

5. With the thermostat removed, but the system sealed everywhere except at the hose you've removed, hold a garden hose up to the radiator hose and allow water to be forced through the system and to exit the bottom of the radiator. Clean water will flow through the engine, through the upper radiator hose and finally through the radiator.

6. Flush the system until the water coming out of the radiator is completely clean.

➡ **Since the thermostat is out, why not take the opportunity to replace it with a new one? The cost is minimal, and will ensure that the cooling system operates properly, eliminating the possibility of overheating.**

7. Install the thermostat in the proper direction, and replace any gaskets or seals. Reconnect the lower radiator hose and or water pump drain plug and refill the cooling system.

FLUSHING BY RUNNING THE ENGINE

1. Drain the cooling system.

❄ CAUTION

Ethylene-glycol antifreeze is highly toxic. It is also cool and green. Some children might think it looks a lot like a soft drink so KEEP IT AWAY FROM THEM. Also, it has a sweet taste and smell which can attract animals, and in sufficient quantity it could kill them, so protect your kids AND your pets from coolant.

2. Install the lower radiator hose and/or the water pump drain screw, as applicable.

3. Fill the cooling system with water through the pressure cap. Then start and run the ATV until it reaches normal operating temperature and the thermostat opens. You can tell when this occurs because the upper radiator hose and the radiator will get hot.

4. Shut the engine **OFF** and drain the cooling system. BE CAREFUL as the water will be VERY HOT.

5. Repeat these steps until the water which is drained comes out completely clean.

6. Install the lower radiator hose and/or the water pump drain screw and refill the cooling system.

REFILLING THE SYSTEM

1. Pre-mix the distilled water and coolant in a container by filling it halfway with one and then topping it off with the other. This way you will be certain to maintain the proper 50/50 ration of coolant to water.

2. Carefully pour the solution in the pressure cap opening in the system.

3. Keep filling the system until the level is at the bottom of the filler neck.

4. Fill the reservoir tank to the UPPER, FULL or HOT mark, as applicable.

5. Crank the engine to see if you will be able to run it without closing the system. If you can (without the coolant spraying all over the place) this is the best way to bleed air and make sure the system is full. If so start and run the engine, adding coolant as the level drops until the level remains steadily at the base of the filler neck.

6. If you cannot run the engine with the cap off, close the system and start the engine. As the system approaches operating temperature the thermostat should open. Then shut the engine **off** and CAREFULLY remove the pressure cap (using a rag to shield you in case you warmed the engine too much). Then add coolant until the level is at the base of the filler neck. Close the system and repeat until the level does not drop when the system is operated.

7. Be sure to clean up any antifreeze or coolant that you have spilled and place the remaining solutions in a CHILD PROOF container (then put it where a child can't get at it).

❊❊❊ CAUTION

Ethylene-glycol antifreeze is highly toxic. It is also cool and green. Some children might think it looks a lot like a soft drink so KEEP IT AWAY FROM THEM. Also, it has a sweet taste and smell which can attract animals, and in sufficient quantity it could kill them, so protect your kids AND your pets from coolant.

Fuel Filters

The fuel filter is designed to do for your carburetor what the air filter does for your engine; keep out particles of dirt and debris. If however, the screen becomes clogged, the flow of gasoline will be impeded. This could cause lean fuel mixtures, hesitation and stumbling, and idle problems.

ATVs almost always come equipped with a screen type filter that is attached to the petcock, either inside or outside the fuel tank. These screens provide the most basic form of filtration for the fuel that enters the carburetor.

As long as you keep from pouring dirty fuel into your tank, the screen should be clean. But, over time, dirt and lint can get into your tank and clog the screen. It should be inspected periodically to prevent clogging, and also to check the screen itself for tears and deterioration.

In addition to the petcock filter screen, most ATVs also come equipped with one or more inline fuel filters. These are usually similar to the old carbureted automotive style filters, consisting of a filter element in a plastic housing with nipples on either end to attach the fuel lines. If your ATV does not come equipped with an inline filter, you may wish to install one, just below the petcock. These filters are readily available at most automotive supply stores. If you do this, you can usually leave the screen in the tank alone until you notice a reduction in the fuel flow (meaning that the screen is clogged). One of the additional advantages of adding an inline filter is that most of them are clear plastic and you can actually see if fuel is filling the filter housing. This is helpful in determining if your in-tank screen is clogged.

INSPECTION AND REPLACEMENT

❊❊❊ CAUTION

For those of you who have led a sheltered life: YOU ARE DEALING WITH A HIGHLY FLAMMABLE SUBSTANCE HERE! Do not allow any open flames, sparks or other sources of combustion anywhere near the work area. Make sure you are working in a well-ventilated area. Protect your skin from gasoline by wearing vinyl gloves. AND DON'T SMOKE!

Petcock Filter Screens

▶ See Figures 76 thru 81

1. Disconnect the fuel line from the carburetor or from the petcock (whichever is easier). If you must remove the line from the petcock itself, obtain

a short length of fuel line (with the same inner diameter as the petcock nipple) to use as a drain hose, then attach it to the petcock. Keep this extra line in your tool kit because it could become VERY helpful on the trail if you or a buddy runs out of gas.

2. Turn the gas to **RESERVE** or, if equipped, to **PRIME** and allow the fuel to drain.

➡If you have a vacuum actuated petcock, turning the valve to the **PRIME** setting (when equipped) will usually allow the tank to drain without applying vacuum to the valve diaphragm. If your ATV does not have a prime setting, or if prime does not allow it to fully drain, then you will need a hand-held pump to apply vacuum to the diaphragm. These pumps are relatively inexpensive, are available at most automotive supply stores and are handy for other things such as brake bleeding (so they are a good investment).

3. If necessary, remove the vacuum line from the back of the petcock and connect a small, hand-held vacuum pump. Gently apply a small amount of vacuum, no more than 10 in. Hg. at first and see if the fuel flows. If no fuel is flowing, check that the petcock valve is in the **RESERVE** position and, if necessary,

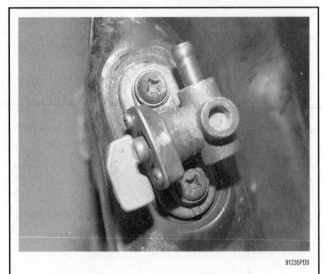

91235PD9

Fig. 76 Most Petcocks are held on by a couple of screws

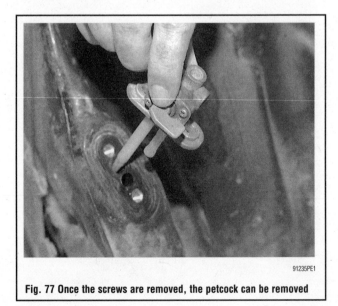

91235PE1

Fig. 77 Once the screws are removed, the petcock can be removed

apply a little more vacuum. Do not apply too much vacuum or you will destroy the valve diaphragm.

4. Once the fuel tank is fully drained, decide if you will be able to remove the petcock with the tank installed. You can on most models, but there is always an exception. If necessary, remove the fuel tank to make things easier. This usually involves removing some plastic and a couple of bolts.

➡If your ATV has an external filter screen on the petcock, it can be unscrewed after the fuel has been drained; make sure that the fuel tank is fully drained, and keep rags handy to contain excess fuel.

5. To remove the petcock from the fuel tank, remove the bolts or screws and carefully withdraw the petcock. If the bolts feel tight, spray them with a pen-

etrant to loosen them. DON'T force the bolts if they do not loosen with moderate force; the metal inserts are molded into the tank and can easily strip out in the plastic.

➡Have a few disposable rags and a small drain pan handy to catch any remaining fuel with may drain from the tank. If possible, position the ATV or the fuel tank so any remaining fuel will not run out.

6. Clean the filter screen with a mild solvent and blow it dry with **low** level compressed air (if available).

7. Inspect the screen for tears, damage or uncleanable clogging. If any of these conditions are found, replace the screen with a new one. The screens are usually press-fit into the petcock.

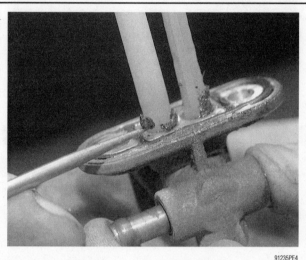

Fig. 78 Clean any debris from the filter screens

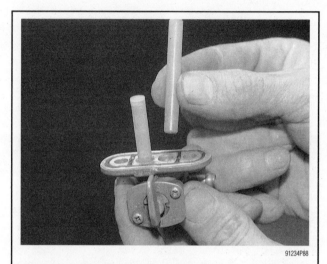

Fig. 80 If the petcock screens are torn, they can be replaced by carefully pulling them out of the petcock

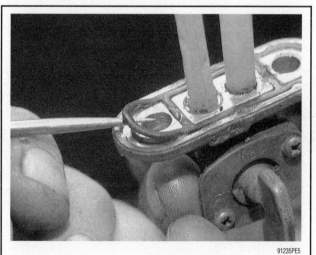

Fig. 79 Make sure to replace the gasket or O-ring on the petcock, or the tank may leak fuel (VERY DANGEROUS!!)

Fig. 81 A close view of one of the petcock screens shows the fine mesh, which filters out dirt and particles before they reach the carburetor

To install:

8. Install the filter screen and petcock assembly using a new O-ring or gasket.

9. Reconnect the vacuum line and/or fuel line(s), as applicable.

10. Carefully refill the tank with a small amount of fuel.

11. Turn the petcock **ON** and check for leaks.

12. If you have a vacuum actuated petcock, start and idle the motor, then recheck for leaks.

13. Once you are certain that there are no leaks, you can completely fill the tank with fuel.

Inline Filters

◗ See Figure 82

On most carbureted vehicles, replacement of the inline filter is a very simple matter or disconnecting the fuel lines from either end and removing the filter. Just remember to shut the fuel petcock **OFF** first. To help prevent making a mess, turn the petcock **OFF**, then idle the motor until the fuel line is empty (it is easy to tell with a see-through filter, but otherwise you may have to run it until the carburetor float bowl or bowls is/are empty.) With the lines and filter empty, you will spill less or no gas removing the filter.

91234PF5

Fig. 82 Most inline filters can be replaced by loosening the clamps on each side and removing the hose

ENGINE TUNE-UP

Once upon a time, riders would have to perform lengthy and sometimes complicated rituals every few thousand miles in order to keep their machines running properly. ATVs of yesterday used components that wore out quickly like ignition points which would have to be replaced and valves which would require adjustment often. In those days of yore, machines could get temperamental if valve, ignition and carburetor adjustments were not performed regularly (and properly).

A tune-up is a sequence of component replacement and adjustment which is designed to restore engine performance which is lost to normal use and wear. Just like the preventive maintenance described earlier, a tune-up should be performed based on time, mileage and your particular pattern of usage. An ATV used in competition will require a tune-up before each race, while a weekend warrior's mount might only need one every few months.

To properly perform a tune-up, you must follow a set order of events. For instance, valve adjustment and ignition timing should always precede carburetor adjustment, since they can both affect engine rpm (which is one of the items you would adjust while working on the carburetors). A typical tune-up could consist of the following items (as applicable):

- A compression test
- Spark plug inspection and replacement
- Valve adjustment
- Ignition timing inspection
- Carburetor idle speed and mixture adjustments
- Vehicle test

But, you should note that the tune-up of yesterday is completely gone from the automotive world and it is slowly, but surely, disappearing from the world of ATVs. Advances in engine management technology (like electronic ignition systems), and low maintenance mechanical components (such as hydraulic lifters) leaves today's rider with not too much to tweak.

The one thing that you CAN count on is that you will have to periodically check and replace your spark plug. As a matter of fact, on some ATVs, that is the sum total of your tune-up, since valve, timing and carburetor adjustments may not be possible or necessary. On other ATVs spark plug replacement is just the beginning. Once again, grab your owner's manual and check for the following items, then perform each of them in the proper sequence (which will usually be in the order we have presented them, although valve adjustment and ignition timing are sometimes reversed).

➡The steps of a tune-up ASSUME that all engine maintenance from fluid to filter changes has been properly performed. If you are performing carburetor or timing adjustments, BE CERTAIN that there are no air or fuel filter problems before proceeding.

Checking Engine Compression

A compression check is a great way to keep an eye on engine condition. But, if you have a new ATV, then you probably won't NEED to do this. Of course, performing a compression check on a new ATV (one that has been broken-in already) is a great way to set the baseline for years to come. You will know what the compression was when new and how to compare that with wear on future readings.

CHECKING COMPRESSION

◗ See Figure 83

An engine compression test is performed by cranking the motor (using the starter) while a pressure gauge is threaded into (or held into) the spark plug port. The gauge will measure the amount of pressure (read as psi or kPa depending on your gauge) which the piston, rings and valves are capable of building.

Compression readings are a fast and effective way to determine engine condition. Although specifications vary greatly from one motor to another, the important thing to watch for in a compression test are changes. Keep track of the readings, noting if they are significantly lower than the previous tune-up.

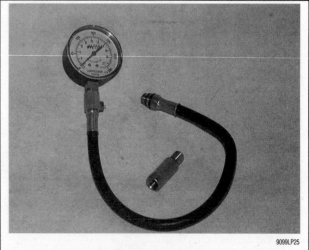

9099LP25

Fig. 83 A compression gauge is a relatively inexpensive tool that can help you determine engine condition

Typically speaking, compression readings should be above 100 psi and no cylinder should be more than 15% lower than the highest reading you have taken (multi-cylinder models).

To obtain a proper reading you should be sure that the engine has been warmed to normal operating temperature (so all components are properly seated). This may be awkward on some ATVs where you will have to run the engine up to temperature, then quickly (but carefully) remove the fuel tank for access to the spark plugs.

If possible, a threaded compression gauge should be used. Threaded gauges are more accurate, since they all but eliminate the possibility of compression leaking out the spark plug threads. This is a common cause for low readings when using a non-threaded, hold-in-place type gauge. Threaded gauges are also easier to use, since they leave both your hands free to do other things, like hitting the starter button.

1. Warm the engine to normal operating temperature.

2. Shut off the fuel supply to empty the float bowl or bowls (this will prevent gasoline from spraying in the cylinder during the compression test. Allow the engine to stall.

3. If your ATV does not have a fuel petcock (or does not have one with a full OFF position), shut the engine **OFF** and drain the float bowl of the carburetor.

4. Disable the ignition system.

➡**Disabling the ignition system can be done in a variety of ways. Check a service manual to find the preferred method for your ATV. It may involve disconnecting the ignition coil primary wiring, removing a relay or fuse, or it may be as simple as using the engine kill switch on the handlebar (since some models will allow the starter to work, but will disable the ignition system when the switch is thrown).**

5. Carefully clean the area around the spark plug bore, then remove the spark plug and set it aside.

➡**If your ATV has more than one cylinder, be sure to label the spark plug wires before removing them.**

6. Install the gauge to the cylinder. When using a threaded gauge, be sure the proper sized adapter is attached, then thread it carefully into the bore.

7. Hold the throttle wide open and crank the motor a few times. If you have an ATV without an electric starter, you will have to give the starter a good, strong kick (or pull) to be sure that you get the highest reading of which the cylinder is capable.

➡**Remember that it is assumed that all maintenance has been performed, meaning that the throttle cable is properly adjusted. If you are in doubt, visually check that the carburetor venturi is fully open before cranking the motor.**

8. Note the compression reading, release the pressure and repeat for that cylinder 1–2 more times to be certain that you have the highest possible reading.

9. Although not all manufacturers provide specifications, most four-stroke engines should have compression readings somewhere above 100 psi. Figures in the 150–160 psi range are not uncommon on high performance machines. Two-stroke motors tend to have lower readings, closer to 110 psi.

10. On multi-cylinder machines, repeat the check for each of the cylinders. Compare the highest readings for each cylinder. Ideally all readings should be within 10% of each other, but a variance of 15% between the lowest and the highest is usually considered the outer limit.

11. If one or more cylinders of the engine read lower than specification, or lower than the recommended percentage of the highest cylinder's reading, you should repeat the test. But, this time, add a tablespoon of fresh, clean engine oil to the cylinder (through the spark plug hole) before taking the readings. If the compression readings come up with the oil added, then it is likely that the piston rings and cylinder walls for that cylinder are worn. If the compression remains low your problem is likely in the head (either a leaking head gasket or problems with a four-stroke engine valve train).

➡**Remember that improperly adjusted valves can lower compression readings, so if the valves are checked and shown to be out of adjustment, you should repeat the test to see if compression will then come up to specification.**

12. On two-stroke engines, keep track of the readings over a series of tune-ups. If the compression increases dramatically, the piston crown and chamber are probably becoming carboned-up and should be decarbonized. This involves removing the cylinder head and cylinder.

LEAK-DOWN TESTS

An even better (and easier) way to check cylinder condition is with the use of a leak-down tester. The only problem to the home mechanic is expense. A leak-down tester is an expensive and specialized tool which is used along with an air compressor. Instead of using the engine to build compression, a leak-down tester pressurizes a cylinder with compressed air and then monitors how much leaks out.

To use a leak-down tester you start by warming the motor and then removing the spark plugs (just like a compression check). But, then you find TDC of the compression stroke the cylinder which is about to be tested (if your ATV has more than one cylinder). At this point the tester pressurizes the cylinder and you watch the gauge to see if it is leaking.

If leaks are found, listen at the tailpipe, oil fill hole and the carburetor. Hissing sounds coming from these places will tell you which components are worn. Sounds coming from the tailpipe only mean damaged exhaust valve(s). Sounds heard at the carburetor or throttle body point to intake valve problems. Sounds coming from the crankcase (such as through an oil fill) indicate a problem with the pistons, rings and cylinder walls. If you have a water cooled ATV, bubbles in the radiator are an indication of head gasket problems.

If you become serious about playing with and/or rebuilding motors, then a leak-down tester may be worth the investment. If not, check your local tool rental shops, they may have one available for a reasonable fee.

Spark Plugs

GENERAL INFORMATION

▶ **See Figure 84**

Unlike automobiles, whose plug life has increased dramatically over the years with the use of high voltage, electronic ignition systems (as opposed to points which were used in days gone by), most ATVs still seem to be hard on their spark plugs. During normal use, the plug gap increases and the sharp edge of the center electrode tends to dull. As the gap increases and the electrode's edge rounds off, the plug's voltage requirement increases. It requires a greater voltage to jump the wider gap and about two to three times as much voltage to fire the plug at high speeds than at idle. The improved air/fuel ratio control of modern carburetors combined with the higher voltage output of modern electronic ignition systems will often allow an engine to run significantly longer on a standard spark plug, but keep in mind that efficiency will drop as the gap widens. As the plugs wear, gas mileage and performance will drop over time. You will know if the plug has been ignored for too long, as the engine may very well start to sputter or miss under load (it can feel a lot like forgetting to turn the petcock right before an ATV starts to hit reserve).

A typical spark plug consists of a metal shell surrounding a ceramic insulator. A metal electrode extends downward through the center of the insulator and protrudes a small distance. Located at the end of the plug and attached to the side of the outer metal shell is the side electrode. The side electrode bends in at a 90° angle so that its tip is just past and parallel to the tip of the center elec-

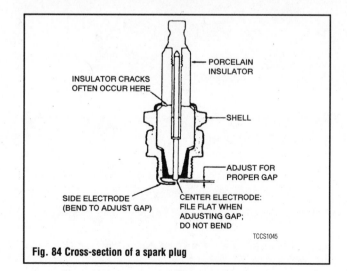

Fig. 84 Cross-section of a spark plug

trode. The distance between these two electrodes (measured in thousandths of an inch or hundredths of a millimeter) is called the spark plug gap.

The spark plug does not produce a spark but instead provides a gap across which the current can arc, which is considered a "spark." The ignition coil produces anywhere from 20,000 to 50,000 volts (depending on the type and application) which travels through the wire to the spark plug. The current passes along the center electrode and jumps the gap to the side electrode, and in doing so, ignites the air/fuel mixture in the combustion chamber.

SPARK PLUG HEAT RANGE

▶ See Figure 85

Spark plug heat range is the ability of the plug to dissipate heat. The longer the insulator (or the farther it extends into the engine), the hotter the plug will operate; the shorter the insulator (the closer the electrode is to the block's cooling passages) the cooler it will operate. A plug that absorbs little heat and remains too cool will quickly accumulate deposits of oil and carbon since it is not hot enough to burn them off. This leads to plug fouling and consequently to misfiring (quite common with two-stroke engines). A plug that absorbs too much heat will have no deposits but, due to the excessive heat, the electrodes will burn away quickly and might possibly lead to preignition or other ignition problems. Preignition takes place when plug tips get so hot that they glow sufficiently to ignite the air/fuel mixture before the actual spark occurs. This early ignition will usually cause pinging (preignition) during low speeds and heavy loads.

The general rule of thumb for choosing the correct heat range when picking a spark plug is: if most of your riding is long distance, high speed travel, use a colder plug; if most of your riding is stop and go, or tight, twisty trails, use a hotter plug. Original equipment plugs are generally a good compromise between the two styles, and most people never have the need to change their plugs from the factory-recommended heat range.

❋ WARNING

Using a spark plug that is not within the proper heat range may cause serious engine damage. Just because the spark plug LOOKS the same doesn't mean that it can be used in your ATV engine. Always use a spark plug within the correct heat range to avoid engine problems.

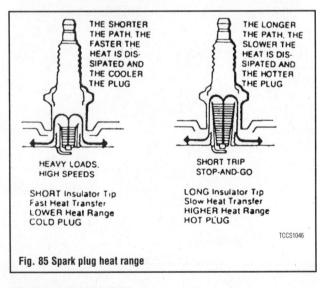

Fig. 85 Spark plug heat range

REMOVAL & INSTALLATION

▶ See Figures 86 thru 91

1. Disconnect the negative battery cable, and if the engine has been run recently, allow the engine to cool.
2. If necessary, remove the gas tank and/or any body plastic which interferes with access to the spark plug.

➡ If you are trying to take a compression reading then you obviously don't want the engine too cool off. BUT, be careful because removing

spark plugs from a hot aluminum cylinder head can cause damage to the threads. If plug removal is difficult, forget the test for now (save your CYLINDER HEAD!!!) and allow the cylinder to cool. Once the cylinder has cooled sufficiently, remove the spark plugs, clean the threads on the plug and give them a good coating of anti-seize paste. Then install the plugs, warm-up the engine and start again. The anti-seize paste should allow you to safely remove the plugs from a hot head (but BE CAREFUL and DON'T FORCE THEM).

3. Carefully twist the spark plug wire boot to loosen it, then pull upward and remove the boot from the plug. Be sure to pull on the boot and not on the wire, otherwise the connector located inside the boot may become separated.
4. Using compressed air, blow any water or debris from the spark plug well to assure that no harmful contaminants are allowed to enter the combustion chamber when the spark plug is removed. If compressed air is not available, use a rag or a brush to clean the area.

➡ Some computer or office supply stores sell cans of compressed air which are used to clean electronic components. If you don't have a compressor or a portable air tank, then one of these can serve the purpose for blowing dirt out of spark plug ports.

5. Using a spark plug socket that is equipped with a rubber insert to properly hold the plug, turn the spark plug counterclockwise to loosen and remove the spark plug from the bore.

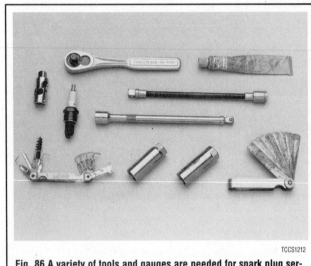

Fig. 86 A variety of tools and gauges are needed for spark plug service

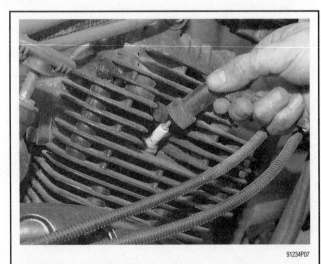

Fig. 87 Always grab the spark plug wire from the boot to avoid damage

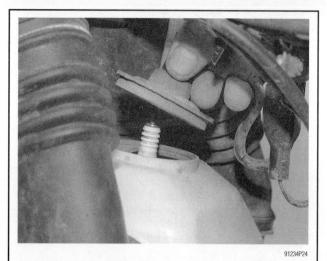

Fig. 88 Forced air-cooled engines may have spark plug boot with an additional seal; be careful not to tear the boot

Fig. 89 Once the boot is removed, use a spark plug socket and a ratchet to remove the plug

Fig. 90 If access is tight, the tool kit supplied with your ATV may be a better choice

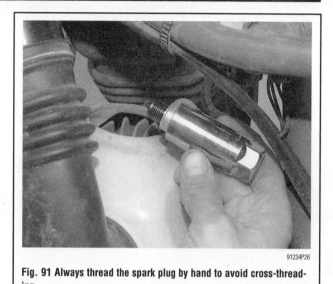

Fig. 91 Always thread the spark plug by hand to avoid cross-threading

➡Remove the spark plug when the engine is cold, if possible, to prevent damage to the threads. If removal of the plug is difficult, apply a few drops of penetrating oil or silicone spray to the area around the base of the plug, then give it a few minutes to work.

❋❋ **WARNING**

Be sure not to use a flexible extension on the socket when removing or installing a spark plug. Use of a flexible extension may allow a shear force to be applied to the plug. A shear force could break the plug off in the cylinder head, leading to costly and frustrating repairs.

To install:

6. Inspect the spark plug boot for tears or damage. If a damaged boot is found, the spark plug boot or boot and wire must be replaced.

7. Using a wire feeler gauge, check and adjust the spark plug gap. When using a gauge, the proper size should pass between the electrodes with a slight drag. The next larger size should not be able to pass while the next smaller size should pass freely.

8. Place a thin coating of anti-seize on the plug threads to make sure they will be easy to remove next time. DON'T FLAKE OUT HERE! If you don't have any anti-seize paste, buy some! It is way too easy to strip out a spark plug hole. Don't overdue it with the paste, a small dab is more than enough.

9. Carefully thread the plug into the bore by hand. If resistance is felt before the plug is almost completely threaded, back the plug out and begin threading again. In small, hard to reach areas, an old spark plug wire and boot could be used as a threading tool. The boot will hold the plug while you twist the end of the wire and the wire is supple enough to twist before it would allow the plug to crossthread.

❋❋ **WARNING**

Always carefully thread the plug by hand to prevent the possibility of crossthreading and damaging the cylinder head bore.

10. Carefully tighten the spark plug. If the plug you are installing is equipped with a crush washer, seat the plug, then tighten about ¼ turn to crush the washer. If you are installing a tapered seat plug, tighten the plug to specifications provided by the ATV or plug manufacturer.

11. Apply a small amount of silicone dielectric compound to the end of the spark plug lead or inside the spark plug boot to prevent sticking, then install the boot to the spark plug and push until it clicks into place. The click may be felt or heard, then gently pull back on the boot to assure proper contact.

12. Unless further checks or adjustments need to be made, install the gas tank or any body plastic if it was removed to access the spark plug easier.

13. Connect the negative battery cable.

SPARK PLUG INSPECTION

◆ **See Figures 92 and 93**

Whenever the spark plug is removed from the engine it should be examined for deposits and wear. Your used spark plugs can lend important clues to engine mechanical and operating conditions.

The best method for checking a spark plug is to inspect it immediately after it has been under typical operating conditions, under load, but WITHOUT allowing the engine to return to idle operation (which could significantly alter what you might find). The best way to check engine condition using the spark plug is to use the following procedure:

1. Go out for a ride (with a helmet and protective gear, of course) and allow the engine to come up to normal operating temperature.

A normally worn spark plug should have light tan or gray deposits on the firing tip.

A carbon fouled plug, identified by soft, sooty, black deposits, may indicate an improperly tuned vehicle. Check the air cleaner, ignition components and engine control system.

This spark plug has been **left in the engine too long,** as evidenced by the extreme gap- Plugs with such an extreme gap can cause misfiring and stumbling accompanied by a noticeable lack of power.

An oil fouled spark plug indicates an engine with worn poston rings and/or bad valve seals allowing excessive oil to enter the chamber.

A physically damaged spark plug may be evidence of severe detonation in that cylinder. Watch that cylinder carefully between services, as a continued detonation will not only damage the plug, but could also damage the engine.

A bridged or almost bridged spark plug, identified by a build-up between the electrodes caused by excessive carbon or oil build-up on the plug.

TCCA1P40

Fig. 92 The condition of used spark plugs can give you a good idea what is happening with your engine

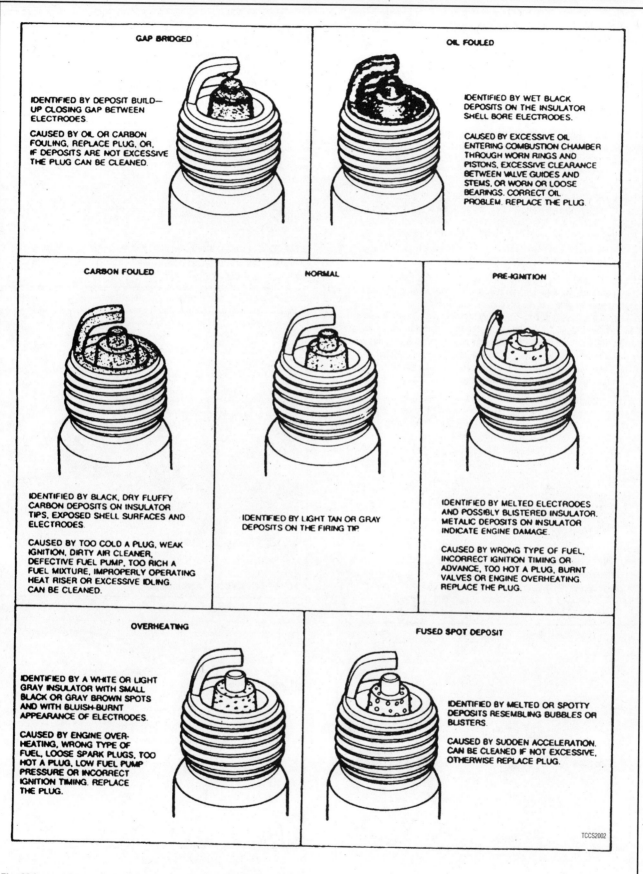

GAP BRIDGED

IDENTIFIED BY DEPOSIT BUILD-UP CLOSING GAP BETWEEN ELECTRODES.

CAUSED BY OIL OR CARBON FOULING. REPLACE PLUG, OR, IF DEPOSITS ARE NOT EXCESSIVE THE PLUG CAN BE CLEANED.

OIL FOULED

IDENTIFIED BY WET BLACK DEPOSITS ON THE INSULATOR SHELL BORE ELECTRODES.

CAUSED BY EXCESSIVE OIL ENTERING COMBUSTION CHAMBER THROUGH WORN RINGS AND PISTONS, EXCESSIVE CLEARANCE BETWEEN VALVE GUIDES AND STEMS, OR WORN OR LOOSE BEARINGS. CORRECT OIL PROBLEM. REPLACE THE PLUG.

CARBON FOULED

IDENTIFIED BY BLACK, DRY FLUFFY CARBON DEPOSITS ON INSULATOR TIPS, EXPOSED SHELL SURFACES AND ELECTRODES.

CAUSED BY TOO COLD A PLUG, WEAK IGNITION, DIRTY AIR CLEANER, DEFECTIVE FUEL PUMP, TOO RICH A FUEL MIXTURE, IMPROPERLY OPERATING HEAT RISER OR EXCESSIVE IDLING. CAN BE CLEANED.

NORMAL

IDENTIFIED BY LIGHT TAN OR GRAY DEPOSITS ON THE FIRING TIP.

PRE-IGNITION

IDENTIFIED BY MELTED ELECTRODES AND POSSIBLY BLISTERED INSULATOR. METALIC DEPOSITS ON INSULATOR INDICATE ENGINE DAMAGE.

CAUSED BY WRONG TYPE OF FUEL, INCORRECT IGNITION TIMING OR ADVANCE, TOO HOT A PLUG, BURNT VALVES OR ENGINE OVERHEATING. REPLACE THE PLUG.

OVERHEATING

IDENTIFIED BY A WHITE OR LIGHT GRAY INSULATOR WITH SMALL BLACK OR GRAY BROWN SPOTS AND WITH BLUISH-BURNT APPEARANCE OF ELECTRODES.

CAUSED BY ENGINE OVER-HEATING, WRONG TYPE OF FUEL, LOOSE SPARK PLUGS, TOO HOT A PLUG, LOW FUEL PUMP PRESSURE OR INCORRECT IGNITION TIMING. REPLACE THE PLUG.

FUSED SPOT DEPOSIT

IDENTIFIED BY MELTED OR SPOTTY DEPOSITS RESEMBLING BUBBLES OR BLISTERS.

CAUSED BY SUDDEN ACCELERATION. CAN BE CLEANED IF NOT EXCESSIVE, OTHERWISE REPLACE PLUG.

TCCS2002

Fig. 93 Inspect the spark plug to determine engine running conditions

2. In an area where you can accelerate to speed, accelerate through the gears at full throttle. With the throttle still wide open, simultaneously hit the engine **KILL** switch while you pull in the clutch or shift into Neutral.

3. Coast to a safe spot and brake to a full stop.

4. Remove the spark plug and examine the deposits to help determine the condition of each cylinder. Compare the plugs to the illustrations and descriptions we have provided.

✴✴ CAUTION

Be very careful not to burn yourself when removing the spark plug from a hot engine. Wear leather gloves that won't melt or catch fire when exposed to the hot cylinder head and exhaust pipe.

5. If the plug insulator has turned white or is burned, the plug is too hot and should be replaced with the next colder one available for your engine.

6. If the plugs you are using are too cold, then you will notice sooty or oily deposits. These deposits could be black or only a dark brown. If found, you should try the next hotter plug. If a hotter plug does not remedy the situation, then suspect an overly rich fuel system, or that your engine is burning oil. A compression or leak-down test would be the next step.

➡ **If your ATV has a two-stroke engine, there is an additional point to be noted regarding spark plug condition. An improper ratio of oil and fuel (whether your engine has oil injection or pre-mixed fuel) can have an effect on the spark plug. One indication of too rich of a fuel/oil mixture is excessive oil deposits on the spark plug tip, otherwise known as fouling. Too little oil mixed with the fuel may cause a lean condition, resulting in a burned plug tip. A lean condition can destroy the piston and cylinder in a two-stroke engine if not corrected. Make absolutely certain that the fuel/oil ratio is correct before making any adjustments.**

7. If the plugs have a damp or oil film over the firing end, a black tip, and a carbon layer over the entire face of the plug, it has been oil fouled. Although you can clean and reuse the plug, it should be replaced. You should also perform a compression or leak-down test to determine the cause of oil fouling.

8. If the plugs exhibit light tan or gray deposits, along with no excessive gap or electrode wear, the engine is running properly and you are using the correct spark plugs.

GAPPING

▶ **See Figures 94, 95, 96 and 97**

If the spark plugs are not going to be replaced, clean the plugs thoroughly. Remember that any kind of deposit will decrease the efficiency of the plug. Plugs can be cleaned on a spark plug cleaning machine, which can sometimes be found in service stations, or you can do an acceptable job of cleaning with a stiff brush. If the plugs are cleaned, the electrodes must be filed flat. Use an

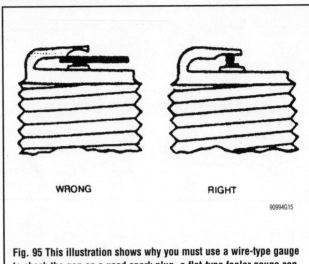

WRONG   RIGHT

90994G15

Fig. 95 This illustration shows why you must use a wire-type gauge to check the gap on a used spark plug, a flat-type feeler gauge can give an incorrect reading

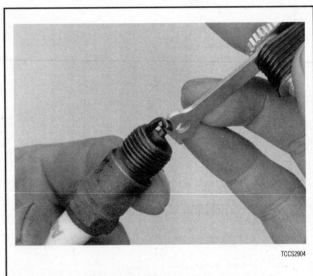

TCCS2904

Fig. 96 Adjusting the spark plug gap

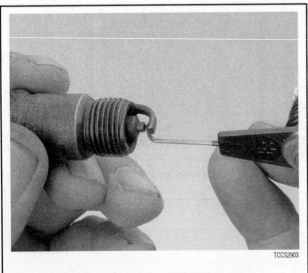

TCCS2903

Fig. 94 Checking the spark plug gap with a feeler gauge

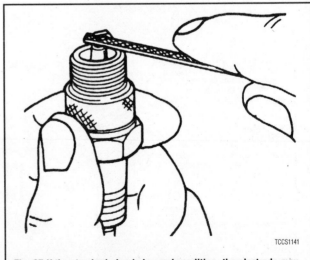

TCCS1141

Fig. 97 If the standard plug is in good condition, the electrode may be filed flat—WARNING: do not file platinum plugs

ignition points file, not an emery board or the like, which will leave deposits. The electrodes must be filed perfectly flat with sharp edges; rounded edges reduce the spark plug voltage by as much as 50%.

Check spark plug gap before installation. The ground electrode (the L-shaped one connected to the body of the plug) must be parallel to the center electrode and the specified size wire gauge must pass between the electrodes with a slight drag.

➡**NEVER adjust the gap on a used platinum type spark plug.**

Always check the gap on new plugs as they are not always set correctly at the factory. Do not use a flat feeler gauge when measuring the gap on a used plug, because the reading may be inaccurate. A round-wire type gapping tool is the best way to check the gap. The correct gauge should pass through the electrode gap with a slight drag. If you're in doubt, try one size smaller and one larger. The smaller gauge should go through easily, while the larger one shouldn't go through at all. Wire gapping tools usually have a bending tool attached. Use that to adjust the side electrode until the proper distance is obtained. Absolutely never attempt to bend the center electrode. Also, be careful not to bend the side electrode too far or too often as it may weaken and break off within the engine, requiring removal of the cylinder head to retrieve it.

CHECKING AND REPLACING SPARK PLUG WIRES

▶ **See Figure 98**

At every tune-up, visually check the spark plug cable for burns cuts, or breaks in the insulation. Check the boot and the nipple on the coil. Replace any damaged wiring.

As wires age, internal strands will break, the connectors on either end may corrode or become physically damaged, and the insulation will break down, allowing for further corrosion and arcing of the spark during use. All of these items add up to a loss of power for your ATV, harder starts, and sometimes to a total loss of spark in the RAIN or under damp, misty conditions.

Every 2 years the resistance of the spark plug wire should be checked with an ohmmeter. If wire is shown to have excessive resistance, it should be replaced. Typically speaking, wire resistance for an electronic ignition system should be below 10,000 ohms. Check a shop manual to see if resistance specifications are available for your model.

To check resistance, disconnect the wire at both ends. Connect the probes of a multi-meter (such as a digital volt ohmmeter or DVOM) set to the 10K or 20K ohm scale to the ends of the spark plug wire. Read the resistance on the meter.

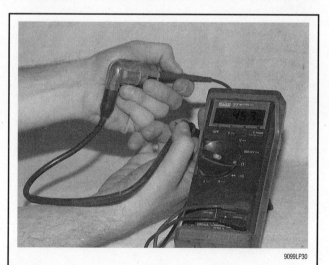

Fig. 98 An ohmmeter can be used to check spark plug wire resistance

Valve Lash

▶ **See Figures 99 and 100**

Two-stroke guys, just keep on moving. Two-stroke engines do not have any valves in the cylinder head to adjust, but you may want to read on anyway, so you can see what you're missing.

Four-stroke cylinder heads use valves to admit the fuel/air mixture into the combustion chamber, to seal the combustion chamber for compression, and to allow the spent exhaust gases to escape. All of these functions are timed using the valve train (camshaft, lifters/shims and sometimes rocker arms and/or pushrods) to occur at the proper times.

In order for the valves to operate properly, they must be adjusted to assure that the full benefit of the camshaft lobe lift is realized, but they also must be able to close fully once the lobe of the camshaft has gone by. Valves are adjusted by increasing or decreasing their LASH, which is the amount of free-play in the valve train when the valve is closed (meaning the camshaft lobe is NOT actuating the shim, pushrod or rocker arm). Valve lash therefore, is basically a gap that exists between components (the valve stem and a rocker arm or a camshaft lobe and a shim depending on the engine design) when the valve is fully closed.

Since valves open and close with every turn of the crankshaft, their movement becomes a blur at engine speeds, which can create a pounding on the entire valve train. As this use wears the components valve lash will tend to change (increase or decrease depending on the model). On some engines, the valve seats and heads will wear slowly, causing the valve to come further into the cylinder head (moving the stem closer to the shim or rocker arm and decreasing valve lash). On other models, the stem, shim or other valve train components will wear, causing the gap to increase.

But whether the valve lash is increasing or decreasing slowly through use doesn't really matter, either one will eventually lead to the valve being out of adjustment, and this will adversely affect engine performance.

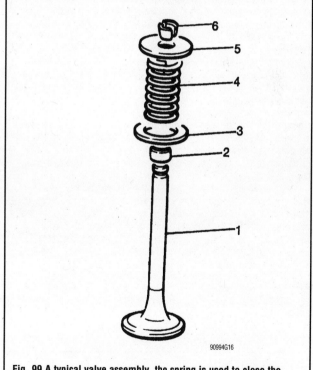

Fig. 99 A typical valve assembly, the spring is used to close the valve, once the rocker arm or shim is no longer pushing downward

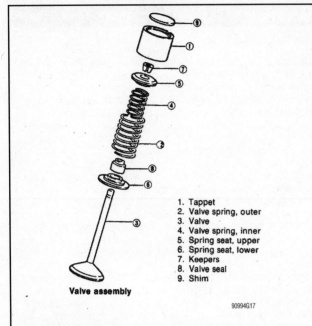

1. Tappet
2. Valve spring, outer
3. Valve
4. Valve spring, inner
5. Spring seat, upper
6. Spring seat, lower
7. Keepers
8. Valve seal
9. Shim

Valve assembly

90994G17

Fig. 100 Another popular valve and spring assembly, this model uses two valve springs

Increased valve lash will not allow a valve to fully open since some of the camshaft lobe lift will be wasted on taking up the excess lash. If an intake valve does not open sufficiently, the full fuel/air charge will not make it into the cylinder and power will be lost during combustion. If an exhaust valve does not open enough, some the exhaust gases will be left in the cylinder, displacing some of the fuel/air mixture which will try to enter the cylinder on the next stroke. Again, the result will be a reduction in engine power.

Decreased valve lash will have a less noticeable effect on engine power, but could have a more devastating effect on your engine. As valve lash is decreased beyond specification, the valve train components may not allow the valve to fully come into contact with the seat. This will prevent the valve from cooling through heat transfer with the valve seat. The term "burnt valve" which you have likely heard someone mention before means that a valve was ruined by heat. A burnt valve will not properly seal the combustion chamber, and can also come flying apart, destroying your piston and cylinder wall. As valve lash decreases, the engine could lose power if valves are held partially open by the valve train (not allowing for proper compression).

You can see from these examples why you would want to keep an eye on your valve lash.

Intake and exhaust valves usually have different specifications, because of the differences in their sizes and jobs. The exhaust valve is usually set a little looser than the intake, because of the harsh environment it lives in (superheated gases pass over it into the exhaust system when it is open). Intake valves have it easy (for a valve) as they are in contact with the cylinder head when they are exposed to combustion gases and temperatures (when they are open, relatively cool air/fuel mixture passes over their surface).

To identify an exhaust or intake valve, look at its position in relation to the rest of the cylinder head. In most cases, the intake valve will be closest to and in alignment with the intake manifold, while the exhaust valve is closest to and adjacent to the exhaust pipe.

ADJUSTMENT

▸ **See Figure 101**

✳✳ CAUTION

Great care must be taken when adjusting the valves. While some small error is permitted on the loose side (which will result in noisy valves and a slight reduction in performance), setting the clearances too tight will often burn the valves.

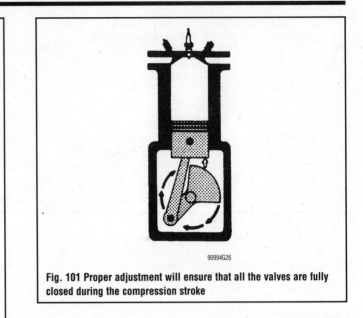

90994G26

Fig. 101 Proper adjustment will ensure that all the valves are fully closed during the compression stroke

With the higher quality metals and components used in modern ATV engines, the need for periodic valve adjustments has often been reduced. This is not to say that it has been eliminated in most cases, but that the maintenance intervals have been increased. What was once a ritual which was as common as the oil change is now more likely a once a year task. It also has been eliminated on some models, thanks to hydraulic lifters.

Be sure to consult your owners manual for recommendations on intervals and model valve lash specifications. The specifications can also sometimes be found on emission labels which are mounted to the ATVs themselves. Although the specific lash adjustment procedures will vary from model-to-model (and you should consult a shop manual before attempting this), there are a few basic designs and points to keep in mind when trying it for the first time.

To begin with, since valve lash is a measurement of the amount of free-play in the valve train, you must be CERTAIN that you always measure it with the valve fully closed. That means that the actuator (shim, pushrod or lifter) for that particular valve MUST be in contact with the BASE portion of the camshaft lobe (NOT THE RAISED AREA). This means that you should turn the crankshaft (which can be done with a kickstarter pedal or with the rear wheels if the transmission is placed in gear and the spark plug is removed to relieve compression) until the cylinder is at Top Dead Center (TDC) of the compression stroke. This is when the cylinder would be ready to fire and the valves would have to be closed.

In almost all cases, valves must be adjusted on a cold engine. This is important since metal components will expand with heat. Specifications for the same valve will be larger when the valve is cold than when it is hot. If a valve is adjusted to a cold specification when it is hot, that adjustment will be far too tight at operating temperatures, which could lead to a burnt valve. Most importantly here, follow the specifications, they should ALWAYS be presented with the information on whether it is a hot or cold spec.

ALSO, some manufacturers will have you retorque the cylinder head before adjusting the valve lash. Check your owners or shop manual for the proper torque sequence, specification and to be certain that this is necessary for your model before proceeding.

ATV engines typically use one of three systems to adjust valve lash:
- **Rocker Arms and Screw-type adjusters**
- **Shims and buckets**
- **Hydraulic valve lifters**

Rocker Arms and Screw-Type Adjusters

▸ **See Figures 102 thru 120**

Probably the most popular form of lash adjustment is a simple screw fitting on the end of a rocker arm. These are especially popular because they usually do not require any special tools to make the adjustments (with the exception of a feeler gauge). They are common on pushrod engines (that don't use hydraulic lifters) and on some overhead cam motors as well.

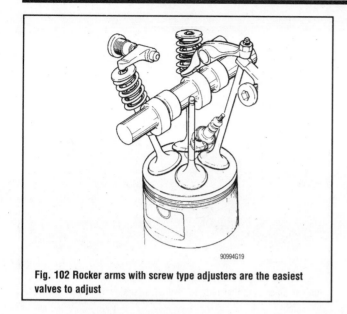

Fig. 102 Rocker arms with screw type adjusters are the easiest valves to adjust

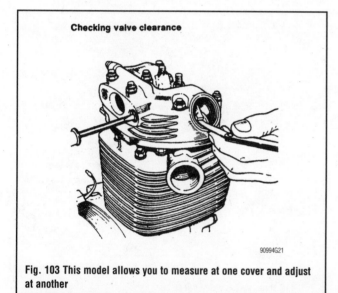

Fig. 103 This model allows you to measure at one cover and adjust at another

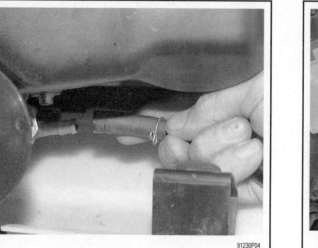

Fig. 104 On most ATVs, removing the gas tank is required to adjust the valves. Turn the petcock OFF, unplug the fuel line . . .

Fig. 105 . . . remove any fasteners . . .

Fig. 106 . . . then lift the gas tank from the ATV and set aside

Fig. 107 Some ATVs have additional components that have to be removed for access to the cylinder head

Fig. 108 Keep track of any additional fasteners

Fig. 111 On most pushrod engines, the timing marks on the alternator can be used to find TDC. Don't confuse the timing mark with TDC

Fig. 109 On ATVs with overhead cam engines, remove the upper sprocket cover . . .

Fig. 112 Remove the valve cover . . .

Fig. 110 . . . and line up the marks on the sprocket for Top Dead Center (TDC)

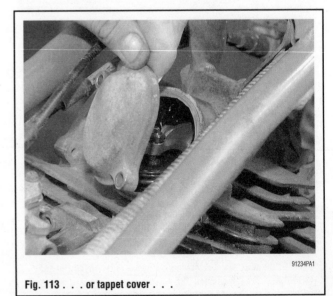

Fig. 113 . . . or tappet cover . . .

Fig. 114 . . . to access the adjusters

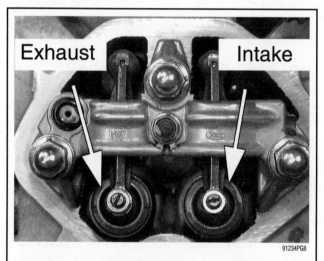

Exhaust   Intake

Fig. 115 Be sure to identify which valve(s) are for intake and exhaust, since they may require different specifications

Fig. 116 With the engine at TDC, insert the proper size feeler gauge between the tappet and the valve. The gauge should fit snugly, with a slight drag

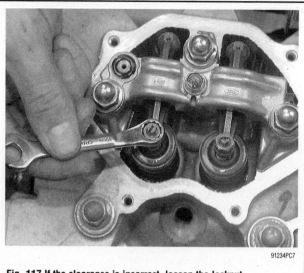

Fig. 117 If the clearance is incorrect, loosen the locknut . . .

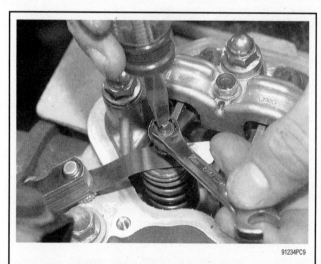

Fig. 118 . . . and turn the adjuster until the lash is correct. Hold the adjuster stationary while tightening the locknut

Fig. 119 Be sure to replace any damaged gaskets or O-rings during assembly to prevent leaks

91234PD3

Fig. 120 When specifications are available, use a torque wrench on engine components to prevent warpage

On most machines with rocker arms and screw-type adjusters, valve lash is adjusted as follows:

1. Place the ATV on a lift or workstand for easier access.

2. Remove the gas tank or any bodywork which interferes with access to the valve cover(s).

3. Remove the spark plug (unless you still haven't installed it from the compression or spark plug condition check) to make the engine easier to turn.

4. Remove the valve adjustment access covers or the valve cover(s), as necessary for access to the rocker arms.

5. Set the cylinder on TDC of the compression stroke, making sure that both valves are fully closed. Unless the valve lash is way out of spec on the tight side, the rocker arms should be a little loose with the cylinder at TDC. If necessary, place the transmission in gear and turn the rear wheel in order to turn the cylinders (this shouldn't be too hard with the spark plugs removed, but BE CAREFUL if you are using a workstand, don't knock it over).

6. If your model requires it, retorque the cylinder head to specification using the proper torque sequence.

7. The proper sized feeler gauge for each valve's specification (remember that the intake and exhaust
valves are usually set at different specs) should slide between the tip of the valve stem and the rocker arm with only a slight drag.

8. If the lash must be adjusted, loosen the locknut and rotate the adjuster until the proper clearance is obtained. Hold the adjuster in position while tightening the locknut, then recheck the valve clearance to be certain that the adjuster did not turn.

9. Repeat the adjustment for each valve, making sure each time that the cylinder is at TDC of the compression stroke.

10. Install the valve cover(s), using a new gasket when necessary.

11. Install the spark plug.

12. Install any bodywork or other components which were removed for access to the valve cover.

13. If raised on a lift or workstand, carefully lower the ATV to the ground.

Shim and Bucket Adjusters

▶ See Figures 121, 122, 123, 124 and 125

Some ATVs, especially many of the high performance models, are equipped with overhead cams and usually NO rocker arms. These motors use shims between the cam lobes and the valve stems to adjust the clearance, and in these instances you will need a micrometer and a selection of shims of the proper thickness in order to adjust the lash.

➡There are 2 basic designs: shim under bucket and shim over bucket. On the shim under bucket designs, the camshaft must be removed in order to access the shims. On most of the shim over bucket designs, the valve spring can be depressed slightly (sometimes using a special tool to lever on the bucket or valve stem only), allowing for shim removal WITHOUT removing the camshaft.

The advantage of these setups include smaller, simplified valve trains with less components to rob the crankshaft of power. The disadvantage is that the camshafts are going to have to be removed in order to adjust the valve lash. Again, you are going to want a good shop manual too make sure that you don't miss something important, like the proper camshaft bearing removal or installation sequence and bolt torques (if you have the shim under bucket design or a shim over bucket on which the shaft must be removed for some reason).

Basically, shim and bucket adjustment involves accessing the cams, measuring the valves and installing new shims (where necessary):

1. Make sure the engine is completely COLD. If you did a compression check earlier and you are done gapping a new spark plug, take a break, grab some lunch, find something to clean, but make sure the engine is COLD.

2. Place the ATV on a workstand or a lift for easier access.

3. Remove the gas tank or any bodywork which interferes with access to the valve cover(s).

4. Remove the spark plug (unless you still haven't installed it from the compression or spark plug condition check) to make the engine easier to turn.

5. Remove the valve cover(s) for access to the valve train.

6. You are going to have to turn the engine over manually in order to set each cylinder at TDC of the compression stroke. Most engines have a cover which can be removed for access to the crankshaft snout. With the cover removed you can turn the crankshaft directly. If you cannot find a cover (or would rather not remove it), you can place the transmission in gear and use the rear wheels to turn the engine (as long as the wheels are off the ground, but be CAREFUL if you are using a workstand or lift not to tip the ATV.)

7. Use a feeler gauge set to check the clearance between the base of each camshaft lobe and its shim (over bucket) or between the lobe and the bucket (shim under bucket). Note the clearances for the intake and exhaust.

8. Once you have measured the lash on all valves (if your engine has a four-valve head) it is time to remove the camshaft (if necessary to access the shims on your engine). Follow your shop manual closely for details on this procedure. Typically this involves the following procedure:

a. Rotate the engine to TDC with all appropriate timing marks aligned.

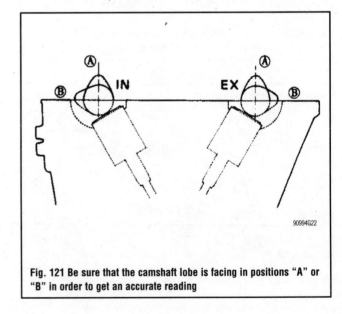

90994G22

Fig. 121 Be sure that the camshaft lobe is facing in positions "A" or "B" in order to get an accurate reading

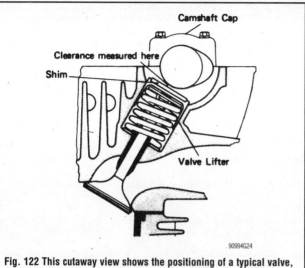

Fig. 122 This cutaway view shows the positioning of a typical valve, camshaft, and shim adjuster (shim OVER bucket design shown)

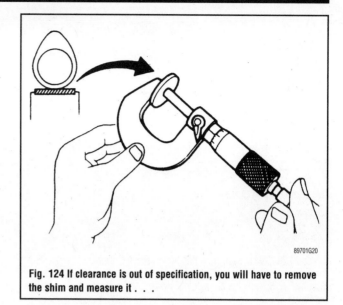

Fig. 124 If clearance is out of specification, you will have to remove the shim and measure it . . .

Fig. 123 With the lobe facing the proper direction, use a set of feeler gauges to determine the valve clearance

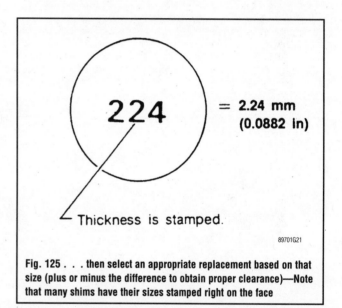

Fig. 125 . . . then select an appropriate replacement based on that size (plus or minus the difference to obtain proper clearance)—Note that many shims have their sizes stamped right on the face

b. Use a small marker or bottle of White Out® to make alignment marks between the camshaft sprockets and the camshaft drive chain (or belt, if applicable). This will assure that you preserve proper valve timing when installing the cam(s).

c. Tie the camshaft timing belt or chain in position (this can often be done using safety wire between the frame and the chain/belt.

d. Place a clean rag over the opening in the timing cover and anywhere else you don't want an errant bolt or small part to fall during your work.

e. Loosen each of the camshaft bearing cap bolts using the proper sequence.

➡BE SURE to properly tag and arrange ALL components which are removed from the valve train including the camshaft bearing caps, bolts and bearings. These should all be installed in the exact same positions from which they were removed. An old baking tray or egg carton works well for this.

f. Remove the bearing caps, then carefully remove the camshafts and sprockets.

➡On most models the camshaft sprockets may need to be removed before the camshaft is removed.

9. Remove and measure each of the valve shims which must be replaced to achieve proper lash. Based on the measurement, calculate what size replacement shims you will need and head on down to the local ATV shop. If the measurement for a cylinder was too tight, then you will need a shim which is that much smaller for that cylinder. If the measurement was too loose, then you will need a shim which is that much thicker.

➡On shim over bucket engines where the camshaft is not removed, use an appropriate tool to gently pry downward on the bucket or the valve stem to provide clearance necessary to remove the shim. In some cases special tools for this are available from the manufacturer. In other cases, tools are available from aftermarket sources, or some automotive tools may do the trick. If in doubt, check with your dealer for advice on how to safely slide the shims from under the camshaft.

10. Position the new shims in place. Make sure each of the valves receive the proper shim that will correct the lash to proper specification. Don't mix them up, or you'll be performing the procedure twice.

11. If removed, install the camshafts, making sure that all of the timing marks have remained in proper alignment. Tighten the bearing caps to specification using the proper torque sequence.

12. Rotate the engine one full revolution, and verify that the valve timing is correct.

13. Install the valve cover(s) and any engine covers which were removed.

14. Install the spark plug.

15. Install any bodywork or other components which were removed for access to the valve cover.

16. Safely lower the ATV from the workstand or lift.

Hydraulic Valve Lifters

▶ **See Figure 126**

You've got hydraulic valve lifters? Well then, boy this is your lucky day. Hydraulic valve lifters are designed to automatically compensate for changing valve lash. They work by using a multi-piece, spring loaded lifter body to maintain zero lash in the valve train (allowing valves to open and close fully regardless of normal wear and tear to the valve train). For this reason, engines with hydraulic valve lifters normally do NOT require any periodic valve adjustments.

It is argued that this design can rob the engine of some power (by loosing a little camshaft lift to hydraulic lifter lash, depending on the design and condition of the lifter). So you will probably see that hydraulic lifters tend to be more popular on models whose primary purpose does NOT involve cutting edge engine performance. Hydraulic lifters provide excellent, long-term ease of maintenance at a reasonable cost to overall engine performance and are quite likely to be found on many utility type models for this reason.

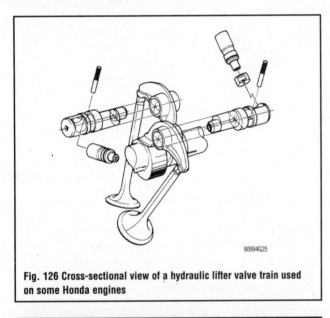

Fig. 126 Cross-sectional view of a hydraulic lifter valve train used on some Honda engines

Ignition Timing

GENERAL INFORMATION

▶ **See Figures 127, 128 and 129**

Ignition timing is the measurement, in degrees of crankshaft rotation, of the point at which the spark plugs fire in each of the cylinders. It is measured in degrees before or after Top Dead Center (TDC) of the compression stroke.

Because it takes a fraction of a second for the spark plug to ignite the mixture in the cylinder, the spark plug must fire a little before the piston reaches TDC. Otherwise, the mixture will not be completely ignited as the piston passes TDC and the full power of the explosion of the fuel will not be used by the engine.

The timing measurement is given in degrees of crankshaft rotation before the piston reaches TDC (BTDC). If the setting for the ignition timing is 5° BTDC, the spark plug must fire 5° before the piston reaches TDC. This only holds true, however, when the engine is at idle speed.

As the engine speed increases, the piston goes faster. The spark plug has to ignite the fuel even sooner if it is to be completely ignited when the piston reaches TDC. To do this, ignition systems have various means of advancing the spark timing as the engine speed increases. On older ATVs, this was accomplished by centrifugal weights on a breaker point rotor. But on modern ATVs with electronic ignition systems, the ignition timing is usually advanced electronically by the control module based on input from engine sensors or vacuum switches.

If the ignition spark was too far advanced (BTDC), the ignition and expansion of the fuel in the cylinder would occur too soon and tend to force the piston

Fig. 127 Timing marks on some engines can be found underneath an inspection cover on the engine case

Fig. 128 Although most engines do not have adjustable timing, the reference markings are helpful for diagnostic purposes

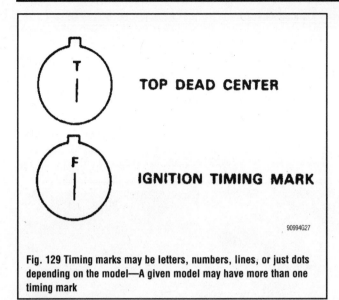

TOP DEAD CENTER

IGNITION TIMING MARK

90994G27

Fig. 129 Timing marks may be letters, numbers, lines, or just dots depending on the model—A given model may have more than one timing mark

down while it is still traveling up. This would cause engine ping (preignition). If the ignition spark is too far retarded, after TDC (ATDC), the piston will have already passed TDC and started on its way down when the fuel is ignited. This would cause the piston to be forced down for only a portion of its travel, resulting in poor engine performance and lack of power.

INSPECTION & ADJUSTMENT

Before transistorized ignitions took over in the late 70's and very early 80's, motorcycle and ATV riders would have to check, adjust and replace their breaker points very frequently. Failure to do so would lead to hard starts and eventual, no starts as the point gap widened or the points eventually became worn or burned beyond service. If you are riding an older ATV with points, then God bless you. But, if it is not a show-able antique, you are crazy. There are many retrofit kits available to convert a points machine over to electronic ignition. Don't listen to those people who are afraid of electronic ignition because "if it breaks I can't just fix it on the trail." Electronic ignition works better and breaks down much less often than mechanical breaker points. As a matter of fact, it is a good thing that those die-hards who insist on keeping points CAN fix them on the trail, because eventually THEY ARE GOING TO HAVE TO.

Every modern ATV is equipped with an electronic ignition system, usually known as transistorized ignition, breakerless discharge or capacitor discharge ignition. On these systems, the mechanical breaker points have been replaced with an ignition module and a signal rotor of some sort. Where the mechanical breaker points were once used to physically break the primary ignition circuit, causing the ignition coil to discharge and fire the secondary circuit, an ignition module now performs that function. The module knows WHEN to perform that function based on a signal received from a signal rotor (usually a magnetized pick-up coil of some sort, which sends signals to the ignition module). The pick-up coil normally sends signals to the module based on changes to a magnetic field caused by notches machined into a part of the crankshaft, or a part turned by the crankshaft. The advantages of electronic ignition include long life (because no mechanical contacts are used to break the primary circuit which could wear like points), along with a significantly higher voltage capacity. The higher voltage is an advantage when it comes to firing plugs with larger gaps or under adverse conditions like oil soaked plugs.

The newer your ATV, the lesser the chance that the ignition timing can or should be adjusted. Although many modern ATVs still have the ability to adjust their ignition timing, it is no longer recommended as a periodic procedure. Timing marks are usually provided ONLY to be used as a check to make sure all ignition components are installed correctly and functioning properly. Check your owners manual for recommendations regarding checking ignition timing.

If your ATV is equipped with timing marks they will usually consist of a notches, dots, or letters that are either machined directly on a part of the crankshaft, or a part which the crankshaft turns such as the alternator rotor. There is usually a cover or plug which can be easily removed to view the timing mark.

Timing procedures vary from one manufacturer to another. In the days of points, the procedures ranged from using a dial gauge or degree wheel to using a test light or continuity checker to set "static timing." This meant timing was often set WITHOUT the engine running. "Dynamic timing" checks were made on some models, using an automotive style stroboscopic timing light (which makes the timing marks appear to stand still due to the effect of the strobe light).

On most modern ATVs, timing checks are designed to use a stroboscopic timing light with an inductive pick-up to perform a "dynamic timing" inspection. The timing light's pick-up is clamped to the spark plug wire and will trigger the timing light each time a pulse is detected in the wire. By pointing the timing light at the timing mark, you can see if it lines up with the appropriate marker or if it centers in the access hole, as required by your particular engine's specifications.

➡Never pierce a spark plug wire in order to attach a timing light or perform tests. The pierced insulation will eventually lead to an electrical arc and related ignition troubles.

Carburetor Adjustments

▶ See Figure 130

Carburetor tune-up procedures will largely depend upon the type of engine, the type of carburetor, what kind of controls are fitted, and ancillary systems, if fitted, such as oil pumps (two-strokes) and the like which operate in conjunction with the carburetor.

Carburetor adjustments generally fall into 2 major categories:
- **Idle Speed**
- **Mixture**

Periodic carburetor adjustments have become another victim of increasing technology. But this can also be attributed to increasing emissions laws that recently have affected the off-road community. Some carburetors on certain ATVs have been fit with sealed and tamper-resistant screws to prevent adjustment to the air/fuel mixtures. Manufacturers tell us that the mixtures are set at the factory and should NOT be touched in the field. So, if you are riding one of these ATVs, and it has not been modified, then chances are that you only need to worry about occasionally adjusting the idle speed.

Carburetor adjustments must always be made when the engine is at operating temperature.

PRE-ADJUSTMENT CHECKS

▶ See Figure 131

Before attempting to make carburetor adjustments, all of the following points should be checked:

1. Carburetor alignment. On flexible mounted units, ensure that the carburetor is vertically oriented, and not tilted sideways. This may effect fuel level and high-speed operation.

2. Cable condition. Check throttle operation, ensuring that the cable(s) are not kinked or binding, and that they are well-lubricated. If the gas tank has been removed and reinstalled, check that it has not trapped or pinched the throttle cables, or that the cables have not been forced to make sharp bends anywhere along their route.

3. Ancillary systems. Carburetor adjustments should be made last after all other systems have been attended to in order to prevent misleading symptoms. Check that the air cleaner is not dirty, the spark plugs are in good condition, valves are correctly adjusted, and the ignition is operating correctly. Also ensure that the gasoline is reasonably fresh, of the correct octane, and that foreign material, such as water or dirt, has been purged from the fuel system. Check fuel filters to make sure that the carburetor is not being starved of fuel.

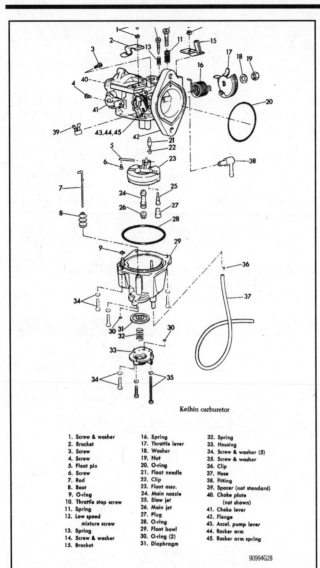

1. Screw & washer	16. Spring	32. Spring
2. Bracket	17. Throttle lever	33. Housing
3. Screw	18. Washer	34. Screw & washer (5)
4. Screw	19. Nut	35. Screw & washer
5. Float pin	20. O-ring	36. Clip
6. Screw	21. Float needle	37. Hose
7. Rod	22. Clip	38. Fitting
8. Boot	23. Float assy.	39. Spacer (not standard)
9. O-ring	24. Main nozzle	40. Choke plate
10. Throttle stop screw	25. Slow jet	(not shown)
11. Spring	26. Main jet	41. Choke lever
12. Low speed	27. Plug	42. Flange
mixture screw	28. O-ring	43. Accel. pump lever
13. Spring	29. Float bowl	44. Rocker arm
14. Screw & washer	30. O-ring (2)	45. Rocker arm spring
15. Bracket	31. Diaphragm	

90994G28

Fig. 130 The typical carburetor is composed of dozens of intricate parts which work together to produce proper air/fuel ratios—they do not respond well to inexperienced and unnecessary tampering

91234P28

Fig. 131 Before making any carburetor adjustments, make sure everything is in working order, and all connections are tight

Cable Adjustment

◆ See Figures 132 and 133

On most ATVs, provision is made for adjusting the throttle cable to compensate for stretching. The adjuster is usually found at or near the throttle lever, on the handlebars. This device should be adjusted so that the thumb lever has a small amount of noticeable free-play. In general, this free-play should amount to about $^{13}/_{16}$–$^{3}/_{8}$ (5–10 mm) at the lever tip before the slides begin to lift or butterflies begin to turn on the carburetor(s).

On certain oil-injected two-strokes, the oil pump cable adjustment must be checked any time the throttle cable is adjusted. It is essential that the oil injection pump is synchronized with the throttle cable for proper injection of oil into the cylinder.

91235PQ7

Fig. 132 Adjusting the throttle cable at the housing (cover removed for clarity)

91234PD7

Fig. 133 The cable and cam on this carburetor should be lubricated periodically for smooth operation

➡After adjustment, turn the handlebars slowly from side to side with the engine idling. Idle speed must not change or the cable is too tightly adjusted or too short. Check routing and adjust as necessary.

IDLE SPEED & MIXTURE ADJUSTMENTS

◆ See Figures 134, 135, 136 and 137

Idle speeds which are recommended by the manufacturer should be adhered to in most cases. The idle running of an ATV engine is usually the most unsatisfactory carburetor range. There are many reasons for this. For one, the quantities of fuel and air which are going into the engine are relatively small, and are controlled by equally small passages. These are more likely to become clogged with dirt or varnish than the much larger jets, (used for off-idle operation) and the mixture will then be upset. Further, the relative quantities of gas and air are more critical at idle. Finally, since the engine is turning slowly, and is not under load, any irregularities in the mixture flow cause an erratic idle which may be irritating.

On most ATVs, a satisfactory idle can be obtained by carefully setting the carburetor(s) idle stop screw to the recommended specifications. As noted above, idle speed should be set to the recommended specification. An idle speed which is too low may cause trouble by making smooth transition to the slow or mid-range circuit impossible. On some ATVs, too low an idle may cause damage to bearings and other moving parts due to the great lapse between power pulses or to oil pressures which drop too low below specified idle.

On the other hand, too high an idle speed may cause the rpm to hang up for a moment or so when the throttle is closed. It may also make engaging the gears noisy or difficult, or result in excessive brake lining wear by negating the effects of engine braking. Because of the low engine speeds involved, minor misadjustments or slightly defective components will be much more noticeable at idle.

Because idle speed and mixture adjustments can vary so greatly with model, year and engine design, no attempt can be made to give them all here. If you need to adjust the mixture, either because your ATV is that old or it is that modified (exhaust systems especially), you should start with a shop manual.

❊❊ CAUTION

REMEMBER that running internal combustion gasoline engines produces CARBON MONOXIDE which can kill you. NEVER, EVER run an engine (even for a short time) in an enclosed area like a shed or a garage. ALWAYS make sure there is plenty of ventilation (meaning that all garage doors and windows are open and, if at all possible, the exhaust pipes are sticking out through them). Better yet, do it on a nice, sunny day, and perform all adjustments outside.

To check and set idle speed on most ATVs:
1. Attach a tachometer to the engine according to the tool manufacturer's instructions. The easiest type to use are the modern tachometers which have an inductive pick-up which you clamp to the spark plug wire. If you don't have a tachometer, you can "guesstimate" the proper idle speed, although it is not nearly as accurate.
2. Start and run the engine until it reaches normal operating temperature.
3. Locate the idle speed stop screw or idle speed adjusting knob. The adjusting knob is usually found on the carburetor itself. On models with dual carburetors, there is usually either a single screw attached to a mechanical linkage which actuates the throttle plates of both carburetors or there may be a

Fig. 135 Another example of an idle speed adjustment screw that can be adjusted by hand—but not as easily, due to the location

Fig. 136 As with idle speed adjustment screws, some mixture adjustment screws are easy to get to . . .

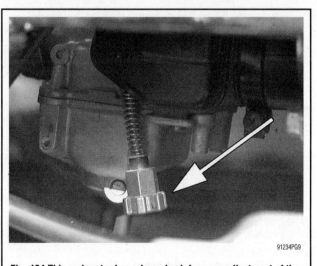
Fig. 134 This carburetor has a large knob for easy adjustment of the idle speed without any tools

Fig. 137 . . . while others may require the use of specialized tools

knurled knob on the end of a cable which is attached to the linkage. It may be necessary to remove a panel to gain access to the throttle adjustment screw.

4. With the engine running and the throttle fully closed, turn the idle speed screw until the proper specified idle has been reached.

5. Open and close the throttle a few times, and watch to see that the idle speed returns to specification. Repeat this once or twice to be certain the idle speed remains within specifications.

6. With the engine still running at idle speed, slowly turn the handle bars from lock-to-lock. If the idle speed increases, even slightly, the throttle cable should be checked for kinks or binding. If none are found, the throttle cable should be adjusted until normal idle speed can be maintained while the bars are turned through their full range of motion.

Mixture Adjustments

On most carburetors, the idle mixture is determined largely by the pilot air screw which controls the amount of air mixing with the idle circuit jets, or the pilot fuel screw, which controls the amount of gasoline passing into the circuit.

Carburetors may be equipped with one or the other of these screws. While exceptions exist, on most carburetors the location of the screw will indicate whether it is an air screw or a fuel screw. Generally pilot air screws are located on the intake side of the carburetor, while most pilot fuel screws are located between the throttle slide and the engine manifold. Most "CV" carburetors use pilot fuel screws.

It is important to know whether you have an "air screw" or a "fuel screw" if you intend to make mixture changes based on spark plug readings or other tests. Turning an air screw in will give a richer mixture, while turning it out will lean the mixture out. For pilot fuel screws, exactly the opposite is true.

Regardless of type pilot screw, settings are given by the manufacturer, and should be adhered to, at least to within certain limits. The pilot screw settings are expressed in turns out from the seated position. The pilot screw's tip is tapered and is mated to an air or fuel passage. To make the adjustment, the screw is turned in gently until you can feel that it is lightly seated, then backed out the given number of turns. For example, if your specification for the pilot

screw setting is "2 ½" that is the number of times that the screw is to be turned.

When turning these screws in, it is best to be very careful, as it is possible to ruin the tapered portion of the screw if it is turned down too tightly.

When adjusting the mixture, always turn the pilot screws out to the given specification, then make any necessary adjustments. It should not be necessary to vary the screw setting more than 1/2 turn from the given setting unless changes have been made to the intake, engine, or exhaust systems. If it is not possible to obtain satisfactory performance with the settings as specified, suspect clogged carburetor passages or air leaks, etc.

Adjusting the pilot screws (air and fuel) usually only affect the mixture within the lower throttle range.

Another adjustment that can be performed to adjust the mixture of fuel and air is changing the position of the jet needle. The jet needle is found inside the carburetor, attached to the sliding throttle valve. In most cases, it is required that the top of the carburetor be removed to access the needle jet. If the mixture needs to be richened, the circlip on the jet needle should be lowered, which would raise it's position. For a leaner mixture, raise the circlip on the jet needle, which will lower the position within the needle jet (the needle jet is the stationary part on the carburetor body, and the jet needle is the part which is attached to the throttle valve.) In most cases, adjustment of the jet needle will affect the air/fuel mixture within the mid-to-upper throttle range.

If you have installed a high-performance exhaust on your ATV, it may require more than adjustments to the carburetor to obtain a proper air/fuel ratio. Changing the main jet of the carburetor is really the best way to adjust the mixture in this type of situation, as opposed to using the adjustments on the carburetor to an extreme. Due to great amount of testing and adjusting involved in re-jetting a carburetor, we at Chilton recommend having a professional perform this type of procedure. A carburetor that is improperly adjusted and or jetted can quickly ruin an engine quickly. (Especially two-strokes which can be ruined in a matter of **seconds** if the mixture is too lean.) Don't take the chance on frying your motor just to save a couple of dollars; take it to a shop who will set up your ATV to run properly.

DRIVELINE MAINTENANCE

Transmission Oil

◆ **See Figures 138 and 139**

Most ATVs with four-stroke transmissions share their oil with the engine. There are however, exceptions. Polaris ATVs for example, have a unique automatic transmission, which separates the engine oil from the transmission oil. If your ATV is like most, you've already changed the transmission oil when you changed the engine oil. However, if your ATV is a two-stroke, or among those with a separate transmission and engine, then read on.

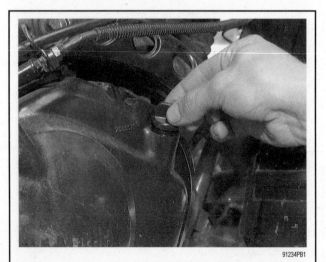

91234PB1

Fig. 138 Most four-stroke ATV engines share engine and transmission oil

On ATVs without cases that share engine and transmission oil, a separate oil change must be performed in order to keep your transmission in top shape. Remember that most ATV transmissions lead a rough life. Most are mounted in close quarters with the engines meaning they get a large amount of the heat from the motor, not to mention the heat from the job they normally perform—transmitting power to the rear wheels.

Like engine oil, transmission gear oil will oxidize over time when exposed to moisture and atmospheric contaminants. Luckily, on ATVs that don't share their oil with the engine, this process is significantly slower because the oil is not exposed to the acids and other nasty byproducts of combustion. But, that doesn't mean you should ignore it. At least annually, you should drain the transmission fluid, check it for unusual wear or excessive emulsification. If either is found, you should perform more frequent inspections or changes to see if there is a problem developing. If you ride in adverse conditions (like rainy weather or a lot of mud), then the fluid level should be checked to make sure too much water didn't find its way in. If the level has gone up (without you adding), you can assume there is too much water in the case and the oil should be changed right away.

SELECTING THE PROPER OIL

ATVs with transmissions that do not share oil with the engine often require special oil for the gears. On some ATVs, the clutch is also of the "wet" type, meaning that it is immersed in oil. Be sure to check whether your clutch is a wet or dry type, as this may have an affect on the type of oil that the transmission requires. Check with your dealer or owner's manual and find out what type and viscosity of oil your ATV's transmission requires.

❊❊ WARNING

Be sure to check your owner's manual for your ATV manufacturer's particular requirements before selecting a gear oil.

If your clutch is of the dry type, then your choices are not as limited. A high quality gear oil of an automotive type can be used. As always, be sure to consult your local ATV dealer or owner's manual for the proper viscosity and type of oil to use in your transmission.

CHECKING YOUR OIL

The fluid level of your transmission is usually checked in one of two ways, either using a dipstick OR a check plug. In both cases the ATV should usually be on a perfectly level surface to assure a proper reading.

Fig. 139 On some two-stroke engines, the only means of checking the level of the transmission fluid is by adding the specified capacity during an oil change

With A Dipstick

If a dipstick is used, the same rules apply as when checking engine oil. If the dipstick is threaded, DON'T rethread it to check the level, but leave it sitting on top of the threads. Remember to pull it out, wipe it off and reinsert it. Then pull it out and hold it vertically. Oil will not magically run up the dipstick. If you hold the dipstick vertically, you will never get a false high reading (unless you are thick enough to hold it upside-down, but then you get what you deserve, right?). If oil is necessary, add it through the dipstick opening, SLOWLY. Remember that these transmissions are usually very compact and a few ounces can make quite a difference on the fluid level. Add slowly, let it sit for a minute and then recheck.

With a Check Plug

Locate the check plug on the side of the engine case. The check plug is usually noted with an arrow or markings on the side of the engine case. Next, remove the check plug from the side of the engine. With the ATV on a fully level surface, a small amount of oil should dribble from the hole. If oil does not come out of the hole, the oil level is low, and oil should be added. If an excessive amount runs out of the case, then the transmission was overfilled OR a lot of moisture has found its way in (and it is time for an oil change).

In most cases, a fill cap will be on the top of the transmission case for adding oil. If there is no cap, chances are that a bolt is used. When adding oil, leave the check plug out, and add oil through the fill hole in the top of the transmission. Add oil slowly; when oil starts to dribble out of the check hole, the oil level is correct.

CHANGING YOUR OIL

As we said, in order to keep an eye on your transmission's health, be sure to change the fluid AT LEAST once a year, or by your manufacturer's recommended mileage intervals (if they are shorter with your riding style).

Like with all oil changes it is best to drain the oil at normal operating temperature. So once again, suit up and go for a ride (not up and down the street!! if you can't ride your ATV near your house, then drain the transmission cold).

You will eventually learn that if you have a lot of fluids to drain you can buy a couple of drain pans and do them all at once.

After a decent ride (10–20 minutes, depending on how warm it is outside, you'll need less time the hotter the ambient temperature), come back in and remove the transmission drain plug. Allow the transmission to drain fully.

➡**MAKE SURE YOU REMOVE THE CORRECT DRAIN PLUG. You don't want to empty your engine oil by accident (If you have a two-stroke, this is impossible). If this should happen, you will probably realize it as the oil is draining (since transmission oil is usually not as black as used engine oil, and it tends to smell different), or at worst when you go to add new transmission oil. Be careful because on some ATVs, it really can be tricky.**

Since transmissions do not usually use oil filters, many transmission drain plugs are equipped with a magnet to attract and hold tiny metal deposits which come off gears in use. Be sure to thoroughly clean the metal paste which has collected on the drain plug magnet. Paste is OK, while little chunks could be bad. If chunks are found, be worried (it might be time to have the transmission professionally checked).

When installing the drain plug, check to see if it uses a crush washer or an O-ring. You might have success reusing either of them and you are usually OK reusing an O-ring, as long as it is not cut or dried out and cracked. BUT, if a crush washer was used, then it is best to replace it (don't try to save a few cents on a washer only to lose a few bucks on oil if it starts leaking). DON'T BE CHEAP !

Clutch Adjustments

MANUAL CLUTCH

▶ See Figure 140

There are several variations of manual clutches used on ATVs. Most of them are multi-disc wet or dry clutches known as the countershaft type because they are mounted on the transmission countershaft which runs at somewhere between one half and one third engine speed. In most cases the clutch is chain or gear driven from the crankshaft. The advantage offered by this configuration is that its low operating speed is conducive to smooth high speed shifting. Its greatest disadvantage is its relatively large mass and frictional area which requires the use of stiff springs (that often require a lot of lever pressure).

A clutch is said to be a "wet-type" if it runs in an oil bath, and a "dry-type" if it does not. The only difference between the two is the type of friction material on the clutch plates. All manual clutches operate basically in same manner, be they wet or dry single or multi-plated. When the clutch lever is actuated, the release worm or lever moves in toward the clutch hub and presses the clutch pushrod against the pressure (spring) plate. The force exerted by the pushrod(s)

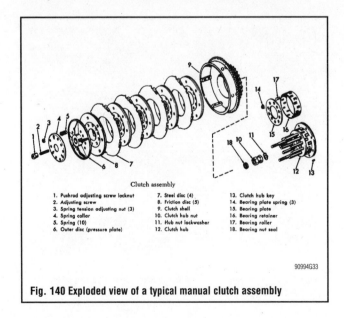

Fig. 140 Exploded view of a typical manual clutch assembly

compresses the clutch springs while moving the pressure plate away from the clutch plates, thereby allowing the plates to disengage and spin freely. When the hand lever is released, a return spring moves the release worm or lever back into its original position and the pushrod(s) is pushed back against its seat by the pressure plate which again presses against the clutch plates causing the clutch to engage.

.Because clutches wear and cables can stretch with use, the clutch must be checked and adjusted periodically to assure proper operation.

INSPECTION & ADJUSTMENT

▶ **See Figure 141**

Incorrect clutch adjustment can cause problems including early clutch failure, clunky shifting, lack of power and difficulty finding neutral. Too much free-play in the cable may not allow the clutch plates to completely separate causing clutch drag (rough shifting and difficulty finding neutral can result). Not enough free-play may cause clutch slippage by keeping the plates from closing fully (which can lead to clutch burning and failure).

Although methods of adjustment vary from machine-to-machine, they are usually set with one or more threaded adjusters on the cable (hydraulic systems are usually self-adjusting, taking additional fluid from the reservoir as the clutch wears). Some models have additional clutch adjustments which must be performed at the engine, so be sure to check your owners manual or a good shop manual to be sure you have the proper techniques and specifications.

You will usually know the your clutch on your ATV is properly adjusted if there is a small amount of free-play at the lever and you are not experiencing any of the symptoms described earlier. By free-play, we mean the distance the lever moves BEFORE resistance is felt. If there is no detectable free-play at the lever (the clutch begins to release as soon as you begin pulling the lever), then you can't be sure the clutch is fully engaging. If there is an excessive amount of free-play you should check the ATV in gear on a level surface. Hold the clutch lever fully against the hand grip and, without holding the brake, rev the engine and see if the ATV wants to creep forward (if it does, then the there is probably too much free-play in the cable and the clutch is not fully disengaging).

On most models the clutch free-play adjustment specification is given in inches or mm as the amount of distance the cable can be pulled back from the lever housing by hand or as the distance the lever travels before resistance is felt. Although specifications vary the gap between the cable and lever housing is usually in the neighborhood of 1/16–1/8 in. (2–3mm). Specifications for measuring lever travel as free-play tend to be a little bit higher, usually more like 3/8–3/4 in. (10–20mm) as measured at the end of the lever. Again, check your owners manual for specifications on your ATV.

Simple free-play adjustments can usually be made at an adjuster on the cable (sometimes at the handlebar end of the cable, and sometimes a short distance down the cable). On many ATVs, there are two cable adjusters, one at each end. On these ATV adjustments should be made at the handlebar end,

unless that adjuster reaches the end of its travel, then you would reset it and instead turn to the adjuster on the engine side of the cable. Other ATVs may have a cable adjustment one and a lever or pivot adjustment at the engine.

Also, pay attention to your ATV manufacturer's recommendations regarding adjustment spec. Some specifications are heat sensitive and must be adjusted either hot or cold.

AUTOMATIC CLUTCH ADJUSTMENTS

▶ **See Figures 142 and 143**

A large majority of ATVs are equipped with an automatic clutch. The automatic clutch is actually composed of two clutches; the first being a centrifugal clutch, and the second being a multi-plate "manual" clutch that is operated by the gearshift lever during gear changes. How does all this work? Well, lets go into some detail about the automatic clutch operation.

The centrifugal clutch, usually mounted on the crankshaft, operates based on engine speed. This clutch is designed to engage at a set speed, which is usually around 2800 rpm. There are weights in the clutch which engage when the rotational speed of the clutch housing overcomes the spring pressure that holds the weights in place. Once the centrifugal clutch is engaged, a direct link of power is achieved, and the ATV will move forward. When the engine reaches the maximum speed for that gear, a larger gear is selected.

91234PD5

Fig. 142 This ATV has the instructions for adjusting the automatic clutch cast into the engine case

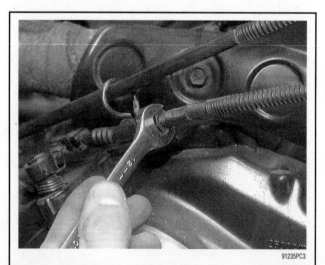

91235PC3

Fig. 141 Keeping the clutch cable properly adjusted is important for proper clutch operation

91234PH3

Fig. 143 Some automatic clutches have more than one adjustment; make sure you adjust the right one!

When the shift lever is operated to change to another gear, the multi-plate manual clutch is momentarily released via linkage at the same time that the next gear is being selected. During this time of a gear shift, the weights of the centrifugal clutch have also momentarily disengaged, since the throttle is released, letting engine speed drop. Once a gear is selected and the shift lever is released, the manual clutch is engaged, followed by the centrifugal clutch engaging when the engine is brought back up to speed with the throttle.

The majority of ATVs with automatic clutch system use this dual set-up with two different types of clutches. Due to the design of the centrifugal clutch, there usually is no need for adjustments to compensate for wear. The "manual" clutch of an automatic clutch-equipped ATV does however, require periodic adjustment.

To adjust an automatic clutch:

1. Locate the clutch adjustment cover on the side of the engine case. Some ATVs might not have a cover; others will have a large circular cover which is threaded, or have two or three bolts or screws holding on the cover.

2. Remove the cover (if applicable) to reveal the adjustment nut and locknut.

3. Loosen the outer locknut with the appropriate wrench or socket.

4. Using a screwdriver or hex wrench (as applicable), loosen the release screw.

5. After the release screw is loosened, slowly tighten it until a slight resistance is felt, and then stop.

6. Depending on your specific ATV, the manufacturer may require another ⅛–¼ turn clockwise or counterclockwise, depending on the model. Most models require slight clockwise rotation of the adjustment screw. However, it is a good idea contact a local dealer or check for the proper specification in a shop manual.

7. While holding the adjustment screw stationary, tighten the locknut. Make absolutely certain that the adjustment screw does not move when tightening the locknut, as this will affect adjustment.

8. Install the cover (if applicable) and test ride the ATV for proper clutch operation.

Automatic Transmission Maintenance

▶ See Figures 144, 145 and 146

Within the ATV industry, the fully automatic transmission is fairly new. The method of providing a constant variable transmission using variable diameter pulleys and a belt has been used in the snowmobile industry for sometime, but Polaris was among the first ATV manufacturers to offer a fully automatic transmission in an ATV. Other manufacturers are starting to produce ATVs equipped with automatic transmissions similar to the Polaris design due to the growing popularity of the concept. Some riders enjoy the "gas and go" style of an automatic transmission, and others, well, find it not well suited for their particular purpose.

Fig. 144 With the cover removed, the mechanicals of the transmission on this ATV can easily be seen

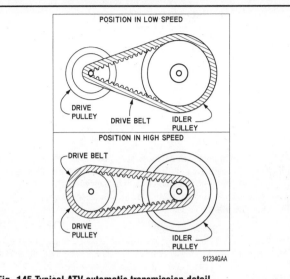

Fig. 145 Typical ATV automatic transmission detail

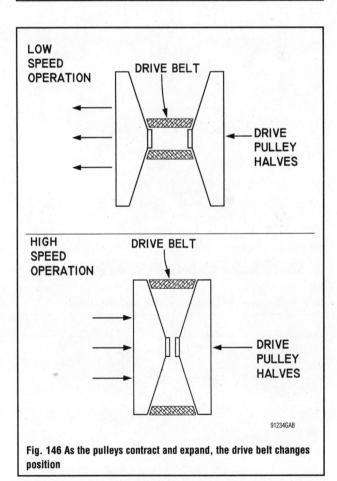
Fig. 146 As the pulleys contract and expand, the drive belt changes position

The automatic transmission on an ATV typically consists of two variable diameter pulleys, and a V-belt. A centrifugal mechanism on each of the pulleys controls the distance between each of the pulley halves. Because of the angle each of the pulley halves, the belt is moved between the pulley halves as they are brought together (or drawn apart), effectively changing the drive ratio between the engine and the wheels. With this mechanism, a smooth, seamless transition from low to high speeds allows the engine to remain in it's peak horsepower range.

INSPECTION AND REPLACEMENT

♦ **See Figures 147 thru 152**

The fully automatic transmission has some unique features that require special attention. The drive belt, which is the heart of the transmission, should always be checked for wear, fraying and cracks on a regular basis. Keeping a close eye on the condition of the belt will avoid major problems on the trail. If your belt breaks, you're not going to be moving anywhere unless you have a tow rope to attach to a buddy's ATV. When inspecting the belt, look for narrow spots, sheared cogs and belt disintegration.

➡The pulleys are precision balanced parts. It is recommended that the pulleys not be disassembled. If your transmission is not functioning properly, and your belt is in good condition, contact an authorized dealer who can diagnose and service any problems occurring in the function of the transmission.

If the belt is damaged in any way, it should be replaced. Usually all that is required to replace the drive belt is to remove the outer cover, push against the inner sheave of the driven pulley, followed by rolling the belt out of the pulleys. When installing a new belt, make sure it is installed with the arrow or markings facing in the proper direction. Do NOT use any chemicals on the belt to try to ease in installation; the belt may slip on the pulleys. Refer to your owner's man-

Fig. 149 Expand the rear pulley by rotating the two halves against each other, and slip off the belt

Fig. 147 To inspect the drive belt, remove the cover screws . . .

Fig. 150 The cracks on this drive belt mean that it is time for replacement

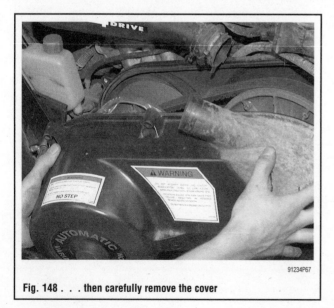

Fig. 148 . . . then carefully remove the cover

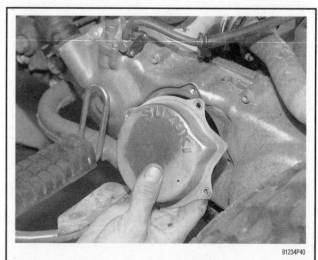

Fig. 151 On this ATV, the belt is enclosed in the engine case; but the cover can be removed for inspection of the belt

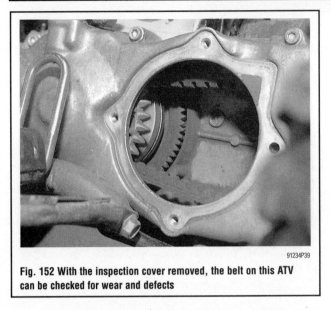

Fig. 152 With the inspection cover removed, the belt on this ATV can be checked for wear and defects

ual or contact a dealer for details regarding your particular ATV, since some models may require partial removal of the engine/transmission case.

Another important aspect concerning the life and condition of the belt is the forced air cooling system that surrounds the pulleys and belt. Check that the blower and ductwork are not clogged. If the ductwork is clogged with debris, the belt may overheat and disintegrate, or be severely damaged.

Shaft Drive

▶ **See Figures 153, 154, 155, 156 and 157**

A growing number of ATVs are equipped with shaft drive. Shaft drive ATVs are increasing in popularity, especially among riders who find the maintenance of the drive chain irksome, and are willing to pay (in weight and in dollars) extra for the reliability of shaft drive.

The driveshaft must transmit power through a 90° angle. The flow of power moves from the engine in approximately a straight line with constant velocity joints allowing the rear axle to move up and down. At the rear axle, however, the power must be turned at right angles from the line of the driveshaft and directed to the axle. This is accomplished by a pinion drive gear which turns a circular ring gear.

Drive units are built quite strongly for the loads they must carry, so it is unlikely that trouble will ever be encountered provided that routine oil changes are carried out on schedule.

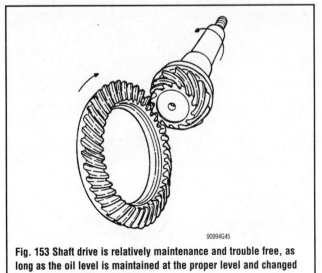

Fig. 153 Shaft drive is relatively maintenance and trouble free, as long as the oil level is maintained at the proper level and changed at the recommended intervals

Fig. 154 On most shaft drive ATVs, the fill plug is found on the top of the drive unit case

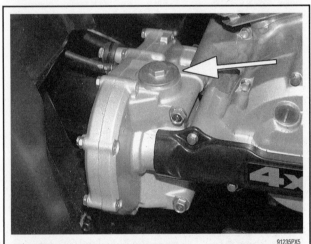

Fig. 155 Note the fill plug on the transfer case of this ATV. Some ATVs with transfer cases require periodic oil changes, similar to a shaft drive unit

Fig. 156 Sometimes fill plugs are not easily accessible, like the front drive unit on this ATV

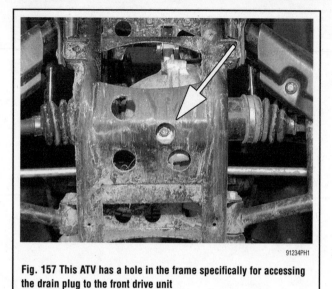

Fig. 157 This ATV has a hole in the frame specifically for accessing the drain plug to the front drive unit

Fig. 158 To check the level, loosen the plug . . .

Most designs use one or more bearings to support the pinion shaft. These are lubricated by the oil in the drive unit. The ring gear is supported by a large ball bearing, which is lubricated by the same method.

Driveshafts may be permanently lubricated and sealed, or may require their own oil changes, depending on the model.

On four-wheel drive ATVs, a transfer case may be used to supply power between the front and rear axles. Depending on the design, a separate oil may be required for the transfer case if it is not lubricated by the engine oil. If your four-wheel drive ATV is equipped with a separate transfer case, chances are that it uses the same type of oil as a shaft drive unit requires. Check with your owner's manual to verify which type of transfer case your ATV is equipped with, and the type of lubricant that it requires.

SELECTING THE PROPER OIL

Most manufacturers recommend using some form of gear oil in their drive-shafts, final drives, and transfer cases, usually a SAE 80 or SAE 90 EP Extreme Pressure (EP) gear oil. Keep in mind that a gear oil viscosity rating does NOT equal an SAE engine oil rating.

Shaft drive units and transfer cases are also good places to use synthetic gear oils. The same extreme operating conditions which occur in a transmission can be found in the final drive, including the high pressure and shear factors on the gears and bearings.

Be sure to check your owner's manual for your ATV manufacturer's particular requirements before selecting a gear oil, as some may have special requirements.

CHECKING YOUR OIL

▶ **See Figures 158, 159 and 160**

Basically, you should treat a shaft drive unit or transfer case in the same manner you would the transmission. The fluid should be checked periodically to make sure that none has leaked out undetected AND to be certain that the level has not increased from moisture that has entered the housing.

Like with most fluid checks, the shaft drive unit or transfer case oils should usually be checked with the ATV on a level surface.

On most models, the fluid level of your shaft drive unit or transfer case is checked with a filler plug. With this method, the level should be up to the bottom of the threads. We say most, because there are some exceptions.

Some ATVs use a self-leveling plug (or check plug) to properly adjust the oil level of the shaft drive unit or transfer case. To check the oil level, remove the check plug and see if any oil dribbles out of the hole. If necessary, add fluid until oil begins to run from the opening. When the oil ceases to flow from the hole, the level is correct.

When checking the fluid level on any shaft drive unit or transfer case, check to see if the fluid has been contaminated from moisture. If an excessive amount

Fig. 159 . . . unscrew it from the housing . . .

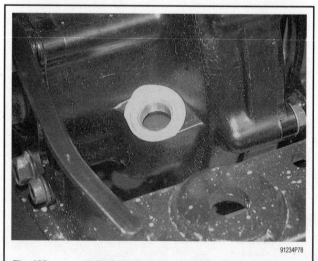

Fig. 160 . . . and check the fluid level. On this ATV, the proper level is at the base of the threads for the plug

runs out of the case, then the unit was overfilled OR a lot of moisture has found its way into the unit. Emulsified or contaminated oil should be changed right away to prevent unnecessary wear or corrosion to the final drive.

CHANGING YOUR OIL

▶ **See Figures 161, 162 and 163**

In order to monitor the health of your shaft drive unit and/or transfer case, be sure to change the fluid AT LEAST once a year, or by your manufacturer's recommended intervals.

Like with all oil changes, it is best to drain the oil at normal operating temperature. If you have enough drain pans, it is good to drain this fluid at the same time you perform engine and transmission.

The warmer the ambient temperature, the easier the fluid will drain from the housing. If the ambient temperature is on the cold side, use a blow dryer to warm up the housing and speed things up a bit.

Since they do not use oil filters, most shaft drive unit and transfer case drain plugs are equipped with a magnet to attract and hold tiny metal deposits which come off gears and splines during use. Be sure to thoroughly clean the metal paste which has collected on the drain plug magnet. Paste is not a problem, don't worry about it. But, if large metal chunks or pieces of the splines are found, be worried (it might be time to have the unit checked by a shop).

Fig. 161 Squeeze bottles are an excellent way to add gear oil to a shaft drive unit

Fig. 162 Make sure that the drain pan is in place BEFORE you loosen the drain plug

Fig. 163 It is a good idea to replace any washers or O-rings on drain and fill plugs to prevent leaks

When installing the drain plug, check to see if it uses a crush washer or an O-ring. You might have success reusing either of them and you are usually OK reusing an O-ring, as long as it is not cut or dried out and cracked. BUT, if a crush washer was used, then it is best to replace it (don't try to save a few cents on a washer only to lose a few bucks on oil if it starts leaking).

Chain Drive

▶ **See Figures 164, 165 and 166**

Final drive by means of a roller chain and sprockets is a very common method of power transmission in ATVs, and has been around for years. The method is cheap, compact, and quite reliable—provided that certain precautions are taken.

In truth, drive chains are remarkable in the amount of punishment that they absorb in the course of normal operation. They must be able to stand the tremendous torque developed by the engine. This torque is not always applied smoothly due to variations in clutch slippage, throttle application, and other factors such as acceleration, deceleration, and gear shifting.

Furthermore, the chain is subjected to varying tension as it rotates since the rear axle is moving up and down on the swing arm. If the engine sprocket was concentric with the swing arm pivot, this tension variation would be minimized, but this is not often the case. Even the motion of the chain around the sprockets themselves puts pressure on the links. The smaller the sprocket, the more ten-

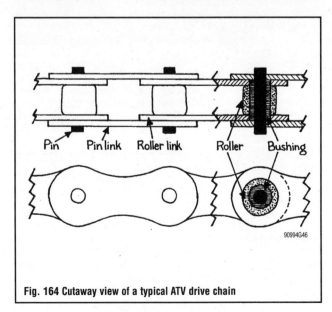

Fig. 164 Cutaway view of a typical ATV drive chain

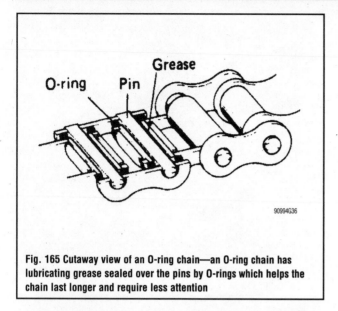

Fig. 165 Cutaway view of an O-ring chain—an O-ring chain has lubricating grease sealed over the pins by O-rings which helps the chain last longer and require less attention

lubricant designed specifically for ATV drive chains is recommended. You will also want a stiff bristled brush and a mild solvent or kerosene to clean the chain (but before buying, check with the ATV or chain manufacturer to see what they recommend as safe for your O-rings). There are some clever devices out there which can be used for chain cleaning and lubrication. Some of the better ones enclose a few links of the chain with a stiff brush for cleaning and have a tube to which you can attach a spray lubricant. You can rotate the chain through these while cleaning and lubricating the chain. But, for seriously neglected chains, a prior hand cleaning is usually recommended and necessary.

➡️To make chain maintenance easier, you are going to want to purchase some form of lift or workstand in order to get the rear wheels off the ground. To properly lubricate and clean a chain you will be constantly turning the rear axle and pushing the ATV back and forth gets tiring (besides you are more likely to rush or skip part of the chain if it is a pain in the butt to clean and lube).

Frequency of cleaning and lubrication is dependent upon the type of lubricant used, riding habits, average speeds, weather conditions, and so on. The rider should check chain condition frequently until he/she finds the maintenance interval compatible with his/her riding style. As in the case of engine oil, maintenance will be necessary at shorter intervals if the chain is subjected to severe use, like riding in heavy mud.

Fig. 166 This ATV uses a chain to transmit power to the front wheels

Fig. 167 A wire brush can be used to clean the sprockets . . .

sion the chain must endure. As if this was not enough, the chain is exposed to dirt, moisture, and exposure to the elements.

It is very wise, therefore, to pay some attention to the chain and its sprockets to ensure a long service life.

Chains are designated using a size (based on ⅛ of an inch) and number of links. The first two numbers of a chain's designation will give you its critical measurements. For instance, on a 420 chain, the 4 refers to the pitch between the pins (⁴⁄₈ of an inch), while the 2 refers to the width of the roller (²⁄₈ of an inch, or better known as ¼ in.).

CLEANING & LUBRICATION

▶ **See Figures 167 thru 180**

Most models now come with permanently lubricated O-ring drive chains, but some still don't. If your ATV does not have an O-ring chain, you should seriously consider adding one when it comes up for replacement. Modern O-ring chains last longer and work better with less maintenance than their non-permanently lubricated counterparts.

The term permanently lubricated is somewhat misleading, because you might think that you could ignore a chain like that. The truth is that ALL chains require periodic cleaning and lubrication in order to fight corrosion and wear.

The first thing you will need to do is buy some supplies. A good brand of

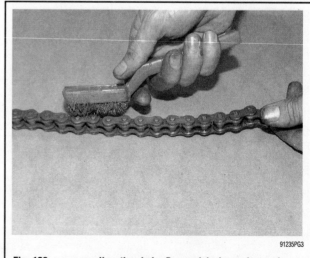

Fig. 168 . . . as well as the chain. Be careful when using a wire brush on an O-ring chain, since the rubber O-rings can be damaged

Before attempting to lubricate, inspect or adjust your chain, you should always clean it thoroughly. The BEST way to clean the chain is to remove it from the ATV so it can be thoroughly cleaned (this will also make inspection easier). But, there is no need to remove the chain from the ATV every 300 miles. If nothing else, remove it for cleaning at least once a year.

➥Models with endless chains (no master link) will require a special tool to break the chain. On all models, removal and installation of the masterlink spring clip should be done with a pliers or a small prytool—to avoid deforming the spring clip.

Having an old chain on hand makes removal somewhat simpler, since the old chain can be attached to one end of the chain on the ATV and pulled through over the engine sprocket, so that it is not necessary to remove the sprocket cover or other components.

To clean the chain, remove heavy deposits of dirt and grease with a stiff brush and suitable solvent (many manufacturers recommend the use of

Fig. 171 . . . and remove it from the master link

Fig. 169 Different brands of chain lubricant all have unique qualities; find one that works best for you

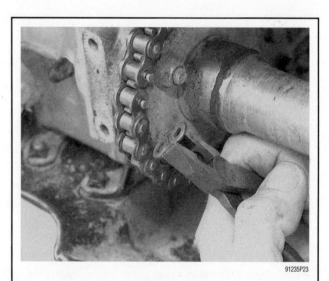

Fig. 172 Next, remove the pin link . . .

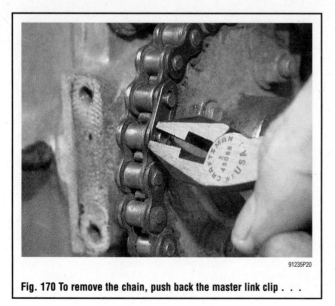

Fig. 170 To remove the chain, push back the master link clip . . .

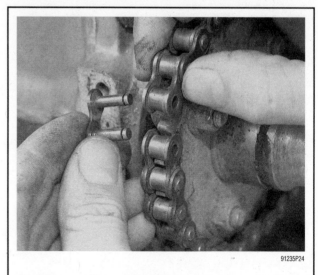

Fig. 173 . . . and separate the chain

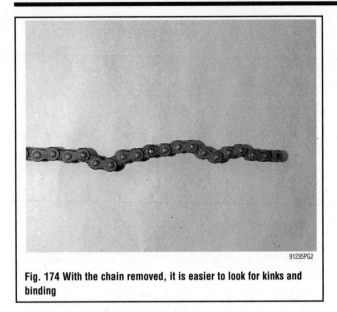

Fig. 174 With the chain removed, it is easier to look for kinks and binding

Fig. 177 . . . then push the pins from the links by twisting the handle on the tool . . .

Fig. 175 To cut a chain to length with a chain breaker, position the tool on the chain . . .

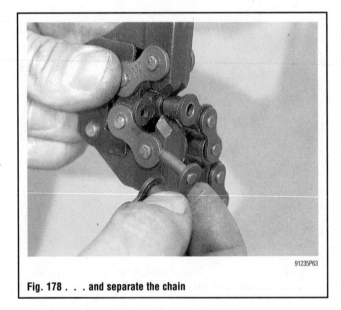

Fig. 178 . . . and separate the chain

Fig. 176 . . . lock it in place . . .

kerosene). If you have removed the chain, soak it in the solvent for 10 minutes or so, then remove it and clean it again with a brush.

Check that each chain link can pivot freely If there are any kinked or binding links which cannot be freed, or if the chain is rusted or has suffered damage from corrosion (such as might happen if it is touched by acid from an incorrectly routed battery overflow tube), replace it. If the chain has been removed for cleaning, take the opportunity to measure chain stretch now, (covered later in this section) this way you won't risk wasting your time lubricating it only to decide it must be replaced.

After cleaning the chain, it is time to oil it. It is your choice whether you would like to oil it now or after it is refitted. There are advantages to both. Oiling the chain while it is removed gives you a good opportunity to hit all of the wear surfaces which can be harder to access when the chain is in place. Of course, it could mean that you have a messy chain to work with when refitting (though if you properly oil and clean the excess off, it should not be a big problem). Of course, if you refit it to the machine first, that will give you an opportunity to warm the bearing surfaces so they better absorb oil (one alternative is to use a hair dryer to warm and oil the chain before installation). The choice is yours.

When installing the chain, note the following points: models which use an endless type chain will require a new masterlink. On other models, the masterlink may be reused if in good condition. Also, check the condition of the masterlink spring clip. Be sure to install the spring clip with the closed end facing the direction of chain rotation. Also, if the clip is "sprung," (meaning that it is

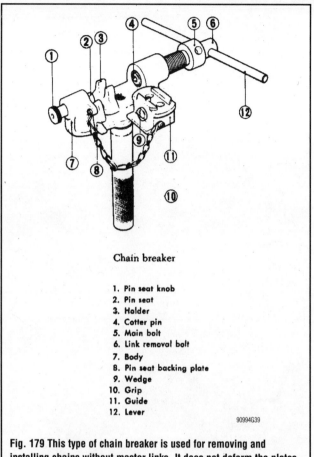

Chain breaker

1. Pin seat knob
2. Pin seat
3. Holder
4. Cotter pin
5. Main bolt
6. Link removal bolt
7. Body
8. Pin seat backing plate
9. Wedge
10. Grip
11. Guide
12. Lever

90994G39

Fig. 179 This type of chain breaker is used for removing and installing chains without master links. It does not deform the plates when pushing out the pins

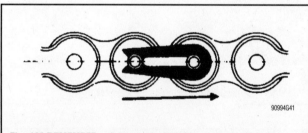

90994G41

Fig. 180 REMEMBER, when you are installing a master link, the CLOSED END must go toward the direction of travel

curved to provide spring tension when installed) the concave side must face the chain.

Next, you can begin applying the chain lube. Be sure to follow the lubricant manufacturer's instructions for use. Many lubes are dispensed in a very fluid state. This facilitates their penetration into the chain. In a few minutes they become thick and sticky, enabling them to adhere to the chain as it spins around the sprockets while riding.

Many people improperly lube chains, wasting too much of their time and lubricant on the outside of the links, where all it can do is help prevent corrosion. It is most important to lubricate in the places that wear occurs most (where there is metal-to-metal contact). Instead of worrying about the rollers (which require little, if any additional lubrication), make sure you get the lubricant between the link side plate where most of the wear occurs.

✳✳ CAUTION

NEVER USE THE MOTOR TO TURN THE REAR AXLE! Should something become caught in the chain or a sprocket you could be seriously injured or killed. Keep you hair, hands and fingers away from the chain and sprockets as much as possible and only turn the wheels by hand.

With rear wheels raised, slowly rotate the axle as you spray the chain lube onto the inside (sprocket side) of the chain side plates. Work on either the right or left side plates, don't try to cover both at one time. Continue to apply the lubricant for two full revolutions of the chain (to be certain nothing was missed). Then switch to the opposite row of side plates (still spraying from the inside of the chain) and continue to lubricate the links for two revolutions. Give the lubricant a few minutes to soak in and thicken.

Once the lubricant has thickened, apply a small amount of solvent to a shop rag and CAREFULLY turn the rear wheels while you wipe the excess lubricant back off. Too much lubricant is going to hold dirt in suspension which will just accelerate wear.

Once the chain is clean and lubricated, adjust it to the proper specification.

INSPECTION & ADJUSTMENT

◗ See Figures 181 thru 194

1. First make a visual inspection of the chain and its sprockets. If the chain is rust red in color, it has probably suffered too long without proper lubrication, and should be replaced as the damage done to the pin bushings (which you cannot see) is already beyond repair. The chain must also be replaced if it has any broken or cracked rollers. If the chain is very dirty, covered with grease and dirt, it should be removed and cleaned (refer to the previous section).

2. Check the battery overflow tube, and ensure that it has been so routed as to avoid the chain completely. White deposits on the links is a sign that sulfuric acid from the battery has come in contact with the chain. If this has happened, the acid has probably damaged one or more of the links. This will weaken them to the point where the chain can no longer be trusted. The chain should be replaced immediately.

3. The drive chain slack is the total up and down movement of the chain

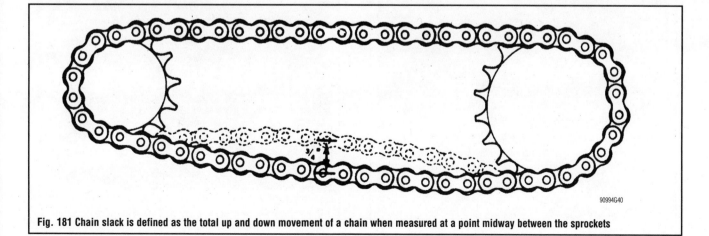

90994G40

Fig. 181 Chain slack is defined as the total up and down movement of a chain when measured at a point midway between the sprockets

Fig. 182 Items like chain guides can easily go unnoticed; inspect them as often as you inspect the chain

Fig. 183 Many ATVs have a label on the chain guard or near the chain which specifies proper chain adjustment

Fig. 184 Some ATVs have chain guards that have to be removed to lubricate the chain

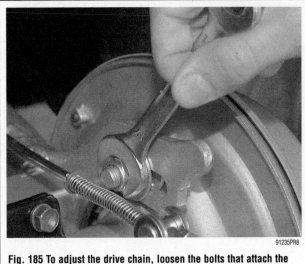

Fig. 185 To adjust the drive chain, loosen the bolts that attach the hub to the swingarm . . .

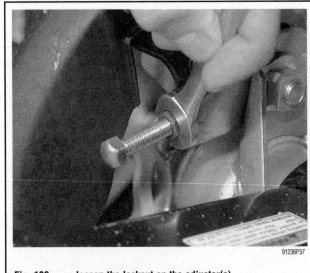

Fig. 186 . . . loosen the locknut on the adjuster(s) . . .

Fig. 187 . . . and turn the adjuster until the chain slack is correct. Then tighten the locknut and the hub-to-swingarm bolts securely

Fig. 188 Here's another type of method for chain adjustment; the eccentric hub is rotated in the swingarm to obtain the correct chain slack. Pinch bolts hold the hub in place

measured at a point midway between the sprockets. The specifications may differ for various machines, but is usually about 25mm (1 in.). Always consult your owner's manual or a shop manual for proper slack.

4. On all machines, however, it is imperative that the chain be clean and well lubricated before checking slack.

5. The chain must be checked for tight spots before making this adjustment. Rotate the wheels slowly and note any variances in chain tension. Tension will always vary slightly, but if the tension varies greatly, it is probable that the chain or the sprockets are worn to the point of replacement. If a tight spot is found, make a mark on the rear sprocket relative to some fixed point. Continue to rotate the wheels. If the chain becomes tight each time the sprocket mark passes the point you chose, the sprocket is warped and should be replaced. If there is no relation between the periods of chain tightness and the rotation of the sprocket, chances are that the chain itself is the problem.

6. Although a chain with an excessive tight spot must soon be replaced, if it must remain in service for a period of time be sure to adjust the chain tension to the given specification at the tight spot. This will probably mean that the chain will have some very loose spots at which it may slap around, but the potential of breaking the chain will be somewhat reduced.

7. If your slack measurement shows that the chain must be adjusted, then use the adjuster nuts on each side of the swingarm to tighten or loosen the chain, as necessary.

→ In order to preserve alignment of the rear axle, ALWAYS turn the adjusters exactly the same amount on each side of the swingarm. Use a deep socket with a line painted on it for reference, and rotate the socket in ½ turns which are easy to judge.

8. Proper alignment of the rear axle is very important for handling as well as for chain and sprocket life. Most ATVs have axle alignment marks on the swing arm, and care should be taken when adjusting the chain that the index on the adjusters are lined up equally. BUT, these marks are not always accurate. If such alignment marks are not fitted or are not trusted, it is possible to align the axle by "eyeballing" it using the front wheels as a reference. Alternately, if there

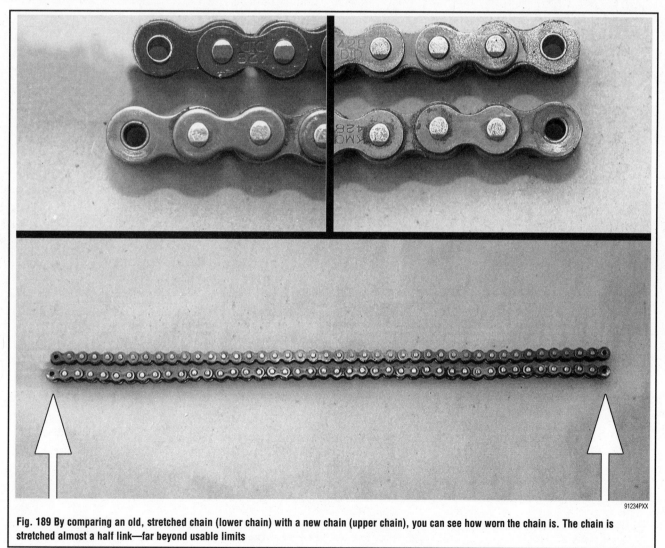

Fig. 189 By comparing an old, stretched chain (lower chain) with a new chain (upper chain), you can see how worn the chain is. The chain is stretched almost a half link—far beyond usable limits

is not too much in the way, you can measure the distance from the swing arm pivot to the center of the axle and make sure it is the same on both sides.

9. Another method of chain adjustment is with the use of eccentric cams. With this method, the axleshaft, mounted off-center within the hub, is rotated in an outer housing (usually the swingarm) to provide a means of adjustment. In most cases, there are pinch bolts that hold the cam in place which have to be loosened to allow the hub to rotate. Rotating the hub within the housing will loosen or tighten the chain, depending on the orientation of the hub within the housing. After the chain is adjusted to specification, make sure that the pinch bolts are tightened securely, since they may be all that holds the hub to the swingarm.

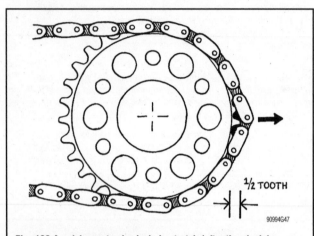

Fig. 190 A quick way to check chain stretch (after the slack is adjusted) is by pulling the chain off the rear sprocket. If you can see more than ½ tooth, then the chain is stretched and should be replaced

10. After adjusting the chain to the manufacturer's specification, check for wear by attempting to pull the chain off the sprocket. If you can see more than ½ of the sprocket tooth at the point this is done, the chain is worn and should be replaced as soon as possible.

11. Other methods of checking the chain for wear involve measuring the chain stretch. This can be done on or off the machine depending on the method you use:

   a. If the chain is off the ATV, stretch the chain out to its full length and measure it. Then compress the links so that the chain is as short as possible, but not bent. Measure the chain again. If the difference between the two measurements amounts to more than 3% of its total length, the chain should be replaced.

   b. If the chain is still installed, you will have to calculate the proper length for a sub-section of the chain (a length that can be measured while it is installed). Do this with the information we provided earlier on chain sizes and their designations. For example, on a 620 chain, the pitch (or distance between pins) is ⅝ in. The distance between 21 pins should equal 20 pitches (20 x ⅝ in.) or 15 in. total. A 3% stretch would allow a maximum length of 15.45 in. across 20 links. If you take a measurement of a longer length across 20 links of a 620 chain, you should replace it.

12. In the event of a worn chain, the sprockets should be inspected closely. A badly worn chain can ruin sprockets, and conversely, badly worn sprockets will quickly wear out a new chain.

13. Check that the sprocket teeth are not hooked. This is the most common sign of a damaged sprocket. Also check for wear on the edges and sides of the teeth. If possible, remove the sprockets, place them on a flat surface and check for warpage. The sprockets must be perfectly flat. If one of the sprockets is worn, it is recommended that both of them be replaced.

14. After lubrication and adjustment, test ride the ATV to check chain operation. If the ATV vibrates at intervals, it could be that the chain is too tight, or that one of the sprockets is warped or worn. Another symptom of a badly adjusted or worn chain or sprockets is noise while coasting. This can be checked by simply rolling the ATV down hill for a short distance.

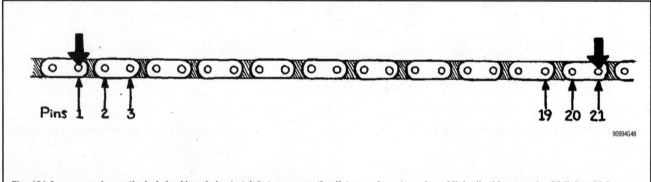

Fig. 191 A more precise method of checking chain stretch is to measure the distance of a set number of links (in this example, 20 links which means the distance between 21 pins) and compare it to specification

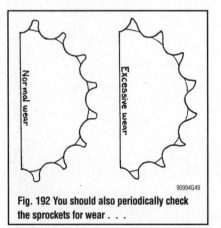

Fig. 192 You should also periodically check the sprockets for wear . . .

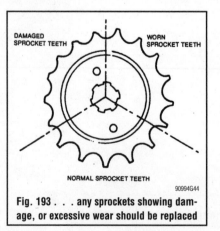

Fig. 193 . . . any sprockets showing damage, or excessive wear should be replaced

Fig. 194 An example of a severely worn countershaft sprocket

5

CHASSIS MAINTENANCE

WHEEL & TIRE MAINTENANCE

Tires

The essence of an ATV is, without a doubt, the tires. The fat, squishy, balloon-like shape allows ATVs to travel over most any surface with ease. A combination of the shape, design, and the low air pressure requirement allows an incredibly wide footprint. Multiply this wide footprint four times, and you have a vehicle that can easily travel in sand, mud, and snow; otherwise known as an All Terrain Vehicle (ATV).

INSPECTION

▶ See Figure 1

The following steps should be done as a minimum before heading out for any ride, no matter how short. They don't take much time and it will help prolong the life of your tires, and maybe even you!

1. Perform a visual check of the tread depth at the center of the tire. Make sure the tire has a reasonable amount of tread left. There are tread depth indicator bars molded into all modern tires. These bars travel the width of the tire and when they are even with the tread blocks, the tread has reached its minimum useful depth. Keep in mind, sufficient tread depth doesn't mean your tires are good, it just means that there is enough tread!

2. Look for cuts and punctures. Glance over the entire tread area and the sidewalls, too. A puncture can be repaired in an emergency with an automotive tire plug kit. However, plugging a tire only works if your tire is of the tubeless type, and should not be considered a permanent fix.

3. Check the sidewalls for signs of dryrot and cracking. Older tires, or those that have been exposed to daylight for extended periods of time (such as ATVs stored outdoors) can start to crack down near the tire bead, where it flexes. Ultraviolet light and ozone can start to degrade the rubber that composes the tire. After a while, these cracks will compromise the integrity of the tire and may cause it to fail. Replace dryrotted tires.

4. Check the tire pressure. We will go into more detail below, but suffice it to say that without the proper air pressure in the tires, you are risking damage to your tires, wheels and the performance of the ATV. Know what your tire pressures should be and keep them there!

5. Check the integrity of the wheels. Look for dents, cracks, gouges and missing chunks. A slightly scraped wheel may just be unsightly, but a wheel with a missing chunk or a bend that exposes the tire bead is dangerous.

6. Check for out of round wheels. With the wheel off the ground and free to spin, rotate the wheel and look for excessive side-to-side movement. The wheel should be almost perfectly straight with only the tiniest amount of wobble allowed (maybe 0.02 in. =[0.5mm=], at best). Also check that the wheel doesn't move up and down as if it had an egg shape. Either of these conditions require the wheel to be replaced with a straight unit.

AIR PRESSURE

▶ See Figures 2, 3 and 4

A tire can support only so much weight by itself. The tire is inflated with air and it is the pressurized air that supports the rest of the weight of the vehicle. The air pressure inside the tire lends rigidity in some amount to the tire and limits how much the tire flexes. If the tire has too little air in it, the rubber will flex too much and eventually heat up. If too much heat is allowed to build up, the rubber can start to degrade, leading to failure of the tire. At the same time, too much air can lead to changes in the way the ATV handles. Either way, the ATV will not maintain stability. Proper air pressure is more than just important, it is imperative!

Your ATV was designed with a certain range of tire pressures in mind. Trust the engineers who designed your ATV; They know what is good for you and it! Your owners manual should have a listing of what pressures to use in what situations. The range of tire pressures can vary; a pound or two in either direction can really be felt. If the chart isn't in your owners manual, you will probably find it on a sticker attached somewhere on your ATV, under a seat or sidecover.

91235PC8

Fig. 2 Make sure that the air pressure between two wheels of the same axle is equal. A slight difference in air pressure can change the size of the tire drastically, and cause alignment problems

91236P30

Fig. 3 To check air pressure correctly, a special low pressure gauge should be used. Usually, the tool kit supplied with your ATV includes one . . .

91235PD6

Fig. 1 If debris gets jammed between the wheel and the tire bead, the wheel should be deflated and cleaned

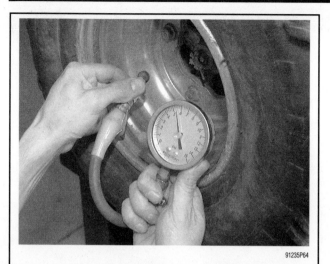

Fig. 4 . . . if not, I would recommend a dial-type gauge for accurate readings and ease of adjustment

❊❊ WARNING

Do NOT overinflate ATV tires, or they will be permanently damaged. If an ATV tire is overinflated, the carcass of the tire will stretch, and will not return to original size. To avoid damage, never exceed the maximum tire pressure written on the sidewall.

Most tire pressures are taken when cold. This means you should check the pressures before you head off. How convenient, since you should check them before a ride anyway! As the tire temperature goes up, so will the pressure. If you check your pressures on a hot tire and then adjust the pressure to what the sticker says, you will actually end up with a pressure lower than specification.

Use a tire pressure gauge of good quality and repeatability. Some inexpensive, pencil type gauges may not be able to provide low enough readings for ATV tires. A special low pressure (0-15 psi) tire gauge should be used to provide the most accurate reading.

If air pressure in a particular tire is low, inflate it to the proper pressure using a hand pump. It is recommended that a high pressure air pump (like at a gas station) NOT be used to fill ATV tires with air. The high pressure can overinflate the tire in only a couple of seconds. If this happens, the tire may be permanently damaged.

Make sure that the tire pressure between both wheels (right and left) are equal. It can take less than one pound of pressure to change the overall diameter of an average ATV tire. If the tires on each side are not of equal diameter, the ATV will pull to one side when riding. Different tire pressures can be used between front and rear tires, (except for some four-wheel drive ATVs) but the pressure between both rear tires and both front tires must be equal.

WHEEL REMOVAL & INSTALLATION

▶ See Figures 5, 6 and 7

Removing a wheel and tire on an ATV is much like removing a wheel and tire on an automobile; you lift the vehicle, remove the lug nuts, and pull the tire off the studs on the hub.

Most ATVs use around three to five fasteners to secure the wheel to the hub. When removing the nuts, be sure not to lose the washers (if equipped). Also, pay close attention to the condition of the lug nuts and the threads on the studs. Replace and damaged parts.

When installing wheels, its not a bad idea to apply a small amount of anti-seize paste to the mounting surfaces between the wheel and hub. This will help to prevent corrosive build-up between the hub and the wheel.

❊❊ CAUTION

Be sure to torque the lug nuts with a torque wrench when installing wheels to prevent the lug nuts from becoming loose. If a wheel were to come off while riding, you could lose control of your ATV and be seriously injured or even killed. Also, using a torque wrench will help prevent the possibility of hub assembly warpage which can occur due to unevenly torqued lugs.

Also, if removing more than one wheel at a time, make sure to mark each wheel so they can be installed in the proper tread direction. Most ATV wheels have "offset" which means that the center of the wheel is not symmetrical with the width. On some ATVs, this can be an advantage, since the wheels can be "flip-flopped" (swapping the left wheel with the right) around to gain additional width at the axle. This can also be an advantage to utilize some aftermarket types of tires that can be used in two directions. Be careful though, since some tires are designed to only operate in one direction. Also, keep in mind that if you do mount a wheel in the opposite direction, the valve stem will be on the

Fig. 5 A large ratchet or breaker bar can be used to tighten and loosen the wheel lug nuts

Fig. 6 Once the lug nuts are removed, lift the wheel from the studs on the hub

Fig. 7 On some ATVs, the wheels can be "flip-flopped" to gain additional width at the axle. Note the tire tread shape has not changed direction

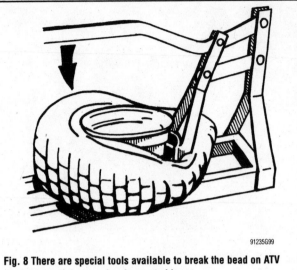

Fig. 8 There are special tools available to break the bead on ATV tires; this model uses a hand-operated lever

Fig. 9 Once the bead is broken loose on both sides of the tire, carefully lift the bead over the edge of the wheel with tire irons

inside of the axle, and may interfere with the brakes, depending on your model. Always check with a dealer or owner's manual, since certain models may be adversely affected.

TIRE CHANGING

▶ **See Figures 8, 9, 10, 11 and 12**

Back in the early days of ATVs, the wheels were of a two-piece design, making a tire change an easy task. Simply remove the wheel from the axle, unbolt the wheel halves, and replace the tire with a new one. In actuality though, there were some problems with this design. An O-ring was used to provide a seal (well, sort of) between the rim halves, which was a constant source of leakage. As ATV technology progressed, one piece wheels prevailed, since the inconvenience of the tools required to change a tire far outweighed the nagging task of constantly refilling the tires with air.

Since ATV tires are tubeless and use extremely low tire pressure, a wheel with a large bead ridge is required to keep the wheel in place during use. This makes changing a tire a difficult task if you do not have a special bead breaking tool. If you do not have a bead breaking tool, don't waste your time trying to change a tire. Take your wheel and tire to a dealer and have them do it for you.

If you are able to spend a few dollars on a bead breaker tool, then you already know its value, and chances are you already know how to change a tire. If you don't have a bead breaker tool, and you want to change or repair tires yourself, buy one of these tools! Yes, you might get lucky and have a bead come loose by walking around the edges of the wheel, but most of the time you'll just end up hurting yourself, or damaging the tire and wheel, or even both.

In addition to a bead breaking tool, you'll need to purchase some suitable tire irons, which are available at any ATV or motorcycle dealer. Tire irons are specifically designed for the job. They are angled to provide good leverage and have

Fig. 10 Some tires may specify a direction of rotation; make sure that the tire is positioned properly on the wheel during installation

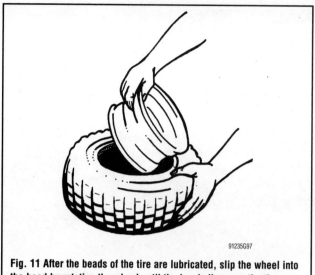

Fig. 11 After the beads of the tire are lubricated, slip the wheel into the bead by rotating the wheel until the bead slips over the tire

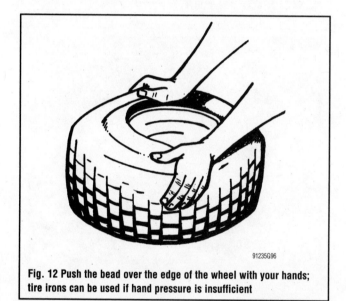

Fig. 12 Push the bead over the edge of the wheel with your hands; tire irons can be used if hand pressure is insufficient

smooth, rounded spoons to prevent damage to the bead. Although some irons may seem small, if you are using the right method they should provide sufficient leverage to get the tire off the rim. There is no acceptable substitute for good tire irons. Attempting to use prybars or other levers for this job is only asking for trouble.

A large sheet of cardboard can also decrease chances of damage to the wheel. Changing the tire on a concrete surface can easily scratch the rim. Changing a tire on the lawn will certainly get dirt or grass into the wheel bearings unless a rag is placed under the hub.

Let's take a look at a basic procedure for changing a tire.

1. Remove the wheel from the ATV.
2. Remove the core from the valve stem and let all of the air out of the tire. Removing the core from the valve stem allows the tire to "breathe" while the bead is being broken loose from the wheel.
3. Using liquid dish detergent or another type of lubricant safe for rubber, lubricate the tire bead and wheel rim flanges. Pressing down on the tire while applying dish detergent will allow the bead area to be lubricated better.
4. Position the wheel in the bead breaking tool. Working on small sections at a time, carefully separate the bead of the tire from the flange on the wheel. Once one side is fully loose, break the other side loose in the same manner.
5. Using tire irons, grab the inside of the tire and lift it over the rim of the

wheel. When lifting the bead of the tire, press down on the opposite side of the tire to force the bead into the smallest part of the wheel. This will help minimize the stretch required to lift the bead over the rim on the opposing side of the tire.

6. Once one side of the bead of the tire is free from the wheel, angle the wheel and pull it away from the remaining bead. Add additional lubricant to help ease the process.

to install:

➡ While the tire is off the wheel, it's a good idea to replace the valve stem. Use diagonal cutters to cut the old one out, and pop a new one into position. It will be much easier if you use a valve stem installation tool, which threads onto the valve stem, allowing you to pull it into place. Make sure to use liquid dish detergent to avoid tearing the rubber.

7. Before installing the tire to the wheel, inspect the bead surface area for rust or scale. Use a wire brush to clean the surface.
8. Using dish detergent, thoroughly lubricate the bead area on both sides of the tire.
9. Locate the directional arrow on the tire, and the valve stem on the wheel. The tire should be positioned on the wheel with the arrow pointed in the direction of rotation, and the valve stem on the outside of the wheel when it is mounted on the ATV.
10. Holding the wheel at an angle to the tire, push the wheel through the tire bead. In most cases, the wheel should slip right into place. If this is difficult, a tire iron may be necessary to ease the bead over the wheel.
11. Once the bead is in position on one side, flip the tire and wheel over and push the other bead over the lip of the wheel with your hands. If you can't push the bead over the lip, use the tire irons to carefully guide it into position. Make sure that you push down on the tire so the opposite side of the bead is in position with the smallest area of the inside of the wheel.

✳ WARNING

Do NOT overinflate the tire when seating the bead, or the tire will be permanently damaged. If an ATV tire is overinflated, the carcass of the tire will stretch, and will not return to original size. Never exceed the maximum bead seating pressure written on the sidewall to avoid damage.

12. After the tire is installed, temporarily inflate it to seat the tire. The tire will have an aligning mark which is a thin line molded into the sidewall and which will appear just above the edge of the rim. This line should be equidistant from the rim edge all the way around the tire. If it is not concentric, the tire is not properly seated. This is sometimes caused by rust on the rim and can often be remedied by thoroughly lubricating the beads.
13. If necessary, a tie-down strap placed around the circumference of the tire and tightened up can help to bulge the tire enough to allow for sufficient air to become trapped in the tire, which will force the beads into position.
14. After the bead is seated, adjust the air pressure to the proper rating.
15. The wheel should be balanced after completing this operation.

WHEEL AND TIRE BALANCING

In **most** situations, ATV tires do not need to be balanced. Most ATVs are not capable of sustaining the high speed required to reveal an out of balance wheel and tire. If your ATV has a "shimmy" or a wobble, chances are the wheel is bent, or the suspension and steering components are worn.

CHECKING WHEEL RUN-OUT

1. Wheel run-out (or out-of-round) can be checked with a dial gauge or a simple pointer. This check can be made with the wheels on the ATV. Before this is done, however, be sure that the wheel bearings are in good condition or misleading results may be obtained.
2. Wheels should be checked for lateral (side-to-side) run-out, and for concentricity (up and down movement). The maximum acceptable variance is typically in the neighborhood of 0.035 in. (0.9mm.) vertically and 0.020 in. (0.5mm) laterally, but check the factory specifications. If either lateral or vertical run-out exceeds this amount, the wheel should be replaced.

BRAKE MAINTENANCE

Brake Fluid

SELECTING THE PROPER FLUID

♦ **See Figure 13**

Selecting the proper brake fluid is as easy as looking on the cover of your master cylinder and reading the DOT type that the manufacturer calls for. You will find the cover calls for DOT 3, 4 or 5 brake fluid. In general DOT 4 fluid can be used in place of DOT 3, but NEVER mix DOT 5 fluid with DOT 3 or 4. While DOT 3 and 4 fluids have the same general chemical properties, DOT 5 is a whole different ball game.

The difference between DOT 3 and 4 is how well the fluid resists boiling. Temperature ratings for DOT 4 are higher than those of DOT 3. DOT 5 fluids have a temperature rating like the DOT 3 and 4 fluids, but they are silicone based, and unless your brake system is designed for DOT 5, do not use it.

Silicone based DOT 5 fluids do not absorb water in the way that DOT 3 and 4 fluids do. Water contamination is what kills brake fluid and since DOT 5 fluid won't absorb moisture, it would seem that DOT 5 is the way to go. Unfortunately, when water gets into a DOT 5 brake system, it forms droplets. If a droplet gets heated to the point of boiling, it will flash into steam and cause all sorts of nastiness that will result in a loss of braking or possibly locking up the brakes. Although DOT 5 fluid is superior to DOT 3/4 fluid, simply flushing the brake system and installing DOT 5 fluid cannot be done without changing every rubber seal within the hydraulic system.

The DOT 3 and 4 brake fluids are hydroscopic meaning they absorb fluid. As the moisture content goes up, the resistance to boiling goes down. This is the reason why it is so important to change and flush brake fluid on a regular basis. It is a good idea to change the fluid at least once a year, maybe more if you do a lot of wet weather riding and use your brakes more severely than the average rider.

The brand of brake fluid isn't very critical as long as you choose a high quality name brand or the manufacturers offering. There are "racing" brake fluids out there, but unless they meet a DOT rating, their use is not recommended. The cost of brake fluid is fairly small compared to the job it performs, so don't skimp on quality here!

Fig. 14 Some ATVs have reservoirs with a sight glass . . .

Fig. 15 . . . or have translucent plastic reservoirs

Fig. 13 Always use new fluid from an unopened bottle

CHECKING BRAKE FLUID

♦ **See Figures 14 thru 20**

Take a quick glance in your owner's manual. You will find exact instructions on how to check your brake fluid. In general, it is as simple as looking at a translucent reservoir or into a sight glass. The trick is finding out if the handlebars need to be turned one way or the other to make an accurate check. Most

Fig. 16 To add fluid to handlebar mounted reservoirs, remove the cap (by unthreading the cover or the retaining screws) . . .

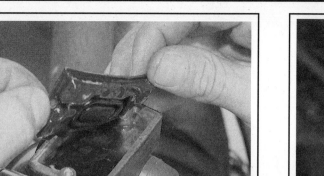

Fig. 17 . . . remove the diaphragm/gasket . . .

Fig. 18 . . . then add fresh brake fluid to top off the reservoir. If necessary, turn the handlebars to make the reservoir level

Fig. 19 Reservoirs with a screw-on cap allow for quicker filling

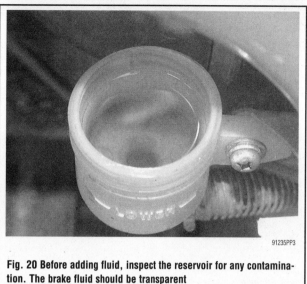

Fig. 20 Before adding fluid, inspect the reservoir for any contamination. The brake fluid should be transparent

likely you will have to turn the handlebars so that the master cylinder is level. On rear brake master cylinders, the reservoirs are either integral with the master or separate, but either way, making sure that the ATV is level will get the fluid level check that you need.

If your ATV doesn't have a translucent reservoir or a sight glass, you may have to take the lid off the reservoir and look down into it to check the level. Be sure to clean off the fill cover before removing it. You don't want any dirt to fall in and contaminate the system.

BRAKE BLEEDING

♦ See Figures 21 thru 26

A mushy feeling at the brake lever or pedal is most often due to air in the lines. This can happen if the fluid level drops too low, or if a line or hose is disconnected for any reason. This requires brake bleeding to remove the air.

Brake bleeding can be done manually, where the fluid is pumped out using the master cylinder, can be performed using a vacuum pump, or by gravity. A vacuum pump sucks the old fluid out through the bleeder. Gravity bleeding allows the fluid to flow out over a period of time. Manual bleeding is the most common method. Vacuum bleeding is very quick, but requires use of a vacuum pump. One small drawback of vacuum bleeding though, is air sometimes is sucked through the threads of the bleeder, and can obscure the vision of real air bubbles in the fluid. Gravity bleeding is the easiest, but it can take a while and might not dislodge stubborn air bubbles.

Certain precautions should be taken when working with brake fluid:
• Brake fluid absorbs moisture very quickly, and then becomes useless. Therefore, NEVER use fluid from an old or unsealed container.
• Do not mix brake fluids of different types.
• DOT 3 or 4 hydraulic disc brake fluid is recommended for almost all ATVs at the time of publication, but you should check your owner's manual to be sure.
• Brake fluid will quickly remove paint Avoid damage to the gas tank and bodywork by placing a protective cover over painted surfaces.

Manual Bleeding

1. To bleed the brake system, obtain a length of transparent plastic hose, the inside diameter of which is such that the hose will fit tightly over the bleed nipple of the brake caliper. Also needed is a small cup or plastic bottle.
2. Place an appropriately sized box-end wrench over the bleeder valve.
3. Fit the plastic hose to the bleed nipple, and put the other end in the cup which should have an inch or so of new brake fluid in it. Be sure that the end of the hose is below the surface of the fluid in the cup.
4. The hose should not have any sharp bends or kinks in it. It should loop up from the bleed nipple, and then down towards the cup.
5. The ATV should be on a level surface. If you're using a workstand or lift, make sure the ATV is completely level.

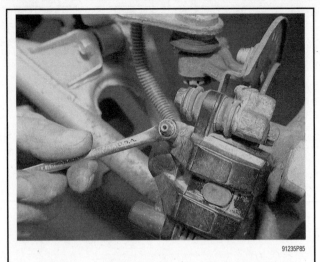

Fig. 21 Always use a box end wrench on the bleeder valve to prevent stripping

Fig. 22 Keep the reservoir topped off during the brake bleeding procedure

Fig. 23 The rubber diaphragm inside reservoirs keeps air from entering the system; after the reservoir is filled, make sure to reset the diaphragm . . .

Fig. 24 . . . which can be done by pushing in on the bellows until they are retracted

Fig. 25 Make sure to keep the rubber caps on the bleeder valves in order to keep dirt and contaminants away from the system

6. Check that the fluid level is topped up to the indicated line.
7. Apply the brake lever slowly several times, then hold it.
8. While holding the brake lever, loosen the caliper bleed nipple. The brake lever will be pulled towards the handgrip (or if a rear brake, will bottom out), and fluid will be forced through the plastic hose. Try to tighten the bleed nipple before the lever bottoms out.
9. Note the brake fluid being forced out of the plastic hose. If there was air in the lines, air bubbles will be noted coming out of the hose.
10. Slowly Pump up the lever again until resistance is felt, then hold it and loosen the nipple as before, again checking the fluid being forced out. When air bubbles no longer issue from the plastic hose, the system is bled.

➡If the fluid level drops too low during the bleeding procedure air could be drawn into the system at the master cylinder, requiring you to start all over again in order to remove all of the air.

11. Be sure that the master cylinder reservoir is kept topped up during the bleeding procedure. Top off when completed.

Vacuum Bleeding

Vacuum bleeding requires the use of a vacuum pump. The pumps can be handheld or driven from a compressed air source. In simplistic terms, a vacuum is applied to the bleeder screw and then the screw is opened. The fluid is

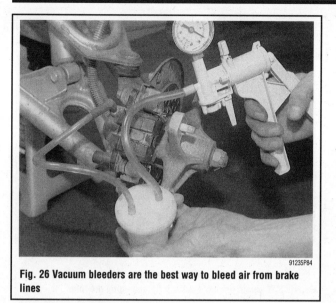

Fig. 26 Vacuum bleeders are the best way to bleed air from brake lines

sucked from the system along with any trapped air. The bleeder screw is tightened when done and the fluid reservoir topped off. If you choose to use this method, follow the directions provided with the vacuum pump. Be careful not to suck all the fluid from the system!

Gravity Bleeding

To gravity bleed a system, simply attach a hose to the bleeder nipple and place the open end in a container. Open the bleeder nipple and let the fluid flow out. Keep the reservoir topped off and check the progress from time to time. The longer you let it go, the more bleeding you have done.

FLUSHING THE BRAKE SYSTEM

The procedure for flushing a brake system is identical to that for bleeding, except that the process should be continued until new brake fluid begins to issue from the plastic hose. Remove as much of the old fluid from the reservoir as possible before you start and top off with new. You will begin by pumping out the old fluid with the lever while adding the new fluid in its place. After the new fluid starts coming out, begin checking for air bubbles and continue until you get a solid flow with no bubbles present.

Brake Lines

INSPECTION

Periodically check condition of the hoses and lines. Be sure that all hoses are arranged as the manufacturer intended, and are properly mounted. Check for abrasion damage. Check banjo fittings for signs of seepage.

Over a period of time, brake hoses tend to get hard and lose their flexibility. They can become prone to cracking both internally and externally. Even a hose that looks good on the outside can be breaking down on the inside leading to restricted flow or trapped pressure in the system.

If you have an older ATV and you have any doubts to the condition of the brake hoses, replace them. There are many choices available in replacement hose; You can buy original equipment hose, aftermarket hoses or high performance braided steel or Kevlar hoses. The choice is yours.

REPLACEMENT

1. Before attacking your ATV's brake hoses or lines, inspect the hoses and compare the replacements with the originals. Make sure they are identical. Hoses that are too short or too long can cause problems with routing or performance.

2. Make a diagram of the brake line and hose routing before you even get your tools out. Note the location of every clip, tab and bracket that the lines go through. If any of them are damaged, get a replacement for it (maybe two).

3. Protect the paint or bodywork near where you will be working as spilled brake fluid can be harmful to surfaces. This is true for DOT 3 and 4 fluids as DOT 5 silicone fluids aren't as reactive to paint, but you should still be careful.

4. Remove the brake fluid from the master cylinder using a siphon or suction bulb.

5. Clean the connections of dirt and crud. This will prevent dirt from entering the system. In the case of flare nut fittings, clean the area between the nut and the tube. This will make spinning the nut off easier.

6. If the hose connection is a flare nut, use a backup wrench on the female side of the connection and a flare nut wrench on the nut itself.

7. Install the new hose or line and route it in the same manner as the original.

8. Make the connections at either end and tighten.

9. Check the lines for interference. Turn the handlebars from side-to-side and make sure nothing binds or kinks.

10. Fill and bleed the system.

11. Apply pressure to the system and check the connections for leaks.

Disc Brakes

INSPECTION

▶ **See Figures 27 and 28**

Disc brake systems need little routine maintenance other than an occasional check on pad wear and fluid level.

1. Pads should be replaced when they are worn to the limit lines. These are cut outs or grooves cut into the friction material and indicate the minimum thickness limit. Other types will have tab wear indicators. For others still, the manufacturer will specify minimum pad thickness. In any case, continuing to use a set of brake pads until all of the friction material is gone from the backing plate should be avoided at all costs, since the brake rotor will be destroyed by contact with the backing plate metal.

2. The master cylinder fluid level is usually inscribed on the master cylinder. The fluid level may drop slightly over a period of time as the pads wear, but this drop will be slight. Do not top up a master cylinder reservoir whose level has dropped slightly due to pad wear, since the level will return to the normal level when new pads are fitted. An exception, of course, will be made if braking effectiveness is reduced due to a low level. By then, air may have been introduced to the system, requiring bleeding.

3. Check the surface of the brake rotor for scoring, grooves, hot spots or

Fig. 27 In most cases, removing the wheel is the best way to inspect disc brakes

Fig. 28 Some calipers have inspection plugs to allow a better view of brake pad wear

Fig. 30 Keep track of any shields or spacers when removing the wheel. This shield prevents rocks from damaging the rotor

any other damage. Check the rotor for warpage. This can be done by sighting the edge of the rotor while spinning the wheel assembly. A dial indicator may be used, but a simple visual test is usually sufficient.

PAD REPLACEMENT

▶ See Figures 29, 30 and 31

Procedures will vary according to the make and model of the ATV, but all have basic points in common:
• When new pads are fitted, avoid hard braking if possible for at least the first few rides to give the new pads a chance to seat themselves.
• Brake fluid and solvents must be kept off the brake pads.
• A few older design calipers must be adjusted periodically. This procedure should be outlined in your shop manual or owner's manual.

There are many different styles of brake calipers, each with a different method of removing the pads. In general, disc brake calipers fall into two categories: fixed, and sliding (or floating).

Sliding and Floating Calipers

Sliding and floating calipers have one or more pistons working on one side of the caliper. When the piston presses the pad against the rotor, the caliper slides over and applies the pad on the opposite side as well. Most of the time

Fig. 31 A comparison of a new brake pad (left) to an old pad (right). These brake pads were toasted!

these calipers will have two rubber bellows on pins from which the caliper body slides; this is the floating type. The sliding type moves on machined areas of the calipers and doesn't use pins.

SLIDING CALIPER

▶ See Figures 32 thru 55

1. Raise and support the ATV for access, then remove the wheel, if necessary.
2. Remove the mounting hardware and pull the caliper off the ATV.
3. Remove the pads from the caliper.
4. Clean the body of the caliper and the surface on which the pads move. Lubricate the sliding surfaces.
5. Remove some brake fluid from the reservoir if the level is at or near the full mark..
6. Compress the piston back into the caliper body with either your hands or with a large pair of pliers. If you're working on a rear disc brake with a mechanical park brake, make sure to back out the adjusting screw.

❊❊❊ WARNING

When compressing the piston back into the caliper body, be very careful not to pinch or damage the dust boot.

Fig. 29 Once the ATV is safely supported, the wheel can be removed to access the caliper

7. Install the new pads and replace the pad retention screw, if equipped. Use non-permanent thread locking compound on the screw.

8. Install the wheel, if removed.

9. Apply the brakes to seat the pads. Pump the lever or pedal until it firms up.

10. Check the level of brake fluid, and top off it if necessary.

11. Bleed the brakes as necessary.

FLOATING CALIPER

▶ **See Figures 32 thru 55**

1. Raise and support the ATV for access, then remove the wheel, if necessary.

2. The caliper must be dismounted to change the pads. Loosen any clamps or brackets holding the brake line to the ATV. This will keep the metal line from being bent or the hose from twisting severely.

3. Unbolt the caliper and pull it off the mounting. Always support the caliper to keep the brake line from being stressed.

4. If equipped, remove the pad retaining pin(s). The pin(s) may be held by a clip or screwed into the body of the caliper.

5. Remove the pads from the caliper.

6. Clean the body of the caliper and where the pads move. Lubricate the surfaces on which the pads slide.

7. Remove some brake fluid from the reservoir if the level is at or near the full mark.

8. Compress the piston(s) back into the caliper body with either your hands or a large pair of pliers. A C-clamp can also be used. If you're working on a rear disc brake with a mechanical park brake, make sure to back out the adjusting screw.

❋❋ WARNING

When compressing the piston back into the caliper body, be very careful not to pinch or damage the dust boot.

9. Install the new pads and replace the pad retention pin with its clip. You may have to slide the caliper to get the holes in the pads to line up with the pins on some designs.

10. Install the caliper and tighten the mounting bolts. Use a threadlocking compound to prevent the caliper bolts from loosening.

11. Install any clips and brackets holding the brake lines or hoses.

12. Apply the brakes to seat the pads. Pump the lever or pedal until it becomes firm.

13. Check the level of brake fluid, and top off it if necessary.

14. Bleed the brakes as necessary.

Fig. 33 . . . then draw the pin bolt out of the pin

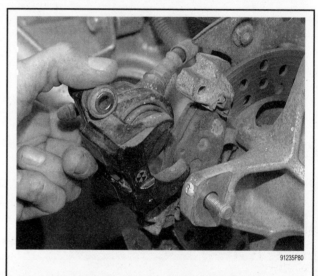

Fig. 34 With the pin removed, the caliper can be tilted back . . .

Fig. 32 After the front wheel is removed, loosen the upper pin bolt . . .

Fig. 35 . . . and removed from the lower pin

Fig. 36 After the caliper is removed, the pads can be withdrawn from the bracket (be sure to note their orientation)

Fig. 39 Once the tabs are bent flat, loosen the pin bolts . . .

Fig. 37 Be careful not to lose any clips or spacers when removing the brake pads

Fig. 40 . . . and draw them out of the caliper

Fig. 38 On this rear brake, the locking tabs that retain the pad pin bolts can be bent back with a small punch

Fig. 41 Once the pad pins are removed, you may need to loosen the upper caliper bracket bolt . . .

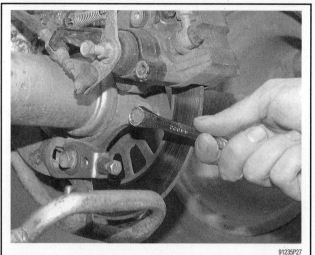

Fig. 42 . . . followed by the lower bolt. Also, on some calipers, you can swing the caliper upward . . .

Fig. 45 . . . keeping track of any spacers

Fig. 43 . . . then tighten up the top caliper bolt to hold the caliper in position

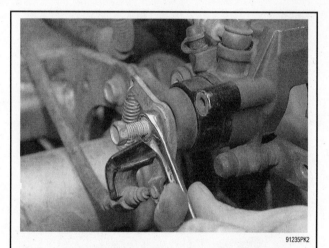

Fig. 46 Before the caliper can be pushed back into its bore, the parking brake mechanism on this rear caliper must be backed away from the piston. to do this, loosen the lever nut . . .

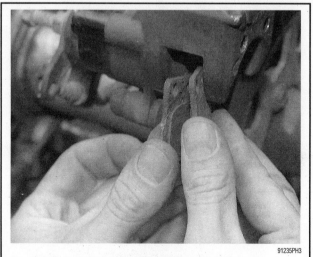

Fig. 44 With the caliper held in position away from the rotor, remove the brake pads . . .

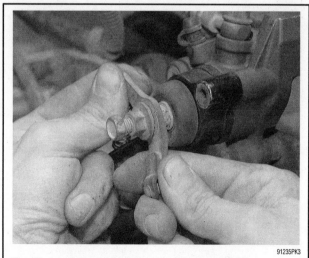

Fig. 47 . . . and move the lever away from the mechanism

Fig. 48 Note the teeth on the lever that activate the piston when the lever is turned; make sure the lever is clear . . .

Fig. 51 Once the piston is retracted, install the new pads

Fig. 49 . . . and loosen the bolt that adjusts to the piston

Fig. 52 Before installation, apply a light coating of anti-seize compound on the pad pins to prevent binding

Fig. 50 CAREFULLY push the piston back into its bore with a C-clamp. If the piston does not move, the adjuster bolt for the parking brake is not fully backed away from the piston

Fig. 53 If equipped, don't forget the locking tab plate when installing the pad pins

Fig. 54 Using a punch and a hammer, fold the tabs over the heads of the pad pins

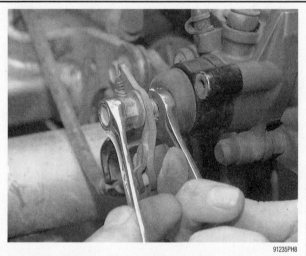

Fig. 55 After the caliper bracket bolts are tightened, adjust the parking brake mechanism

Fixed Calipers

Fixed calipers can be identified by having opposed pistons. A fixed caliper doesn't move during brake application. Fixed calipers are firmly bolted to the suspension and have no moving portion as does a sliding or pivoting caliper.

Fixed calipers come in two basic flavors: open back and closed back. Open back calipers have an opening from which the brake pads are removed and installed. Closed back calipers require the removal of the caliper to change the brake pads.

There are many different fixed calipers mounted on ATVs, but they all change the pads in a similar fashion.

OPEN BACK

▶ See Figure 56

1. Raise and support the ATV for access, then remove the wheel.
2. Remove the caliper dust cover to expose the tops of the pads and the pad retaining pins
3. The pad retaining pins will either have to be knocked out with a punch from the back side, unthreaded, or just or driven out with a punch after a retaining clip is removed.
4. After removing the pins, remove the spring from the caliper. This spring keeps the pads retracted when the brakes aren't applied and also keeps the pads from rattling. Make a note of how the spring fits.

5. Remove some brake fluid from the reservoir if the level is at or near the full mark.
6. Remove the pads and press the pistons back into their bores with a C-clamp or pliers. If the opposite piston pushes out while you push in the other one, place a pad or piece of wood between it and the rotor to keep it from moving out. Do not pry on the rotor when pushing in the piston as you can bend or crack it.
7. Clean the caliper of brake dust and road grime. Dirt can prevent proper action of the caliper.
8. Drop in the new pads and align the holes for the pad retaining pin.
9. Install the spring and the pad retaining pins. The spring may be held under the pins in some designs.
10. Pump up the brakes until you see the pads compress against the rotor. Check that both sides apply at the same time.
11. Install the dust shield.
12. Check the level of brake fluid and top off. Bleed the brakes as necessary.

CLOSED BACK

1. Raise and support the ATV for access, then remove the wheel.
2. The caliper must be dismounted to change the pads. If necessary, loosen the clamps or brackets holding the brake line. This will keep the lines from being bent or the hoses from twisting severely.
3. Unbolt the caliper and pull it away from the mounting . Support the caliper so it doesn't hang on the brake line.
4. Remove the pad retaining pin(s). A pin may be held by a clip or screwed into the body of the caliper.
5. Remove the pads from the caliper.
6. Clean the body of the caliper and the surfaces on which the pads move.
7. Remove some brake fluid from the reservoir if the level is at or near the full mark.
8. Using a C-clamp, compress the pistons back into the caliper body. Don't force the piston; moderate force should be all that is required. If you're working on a rear disc brake with a mechanical park brake, make sure to back out the adjusting screw.

✳ WARNING

When compressing the piston back into the caliper body, be very careful not to pinch or damage the dust boot.

9. Install the new pads.
10. Install the pad retention pin(s) with its clip or by screwing them in place.
11. Install the caliper on the ATV and tighten the mounting bolts. Use a threadlocking compound to prevent the caliper bolts from loosening.
12. Install the clips and brackets holding the brake lines or hoses.
13. Apply the brakes to seat the pads. Pump the lever or pedal until it gets firm.

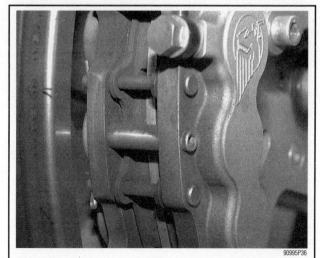

Fig. 56 An example of an open back fixed caliper. Note the pins that retain the pads

14. Check the level of brake fluid, and top it off if necessary.
15. Bleed the brakes as necessary.

Drum Brakes

INSPECTION & ADJUSTMENT

▶ **See Figures 57 thru 69**

Drum brakes are becoming a rarity. They were once used on almost every ATV, but discs have taken over most braking duties. You will find some ATVs with rear drums, but front drums can usually only be found of some lighter and less expensive models.

1. Drum brakes are operated by either cable or rod. In most cases, front brakes have cable adjusters at the brake plate and at the hand lever. Rear brakes usually have an adjuster at the brake plate. Generally, brake adjustment should be maintained so that the brake hand lever or brake pedal has about 1 in. (24.5mm) of movement before the linings contact the drum. In the case of rod-operated rear brakes, this adjustment should be made with a rider sitting aboard. The reason for this is that the movement of the swingarm may vary the distance between the brake cam and the pedal pivot, thereby changing the brake adjustment as the machine is operated.

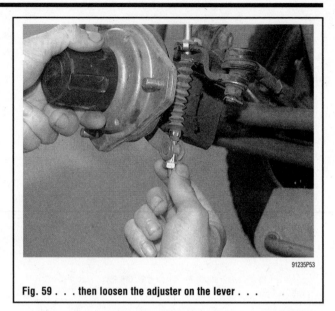

Fig. 59 . . . then loosen the adjuster on the lever . . .

Fig. 57 Some ATVs have inspection holes for checking the shoes for wear

Fig. 60 . . . followed by removing the dust cap . . .

Fig. 58 If your ATV does not have inspection holes on the drum, the drum must be removed for inspection. First, remove the wheel . . .

Fig. 61 . . . to access the spindle nut. Note the paint markings on the nut; align the marks when tightening the nut to obtain proper torque

Fig. 62 Using needlenose pliers, straighten the cotter pin . . .

Fig. 65 . . . keeping track of any washers . . .

Fig. 63 . . . then pull the cotter pin out of the spindle

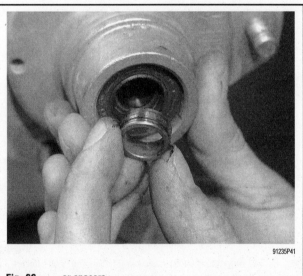

Fig. 66 . . . or spacers . . .

Fig. 64 Loosen and remove the spindle nut . . .

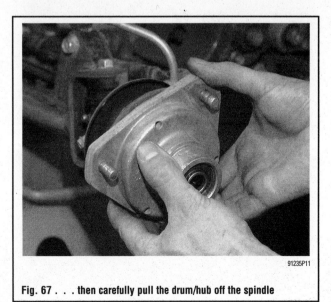

Fig. 67 . . . then carefully pull the drum/hub off the spindle

Fig. 68 With the hub removed, the condition of the shoes and hardware can easily be checked

Fig. 69 This drum has the maximum diameter marked inside for reference; if the diameter exceeds the limit, it should be replaced

2. On front brakes, the rough adjustment is usually made at the brake plate, with more precise adjustments made at the hand lever.

3. Twin-leading shoe brakes are fitted with a linkage connecting the two cams, and the linkage may not need routine adjustment unless the brake plate has been disassembled or new shoes have been fitted. One type of the linkage has both brake levers connected with a cable and the levers are pulled together when the brake is applied. This type is self-adjusting. A more common method is to have the brake cable connected to one brake lever, the remaining lever being connected to the first by means of a rod and clevises. The rod is usually threaded as a means of varying the length to make an adjustment.

4. To check the adjustment, disconnect the rod at the main brake lever. There is usually a retaining clip or cotter pin at the clevis pin. Apply the brake hand lever until the shoe contacts the drum. Holding this position, apply the secondary brake lever with your hand until that shoe contacts the drum. The clevis holes should line up at this point. If they do not, lengthen or shorten the brake rod so that the holes align.

5. Some drum brakes have wear indicators fitted to the brake cam. In most cases these consist of arrows. If the arrows align when the brake is applied, the brake linings are worn to the point of replacement.

6. Brakes not fitted with indicators can be checked with the wheel in place. When the brake is applied, the angle formed by the brake rod or cable and the brake lever should not exceed 90 degrees. After this point, braking effectiveness will be reduced.

7. Wear of brake linings can be checked with the linings in place. Be sure to measure brake lining thickness at the thinnest point. On riveted brakes, measure the distance from the top of the rivets to the lining surface.

8. On brakes without wear indicators, an occasional check of lining thickness is recommended. Minimum allowable lining thickness is usually given by the manufacturer. It is approximately 0.08 in. (2.0 mm) measured at the lining's thinnest point, but this value is only a generalization, and the exact figure must be obtained from your owner's manual or shop manual, as it differs from one model to another. On machines with riveted brake shoes, the thickness of the lining must be measured from the top of the rivets. On bonded shoes, it is measured from the surface of the shoe casting.

9. During inspection, be sure to check the linings for grooves, scoring, or other signs of unusual wear. Most damage of this sort is caused by particles of dirt, which have entered the brake drum. If badly scored, the shoes must be replaced. If the shoes are scored, the drum should be checked for the same type of damage. Make sure that there is no oil or grease present of the linings. Oil-impregnated linings must be replaced. If the linings show this condition, determine the source of the lubricant: defective wheel bearing grease seals, excessive chain lube, etc.

10. The drum should be checked for concentricity. An out-of-round condition is usually noticeable as an on-off-on feeling when the brake is applied while riding. With the wheel assembly mounted on the machine, spin the wheel while applying the brake very lightly. The rubbing noise of the brakes against the drum should be heard for the entire revolution of the wheel.

11. An out-of-round condition and most scoring can be removed by having the drum turned on a lathe. This operation should be entrusted to a qualified specialist with the proper equipment. Usually, the wheel bearings will have to be removed so that the wheel can be connected to the lathe.

SHOE REPLACEMENT

▶ **See Figures 70 thru 76**

The following procedure is to be considered a general guide to inspecting and servicing a drum brake assembly. The procedure may vary in detail depending upon the design of the brake assembly in question.

1. Remove the wheel from the ATV, followed by the removal of the hub/brake drum.

2. If the linings are usable, rough up their surface with sandpaper. Then clean them with alcohol or lacquer thinner. Polish the brake drum surface, removing any rust or dirt and clean the drum thoroughly.

3. To disassemble the brake plate, remove the shoes. On some models, this is possible simply by grasping both shoes and folding them towards the center of the brake plate. Other models, however, are fitted with retainers or guards. Remove any cotter pins and washers from the brake cam(s), then remove the shoes.

Fig. 70 A pry tool can be used to lift the shoes from the pivot on models without hold-down springs

Fig. 71 Once the shoes are free of the pivot, they can easily be removed

Fig. 72 Although the brakes on this ATV are simple, some ATVs can have complicated braking systems, and it is a good idea to carefully lay out the parts in the order they are removed

Fig. 73 The felt gasket on this brake drum/hub is used to keep debris from getting inside the drum. Be sure to inspect and replace any damaged seals or gaskets

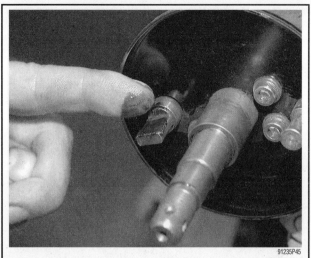

Fig. 74 Lightly grease the cam and pivot points of the brake shoes before assembly

Fig. 75 Once the shoes and hardware are in place, lightly grease the spindle before installing the hub

Fig. 76 Always use a torque wrench on the spindle nut to provide proper preload for the wheel bearings

➡ **The plurals throughout this procedure refer to the twin leading shoe brakes.**

4. To remove the cam(s) from the brake plate, remove the brake lever pinch bolt(s). Most brake levers are fitted on splines and will have to be pried off carefully. After the lever is removed, the brake cam can be tapped or pushed out of the brake plate. Note any dust seals or washers on the brake cam.

5. Check that the brake lever pinch bolts are not bent. This can easily happen if they are overtightened. Replace any bolts in this condition. Inspect the brake lever splines and replace the lever(s) if these are worn or stripped.

6. Inspect the splines on the brake cam(s). These should be in good condition. Check that the brake cam(s) are not bent and that they can rotate freely in the brake plate passage. If it will not, use a fine grade of sandpaper on the camshafts and the surface of the brake plate passage.

7. Clean the cam(s) thoroughly in a solvent to remove any old grease, rust, or corrosion. Use sandpaper or emery cloth to polish the cams. Clean off any residue; before reassembly, smear the cams lightly with chassis grease.

8. Inspect the brake plate for cracks or fractures, and replace it if necessary.

9. On twin-leading shoe brakes, the brake plate linkage should be checked. The connecting rod is secured to each brake lever by a clevis pin and cotter pin or clip. They should be checked for wear, especially on high mileage machines, and replaced if necessary.

10. Check the condition of the brake springs, noting any twisted or fatigued hooks. Replace any broken, rusted, or old springs with new ones.

11. Clean all metal parts thoroughly with a suitable solvent, making a special effort to remove the dust and built-up dirt from the backing plate.

12. When reassembling the brake plate, note the following points:

   a. Ensure that the brake cams are lubricated with chassis grease.

   b. The use of new dust seals is recommended.

   c. Lubricate the brake shoe pivot points with a little grease.

   d. Install the shoes as on removal. Hook them together with the springs, and fold them down over the brake cam(s) and pivot(s). Install new cotter pins to the pivot points.

   e. When installing the brake lever on the brake cam, be sure that the punch marks on the lever and cam align, if applicable.

STEERING & SUSPENSION MAINTENANCE

Suspension Pivot Points

INSPECTION AND MAINTENANCE

Front A-arms

▶ **See Figures 77 thru 82**

The majority of ATVs use bushings for the pivot points of the front suspension. As with most automotive applications, suspension bushings consist of a metal shell, a rubber bushing, and an inner metal sleeve. The rubber is bonded to the metal, so the rubber actually flexes around the inner and outer sleeves. This design allows for some cushioning of the suspension, and also eliminates the need for maintenance. However, the constant flexing of the rubber can cause it to tear, or lose its bond to the metal sleeve.

When inspecting the front A-arm mounts, look for torn or bulged rubber from the side of the bushing where it attaches to the frame. With the ATV on a lift or workstand to lift the wheels from the ground, grab the front wheel and rock it in a front-to-back motion. Be careful not to knock the ATV from the lift. Look for excessive movement from the pivot points. If movement seems to be excessive, the bushings will have to be replaced. Unfortunately, bushings of this design usually require them to be pressed out of the A-arm.

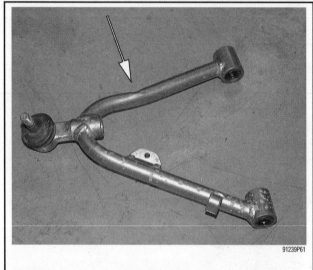

Fig. 78 A bent A-arm can cause accelerated wear of the bushings

Fig. 77 Look for excessive movement or torn rubber on the front A-arm bushings

Fig. 79 Rubber seals on ball joints should be checked for cracking or splitting periodically

Fig. 80 On some ATVs, the ball joint is bolted to the A-arm, and can be replaced separately

Fig. 81 Sometimes the best way to inspect ball joints is by separating the spindle from the ball joint

Fig. 82 With the spindle removed, rotate the stud; it should be smooth, but take moderate force to move back and forth

If your ATV has urethane or plastic bushings, then chances are that it contains fittings on the pivot points to lubricate the suspensions. Simply attach the grease gun to the fitting, and pump in fresh grease until the old grease begins to seep from the bushing pivot. If there aren't any fittings for greasing the bushings, they will have to be disassembled periodically for lubrication. If you're not up to the task, a dealer can perform this procedure for you.

Urethane or plastic bushings don't provide as much flex as rubber bushings do, so when you're inspecting them, there should not be any play in the bushings. If you can feel a "clunking" when you rock the A-arms from side-to-side, the bushings are worn and must be replaced.

If your urethane or plastic bushings are worn and require replacement, they can be replaced by tapping the old ones out with a blunt-tipped punch, and pushing in new ones. Don't forget to grease the inner sleeve before assembly.

Rear Swingarm

▶ See Figure 83

Swingarms are usually attached to the frame by means of a heavy shaft which may ride in bushings or needle bearings. Wear to these bushings is the prime trouble spot of the swingarm.

To check your swingarm bushings or bearings for wear, proceed as follows:

1. Lift the rear wheels from the ground, or place the ATV on a workstand or lift.

2. Grasp the legs of the swingarm and attempt to move it from side-to-side. Any noticeable side-play will indicate that the swingarm bushings or bearings need replacement.

3. Bushings are usually press-fit in swingarms, and, if worn, they should be driven out and replaced with new ones. Do not remove pressed-in bushings unless you intend to replace them, since they will be ruined by the removal process.

➡️**If your ATV is shaft driven, there may be a requirement for special tools to remove the rear swingarm from the frame. Consult a dealer or shop manual for more information on your specific ATV.**

4. When disassembling a swingarm bushing, make careful note of how each component is installed as placement of shims, bushings, sleeves, etc., is critical. Bushings should be lubricated according to manufacturer's instructions. Most have a grease fitting on the swingarm shaft to facilitate the operation, while others must be lubricated by hand. After a rebuilt swingarm is installed, tighten the shaft nut (if fitted) to the properly torque, and check for free movement of the swingarm. Movement should be relatively free (not loose) and noiseless.

5. New bushings should be checked carefully before installation. Be sure they are the correct ones for your machine, and that any lubrication holes or grooves are lined up correctly when installing them into the swingarm.

Fig. 83 Some ATVs have grease gun fittings on the swingarm, making lubrication easy

Steering Linkage

INSPECTION

▶ See Figures 84, 85, 86, 87 and 88

A typical steering linkage setup on an ATV consists of a steering shaft, (which attaches the handlebars) tie rods, and spindles, which attach to the suspension linkage. Every time you turn the handlebars, these parts work together to turn your wheels so your ATV goes in the direction that you want it to.

Inspection of the steering linkage should be performed on a regular basis. Along with the brakes, steering input is essential for safety.

The front of the ATV should be lifted from the ground to inspect the steering linkage. While turning the handlebars from side-to-side, there should not be any binding or resistance. If everything is moving smoothly, check for wear of the bearings and bushings. Clunking or excessive play generally means that something is worn out. Having another person turn the handlebars while you look for play in the bushings or bearings can speed up the process.

The tie rods can be checked by grabbing and twisting the wheel from side-to-side. If there is any clunking or play, they are worn out and should be replaced. Grabbing the wheel and rocking the wheel vertically (assuming the wheel bearings are in good condition) will test the spindle for any excessive clearance. Usually, spindles are not adjustable, and will require replacement if they are found to be worn.

Again, this is something that an ATV dealer or service center can perform if you are uncomfortable with tearing apart your ATV. If you don't mind turning a few wrenches, parts like spindles and tie rods can easily be replaced.

To help gain a better view of the front alignment, stand the ATV up on end (making sure to follow the manufacturer's instructions regarding doing this) and set the handlebars straight. Standing back a few feet from the ATV, make a rough observation of the angle of the tires. Most ATVs require a small amount of toe in (meaning the front wheels point inward slightly) or in some cases, no toe at all. If things are out of alignment, a tape measure and a straight edge can be used to measure the settings. Your ATV dealer or service center can give you detailed information about the correct alignment settings for your specific ATV.

If you find that parts of your steering linkage are worn, and you want to replace them yourself, there are some important guidelines to follow:

• When disassembling suspension parts, replacement of all fasteners is recommended. Suspension and steering fasteners are critical components. If a fastener were to fail, you could be seriously injured or even killed. Don't take the chance—spend a few extra dollars and buy all new nuts and bolts.

• If you are only replacing a tie rod end, mark the threads with paint after the locking nut is backed off. This way, you can count the number of threads and install the new one in the proper position.

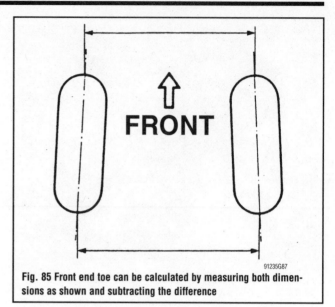

Fig. 85 Front end toe can be calculated by measuring both dimensions as shown and subtracting the difference

Fig. 86 When the wheels are turned to one side, one wheel should turn outward more than the other

Fig. 84 Standing the ATV on end will allow a better view of the alignment of the front wheels

Fig. 87 Steering shaft pivot points should be checked periodically for wear

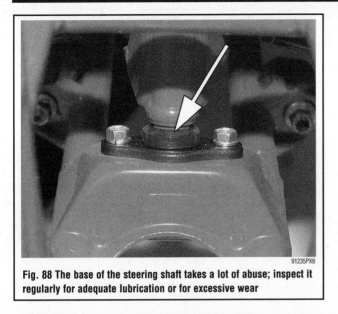

Fig. 88 The base of the steering shaft takes a lot of abuse; inspect it regularly for adequate lubrication or for excessive wear

Fig. 89 If possible, use line wrench (left) on the tie rod end locknut to prevent stripping

• When replacing tie-rods, measure the length of the old tie rod and adjust the new one to the same length. This will avoid any problems with alignment when the new tie rod is installed.

• Use a good quality liquid locking compound on suspension fasteners as a safety measure. Most suspension fasteners use locking washers and nuts; a dab of thread lock on the threads will help to keep things secure.

LUBRICATION

Due to the variances in steering linkage, no procedures are given here; only generic guidelines are given.

Lubricating the steering linkage can be as simple as applying a grease gun to a zerk fitting or be as tedious as disassembling the whole unit. If your ATV doesn't have grease fittings, the steering shaft and spindles will have to be removed to be able to apply new grease. As with suspension fasteners, always replace any fasteners removed for lubrication with new ones.

Tie rods may or may not have fittings. If not, they are maintenance free and do not require lubrication. If the rubber boot is torn, the tie rod end life span will be seriously shortened. Dirt and mud will cling to the exposed grease and grind away at the metal. Usually a torn boot on a tie rod end cannot be replaced separately; the tie rod end must be replaced as a unit.

REPLACEMENT AND ADJUSTMENT

▶ See Figures 89 thru 98

Your ATV comes from the manufacturer with the correct alignment setting. In most cases, there is no reason to change the alignment, except to compensate for wear of the linkage components. If you have inspected your steering linkage and found a tie rod end to be worn, it can be easily replaced.

Usually, a tie rod end has a tapered stud with a nut that mounts to the spindle. To remove a tie rod end:

1. First, remove the locknut on the threaded portion of the tie rod.

2. Next, mark the position of the relationship of the tie rod end and the threaded portion of the tie rod with a paint marker or other suitable means. By doing this, you'll avoid any major deviations from the original alignment settings.

3. Now the nut that secures the tie rod end to the spindle can be removed. Some ATVs might use a cotter pin with a castellated nut, and others might use a self-locking nut. Remove the cotter pin, if equipped.

4. After the nut is removed, gently tap on the area of the spindle where the stud of the tie rod protrudes. If the tie rod does not break free, a tie rod puller tool may be necessary for removal. Also, liberal use of a good penetrating oil will help the removal process.

5. Once the tie rod end is free, it can be unscrewed from the tie rod.

6. Upon replacement, thread the tie rod on until it reaches the markings placed on the threads.

Fig. 90 Loosen the locknut . . .

Fig. 91 . . . then mark the threads (for reference) on the tie rod end and tie rod . . .

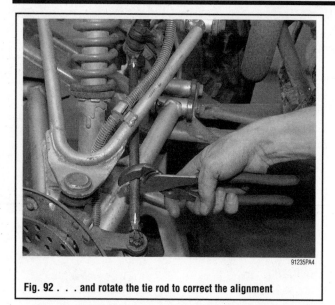

Fig. 92 . . . and rotate the tie rod to correct the alignment

Fig. 95 . . . but avoid using a hammer to drive the stud out of the spindle or other suspension components might be damaged!

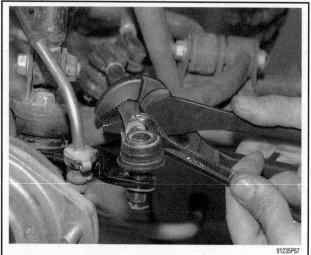

Fig. 93 Once the alignment is adjusted, hold the tie rod end while tightening the locknut

Fig. 96 If you plan to reuse a tie rod end, always use a tie rod end separator to avoid damaging the threads on the stud

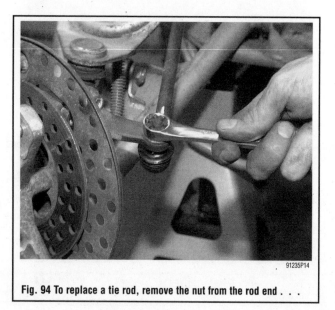

Fig. 94 To replace a tie rod, remove the nut from the rod end . . .

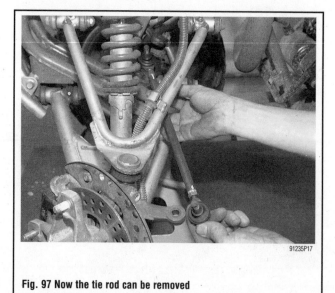

Fig. 97 Now the tie rod can be removed

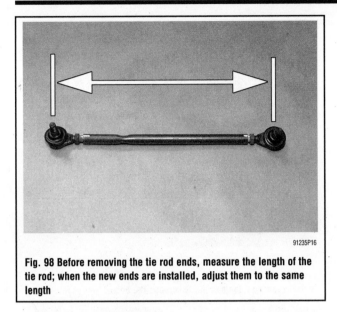

Fig. 98 Before removing the tie rod ends, measure the length of the tie rod; when the new ends are installed, adjust them to the same length

Fig. 99 To adjust the preload on most shocks, a spanner wrench is required

7. Install the stud into the spindle, and torque the nut to the specification required by the ATV manufacturer.

8. If a cotter pin is used, replace it with a new one. When installing a new cotter pin, push the pin through the hole in the stud and through the castellated nut, then bend the ears to hold the pin securely. It is most common for mechanics to bend one of the ears back over the nut, parallel to the direction the pin was inserted. the other ear is usually bent slightly around the circumference of the nut and cut short (leaving just enough of the bend to hold it in position).

9. When you are satisfied that the rod is properly installed and adjusted, tighten the locknut on the threaded portion of the tie rod.

➡️**If your ATV is pulling to one side, and "feels" out of alignment, chances are the air pressure in the tires is incorrect. A small difference in pressure between the rear tires can drastically affect the overall size of the tire. Make sure the tires are of the same air pressure and diameter before performing any alignment adjustments.**

Shock Absorbers

◆ **See Figures 99, 100 and 101**

Most ATVs have some basic form of adjusting the shocks for a softer or stiffer ride. For improved ride characteristics, the ride height (or preload) should be adjusted for your weight. If the ATV sits at the top of its suspension travel, the ride will be harsh, since the suspension can only travel upwards because the shocks are already at the top of their stroke. With you aboard, and the suspension adjusted properly, the ATV should sit approximately one third of the total length of the suspension travel. For example, if the total suspension travel of your ATV is around nine inches, the shocks should be compressed around three inches with you aboard. This will allow your suspension to operate in **both** directions, smoothing out the terrain as you ride.

Avoid that urge to grab that tool and crank those springs as tight as they'll go! With some testing, you'll find that the suspension doesn't need to be nearly as stiff as you might think. The notion that "the higher it sits, the better" is far from reality. A supple and compliant suspension will not only make the ATV handle better, but will keep you from being pounded by every crack and crevice that you ride over.

ADJUSTING PRELOAD

There are two ways of adjusting shocks for preload. The first method uses a notched collar which rotates around the shock body. The notched collar is part of the lower spring perch. When the tube is rotated, the graduations on the tube increase the amount of tension, or preload, on the spring.

The second type of method uses a threaded adjuster on the shock body. There are usually two threaded rings; one is the spring perch and the other is a locking nut. To adjust the preload, back off the locknut, and twist the spring perch to increase or decrease the preload. After the preload is correct, make sure to tighten the locknut.

Fig. 100 Most ATV shocks use notched adjusters . . .

Fig. 101 . . . although some sport-oriented ATVs have threads, allowing for more refined adjustment

In most cases, the spanner required to change the preload is included the tool kit that comes with your ATV. Use the wrench to twist the tube in order to change the preload. Don't use a screwdriver or punch to move the adjuster. You can damage the adjuster by not using the proper tool.

ADJUSTING SHOCK RATES

Some ATVs (usually sport or high-performance models) have adjustments for tuning the compression and rebound rates of the shock, as well as a means of adjusting the preload. These adjusters can be found on the shock itself or in some cases, on the fluid reservoir. For optimum performance, the compression and rebound adjustments should be adjusted **after** the preload has been set properly.

Compression adjustment will affect how fast the shock travels upward, or compresses. Rebound adjustment will affect how fast the shock returns from compression (how fast the suspension bounces back). Make adjustments in small increments, to avoid losing track of your previous settings. Most adjusters "click" between adjustments, so it is easier to keep track of things. If there is no clicking mechanism, keep track of the number of turns you make. Most of the time the adjustment to the shock will take a little time to take effect; fine tuning the compression and rebound should be done on the trail.

INSPECTION

The only periodic MAINTENANCE that should be necessary for your shock absorbers is to perform a visual inspection. Make sure that no fluid is leaking from the shock. A trickle of oil or a thick coating of oily residue (that cannot be traced to another source) is an indication that the shock has lost one or more of its seals. Since the shock depends on fluid under pressure in order to accomplish its job, once a seal is lost, the shock can no longer function properly and the axle set (the shocks on both sides of that axle) must be replaced.

During a visual inspection you should take time to examine the mounting fasteners, to make sure they are tight and undamaged. Also, take a moment to inspect the spring for damage in the form of cracks along the coils. Damaged components should always be replaced to assure that you have a safe and dependable ATV suspension.

Wheel Bearings

▶ **See Figures 102 thru 114**

The wheel bearings on your ATV are subjected to a lot of abuse. Tremendous loads are placed on them during acceleration, braking and cornering. Despite these constant demands, wheel bearings have a long service life. If the ATV is not abused, the bearings can last the life of the ATV and may never require replacement.

There are two primary reasons that wheel bearings wear out. The first culprit is lack of lubrication. When metal-to metal contact occurs, friction begins to build up heat. The balls (or rollers) of the bearing grind away, slowly destroying

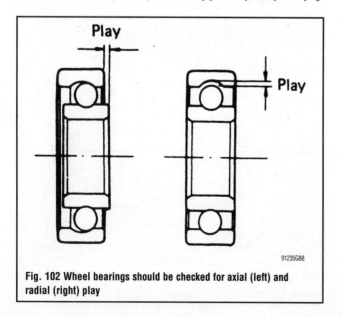

Fig. 102 Wheel bearings should be checked for axial (left) and radial (right) play

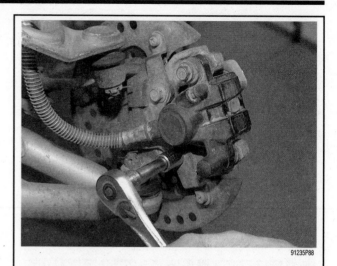

Fig. 103 On ATVs equipped with disc brakes, the caliper will need to be removed from the spindle to remove the hub

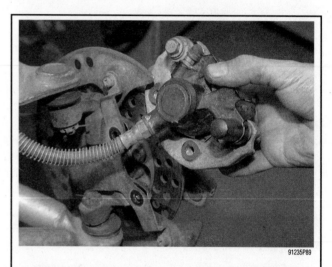

Fig. 104 Once the caliper bolts are removed, slide the caliper from the rotor, and set aside; use wire to support it if necessary

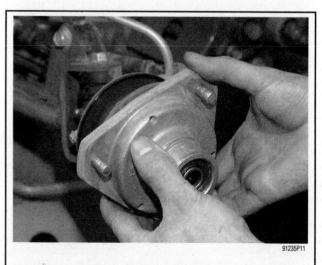

Fig. 105 If your ATV has drum brakes, simply remove the spindle nut and slide the drum/hub from the spindle

themselves, and the races that they ride on in the process. When this wear occurs, the diameter of the balls (or rollers) decreases, and excessive clearance develops between the inner and outer races, then the bearing becomes worn and unusable. The second cause for bearing wear is contamination. Granted, most ATVs use sealed bearings these days, but riding in a lot of water and mud can still cause problems. Water can be literally sucked into the hub because of the vacuum created when the heat in the hub is suddenly cooled by water. Even the best seals can leak under these circumstances. When water enters the hub, it not only contaminates the grease in the bearing, but can also carry dirt and grit, which will quickly destroy the bearing.

Regular inspection of the wheel bearings can help to avoid potential hazards. If a front wheel bearing were to heat up and seize onto the spindle (yes they can get that hot) the spindle could shear off, causing you to lose control of your ATV. Combine the loss of a wheel and traveling at moderate speed; you could be seriously injured. Don't neglect inspecting your ATV's wheel bearings—your life might depend on it.

BEARING INSPECTION

There are two ways of inspecting the wheel bearings. The first, and by far the easiest, is to simply lift the front (or rear) of the ATV and rock the wheels from side-to-side. Feel for a clunking or looseness; there should be virtually zero play. Now keep in mind that your suspension and steering linkage should be in top

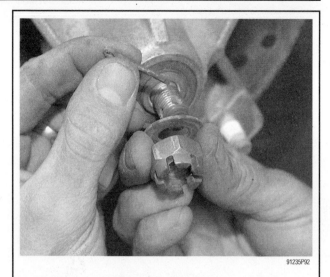
Fig. 108 Keep track of the order in which fasteners . . .

Fig. 106 A large socket is the best tool to use for removing the spindle nut

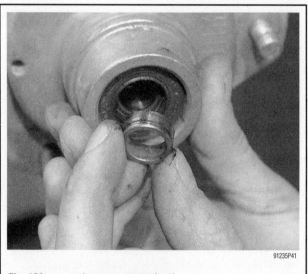
Fig. 109 . . . and spacers are removed . . .

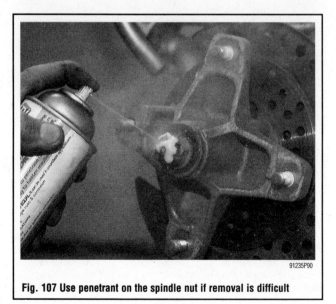
Fig. 107 Use penetrant on the spindle nut if removal is difficult

Fig. 110 . . . then slide the hub off of the spindle

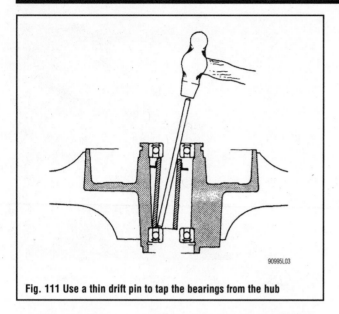

Fig. 111 Use a thin drift pin to tap the bearings from the hub

Fig. 112 Grease seals can be pried from the hub to access the wheel bearings

Fig. 113 Always use a torque wrench to tighten the spindle nut

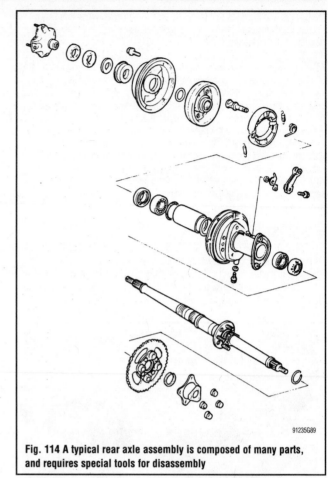

Fig. 114 A typical rear axle assembly is composed of many parts, and requires special tools for disassembly

condition; you can easily mistake a bad wheel bearing for a worn out ball joint or tie rod. If you do feel looseness, determine that it is in fact the wheel bearing. There's no sense in replacing a perfectly good wheel bearing if you don't have to.

The second method involves removing the hub to visually inspect the bearings and the grease. Now of course, if your ATV has sealed bearings, this is a waste of time, because there's nothing to look at! But if your ATV has separate seals that attach to the hub, you'll be able to get a good look at the bearings and the grease by removing the seals. You'll have to wipe away the grease so you can look closely at the surfaces of the balls and races. Look for a blue tint on the balls and races; this would indicate that the bearing has been subjected to extreme heat (known as scalding), and will fail soon. Even if the bearing doesn't FEEL like it is bad, scalding of the bearing will fail quickly because the temper (hardness) of the balls and races is destroyed by heat.

In addition to checking for the bearing overheating, closely inspect the grease for grit and dirt. Rub a small amount between your fingers and feel for debris that may be too small to see. If the grease has a milky color, odds are that water has made its way into the hub. Be sure to remove the grease completely and replace it with fresh grease of the type that the manufacturer of your ATV recommends for the wheel bearings.

Inspecting the bearings visually is a good idea, even if the preliminary test shows they're in good shape. Of course this requires the bearings to be cleaned and repacked with fresh grease.

BEARING ADJUSTMENT

Front

Because of the design of the bearings on most ATVs, they are not adjustable to compensate for wear. When the bearings become worn, they should be replaced with new ones. In most cases, this applies to both two-wheel drive and four-wheel drive ATVs. You can, however, check the spindle nut (or the stub axle nut, on 4x4 models) for proper torque. Because every ATV is different, each manufacturer has a different requirement for the torque value of the spindle nut (or axle nut). Refer to a shop manual specifically for your ATV for proper torque values.

Some older ATVs that use tapered roller bearings (like an automobile) that can be adjusted by simply loosening or tightening the axle nut. With bearings of this type, remove the cotter pin, turn the castellated axle nut until the play in the wheel cannot be felt. Overtightening the bearings will cause them to fail quickly. Turn the axle nut until the castellated end aligns with the opening in the axle, and install a new cotter pin. Using a wrench on wheel bearings of this type is not normally required.

Rear

As with the front wheel bearings, the rear bearings on most ATVs usually do not require adjustment. The reason for this is because rear axle bearings are usually needle-type, or roller type. Usually, the bearings are pressed into a carrier which attaches to the swingarm, or in some cases, is integrated into the swingarm.

➡**Servicing the rear axle bearings on most ATVs requires the use of special tools. If you have performed a preliminary inspection on your rear axle bearings, and have found them to be worn, discuss your options with a service center. It may be easier to have a dealer or repair shop install them for you, as rear axle bearing replacement can be a difficult and time consuming task. If you want to replace them yourself, a dealer or repair shop will be able to give you the details regarding replacement, and recommend the special tools (hydraulic press, special sleeves) required.**

REPACKING THE BEARINGS

▶ **See Figures 115 and 116**

The following procedures are for non-sealed bearings. Sealed bearings require no maintenance. Check in your owners or shop manual for the type installed in your ATV.

Each wheel typically has two bearings which in most cases are press-fit into the hub and are separated by a spacer tube. Some wheels use threaded retainers or perhaps circlips to secure one or both bearings. Grease seals are usually fitted to both sides of the hub to keep the bearing grease in and dirt and moisture out. In the case of rear axles, there are usually two bearings, which are enclosed in the swingarm, and a grease seal on each side.

➡**Bearings should always be replaced in pairs.**

Removal of the bearings is obviously necessary for replacement and is also required for thorough cleaning and repacking. Keep in mind that removing the bearings from the hub may damage them, so you're better off replacing the bearings while things are apart.

➡**You should note that the removal process may ruin ball bearings that they are press-fit in the hub and must be driven out. This is especially**

Fig. 115 The rear axle hub on this ATV has a grease fitting for easy bearing lubrication

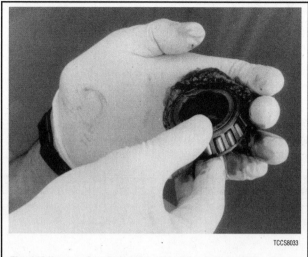

Fig. 116 If your axle or hub does not contain a grease fitting, then the bearings must be removed and repacked by hand

true on high-mileage machines. In addition, grease seals should always be replaced with new ones if they are removed. Tapered bearings do not require driving out, since the outer race is pressed into the hub.

A basic procedure is given here for repacking and or replacing the front wheel bearings. As always, consult a factory service manual for details pertaining to your particular ATV. Things like torque specifications and removal procedures may be specific for your ATV. If you have any questions, always follow the factory manual instructions to avoid problems.

1. Remove the wheel from the ATV.
2. If your ATV is equipped with disc brakes, remove the caliper from the spindle and support it safely. After the caliper is removed, be sure not to apply the brake lever; the piston in the caliper will be pushed from its bore, and will have to be disassembled for repair. Better yet, shove a small piece of fuel hose between the brake pads to prevent any accidents.
3. Remove any dust cover or cap from the spindle nut.
4. Using needlenose pliers, remove the cotter pin, if equipped.
5. Remove the spindle nut, keeping track of any washers or spacers that may follow.
6. The hub should slide off the axle with a moderate pull; use a rubber mallet if things are sticky.
7. Pry out the grease seals from the hub, if equipped. ATVs with tapered-roller bearings use the seals to hold the bearings, and once the seals are removed, the bearings will come out.
8. Remove any retainers or circlips from the hub. Note that some threaded retainers are left-hand thread. Be cognizant of situations such as this, and check your shop manual to be sure.
9. Wheel bearings are driven out with a drift in most cases. It is sometimes helpful to heat the hub very gently to facilitate removal. Heating the hub in boiling water is one way to do this. Some manufacturers specify that the hub should not be heated to more than 212° F (100° C).
10. The best way to remove wheel bearings is to tap around the outer race with a punch and hammer. In some instances a slight movement is all that is necessary, and the bearings will be free. If this is not possible, the bearing can be removed by reaching through the hub with a long punch. Try to move the spacer tube to one side so that a good surface for the punch to drive against can be obtained. Tap the bearing out evenly, alternating your blows around the circumference of the race.
11. Once one bearing is removed, you can take out the spacer tube. If this is only a routine repacking, leave the other bearing in place if possible. As noted, removal risks ruining the bearings, and repacking is possible with one removed.
12. Remove old grease from the hub and the bearings with a solvent. After the bearing is clean, lubricate it with oil and check for smooth rotation. Any roughness, binding or clicking sounds which appear indicate that both bearings should be replaced. Place each bearing on a known flat surface and hold the outer race firmly in place. Attempt to move the inner race back and forth. Little or no movement should be noted, or a worn bearing is indicated.
13. Repack bearings with a good grade of wheel bearing grease of the type

recommended for your ATV. Grease should be pressed into the bearing until it is full. Place a quantity of grease into the hub as well. Keep in mind that grease on the hub not only lubricates the bearings, it provides a means of heat transfer to keep things cool.

14. Bearings should be installed by tapping them into place using a bearing driver tool or properly sized socket. Tap on the outer bearing race only. Drive the bearing in squarely and evenly. Do not allow the bearing to become cocked while entering the hub. If a retainer or circlip is fitted to one side of the hub, the bearing on that side should be installed first. After the bearing is installed, fit the retainer or circlip. This will ensure proper location of the bearing to ease fitting the other one.

➡**Bearings that have one side sealed are always installed with the sealed side facing outward.**

15. Install new grease seals. A large flat block of wood or the smooth round end of an appropriately sized socket works well for driving in new seals. Of course, a seal driver really works better (Lisle® along with other specialty tool companies make some relatively inexpensive sets). Place the block against the seal, and using a hammer, tap the block of wood and drive in the seal. Try to keep the seal as straight as possible during installations; distorting the seal might cause leakage.

16. Place the hub onto the spindle, and install the spacers and washers in their original locations.

17. Install the axle nut, tighten it to the torque specification recommended by the manufacturer. Proper bearing preload is essential for a long service life.

18. If equipped with a cotter pin, install a new one and secure it properly.

19. Install the caliper to the spindle, and tighten it securely.

20. Install the wheel and check for play.

CABLE AND CONTROL LINKAGE MAINTENANCE

Control Cables

INSPECTION

▶ **See Figures 117 thru 124**

Inspecting the cables for kinks, fraying and contamination is important for proper operation, as well as safety. If a cable were to break on the trail, you could be left without a clutch, or worse, brakes. By inspecting your ATV's operating cables on a regular basis, problems of this nature can be avoided.

LUBRICATION

▶ **See Figures 125, 126 and 127**

➡**Do not lubricate Teflon lined cables as the cable is designed to be self lubricating. Adding lubricant will only cause problems. Check your owner's manual or with your ATV's manufacturer (or even the cable manufacturer, if you can find them) to see what type you have.**

Fig. 119 On some ATVs, cables have "splitters" that convert a single cable into a double cable

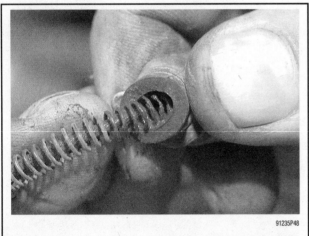

Fig. 117 Cables should inspected frequently for signs of contamination. Rust has set in on this cable from water in the housing

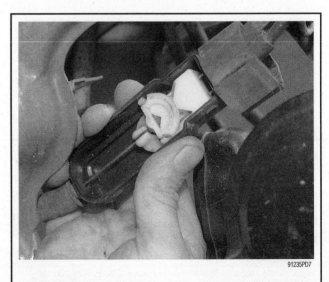

Fig. 120 Check the splitter for any signs of wear or contamination

Fig. 118 Some cables are adjusted by hand with thumb wheels . . .

91235PL2

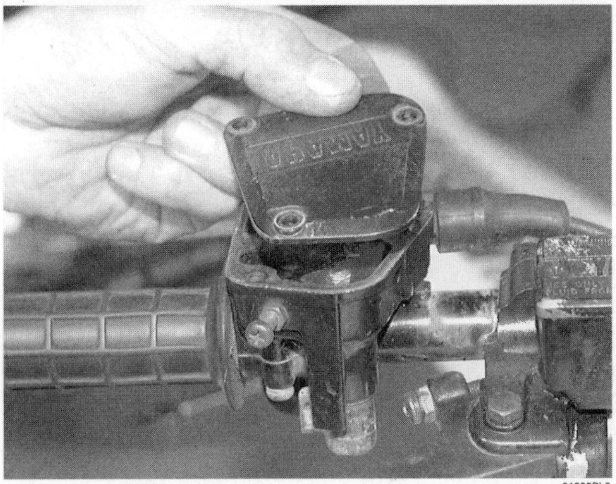

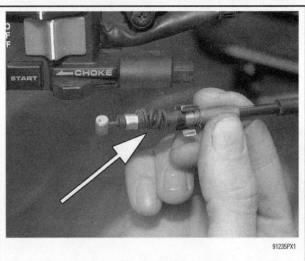

Fig. 121 To inspect the throttle mechanism, unscrew the cover . . .

91235PX1

Fig. 124 Keep an eye on rubber boots; if they crack or tear, cable life will be severely shortened due to contamination

91235PL3

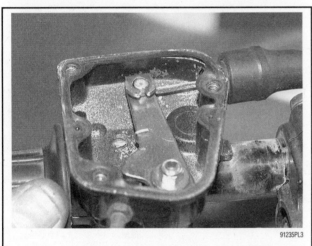

Fig. 122 . . . and look for any signs of wear or contamination. Once the cover is removed, the cable can be removed for lubricating, as well as the lever pivot

91230P14

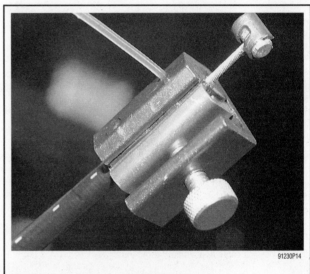

Fig. 125 An example of a cable lubrication tool

91235PQ4

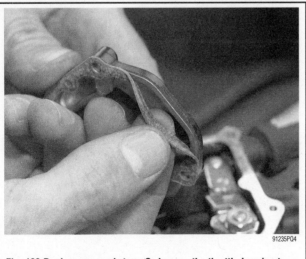

Fig. 123 Replace any gaskets or O-rings on the throttle housing to ensure a watertight seal

91235PW9

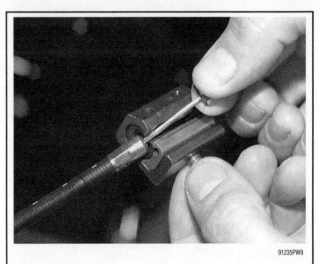

Fig. 126 Once the cable is removed from the lever, position the tool onto the cable . . .

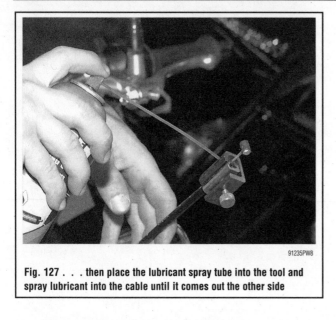

Fig. 127 . . . then place the lubricant spray tube into the tool and spray lubricant into the cable until it comes out the other side

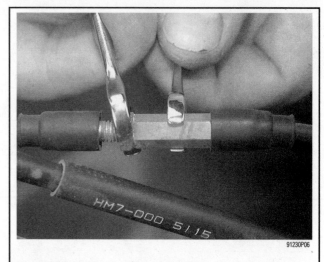

Fig. 129 Most cables on ATVs have a means of adjustment to compensate for stretching and component wear

1. Disconnect the cable and drip cable lubricant down the housing. There are special cable lubricating fittings that make this easier and neater. Add lubricant until it runs out of the other end of the cable.

2. Lubricate the ends of the cable with grease where they connect to the controls and levers. A dab of grease at the cable openings will help prevent the entry of dirt and moisture into the cable.

ADJUSTMENT

▶ **See Figures 128 thru 133**

The majority of control cables all have some form of adjustment to compensate for the natural stretching of the cable and wear of parts, like brake shoes. In most cases, a threaded adjuster on the lever perch is used for cable adjustment. Most are the "thumbwheel" type, meaning that they can be operated by hand. Other adjusters are usually hex-shaped, and require a wrench for adjustment. In addition to the adjuster on the lever, an adjuster is usually found on the other end of the cable where it activates the brake lever (or carburetor).

➥When making cable adjustments at the perch, always position the threaded adjuster with the slot facing downward. If the slot is facing upward, dirt and water can accumulate and enter the cable.

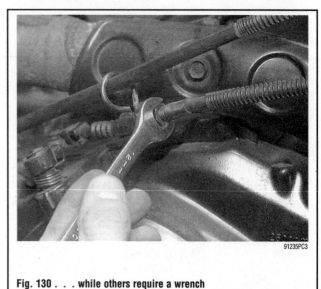

Fig. 130 . . . while others require a wrench

Fig. 128 The rear brake on this ATV has a bolt for cable adjustment

Fig. 131 Some throttles have an adjustable stop for positioning the lever

Fig. 132 To position the lever, loosen the locknut, and turn the adjustment screw while holding the locknut in position, then tighten the locknut while holding the adjustment screw

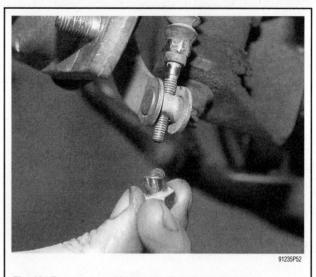

Fig. 134 To remove a cable, remove the adjustment nut . . .

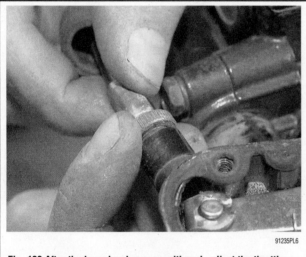

Fig. 133 After the lever has been repositioned, adjust the throttle cable accordingly

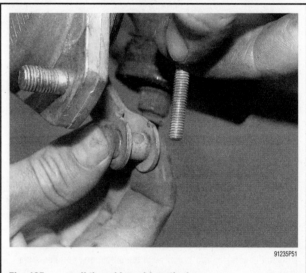

Fig. 135 . . . pull the cable end from the lever . . .

The the threaded adjusters on a lever perch (or lever, in the case of a thumb throttle) can be used for keeping cables adjusted properly in most cases. However, if the adjuster is at the end of it's threading, screw the perch adjuster all the way in, then adjust the cable at the other end. By doing this, the perch adjuster can be used for more convenient adjustments. If a cable is reaching the end of the threads on both adjusters, its likely that the cable is stretched beyond it's useable limits, and should be replaced.

REPLACEMENT

▶ **See Figures 134, 135, 136, 137 and 138**

Cable replacement usually involves disconnecting the ends, and removing any necessary clamps, straps, or anything else that retains the cable. Some cables can be simple to replace, while others, like carburetor cables, may require removal of the gas tank, or the fenders.

When replacing a cable, always make sure that is routed properly. Before removing the old cable, note the routing. Be sure to route the new cable in the same manner to avoid any problems with chafing or kinking. Once the cable is replaced, turn the handlebars from side-to-side, and check for any problems. There should not be any binding when the lever (or throttle) is operated.

Fig. 136 . . . and lift the cable through the slot in the bracket

Fig. 137 Next, remove the lever pivot bolt . . .

Fig. 139 Most brake and clutch levers are held in place by a single pivot bolt

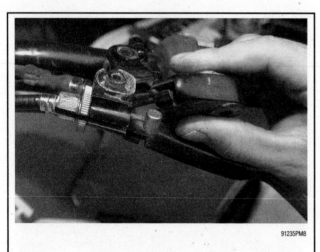

Fig. 138 . . . and unhook the lever from the cable end. Align the slots in the adjuster and locknut with the perch, and pull the cable through

Fig. 140 With the lever removed, lubricant can easily be applied to the lever pivot area . . .

Shifter/Brake Linkage

INSPECTION AND LUBRICATION

▶ See Figures 139, 140, 141, 142 and 143

Any linkage on the ATV including the handlebar levers and shifter linkage need to be lubricated on a regular basis. Lubrication of shifter and brake linkage is essential for safe operation, as well as preventing excessive wear.

1. Check the condition of the pivots and wear areas. Replace any severely worn components.

2. Clean any accumulated dirt and grit from the pivoting surfaces of the linkage.

3. If necessary, remove the lever pivot bolt to allow better access to the bushing.

4. Apply oil or light grease to all bushings and sliding surfaces. Anti-seize compound can also be used.

5. If the linkage is equipped with grease fittings, use an appropriate grease gun with the lubricant specified by the manufacturer.

Fig. 141 . . . and to the pivot bolt

Fig. 142 When tightening the pivot bolt, be careful not to over-tighten it, or the lever may bind

Fig. 144 The actuator rod on this rear brake is threaded for adjust-ment

Fig. 143 Levers can be repositioned by loosening the screws on the perch

Fig. 145 If you are having problems getting your boot under your ATV's shift lever . . .

ADJUSTMENT

♦ See Figures 144, 145, 146, 147 and 148

As with cables, most shifter and brake linkage usually have a means of adjustment to compensate for wear. Adjusters usually consist of a threaded rod, with the adjustment being accomplished by turning a nut or a rod end.

Make sure enough free play in the linkage when making adjustments. Check with your owner's manual or a dealer to obtain the proper amount of free play that your ATV's shifter or brake linkage requires.

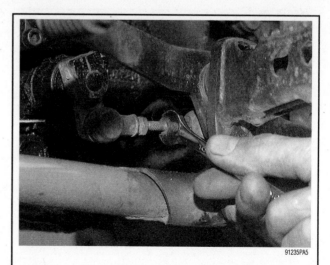

Fig. 146 . . . the position of the shift lever on some ATVs can be adjusted

Fig. 147 Some hydraulic brake levers have an adjustment screw. To adjust the screw, loosen the locknut . . .

Fig. 148 . . . hold the locknut stationary while adjusting the screw. Then hold it in position while tightening the locknut

ELECTRICAL SYSTEM MAINTENANCE

Battery

The battery is the heart of an ATV in many ways. Face it, without a battery we would all be stomping away at kickstarters or pulling away thinking that there had to be a better way to start the engine! The battery gets the beast going in the morning, and acts a mediator for the electrical system. All of you racer types have probably chucked your battery to save weight, but read on; you might be putting one back in soon.

The battery is like a pet goldfish; it needs little to keep it alive, but it has a limited life. Feed it properly and keep its environment clean and it will live as long as it can. Neglect or abuse it and you will find it belly up at the most inopportune times.

CHECKING FLUID LEVEL

♦ See Figures 149 thru 155

Most batteries, up until recently, have been classified as "wet cells" meaning that the electrolyte in the unit has been in liquid form and the level of fluid had to be topped off at times. All ATV and motorcycle type batteries uses two dissimilar materials with some type of electrolyte between them. Wet cell batteries

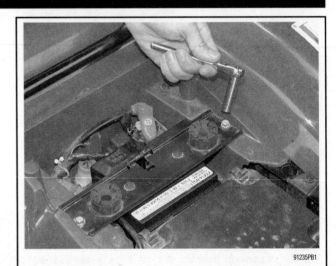

Fig. 150 This ATVs has a bracket which holds the battery in place. Loosen the bolts . . .

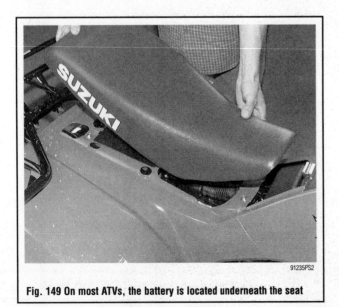

Fig. 149 On most ATVs, the battery is located underneath the seat

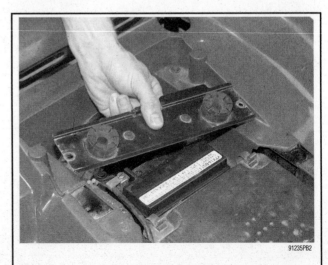

Fig. 151 . . . and remove the bracket for access to the filler caps

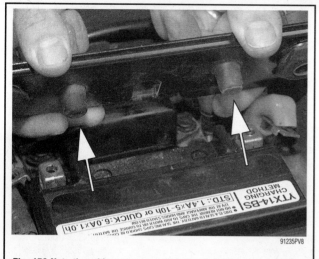

Fig. 152 Note the rubber spacers on this bracket; they help hold the battery in place

Fig. 153 Once the bracket is removed, the wires can be unbolted from the terminals . . .

Fig. 154 . . . and the battery can be lifted out

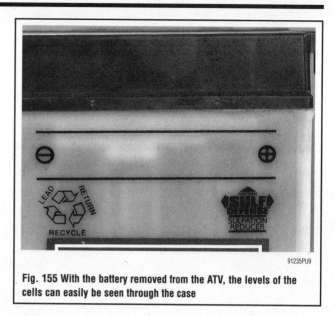

Fig. 155 With the battery removed from the ATV, the levels of the cells can easily be seen through the case

that we need to check are what most of us are used to, but recent advances have brought maintenance-free sealed batteries to the ATV world. Sealed batteries make routine electrolyte checking unnecessary.

Standard batteries can have some of the electrolytes water portion dissipate with time. Water is needed to bring the level back up to the proper point.

All batteries have some type of electrolyte in them, but sealed batteries recycle the fluid in them and don't lose it to the atmosphere as a standard battery would. As a result, you do not need to check the fluid level in a sealed battery.

Standard batteries will have a level range marked on the case. There will be a high and low level mark. They may have the words "High" and "Low" marked on them or just be a set of parallel lines. If there are no lines, there will be a level tab in the inside of the filler hole.

1. The level of the electrolyte must be maintained between the lines or up to the level tab. Check in all six cells, not just an end one. Some ATVs will require that a side panel be removed or the battery removed from the ATV completely to see all six cells.

2. If the fluid needs to be topped off, gain clear access to the top of the battery and clean the top with a clean rag to remove any dirt.

3. Remove the cell cap and use a small funnel to add distilled water to the cell. Bring the level up to the mark. Do not use battery acid or the balance of the electrolyte will be effected. Fill only to the mark; Do not overfill.

➡Only pure, distilled water should be used as regular water contains minerals and chemicals which can contaminate the battery.

4. Do this to all the cells that need it and replace the caps tightly.

TESTING THE BATTERY

Batteries typically test themselves by failing on us! To prevent this from happening, we can test the electrolyte and voltage to give us an idea about what is happening inside the battery.

1. With the engine not running, the battery voltage should be 12.6 volts minimum (12 volt system) or 6.3 volts (6 volt system). If the voltage is lower than this, charge the battery and let sit off the charger for 3 or 4 hours. Recheck the voltage. If the voltage is still low, the battery is bad. If the battery holds the voltage, look for problems with the charging system.

2. If the battery allows for individual cells to be checked (rare nowadays), each cell should read a minimum of 2.1 volts. If nothing else, all the cells should read about the same. If one is lower than the rest, replace the battery.

3. Remove the caps to the battery and test the electrolyte with a hydrometer. The hydrometer will indicate the state of charge in each cell by measuring the specific gravity of the electrolyte. Read the instructions that came with the hydrometer to learn how to interpret the scale on the tool. Some have floating balls and others have pointers. All the cells should have similar readings otherwise you will need to replace the battery due to a dead cell.

CLEANING THE BATTERY

After a hard ride, I'm sure you like to get cleaned up and brushed off. So does your battery! OK, so you don't have to do it after every ride, but cleaning your battery and connections needs to be on your list of scheduled maintenance items.

1. Remove the battery and clean the outer casing with a solution of baking soda and water. Baking soda will neutralize acid. Make sure the caps are on good and tight.

❊❊ WARNING

NEVER let even a small amount of the baking soda solution enter the battery through any means. Baking soda is a "basic" substance (meaning that on the PH scale it is the opposite of an acid). Acids and bases will neutralize each other when combined, that is why you use it to clean the outside of the battery and the area surrounding the battery in the first place. Should some of the solution make it inside the battery, the electrolyte will be ruined.

2. Clean the battery connections and terminals with the same baking soda and water solution. Inspect the cables for frayed ends and corroded wires.

3. Still using the solution, clean the battery tray. Inspect the tray for damage and corrosion. If the tray is rusty (metal trays), consider cleaning it and repainting it. If the corrosion isn't fixed, the battery tray will not live a long life.

4. Install the battery and use some terminal protection gel on the connections. You can buy this at any auto parts supply and it will help keep the white powder from attacking for a while.

SELECTING & PREPPING A REPLACEMENT

Since a dead battery can take all the fun out of riding, you want to use a good quality battery in your ATV at all times. Batteries can get expensive, but if you take good care of your battery, it should last for many seasons.

Use a high quality battery. You can't go wrong with the factory supplied battery, but they tend to be expensive. You can go with the aftermarket, but find out from your riding pals what brands they have had good luck with. Yuasa® batteries are an excellent replacement for a stock battery, and in some cases, better than

what the manufacturer supplies. Yuasa offers batteries for almost every ATV and motorcycle application on the planet, so you're bound to find one for your ATV.

Find the proper sized battery both physically and in terms of power. The battery needs to fit well in the stock battery tray and to be held by the battery hold-downs, plus the terminals must match. The battery needs to have at least (or more capacity, if your ATV has electrical accessories) the electrical capacity of the original. Most ATV batteries are rated in amp hours. This number will be printed on the case of the battery or in the literature that came with the battery.

If you are searching for a new battery for your ATV, consider replacing a conventional battery with a maintenance-free sealed unit. The price of a sealed battery may be higher than a conventional unit, but the benefits by far outweigh the additional cost.

If you decide to buy a new battery from a mail order warehouse, chances are it will be shipped to you with the electrolyte in a separate container. In most cases, this is true whether you buy a sealed maintenance-free battery, or a conventional battery. Keeping the battery dry indefinitely extends it's shelf life, and also ensures that the battery is "new" when it is received. Of course this is requires that you, the consumer, add the electrolyte to the battery. This is a simple procedure, and in the case of the batteries that were supplied to us by Yuasa®, complete instructions were provided to make things easier. We have shown filling both conventional and maintenance-free batteries just to give you an idea of what is involved with setting up a new battery.

➡**After filling a new battery with electrolyte, it should be charged to full capacity before placing the battery back into the ATV. Some maintenance-free batteries may not require an initial charge, but in most cases, a new battery must be charged before use. Failure to charge a new battery will permanently decrease the power output, and severely shorten it's service life. Always follow the instructions that come with a new battery regarding charging procedures. Improper setup will ruin a new battery.**

Conventional Battery

▶ **See Figures 156 thru 162**

1. Remove the cell caps on the new battery.
2. Cut the tip from the plastic bottle and place the filler tube onto the tip.

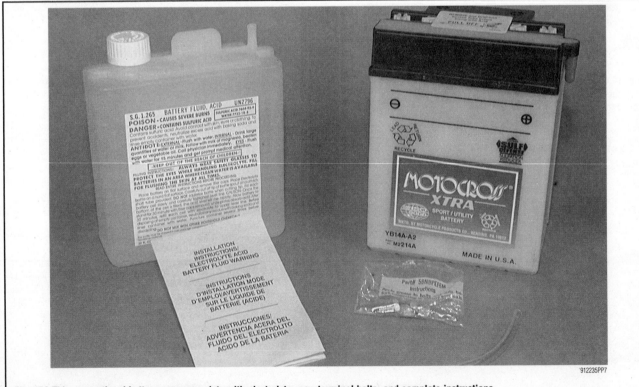

Fig. 156 This conventional battery came complete with electrolyte, new terminal bolts, and complete instructions

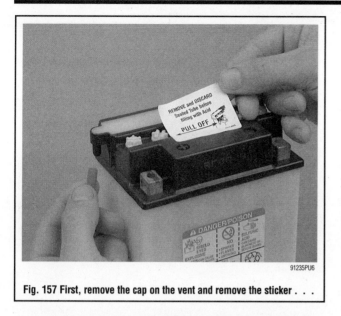

Fig. 157 First, remove the cap on the vent and remove the sticker . . .

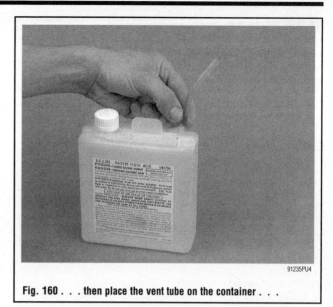

Fig. 160 . . . then place the vent tube on the container . . .

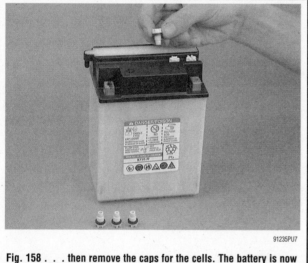

Fig. 158 . . . then remove the caps for the cells. The battery is now ready for electrolyte

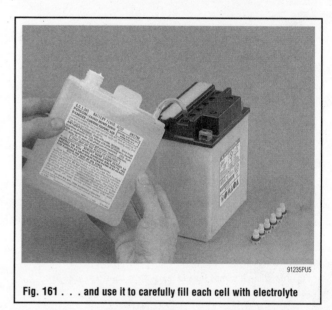

Fig. 161 . . . and use it to carefully fill each cell with electrolyte

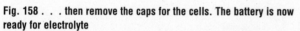

Fig. 159 Cut the cap off the electrolyte container . . .

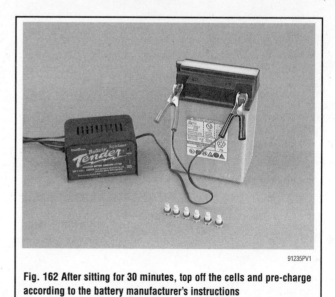

Fig. 162 After sitting for 30 minutes, top off the cells and pre-charge according to the battery manufacturer's instructions

✳✳ **CAUTION**

When handling electrolyte, always wear eye protection. Electrolyte is a caustic acid, and can cause blindness if it comes in contact with your eyes.

3. Place the filler tube in a cell, and slowly tip the bottle, allowing the electrolyte to fill the cell. Repeat with all of the cells.

4. Let the battery sit for 15-20 minutes, and check the level of each cell. Top off the level of any low cells.

5. Let the battery sit (without the caps installed) for 30 minutes.

6. Attach a battery charger to the new battery, and charge it for the time specified by the manufacturer. This is a very important step; make absolutely certain that the battery has fully charged before use.

Maintenance-free Battery

◆ See Figures 163 thru 170

1. Remove the plastic or metal foil seal that covers the cell caps.

2. Remove the plastic caps on the electrolyte bottle. Do not discard the cap; it is the cap for the cells of the battery.

3. Align the tips of the electrolyte bottle with the cells; then press down on

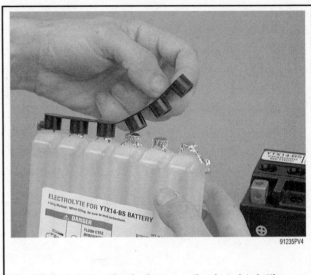

Fig. 165 Next, remove the plastic caps on the electrolyte bottle

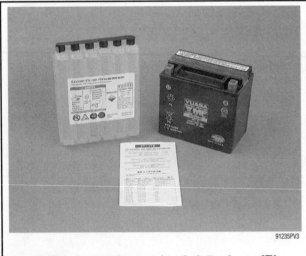

Fig. 163 When it comes time to replace the battery in your ATV, sealed batteries make an excellent replacement

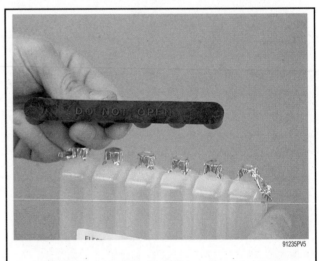

Fig. 166 On this battery, do not discard the caps, for they serve as the sealing caps in service

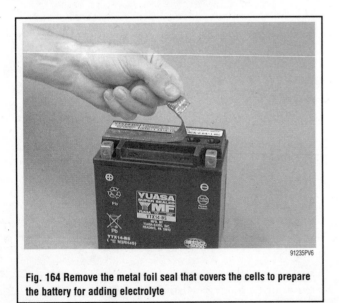

Fig. 164 Remove the metal foil seal that covers the cells to prepare the battery for adding electrolyte

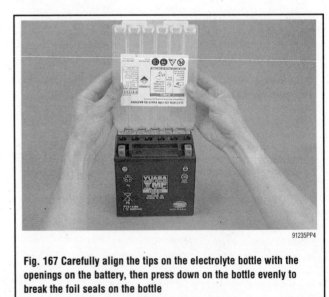

Fig. 167 Carefully align the tips on the electrolyte bottle with the openings on the battery, then press down on the bottle evenly to break the foil seals on the bottle

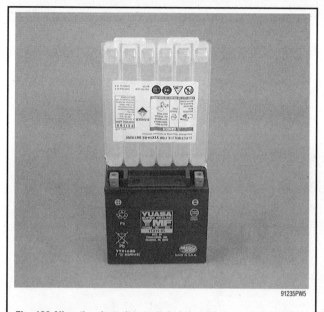

Fig. 168 Allow the electrolyte to drain into the cells until the bottle is completely empty

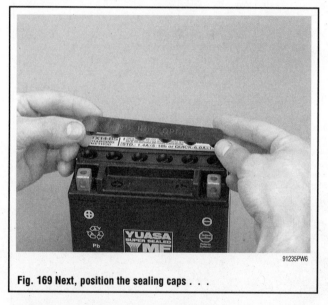

Fig. 169 Next, position the sealing caps . . .

the electrolyte bottle, breaking the foil seals on each of the tips. This should be done in a quick motion to avoid spilling electrolyte. from the bottle.

✳✳ CAUTION

When handling electrolyte, always wear eye protection. Electrolyte is a caustic acid, and can cause blindness if it comes in contact with your eyes.

4. Allow the bottle to empty into the cells. Once the cells are full, let the battery sit for 30 minutes.
5. Charge the battery as the manufacturer specifies. As stated earlier, some maintenance-free batteries may not require a charge.
6. Install the caps onto the top of the battery.

Fig. 170 . . . and firmly press them into place. The battery is now permanently sealed and ready for use

CHARGERS

▶ See Figures 171 and 172

There will be a time in your ATV's life that it will need to have some extra help in the form of a battery charger. When looking for a charger for your car, almost any will do, but an ATV is a different animal. An ATV battery is quite a bit smaller than a car battery and its needs are different.

If you use a car battery charger on an ATV battery, you can boil out all the electrolyte and kill it. The charging requirements for the battery are much lower and are in the range of 2 amps or less. If you have no choice and have to use a car battery charger, choose the lowest power range (typically 2 amps) and check the battery often during the charge. If it is getting hot or bubbling excessively, remove it from the charger.

The best bet for charging an ATV battery is using a specialized ATV and motorcycle battery charger. Probably the most convenient is a smart charger such as the Deltran Battery Tender®. This type of charger will provide a low charging rate (say something around 1.25 amps) until the battery is completely charged and then switch to a safe storage rate. This storage rate will keep the battery at peak condition indefinitely and not harm the battery. This is a great feature for seasonal riders, since you can leave the battery plugged into the charger until you are ready to ride.

✳✳ CAUTION

USE EXTREME CARE when charging a battery. The process that occurs when charging or discharging a battery allows explosive hydrogen gas to escape from the electrolyte. Any source of ignition (including sparks or open flame) could case a violent explosion of the battery and casing. Besides the normal dangers associated with an explosion, this would also shower the surrounding area with hydrochloric acid. Obviously this could seriously injure or possible even kill anyone within close vicinity of the battery.

Be careful of low priced battery chargers with questionable monitoring circuits. They may not have the smarts to keep your battery from overcharging and boiling off. If you chose a low priced unit, keep an eye on the battery to make sure it is doing OK and not getting hot or off gassing too much.

Some battery chargers come with a harness that you can connect directly to you battery and plug in the charger instead of having to use big clips on the terminals. Some chargers will have a plug that will match the accessory power port on the ATV. If your ATV doesn't have a power port, it is easy to attach one.

Fig. 171 The Battery Tender® from Deltran allows for continuous charging without the fear of damaging the battery

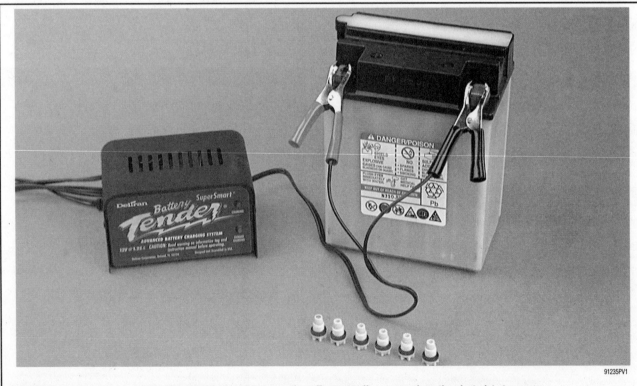

Fig. 172 When charging a conventional battery, be sure to remove the cell caps to allow gasses from the electrolyte to escape

Light Bulbs

Visibility is of paramount importance to an ATV rider at night. If you can't see the terrain ahead, then you are in deep trouble. If other riders cannot see you, you can be in even more trouble.

REPLACEMENT

Headlights

◆ **See Figures 173, 174, 175 and 176**

Headlights come in two general camps: either a sealed beam unit, or a reflector/bulb combination. The latter is the more popular technology as it provides better lighting.

Sealed beam bulbs get replaced as a unit, reflector and all. Reflector/bulb type lamps just need the bulb to be replaced. Most sealed beams can be replaced by an H4 type reflector/bulb lamp unit from the aftermarket. These units will provide superior lighting and replaceable bulbs with a choice of wattage.

The headlight can be held by a retaining ring or in a nacelle or maybe it will be built into the fender. There are about as many different mounting schemes as there are ATVs.

Fig. 175 Once the headlight has been removed from the bracket, the lens can be separated from the bucket . . .

Fig. 173 Remove the headlight bolts . . .

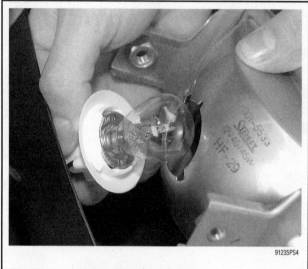

Fig. 176 . . . and the bulb can be accessed

1. If the headlight is held by a retaining ring, remove the ring and pull the lamp forward.
2. If the lamp is held in a nacelle, you may have to remove the nacelle to access the wiring and plug for the lamp.
3. Disconnect the plug from the back of the bulb.
4. If the lamp is a sealed beam unit, remove the lamp. If the lamp is a separate bulb, pull of the rubber cover and unclip the retainer. Pull the bulb out of the housing.
5. Replace the sealed beam with a new bulb and plug in the connector. Install the retaining ring. If you are replacing just a bulb, be sure **not to touch the glass on the new bulb** with your skin or the life of the bulb will be severely reduced. If the bulb was touched, clean it with alcohol and a lint-free wipe. Install the retainer and rubber cover.
6. Install any removed parts and check the aim of the light. Adjust if needed.

Running lights

◆ **See Figures 177, 178, 179 and 180**

Most bulbs for running lights (tail lights) are held in the reflectors under the lens and simply removing the lens gains you access to the bulb. The lens may be held on by a screw or two or possibly the lens just pries off. Sometimes the entire housing will have to be removed from the ATV and disassembled to get at the bulb. I have seen housings held by screws, bolts or thumbscrews.

Fig. 174 . . . and carefully pull the headlight away from the bracket

Fig. 177 To change a common running light, unscrew the lens . . .

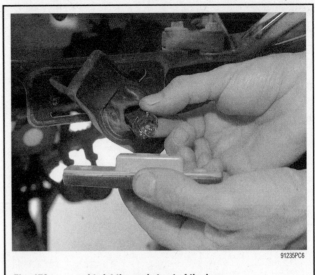

Fig. 179 . . . and twist the socket out of the lens

Fig. 178 . . . then separate the rubber backing . . .

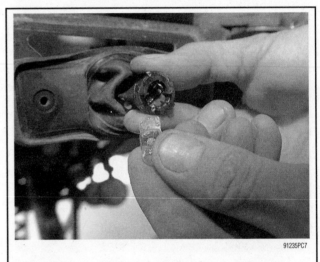

Fig. 180 Once the socket is free, simply pull the bulb out of the socket

1. Remove the lens or housing. The mounting screws can be hidden behind a piece of bodywork or buried in a tail housing. Look for screws, bolts or thumbscrews that will need to be removed.

2. Remove the bulb from the socket.

3. Check the socket for corrosion or damage. Light corrosion can be removed by cleaning with a contact cleaner available at auto parts stores or electronics stores. Heavy corrosion may require replacement of the socket or maybe the entire housing if the socket isn't available separately.

4. Clean the interior of the reflector, removing the dust and dirt that accumulates there.

5. Clean the lens with soapy water and dry before installation.

6. Replace the bulb with a proper part. Be careful that you install the proper wattage and size bulb, otherwise the light may not work correctly or could damage the socket and lens. You may want to use a dab of dielectric grease to protect the socket from corrosion.

7. Install the lens and housing. Check the bulb for proper operation.

6

PREPARING
TO RIDE

PRE-RIDE CHECK

▶ **See Figures 1 thru 6**

Before you go tearing off into the woods, take a little time and inspect your ATV. It's easy to get excited when you've pulled into your favorite riding area and see others having fun on their ATVs; you probably want to be quick to join in on the fun. But wait!! Did you remember to fuel up? Are your tires inflated properly? When **was** the last time you checked your oil? It's so easy to forget all of these important things when you've driven for hours to get to your favorite riding area, and all you'd like to do is get your ATV off the trailer and get geared up to ride. The LAST thing that you want to be bothered with is inspecting the mechanicals of your ATV. You want to RIDE!!

When it comes to riding ATVs, one point is always stressed: SAFETY. There are so many different aspects of safety when it comes to riding ATVs—safely transporting your ATV, courteous riding, crossing adverse terrain, performing maintenance, and the list goes on.

Inspecting your ATV before riding it is probably one of the most neglected forms of safety. By inspecting your ATV before you ride, you are taking precautions to ensure that your ATV is functioning properly, and this affects the safety of both you AND the riders around you. Finding out that your brakes are not properly adjusted **after** you're heading down a steep hill can get pretty scary!

Fig. 3 The debris in the bead of this tire may cause leakage if left unattended

Fig. 1 Before speeding off onto your favorite trail, take a couple minutes and inspect your ATV

Fig. 4 When was the last time you cleaned the air filter?

Fig. 2 Frequent inspection of components (like this drive belt) will help prevent any unexpected problems from leaving you stranded

Fig. 5 In addition to keeping mechanical brakes properly adjusted, make sure the reservoirs of hydraulic brakes are kept full

Fig. 6 Always use fresh fluid to top off brake fluid reservoirs

Fig. 8 Notice how much taller the tire is on the right; a couple pounds of air pressure can cause handling and alignment problems

With a little bit of care and time, we can make our riding experience much more fun as well as safe. A few moments before each ride is all that is necessary to help reduce the chance of running into a bad situation. It isn't hard, and with some practice and discipline, it becomes an integral part of the ATV riding experience.

Things To Look For

If you keep up on your ATV maintenance, the pre-ride check should be short and sweet. In general, the check includes items which effect safety and driveability. You will look at items like your tires, oil level, coolant level, brake pads, lights and controls. Depending on the ATV, the actual items may change as appropriate (check your owner's manual), but use the following list as a guide:

TIRES

▶ See Figures 7, 8 and 9

Check the tire pressure and the condition of the wheel/tire combination. If the tire pressure is not correct, adjust it to specification. Without the proper tire

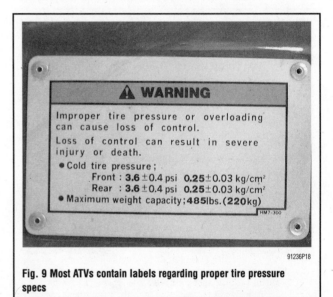

Fig. 9 Most ATVs contain labels regarding proper tire pressure specs

pressure, the ATV can pull to one side, become unstable, or the tire itself may be damaged. By checking the pressure every time you ride, you will find trends; If the pressure stays mostly even every time you check it and then one day it is way down, you will be alerted that another problem may exist, like a puncture or cracked wheel. While down on your knees checking the pressure, look for damage to the tire and wheel. You might spot a crack or tear in the sidewall that could develop into a serious leak.

OIL LEVEL

▶ See Figures 10, 11, 12 and 13

An engine of any type uses oil to lubricate and cool itself. Most ATVs provide some type way to check of the oil level, such as a dipstick or sight glass. Read your owner's manual or refer to Section 4 of this manual to help decide how the level is to be read. To avoid problems, keep your oil level topped off at all times.

A low oil level could slowly ruin your engine, while a very low level could lead to a dangerous engine seizure. At best an engine seizure would cost you a lot of money for rebuild or repair, but it could also strand you in the middle of nowhere or cause a serious accident. Bottom line: KEEP AN EYE ON YOUR ENGINE OIL LEVEL.

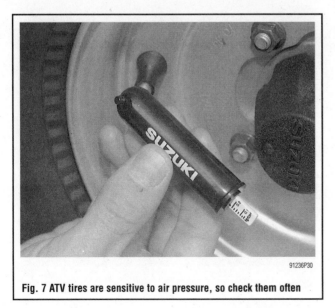

Fig. 7 ATV tires are sensitive to air pressure, so check them often

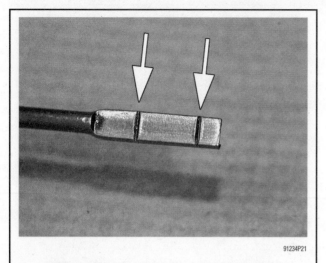

91234P21

Fig. 10 Keep the oil level between the marks on the dipstick to avoid engine damage

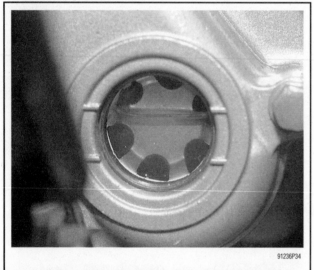

91236P34

Fig. 11 Engines with a sight glass are easier to keep an eye on

91234PH4

Fig. 12 If the level is low, top off the engine with fresh oil

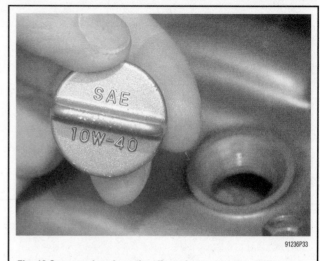

91236P33

Fig. 13 Some engines have the oil requirement on the oil fill cap, or sometimes on the engine case

COOLANT

♦ See Figures 14, 15, 16 and 17

✳✳ CAUTION

Never open, service or drain the radiator or cooling system when hot; serious burns can occur from the steam and hot coolant. Also, when draining engine coolant, keep in mind that cats and dogs are attracted to ethylene glycol antifreeze and could drink any that is left in an uncovered container or in puddles on the ground. This will prove fatal in sufficient quantities. Always drain coolant into a sealable container.

If your ATV is water cooled, take a peek at the coolant level in the reservoir. Coolant has a mysterious way of slowly disappearing over a period of time, so even if you don't have any visible leaks, your coolant level may be low. You may spot a slow leak by having to add coolant on a regular basis even if it doesn't leave any drips on the floor.

91236P42

Fig. 14 Just like the engine oil, keep the level of the coolant between the MAX and MIN lines

Fig. 15 If the coolant level is low, always add coolant to the reservoir first (if equipped)

Fig. 16 If the reservoir is completely empty, check the level in the radiator. It should be up to the base of the filler neck

Fig. 17 To avoid making a slippery mess, always use a funnel to add coolant

CABLES AND CONTROLS

▶ **See Figures 18, 19, 20 and 21**

It is real bummer to have a throttle or clutch cable snap during a ride. Look at the cable ends for fraying and damage. If your levers are stiff and sticky feeling, chances are that the cable is in need of lubrication. Also, make sure that the shifter and brake levers aren't bent or binding. It is not uncommon for linkage to rattle apart from time to time. The occasional rock or branch can do damage to the levers and linkage, so beware.

One item that often goes overlooked is the protective rubber boot found at the ends of many cables. This boot is used to keep dirt and moisture from the otherwise unprotected cable end. If the boot becomes damaged with cracks or tears, or if the boot stretches over time, allowing contaminants access to the cable, it is no longer performing its job and should be replaced. If allowed to go unrepaired, it is likely that the cable will suffer a sudden and total loss of operation when it is least expected. This is because of wear and corrosion that will occur on the pivot or sliding point at the cable end. If you don't want to get stranded because of a torn boot, then give a quick visual check before each ride and it won't go unnoticed.

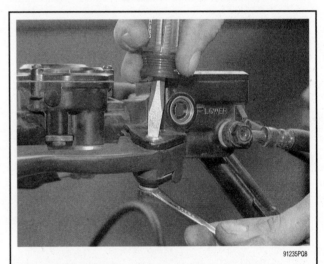

Fig. 18 Keep lever pivots adjusted properly to avoid binding or excessive looseness

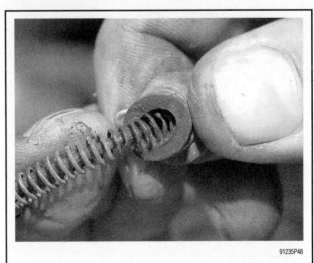

Fig. 19 If cables feel tight or bind, suspect rust or mud inside the cable. Cables in this condition can break at any time on the trail

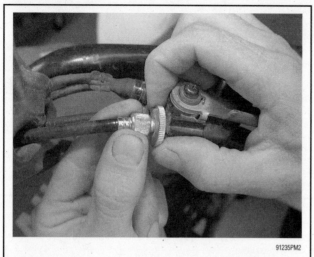

Fig. 20 The cables are designed for quick adjustment without tools—use them often to keep cables adjusted properly

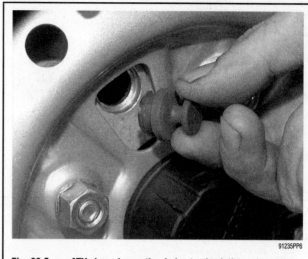

Fig. 22 Some ATVs have inspection holes to check the wear on the brake lining

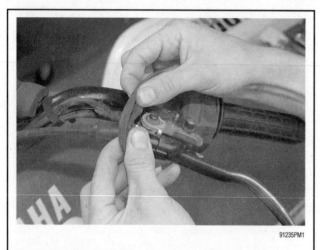

Fig. 21 The rubber boot that covers the lever perch keeps the adjusters free from debris—keep an eye on these boots and replace them if they become damaged.

Fig. 23 Disc brakes usually require wheel removal for inspection; inspect them periodically for wear

BRAKE PADS AND SHOES

▶ See Figures 22 and 23

Some ATVs have brake pads that are easily seen and can be checked with a glance. Look for enough material left on the pad for your ride. Drum brakes aren't as easy if they don't have wear indicators on the linkage, but if there is an inspection opening, use it! Front brakes are more critical on most ATVs due to the forward weight transfer that occurs during braking.

CHAIN OR SHAFT DRIVES

▶ See Figures 24, 25 and 26

Your ATV has either a chain or shaft drive. If equipped with a drive chain, take a look at the slack in the chain and make sure that it isn't excessive. Look for kinked portions of the chain and signs of reddish rust on the side links. Check the sprockets for damage while you have your nose down that far.

If your ATV is shaft drive, look for leakage from the axle seals or drain plug.

Fig. 24 This chain is TOASTED!! Don't let this happen to you; lube your ATV's chain regularly

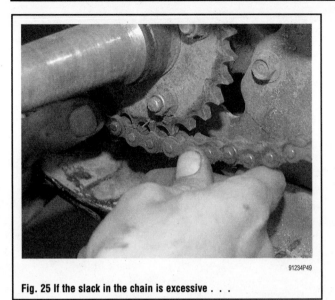

Fig. 25 If the slack in the chain is excessive . . .

Fig. 27 If a headlight is burned out . . .

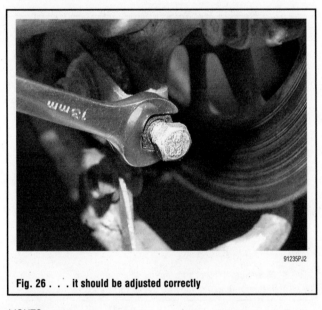

Fig. 26 . . . it should be adjusted correctly

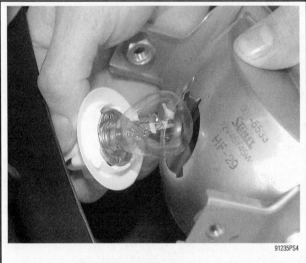

Fig. 28 . . . it can be easily repaired by replacing the bulb

LIGHTS

▶ **See Figures 27, 28 and 29**

If your riding adventures carry you into the evening hours, make sure to check that all your lights work. (Getting caught in the dark a long ways from camp can be a real downer). This includes the headlamp (high and low beams) and the taillight(s). It is also worth the time to make sure all your warning lights on the instrument pad light up when you turn on the key because you don't want to find out the hard way that your oil pressure light is burned out!

BATTERY ELECTROLYTE

▶ **See Figure 30**

Check the battery for the proper level of electrolyte. Most ATVs have the battery right underneath the seat. If you can check it easily, make it a habit to do so. If it isn't easy to see, make it part of your regular maintenance routine. If your battery bails out on you in the middle of nowhere, you might be pulling on that back up starter (or if you don't have one, looking for a hill to push-start it!)

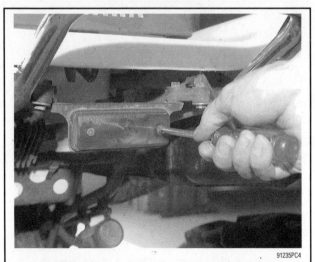

Fig. 29 Taillights are also easily replaced by unscrewing the lens and replacing the bulb

Fig. 30 Keep an eye on the electrolyte level in the battery. Keeping the level correct will ensure proper output

LEAKS

Look over the engine and driveline for obvious leaks. A small leak now may turn into a gusher just as you are entering a turn. It is also a good way to keep a tab on the mechanical condition of your ATV. If things have always stayed dry, and now there's a sheen of oil on the crankcase, you have a problem that you need to look into.

AND THE LAST CHECK!

▶ See Figure 31

We all know that sometimes it just isn't possible to do all the items in the list. In this (hopefully rare) case, pick the most important items such as tire pressure, oil level and FUEL LEVEL. If you have been looking at all the items in the above list on a continuing basis, you should have a good feel for the overall condition of the ATV and skipping an item or two shouldn't hurt once in a while. It still is very much a good idea to always check these items when you head out for your first ride of the day, and some of the more basic items (oil level, fuel level, etc.) a few more times during a long ride. If you miss one item on that list and it causes you a problem, it is all on you. ATV riding should be fun, but the responsibility of riding is great, and you should respect that, just not for you, but for your fellow riders.

Fig. 31 This guy is really happy, because he has inspected his ATV and is ready to hit the trail

Tools For The Trail

If your ATV breaks down in the middle of nowhere, having some basic hand tools to use may be all that is necessary to get you going again. If the spark plug rattles loose when you're miles from camp, a spark plug socket can really come in handy. Carrying tools on your ATV (or on your person) can get a little cumbersome, though. By carrying only the tools (and parts) that you need, hauling around a complete 110 piece Craftsman tool set will be all but eliminated, and you'll still have all of the tools you need to make trailside repairs.

ESSENTIALS

▶ See Figures 32, 33, 34, 35 and 36

There are some tools that are essential to carry with you at ALL times. The first is the tool kit that comes with your ATV when it is purchased. If you have bought your ATV used, and it did not come with a tool kit (usually in the form of a small bag under the seat, or in a compartment in the rear), it would be a good idea to buy a new one from a dealer. Make sure the tool kit is specifically for your ATV; other tool kits may not have some special tools that fit the fasteners on your ATV.

The original tool kit that was provided with your ATV has most of what you'll need to make repairs in a tight situation. Granted, the tools aren't usually of top

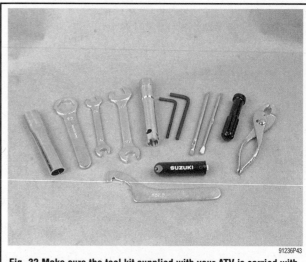

Fig. 32 Make sure the tool kit supplied with your ATV is carried with you at all times—it can really help you out in a pinch

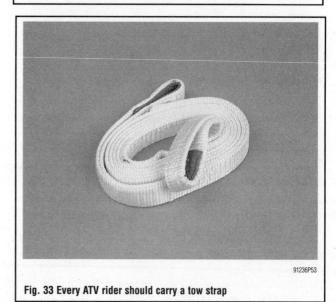

Fig. 33 Every ATV rider should carry a tow strap

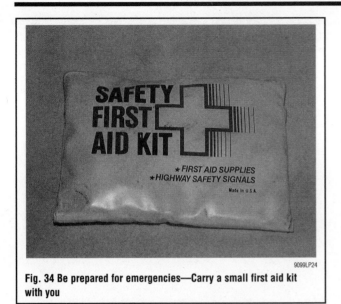

9099LP24

Fig. 34 Be prepared for emergencies—Carry a small first aid kit with you

91236P70

Fig. 35 Since ATVs don't carry spares, a tire plug kit is another essential tool for the trail

91239P18

Fig. 36 Make sure that you have extra fuses

notch quality, but they can really help in a pinch. Most factory tool kits come with a spark plug tool, pliers, a screwdriver with changeable tips, and a couple of wrenches, which fit the most common fastener sizes on your ATV.

In addition to carrying the basic tool kit, a tire plug kit should be considered an essential tool. A tire plug kit (with cartridges for filling the tire) are crucial to carry on long trips, since ATVs don't carry spare tires like 4x4s. Make sure that the cartridges for refilling a tire are easily removed from the valve stem though. Don't forget, ATV tires use little air pressure (less than 15 psi, in most cases). There are also many types of tire sealants that can prevent air leaks from small punctures, but substituting sealant for a tire plug kit is not recommended. Most tire sealants only work for small punctures. Just remember though—tire plugs should be considered a temporary fix. A plugged tire should be properly patched from the inside. An ATV dealer should be able to do this for you.

In the case that your ATV breaks down and the tools you do have can't be used for repairs, a tow strap can really come in handy. A buddy or good Samaritan can haul you back to camp if you've got a tow strap with you. Make sure the tow strap is of good quality, and it is long enough to provide enough distance between vehicles when towing. Since the tow strap will most likely be stored in the compartment under the seat, a nylon tow strap would be a better choice, since a canvas strap might get moldy and rot over time.

Another essential tool to carry on every ride is a small first aid kit. If you look around, you can find one that will fit perfectly in the tool compartment of your ATV. Make some measurements, and head on down to the local camping supply. First aid kits come in all shapes and sizes, so you should be able to find something that doesn't occupy too much room, and can still be of use in case of an emergency on the trail.

OTHER ITEMS TO CONSIDER

There are so many useful things to carry with you on a ride that can pull you out of trouble. Here is a list of additional items that you should have that can save the weekend. Some of these items may be a bit extreme, but hey, it can't hurt to be a little over-prepared.

- Spare bottle of water
- Spark plugs
- Locking pliers with cutters
- Bailing wire
- Duct tape
- Nylon tie wraps (wire-ties)
- Extra throttle and brake cables
- A few feet of spare fuel line (good for siphoning or repair)
- A knife
- Small flashlight
- Toilet paper
- Packaged beef jerky
- Matches or a lighter
- Compass
- Flares

On chain drive models consider carrying these items as well:

- Extra master links
- Extra lengths of chain
- Compact chain breaker

This list is generic, and applies to just about anyone who ventures off into the wilderness on (or in) motor vehicles. Over time, you'll probably amass your own custom collection of tools and supplies that apply to your ATV.

If you pack up everything tight enough, most of these items can fit into a small gear bag that can be attached to your waist. But if you don't want to be hassled with a bag, consider the compartment below your seat. If it is large enough, everything can be made to fit.

The benefits of carrying these items far outweighs the extra weight added to your ATV. If a buddy breaks down, you might have the extra tools and supplies to help out.

Many cross-country racers and desert racers attach tools and supplies over various areas of their ATVs. For instance, an extra throttle cable can be tie-wrapped to a frame rail, where it can easily be accessed in an emergency. You can do the same with other tools and supplies. Look for little nooks and crannies to stash parts and supplies, and use appropriate means to secure them. Make sure water and mud aren't going to ruin anything, though. You'll be glad that you went through the extra effort to carry extra tools, parts and supplies; sooner or later you'll be using SOMETHING!!

PLANNING A TRIP

Planning ahead for a day ride, weekend, or camping/hunting trip all have one thing in common: BEING PREPARED. After all, it would be safe to say that there won't be an ATV shop nearby, or a local camping supply store. Of course this all depends on the location of your riding area. You might be lucky enough to have a convenience store that sells gasoline and soda a few miles down the road. But even then, being prepared will save the inconvenience of having to pick up supplies in the middle of your fun-filled weekend.

Preparing for a weekend ride or ATV camping trip can become really hectic and unorganized if you wait until the last minute to round everything up for packing. Its a good idea to make a complete list a few days **before** you get ready to pack everything. Go over the list with your riding buddies; they might think of items that you've overlooked. This way, when it comes time to pack up your truck, trailer and/or ATVs, you can check off the list as you go along, and ensure that everything that you had planned to bring along actually gets loaded up.

There's nothing worse than driving for hours to a riding area, and realizing that you forgot your HELMET, or even worse, the KEY to your ATV. We've all forgotten to bring things along from time-to-time, but forgetting something really important can absolutely RUIN your weekend. Don't let this happen to you! Having everything that you need for the weekend will make things much more enjoyable.

What To Bring

♦ **See Figures 37, 38 and 39**

Discussing in detail what to bring along on an ATV camping trip could be a separate book in itself, since the intended plans of your trip can vary so greatly. Just heading out to your favorite riding area for the weekend? Or are you planning a week long excursion in the wilderness and packing all of your camping gear on your ATV? Going hunting?

Whatever your plans are, there are some things to bring along that are common to all types of riding. Items like extra fuel, oil, and spare parts are just about essential to bring along for any trip. Earlier in this section, tools and supplies to carry on an ATV are discussed in detail. However, extra tools, supplies, and other items that are too big to carry on your ATV can be brought along and kept in your tow vehicle in case of an emergency. In addition to these items, there are some basic items listed below that should always be brought along on any trip.

ESSENTIAL ITEMS

♦ **See Figures 40 and 41**

One of the most important items is WATER. Sounds obvious, but it requires some forethought if you haven't done any long rides on your ATV before.

90996P95

Fig. 38 There are also ultra-compact tents available, like this one that measures only 6x16 inches when broken down

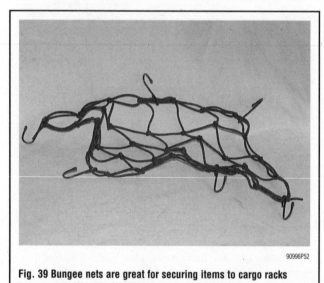

90996P52

Fig. 39 Bungee nets are great for securing items to cargo racks

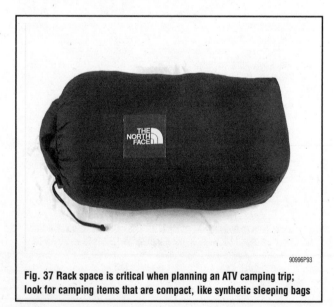

90996P93

Fig. 37 Rack space is critical when planning an ATV camping trip; look for camping items that are compact, like synthetic sleeping bags

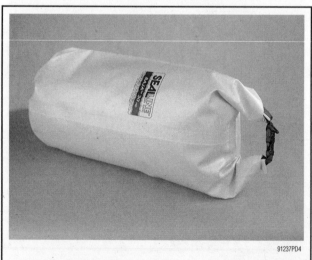

91237PD4

Fig. 40 For weekend camping adventures, dry bags are essential for keeping food and supplies safe from inclement weather

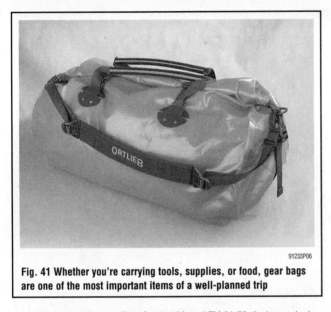

Fig. 41 Whether you're carrying tools, supplies, or food, gear bags are one of the most important items of a well-planned trip

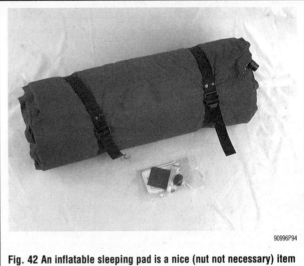

Fig. 42 An inflatable sleeping pad is a nice (nut not necessary) item to bring along on a camping trip

According to the U.S. Army Field Survival Manual FM 21-76, the human body needs at least 2 quarts of water a day in cold climates where your perspiration and loss of body fluids are lower than when in hot climates. For warm weather and ATV travel, a minimum of 1 gallon of water per person per day is suggested. The water should be commercially available bottled water or from your home tap. If you run out of water, and have to drink from streams, lakes or ponds, always treat it with water purification tablets, or boil for at least 5 minutes before drinking.

Plenty of food is essential to bring along also. This can be just as critical as water. Dried and canned food is best to bring along, since space and weight requirements are so critical. Of course, if you are setting up camp for the weekend, and regularly returning to camp after a ride, ice chests will be your best bet. Just like water, you can never bring enough food along. A riding trip can become a miserable experience if you run out of food, so be sure to bring plenty.

Depending on the time of year, bringing extra clothing along is a good idea. Even during the warmer months of the year, a cold snap can move in overnight. If you didn't bring along an extra jacket or thermal underwear, things could get really miserable. A lot of the newer off-road riding jackets have the unique feature of folding up into themselves, and being worn like a belt. These jackets are really practical since you can start off on a ride with the jacket on in the cool morning hours, and take it off at high noon, fold it up and wear it around your waist. These jackets allow you to have the best of both worlds.

In addition to bringing extra clothing for cold weather, bring clothing and gear for wet weather. If the weather suddenly takes a turn for the worst, you'll be prepared to deal with rain. There are camping equipment manufacturers that make clothing and gear bags specifically for wet weather. Jackets with Gore-Tex® fabric will keep you nice and dry, and still provide adequate ventilation. Many different types of camping gear (tents, backpacks, etc.) are made from these types of materials.

ADDITIONAL ITEMS

▶ See Figures 42 and 43

As stated earlier, the type of riding you do will dictate exactly what type of gear to bring along. If you haven't gone hunting on your ATV before, but would

Fig. 43 In addition to gear bags, other cargo-carrying accessories can really help to organize items to bring along for a trip

like to, talk with other hunters and get the details on specialized hunting products for ATVs. There are loads of aftermarket companies that make gear and accessories that can make hunting with an ATV more enjoyable. Camouflage covering kits, gun scabbards and racks, tinted lenses for goggles and gear bags are just some of the items that can enhance the hunting experience. If you are into long trail expeditions, 4x4 clubs will have tons of information on compact camping gear, winches, wet weather gear bags and accessories, etc. You can also obtain detailed maps of trails and forest areas from 4x4 clubs, which can be really useful for trail exploration. If playriding at the closest riding area is what you're into, your local motorcycle and ATV dealer will be able to tell you which area is closest to you. Most importantly, you can meet other riders an discuss important items to bring along with you to make your weekend fun and carefree.

RIDING SAFELY

▶ **See Figures 44 thru 51**

In recent years, the popularity of ATVs has skyrocketed. Along with the rise in popularity, ATV related injuries and deaths have risen substantially. Years ago, three-wheeled ATVs were completely banned because of the high injury and death rate involved with their use. Even now, four-wheeled ATVs are under the watchful eye of the government.

The problem is the perception of ATVs as being "easy to ride" and "safe to ride". This false perception of safety lures inexperienced riders into a false sense of security. Most of these naive riders usually hop onto a borrowed ATV without any safety equipment or training, and some end up getting seriously injured or even killed. A large portion of ATV related injuries and deaths happen to children. Often times young children end up riding full-sized ATVs, with absolutely no parental supervision or any safety gear, and are seriously injured. Please, if you have children, **educate** them about riding safely. Make sure they wear appropriate safety gear, and obey the warning labels on ATVs regarding age limits. The only way to ensure a future for ATV recreation and sports is RESPONSIBILITY. Don't let friends and children become another government statistic.

Whenever you ride, ALWAYS wear all of your safety gear. The minimum recommended gear would be a helmet, goggles, gloves, long sleeve shirt or jersey, pants, and boots that at least cover the ankle. No matter how good of a rider you

Fig. 46 Warning labels are attached to ATVs for a reason—your safety!

Fig. 44 No matter what kind of riding you do . . .

Fig. 47 ATVs are not meant to carry passengers

Fig. 45 . . . proper safety gear is essential for safety

Fig. 48 Again . . . NO PASSENGERS !!!

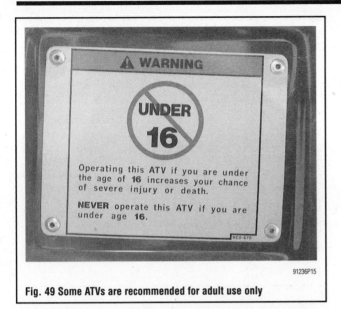

Fig. 49 Some ATVs are recommended for adult use only

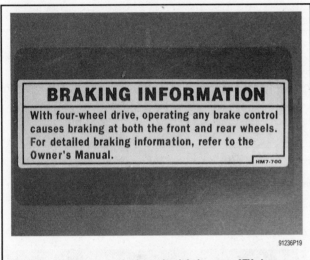

Fig. 50 In addition to standard warning labels, some ATVs have special characteristics that should be brought to the operator's attention

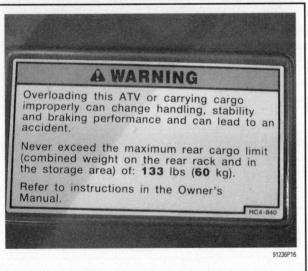

Fig. 51 Be careful not to exceed the capacity of cargo racks

may be, accidents WILL happen, and wearing proper gear will protect you if something were to happen.

Fighting Back Against Land Closure

Off highway recreation has recently come under attack. The rise in public awareness about pollution and the environment in recent years have caused the off-road community to come under close scrutiny. In a panic-stricken frenzy, environmental extremists are now pushing hard for land closures from the public to "conserve and protect" wilderness areas. With the powerful influence of the media, environmental extremists sometimes misrepresent the off-roading community as careless and destructive to the environment. This slanderous representation of the off-road community is used to gain support from the uninformed public about off-road recreation of all kinds. Such environmental extremists continue to threaten our sports, our recreation, and to some of us, our jobs. It all comes down to this: the off-road community has gained a bad reputation in the eyes of the general population.

There are ways we can fight for our rights to public land as United States citizens. You can help stop closures and unreasonable restrictions on public land. Rights organizations, such as the Blue Ribbon Coalition, fight for our rightful access to public land for off-road recreation of all kinds. The Blue Ribbon Coalition regularly travels to Washington D.C. to speak on behalf of the off-roading community, and uses the judicial system and legislative system to fight for your right to land access.

If you care about keeping your riding area open, join the Blue Ribbon Coalition, and become involved in standing up for your rights as an off-road recreationalist. The Blue Ribbon Coalition will also provide detailed information on how you can make a difference in your local riding area, as well as keep you informed on a national level. Motorcyclists, snowmobilers, ATV riders, four-wheel drive enthusiasts, outdoorsmen, watersport and equestrian recreationalists join the Blue Ribbon Coalition for the common cause of keeping our land from being locked up. These groups all join together and oppose misinformation campaigns and promote reasonable and responsible use of public resources.

There are also many rights groups that also operate on a local level which help fight land closures. By joining these clubs and coalitions, you will not only do your part to keep your riding area open, you may meet new riding partners, and make new friends. The main thing is to get involved. If we don't fight for our rights, they will eventually be taken away and there will soon be nowhere to ride. This is no joke—thousands of acres of public land all over America are **already** closed.

If you're a "regular" at your favorite riding area, Contact the local U.S. Forest Service district, and consider becoming a steward. You'll have to do a little work, (like pruning trees, picking up litter, etc.) but the local rangers will greatly appreciate your efforts, and you will help project a positive image for the ATV community. Sacrificing a small amount of your time to maintain your local riding area will ensure a place to ride in the future. Encourage your friends to join, and you'll have so much fun that you'll forget that it's a job.

Many of us have witnessed fellow ATV riders acting foolishly and carelessly at our favorite riding areas. When an extremist group is working hard to fight for a land closure, a few seconds of video tape or pictures of ATV riders riding carelessly, littering, or having complete disregard for the environment is all they need to sway a congressman or a news reporter. Unfortunately, the small handful of ATV riders who act like idiots are the people who are ruining the reputation of the off-road community. Do everyone a favor and DON'T BE ONE OF THOSE PEOPLE !!!!!

Showing respect for the environment and "treading lightly" are essential to project a positive image for the off-road community. By riding in a responsible and mature manner, we can ensure that the opposition will be unable to slander and misrepresent us all. So get off your duff and **get involved!!**

Tips For The Trail

▶ See Figure 52

Here's a list of tips and pointers for camping and riding your ATV. Remember—the rules and etiquette are for consideration and fun for all, not to make things miserable for ATV riders. Do your part and be a responsible ATV rider; set an example for others. This is the ONLY way that we can keep riding areas open.

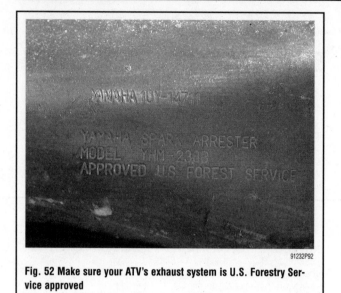

91232P92

Fig. 52 Make sure your ATV's exhaust system is U.S. Forestry Service approved

ON THE TRAIL

• Take an ATV safety course—they're usually free of charge when you purchase a new ATV.

• Don't be fooled into thinking that ATVs are "easy to ride". You can be seriously injured or even killed riding an ATV.

• Don't drink and ride. In certain areas, you can be convicted of a DUI the same as if you were driving an automobile.

• Always observe and obey the age limit tags and labels placed on ATVs. They are placed there for your own safety.

• Use your brain when you ride—always wear a helmet, full eye protection, boots and protective clothing whenever you ride.

• Always offer assistance to somebody in need of it. And always be prepared for medical emergencies with a good first aid kit.

• Make sure your exhaust system has an approved spark arrestor. To ride in most U.S. Forest areas, a spark arrestor is required.

• Regardless of whether you are heading off into the woods for a week on a hunting adventure, or checking out that hill on the other side of your camping area, LET SOMEONE KNOW WHERE YOU ARE GOING. Someone who knows where you're going and when you're planning on returning can suspect trouble if you don't return when planned, and can take action to locate you.

• Stay on designated road and trails or other areas open for use.

• When approaching an ATV that is coming up a hill, they have the right of way. If it's a steep long climb, pull off to the side, and let him pass you before proceeding. Stopping on a long uphill can cause you to lose traction and control.

• If you turn a corner or crest a hill, and there's another ATV (or other vehicle) coming straight toward you, turn to the right while slowing down. Your counterpart is supposed to do the same.

• When approaching riders on horseback, pull off to the side of the trail, stop your engine, and take off your helmet. Horses are easily spooked; by taking off your helmet and standing next to your ATV, a horse can recognize you as a human.

• Never blaze your own trail. Most off-road riding areas seriously frown on this, and doing so might get you permanently barred from any future visits.

• Always ride with one or more buddies. If an accident were to happen, another can assist or go for help.

AT THE CAMPSITE

• Use existing campsites whenever possible.

• Only build fires in designated areas using a strong fire ring to contain the coals. Remember that hot coals can easily ignite falling branches and leaves. A fire should never be left unattended and all coals should be thoroughly wetted once you are through with it.

• Pack out what you pack in.

• Let others enjoy the outdoors in peace. Don't play loud music. Maybe you like Molly Hatchet blasted at top volume, but that's not what others come to nature to experience. Be considerate to others, and be aware of your presence.

• Pick up any litter you find, even if it's not yours!

• Leave gates to trails and roads as you find them.

• Obtain a map of the area you wish to explore and determine which areas are open for use.

• Contact the land manager for area restrictions and if crossing private property, be sure to ask permission from the land owner.

• Remember, designated wilderness areas are reserved for the most primitive outdoor adventure.

• The TreadLightly! Guide to Responsible Off-Roading contains detailed and informative information when riding into the great outdoors. You can refer to this guide for additional tips and details.

TRANSPORTING YOUR ATV

Getting your ATV to your favorite riding area can become quite a hassle if you don't have a trailer or a truck. If you have a truck, chances are that your ATV will fit into the bed quite nicely. If you can't make your ATV fit into a truck bed, a trailer is your only alternative. (unless you consider selling your ATV for a smaller one!) If you have more than one ATV (you're bringing the whole family out) a trailer that can haul a quantity of ATVs would be your best choice.

Trucks

▶ See Figures 53, 54 and 55

The majority of ATVs will fit into the bed of a pickup truck. Getting your ATV into your pickup truck can be a daunting task though, especially if your ATV is a heavier four-wheel drive model.

Before you attempt to put your ATV into the back of your pick-up, get the tape measure. Start taking measurements of the ATV and the bed of your truck. If you have determined by measurement that the ATV will indeed fit, next you will have to get it up into the bed.

The best way (read: SAFEST) way to do this is with specialized loading ramps. The Ramp Master® makes an excellent lightweight aluminum ramp that will allow most all ATVs to be safely loaded into the bed of a truck. The ramps also come with safety cables that are adjustable, so they can be fitted to most any truck. Once the safety cables are in place, you can roll the ATV onto the

91237P26

Fig. 53 This lightweight aluminum loading ramp, made by The Ramp Master® allows an ATV to be easily loaded into a truck

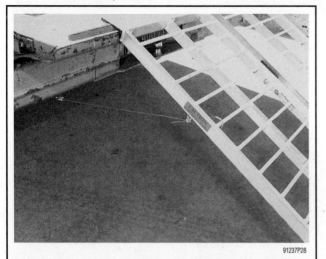

Fig. 54 These foldable ramps also feature adjustable safety cables that attach to the bumper and prevent the ramp from slipping

Fig. 56 This lightweight trailer, made by Load Rite® is perfect for hauling ATVs and snowmobiles

Fig. 55 Once the ramp is secured with the safety cables, the ATV can be safely rolled up the ramp and into the truck bed

Fig. 57 This trailer pivots on the axle, allowing loading without ramps. To prepare the trailer for loading, remove the lock on the pin . . .

truck bed. If you choose, you can actually ride the ATV onto the truck, but be EXTREMELY CAREFUL when doing this. Because of the sharp incline of the ramp, you could cause the ATV to "wheelie" and flip over on you. Unless you are an experienced rider, DO NOT ATTEMPT TO RIDE THE ATV UP THE RAMP. You can be seriously injured or even killed.

Your loading ramp should fit underneath your ATV. Once everything is in place, things like gear bags and other gear can be loaded around the edges. Make sure everything is secure, and use bungee cords or nets to keep things from falling out.

Trailers

▶ See Figures 56 thru 62

There are a large selection of trailers available that could be used for safely transporting your ATV, all different shapes, sizes and price tags. Anything from a small 4x8 trailer for one ATV to a specialized double axle two-level trailer for hauling eight ATVs is available. Now of course, the latter would require a truck or van equipped with specialized towing equipment. Load Rite® makes an excellent lightweight aluminum trailer that is well-suited for ATVs and snowmobiles, and is light enough to be towed by a car, if equipped with the proper towing equipment.

The many aspects regarding towing and trailers are complex; to discuss

Fig. 58 . . . pull out the pin, and tilt the trailer deck downwards . . .

91236P26

Fig. 59 . . . carefully position the ATV . . .

91236P27

Fig. 60 . . . slowly proceed up the deck surface . . .

Fig. 61 . . . until the deck starts to level out . . .

Fig. 62 . . . perfect! Install the deck retaining pin, and secure the ATV to the deck with tie-downs

everything in detail could easily consume this entire book. However, some basic issues are discussed here to help gain a better understanding about towing and trailers.

TOWING CAPACITY

Before you decide to buy a trailer to tow your ATV, there are several things to consider. The first is the towing ability of your vehicle.

The towing capacity of your vehicle (along with your wallet) will ultimately dictate the type of trailer and quantity of ATVs that you can safely tow.

Tow ratings on modern cars and trucks can range from "not recommended for towing" for a small car to 10,000 pounds for a large truck. Information regarding towing capacity can usually be found in the vehicle owner's manual.

If you are able to equip your car for towing, it would be safe to say that one ATV and a trailer would be about the most that small cars can handle.

HITCHES

Once that you have determined your vehicle is suitable for towing ATVs on a trailer, a hitch will have to be mounted to your vehicle. Tow hitches are available in different configurations and for a variety of uses. However, we'll look only at those popularly used for towing recreational trailers. We'll also discuss the accessories needed for their safe and proper use.

Hitch Classifications

Automotive manufacturers' tow rating requirements will often list certain types of hitches. Normally, the requirements will be for either "weight distributing," "frame mounted," or "deadweight". Also, manufacturers do not recommend towing with certain hitches. You can tow a lighter load with a heavier hitch, but you can't safely tow a heavier load with a lighter hitch. Before making a hitch selection, however, you need to know your total towed load. This can be calculated by adding the weight of your ATV(s), the trailer, and estimating the weight of your accessories and gear.

Four basic classifications are given to conventional hitches: Class I (up to 2000 pounds), Class II (2000 to 3500 pounds), Class III (3500 to 5000 pounds) and Class IV (5000 to 10,000 pounds). Hitch makers have also begun to use the designation of Class V to indicate a heavier duty hitches designed for those who do not want or need to use a weight distributing hitch. Most hitches are considered to be weight carrying (also called "deadweight"), which means they support all of the trailer tongue weight. These are the most popular hitches used to tow light or medium loads (most ATVs). Hitches are rated for Gross Trailer Weight (or GTW) and Tongue Weight (or TW). Many Class III and Class IV hitches have weight distributing capabilities, which means they can be used to distribute tongue weight to the front of the tow vehicle and to the trailer to relieve overweight conditions at the rear of the tow vehicle.

CLASS I HITCHES

The smallest hitch is a Class I, and is meant for loads less than 2000 pounds (most ATV trailers fall into this category). It comes in three basic types: a bumper mount (not really used these days), a bumper/frame mount (for most modern cars) and as part of a step bumper on a truck. Step bumpers found on trucks don't always have tow ratings, though. Even though a step bumper may have a hole for a hitch ball, the bumper itself may not be strong enough to handle a bouncing tongue load. Before you run off to the auto parts store to buy a hitch ball, be sure the bumper is properly constructed for towing and that it has a tow rating stamped into the metal. Some automotive and aftermarket manufacturers offer replacement step bumpers with high tow ratings.

CLASS II HITCHES

Class II hitches are frame-mounted, which means they connect to the frame or structural crossmembers of the vehicle, not to the bumper. They are rated to tow up to 3500 pounds. Some vehicles may need extra bracing installed to the chassis to help support this type of hitch. On a unibody vehicle, for example, the hitch is bolted to sheetmetal, rather than to a heavy gauge, steel frame. Without extra support, the bolts can pull away from the sheetmetal. Factory installed hitches usually have an extra metal plate for support when the tow package is ordered, as do kits from the better hitch manufacturers.

There are a few variations regarding Class II hitches. One has a ball mount

permanently built into the hitch assembly. Some use a receiver, which has a removable ball mount that fits into a square hole. Receiver hitches come in two ball mount sizes. On a receiver hitch, the ball mount is the shank that holds the hitch ball and fits into the receiver. This ball mount shank can be either 1 5/8 or 2 inches square. The smaller shank size is used with a mini hitch, which has a tow rating limited to 3500 pounds. The smaller mini hitch allows better ground clearance and is more easily hidden under the vehicle than a full size hitch.

CLASS III AND IV HITCHES

Class III (up to 5000 pounds) and Class IV (up to 10.000 pounds) hitches are necessary for heavy duty towing. This is a weight category for which you will probably need a specially equipped truck and a frame mounted, receiver hitch. Also, in this weight range you'll be getting into very heavy tongue weights, which can drastically affect the way your vehicle handles. A 500 pound tongue weight may not sound like a lot, but that weight takes on a different perspective when it's pushing down on a hitch ball that might be six feet behind the rear axle. This creates a six foot long lever that lifts the front steering wheels of the tow vehicle, drops the front of the trailer and results in sloppy steering, bounce, and sway at the back of the vehicle and at the trailer. Suspension aids may help, but the most successful way to offset this leverage action is with the use of a weight distributing hitch.

CLASS V HITCHES

These are large, heavy gauge steel hitches designed for large trucks high tow ratings. Their primary purpose is to allow towing without having to use a weight distributing hitch. Class V hitches are often referred to as "dead weight hitches."

Weight Distributing Systems

A weight distributing system spreads tongue weight over the front and rear axles of the tow vehicle and the trailer axle(s). With a 500 pound tongue weight, for example, The weight can be redistributed so that 200 pounds of that weight is on the front axle, 200 on the rear axle and 100 on the trailer axle(s). The result is a stable, controllable tow vehicle and trailer.

The weight distributing system consists of a frame mounted platform and spring bars (also called equalizing bars) that attach to a special ball mount assembly and to the trailer frame. A special ball mount is needed because it mates with the receiver and has sockets into which the spring bars are inserted. The weight distributing ball mount is also adjustable. It is especially important to set the hitch ball angle and to raise or lower the hitch ball to properly set spring bar the height. Two spring bars are usually used on each side of the ball mount. The spring bars have chains connected at the trailer end, which attach to brackets on the trailer tongue. The length of the chains actually distribute the tongue weight as they are raised or lowered to put tension on the spring bars.

Hooking and unhooking the system only takes a couple of minutes, but some don't like to have to deal with the extra complication of hooking up a weight distributing system. A trailer dealer will be able to discuss with you at length the details of weight distributing systems.

TONGUE WEIGHT

▶ See Figure 63

Tongue weight is defined as the weight from the trailer that is applied to the hitch ball. This can vary considerably, depending on the number of ATVs and how the trailer is loaded. Excessive tongue weight will cause the rear of the tow vehicle to sag considerably, and handling will be adversely affected. Tongue weight can be too light also, affecting handling.

When you are buying a trailer, discuss with the salesman what you plan to tow, and what you're going to tow it with. This should help to answer most of your questions about the proper tongue weight for your vehicle.

HITCH BALLS

Hitch balls comes in three basic sizes: 7/8 inches (up to 2000 pounds; sometimes more), 2 inches (up to 6000 pounds) and 2 5/16 inches (up to 10,000 pounds or more). Most importantly, be sure the ball is the proper size for the trailer. A ball that is too small will cause the coupler to bounce loose. Some hitch balls have extended bases and shanks for special purposes. The base and shank of a hitch ball can have significant effects on weight rating. Also, some shanks may be slightly undersize or oversize. On step bumper

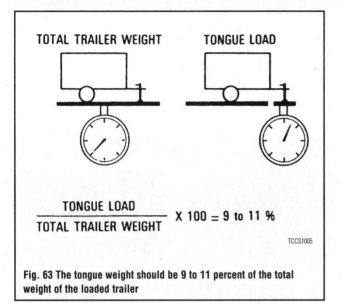

TONGUE LOAD / TOTAL TRAILER WEIGHT × 100 = 9 to 11 %

TCCS1005

Fig. 63 The tongue weight should be 9 to 11 percent of the total weight of the loaded trailer

hitches especially, be sure the shank (in American measurements) conforms to the hole (which may be in a metric equivalent, especially on some foreign trucks).

A frequently overlooked requirement for hitch balls is the torque recommendation for the mounting nut. The general rule of thumb for proper torque is 85 ft. lbs. (116 Nm) for Class I, 105 ft. lbs. (143 Nm) for Class II, 235 ft. lbs. (320 Nm) for Class III and 300 ft. lbs. (408 Nm) for Class IV.

WIRING A TRAILER TO YOUR VEHICLE

By law, a trailer must have running lights (taillights and/or marker lights), turn signals and brake lights. The electrical system of the tow vehicle must be tapped into to provide power and signals to the trailer lights. But other laws may apply based on where and what you will be towing. Be sure to check with the local authorities for other requirements in your area.

Connectors

Most small trailers use a four-way connector. One pin in the connector transfers power to the running lights, two others power the turn signals and brake lights. The fourth pin is for ground. The wiring on these flat, four way plugs is usually based on a standard color code. Brown is for taillights and side marker lights. Yellow is for the left turn signal and brake light. Green is for the right turn signal and brake light. White is for ground. Round, four way plugs don't always have a consistent color code, so you may have to figure it out by using a troubleshooting light.

A trailer electrical connector is often included when you buy a new vehicle with a "Towing Package." However, a connector can easily be fitted to most any tow vehicle for operating the trailer lights.

Adapters

If your vehicle does not have a towing package, an adapter can be used to tap into the vehicles wiring to provide the necessary signals to a trailer. Most trailer dealers and hitch installation centers will carry a line of easily installed, in-line adapters. These adapters typically consist of a 3 ended wiring harness, two ends of which attach to the male and female sides of your tow vehicle's tail light wiring. The third end of the harness is simply a breakout of those tail light wires and is connected to the trailer. Installation is usually a simply matter of locating the harness under the rear of your tow vehicle, carefully undoing the factory connector, then installing the adapter to either end of the factory harness. Just be sure that you use wire ties to safely tuck the adapter out of harm's way, while still leaving a sufficient amount of free wire so that it can connect to the trailer harness. If no adapter kit is available for your tow vehicle, you might have to solder or modify the wiring harness of your vehicle. If you aren't real savvy with electrical items, it may be better to have a dealer or hitch installation center modify your harness for you.

Flashers

The standard flasher that comes with most vehicles is not designed to operate more than the vehicle's lights, so it can overload when a trailer electrical system is connected to the vehicle. This overloading causes the tow vehicle and trailer turn signals to flash rapidly and faintly. Additionally, the dashboard turn signal indicators will also flash quickly and faintly to alert you that a stronger flasher is needed.

Changing to a heavy-duty flasher will usually solve this problem. Be sure you get the right heavy-duty replacement by reading the packaging carefully to make sure it is designed for trailering applications. Many foreign vehicles come with heavy duty flashers.

The flasher is usually located under the dashboard. On most new vehicles, it is connected to the fuse box and simply pulls out. If you have trouble finding it, check your owner's manual or even the cover of the fuse box itself (as most fuse boxes are labeled these days). You might also want to refer to a Chilton Total Car Care manual for your model.

Securing Your ATV For Transport

▶ **See Figures 64 thru 69**

Whether you are transporting your ATV in a truck or on a trailer, it is equally important to secure it properly. The best way to do this is with specialized ATV

91236P62

Fig. 64 An example of an ATV properly secured to a trailer

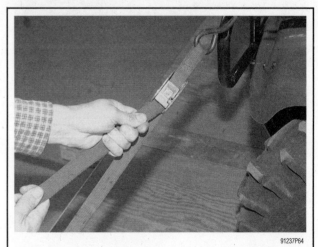

91237P64

Fig. 65 Some motorcycle/ATV tie-downs have a cam mechanism that allows a one-way action, allowing the suspension to be compressed by simply pulling on the strap

and motorcycle tie-downs. ATV and motorcycle tie-downs are designed to allow the compression of the suspension to prevent the ATV from bouncing around on the trailer or in the back of a truck. Using other means of securing the ATV (rope, bungee cords, etc.) is a sure way to get yourself in serious trouble.

To safely secure an ATV, a minimum of four tie-downs should be used; one on each corner. The racks on utility-type ATVs are usually a good place to hook the tie-downs. If your ATV is a sport-type and does not have racks, the handlebars and the rear grab bar are the best places to hook the tie-downs. Make sure

the suspension is compressed as far as possible when the tie-downs are tightened. if not, the suspension of the ATV could compress when you hit a large bump or dip in the road, and the tie-down may come unhooked. To keep this from happening, you can use duct tape to wrap around the ends of the hooks after they are attached. Or, if your tie-downs are long enough, you can tie the excess of the strap around the hook to prevent it from coming off. It is VERY important to fully compress the suspension to keep slack from developing during towing.

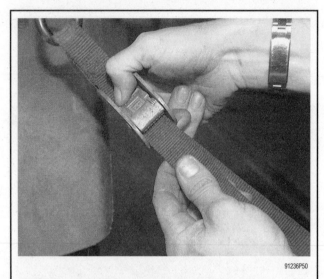

Fig. 66 To release this tie-down, press the lever on the cam

Fig. 68 For added safety, a thin strip of duct tape can be used on each hook to prevent it from coming off the ATV during transport

Fig. 67 An ATV is properly secured when the suspension is compressed evenly on all four corners. If necessary have an assistant push down on the front and rear of the ATV to tighten the tie-downs

Fig. 69 The remainder of the tie-down should be tied as an added safety measure

7

ACCESSORIZING YOUR ATV

ACCESSORIZING YOUR ATV

♦ See Figures 1, 2, 3 and 4

This section is designed to help you choose the proper accessories to help your ATV better suit your riding needs. The goal here is familiarize you with what options are available when it comes to buying accessories and with what features you should look for in them.

When looking at modifying your ATV with accessories, you have to determine your goals. Are you trying to make your ATV a little more versatile? Are

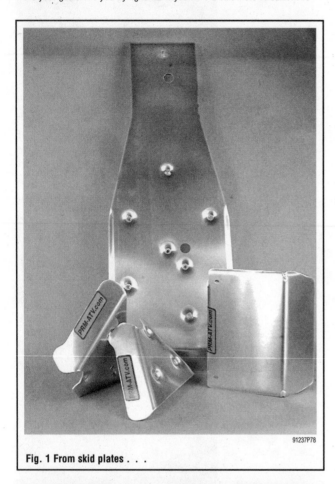

Fig. 1 From skid plates . . .

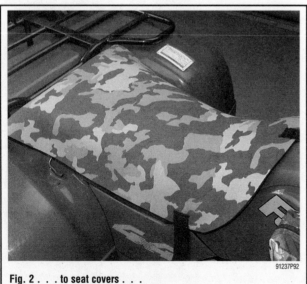

Fig. 2 . . . to seat covers . . .

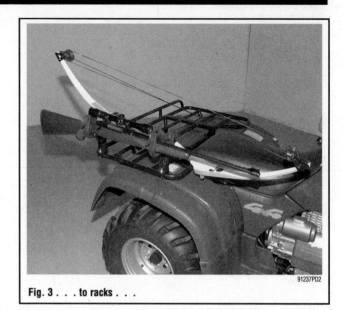

Fig. 3 . . . to racks . . .

Fig. 4 . . . to drink holders and tank bags, there is an endless supply of accessories available to customize your ATV

you looking into making your ATV go faster? Looking for ways to make maintenance easier? Or maybe just a few small accessories to individualize your ATV? Whatever your specific goals are, this section should help you learn what to look for when choosing accessories.

To really get a good idea of the selection of accessories available for your ATV, pick up a couple copies of ATV magazines or catalogs. Page through them, and you'll be amazed; tons of accessories just waiting to be bolted to your ATV. You will find skidplates, axles, wheels, tires, winches, racks, shocks, bags, exhaust systems, air filters, and tons of other neon or camouflage colored doo-dads.

Down to business: Make a list of what you want your ATV to do. Okay, now that you have that, make a list of possible accessories that will help you achieve your goals. Decide if any of the accessories may degrade other aspects of your riding that you aren't willing to sacrifice and cross them off the list.

The nice thing about ATVs and the aftermarket is that you can get almost anything you want. Take your list to your dealer, the local ATV and motorcycle shop or call one of the catalog houses. They will help you with obtaining the stuff you want. Keep in mind that the manufactures often have accessories for your ATV that fit and work as the factory intended. You don't have to hit the aftermarket for everything!

What types of accessories may I want on my ATV? Let's look at some of the different types of riders and what they may outfit their ATV with.

• The hunter/camper might want a camouflage cover for the entire ATV, specialized racks for carrying deer, large gear bags for carrying hunting and camping gear, a rifle/bow rack or scabbard, a winch, and skid plates.

• The sport rider might look for high-performance parts, like air filters, exhaust systems, suspension components, heavy-duty bumpers, nerf bars, and aluminum wheels.

• The utility/farmer would look for things like rack extensions, winches, plows, fender extensions, and small trailers.

There are many different needs and even more solutions. Ask the guys at your local ATV shop what they think will best suit your needs. They may show you that the manufacturer already makes something that you want. You can also call the catalog houses, as they answer questions all day long and can help point out your choices.

We have chosen examples of accessories from some of the industries known leaders (and in some cases from lesser known but just as high quality manufacturers), and we would like to thank the manufacturers again for their help with the production of this section. That is not to say the brands pictured here are your only options. However it is to say that they are VERY GOOD examples of the high quality accessories that are available, and as such are excellent standards for comparison with the accessories you look at when deciding on a purchase.

Air Filters

HOW TO SELECT

▶ **See Figures 5 thru 10**

Purchasing an aftermarket air filter may not be one of your top priorities if you aren't really into hot-rodding your engine. But since the air filter on an ATV is one of the most continually maintained items, they can wear out quickly from constant washing.

If you are headed to the dealer for a new air filter, you might be shocked at the price for it when you get there. OEM parts are usually pretty costly to replace. This is where the aftermarket air filter comes in.

➡ **Avoid using air filters which require removal of the air box. If you operate the ATV in wet weather, water can easily be ingested into the engine. Open air filters are recommended for racing only.**

There are a handful of aftermarket companies that offer replacement air filters for ATVs. K&N® makes one of the most reputable and high quality aftermarket air filters around. K&N® uses a cotton gauze supported in a mesh screen to provide superior performance to foam type air filters.

One of the best things about a K&N® filter is how easy it is to clean and re-oil. Simply wash the filter in the special K&N® air filter cleaner, let the filter dry

Fig. 6 Foam filters can become clogged with dirt quickly, robbing the engine of horsepower

Fig. 7 K&N's Power Kit for ATVs comes with everything you need for installation and maintenance

Fig. 5 The K&N filter (left) offers more airflow than the stock unit

Fig. 8 Although K&N filters require special cleaner and oil, these products allow for easier maintenance

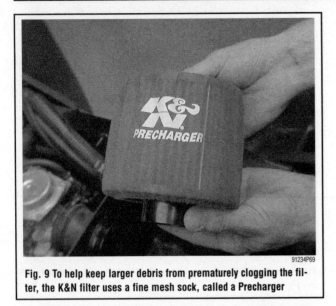

Fig. 9 To help keep larger debris from prematurely clogging the filter, the K&N filter uses a fine mesh sock, called a Precharger

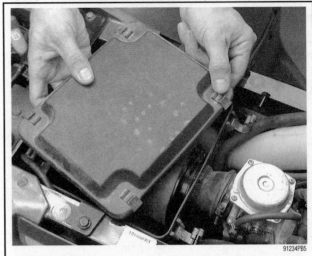

Fig. 11 To install the K&N filter, remove the air box lid, and remove the stock filter . . .

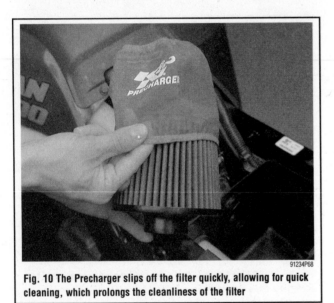

Fig. 10 The Precharger slips off the filter quickly, allowing for quick cleaning, which prolongs the cleanliness of the filter

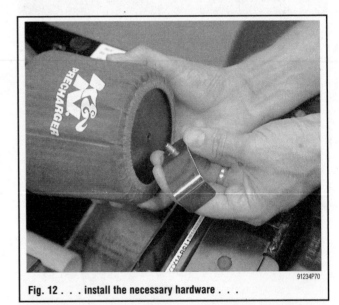

Fig. 12 . . . install the necessary hardware . . .

(which may take up to 24 hours), and apply the K&N oil to the filter. The filter needs very little oil to work properly, so a small amount is all that is required which will allow the oil to wick through the cotton gauze. Once the filter element is oiled, let it sit for a while (preferably 24 hours) to allow for the oil to soak in evenly. Before installing the element, check for any light spots indicate a dry area, and should be touched up with a small amount of oil. Excessive oil in the element will actually restrict air flow, and will drip oil inside the air box.

K&N® air filters offer two advantages over stock air filters. First, the cotton gauze is more effective at trapping fine dirt particles than a foam filter. This will make your engine last longer, as well as keep the passages in your carburetor from getting clogged, which can cause major engine problems. Second, the engine will be able to breathe easier, which will improve the output of your engine.

K&N® now offers "Power Kits" which include an air filter, cleaner, oil, and a kit to recalibrate the settings on your carburetor. Using the carburetor recalibration kit (which consists of a needle and larger jets) in conjunction with the air filter will provide a significant increase in overall engine performance.

HOW TO INSTALL

♦ See Figures 11, 12 and 13

Installing an aftermarket air filter on your ATV is (in most cases) just like removing and installing the original one on your ATV. Usually, air filters are

Fig. 13 . . . and clamp the filter in place. The filter is a direct replacement of the stock filter

accessed by removing the seat, and unscrewing or removing clips that hold air box lid in place. Once the stock air filter is removed, thoroughly clean the air box. Be careful not to get any dirt or debris in the carburetor inlet. Once the air box is clean, install the new aftermarket filter element. Sometimes air filters come pre-oiled and ready to go, and in some cases, oiling the filter before installation is necessary. Make sure that the filter lip is in place around the car- buretor inlet, and clamp it in place. Install the air box lid, followed by the seat. All done!! Next time you ride, you'll probably notice a little more power from your engine.

CLEANING

▶ **See Figures 14, 15, 16 and 17**

1. Carefully remove the filter element from the air box.
2. After the filter is removed, tap the element to dislodge any large chunks of embedded dirt. A soft bristle brush can also be used.

➡**If complete cleaning of the element is not practical at this time, re-oil the element and place it back into service.**

3. Spray K&N air filter cleaner liberally onto the entire element, then let soak for 10 minutes.

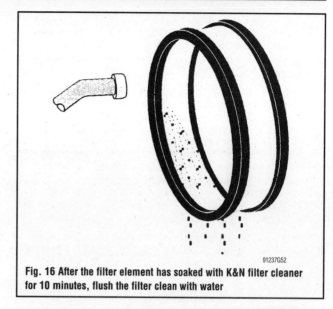

Fig. 16 After the filter element has soaked with K&N filter cleaner for 10 minutes, flush the filter clean with water

Fig. 14 A paint brush makes a good tool for cleaning loose dirt and debris before cleaning

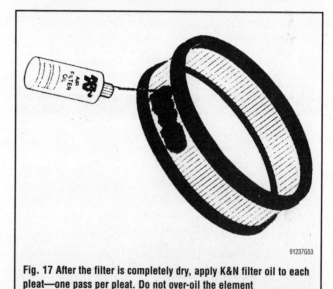

Fig. 17 After the filter is completely dry, apply K&N filter oil to each pleat—one pass per pleat. Do not over-oil the element

> ❊❊ **WARNING**
>
> **Using any other method of cleaning your K&N filter such as using gasoline, parts cleaning solvents, strong detergents, or steam cleaning can cause permanent damage.**

4. After the filter element has soaked with cleaner for 10 minutes, rinse it thoroughly with low pressure water. Always flush the element from the inside outward. This helps remove the dirt, instead of drive it into the filter.

> ❊❊ **WARNING**
>
> **Do NOT use compressed air, heat dryers, or open flame to dry the filter element. Excess heat will shrink the cotton gauze.**

5. Once the filter element has been cleaned, allow it to dry naturally. This can take up to 24 hours, depending on the ambient temperature and humidity.

> ❊❊ **WARNING**
>
> **Never use a K&N air filter without oil. (The filter will not stop the dirt without the oil.)**

Fig. 15 After cleaning any loose dirt, spray the entire filter element with K&N filter oil

6. Before oiling the freshly cleaned filter element, make certain that the filter is completely dry. If the filter element is wet, the water in the gauze will not allow the oil to penetrate.

✳✳ WARNING

Use only K&N formulated air filter oil. K&N air filter oil is a compound of mineral and animal oil, with red dye added to show where the oil is applied on a clean filter element. NEVER USE automatic transmission fluid, diesel fuel, motor oil, WD-40, or other light weight oils on your K&N filter.

7. Apply K&N filter oil to the element. If using spray K&N air filter oil, lightly spray oil down into each pleat, making one pass per pleat. Squeeze bottle application is similar—squeezing one pass of oil into each pleat. DO NOT APPLY TOO MUCH OIL! Applying too much oil is not only unnecessary, but the filter will drip oil. Once the filter is oiled, let it sit for at least 20 minutes.

➡**If possible, let the filter sit overnight on a paper towel. This will allow the filter oil to completely permeate the element, providing the best filtration. If the filter was slightly over-oiled, the paper towel will help contain any oil run-off.**

8. If there are still white spots on the filter element, apply oil as necessary to fill the areas.

9. Once the filter element is cleaned and oiled, it can be installed. Make sure the element seats properly in the filter case. Tighten all the nuts, bolts, screws or clips to factory specifications.

10. Affix the "Do Not Discard" sticker to the filter case or lid (included with every K&N replacement element). Make sure you put the sticker in a highly visible place to alert your mechanic that the filter element is not disposable.

Skid Plates

HOW TO SELECT

▶ **See Figures 18 thru 24**

Most ATVs come equipped from the manufacturer with skid plates. However, the stock skid plates can get beat up quickly if you do a lot of riding in rocky areas, or

Fig. 19 The stock skid plates offer very little protection, and leave the frame exposed to the elements

Fig. 20 With custom skid plates, the underside of this ATV is fully protected from rocks and debris

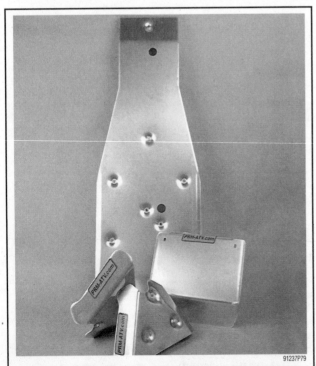

Fig. 18 Skid plates offer substantial protection to the underside of an ATV, and add a trick, customized appearance

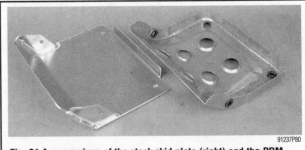

Fig. 21 A comparison of the stock skid plate (right) and the PRM unit

may be just plain wimpy, which is an excellent excuse to replace them with some trick aluminum units. Aftermarket manufacturers quickly came up with skid plates that were stronger and offered more protection than their OEM counterparts.

If you're in the market for skid plates, there are some important features to be considered. Things like holes for the drain plugs are nice touches, but most importantly, look for smooth, high quality welds, thick gauge aluminum, and factory mounting points. Unless, of course, the idea of drilling holes in your frame

Fig. 22 The PRM skid plate (top) is twice as thick as the stock unit

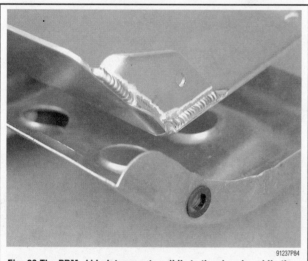

Fig. 23 The PRM skid plate mounts solidly to the chassis, while the stock unit is rubber mounted

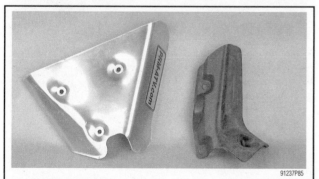

Fig. 24 The stock plastic A-arm plate (right) is a far cry from the heft of the PRM plate (left)

doesn't bother you. Chances are, if you have to break out the drill, the skid plates aren't of high quality. As the old saying goes, "you get what you pay for."

One company that we found that makes ultra-beefy skid plates is PRM Products. PRM makes skid plates for a large variety of ATVs and also makes lightweight bumpers and grab bars. PRM outfitted our Honda Foreman 400 4x4 with aluminum A-arm skid plates, a front bumper skid plate, and an underside chassis plate.

As you can see from the photos, the stock skid plates don't offer close to the same protection as the PRM set. The extra protection from these skid plates will help ensure full protection of the underside of an ATV, preventing such disasters as punching a hole in the engine crankcase. (Replacing an engine case can cost you substantially.) The first time you skid over a big rock or tree stump, the skid plates pay for themselves, since they protect the crankcase, the frame, and the suspension from dings and scratches. Plus, they look really trick!

HOW TO INSTALL

▶ **See Figures 25 thru 43**

To install our PRM skid plates, the stock ones need to first be removed. To make the whole removal and installation process a lot easier, we stood our ATV on its back wheels. Be sure to check with your owner's manual if this can be done with your particular ATV. On some models, the battery may have to be removed in order to do this. If the battery in your ATV is not a sealed type and you stand your ATV on end, acid could leak from the battery, causing damage to the plastic and paint on your ATV.

Once the ATV is on end, removal of the stock skid plates is basic; unbolt them from the chassis and set them aside. Next, trial fit the individual pieces, making sure that the holes align. It took us a while to figure out how everything bolted together, since the A-arm plates are shaped so much differently than the stock pieces. Once we had everything sorted out, we started bolting them in place.

The PRM skid plates use some of the stock mounting locations, as well as using backing plates to sandwich the skid plate onto the chassis. The benefits are twofold; the skid plate pieces are better secured to the ATV, and no drilling or cutting to ATV itself is required for mounting. This is a real advantage, because if you decide to sell your ATV someday, The skid plates can be removed and be replaced with the stock pieces, and everything will be as stock as the day it rolled off the showroom floor.

Fig. 25 Standing the ATV on end made installing the skid plates much easier

Fig. 26 Once the ATV was on end, we removed the A-arm plates . . .

Fig. 29 Before we used the stock skid plate for a frisbee, these rubber grommets had to be removed . . .

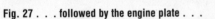

Fig. 27 . . . followed by the engine plate . . .

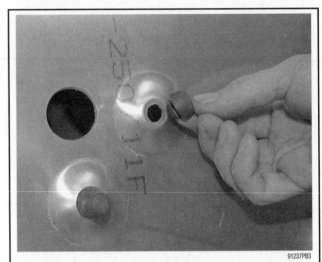

Fig. 30 . . . and installed on the new skid plate. The grommets keep the skid plate from rubbing against the engine case

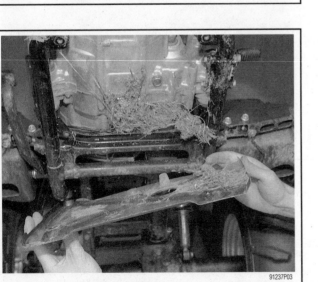

Fig. 28 . . . which had a lot of dirt and brush behind it (This is one small disadvantage of skid plates)

Fig. 31 It took a while to figure out exactly how the A-arm plates mounted, since they are shaped differently than the stock units

Fig. 32 These small triangular plates are used to secure the plate to the A-arm without drilling or welding

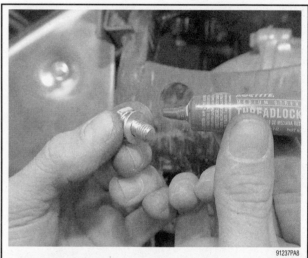

Fig. 35 After the A-arm plates were installed, the front plate was up next. It attached in the same places as the stock unit, but without the rubber grommets

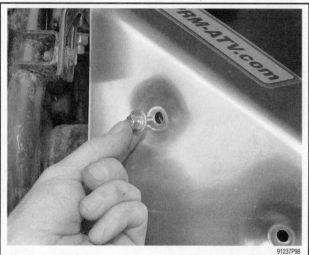

Fig. 33 Once the position of the arms was determined, the fasteners were installed . . .

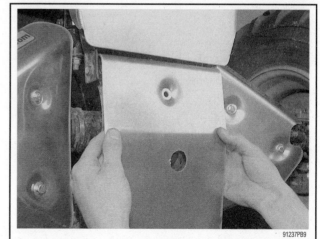

Fig. 36 It is a good idea to use locking compound on the skid plate fasteners to keep things secure

Fig. 34 . . . and tightened securely

Fig. 37 The main plate was the final piece to be installed. As with the A-arm plates, it took a while to figure out all of the mounting points

Fig. 38 This trick little bracket fits perfectly in the frame to provide an additional mounting point for the main plate . . .

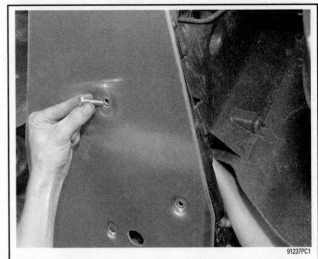

Fig. 41 Holding the plates in position while threading the bolts was a little bit tricky

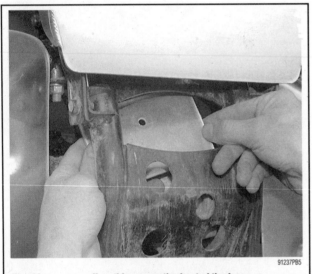

Fig. 39 . . . as well as this one on the front of the frame . . .

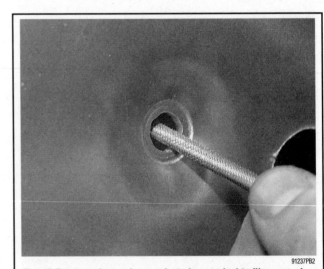

Fig. 42 Due to variances in manufacturing, we had to file some of the mounting holes on the plates to make everything align right

Fig. 40 . . . and another at the rear of the frame, near the engine

Fig. 43 With everything in place, our ATV looks ready for some serious rock crawling action

There was a minor glitch in our otherwise basic bolt-on installation though. Due to variations in the manufacturing of the skid plates, some minor filing of the mounting holes was required to get things to align perfectly. A small "rat tail" file worked perfectly to help size up the mounting holes.

Also, a couple drops of medium strength thread locking compound on the mounting bolts isn't a bad idea, either. If a skid plate were to come lose while blazing down the trail, you might not even notice it coming off. It might be hours before you or one of your riding buddies notice your ultra-trick skid plate is gone, and it might be a long time back-tracking to find it.

Once you have everything in place, you are ready to head out for a ride, and find the roughest, rockiest trail you can find. Happy trail bashing!!

Winches

HOW TO SELECT

▶ **See Figures 44 and 45**

Years ago, nobody really thought of putting a winch on an ATV. However, the adaptation of four-wheel drive to ATVs introduced a new genre. Suddenly, the ATV was no longer only a fun, recreation toy, but a heavy-duty workhorse capable of handling the kind of jobs that are normally reserved for 4x4 trucks.

Fig. 44 Warn® winch kits come with everything you'll need for an easy installation

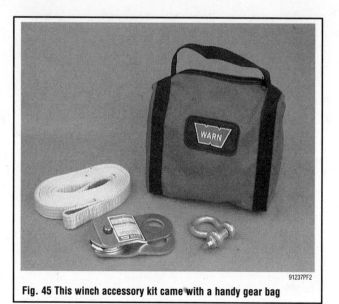

Fig. 45 This winch accessory kit came with a handy gear bag

For serious trail exploration and utility work, a winch is an indispensable accessory. A winch can help to pull your ATV out of a deep, mud-soaked trench, move a big log or a rock, or even pull a buddy up a hill. At some riding areas, you might have to leave your ATV for dead if you aren't equipped with a winch to pull you out of trouble.

When it comes to winches, Warn® is the industry leader. When 4x4 utility ATVs were gaining popularity, Warn® was one of the first manufacturers to produce winches specifically for ATV use. Regular automotive winches can be adapted for use on ATVs, but the extra weight and complication of fabricating mounting brackets is usually more hassle than it is worth. Warn® makes winch kits for just about every ATV made today, even two-wheel drive models. The majority of these kits are "bolt on" and do not require any welding or major fabrication to install.

HOW TO INSTALL

▶ **See Figures 46 thru 73**

Warn® supplied us with an A2000 winch, accessory kit, and mounting hardware for our Honda Foreman 4x4. The mounting hardware made things easy, since there wasn't any welding necessary. There was still some lengthy (but fairly easy) work involved, though.

Installing a winch can be somewhat of a time-consuming project. In the case of our particular ATV, removing the front accessory rack and fender assembly was required. The reason for this is because the winch is mounted on the frame behind the front bumper. For installation, this was a pain, but in the long run, having the winch behind the bumper is a better mounting area, since it is out of harm's way, and protected by the bumper.

This procedure is for our Honda Foreman 400 4x4, but will give you the idea of what is involved in mounting a winch to an ATV.

Our winch installation kit included the following items:
- Warn® A2000 winch
- Winch mounting plate
- Fairlead mounting plate
- Fairlead
- Power solenoid
- All necessary wiring
- Winch control switch
- Cable hook
- Snatch block
- Tow strap
- Shackle
- Accessory carrying case
- All necessary fasteners
- Instruction and Operator's manual

As you can see, Warn® supplies literally everything that's required for installation, except for the tools!

Let's look at the details regarding our winch installation:

1. After confirming that all the required parts and hardware were included in our kit, We started things off by preparing our ATV for the installation process. This included removing the seat, the front cargo rack, and the entire front fender assembly. This was a simple task, but was a little intimidating, since it seemed as though we were ripping the ATV apart!

2. Once we stripped everything away that was required for installation of the winch, we got down to business. The first thing we did was attach the winch onto the mounting plate. We decided to use a little bit of thread locking compound on the bolts, as an added precaution. Then we used a torque wrench and tightened the bolts to 12 ft. lbs. (16 Nm) as required.

3. Once the mounting plate was attached to the winch, the assembly was ready to be attached to the frame. In our installation, four "U" bolts are used to secure the plate to the frame. Things were starting to look good at this point.

4. Now that the winch was secured to the frame, attaching the fairlead to the front bumper was next. First we attached the mounting strip to the bumper (using the same type of U-bolts that attached the winch mounting plate) and then bolted the fairlead to the bracket.

5. Now that all the fun work was done, installing the electrical wiring was next in line. The Warn® winch uses a solenoid as a safety feature, which disconnects the winch from the battery when the key is not in the ignition switch. We had to find a suitable location for the solenoid, which happened, in our case, to be underneath the seat. We customized the installation of the solenoid a bit, to avoid having to perform yoga to get to the mounting bolts, and also to provide a

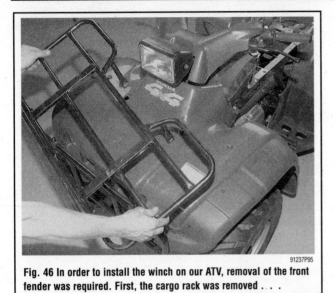

Fig. 46 In order to install the winch on our ATV, removal of the front fender was required. First, the cargo rack was removed . . .

Fig. 47 . . . then the gas tank cover . . .

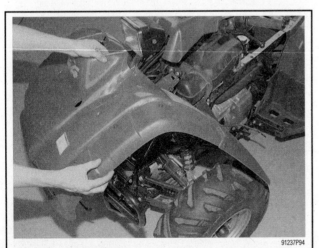

Fig. 48 . . . and finally, the fender itself. Although it may look complicated, it actually was simple, and just required removing a few fasteners

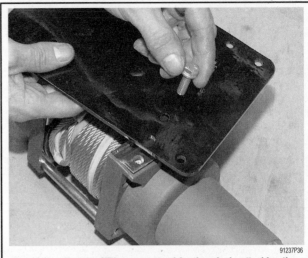

Fig. 49 Now that the ATV was prepared for the winch, attaching the mounting plate to the winch was next on the list

Fig. 50 The bolts had to be tightened before the winch and mounting plate were attached to the frame

Fig. 51 The winch and mounting plate are attached to the frame with U-bolts

Fig. 52 Once the winch and mounting plate were attached to the frame, we used a drop of green threadlocking compound on the bolt threads to keep them from loosening

Fig. 53 The winch attached securely to the frame

Fig. 54 The mounting plate for the fairlead (cable guide) attaches to the frame in the same manner as the winch mounting plate

Fig. 55 With the hardware installed, the electrical connections were next. We decided to mount the solenoid underneath the seat, safe from the elements

Fig. 56 We decided to customize the mounting of the solenoid, to make access to the mounting bolts easier to access

Fig. 57 This left some small holes, so some silicone was used to seal things up

Fig. 58 The solenoid is securely mounted, and out of the way

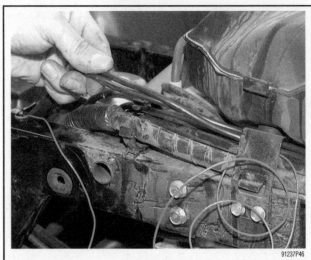

Fig. 61 We used the existing wiring retainers for routing the power wires to the front of the ATV

Fig. 59 Now that the solenoid was mounted, routing and connecting the wires was next

Fig. 62 The solenoid with all of the connections in place. Note the boots covering the connections; they help keep the terminals from corroding

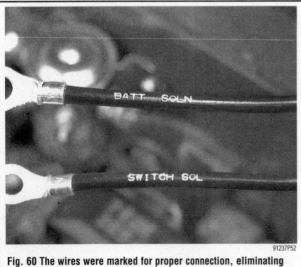

Fig. 60 The wires were marked for proper connection, eliminating any confusion. This made connecting the wires a piece of cake

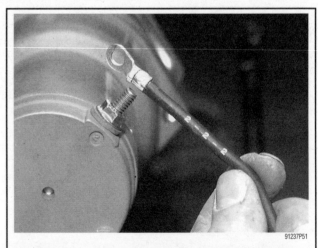

Fig. 63 With the wiring completed at the rear of the ATV, connecting the wires up front was next. Note the number "2" on the wire, and the winch also marked "2"

Fig. 64 Just like the connections on the solenoid, rubber boots on the winch connections help prevent corrosion

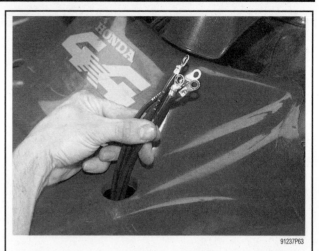

Fig. 67 The final task was connecting and mounting the winch control switch. To avoid drilling holes in the fender, we routed the wires through the rack mount opening

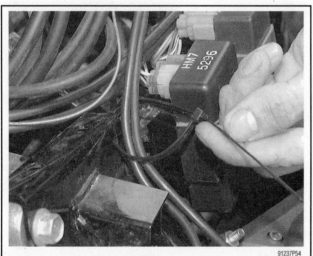

Fig. 65 To keep the wires from chafing, we used nylon tie-wraps to hold the power lines to the winch

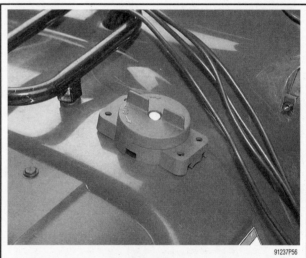

Fig. 68 The control switch can be mounted on the cargo rack, or on the fender. Mounting the switch on the fender required drilling . . .

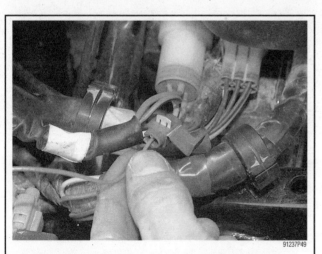

Fig. 66 A special connector (supplied with the kit) was used to splice into the ignition switch. This wire supplies voltage to the solenoid when the key is in the ON position

Fig. 69 . . . so we decided to mount it on the cargo rack instead

Fig. 70 Before mounting the switch, the wires must be connected. Note the markings on the wires and the switch to ensure proper connection

Fig. 72 With everything installed, the cable was ran through the fairlead, and the hook was attached

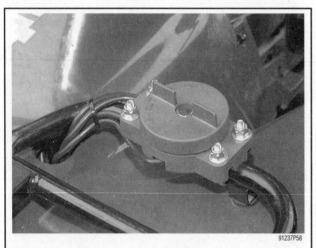

Fig. 71 The finished product. Like the winch and fairlead plates, the switch uses U-bolts for attachment. Note the tie-wrap and discrete wire routing

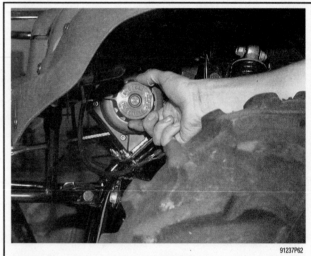

Fig. 73 The spool can be unwound manually by reaching through the fender and turning the knob

sturdy means of attaching the solenoid to the plastic. This involved making a couple of holes in the plastic, but they were easily sealed with silicone.

6. Once the solenoid was in place, running the wires was next. The wires are marked for easy installation, so we sorted them out, and started running the wires along the chassis from the battery to the winch. We followed the route of the factory wiring harness, and threaded the wires in place. We also used some nylon tie-wraps (included with the kit) to secure the wires to the chassis. The installation manual included an easy-to-read diagram for proper connection of the wires.

✳✳ WARNING

When routing the power wires, make sure route them in a manner so they do not come in contact with any moving parts, like the front springs or steering head. If a power wire were to become pinched, or wear through the plastic covering to the bare metal strands, an short could occur and cause serious electrical damage to the ATV.

7. Before we installed the front fender and plastic assembly, we tested out the operation of the winch by temporarily hooking up the control switch. After double-checking all of the connections with the diagram in the manual, we

turned on the ignition switch, and Viola! everything worked just fine. We were startled at how loud the solenoid was when it was energized, though.

8. Now that we confirmed that everything was working properly, we cut the rubber band on the winch spool and pulled the cable through the cable guide, (called a fairlead) on the front bumper. After attaching the hook, we installed the front fender assembly.

9. Instead of drilling a hole in the fender for the winch control switch wires to go, we discovered that they could be routed through an opening in the fender for the cargo rack attachment points. After the wires were pulled through, we carefully installed the cargo rack.

10. Once the cargo rack was bolted in place, the only item left to take care of was mounting the switch. We decided to mount the winch control switch on the front cargo rack instead of drilling holes in the fender for mounting. Of course, mounting the switch on the fender might have been better, since anything placed on the racks in the future would interfere with operation of the switch. The instruction manual stressed the importance of proper wire routing, so we made sure that all of the switch wires were secure by using nylon tie-wraps to hold them to the frame.

11. Once all the wiring was secured, we gave everything another try. Of course everything worked just fine, and our winch installation was a success.

⁎⁎ CAUTION

Use of heavy leather gloves is recommended for handling of the winch wire.

→After a new winch is installed, Warn® stresses the importance of unwinding the cable until only five wraps of wire are on the spool, and then winding in the entire length of the wire under a 500 pound load. You can accomplish by unwinding the spool as required, and attaching it to a large tree. Then, operate the winch and pull the ATV toward the tree (using only the power of the winch) until all of the cable is taken in on the drum. For optimal winding, the ATV should be pulled up a slight incline. This will ensure proper stretching of the wire, and will create a tight wrap around the drum, which will prevent damage during later use.

Rifle And Bow Racks

HOW TO SELECT

▶ **See Figures 74, 75, 76, 77 and 78**

For ATV riders who are into hunting, fishing, and field work, rifle and bow racks are just about indispensable. Most ATV riders would think of "gun racks" as something that wouldn't be of any benefit unless they are into hunting. This is far from the truth! Rifle and bow racks allow for easy transport of just about any long, thin, stick-shaped object. Let's go through a list of goodies that you could tote around with a rifle rack:

- Rifles
- Bows
- Fishing rods
- Shovels
- Rakes
- Axes

Well, you get the idea. Just about any stick-shaped object can be carried with a rifle rack. The point is that rifle and bow racks can actually be quite versatile, and can be used for more than carrying rifles.

There are several different types of racks that are available for carrying rifles. Some are of the enclosed kind, which are known as scabbards. These are great for protecting that family heirloom 12 gauge shotgun from scratches and other damage during transport on your ATV, but probably won't be able to carry anything else besides rifles.

The other type of rifle and bow rack is the open type. These are much lower in price, and can be used for carrying other items besides rifles. All-Rite Products® supplied us with a few fine examples of rifle and bow racks which are pictured here.

All-Rite's Fin Grip® rack has special rubber "fins" which help to hold items in place during transport. This unique feature is a real advantage to riders who

Fig. 75 There are also specialized products available for carrying rifles

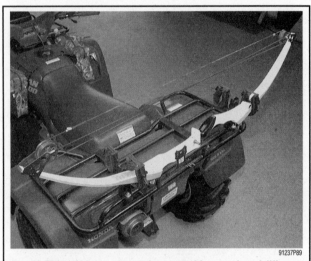
Fig. 76 Rifle and bow racks can be mounted in a number of different positions on an ATV, so they can be situated to your liking

Fig. 74 Rifle and bow racks are essential accessories for hunting

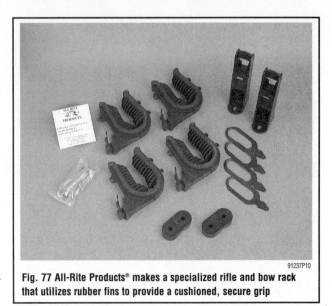
Fig. 77 All-Rite Products® makes a specialized rifle and bow rack that utilizes rubber fins to provide a cushioned, secure grip

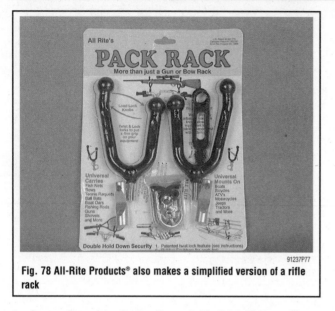

Fig. 78 All-Rite Products® also makes a simplified version of a rifle rack

Fig. 80 . . . or mounted on a tube (such as a cargo rack) with an adapter plate

travel over really rough terrain, since the constant jarring could cause a rifle or bow to shift when using other types of racks. Other types of racks are more generic, and don't provide the specialized carrying of bows and rifles.

HOW TO INSTALL

♦ See Figures 79 thru 90

As with most rifle and bow racks, there are several ways to mount them to an ATV. The best (and easiest) way to mount them is on the cargo racks on the front or rear of the ATV. Some racks can also be mounted on the handlebars.

Once you've found a suitable position for your rifle and bow racks, pre-assemble any required components, as necessary. Next, install the U-bolts around the cargo rack, and place the rifle rack half onto the ends of the U-bolt. Don't fully tighten the bolts quite yet, though. Wait until you have both sides of the rack in position, and make sure that your bow or rifle will fit between the rack spacing properly. Once you have everything where it should be, tighten the nuts securely. Your rifle and bow rack is ready to go!

➥Make sure that the rifle or bow does not interfere with any operational controls of the ATV when placed in the rack.

You might decide that the location of the racks doesn't suit you after they are mounted; this is no big deal, since most racks are really easy to remove and install. The only exception to this is if you have composite cargo racks on your

Fig. 81 A U-bolt is used for securing the rack post to the tube

Fig. 79 The All-Rite racks feature two styles of mounting—they can be bolted to a flat surface . . .

Fig. 82 Locking nuts are used on the U-bolts to keep the racks from vibrating loose

Fig. 86 Make sure the tab on the support snaps inside of the mounting post

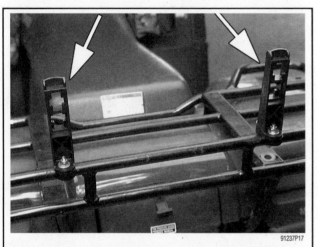

Fig. 83 Once the rack posts were positioned to our liking, we tightened the nuts, being careful not to overtighten them, since the posts are made of plastic

Fig. 84 Make sure the posts are both mounted in the same direction, since there are two different mounting locations for the supports

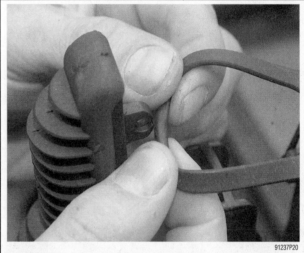

Fig. 87 The last thing to do was to snap the rubber straps onto the supports

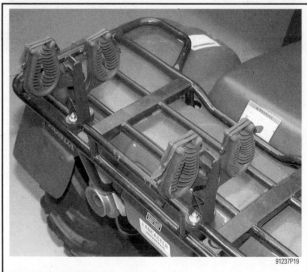

Fig. 85 Once the posts were secure, attaching the supports was a matter of simply snapping them into the posts

Fig. 88 The rack is ready to go!

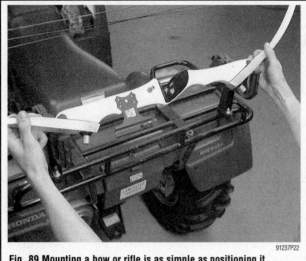
Fig. 89 Mounting a bow or rifle is as simple as positioning it between the supports . . .

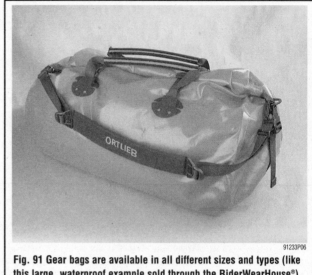
Fig. 91 Gear bags are available in all different sizes and types (like this large, waterproof example sold through the RiderWearHouse®)

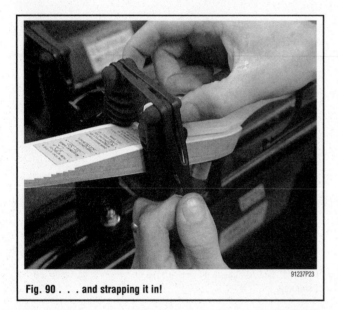
Fig. 90 . . . and strapping it in!

Fig. 92 There are also gear bags designed for specific applications—this tank bag and drink holder are available from Innovative Products®

ATV, since you'll have to drill holes into the rack to reposition them. Keep this in mind when you are installing rifle and bow racks.

Gear Bags

HOW TO SELECT

▶ **See Figures 91 thru 99**

Gear bags aren't really a big priority for a lot of ATV riders, but once you've spent a couple weekends riding, you will quickly learn the importance of having gear bags to put all of your stuff into. Gear bags are great for organization, protection, and convenience.

The first thing you need to decide is the exact use of your gear bag. Do you just need something to stuff your weekend gear into, or are you looking for heavy duty bags to carry camping gear? Do you want waterproof bags to keep rain and mud off your gear? Do you want to maximize the carrying capacity of your ATV? Just looking for something to put all your little things into that fits onto your ATV? The choices are endless.

We obtained a couple of samples of different types of gear bags to show a little of what is available. New gear bags are constantly being introduced for ATVs, motorcycling and camping, each bag with various specialized purposes.

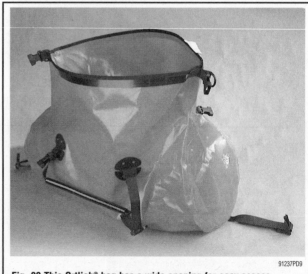
Fig. 93 This Ortlieb® bag has a wide opening for easy access

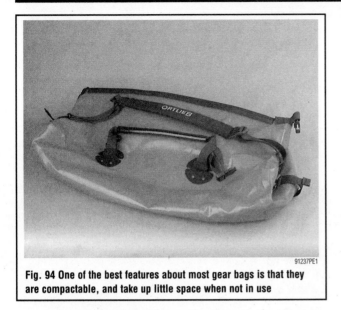

Fig. 94 One of the best features about most gear bags is that they are compactable, and take up little space when not in use

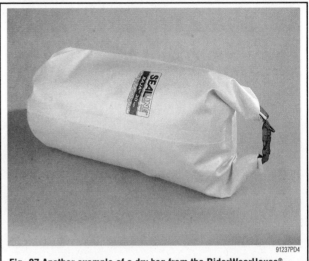

Fig. 97 Another example of a dry bag from the RiderWearHouse® catalog—great for ATV riders who ride in inclement weather

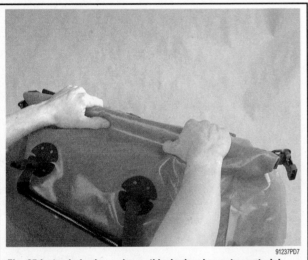

Fig. 95 Instead of using a zipper, this dry bag has extra material that is rolled up . . .

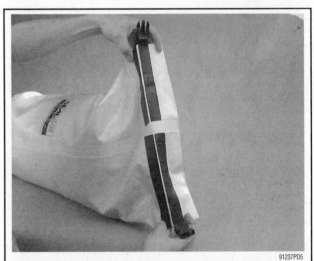

Fig. 98 Like most dry bags, this one rolls up tightly instead of using a zipper to keep the contents dry

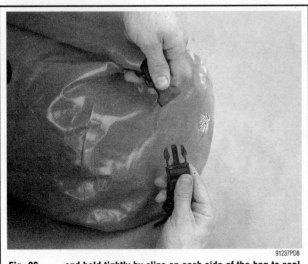

Fig. 96 . . . and held tightly by clips on each side of the bag to seal out water (and keep the contents in)

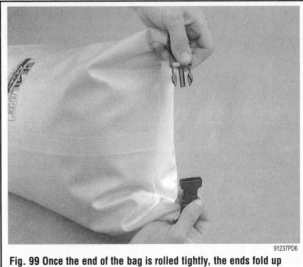

Fig. 99 Once the end of the bag is rolled tightly, the ends fold up and connect together with a plastic clip

What we have shown here is only a small portion of what is available, but to get more ideas, go to ATV, motorcycle and camping dealers, catalogs or suppliers.

Innovative Products, Inc.® supplied us with a handy tank bag. This is a great accessory bag that fits just about all ATVs. If you don't want to use it as a tank bag, the straps can be disconnected, and you can mount it onto a cargo rack. The possibilities are endless as to what you can haul around in it. Tools, hunting supplies, food, cameras, binoculars, gloves, you name it! A small tank bag like this can be useful for just about any type of ATV rider. Overall, this tank bag is a great all-around addition to any ATV.

We also were supplied with a seat cover and a really cool drink holder, which was also from Innovative Products, Inc.® This insulated drink holder has a hook and loop fastener just like the tank bag. This makes the drink holder really handy since you can place it just about anywhere you want to on your ATV, or even on yourself. As with the tank bag, the drink holder can be adapted to carry around just about anything that you can manage to stuff inside.

There are tons of other unique gear bags, including gear bags which are shaped to fit onto the cargo racks of an ATV. Innovative Products, Inc.® also makes specialized bags that are shaped to fit cargo racks. Bags like this have the benefit of easy access to the contents, since bungee cords or rubber straps aren't required to hold them in place. On the other hand, they might be cumbersome to carry around when they're not mounted on the ATV.

Another type of gear bag that should be of major interest to ATV riders are dry bags. Dry bags were originally developed for whitewater rafters, but work out really well for ATV riders who spend any amount of time in wet weather. Dry bags are made from vinyl or rubber coated canvas, and have sealed seams to keep the contents inside the bag dry. Most dry bags are of the "roll closing" type, which eliminate leaky zippers.

Seal Line® and Ortlieb Waterproof Outdoor Gear® are two large manufacturers of dry bags that were sent to us by RiderWearHouse®. These fine examples of dry bags are just a portion of the large selection of different styles available. The unique way that they fold up helps to keep water from entering the bag. Dry bags such as these pictured here can easily be strapped onto the cargo racks of an ATV, and carried around the campsite later. Things that are important to keep dry, such as food, extra clothing, sleeping bags, etc. can be safely stored in a dry bag. If you're into camping trips with your ATV, these dry bags are the way to go.

Workstands

HOW TO SELECT

▶ **See Figures 100 thru 106**

Simple maintenance like lubricating chains and changing wheels can be a real pain without a workstand. Sure, you can use a milk crate or paint bucket to lift the wheels from the ground, but do you always want to be crawling around on the garage floor? (you should answer NO) After performing basic maintenance on your ATV on the garage floor a few times, you'll quickly learn the value of a workstand.

There are several types of lifts and workstands available for ATVs. Some lift only the rear axle, and others lift the whole ATV, but only a foot or two from the ground. These can be convenient and easy to use, but just like using a milk crate, you'll be constantly bending over when working on your ATV. The best type of workstand to get is one that will support your ATV at a reasonable work height.

One workstand that we found which provided a good work height is available from James Lucky Enterprises®. This lightweight, portable lift is great if you don't have a lot of space in your garage, since it folds flat. It is also light weight, so it can also be brought along for the weekend to make things like changing wheels and chain lubrication a piece of cake.

The JL workstand is really easy to use. The first thing that needs to be done before you use the lift is to set the cleats on the workstand to fit your ATV. Stand the ATV on the back wheels (remembering to remove a Non-Sealed battery first!), so you can have easier access to the lower portion of the frame. It is essential that the cleats are adjusted properly, since they help to stabilize the ATV when you lift it onto the workstand. The cleats should be adjusted on the frame to keep the ATV from sliding from side-to-side. The cleats slide back and forth, and are held in place by pinch bolts. Once the cleats on the lift are adjusted properly, carefully lower the ATV onto the stand as shown in the photo sequence. At this point, both ends of the lift should be touching the frame, with the back legs of the lift touching the ground. Having a buddy help out will make things a lot easier. Once you get to this point, simply pull the front end of the

Fig. 100 Yes, jack stands or milk crates can be used to lift your ATV from the ground, but they don't always provide a comfortable work height

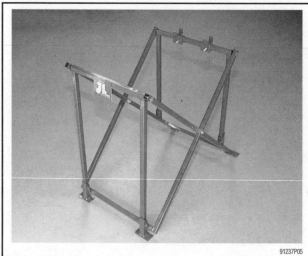

Fig. 101 This lightweight ATV workstand is available from JL Enterprises®

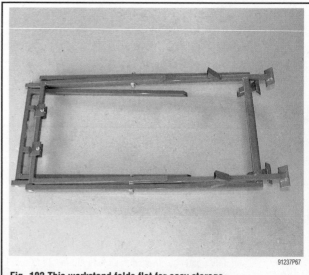

Fig. 102 This workstand folds flat for easy storage

Fig. 103 Stand the ATV on end, adjust the cleats to fit the frame

Fig. 104 With the stand resting against the frame, carefully tilt the ATV forward . . .

Fig. 105 . . . until the ATV is level, then you're ready to work!

Fig. 106 To lower the ATV from the stand, tilt it back and carefully lower it onto the back wheels, then remove the stand

ATV down, being careful not to slam everything down. (It might take you a couple of tries before you're graceful at it). You're now ready to work!

Once you are ready to ride your ATV, simply tilt it and the stand to lower the back wheels to the ground. Just like lifting the ATV up on the stand, lowering it smoothly might take a little practice. You might want to try it out a few times in private so you don't look stupid when you show your friends your new workstand. Once you get good at it, invite your buddies over, and show them why they need a real workstand!

Overall, the JL workstand is a great value. The ease of working on your ATV at a reasonable height is well worth the price. This workstand works with most all two-wheel drive ATVs; be careful with some of the larger 4x4s though, as they might be too heavy for the lift. If you have any questions, check with the lift manufacturer before use.

Grips

HOW TO SELECT

▶ **See Figures 107 and 108**

Any part of the ATV which your body comes in contact can be considered a vehicle interface. Changing any of these vehicle interface items, they can drastically affect the way your ATV "feels" when you ride.

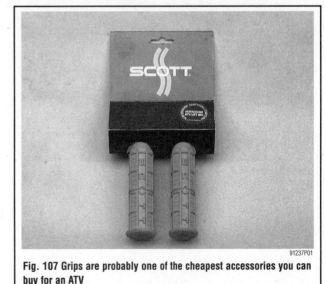

Fig. 107 Grips are probably one of the cheapest accessories you can buy for an ATV

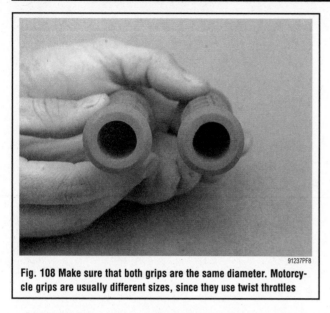

Fig. 108 Make sure that both grips are the same diameter. Motorcycle grips are usually different sizes, since they use twist throttles

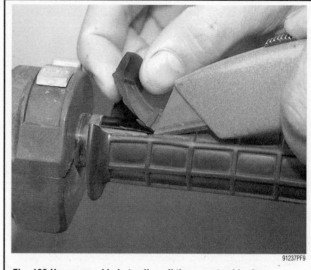

Fig. 109 Use a razor blade to slice off those nasty old grips

Fig. 110 Good ol' fashioned dish soap works well for installing new grips. You can mix it with water, or use it full strength

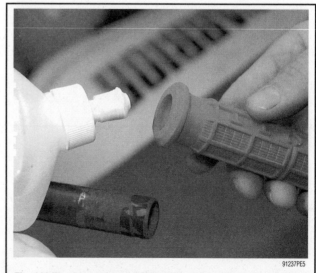

Fig. 111 We chose to use it full strength on our grips

Granted, installing a set of grips on your ATV isn't really an accessory, but more of a long-term maintenance item. Depending on how much you ride though, your grips will wear out and require replacement at some time in the life of your ATV. On the other hand, replacing the stock grips because you don't like their feel could be considered accessorizing.

There are a ton of companies that make aftermarket grips for ATVs. They all have unique features, which may or may not appeal to you. Your local ATV and motorcycle dealer will most likely have a large inventory of grips for you to select. There is one item of importance that must be noted when looking for a new set of grips, though. Make sure that the grips are both of the same inner diameter. Since motorcycles use twist throttles, the right grip will have a larger inner diameter than the left. Motorcycle grips won't work on your ATV unless you buy two of the same pair of grips, and use the two left grips.

As with items like air filters and tires, aftermarket versions of the OEM parts are going to be cheaper, and in some cases, may perform better.

If you like the grips that came with your ATV, and you've just GOT to have them, then you're in luck. Your local dealer will have the Original Equipment Manufacturer (OEM) grips available, whether they're in stock or have to be ordered. Just don't kill the parts guy when he tells you how much they cost!

HOW TO INSTALL

♦ See Figures 109 thru 116

Before you can put on a new pair of grips, you gotta hack the old ones off. This doesn't mean with an axe, though! A carpet or utility knife should work just fine. Make a slice down the length of the grip, and peel it away from the handlebars. Once the old grips have been cut off, chances are that there will be some rust and scaled paint on the handlebars where the grips were. Be sure to neutralize any rust, and clean the handlebars with some light sandpaper to provide a smooth surface for the new grips.

There are a zillion different methods people have come up with for installing a pair of grips. Everything from carburetor cleaner to trim adhesive. One of the easiest (and safest) ways to install a pair of grips onto your handlebars is with good ol' fashioned dishwashing soap as a lubricant.

Just squirt a little inside the grip, and rub it around with your finger. While you're at it, put a little on the handlebar end too. Don't get too carried away with the soap, because the more that you put on, the longer it will take to dry. (Remember, you only need enough to get the grips in place.) Once everything is lubed up, simply push the grip onto the handlebar end. Position the grips how you want them, and let the soap dry. Be sure to plan ahead here; the soap might take up to 24 hours or more to dry out, depending on the type of soap and how much you used to install the grips.

Once the soap is dry, the friction of the rubber against the handlebars should hold them in place. If you find that the grips move around, you can use safety wire to hold them in place. This is an old trick that motocross racers used to do to keep their grips from coming off during a race. Over the years, most aftermar-

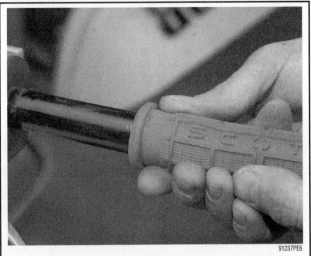

Fig. 112 Once you've lightly coated the handlebar end and the inside of the grip, simply slide it onto the handlebar

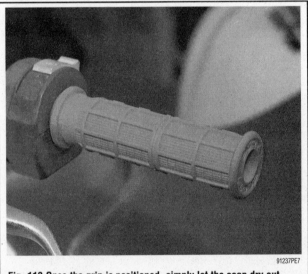

Fig. 113 Once the grip is positioned, simply let the soap dry out

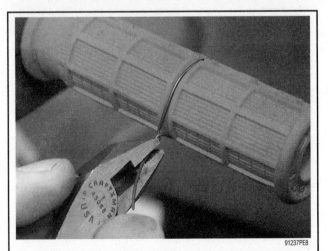

Fig. 114 For additional holding power, the grips can be safety wired in place. The groove on the grip is designed specifically for this purpose

Fig. 115 After the wire has been twisted (not too tightly, or the wire might cut the grip) hook the wire around . . .

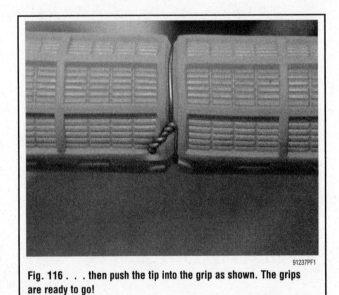

Fig. 116 . . . then push the tip into the grip as shown. The grips are ready to go!

ket grip companies adapted this practice, making "safety wire grooves" that are molded into the grips.

To make use of these grooves, grab some safety wire and some pliers, then wrap the wire around the groove in the grip. Using the pliers, twist the wire as shown to provide some tension on the grip. Be careful not to twist the wire too much, otherwise the wire will break or might cut the grip. Once the wire is twisted, cut off the excess, leaving about ⅜ of an inch of twisted wire. Bend the tip of the wire, and push the tip into the grip.

There are two important things to be noted when using safety wire on grips. The first is not to twist the wire too tightly around the grip, since it may pinch the grip and actually cut it. The second, (and most important) is to position the safety wire so the twisted portion is NOT on the portion of the grip where the palm rests.

✳✳ CAUTION

Position the safety wire so the twisted portion is not underneath your hand when resting on the grip.

If you don't like the idea of using wire on your grips to hold them in place, there is "grip glue" which is available from most ATV and motorcycle shops. This can make installation a little more difficult (since glue is not always the best lubricant), but the grips will stay on well after the glue dries. Follow the directions on the bottle

Exhaust Systems

♦ See Figure 117

There are many reasons to replace the stock exhaust system on your ATV. Maybe yours is rusted out and you wanted something different. Possibly you want a little more rumble to make you grin. Most aftermarket pipes can help you reduce the weight of your ATV, sometimes by as much as 10 pounds (44 kilos) or more!

➡**Keep in mind that some aftermarket exhaust systems are not United States Forestry Service (U.S.F.S.) approved, and may not have a spark arrestor. Most all U.S.F.S. riding areas require an approved spark arrestor.**

There are many different styles of replacement exhaust systems. Some systems are simply replacement mufflers that "slip on" to the existing factory pipes. These are the simplest systems. Other systems replace the entire set of pipes from the cylinder head back. Some of these systems resemble the stock systems, but use bigger pipes or have some other sort of difference. Other systems may be completely different from the stock system. You have to be careful with systems like these as you may block easy access to maintenance items.

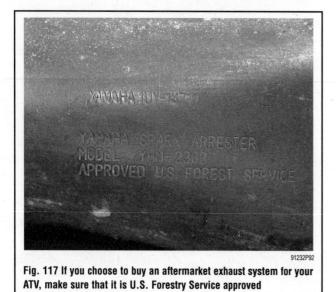

Fig. 117 If you choose to buy an aftermarket exhaust system for your ATV, make sure that it is U.S. Forestry Service approved

HOW TO INSTALL

♦ See Figure 118

One of the biggest concerns when replacing an exhaust system is how much effect it is going to have on the tuning of the engine. Simply bolting a muffler to your ATV is not all with which you have to concern yourself. Replacement exhaust systems from the aftermarket or performance arm of the manufacturer will typically have higher rates of flow than the stock systems. This helps performance if your engine is tuned to take advantage of it. If you don't tune the engine and adjust the mixture, chances are that you will cause the engine to run lean. A lean running engine will run hot and eventually damage itself. Low restriction pipes equal higher flow of gases through the engine. Higher flow of gases means you need more air coming into the engine. More air means more fuel that the engine can burn. The end result is that you have to rejet your carburetor to make things right.

Talk to the manufacturer of the system you intend to use. They will be able to give you an idea about what modifications to the carburetion will have to be done. Sometimes they can give you specific changes and might be able to supply a jetting kit matched to the exhaust system. If they don't have that, they can give you some guidance as to typical setting to use as a baseline. If you have done extensive modifications to your engine, the manufacturer may not be able to help you as they can't possibly know every combination of parts that can be

Fig. 118 Be prepared to make adjustments and/or modifications to your ATV's carburetor if you buy an aftermarket exhaust system

bolted to an ATV. In this case, a shop familiar with your type of ATV may have already done a similar modification and can help you get your ATV dialed in.

1. Once you have figured out what you will with your fuel mixture, now you can start thinking about actually installing the exhaust system. Look through the manufacturers instructions. They should give you a list of parts you will need during the job. If they say to reuse any parts, like gaskets, you may want to pick up new ones just in case the old ones are damaged during the removal process.

2. Before removing any bolts, hold up the new exhaust system to the ATV and try to look for all the places the new system will mount. Look for the way the pipes attach to each other. Check that the pipes and mount will match up. Most quality manufacturers test fit their products so you don't have to do any modifications to the system. Sometimes you will find that the lower priced systems out there require a fair bit of modification to get them to fit. You usually get what you pay for.

3. If you are sure everything will fit fine and you have all the parts you need, it is time to remove the old system. This can be a real pain, as old exhaust system hardware tends to fuse itself together over a period of time. Liberal doses of rust penetrating lubricant can help break free some of the more stubborn fasteners. Sometimes nothing short of a torch will help free things up, just be careful not to damage anything in the process. Loosen all the connections and mounting bolts.

4. Some ATVs require that other parts be removed for access to the exhaust system. Some or all plastic, engine guards, brake levers, foot boards, etc. may need to be removed or moved out of the way.

5. When you have removed the mounting fasteners and disconnected the pipes, be ready to drop the old system. Be careful as the old system may be quite a bit heavier than it may seem, but hey, isn't that one of the reasons you are changing it? Aluminum usually looks cooler than steel, anyway.

6. With the old system removed, this is a great time to inspect the mounting tabs on the frame and any areas that are normally covered by the exhaust system. Check for rust and corrosion. Clean and paint any areas that may need it. Check the threads on the cylinder head where the pipe attaches to; often these threads get buggered up due to the high heat encountered at an exhaust port. Check the inside of the exhaust port for excessive carbon or for signs of burning valves. You might catch a problem before an engine teardown is needed. If you are only installing a slip on muffler, check that the end of the pipe is still round and not squashed out of shape. A small pipe expander can help round out a damaged pipe.

7. Test fit the new exhaust system. Put everything into place, but don't tighten anything yet. Check for clearances at the brake lines and levers, chassis tubes, plastic and other accessories. If there are clearance problems, you might have to bend some mounting tabs or fabricate spacers.

8. Once you are convinced that everything is as it should be, you can install the new gaskets, put anti-seize paste on fittings and get set to bolt everything down. Check your instructions to see if there are any sequences that you

have to follow when tightening the various part of the system. Chance are that you need to start closest to the engine and work your way back. While doing this, keep checking the system alignment as it can change as things snug up.

➡️**You normally tighten exhaust system fasteners working from the engine to the rear of the system. This allows the system to settle into proper alignment with the vehicle as the fasteners are tightened.**

9. With the system completely bolted down, reinstall anything that had to come off in the process. Tighten the fasteners properly and use thread locking compounds where appropriate.

10. If your carburetor will need readjustment or rejetting, do this now, before firing up the engine. Once it is complete, check for any fuel leakage before starting the ATV.

11. Ok, now that you have everything done, fire it up! Check for leaking connections, and tighten them up. Run the engine for a while and recheck the connections once they have cooled back down. They may need retorquing. The next time you go for a ride, keep an eye on the exhaust fasteners, since things might rattle loose. After a couple of good long rides, go over all of the fasteners and snug things up.

Shocks And Springs

▶ **See Figure 119**

Most people who drive cars never think twice about the suspension holding their car up. But since ATV riders spend so much time riding on rough surfaces, suspension is always a topic of conversation.

If only you are on the ATV, it will handle in one fashion, but add a stack of camping gear or start hauling stuff around, and the ATV can turn into something completely different. Adjustment of the original suspension can only compensate for so much, and in some cases, may not compensate enough. This is where aftermarket shocks and springs can be of great benefit.

Fig. 119 Shocks are an essential part of your ATV; changing them can drastically change handling characteristics

HOW TO SELECT

There are many reasons to change the suspension on an ATV. Sometimes the reason is handling and performance; The rider wants to have more control at speed. They may want to stiffen up the chassis so it becomes more reactive and predictable.

ATV manufacturers have to build machines that will meet the needs of most, but can't really make an ATV that will meet the desires of all. Certain compromises have to be made so the greatest amount of people will be able to ride the ATV. It's great if the stock suspension happens to work for you, but a lot of the time, the ATV can be made better with a few tweaks. Sometimes simply replacing worn out stock components can make an ATV handle like new. But why not

take the chance to replace the equipment with some high class suspension componentry?

In general, you can replace either the dampers or the springs in either the front suspension or rear. The front suspension usually has one shock and spring per side, and the rear suspension typically has a single shock, which supports the rear swingarm. In some cases, there may be a pair of them, depending on the type of suspension setup.

It is recommended that the front and rear suspensions be modified at the same time with matched components. If you only modify one end of the ATV, the suspension can be adversely effected (since the front and rear suspensions interact with each other while the vehicle is moving) and the ATV will not handle in a proper manner. Ask the retailer or manufacturer of the suspension for their recommendations as to what would be appropriate for the ATV to do the modification correctly.

You have to decide what your goals are in the suspension modification game. If you are looking for better handling or better control of the ATV under extreme loads, you will be aiming for a different set up than the person who wants to make their suspension smoother over the rough stuff. If you are trying to solve a particular suspension problem, check with the suspension manufacturers. They probably have already figured out the solution and have it ready to install.

Most stock suspensions have a minimum of adjustments. They usually come with a preload adjustment and sometimes a damping adjustment. Aftermarket suspensions come with a full range of possibilities. Some aftermarket suspensions resemble the stock pieces, but may have a few little tweaks or maybe better performance.

Other aftermarket suspensions come with enough dials, wheels, adjustments and doodads to keep the most techno-oriented rider happy. There are rear shocks for ATVs that have hydraulic (not the typical ramp and peg) preload adjustment, compression damping adjustments, rebound damping adjustment, and remote gas filled reservoirs. All of these adjustments don't usually come cheap, though, and aren't really necessary except for heavy-duty racing applications.

Check with your dealer to find out what they recommend for suspensions. They have a lot of experience with your type of ATV. Also check with other people who ride your type of ATV and do your type of riding. They can offer some personal insights. Call the manufacturers and find out what they have to offer. They may already offer the suspension you need, and may have it ready to go, packed up in a box.

HOW TO INSTALL

▶ **See Figure 120**

Most shock/spring assemblies are relatively easy to get at and that is what this procedure describes. Some shocks are buried in the bowels of the ATV and

Fig. 120 Most shocks and springs are only held on by two bolts, making removal and installation a piece of cake

require some major disassembly to get at them, but once you are there, removal or installation should basically be the same. Refer to a repair manual for shock replacement details about your particular ATV.

1. Raise the ATV so all the weight is off of the wheels and the suspension is hanging at full travel. Use a workstand or other means to support the ATV.

2. Remove any components that may be in the way of removing the shock. Items that may need to be removed include: plastic, racks, exhaust systems, side panels and other various items.

3. Remove the upper and lower mounting hardware. Keep track of the washers and spacers that may come off with the shock.

4. When the shock bolts are removed, be prepared for the suspension to drop downwards. Using a tie-down attached to the suspension arm will help to keep from stretching the brake lines.

5. Install the new shock, using the supplied mounting hardware. New performance shocks may be equipped with spherical bearings in place of the original rubber bushings. There may be spacers used that aren't used in the original mounting scheme. The installation instructions will show the proper mounting. Tighten the mounting hardware. Also, it is not a bad idea to use threadlocking compound on the mounting fasteners.

6. Install any parts that may have had to come off to gain access to the shocks.

7. Do the basic adjustment to the shocks to get baseline. Most manufacturers will have guidelines regarding adjustment and tuning of the shocks. In the absence of specific instructions, adjust the spring preload so the sag (the difference in length of the shock when loaded and unloaded) is approximately around 30 percent of the total travel of the suspension. Turn all the damper adjustments to the default setting as determined by the manufacturer.

8. Test ride the ATV and make adjustments as needed.

9. Refer to section 5 for additional information regarding setting up the suspension.

8

CLEANING YOUR ATV

CLEANING YOUR ATV

♦ **See Figure 1**

In order to keep your ATV in good mechanical condition, it is important to keep it clean. This way you can find and correct (or prevent) problems that might be unseen beneath the surface of mud, dirt and other various debris that can collect quickly after a couple of rides.

If you ride your ATV in muddy areas, keeping your ATV clean is especially important. Mud and dirt can hide serious problems, such as a cracked frame. Mud caked underneath the fenders on your ATV can also cause the plastic to crack, from the extra weight that the mud places on the plastic. If left to dry out on the plastic, mud (in certain geographical areas) can permanently stain the plastic. In general, if you ride in a lot of mud, you should thoroughly hose your ATV down with fresh water after every ride.

ATV riders who ride in the desert have a different dilemma to deal with: Dust. Everything from the air cleaner to your cables can be adversely affected by dust. Since dust becomes airborne, it can attach itself just about anywhere on an ATV, and that can make cleaning a real hassle. As with mud, even a thin layer of dust can become an abrasive on your ATV's plastic. Dragging a boot or pant leg across a fender can grind dust particles into the plastic, leaving marks, and eventually dulling the surface.

Every time you wash your ATV, you'll get a chance to closely inspect it for any problems that may have developed since the last washing. While scrubbing away, it is easy to quickly glance over the mechanicals, looking for kinked cables, loose nuts and bolts, and worn out components. This is a prime example of preventative maintenance which can help to avoid problems on the trail.

In addition to helping to keep your ATV in good mechanical order, washing your ATV on a regular basis will also help keep it looking good. An ATV that is kept clean will hold a higher value than a muddy, sloppy one, should you ever decide to part ways with your ride. If a potential buyer sees a clean ATV, they will often assume that it was maintained properly too (which will hopefully be true in your case, thanks to this book. You are following my instructions, right?).

Basic Washing

♦ **See Figures 2, 3, 4 and 5**

Well, washing your ATV sounds pretty easy, right? Quite honestly, it is. The same rules apply to washing an ATV as with washing an automobile. After the ATV is thoroughly wet, start at the top and work your way down, while rinsing often. But there are some important issues to discuss which will make scrubbing off the dirty stuff a little easier. Let's take a look at some tips to washing your ATV:

• Since the engine and all the related controls are exposed to the elements, we need to keep an eye out for potential problem points. For example: you don't want to spray some heavy duty solvent on the engine to find out later you just doused the electronic control unit for the ignition with water and cleaner! Avoid electronic parts and switches when spraying direct streams of water.

• Don't use a high pressure cleaning wand to spray your ATV; Water and cleaner can be forced past seals and gaskets into lubricants or other areas not tolerant of water. Use only a low pressure garden hose or equivalent to remove mud and dirt.

• Always use duct tape or other means to cover the tip of the exhaust pipe to keep water from getting into the engine.

• Cleaning the radiator: If your ATV is water-cooled, make sure to thoroughly wash the mud and dirt from the radiator core. A radiator that is clogged with mud and debris will not be able to cool the engine, since air cannot flow through the cooling fins of the radiator core. Medium water pressure should be able to free most of the dirt and debris from the core of the radiator. Use a toothpick to remove any small pieces of dirt or other debris which might remain lodged in the radiator core.

• If you are using a biodegradable degreaser, let it soak for a couple of minutes before washing it off. Make sure not to let the degreaser dry before you get a chance to rinse it away, since it may leave stains or streaks.

• With your hose's nozzle adjusted to medium spray, thoroughly wet the

91238P05

Fig. 1 Keeping your ATV clean is easy once you have the basics

Fig. 2 Check the airbox drain for debris; a clogged drain could lead to water in the engine

Fig. 4 Make sure items like brake cylinders are sealed completely before washing your ATV

Fig. 3 Standing the ATV on end can make washing a lot easier, especially if it's muddy

Fig. 5 Pay close attention to areas which are prone to collecting dirt and mud

entire ATV, washing off loose grit, dirt, and pollutants. If your ATV is REALLY muddy, concentrate on hosing off all of the mud and grit first. The more mud and dirt that you can manage to remove with water alone will help to avoid scratching the plastic.

• Soak towels thoroughly in sudsy wash solution. Use minimum application pressure. The sudsy solution acts as a lubricant between your wash cloth and the finish. The aim is to loosen mud, dirt and pollutants, float them off the surface, and hold them in suspension within the solution. Floating them off prevents them from scratching the finish. Dunk the cloth frequently in your bucket of wash water to get rid of suspended, potentially abrasive particles. Work with a clean, sopping wet cloth, heavy with solution. While application in a circular motion is easier, and for most detailers more natural, a forward-backward motion is better because it does not leave circular swirl marks in the plastic.

• Rinse well with a medium spray from the hose, flooding areas to float particles off.

• Dry with clean, non abrasive cotton cloths, preferably terry towels, or with a soft chamois.

• As you dry, be sure not to let any water droplets remain, because they'll leave spots behind. Don't neglect to dry wheels and chrome. If any dirt comes off on your drying cloth, you didn't wash the finish well enough.

• Do not wash and detail your ATV in the sun. Soapy water will dry out faster than you can rinse it off, especially in the summer months.

• As previously mentioned, do your best to keep water away from electrical connections. Even a small amount of water can get into a connector and quickly corrode the terminals.

✷✷ WARNING

Using high water pressure to clean radiator fins and oil cooler fins can cause serious damage. Only use low pressure to safely clean mud and debris from the fins.

TOOLS AND CHEMICALS

Now that we have gone over some washing tips, let's discuss the tools and chemicals that make cleaning your ATV easier.

Tools

▶ **See Figures 6 thru 11**

A soft wash towel or rag is the best tool for washing dirt off of plastic. A terrycloth rag works well, since it can hold soapy water. Cotton rags, like the kind that service stations use, might be a little harsh on plastic. Wash mitts can also be used. The important thing here is to look for something that is not going to be abrasive to plastic and paint (like most sponges).

Brushes of all different sizes and types make great tools for hard-to-reach places. Most auto supply stores or hardware stores will have a large selection of brushes. Just like wash rags, it is important to look for brushes with soft bristles that aren't going to scratch paint and plastic. Even brushes that are going to be used for cleaning around axles can't be too stiff, since the seals

can be damaged. When choosing a scrub brush, rub the bristles on the back of your hand. If the bristles on a brush feel stiff in the palm of your hand, imagine what it can to the paint and plastic on your ATV. A stiff scrub brush will work great for removing mud on tires, but might scratch the paint on the frame.

> **✳✳ CAUTION**
>
> **ALWAYS wear adequate eye protection (goggles or safety glasses) when using compressed air to clean your ATV.**

Compressed air is an excellent tool for cleaning an ATV. before you wet down the ATV for washing, use an air nozzle to blow off any loose dirt and debris that has accumulated in the cracks and crevices of the frame. If you ride in dusty areas, compressed air is really useful, since dust built up in hard-to-reach areas can be blown clean. Of course you'll need to have a source of compressed air, whether it's a portable air tank or a small compressor. An air nozzle can usually be purchased at an auto supply or hardware store.

91238P15

Fig. 6 Brushes of assorted sizes are really helpful for cleaning mud out of nooks and crannies

91238P14

Fig. 7 An adjustable nozzle for a garden hose is excellent for controlling water pressure, making heavy mud removal easier

91238P23

Fig. 8 Compressed air is an excellent tool for getting rid of loose debris

Fig. 9 A light grade abrasive pad works great for removing dirt and grit from stainless steel . . .

Fig. 10 . . . and really shines it up too!

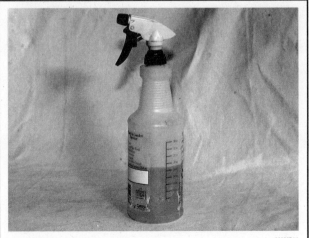

Fig. 11 Spray bottles are a good way to apply cleaners and other products

☀☀ WARNING

Don't overuse the compressed air as a cleaning tool or you will risk blowing the paint right off the surface of the metal. Keep the air pressure down—it doesn't take much to blow away loose dirt and foliage. Compressed air can also turn a little dirt into a sand blasting material (which will remove or scratch paint).

Other tools for washing can vary according to your particular ATV. For instance, if your ATV is water cooled, toothpicks are really useful for dislodging dirt and pebbles from the cooling fins in your radiator. As previously mentioned, using high pressure water (like from a car wash) can ruin the cooling fins on the radiator core. Even when using toothpicks, care should be taken to avoid bending and distorting the fins. NEVER use a metal pick or screwdriver to clean dirt from your radiator! You could easily slip and puncture the radiator. If you have ever had to replace a radiator on a car or truck, then you already know how expensive they can be. Just imagine the price of a new radiator from the dealer for your ATV!

Duct tape is an excellent tool for ATV washing, too. "Yeah, right" you're thinking. Seriously, though, duct tape can help you avoid major problems by sealing off your exhaust system, or even your intake snorkel on your air box. Sucking water into your engine can destroy it if enough manages to get into the combustion chamber. Unlike air, water does not compress. Let's say you've just finished washing your ATV, and water managed to fill up the air box without you knowing. You hit the start button, and Wham!! A bent connecting rod, cracked piston, head or case. Taking the extra precaution of closing off the intake and exhaust openings can save your engine. If you don't want to use duct tape, rubber plugs or even a cork can be utilized. Obviously, make sure that a watertight seal can be obtained.

Chemicals

▶ See Figures 12, 13, 14, 15 and 16

Everybody has their own favorite chemicals for washing their car or truck, and will probably use the same chemicals when they wash their ATV. If you have your favorites, by all means, have at it. However, there are a few considerations that you should keep in mind when selecting cleaning and detailing chemicals.

Dishwashing soap is great for breaking down grease, but can be a little harsh on plastic. Just like dish soap dries out your hands, it also dries out plastic, making it hard and brittle over time. Plastic that is not flexible will crack if bent or flexed. The safe way to go would be to buy "car washing soap" which can be purchased at any auto parts store. Car washing soap is specially formulated to safely remove dirt without damaging paint, or stripping away a good wax job. Granted, most of the surface of your ATV is plastic, but car washing soap won't dry out your ATV's plastic like dish soap can.

Biodegradable degreasers can also be used for washing your ATV. Just be careful about diluting it properly, since full strength use can, in some cases, stain plastic (especially white). In general, degreasers should not be used on plastic, though. If you want to use a particular biodegradable degreaser, try it out on the underside of a fender or something and make sure a stain isn't left behind.

Heavy duty engine degreasers should be used carefully, since most are solvent based, and can ruin and discolor paint. Just like soap, it is really important not to let the degreaser dry out before you get a chance to hose it off. Also, when applying degreaser to an engine, be careful not to let it splatter onto the plastic. Most heavy duty engine degreasers will stain plastic, especially if it is a light color.

One of the most versatile products for your ATV is WD-40®. This stuff should be your best friend if you own an ATV. It can be used as a lubricant, cleaner, and a polish. That hazy film on your engine can by brought to a glossy shine by simply spraying it down with WD-40. Now, most of you are thinking, "Yeah, that's great, but the first time I head down the trail, my engine will be a dust magnet because it is covered with WD-40." Well, actually, you are right. BUT, the next time you wash your ATV, you'll notice how easy it is to clean. It's a trade-off, and it may not be worth it to you. Give it a try and find out if it works for you. As with any product, test it out on a small, inconspicuous area and make sure it doesn't turn into a science experiment.

Talk to other riders, and ask them what kind of chemicals they use to help keep their ATVs clean. A lot of "home brewed" products can work quite well if used carefully. A word of caution, though. If you are unsure about how a product will affect your ATV, test it out on something else that is not of value before

90998P06

Fig. 12 Automotive car wash concentrate is not as harsh on plastic as dish soap

912338P16

Fig. 13 Since ATVs have so much plastic, it makes sense to use a quality plastic and rubber protectant to keep things looking good

91238P13

Fig. 14 WD-40 works well to keep mud from sticking to fenders

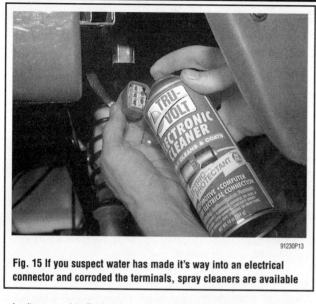

Fig. 15 If you suspect water has made it's way into an electrical connector and corroded the terminals, spray cleaners are available

Fig. 16 Engine degreasers work great for removing grease and grit, but may attack plastic and aluminum

using it on your ride. For instance, one rider heard through the grapevine that Raid® bug spray makes a great low-priced engine degreaser. Well, he tried it out on his engine, and some of the paint was eaten away. The point is here is that you have to be careful when using a product for something which it was not meant.

Plastic

▶ See Figures 17, 18 and 19

Overall, the plastic on your ATV is incredibly durable. It is safe to say that most ATVs would look awful if all of the plastic was made of metal; just imagine how dented and scratched up your ATV would look after just a couple of rides! One of the best things about plastic fenders is that the color is molded into the plastic. If you scratch up your fenders on tree branches, at least the scratches are the same color. But even then, your fenders can get downright ugly looking if they are gouged up.

Most plastic has the color molded into it, and simply cleaning with a soapy water solution and a non abrasive cloth will keep it looking good. The trick is not to scratch the surface during cleaning. If the surface does get scratched, a good commercial plastic polish will help get light scratches out and restore the looks of the piece.

Since the plastic on your ATV covers most of the vehicle, taking good care of it will help keep your ride looking new. If you are careful when riding and washing your ATV, the plastic can maintain its showroom shine for quite a while. Keeping it clean will help it from becoming scratched, but even then, over time the plastic will eventually lose its luster. There are products available to help bring back the shine of your ATV's plastic should things start to look hazy.

Plastic can be restored using plastic polishes and scratch removers. Any well stocked auto parts store or your local ATV and motorcycle dealer will carry such products. There are different grades of products to match the severity of the damage to the plastic.

Some plastic polish products are designed for maintenance type use, helping

Fig. 17 Sometimes you'll just have to live with scratches like these, since little can be done to remove them

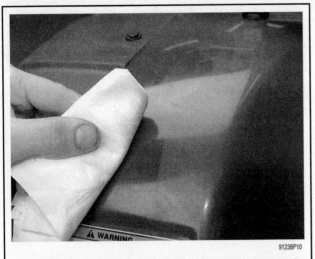

Fig. 18 Dried out, scratched plastic can be rejuvenated with a good application of plastic protectant

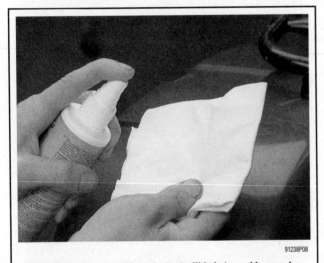

Fig. 19 Using a rag to apply protectant will help to avoid excessive overspray

to keep the tiny scratches polished out of the plastic. Others are for heavier damage and to reclaim deeply scratched surfaces (which is more for repair than maintenance). Follow the instructions on the bottle exactly. Some manufactures are very specific in the use of their products and recommend that their entire system of products be used since each one is matched to the next.

If you own an older ATV, and the plastic is beyond repair, there are some

products that can help to improve the luster. Most of these are "home remedies" and aren't products intended for use on plastic. Nevertheless, some of these products can help to spruce up an older ATV.

Vinyl floor cleaners, such as Mop n' Glo® can help restore the luster to dingy, dull plastic. Experiment with different ways of applying it to the plastic, such as wiping it on with a rag, or using a spray bottle. Just make sure to do this on an area of the plastic that is not easily seen before applying it all over your ATV. Some plastics can react differently, so make sure to test it out before you go too far.

Another product to help shine up dull plastic is WD-40®. Spray it onto a clean rag and wipe a small spot on the plastic. The WD-40 fills the scratches in the surface, and the lubricant gives a luster to the plastic. If you buff the surface with a dry cloth, most of the "greasiness" can be removed. If your ATV has white plastic, make sure that it is clean before attempting to do this, since the WD-40 can smear the dirt around, making things look even worse.

➡ **You can also use WD-40 as an anti-mud coating on the inside of your fenders. After your ATV is clean, coat the inside of the fenders liberally, and allow it to evaporate. The lubricating properties of the WD-40 will help to combat dirt from sticking to the plastic.**

One more thing about plastic. Although this should be considered a last-ditch effort, fine grit scouring pads (like 3M Scotch-Brite®) can be used on old, scratched (we're talkin' really OLD, DRIED OUT, and SCRATCHED) plastic to remove stains and ground-in dirt. Using a scouring pad might scratch the plastic even more, but you'll be able to get those mud stains off of your plastic. Use caution here, since darker plastics might take on a white-colored haze from the abrasiveness of the scouring pad. Once you have the surface clean of stains and marks, applying Armor-All® or other plastic protectant can help to put a little shine into the plastic after it has been scoured down.

Painted Surfaces

▶ **See Figure 20**

The surfaces of the average ATV that are painted are usually the frame, suspension, and in some cases, the engine. The primary reason that these surfaces are painted is not for decorative reasons, but for protection against corrosion. Just imagine how fast your frame would rust if it wasn't painted! Of course, there is nothing wrong with putting a little color into that corrosion protector on your frame known as paint.

Depending on where you ride your ATV, the frame, suspension, and other painted surfaces can quickly become scratched and chipped. Not only does this look bad, but rust can quickly set in on those scratches and nicks, since the metal becomes exposed. Once rust sets in, it can creep under the paint, and quickly spread, eventually affecting the structural integrity of the entire component.

To keep rust from setting in, touching up the scratches and chips on your ATV's painted components is essential. You can buy touch-up paint from your local ATV dealer, or head down to your nearest auto parts store and find a color that best matches the component in need of touch-up.

Here's a basic procedure for touching up scratches and nicks on painted surfaces.

Materials needed:
- All-purpose cleaner or car wash solution
- color-matching touch-up paint

Fig. 20 Touching up those scratches on your ATV's frame will help prevent rust from setting in

- Artist's brush
- Extremely fine wet-sanding paper (at least 600 grit)
- Masking tape (optional, depending on scratch size and location)
- Cotton swab
- Glaze
- Wax

Steps:

1. Thoroughly clean the nicked or scratched area, using a cotton swab wetted with all-purpose cleaner or car wash solution. If rust has set in, the best thing to do is sand it off with medium grit sandpaper, and treat the bare metal with a rust converter.

2. After the surface is clean and dry, apply a dab of paint to the nick using a modeler's or artist's brush. (Some detailers use the tear-off end of a match from a matchbook.) Apply enough thin layers (coats) of color-matching paint so that the surface of the touch-up is level with, or slightly higher than, the surface of the surrounding finish. If the surface of the touch-up is not even with, or slightly above the surface of the surrounding finish, repeat the dab-and-dry cycle until it is.

3. Wait at least a day or more, (or even a week) to let the touch-up paint thoroughly dry. Actual drying time depends on the ambient temperature and the humidity. Paint takes far longer to dry completely than most people believe, so be patient.

4. When you are sure the touch-up is dry, it can be carefully leveled (if it is not already level) with the surface of the surrounding finish. Rub the spot gently and only enough to bring it level, using a very small piece of 600 grit (or finer) wet-sanding paper.

5. Next, apply glaze to fill in any scratches left by the sandpaper. Then wax and buff the touch-up and a small area surrounding it. If you take your time, the scratch can be blended in so well that it may be hard to detect.

If the scratches and nicks on the painted components don't bother you looks-wise, simply spraying the scratched surface with rust converter will help to keep rust from forming. Spray paint can also be used, but if the exposed metal in the scratches is not treated with anti-rust primer or rust converter, rust may make its way back through to the surface.

The important thing is to keep the steel parts of your ATV covered with paint of some type to prevent rust from forming. As previously mentioned, if left untouched, rust can really eat into the metal, eventually weakening the component.

Rubber

♦ **See Figure 21**

Rubber items on your ATV, such as lever boots, or shaft drive boots, can be spruced up with a light coating of a rubber and vinyl treatment, such as Armor-All®. Rubber and vinyl treatments will keep the rubber moist and supple, which can help to slow cracking and aging. On small areas, spray a rag down, and carefully wipe down the part that you want coated. This way, overspray won't get all over the place and make a mess. Be careful not to get any overspray on your grips! A smooth, glossy grip might look nice, but it can be really hard to hold onto.

If you really like to dress up your ATV after washing, using a tire dressing on your tires can help to put the finishing touches on your ride. Dousing your tires with Armor-All® will make your ATV look like it just came off of the showroom floor, but won't do you any good once you hit the dirt. But if you like to really go the extra mile and impress your friends next time everyone's hanging out in the garage, then spray them down thoroughly, and let them soak for a while. Then use a rag to wipe off the excess. Just think of how easy it will to be to slide around in the garage! Seriously, though, be careful when you are loading your ATV on the trailer, since the tires will be really slippery.

If you aren't into Armor-All, there are other products available which can be used to dress rubber and vinyl. Some are formulated differently than others, so you might want to try out a few different brands and find out what works best for you.

Aluminum

The use of aluminum is becoming more common for components on ATVs, mostly to cut down on excess weight. In addition to being lighter than steel, aluminum also is much more resistant to corrosion. Because of aluminum's natural resistance to corrosion, manufacturers sometimes leave components unfinished. Depending on how you look at it, this can be an advantage, or just another thing to tend to when washing and cleaning your ATV.

Although bare aluminum does not rust like steel, it can become oxidized over time if neglected. Oxidized aluminum has a gritty whitish dust on the surface. This can be removed with a scouring pad, or if it is really oxidized, sandpaper. Once the surface is smooth, An aluminum polish should be used to remove

Fig. 21 Treating rubber parts like this shaft drive boot will help to avoid cracking

scratches left behind by the sandpaper or scouring pad. Although the surface oxidation is easily removed, there may be pitting of the surface. Not much can be done to remove heavy pitting, except sanding or grinding it away.

As with steel, the best way to keep aluminum from oxidizing is with paint or anodizing. The aluminum engine cases on most ATV engines are painted to prevent corrosion. Other aluminum items, like swingarms or wheels, may be "clear coated" with clear paint to prevent premature corrosion.

Distinguishing the difference between bare and clear coated aluminum can be a perplexing task. If the aluminum component is question is colored, chances are that is anodized (a translucent form of clear coating) and is definitely coated. If the aluminum component in question looks rough, but feels smooth, chances are that it also is clear coated. If you look really close, you might be able to see the clearcoat on the aluminum. Smooth looking surfaces, though, are the most difficult to identify. Polished bare aluminum can have a chrome-like appearance, but even then, may be clear coated. Sometimes smoothly machined and clear coated components, like wheels, can give the appearance of highly polished bare aluminum. If you just can't tell if the surface is coated or bare, call a dealer and ask if the manufacturer of your ATV clearcoated the component in question, or take a look in your owner's manual. Most have warnings about the finish on the wheels or other surfaces.

✳✳ WARNING

If your wheels or swingarm (or any other aluminum component) is clearcoated, DO NOT use aluminum polish! This will damage the finish considerably. Aluminum polish is only for bare aluminum. Coated aluminum surfaces (paint, anodized, or powder coat) should be treated just like a painted surface.

By keeping bare aluminum surfaces clean and smooth, oxidation can be avoided. Using aluminum polish is the easiest way to keep unfinished aluminum surfaces smooth and clean. The best part about polishing bare aluminum is that with a little elbow grease, a chrome-like luster can be achieved. Occasional touch-up polishing will be required to keep things looking good, though. But, just like washing your ATV, the more you keep up on it, the easier it becomes.

Most aluminum polishes and compounds are applied like wax—rub a small amount of paste with a soft rag, wait for it to haze, and buff with a clean, soft cloth. But, make sure to read the directions on the can, since there may be specific steps or techniques for a particular product.

Vinyl Seat Covers

▶ See Figure 22

The seat covers on most ATVs are made from vinyl. Basic washing will clean vinyl, but just like plastic, constant washing can dry out vinyl. When vinyl dries out, it becomes brittle, and can crack and tear. To compensate for the drying action of washing, a vinyl and plastic treatment should be used.

After your ATV has been washed, spraying a rag and using it to wipe your seat is all that is required to keep your seat cover in good condition.

A word of caution though. Don't wipe down your seat right before you plan to ride, since most vinyl treatments will make your seat a little slippery. This can be a little annoying, or even downright dangerous. Wait until your ATV is not going to be ridden for a few days before applying vinyl treatment to your seat. This will give the vinyl treatment time to soak into the cover.

91238P21

Fig. 22 Seats can also be kept clean and supple with an occasional application of protectant

9

BASIC TROUBLE-SHOOTING (HOW YOUR ATV WORKS)

TROUBLESHOOTING YOUR ATV

Even with the best maintenance, an ATV can sometimes fail to perform as hoped. Your ATV may refuse to start, or it may stop running properly. You may have a problem with it's handling, or maybe one of your accessories stops working. Keep in mind that an ATV is a mechanical device subject to wear and failure. With proper maintenance and care, most problems can be avoided, but once in a while a gremlin can sneak up and bite you. In this section we will look at some of the ways you can troubleshoot problems you may encounter on your ATV and get it back in tip-top shape.

To borrow from The Motorcycle Safety Foundation (MSF) the word "SIPDE" stands for "Scan," "Identify," "Predict," "Decide, " and "Execute." This is the mantra a motorcycle or ATV rider should be repeating every second they are riding. By performing "SIPDE" an ATV rider can keep a clear view of what is going on around them while riding. This SIPDE concept can be applied to troubleshooting your ATV.

Fixing a problem should not be a hit or miss proposition. By charting a plan of action using all the information available to you, the process of troubleshooting should be straightforward, if not easy. The biggest mistake people make when trying to figure out a problem is not taking an organized approach to it, choosing instead to guess at the solution.

The Basic Steps Of Troubleshooting

Many hours and dollars were spent designing your ATV. Some of the worlds best engineers make their livings designing our source of enjoyment. They used standard engineering practices to design them and by keeping this in mind, we can use the same type of thought patterns to fix them.

1. **Scan:** Look the machine over. Are there any obvious problems? Are there any parts out of place or hanging off? Are all the connectors fitted tightly? Is there fuel in the tank? Are any wires disconnected? Are there fluids leaking from anyplace they shouldn't (or in any amounts more than usual!)? Is the battery charged? These are all items that can be done at a glance. The "Scan" por-

tion of troubleshooting should be part of your pre-ride check and by keeping a close eye on your ATV, you might catch something that may become a problem later. You would be amazed at how many problems present themselves with just a good looking over. Never skip this step!

2. **Identify:** What may cause this type of problem? For example: If the ATV won't start, there is no need to check chain slack. Try to narrow down your search. Was the machine making a noise? Ask yourself what might possibly make that kind of noise and start looking in that area. Did you smell something like burning oil or spilled gasoline? Look for areas that contain those fluids. The idea is to eliminate as many potential areas as possible so your search becomes smaller. Remember that the engineer who designed your ATV took it one part at a time; You should also.

3. **Predict:** Now that you have identified the most likely area to explore, it is time to dig a bit deeper. Now it is time to pull out the tools and testers to see if you were right. Pick an area or item that seems to be the most likely culprit. You have been using logic as your detective and now the suspect is in sight. Start testing your assumptions and see if you choose wisely.

4. **Decide:** Did your tests conclude that the item you just tested was the guilty party? Is the problem identified? Can you go onto repairing the problem or is further narrowing required? Will this fix the problem or just cure the symptom? These are things you need to think about. Many times people just fix some symptoms without actually curing the underlying cause. Replacing a tire may fix a wobble caused by uneven wear, but what caused the uneven wear? Make sure you have reached the root of the problem.

5. **Execute:** Go ahead! Fix that problem! You may be able to fix the problem right in your own driveway or on the side of the road, but maybe you can't and will need professional help. Either way, you have figured out what the problem is and you can decide what direction you want to go.

In the rest of this section we will explain how the various systems of an ATV work in order to help you troubleshoot your problems.

POWERTRAIN THEORY & DIAGNOSIS

Before you try to determine what's wrong with your engine you should know how it works when everything is right.

Piston Port Two-Stroke Engines

▶ **See Figures 1, 2, 3 and 4**

The simplest type of ATV engine is the piston port two stroke single which only has three main moving parts. The ports are located in the cylinder wall and are opened and closed by the piston's movement. Their functions are:

1. Intake port—admits fresh fuel mixture from the carburetor into the crankcase.

2. Transfer ports—provide passages for the mixture between the crankcase and combustion chamber. These are also known as scavenging ports.

3. Exhaust port—releases burned gases from the combustion chamber into the exhaust pipe.

Basically, this is what happens during a 360 degree rotation of the crankshaft, beginning with the piston at top dead center (TDC):

• **Downstroke**—the piston descends from the previous cycle and exposes the exhaust port, jetting out the expanding burned gases. Simultaneously, the piston's downward movement compresses the fuel mixture from the previous cycle in the airtight crankcase.

As the piston continues to descend, it also exposes the transfer ports. The compressed mixture waiting in the crankcase now rushes through the ports and fills the combustion chamber, while at the same time sweeping any remaining burned gases out the exhaust port.

• **Upstroke**—after reaching its lowest point of travel, the piston begins to ascend and closes off the transfer ports. At the same time, the piston's upward

movement creates a partial vacuum in the crankcase. As the piston continues to ascend, it closes off the exhaust port and begins to compress the mixture in the combustion chamber.

Meanwhile, the bottom of the piston exposes the intake port and a fresh fuel mixture is sucked into the crankcase. When the piston approaches top dead center, ignition occurs and the piston once again descends to begin another cycle. As described, ignition occurs once every 360 degrees or, more appropriately, once every two strokes of the piston (one down and one up). Hence, the term two-stroke engine.

A recent improvement in piston port design is the five-port cylinder, and the main difference between it and the conventional type lies in the five-port cylinder's more efficient exhaust sweep.

The earlier Schnuerle loop scavenging system has two transfer ports that aim streams of fresh mixture toward the back of the cylinder; this sweeps out most of the remaining exhaust gases, but leaves one area untouched in the middle of the combustion chamber. The five-port system, on the other hand, has two additional auxiliary transfer ports. These extra ports direct a small charge of fresh mixture right at the dead spot and force it out the exhaust port. This complete exhaust sweep creates more space for the incoming mixture, and, as a result, the engine has more low and mid-range power, runs cooler, and consumes less fuel.

A newer style of two-stroke port engineering is the seven-port cylinder used in conjunction with a reed valve. The die-cast aluminum valve consists of a block with flexible stainless steel reeds that open and close the intake port. The reeds are actuated by crankcase vacuum and, therefore, admit only the necessary amount of fuel. When combined with the improved scavenging ability of the seven-port cylinder, the valve helps reduce fuel consumption, increase low-end pulling power, and flatten out the horsepower and torque curves.

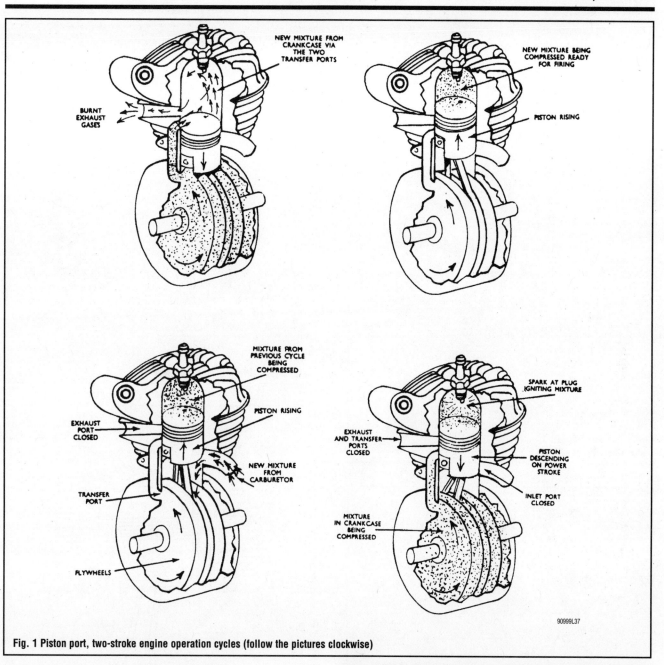

NEW MIXTURE FROM CRANKCASE VIA THE TWO TRANSFER PORTS

BURNT EXHAUST GASES

NEW MIXTURE BEING COMPRESSED READY FOR FIRING

PISTON RISING

MIXTURE FROM PREVIOUS CYCLE BEING COMPRESSED

PISTON RISING

EXHAUST PORT CLOSED

NEW MIXTURE FROM CARBURETOR

TRANSFER PORT

FLYWHEELS

SPARK AT PLUG IGNITING MIXTURE

EXHAUST AND TRANSFER PORTS CLOSED

PISTON DESCENDING ON POWER STROKE

INLET PORT CLOSED

MIXTURE IN CRANKCASE BEING COMPRESSED

90999L37

Fig. 1 Piston port, two-stroke engine operation cycles (follow the pictures clockwise)

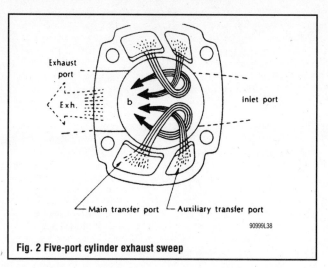

Exhaust port

Exh.

b

Inlet port

Main transfer port — Auxiliary transfer port

90999L38

Fig. 2 Five-port cylinder exhaust sweep

Rotary-Valve Two-Stroke Engines

♦ See Figure 5

The rotary-valve two-stroke operates on the same basic principles as the piston-port type, but is constructed differently and offers some distinct advantages.

The valve itself is a resin hardened fiber disc with a cutaway section along its circumference. The disc is mounted directly to the end of the crankshaft and is enclosed within a narrow sealed chamber located between the crankcase and the carburetor. As the valve rotates, the cutaway section exposes the port and allows the fresh fuel mixture to be sucked into the crankcase. Then, when the cutaway section ends, the port is sealed by the disc and no more mixture can enter.

What is the advantage? In the piston port system the intake port is located in the cylinder wall along with the transfer and exhaust ports. Therefore, intake timing (when the port opens and closes) is dictated by the piston skirt and limited by the size and position of the other ports. In the rotary-valve type, on the other hand, the intake port is located in the side of the crankcase, and intake timing is determined by the position (on the disc) and duration of the valve cutaway.

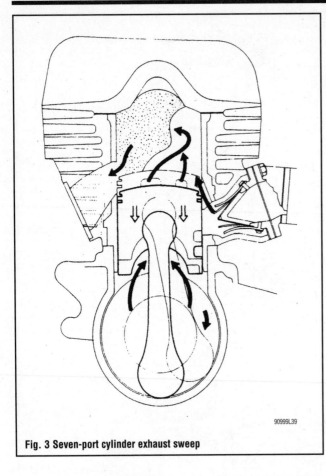

Fig. 3 Seven-port cylinder exhaust sweep

90999L39

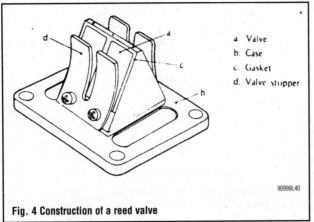

a. Valve
b. Case
c. Gasket
d. Valve stopper

Fig. 4 Construction of a reed valve

90999L40

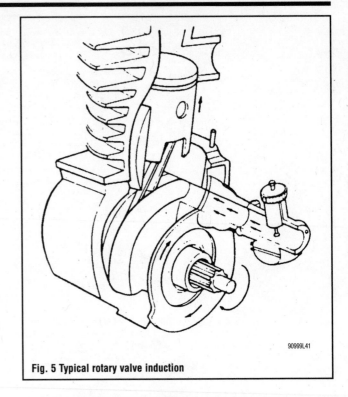

Fig. 5 Typical rotary valve induction

90999L41

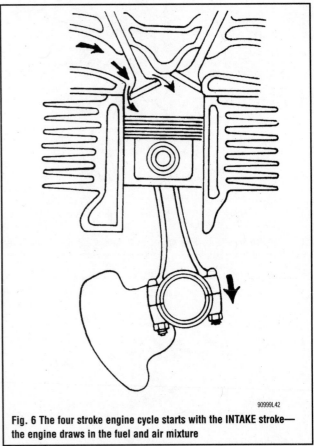

Fig. 6 The four stroke engine cycle starts with the INTAKE stroke—the engine draws in the fuel and air mixture

90999L42

This independence from piston control and cylinder design complications allows intake timing to be set, and easily adjusted, for optimum engine breathing. As a result, the engine has greater flexibility and delivers more power throughout a wider range.

Pushrod Four-Stroke Engines

♦ See Figures 6 thru 9

The four-stroke engine requires four complete strokes of the piston to complete one power cycle. During the intake stroke the intake valve opens and the fuel mixture is drawn into the cylinder as a result of the sudden vacuum created in the combustion chamber. As the piston moves toward the top of its travel on the compression stroke, both valves are closed and the fuel/air mixture is compressed. The spark plug fires and ignites the charge. The resulting combustion forces the piston down in the power stroke. As the piston moves

down toward its lowest point of travel, the exhaust valve opens, and as the action of the flywheel sends the piston back up on the exhaust stroke, the remains of the previous charge are forced out past the exhaust valve. Just before the piston reaches the top of its travel, the intake valve opens and the exhaust flow induces the intake flow which continues while the exhaust valve

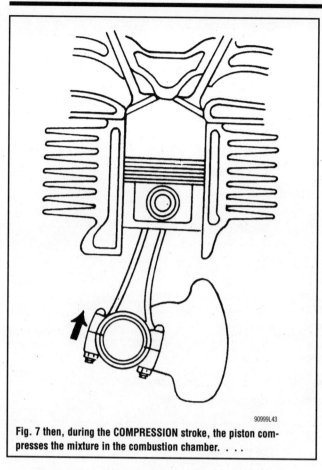

Fig. 7 then, during the COMPRESSION stroke, the piston compresses the mixture in the combustion chamber. . . .

90999L43

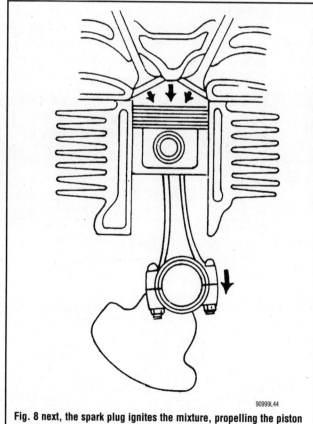

Fig. 8 next, the spark plug ignites the mixture, propelling the piston downwards on the POWER stroke

90999L44

Fig. 9 and when the piston returns upward, the EXHAUST stroke forces the burnt gases out of the exhaust valve

90999L45

closes. The process then repeats itself since each of the four cycles has been completed.

The basic valve train of four-stroke engines consists of camshaft driven pushrods which actuate rocker arms, which in turn, operate the valves. The camshaft can be driven directly by the crankshaft through gears which reduce the rate of rotation to 1/2 the engine speed. Cams can also be chain driven off the crank.

Overhead Camshaft Four-Stroke Engines

♦ **See Figures 6 thru 9**

This is the most common of most ATV engines. Overhead cam engines are those which have the cam mounted above the valves.

The cam or cams ride in the cylinder head supported by plain bearings, usually with inserts, but sometimes directly on the alloy head casting itself, or on ball or roller bearings.

The cam(s) may be driven by chain which necessitates the fitting of a chain tensioner somewhere. Both single and duplex chains are used. Other types of cam drives include spur gears, shaft and bevel gears, and reciprocating rods.

Chain-driven overhead cams predominate since this method is cheaper, quieter, and more compact than other methods, but as noted, a tensioner is necessary to compensate for stretching of the chain. Tensioners are sometimes fully automatic, relying on oil pressure to function, but more often they are simply mechanical devices which must be set by hand. Usually the tensioner will have a spring-loaded arm which, when released, will push against the chain, and a bolt is then tightened to secure it in this position.

Single overhead cam engines use rocker arms to actuate the valves, while more sophisticated dual overhead cam engines may have the cams located directly above the valve stems, obviating the need for any intermediate device. The chief drawback of this latter method is the difficulty of valve adjustment, which must be done with precisely measured shims, but the advantage is in the higher rpm obtainable, and the longer interval between valve adjustments. There are dual overhead cam engines that use threaded adjusters, but they are not the norm.

The advantage of an overhead cam design is that the reduced weight of the valve train allows the engine to turn higher rpm. In addition to this, overhead cam engines have much less valve floating problems than pushrod engines (floating is when the engine begins to turn faster than the valves can operate). The only disadvantage of an overhead cam design is that it necessitates a tall engine which raises the center of balance and makes designing a well handling frame more difficult.

ENGINE TROUBLESHOOTING

Problem	Possible Cause	Inspection/Remedy
Abnormal engine noise	Piston slap; piston-to-cylinder wall clearance too great	Check clearance
	Excessive valve clearance	Adjust
	Excessive carbon in combustion chamber	Decarbonize
	Maladjusted or worn cam chain; worn cam sprocket	Adjust or replace
	Knock (especially noticeable at idle): worn connecting rod big end bearing	Replace
	Worn connecting rod small end bearings or wrist pin	Replace
	Rumble at idle developing into whine at high rpm: crankshaft main bearings worn or damaged	Replace
	Defective or worn transmission gears or shaft bearings	Inspect and replace worn parts
	Pinging or spark knock: timing too advanced; low quality fuel; excessive carbon buildup in combustion chamber	Adjust ignition timing; use better quality fuel; clean cylinder head chamber
Engine fails to start, but has spark at the plug	No fuel in the tank; fuel petcock closed or clogged; fuel line clogged	Refuel; turn on or clean petcock; check for fuel at carbs; clean and blow out fuel lines
	Engine flooded	Remove spark plugs and crank engine to blow out excess fuel
	Crankcase flooded (2-stroke)	Remove spark plug, shut off petcock and crank engine
	Ignition timing incorrect	Reset timing
	Improper fuel/oil ratio (2-stroke)	Drain tank and refill with correct mixture
	Low or no compression	Blown head gasket; warped head; worn or damaged crankshaft seals; poor seal at crankcase mating surface (2-stroke); worn piston rings; worn cylinder bore; bad valves
	Carb adjustments wrong	Adjust carb; check float height
Engine fails to start (no spark at plug)	Ignition switched off	Turn on ignition
	Kill switch off	Reset
	Spark plug worn or fouled	Clean or replace
	Spark plug heat range too cold	Replace with proper spark plug
	Spark plug gap too wide	Reset the gap
	Spark plug resistor cap defective	Replace cap
	Plug lead defective or damaged	Replace
	Ignition coil defective	Replace
	Condenser defective (points type ignition)	Replace
	Points worn, dirty or damaged	Replace
	Points wire disconnected	Reattach and check connections

91239C03

ENGINE TROUBLESHOOTING

Problem	Possible Cause	Inspection/Remedy
Engine fails to start (cont.)	Dead battery	Recharge or replace battery
	Blown fuse, circuit breaker or fusible link	Replace or reset
	Loose or corroded battery terminals	Clean and secure the connections
Engine is hard to start	Worn, dirty or improperly gapped plug; improper heat range (too cold)	Clean or replace plugs with proper heat range
	Points dirty, pitted or out of adjustment	Replace and adjust
	Carburetor idle settings wrong; pilot air or fuel passages clogged	Adjust idle settings or clean carburetors
	Battery low	Recharge or replace battery
	Ignition timing out of specification	Adjust
	Spark plug lead cracked or dirty	Replace
	Loose or intermittently grounded wires at coil, points or connectors	Check connections and condition of wiring
	Defective coils or condensers	Replace
	Valves adjusted too tightly	Adjust
	Worn internal engine component	Rebuild engine
Engine starts but refuses to run	Fuel feed problem	Check fuel supply; check petcock, lines, carburetor for blocked passages; fuel tank vent
	Valve clearance incorrect	Adjust
	Ignition timing incorrect	Adjust
	Spark plug too cold or worn	Replace with proper heat range plug
Engine idles poorly and misfires under acceleration	Incorrect carburetor adjustment	Adjust
	Spark plug dirty, worn or incorrect gap	Clean or replace spark plug
	Poor wiring connections in ignition circuit	Check connections at each ignition component
	Defective ignition coil or condenser	Replace
	Ignition timing incorrect	Adjust
	Air leak at carburetor manifold	Fix leak
	Water in carburetor or tank	Drain carburetor float bowl or drain fuel tank
	Carburetor main jet clogged	Remove and clean
	Fuel tank vent clogged	Clean
	Petcock clogged	Clean
	Float bowl level too low	Adjust float height
Spark plug fouls repeatedly	Plug gap too narrow	Adjust to proper gap
	Plug heat range too low for conditions	Fit a higher heat range plug
	Fuel mixture set too rich	Adjust fuel mixture
	Too much oil in fuel (2-stroke)	Check ratio or mixing pump
	Piston rings worn	Replace
Engine surges or runs unevenly at standard throttle opening	Air leak at carburetor manifold	Check for leaks and fix
	Partial seizure of engine due to overheating	Determine reason for overheating and fix

91239C04

ENGINE TROUBLESHOOTING

Problem	Possible Cause	Inspection/Remedy
Engine breaks up or misfires while running	Dead battery	Recharge or replace battery
	Loose or intermittent connections in ignition circuit	Check connections
	Carburetor float level incorrect	Check float height and that the needle valve is seating
Loss of compression or power	Holed or damaged piston	Replace
	Piston partially seizing	Determine cause and fix
	Worn piston rings	Replace
	Blown or leaking head gasket	Replace
	Muffler or exhaust port clogged with carbon (2-stroke)	Decarbonize
	Clogged air filter	Clean or replace
Poor low speed operation	Incorrect ignition timing	Adjust timing
	Bad points	Replace
	Defective coil or condenser	Replace
	Carburetor float level incorrect	Adjust
	Pilot screw not adjusted properly	Adjust carburetor
	Spark plug gap too large	Adjust
Poor high speed operation	Ignition timing incorrect	Adjust
	Spark plug gap too small	Adjust
	Defective ignition coil	Replace
	Carburetor float level incorrect	Adjust float level
	Low compression	Check engine mechanical condition and repair
	Engine carbon fouled	Decarbonize
	Exhaust pipe loose at engine	Tighten connection
	Weak breaker points spring	Replace points
	Air cleaner dirty or clogged	Clean or replace
Engine partially seizes or slows after high speed operation	Spark plug too hot	Use colder range plug
	Piston seizure	Determine cause and repair
	Fuel mixture too lean	Adjust carburetor
	Insufficient lubricant in fuel mixture (2-stroke)	Check mixture ratio or oil mixing pump
	Air leaks at carburetor manifolds	Repair leaks
Engine overheats	Engine is carbon fouled	Decarbonize
	Water pump not working	Repair
	Radiator clogged internally	Replace
	Loss of coolant	Repair leak and fill with proper coolant
	Ignition timing too retarded or too advanced	Adjust
	Cooling fins clogged with dirt	Clean
	Air/fuel mixture too lean	Adjust

91239C05

ENGINE TROUBLESHOOTING

Problem	Possible Cause	Inspection/Remedy
Engine detonates or preignites	Spark plugs too hot for application	Replace with cooler spark plugs
	Ignition timing too advanced	Adjust
	Insufficient oil in fuel (2-stroke)	Check mixture ratio or oil mixture pump
	Air/fuel mixture too lean	Adjust
	Air leaks at carburetor manifolds	Fix
	Engine carbon fouled	Decarbonize
	Fuel octane too low	Use higher octane fuel
Engine backfires	Ignition timing too advanced	Adjust
Rapid piston and cylinder cylinder wear	Ineffective air cleaner	Replace
	Excess fuel washing cylinder walls	Adjust mixture leaner
Popping at muffler after shutting off throttle	Mixture too lean	Adjust idle circuit and float level. Check for air leaks.
Exhaust smoke accompanied by oil consumption	Too much oil in engine	Set to correct level
	Worn rings or bore	Rebuild
	Worn valve guides or seals	Replace
	Scored cylinder	Bore to oversize
Black smoke from exhaust pipes	Excessive carbon buildup in engine	Decarbonize
	Overly rich mixture	Adjust carb
	Obstructed air cleaner element	Install new element
	Malfunctioning choke mechanism	Repair the mechanism
Piston seizure	Low oil level	Maintain oil at proper level
	Engine overheating due to too advanced ignition timing, insufficient valve clearance, stuck valves	Check settings
	Insufficient oil	Check oil pump
Burned valves	Clearances adjusted too tightly	Replace valves; check guides; maintain adjustment
	Overly lean mixture	Adjust carb; inspect fuel delivery system for
	Timing too retarded	Adjust
Bent valves or broken valve guides	Valve hitting piston because of over-revving the engine, or weak valve springs	Check top end components; inspect for incorrect valve timing
Bad connecting rod bearings	Insufficient or contaminated oil	Check oil, filter, and oil pump
	Over-revving engine	Abide by tachometer red line
	Extended use of the engine with ignition timing too advanced, high-speed misfire etc.	Adjust ignition timing; fix misfire problem
Bad crankshaft bearings	Insufficient or contaminated oil	Change oil and filter when directed
	Over-revving engine	Abide by tachometer red line
	Extended use of the motorcycle with one weak or misfiring cylinder	Fix misfire problem

91239C06

ENGINE TROUBLESHOOTING

Problem	Possible Cause	Inspection/Remedy
Worn cam lobes or bearings	Insufficient or contaminated oil	Maintain oil at proper level; change filter when directed
	Failure to allow engine sufficient warm-up	Allow additional warm-up when starting cold engine
	Defective oil pump or clogged oil passages in engine	Replace
Worn cylinder and rings	Damaged or leaking air cleaner	Replace element; secure connections
	Low oil level or contaminated oil	Maintain oil at proper level; change oil and filter at proper intervals
	Defective oil pump	Replace
	Failure to allow engine sufficient warm-up	Allow at least one minute for warm-up when starting cold engine

91239C07

TRANSMISSION TROUBLESHOOTING

Problem	Possible Cause	Inspection/Remedy
Clutch slips	Release mechanism improperly adjusted	Readjust
	Release worm and lever sticking	Check cable for binding, and lever spring for damage
	Clutch spring tension too loose	Readjust progressively, and evenly, until proper
	Worn or damaged clutch spring(s)	Replace as necessary
	Friction discs or steel plates worn, warped, or oil impregnated	Replace as necessary
	Distorted pressure plate	Replace as necessary
Clutch drags	Release mechanism incorrectly adjusted	Readjust
	Release worm and lever, or throwout bearing, excessively worn or damaged	Replace as necessary
	Clutch spring tension too tight	Readjust
	Friction discs gummy and sticking	Replace as necessary
	Steel plates or pressure plate warped or damaged	Replace as necessary
	Clutch sprocket keys excessively worn or damaged	Replace as necessary
Clutch chatters	Clutch disc rivets loose	Replace as necessary
	Pressure plate excessively flattened	Replace as necessary
	Excessive play in the clutch drive chain	Replace worn components
	Bad clutch hub bearing	Replace as necessary
Grinding when shifting	Clutch drags	Consult the Clutch Drags section
	Worn gear dogs	Replace as necessary
	Worn shifter mechanism (ie. distorted selector forks or worn shift drum or cam)	Replace as necessary
	Bad transmission shaft bearings	Replace as necessary
	Worn transmission shafts	Replace as necessary
	Foreign objects in the gearbox	Flush out gearbox
	Idle speed too high	Adjust
	Excessive oil level in the primary case	Drain and refill according to specifications
	Transmission oil too heavy for conditions	Drain and refill with lighter oil
	Insufficient or diluted gearbox oil	Drain and refill

91239C08

TRANSMISSION TROUBLESHOOTING

Problem	Possible Cause	Inspection/Remedy
Transmission pops out of gear	Shifter rods improperly adjusted or damaged	Readjust or replace as necessary
	Shifter forks improperly adjusted or damaged	Readjust or replace as necessary
	Insufficient shifter spring tension	Replace as necessary
	Worn or damaged gear dogs	Replace as necessary
	Worn transmission shaft splines	Replace the shafts as necessary
	Worn, damaged, or improperly adjusted shifter mechanism or linkage	Replace or adjust as necessary
Hard shifting	Clutch drags	Consult the Clutch Drags section
	Worn, damaged, or maladjusted shifter mechanism	Readjust or replace as necessary
	Worn or damaged gear dogs	Replace as necessary
	Worn return spring	Replace as necessary
	Improper mainshaft and countershaft alignment	Replace as necessary
	Transmission oil too heavy for conditions	Drain and refill with a lighter oil
Excessive gear noise	Excessive gear backlash	Replace the worn components as necessary
	Worn or damaged transmission shaft bearings	Replace as necessary
	Worn or damaged gears	Replace as necessary
Foot shifter operates poorly	Worn, damaged, or maladjusted shifter mechanism	Replace or readjust as necessary
	Worn or damaged shift lever return spring	Replace as necessary
	Galled, gritty, or damaged shifter bearing surface	Repair or replace as necessary
	Gritty shifter mechanism	Thoroughly clean out mechanism
	Bent or distorted shifter shaft	Replace as necessary
	Bent shifter lever which contacts engine case	Repair or replace as necessary
Manual starter slips or fails to engage	First tooth on gear badly worn	Replace as necessary
	Damaged ratchet pinion teeth	Replace as necessary
	Broken, worn, or improperly meshed gear teeth	Replace as necessary
	Broken return spring	Replace as necessary
	Grit on on ratchet mechanism	Thoroughly clean out mechanism
	Worn or damaged ratchet mechanism	Replace as necessary
Chain whine	Chain too tight	Adjust chain correctly
	Chain rusted or kinking	Lubricate or replace chain
Chain slap	Chain too loose	Adjust chain correctly
	Bent chain guard	Repair chain guard so chain rotates freely
Accelerated chain and sprocket wear	Sprockets improperly aligned	Align sprockets
	Rear axle out of alignment	Align axle
	One or both sprockets slightly damaged	Replace sprockets and chain
	Chain worn or damaged	Replace chain and sprockets
	Chain insufficiently lubricated	Keep chain lubricated thoroughly

FUEL SYSTEM THEORY & DIAGNOSIS

▶ See Figures 10, 11, 12, 13 and 14

The fuel system on almost all ATVs is made up of a carburetor(s), fuel filter and occasionally an oil injection pump (two-strokes). The following information encompasses the great majority of components currently in use.

Most basically stated, a carburetor mixes air and fuel to form a combustible mixture. Air passes over an opening, drawing gasoline up and into the air stream. The gasoline is atomized as it is sucked from the opening. A throttle plate blocks the airflow to adjust the speed of the engine.

A carburetor works due to the "venturi effect." A venturi is a passage with a constricted section through which a fluid moves (in this case the fluid is the air). As the air flows through the constriction, the velocity increases (it speeds up) and the pressure goes down. It is this lower pressure that draws the gasoline through the opening.

In real life, there must be multiple ways of adjusting the rate of fuel delivery to match the needs of the engine. As a result, the carburetor can have many different circuits and components. If you wish to know more about this subject, brace yourself and read on. Otherwise, skip to the section about accessories and be happy. Carburetors aren't for the faint-at-heart!

Fig. 11 The carburetor is an essential part of an engine—it provides the proper mixture of air and fuel at varying engine speeds

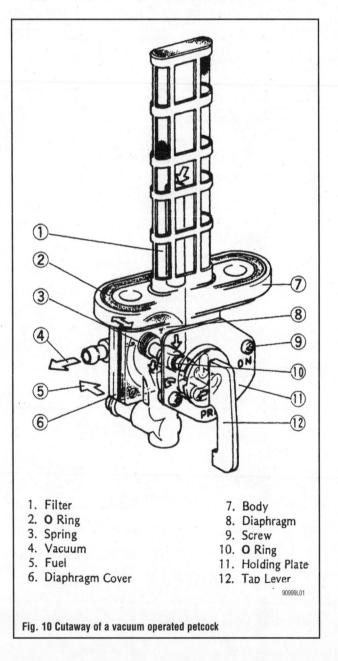

1. Filter
2. O Ring
3. Spring
4. Vacuum
5. Fuel
6. Diaphragm Cover
7. Body
8. Diaphragm
9. Screw
10. O Ring
11. Holding Plate
12. Tap Lever

90999L01

Fig. 10 Cutaway of a vacuum operated petcock

Fig. 12 Contamination is a carburetor's worst enemy—the filters on this fuel tank petcock are essential for keeping foreign matter out of the carburetor

CONSTRUCTION

▶ See Figures 15, 16 and 17

Most carburetors consist of a one-piece body cast from cheap pot metal, although some "racing" units are made from more expensive materials such as magnesium. The body incorporates a bore for the movement of the throttle slide, the venturi, and provides a mounting point for various fuel and air jets.

The body is drilled with a number of fuel and air passages. Among these are the primary air passage, pilot air passage, and pilot outlet or by-pass.

The primary air passage can usually be found just beneath the carburetor intake, and is drilled through to the needle jet. The air taken in through this passage helps to atomize, or mix, the gasoline passing through the needle jet before it enters the venturi. Unless the gasoline is atomized, raw fuel will reach the combustion chamber, resulting in wet-fouled spark plugs, inefficient combustion, and generally poor operation.

The pilot air passage is located alongside the primary air passage on most carburetors. The air taken in through this drilling is used for idle and low-speed operation.

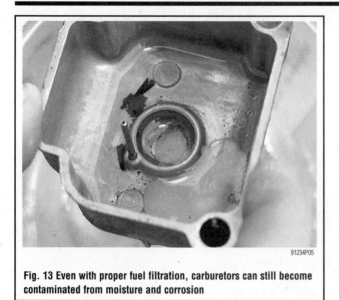

Fig. 13 Even with proper fuel filtration, carburetors can still become contaminated from moisture and corrosion

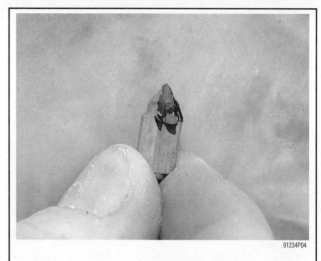

Fig. 14 This needle valve has been coated by varnish deposits, and will not seal the fuel inlet valve, causing the float bowl to overflow

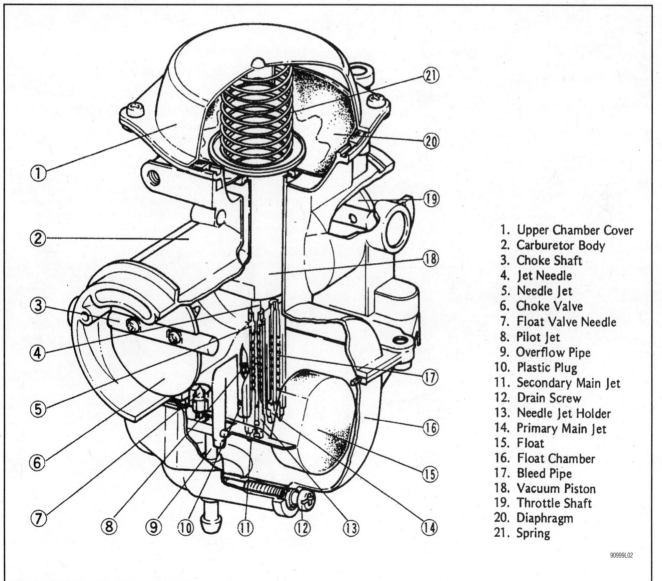

1. Upper Chamber Cover
2. Carburetor Body
3. Choke Shaft
4. Jet Needle
5. Needle Jet
6. Choke Valve
7. Float Valve Needle
8. Pilot Jet
9. Overflow Pipe
10. Plastic Plug
11. Secondary Main Jet
12. Drain Screw
13. Needle Jet Holder
14. Primary Main Jet
15. Float
16. Float Chamber
17. Bleed Pipe
18. Vacuum Piston
19. Throttle Shaft
20. Diaphragm
21. Spring

Fig. 15 This is a typical CV type carburetor

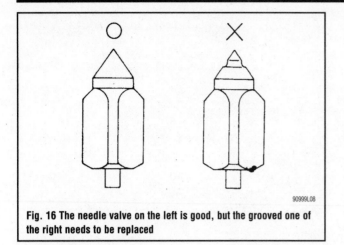

Fig. 16 The needle valve on the left is good, but the grooved one of the right needs to be replaced

The pilot outlet is a very small drilling which can be seen on the engine side of the throttle slide bore. The fuel/air mixture for idling passes through here and then to the engine.

The carburetor body also has a place for the attachment of the float bowl. The float bowl houses the float assembly and carries the carburetor's gasoline supply. A part of the float assembly is the float valve which usually consists of a small needle and a needle seat.

The float rises and falls according to the amount of gasoline in the float bowl, alternately pressing the needle against its seat and releasing it, thus controlling the fuel flow. The float bulbs may be made of various materials. Most early carburetors used brass bulbs, but plastic has been used more frequently in recent years. Float needles can be plastic, brass, or neoprene-tipped brass, the last proving most effective. Needle seats are almost always brass, and on most carburetors can be unscrewed for cleaning or replacement.

The great majority of modern carburetors mount the float bowl directly beneath the carburetor body. In this position the fuel supply surrounds the main jet ensuring an accurately metered supply of fuel during acceleration, braking, or banking to either side. This type of carburetor is usually known as "concentric." Not all carburetors were constructed in this manner, and separate float bowl carburetors were the rule for many years.

The throttle slide is the chief metering component of the carburetor. It is controlled directly by the throttle cable which runs to the twist grip on direct-control type carburetors. On "CV" units, the throttle cable opens and closes a throttle plate, and the slide itself opens and closes by venturi vacuum (this is explained later).

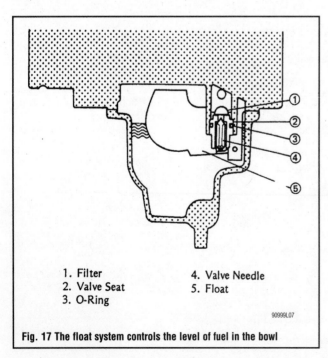

1. Filter
2. Valve Seat
3. O-Ring
4. Valve Needle
5. Float

Fig. 17 The float system controls the level of fuel in the bowl

The throttle slide determines the size of the carburetor venturi and therefore meters the amount of air in the fuel/air mixture at most of the operating range. Additionally, the needle or jet needle is attached to the slide. This needle works in conjunction with the needle jet and determines the amount of gasoline allowed to pass into the engine primarily in the mid-range.

The throttle slide is cylindrical in most carburetors, although there are examples of "square slides" such as used by some Dell `Orto carburetors. The slide has a cutaway at the intake side of the carburetor to allow the entry of air in sufficient quantities to mix with the gasoline when the throttle is closed. The higher the cutaway, the leaner the mixture will be when the slide is just opened. If the size of the cutaway is not matched to the other metering components and the particular needs of the engine, the transition from idle to the main metering system will be greatly impaired. This is a particularly critical period, since the load on the engine is changing as the clutch is engaged, and smooth starts from a dead stop must be considered a matter of safety in many cases.

Formerly, throttle slides were cast from the same material as the carburetor body, but this was found to cause greatly accelerated wear on both slide and body. Today, the slide is commonly steel, often chromed, bringing wear into more acceptable limits. In CV carburetors, where the slide must be moved by venturi vacuum, the slides must be light in weight, so light alloys are used.

OPERATION

The operation of a practical carburetor can best be described by dividing it into five circuits, and the components which control each one.

Direct-Control Carburetor

▶ **See Figures 18 and 19**

STARTING CIRCUIT (0% THROTTLE OPENING)

▶ **See Figure 20**

The engine needs a rich mixture for starting when cold. Since this need is only temporary and the mixture must be balanced when the engine warms up, a manually operated "choke" is incorporated into most carburetors and is controlled by the operator.

There are various ways of creating this rich mixture. The most simple is to reduce the amount of air available to the carburetor by closing off the mouth with a plate. This method is most often found on Hondas and on some others as well.

On some units, a temporary rich mixture is obtained by flooding or overfilling the float bowl. "Ticklers" are provided on the carburetor. When pushed, they depress the float, allowing the float needle to rise from its seat. The fuel level in the float bowl then exceeds its normal level and rises through the jets into the venturi where it provides a rich starting mixture.

Other carburetors, such as Mikuni and Dell `Orto use a refined version of the tickler. A starter jet is fitted which is activated by a cable or lever. When activated, the jet is opened (in most cases a spring-loaded plunger does the open-

Fig. 18 A variation of the CV carburetor, the direct-control type, can be identified by the cable entering at the top of the carburetor

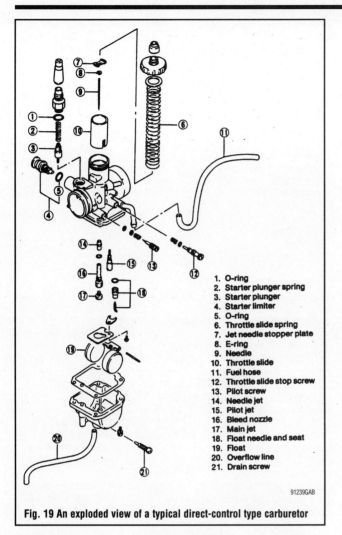

1. O-ring
2. Starter plunger spring
3. Starter plunger
4. Starter limiter
5. O-ring
6. Throttle slide spring
7. Jet needle stopper plate
8. E-ring
9. Needle
10. Throttle slide
11. Fuel hose
12. Throttle slide stop screw
13. Pilot screw
14. Needle jet
15. Pilot jet
16. Bleed nozzle
17. Main jet
18. Float needle and seat
19. Float
20. Overflow line
21. Drain screw

91239GAB

Fig. 19 An exploded view of a typical direct-control type carburetor

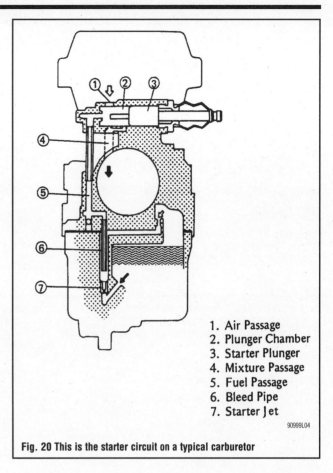

1. Air Passage
2. Plunger Chamber
3. Starter Plunger
4. Mixture Passage
5. Fuel Passage
6. Bleed Pipe
7. Starter Jet

90999L04

Fig. 20 This is the starter circuit on a typical carburetor

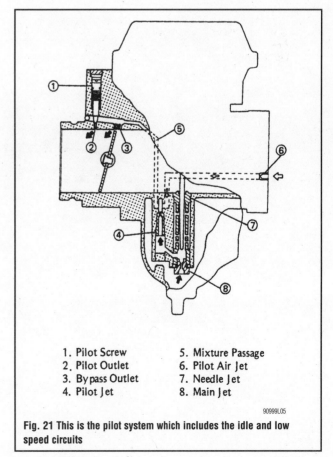

1. Pilot Screw
2. Pilot Outlet
3. Bypass Outlet
4. Pilot Jet
5. Mixture Passage
6. Pilot Air Jet
7. Needle Jet
8. Main Jet

90999L05

Fig. 21 This is the pilot system which includes the idle and low speed circuits

ing and closing), and fuel from the float bowl can bypass the normal fuel jets and pass into the carburetor bore. This is also true for some CV type crabs.

Once the engine is started and warmed up, the choke is switched off, and the fuel/air metering is turned over to the idle circuit components.

IDLE CIRCUIT (0–⅛ THROTTLE OPENING)

▶ See Figure 21

At idle, under normal operating conditions, the engine requires very little fuel and air. It does, however, require more accurate metering than pure venturi action can provide while the engine is turning relatively slowly and intake air velocity is low.

The idle circuit on most popular carburetors consists of a pilot jet, pilot air passage, and the throttle slide.

Fuel is provided by the float bowl. The amount of fuel is metered by the pilot jet, while air is taken in through the carburetor venturi and passes under the throttle slide (which is almost, but not quite closed at this point).

Because the idle mixture is so crucial, it is possible to adjust the mixture to compensate for changing conditions so that a good idle is always maintained. For this reason a pilot screw is fitted to most carburetors. The pilot screw is really a tapered needle and is fitted to an air or fuel passage. Turning the screw in or out will change the amount of fuel or air allowed to pass, and hence the mixture. On some carburetors the pilot screw is fitted directly to the pilot air passage and is sometimes called the "pilot air screw." On carburetors of this type, the amount of fuel entering the idling engine is determined by the size of the pilot jet alone, and the amount of air is varied to meet changing conditions.

On other types of carburetors, it is the amount of air which is fixed by the size of the pilot air passage. On these carburetors, the pilot screw changes the amount of fuel passing into the engine.

In operation, piston suction creates a low-pressure area behind the throttle slide. To equalize this low pressure, air rushes through the pilot air passage, mixes with fuel from the pilot jet. This mixture is bled into the carburetor's intake tract through the pilot outlet. The air coming in under the throttle slide is added to this mixture and delivers it to the combustion chamber.

LOW-SPEED CIRCUIT (⅛–¼ THROTTLE OPENING)

This circuit uses the same components as the idle circuit. There is, however, an increase in the airflow as the throttle slide rises, and in fuel flow as the needle begins to come out of the needle jet. This effects a transition to the mid-range circuit, since the increased amounts of fuel and air delivered by the needle jet and the venturi overshadow the smaller amounts coming from the pilot outlet, eventually eliminating the idle circuit from the metering system.

MIDRANGE CIRCUIT (¼–¾ THROTTLE OPENING)

♦ See Figure 22

In this circuit, air is supplied by two sources: the venturi and the primary air passage. The more important reason for the air going through the primary air passage, however, is that it mixes with the gasoline in the needle jet (the needle jet has a number of holes drilled in it), and this helps to atomize the fuel before it enters the venturi.

Fuel is supplied by the float bowl and metered by the needle jet and needle. The needle jet on most carburetors is located just above the main jet and works in conjunction with the needle suspended from the throttle slide.

As the slide rises, the air flow through the carburetor is increased, and at the same time the tapered needle allows more and more fuel to pass through the needle jet.

HIGH-SPEED CIRCUIT (FULL THROTTLE)

The throttle slide has been lifted clear of the venturi, and no longer controls the amount of air. By the same token, the needle has lifted out of the needle jet, and no longer controls the fuel supply.

Venturi action takes over completely. The amount of air sucked into the engine is determined by the size of the venturi, and the amount of fuel delivered by the size of the main jet. The only other part of the system which still has a

significant effect is the primary air passage which continues to aid fuel atomization.

It should be understood that the operating ranges of the various metering circuits overlap somewhat, so there is a gradual, rather than an abrupt, transition from one to another as the throttle is operated.

The relative independence of the various circuits, however, should explain why it is fruitless to make random changes in carburetor settings without first determining the nature of the problem, and the range in which it occurs.

ACCELERATOR PUMPS

Some direct-control carburetors used on four-stroke motors incorporate accelerator pumps which squirt a stream of raw gasoline into the venturi whenever the throttle is opened. The pumps usually consist of a throttle slide-activated plunger which takes fuel directly from the float bowl, bypassing the normal metering components.

Accelerator pumps are incorporated to aid the transition from the idle system to the main metering system. Throttle response is therefore much improved. One disadvantage of the system, however, is that it may have an adverse effect on fuel economy (especially if you "goose" the throttle often).

Constant-Velocity Carburetors

♦ See Figure 23

The constant-velocity carburetor is basically the same as the direct-control type carburetor, except that the throttle twist-grip is not connected directly to the throttle slide, Instead, in the CV carburetor, the throttle grip and cable are connected to a throttle plate located between the intake manifold and throttle slide. As the throttle plate is opened, the manifold vacuum evacuates air from the top of the slide chamber through a passage in the slide. Consequently, on demand from the engine, the slide is raised and more air is admitted, and the tapered needle is proportionally lifted out of the jet tube to admit more fuel.

The term "constant-velocity" (or constant vacuum) refers to the speed of the air passing over the main jet tube and the vacuum in the carburetor throat which remains constant due to the movement of the piston in relation to the vacuum.

As the engine demands more air and the manifold vacuum increases, the slide responds by lifting in proportion to the vacuum. Thus the carburetor air speed and vacuum remain constant, because an increase in vacuum means an increase in slide lift, which in turn increases the amount of air passing through the carburetor by altering the size of the air passage (venturi), and compensating for the increased engine demands with a larger flow of air.

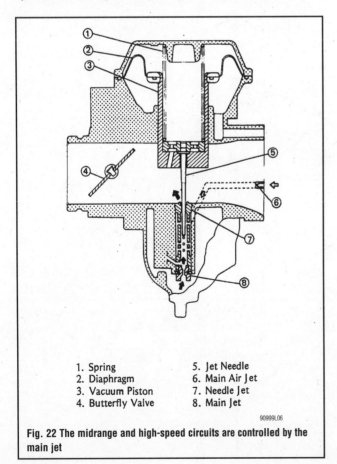

1. Spring
2. Diaphragm
3. Vacuum Piston
4. Butterfly Valve
5. Jet Needle
6. Main Air Jet
7. Needle Jet
8. Main Jet

90999L06

Fig. 22 The midrange and high-speed circuits are controlled by the main jet

91234PD6

Fig. 23 CV carburetors can be identified by the flat vacuum diaphragm housing on the top of the carburetor

Throttle-Plate Carburetors

The "throttle-plate" carburetor is similar in theory to the throttle-slide types described above except, of course, that there is no moving slide, In its place is a flat plate which pivots as the twist-grip is rotated to increase the size of the carburetor throat and allow progressively more of the fuel/air mixture to enter the combustion chamber.

Unlike the throttle-slide carburetors described above, the throttle-plate units do not usually have well defined mid-range circuits, and are best described by breaking the operation down into "low-speed" and "high-speed" circuits.

STARTING CIRCUIT

A choke plate on the intake side of the carburetor closes off the mouth to yield a rich mixture needed for starting. A hole in the choke plate allows some air to enter to prevent flooding the engine. In addition, an accelerator pump is fitted which injects a stream of gasoline into the venturi when the throttle is opened.

LOW-SPEED CIRCUIT

There are three or four idle discharge holes located at the top engine side of the venturi. The main idle discharge hole is variable in size as it works in conjunction with a tapered idle adjusting needle. At idle, the throttle plate stop screw holds the throttle plate open just enough so that this passage is able to discharge its fuel into the engine.

CARBURETOR TROUBLESHOOTING

Problem	Possible Cause	Inspection/Remedy
Carburetor floods repeatedly	Float set too high	Adjust
	Float needle sticking	Remove float bowl and clean needle and seat
	Float needle or seat worn or damaged	Replace as necessary
	Float sticking due to misalignment	Correct
	Fuel petcock left open with engine shut off	Shut off the fuel after stopping the engine
	Float punctured	Replace
Idle mixture too lean	Pilot jet too small	Replace with larger jet
	Worn throttle slide	Replace
	Pilot screw out of adjustment	Adjust
Idle mixture too rich	Pilot jet too large	Replace with smaller jet
	Dirt or foreign matter in idle passage	Dismantle and clean carburetor
	Pilot screw out of adjustment	Adjust
Lean mixture at sustained mid-range speeds	jet needle set too lean	Reset needle clip at lower notch
	Needle or main jet clogged	Remove and clean jets
	Intake manifold air leak	Find leak and rectify
Lean mixture at sustained high-speeds	Main jet too small	Replace with larger jet
	Main jet clogged	Remove and clean
	Float level too low	Remove float and adjust level
Lean mixture during acceleration	Jets clogged	Remove and clean
	Damaged or worn throttle slide	Replace
	Float level too low	Adjust float height
Lean mixture throughout throttle range	Fuel filters clogged or dirty	Remove and clean
	Gas cap vent blocked	Blow clear
	Damaged or worn throttle slide	Replace
	Air leaks at carb manifold	Find leak and rectify
Rich mixture at sustained mid-range speeds	Air cleaner dirty	Clean or replace
	Main jet too large	Replace with smaller jet
	Carburetor flooding	See above
	Needle or needle jet worn	Replace
Rich mixture at sustained high-speeds	Main jet too large	Replace with smaller size jet
	Carburetor flooding	See above.
	Air cleaner dirty	Replace or clean
Rich mixture throughout range	Carburetor flooding	See above
	Air cleaner dirty	Replace or clean
Erratic idle	Air leaks	Determine source and rectify
	Dirty or blocked idle passages	Clean carburetor
	Idle settings incorrect	Adjust to specifications
	Damage to pilot screw	Replace
	Worn or damaged O-rings or gaskets	Rebuild carburetor

Drawn by piston suction, gasoline rises from the float bowl through the idle tube. As the fuel passes the idle discharge holes, air is drawn in and mixed with it.

The mixture is then bled into the intake port through the idle hole. The mixture is determined by the idle adjusting needle. If the needle is turned in, the mixture will be leaned, and it will be richened if the needle is turned out.

As the throttle is opened slightly, the other idle discharge holes are exposed in turn, each allowing progressively more fuel and air into the intake port.

Eventually, the throttle plate is opened enough so that engine suction is powerful enough to draw gasoline from the main discharge tube and the transition to the high-speed circuit begins.

ELECTRICAL THEORY & DIAGNOSIS

Basic Electrical Theory

▶ See Figure 24

For any 12 volt, negative ground, electrical system to operate, the electricity must travel in a complete circuit. This simply means that current (power) from the positive terminal (+) of the battery must eventually return to the negative terminal (-) of the battery. Along the way, this current will travel through wires, fuses, switches and components. If, for any reason, the flow of current through the circuit is interrupted, the component fed by that circuit will cease to function properly.

Perhaps the easiest way to visualize a circuit is to think of connecting a light bulb (with two wires attached to it) to the battery—one wire attached to the negative (-) terminal of the battery and the other wire to the positive (+) terminal. With the two wires touching the battery terminals, the circuit would be complete and the light bulb would illuminate. Electricity would follow a path from the battery to the bulb and back to the battery. It's easy to see that with longer wires on our light bulb, it could be mounted anywhere. Further, one wire could be fitted with a switch so that the light could be turned on and off.

The wiring circuit on an ATV differs from this simple example in two ways. First, instead of having a return wire from the bulb to the battery, the current travels through the frame of the ATV. Since the negative (-) battery cable is attached to the frame (made of electrically conductive metal), the frame of the vehicle can serve as a ground wire to complete the circuit. Secondly, most ATV circuits contain multiple components which receive power from a single circuit. This lessens the amount of wire needed to power components on the ATV.

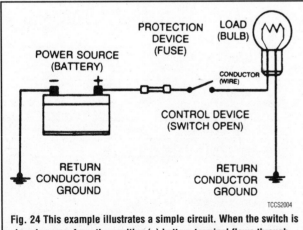

Fig. 24 This example illustrates a simple circuit. When the switch is closed, power from the positive (+) battery terminal flows through the fuse and the switch, and then to the light bulb. The light illuminates and the circuit is completed through the ground wire back to the negative (-) battery terminal. In reality, the two ground points shown in the illustration are attached to the metal frame of the vehicle, which completes the circuit back to the battery

HOW DOES ELECTRICITY WORK: THE WATER ANALOGY

Electricity is the flow of electrons—the subatomic particles that constitute the outer shell of an atom. Electrons spin in an orbit around the center core of

HIGH-SPEED CIRCUIT

The high-speed circuit begins when all idle discharge holes are exposed, and can no longer supply sufficient gasoline and air for the engine's needs.

As the throttle plate is opened the velocity of the incoming air passing through the venturi is increased, and, as this happens, this air exerts an increasingly powerful suction on the gasoline in the discharge tube just below the venturi. This gasoline is already partially atomized by the air drawn through the well vent.

When the throttle is fully opened, the amount of air in the mixture is determined by the size of the carburetor venturi and the amount of fuel by the size of the main jet.

an atom. The center core is comprised of protons (positive charge) and neutrons (neutral charge). Electrons have a negative charge and balance out the positive charge of the protons. When an outside force causes the number of electrons to unbalance the charge of the protons, the electrons will split off the atom and look for another atom to balance out. If this imbalance is kept up, electrons will continue to move and an electrical flow will exist.

Many people have been taught electrical theory using an analogy with water. In a comparison with water flowing through a pipe, the electrons would be the water and the wire is the pipe.

The flow of electricity can be measured much like the flow of water through a pipe. The unit of measurement used is amperes, frequently abbreviated as amps (**a**). You can compare amperage to the volume of water flowing through a pipe. When connected to a circuit, an ammeter will measure the actual amount of current flowing through the circuit. When relatively few electrons flow through a circuit, the amperage is low. When many electrons flow, the amperage is high.

Water pressure is measured in units such as pounds per square inch (psi); The electrical pressure is measured in units called volts (**v**). When a voltmeter is connected to a circuit, it is measuring the electrical pressure.

The actual flow of electricity depends not only on voltage and amperage, but also on the resistance of the circuit. The higher the resistance, the higher the force necessary to push the current through the circuit. The standard unit for measuring resistance is an ohm (Ω). Resistance in a circuit varies depending on the amount and type of components used in the circuit. The main factors which determine resistance are:

• Material—some materials have more resistance than others. Those with high resistance are said to be insulators. Rubber materials (or rubber-like plastics) are some of the most common insulators used in vehicles as they have a very high resistance to electricity. Very low resistance materials are said to be conductors. Copper wire is among the best conductors. Silver is actually a superior conductor to copper and is used in some relay contacts, but its high cost prohibits its use as common wiring. The wiring on most all ATVs is made of copper.

• Size—the larger the wire size being used, the less resistance the wire will have. This is why components which use large amounts of electricity usually have large wires supplying current to them.

• Length—for a given thickness of wire, the longer the wire, the greater the resistance. The shorter the wire, the less the resistance. When determining the proper wire for a circuit, both size and length must be considered to design a circuit that can handle the current needs of the component.

• Temperature—with many materials, the higher the temperature, the greater the resistance (positive temperature coefficient). Some materials exhibit the opposite trait of lower resistance with higher temperatures (negative temperature coefficient). These principles are used in many of the sensors on the engine.

OHM'S LAW

There is a direct relationship between current, voltage and resistance. The relationship between current, voltage and resistance can be summed up by a statement known as Ohm's law.

Voltage (E) is equal to amperage (I) times resistance (R): $E = I \times R$

Other forms of the formula are $R = E/I$ and $I = E/R$

In each of these formulas, E is the voltage in volts, I is the current in amps and R is the resistance in ohms. The basic point to remember is that as the resistance of a circuit goes up, the amount of current that flows in the circuit will go down, if voltage remains the same.

The amount of work that the electricity can perform is expressed as power. The unit of power is the watt (w). The relationship between power, voltage and current is expressed as:

Power (w) is equal to amperage (I) times voltage (E): $W = I \times E$

This is only true for direct current (DC) circuits; The alternating current formula is a tad different, but since the electrical circuits in most ATVs (and cars, for that matter) are DC type, we need not get into AC circuit theory.

Electrical Components

POWER SOURCE

Power is supplied to an ATV by two devices: The battery, and the alternator. The battery supplies electrical power during starting or during periods when the current demand of the ATV's electrical system exceeds the alternator output capacity . The alternator supplies electrical current when the engine is running. Just not does the alternator supply the current needs of the ATV, but it recharges the battery.

The Battery

In most modern vehicles, the battery is a lead/acid electrochemical device consisting of three or six 2 volt subsections (cells) connected in series, so that the unit is capable of producing approximately 6 or 12 volts (respectively) of electrical pressure. Each subsection consists of a series of positive and negative plates held a short distance apart in a solution of sulfuric acid and water.

The two types of plates are of dissimilar metals. This sets up a chemical reaction, and it is this reaction which produces current flow from the battery when its positive and negative terminals are connected to an electrical load. The power removed from the battery is replaced by the alternator, restoring the battery to its original chemical state.

The Alternator

On some ATVs there isn't an alternator, but a generator. The difference is that an alternator supplies alternating current which is then changed to direct current for use on the ATV, while a generator produces direct current. Alternators tend to be more efficient and that is why they are used.

Alternators and generators are devices that consist of coils of wires wound together making big electromagnets. One group of coils spins within another set and the interaction of the magnetic fields causes a current to flow. This current is then drawn off the coils and fed into the ATV's electrical system.

GROUND

Two types of grounds are used in ATV electric circuits. Direct ground components are grounded to the frame through their mounting points. All other components use some sort of ground wire which is attached to the frame or chassis of the vehicle. The electrical current runs through the chassis of the vehicle and returns to the battery through the ground (-) cable. If you look, you'll see that the battery ground cable connects between the battery and the frame or chassis of the vehicle.

➡️**It should be noted that a good percentage of electrical problems can be traced to faulty grounds.**

PROTECTIVE DEVICES

▶ **See Figures 25, 26, 27, 28 and 29**

It is possible for large surges of current to pass through the electrical system of your ATV. If this surge of current were to reach the load in the circuit, it could burn it out or severely damage it. It can also overload the wiring, causing the harness to get hot and melt the insulation. To prevent this, fuses, circuit breakers and/or fusible links are connected into the supply wires of the electrical system. These items are nothing more than a built-in weak spot in the system. When an abnormal amount of current flows through the system, these protective devices work as follows to protect the circuit:

• Fuse—when an excessive electrical current passes through a fuse, it "blows" (the conductor melts) and opens the circuit, preventing the passage of current.

Fig. 25 Most ATVs use fuses to protect the electrical circuits in the event of a component failure

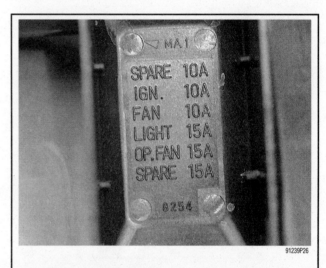

Fig. 26 The inside of this fuse box cover lists the ratings of each fuse—always replace a fuse with one of the same rating

Fig. 27 The fuse panel on this ATV has small clips that hold the fuses in place

Fig. 28 Sometimes checking the fuses involves having to remove them to allow for a better look

Fig. 29 On some larger circuits, fusible links may be used

• Circuit Breaker—a circuit breaker is basically a self-repairing fuse. It will open the circuit in the same fashion as a fuse, but when the surge subsides, the circuit breaker can be reset and does not need replacement.

• Fusible Link—a fusible link (fuse link or main link) is a short length of special, high temperature insulated wire that acts as a fuse. When an excessive electrical current passes through a fusible link, the thin gauge wire inside the link melts, creating an intentional open to protect the circuit. To repair the circuit, the link must be replaced. Some newer type fusible links are housed in plug-in modules, which are simply replaced like a fuse, while older type fusible links must be cut and spliced if they melt. Since this link is very early in the electrical path, it's the first place to look if nothing on the vehicle works, but the battery seems to be charged and is properly connected.

✳✳ CAUTION

Always replace fuses, circuit breakers and fusible links with identically rated components. Under no circumstances should a component of higher or lower amperage rating be substituted.

SWITCHES & RELAYS

▶ **See Figures 30 thru 37**

Switches are used in electrical circuits to control the passage of current. The most common use is to open and close circuits between the battery and the various electric devices in the system. Switches are rated according to the amount of amperage they can handle. If a sufficient amperage rated switch is not used in a circuit, the switch could overload and cause damage.

Some electrical components which require a large amount of current to operate use a special switch called a relay. Since these circuits carry a large amount of current, the thickness of the wire in the circuit is also greater. If this large wire were connected from the load to the control switch, the switch would have to carry the high amperage load and there would be an increased size of the wiring harness. To prevent these problems, a relay is used.

Relays are composed of a coil and a set of contacts. When the coil has a current passed though it, a magnetic field is formed and this field causes the contacts

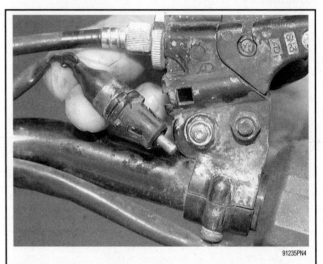

Fig. 30 Sometimes switches are used for safety purposes—like this switch on the brake lever that will not allow the starter to engage without the lever being pulled in

Fig. 31 The control switches on the handlebars on this ATV can be easily accessed by unscrewing the two halves

Fig. 32 Sometimes switches don't reveal themselves easily—neutral position switches and reverse switches are usually screwed into the engine case

Fig. 33 Using a multimeter is the best way to test for a properly functioning switch

Fig. 34 Relays are found in various locations—this ATV has them mounted on the frame

Fig. 35 These relays are mounted inside weatherproof rubber covers

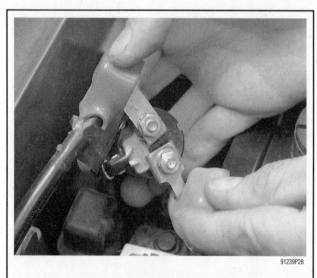

Fig. 36 Most all ATVs with electric starters use a large relay

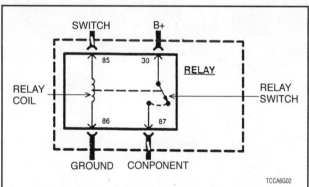

Fig. 37 Relays are composed of a coil and a switch. These two components are linked together so that when one operates, the other operates at the same time. The large wires in the circuit are connected from the battery to one side of the relay switch (B+) and from the opposite side of the relay switch to the load (component). Smaller wires are connected from the relay coil to the control switch for the circuit and from the opposite side of the relay coil to ground

to move together, completing the circuit. Most relays are normally open, preventing current from passing through the circuit, but they can take any electrical form depending on the job they are intended to do. Relays can be considered "remote control switches." They allow a smaller current to operate devices that require higher amperages. When a small current operates the coil, a larger current is allowed to pass by the contacts. Some common circuits which may use relays are the horn, headlights, starter, electric fuel pump and other high draw circuits.

LOAD

Every electrical circuit must include a "load" (something to use the electricity coming from the source). Without this load, the battery would attempt to deliver its entire power supply from one pole to another instantly. This is called a "short circuit." All this electricity would take a short cut to ground and cause a great amount of damage to other components in the circuit by developing a tremendous amount of heat. This condition could develop sufficient heat to melt the insulation on all the surrounding wires and reduce a multiple wire cable to a lump of plastic and copper.

WIRING & HARNESSES

▶ **See Figures 38 and 39**

The average ATV contains yards of wiring, with hundreds of individual connections. To protect the many wires from damage and to keep them from becoming a confusing tangle, they are organized into bundles, enclosed in plastic or taped together and called wiring harnesses. Different harnesses serve different parts of the vehicle. Individual wires are color coded to help trace them through a harness where sections are hidden from view.

ATV wiring or circuit conductors can be either single strand wire, multi-strand wire or printed circuitry. Single strand wire has a solid metal core and is usually used inside such components as alternators, motors, relays and other devices. Multi-strand wire has a core made of many small strands of wire twisted together into a single conductor. Most of the wiring in an ATV electrical system is made up of multi-strand wire, either as a single conductor or grouped together in a harness. All wiring is color coded on the insulator, either as a solid color or as a colored wire with an identification stripe. A printed circuit is a thin film of copper or other conductor that is printed on an insulator backing. Occasionally, a printed circuit is sandwiched between two sheets of plastic for more protection and flexibility. A complete printed circuit, consisting of conductors, insulating material and connectors for lamps or other components is called a printed circuit board. Printed circuitry is used in place of individual wires or harnesses in places where space is limited, such as in instruments.

Since electrical systems can very sensitive to changes in resistance, the selection of properly sized wires is critical when systems are repaired. A loose or corroded connection or a replacement wire that is too small for the circuit will add extra resistance and an additional voltage drop to the circuit.

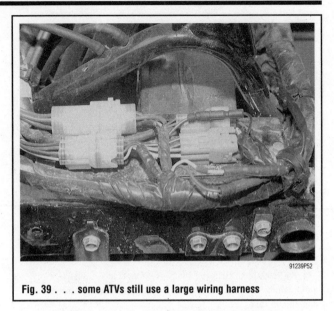

Fig. 39 . . . some ATVs still use a large wiring harness

The wire gauge number is an expression of the cross-section area of the conductor. ATV from countries that use the metric system will typically describe the wire size as its cross-sectional area in square millimeters. In this method, the larger the wire, the greater the number. Another common system for expressing wire size is the American Wire Gauge (AWG) system. As gauge number increases, area decreases and the wire becomes smaller. An 18 gauge wire is smaller than a 4 gauge wire. A wire with a higher gauge number will carry less current than a wire with a lower gauge number. Gauge wire size refers to the size of the strands of the conductor, not the size of the complete wire with insulator. It is possible, therefore, to have two wires of the same gauge with different diameters because one may have thicker insulation than the other.

It is essential to understand how a circuit works before trying to figure out why it doesn't. An electrical schematic shows the electrical current paths when a circuit is operating properly. Schematics break the entire electrical system down into individual circuits. In a schematic, usually no attempt is made to represent wiring and components as they physically appear on the vehicle; switches and other components are shown as simply as possible. Face views of harness connectors show the cavity or terminal locations in all multi-pin connectors to help locate test points.

CONNECTORS

▶ **See Figures 40, 41 and 42**

Three types of connectors are commonly used in ATV applications—weatherproof, molded and hard shell.
- Weatherproof—these connectors are most commonly used where the connector is exposed to the elements. Terminals are protected against moisture and dirt by sealing rings which provide a weathertight seal. All repairs require the use of a special terminal and the tool required to service it. Unlike standard blade type terminals, these weatherproof terminals cannot be straightened once they are bent. Make certain that the connectors are properly seated and all of the sealing rings are in place when connecting leads.
- Molded—these connectors require complete replacement of the connector if found to be defective. This means splicing a new connector assembly into the harness. All splices should be soldered to insure proper contact. Use care when probing the connections or replacing terminals in them, as it is possible to create a short circuit between opposite terminals. If this happens to the wrong terminal pair, it is possible to damage certain components. Always use jumper wires between connectors for checking circuits.
- Hard Shell—unlike molded connectors, the terminal contacts in hard-shell connectors can be replaced. Replacement usually involves the use of a special terminal removal tool that depresses the locking tangs (barbs) on the connector terminal and allows the connector to be removed from the rear of the shell. The connector shell should be replaced if it shows any evidence of burning, melting, cracks, or breaks. Replace individual terminals that are burnt, corroded, distorted or loose.

Fig. 38 Although integrated circuits and solid state technology greatly reduce the need for wiring . . .

TCCA6P03

Fig. 40 Hard shell (left) and weatherproof (right) connectors have replaceable terminals

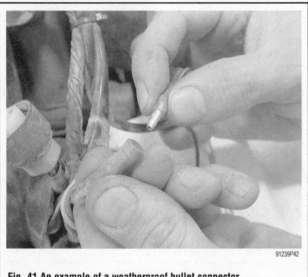

91239P42

Fig. 41 An example of a weatherproof bullet connector

91239P53

Fig. 42 If you look closely, you can see the rubber gasket on the inside of the female connector

Test Equipment

Pinpointing the exact cause of trouble in an electrical circuit is most times accomplished by the use of special test equipment. The following describes different types of commonly used test equipment and briefly explains how to use them in diagnosis. In addition to the information covered below, the tool manufacturer's instructions booklet (provided with the tester) should be read and clearly understood before attempting any test procedures.

JUMPER WIRES

❊❊ CAUTION

Never use jumper wires made from a thinner gauge wire than the circuit being tested. If the jumper wire is of too small a gauge, it may overheat and possibly melt. Never use jumpers to bypass high resistance loads in a circuit. Bypassing resistance, in effect, creates a short circuit. This may, in turn, cause damage and fire. Jumper wires should only be used to bypass lengths of wire or to simulate switches.

Jumper wires are simple, yet extremely valuable, pieces of test equipment. They are basically test wires which are used to bypass sections of a circuit. Although jumper wires can be purchased, they are usually fabricated from lengths of standard automotive wire and whatever type of connector (alligator clip, spade connector or pin connector) that is required for the particular application being tested. In cramped, hard-to-reach areas, it is advisable to have insulated boots over the jumper wire terminals in order to prevent accidental grounding. It is also advisable to include a standard automotive fuse in any jumper wire. This is commonly referred to as a "fused jumper." By inserting an in-line fuse holder between a set of test leads, a fused jumper wire can be used for bypassing open circuits while still protecting the circuit. Use a 5 amp fuse to provide protection against voltage spikes.

Jumper wires are used primarily to locate open electrical circuits, on either the ground (-) side of the circuit or on the power (+) side. If an electrical component fails to operate, connect the jumper wire between the component and a good ground. If the component operates only with the jumper installed, the ground circuit is open. If the ground circuit is good, but the component does not operate, the circuit between the power feed and component may be open. By moving the jumper wire successively back from the component toward the power source, you can isolate the area of the circuit where the open is located. When the component stops functioning, or the power is cut off, the open is in the segment of wire between the jumper and the point previously tested.

You can sometimes connect the jumper wire directly from the battery to the "hot" terminal of the component, but first make sure the component uses 12 volts in operation. Some electrical components, such as fuel injectors or sensors, may be designed to operate on about 4 to 5 volts, and running 12 volts directly to these components will cause damage.

TEST LIGHTS

▶ See Figure 43

The test light is used to check circuits and components while electrical current is flowing through them. It is used for voltage and ground tests. To use a 12 volt test light, connect the ground clip to a good ground and probe wherever necessary with the pick. The test light will illuminate when voltage is detected. This does not necessarily mean that 12 volts (or any particular amount of voltage) is present; it only means that some voltage is present. It is advisable before using the test light to touch its ground clip and probe across the battery posts or terminals to make sure the light is operating properly.

❊❊ WARNING

Do not use a test light to probe electronic ignition, spark plug or coil wires. Never use a pick-type test light to probe wiring on computer controlled systems unless specifically instructed to do so. Any wire insulation that is pierced by the test light probe should be taped and sealed with silicone after testing.

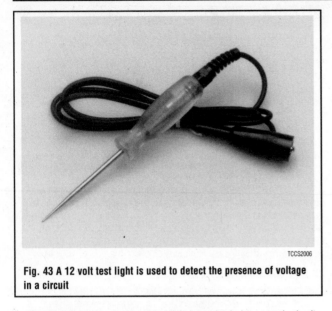

Fig. 43 A 12 volt test light is used to detect the presence of voltage in a circuit

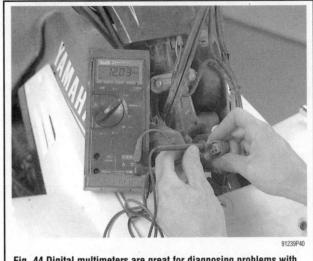

Fig. 44 Digital multimeters are great for diagnosing problems with electrical circuits

Like the jumper wire, the 12 volt test light is used to isolate opens in circuits. But, whereas the jumper wire is used to bypass the open to operate the load, the 12 volt test light is used to locate the presence of voltage in a circuit. If the test light illuminates, there is power up to that point in the circuit; if the test light does not illuminate, there is an open circuit (no power). Move the test light in successive steps back toward the power source until the light in the handle illuminates. The open is between the probe and a point which was previously probed.

The self-powered test light is similar in design to the 12 volt test light, but contains a 1.5 volt penlight battery in the handle. It is most often used in place of a multimeter to check for open or short circuits when power is isolated from the circuit (continuity test).

The battery in a self-powered test light does not provide much current. A weak battery may not provide enough power to illuminate the test light even when a complete circuit is made (especially if there is high resistance in the circuit). Always make sure that the test battery is strong. To check the battery, briefly touch the ground clip to the probe; if the light glows brightly, the battery is strong enough for testing.

➡ A self-powered test light should not be used on any computer controlled system or component. The small amount of electricity transmitted by the test light is enough to damage some electronic components.

MULTIMETERS

▶ See Figure 44

Multimeters are an extremely useful tool for troubleshooting electrical problems. They can be purchased in either analog or digital form and have a price range to suit any budget. A multimeter is a voltmeter, ammeter and ohmmeter (along with other features) combined into one instrument. It is often used when testing solid state circuits because of its high input impedance (usually 10 megaohms or more). A brief description of the multimeter main test functions follows:

• Voltmeter—the voltmeter is used to measure voltage at any point in a circuit, or to measure the voltage drop across any part of a circuit. Voltmeters usually have various scales and a selector switch to allow the reading of different voltage ranges. The voltmeter has a positive and a negative lead. To avoid damage to the meter, always connect the negative lead to the negative (-) side of the circuit (to ground or nearest the ground side of the circuit) and connect the positive lead to the positive (+) side of the circuit (to the power source or the nearest power source). Note that the negative voltmeter lead will always be black and that the positive voltmeter will always be some color other than black (usually red).

• Ohmmeter—the ohmmeter is designed to read resistance (measured in ohms) in a circuit or component. Most ohmmeters will have a selector switch which permits the measurement of different ranges of resistance (usually the selector switch allows the multiplication of the meter reading by 10, 100, 1,000

and 10,000). Some ohmmeters are "auto-ranging" which means the meter itself will determine which scale to use. Since the meters are powered by an internal battery, the ohmmeter can be used like a self-powered test light. When the ohmmeter is connected, current from the ohmmeter flows through the circuit or component being tested. Since the ohmmeter's internal resistance and voltage are known values, the amount of current flow through the meter depends on the resistance of the circuit or component being tested. The ohmmeter can also be used to perform a continuity test for suspected open circuits. In using the meter for making continuity checks, do not be concerned with the actual resistance readings. Zero resistance, or any ohm reading, indicates continuity in the circuit. Infinite resistance indicates an opening in the circuit. A high resistance reading where there should be none indicates a problem in the circuit. Checks for short circuits are made in the same manner as checks for open circuits, except that the circuit must be isolated from both power and normal ground. Infinite resistance indicates no continuity, while zero resistance indicates a dead short.

✳✳ WARNING

Never use an ohmmeter to check the resistance of a component or wire while there is voltage applied to the circuit.

• Ammeter—an ammeter measures the amount of current flowing through a circuit in units called amperes or amps. At normal operating voltage, most circuits have a characteristic amount of amperes, called "current draw" which can be measured using an ammeter. By referring to a specified current draw rating, then measuring the amperes and comparing the two values, one can determine what is happening within the circuit to aid in diagnosis. An open circuit, for example, will not allow any current to flow, so the ammeter reading will be zero. A damaged component or circuit will have an increased current draw, so the reading will be high. The ammeter is always connected in series with the circuit being tested. All of the current that normally flows through the circuit must also flow through the ammeter; if there is any other path for the current to follow, the ammeter reading will not be accurate. The ammeter itself has very little resistance to current flow and, therefore, will not affect the circuit, but it will measure current draw only when the circuit is closed and electricity is flowing. Excessive current draw can blow fuses and drain the battery, while a reduced current draw can cause motors to run slowly, lights to dim and other components to not operate properly.

Troubleshooting Electrical Systems

▶ See Figure 45

When diagnosing a specific problem, organized troubleshooting is a must. The complexity of a modern ATV demands that you approach any problem in a logical, organized manner. There are certain troubleshooting techniques which are standard:

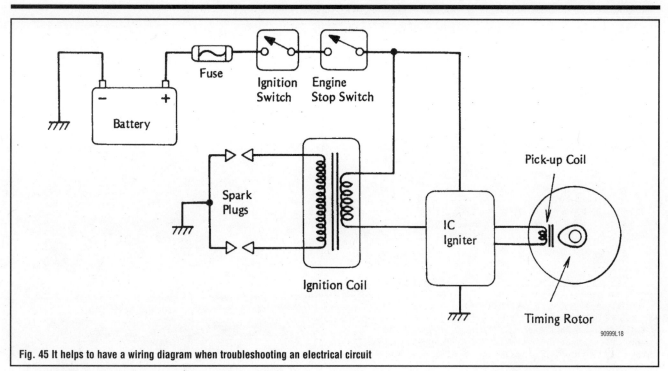

Fig. 45 It helps to have a wiring diagram when troubleshooting an electrical circuit

• Establish when the problem occurs. Does the problem appear only under certain conditions? Were there any noises, odors or other unusual symptoms?

• Isolate the problem area. To do this, make some simple tests and observations, then eliminate the systems that are working properly. Check for obvious problems, such as broken wires and loose or dirty connections. Always check the obvious before assuming something complicated is the cause.

• Test for problems systematically to determine the cause once the problem area is isolated. Are all the components functioning properly? Is there power going to electrical switches and motors. Performing careful, systematic checks will often turn up most causes on the first inspection, without wasting time checking components that have little or no relationship to the problem.

• Test all repairs after the work is done to make sure that the problem is fixed. Some causes can be traced to more than one component, so a careful verification of repair work is important in order to pick up additional malfunctions that may cause a problem to reappear or a different problem to arise. A blown fuse, for example, is a simple problem that may require more than another fuse to repair. If you don't look for a problem that caused a fuse to blow, a shorted wire (for example) may go undetected.

Experience has shown that most problems tend to be the result of a fairly simple and obvious cause, such as loose or corroded connectors, bad grounds or damaged wire insulation which causes a short. This makes careful visual inspection of components during testing essential to quick and accurate troubleshooting.

Testing

OPEN CIRCUITS

▶ **See Figure 46**

This test already assumes the existence of an open in the circuit and it is used to help locate the open portion.

1. Isolate the circuit from power and ground.
2. Connect the self-powered test light or ohmmeter ground clip to the ground side of the circuit and probe sections of the circuit sequentially.
3. If the light is out or there is infinite resistance, the open is between the probe and the circuit ground.
4. If the light is on or the meter shows continuity, the open is between the probe and the end of the circuit toward the power source.

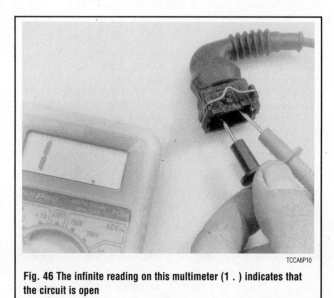

Fig. 46 The infinite reading on this multimeter (1 .) indicates that the circuit is open

SHORT CIRCUITS

➡**Never use a self-powered test light to perform checks for opens or shorts when power is applied to the circuit under test. The test light can be damaged by outside power.**

1. Isolate the circuit from power and ground.
2. Connect the self-powered test light or ohmmeter ground clip to a good ground and probe any easy-to-reach point in the circuit.
3. If the light comes on or there is continuity, there is a short somewhere in the circuit.
4. To isolate the short, probe a test point at either end of the isolated circuit (the light should be on or the meter should indicate continuity).
5. Leave the test light probe engaged and sequentially open connectors or switches, remove parts, etc. until the light goes out or continuity is broken.

6. When the light goes out, the short is between the last two circuit components which were opened.

VOLTAGE

This test determines voltage available from the battery and should be the first step in any electrical troubleshooting procedure after visual inspection. Many electrical problems, especially on computer controlled systems, can be caused by a low state of charge in the battery. Excessive corrosion at the battery cable terminals can cause poor contact that will prevent proper charging and full battery current flow.

1. Set the voltmeter selector switch to the 20V position.
2. Connect the multimeter negative lead to the battery's negative (-) post or terminal and the positive lead to the battery's positive (+) post or terminal.
3. Turn the ignition switch **ON** to provide a load.
4. A well charged battery should register over 12 volts. If the meter reads below 11.5 volts, the battery power may be insufficient to operate the electrical system properly.

VOLTAGE DROP

When current flows through a load, the voltage beyond the load drops. This voltage drop is due to the resistance created by the load and also by small resistance's created by corrosion at the connectors and damaged insulation on the wires. The maximum allowable voltage drop under load is critical, especially if there is more than one load in the circuit, since all voltage drops are cumulative.

1. Set the voltmeter selector switch to the 20 volt position.
2. Connect the multimeter negative lead to a good ground.
3. Operate the circuit and check the voltage prior to the first component (load).
4. There should be little or no voltage drop in the circuit prior to the first component. If a voltage drop exists, the wire or connectors in the circuit are suspect.
5. While operating the first component in the circuit, probe the ground side of the component with the positive meter lead and observe the voltage readings. A small voltage drop should be noticed. This voltage drop is caused by the resistance of the component.
6. Repeat the test for each component (load) down the circuit.
7. If a large voltage drop is noticed, the preceding component, wire or connector is suspect.

RESISTANCE

♦ See Figure 47

❋❋ WARNING

Never use an ohmmeter with power applied to the circuit. The ohmmeter is designed to operate on its own power supply. The normal 12 volt electrical system voltage could damage the meter!

1. Isolate the circuit from the vehicle's power source.
2. Ensure that the ignition key is **OFF** when disconnecting any components or the battery.
3. Where necessary, also isolate at least one side of the circuit to be checked, in order to avoid reading parallel resistances. Parallel circuit resistances will always give a lower reading than the actual resistance of either of the branches.
4. Connect the meter leads to both sides of the circuit (wire or component) and read the actual measured ohms on the meter scale. Make sure the selector switch is set to the proper ohm scale for the circuit being tested, to avoid misreading the ohmmeter test value.

Wire and Connector Repair

Almost anyone can replace damaged wires, as long as the proper tools and parts are available. Wire and terminals are available to fit almost any need. Even

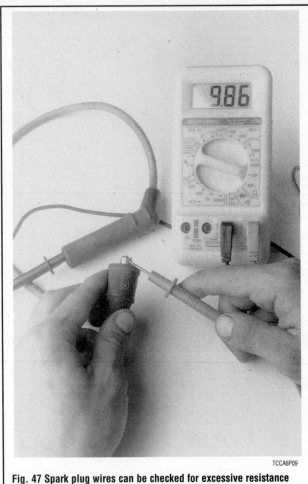

TCCA6P09

Fig. 47 Spark plug wires can be checked for excessive resistance using an ohmmeter

the specialized weatherproof, molded and hard shell connectors are now available from aftermarket suppliers.

Be sure the ends of all the wires are fitted with the proper terminal hardware and connectors. Wrapping a wire around a stud is never a permanent solution and will only cause trouble later. Replace wires one at a time to avoid confusion. Always route wires exactly the same as the factory.

➡**If connector repair is necessary, only attempt it if you have the proper tools. Weatherproof and hard shell connectors require special tools to release the pins inside the connector. Attempting to repair these connectors with conventional hand tools will damage them.**

Reading Wiring Diagrams

♦ See Figures 48 thru 53

For many people, reading wiring diagrams, or schematics, is a black art. It isn't as bad as it seems, since wiring diagrams are really nothing more than connect-the-dots with wires!

If you look at the sample diagrams, you will see that they contain information such as wire colors, terminal connections and components. The boxes may contain information such as internal configurations as would be handy to figure out what is going on inside a relay or switch.

There is a standard set of symbols used in wiring diagrams to denote various components. If the wiring diagram doesn't provide a reference for the symbols, you should be able to pick out their meanings from other information given.

The wiring diagram will use abbreviations for wire colors. There will be a chart somewhere in the wiring diagram or in the manual you are using to decode them.

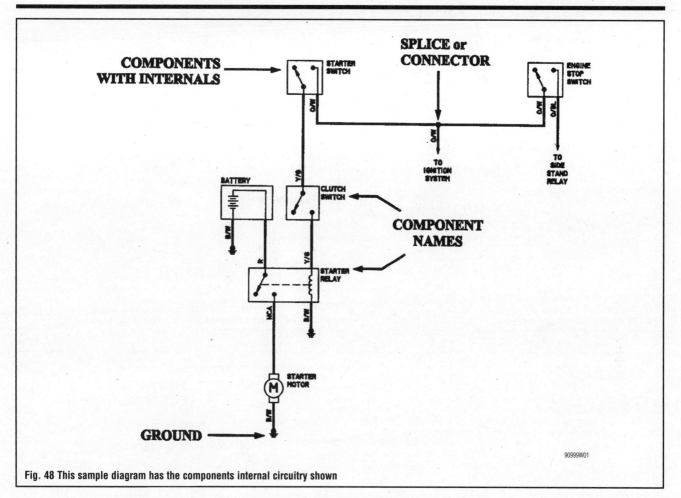

Fig. 48 This sample diagram has the components internal circuitry shown

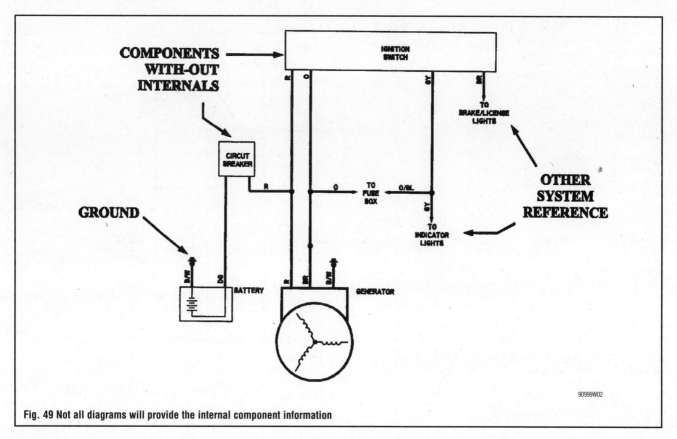

Fig. 49 Not all diagrams will provide the internal component information

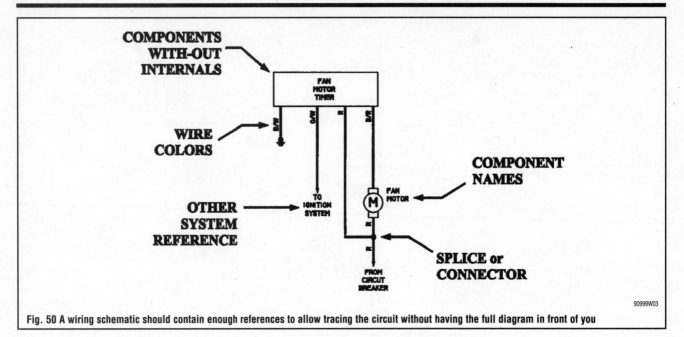

Fig. 50 A wiring schematic should contain enough references to allow tracing the circuit without having the full diagram in front of you

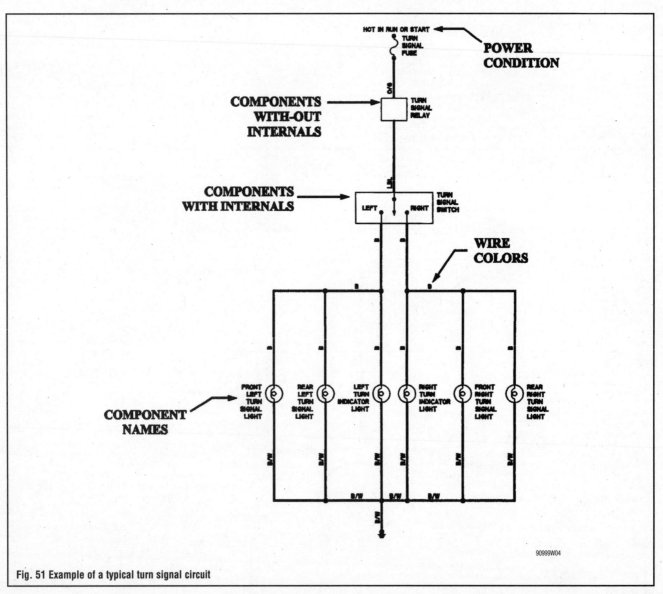

Fig. 51 Example of a typical turn signal circuit

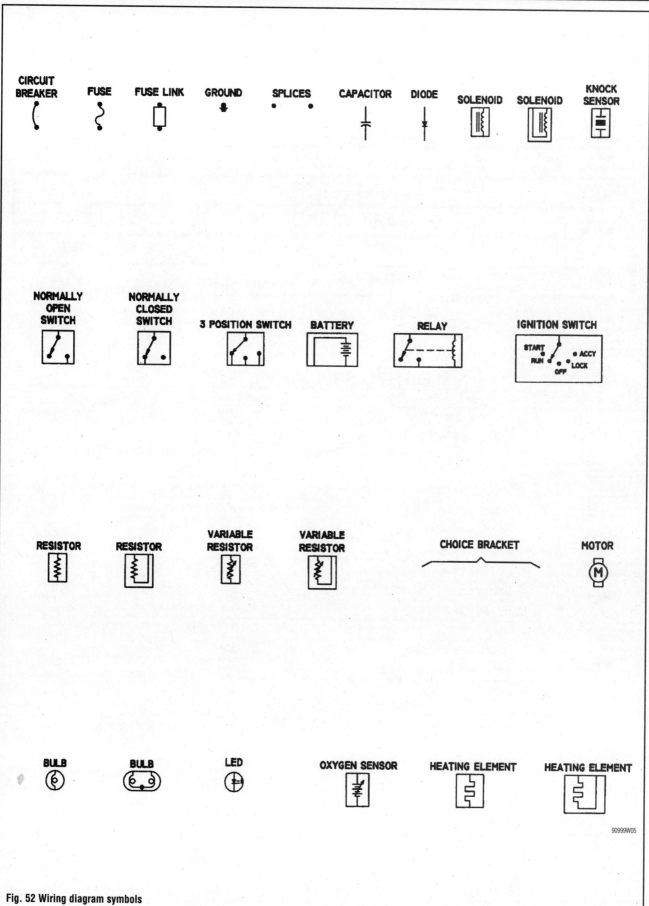

Fig. 52 Wiring diagram symbols

90999W05

BLACK	B	PINK	PK
BROWN	BR	PURPLE	P
RED	R	GREEN	G
ORANGE	O	WHITE	W
YELLOW	Y	LIGHT BLUE	LBL
GRAY	GY	LIGHT GREEN	LG
BLUE	BL	DARK GREEN	DG
VIOLET	V	DARK BLUE	DBL
TAN	T	NO COLOR AVAILABLE	NCA

90999W06

Fig. 53 Examples of some wire color abbreviations

ELECTRICAL TROUBLESHOOTING

Problem	Possible Cause	Inspection/Remedy
Battery does not charge	Defective battery	Test each cell. Replace if shorted cell(s) are evident
	Battery electrolyte level low	Top up
	Broken or shorting wires in charging circuit	Check continuity and condition of insulation on all wires
	Loose or dirty battery terminals	Clean terminals and secure connections
	Defective voltage regulator	Test and replace if necessary
	Defective alternator	Replace
	Defective silicon diode	Replace
Excessive battery charging	Defective battery (shorted plates)	Replace battery
	Voltage regulator not properly grounded	Secure
	Regulator defective	Replace
Unstable charging voltage	Intermittent short	Check wiring for frayed insulation
	Defective key switch	Replace
	Intermittent coil in alternator	Replace

91239C01

ELECTRICAL TROUBLESHOOTING

Problem	Possible Cause	Inspection/Remedy
Electric starter spins, but engine does not	Broken starter clutch	Replace
Starter does not turn over but warning lights	Low battery, or battery connections loose or corroded	Charge or replace battery; clean and tighten terminals
dim when starter button is pushed, or engine turns over slowly	Starter armature bushings worn	Replace starter
Clicking sound when starter button is pushed;	Battery low, or terminals loose or corroded	Charge or replace battery; clean and tighten connections
engine does not turn over	Defective starter solenoid	Replace
Nothing happens when the starter button is pushed	Loose or broken connections in starter switch or battery leads	Check switch connections; check battery terminals; clean and tighten battery leads
Engine turns over	Low or dead battery	Recharge or replace battery
slowly when starter button is pushed (cold weather)	Engine oil too thick	Use correct viscosity oil
No spark or weak	Defective ignition coil	Replace
spark	Defective spark plug	Replace
	Plug lead(s) or wires damaged or disconnected	Check condition of leads and wires; check all connections
Breaker points pitted or burned	Defective condenser	Replace points and condenser
Carbon-fouled spark	Mixture too rich	Adjust carburetor; check air cleaner
plug	Plugs too cold for conditions	Use hotter plug
	Idle speed set too high	Adjust carburetor
Oil-fouled spark plug	Worn rings, cylinders, or valve guides (four-stroke)	Rebuild
	Badly adjusted oil pump cable (two-stroke)	Adjust
	Fuel/oil mixture incorrect	Replace fuel/oil of proper ratio
Spark plug electrode	Spark plug too hot for conditions	Use colder plug
burned or overheated	Engine overheating	See above
	Ignition timing incorrect	Adjust
	Mixture too lean	See above

91239C02

SUSPENSION THEORY & DIAGNOSIS

Front Suspension

♦ See Figures 54, 55 and 56

Front suspensions on most ATVs can be broken down into three types: Parallel A-arm, MacPherson strut, and single swingarm.

Of the three types, parallel A-arm suspension is the most common type. This type of suspension is superior for high performance, and allows for long length travel. Since the upper and lower arms remain parallel to each other (for the most part) throughout the travel of the suspension, the wheel remains vertical. This results in a smooth riding, stable ATV.

Recently, MacPherson strut suspension (borrowed from automotive technology) has been adapted for use on ATVs. Like parallel A-arm suspension, the wheel remains vertical throughout the length of the strut travel. MacPherson strut is a simple, compact design, and uses fewer moving parts than a parallel A-arm. However, due to the geometry of the MacPherson strut design, travel is limited. This type of suspension is most commonly used on utility-type ATVs.

Single swing arm front suspensions are usually found on junior-sized ATVs, and other low cost economy models. This type of suspension is relatively simple, and resembles a MacPherson strut. Unlike the MacPherson strut though,

Fig. 54 Double A-arm suspension is the most common type of front suspension on ATVs

Fig. 55 An example of a MacPherson strut front suspension

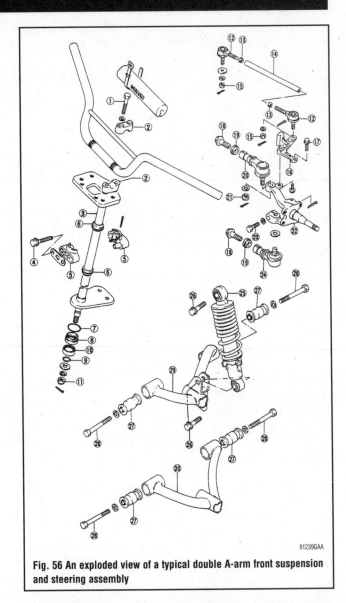

Fig. 56 An exploded view of a typical double A-arm front suspension and steering assembly

the wheel is attached to the swing arm, and follows the arc of the movement of the arm. Because of this movement, the angle of the wheel contacting the ground changes significantly in relationship to the suspension travel. This type of suspension is usually limited in travel, in order to keep the wheel angle from becoming extreme.

Rear Suspension

♦ See Figures 57, 58 and 59

Most ATVs use a basic swing arm with one or two shock absorbers. Derived from motorcycle suspensions, this design has been used for years on ATVs, mainly because of simplicity and strength.

There are only four connecting points for an average swing arm rear suspension: the pivot point which attaches the swing arm to the frame, and the two points which attach the shock absorber to the frame and the swingarm itself. Some high performance ATVs use a progressive rate linkage to attach the shock to the swingarm, and others use two shocks. Of course this increases the amount of connecting points to the frame, but the basic design is still there.

Since the one-piece axle bearing housing is directly attached to the swing arm, and the axle is rigid, both wheels follow the same movement. If one wheel hits a bump and compresses the suspension, the opposite wheel follows the same path as the other wheel. This can cause some instability at high speeds,

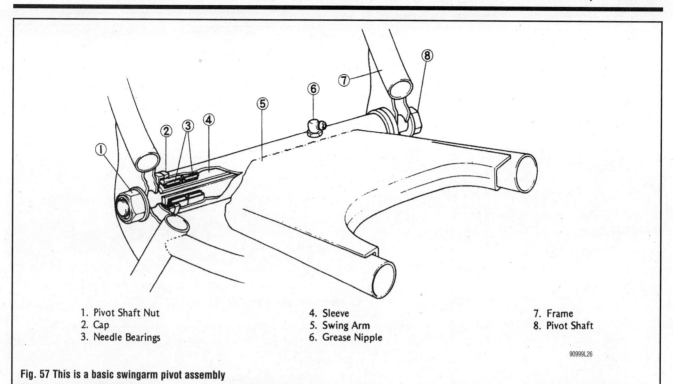

1. Pivot Shaft Nut
2. Cap
3. Needle Bearings
4. Sleeve
5. Swing Arm
6. Grease Nipple
7. Frame
8. Pivot Shaft

90999L26

Fig. 57 This is a basic swingarm pivot assembly

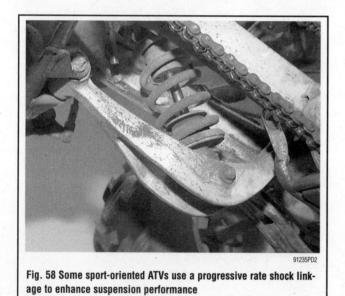

91235PD2

Fig. 58 Some sport-oriented ATVs use a progressive rate shock link-age to enhance suspension performance

since the wheels cannot operate independently of each other. Additionally, high loads are placed on the swing arm pivot.

Recently, ATV manufacturers have designed more complex suspensions which resemble the front suspensions on ATVs, to allow for independent travel of the rear wheels. These types of suspensions allow for a smoother ride, but can add weight and complexity to an ATV.

Shock Absorbers

Whether an ATV is equipped with coil-over shock absorbers, or MacPherson struts, the shock absorber itself performs the same function—control the rate of spring oscillation.

Let's discuss the operation of a shock absorber. The compression stroke of the shock absorber begins when it receives a load compressing both the outer spring and the shock hydraulic unit itself. The cylinder, which contains fluid, rises along the piston rod, causing pressure on the oil beneath the piston. This slows or "damps" the rate of compression. The oil flows through the piston ori-

fice and enters the space above the piston after pushing up the non-return valve held down by a valve spring. At the same time, a small amount of the oil is forced through a base valve, and then another base valve, and enters the chamber between the cylinder and the shock outer shell. When the cylinder, rising along the piston rod, meets the rubber bumper at the top of the rod, the compression ends.

The tension of the spring mounted on the shock absorber eventually forces the shock absorber to extend to it's normal or static length. The cylinder moves down along the piston rod; the oil which had been forced above the piston returns through the piston orifice and through the piston valve to the space beneath the piston. The oil which had been forced between the cylinder and the outer shell also returns to the reservoir beneath the piston after passing through a base valve. The oil resists the attempt of the outer spring to return suddenly to its normal length. This is known as rebound damping.

Some ATVs use a combination gas/oil shock instead of the oil type just described. They function similarly, except pressurized nitrogen helps prevent the oil from cavitating (foaming) during periods high shock movements. Usually these type of shocks have a separate reservoir that is separate from the shock. High-performance ATVs usually come equipped with this type of shock absorber.

Almost all production ATV shock absorbers are sealed, and cannot be disassembled. In fact, on some models, it is dangerous to attempt to do so, since they contain high-pressure gas.

If the shock leaks oil, looses its damping ability, is damaged through collision or extreme use, both units should be replaced. The springs, however, should have a longer life, and in most cases last the life of the ATV .

Suspension Troubleshooting

◆ **See Figures 60, 61 and 62**

In most cases, any problems that arise with suspension systems can be traced to worn parts. Pivot bearings or bushings, ball joints, and shock absorbers all wear out over time, and should be inspected frequently to avoid problems. In some cases, squeaking or binding suspensions may just be in need of lubrication.

Shock absorbers that lose their dampening function may be broken internally, or may be leaking. Of course any problems like this can only be repaired by replacement, since shock absorbers cannot (in most cases) be disassembled.

Use the Chassis Troubleshooting chart to help narrow down the possible causes of any suspension problems on your ATV.

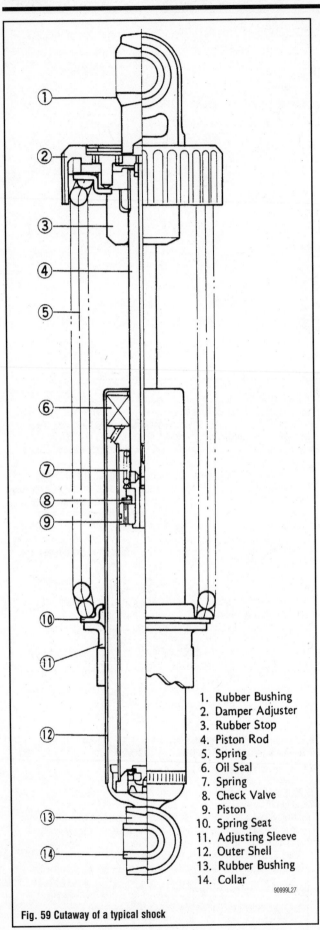

1. Rubber Bushing
2. Damper Adjuster
3. Rubber Stop
4. Piston Rod
5. Spring
6. Oil Seal
7. Spring
8. Check Valve
9. Piston
10. Spring Seat
11. Adjusting Sleeve
12. Outer Shell
13. Rubber Bushing
14. Collar

90999L27

Fig. 59 Cutaway of a typical shock

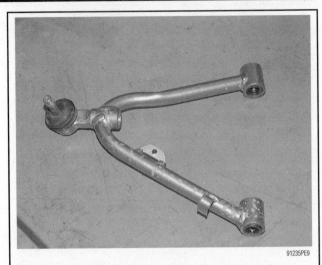

91235PE9

Fig. 60 A bent A-arm can cause a number of problems, such as pulling to one side, and excessive tire wear

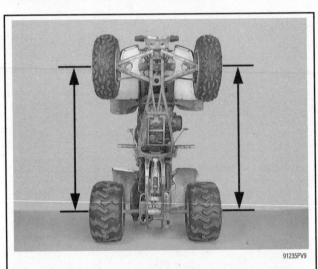

91235PV9

Fig. 61 If the distance between the front and rear axles is not the same on both sides, the ATV will not track in a straight line, and may become unstable at moderate speed

91235PC8

Fig. 62 If you are suspecting alignment problems with your ATV, make sure that the air pressure in the tires is equal on both sides

CHASSIS TROUBLESHOOTING

Problem	Possible Cause	Inspection/Remedy
Excessive vibration	Loose, broken, or worn motor mounts	Secure, replace, or repair motor mounts
	Loose axle nuts	Secure axle nuts
	Excessive hub bearing play	Adjust or replace hub bearings
	Wheels out of true or damaged	Straighten or replace wheel
	Tires overinflated	Check air pressure with tires cold
	Tire and wheel unevenly balanced	Balance wheels
	Worn steering head bearings	Adjust or replace bearings as necessary
	Worn rear shock bushings or shocks	Replace shocks or bushings as necessary
	Swingarm bushings too tight or too loose	Adjust bushings as directed by manufacturer
	Excessive front end loading	Remove excessive weight from front end
	Cylinder head bracket loose or broken (models on which head and frame are attached)	Secure or repair cylinder head bracket
	Broken or bent frame, or swingarm	Repair or replace damaged components
	Chain badly worn, insufficiently lubricated, or too tight	Replace, lubricate, and/or adjust chain
	Incorrectly assembled clutch mechanism	Inspect and repair clutch as necessary.
	Excessively worn crankshaft	Repair or replace crankshaft assembly
Uncertain or wobbly	Worn or bad hub bearings	Adjust or replace bearings
	Bent A-arms or swing arm	Repair or replace damaged components
	Worn swing arm bushings	Adjust or replace bushings
	Wheels improperly aligned	Check alignment of wheels
	Tires improperly seated on wheel	Seat tire so bead is even all around
	Tires unevenly worn	Replace tires as necessary
	Loose front wheel	Secure wheel
	Faulty right or left shock	Replace shocks as a set
Pulls to one side	Incorrectly adjusted drive chain	Adjust as necessary
	Air pressure not adjusted evenly between wheels	Adjust as necessary
	Wheels improperly aligned	Align wheels as necessary
	Incorrectly balanced tires and wheels	Balance wheels as necessary
	Defective steering head bearings	Adjust or replace bearings as necessary
	Bent or damaged A-arms, frame, or swingarm	Repair or replace damaged components
Heavy or stiff steering	Bent or damaged steering stem or frame neck	Repair or replace damaged components
	Bad steering head bearings and/or races	Replace or adjust bearings as necessary
	Front tire pressure too low	Adjust as necessary
	Incorrect damper adjustment	Adjust as necessary

91239C11

CHASSIS TROUBLESHOOTING

Problem	Possible Cause	Inspection/Remedy
Worn shock absorbers	Faulty damper unit	Replace shocks as a set
	Wrong spring in use	Replace springs as necessary
	Shocks adjusted incorrectly	Adjust shocks as necessary
	Faulty damper valve	Replace shock absorbers as a set
Stiff shock absorbers	Wrong spring in use	Replace springs as necessary
	Faulty damper unit	Replace as necessary
	Shocks incorrectly adjusted	Adjust shocks as necessary
Wheel rotates out of true	Excessive hub bearing play	Adjust or replace bearings
	Deformed wheel	Repair or replace as necessary
	Loose swingarm bushings	Adjust as necessary
	Drive chain too tight	Adjust chain as necessary
	Bent frame, A-arm or swingarm	Repair or replace damaged components

91239C12

BRAKE SYSTEM THEORY & DIAGNOSIS

Operation

DISC BRAKES

▶ **See Figures 63, 64, 65, 66 and 67**

Disc brakes are all quite similar in operation. The main components of a disc brake system are the master cylinder, the caliper; and the disc or rotor.

The master cylinder is mounted on the handlebar for front disc brakes, or on the chassis for rear wheel discs. The master cylinder contains a fluid reservoir, a piston assembly for applying hydraulic pressure to the system, and a lever for moving the piston assembly.

The calipers are mounted on the spindles for front discs, or the swing arm for rear disc brakes. The caliper houses the brake pads which bear against the disc when pressure is applied.

There are several types of calipers. One kind consists of a rigidly mounted (fixed) caliper with two (or multiples of 2) moveable pistons, one on each side of the disc. Fluid pressure is applied to both pistons, they, in turn, push their respective pads against the disc.

Another type of caliper is the "sliding caliper" type. As opposed to the fixed caliper described above, this assembly mounts the caliper to a bracket by means of sliding shafts. There is typically only one piston, and when pressure is

Fig. 63 A typical hydraulic disc brake assembly

91235P75

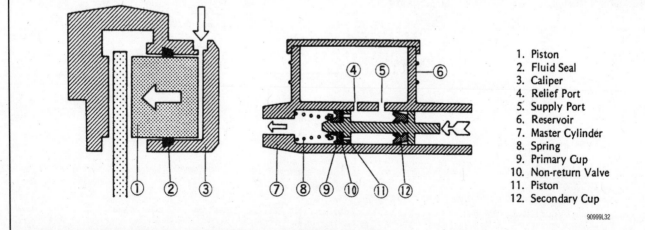

1. Piston
2. Fluid Seal
3. Caliper
4. Relief Port
5. Supply Port
6. Reservoir
7. Master Cylinder
8. Spring
9. Primary Cup
10. Non-return Valve
11. Piston
12. Secondary Cup

Fig. 64 When brakes are applied, fluid is forced from the master cylinder to the caliper

90999L32

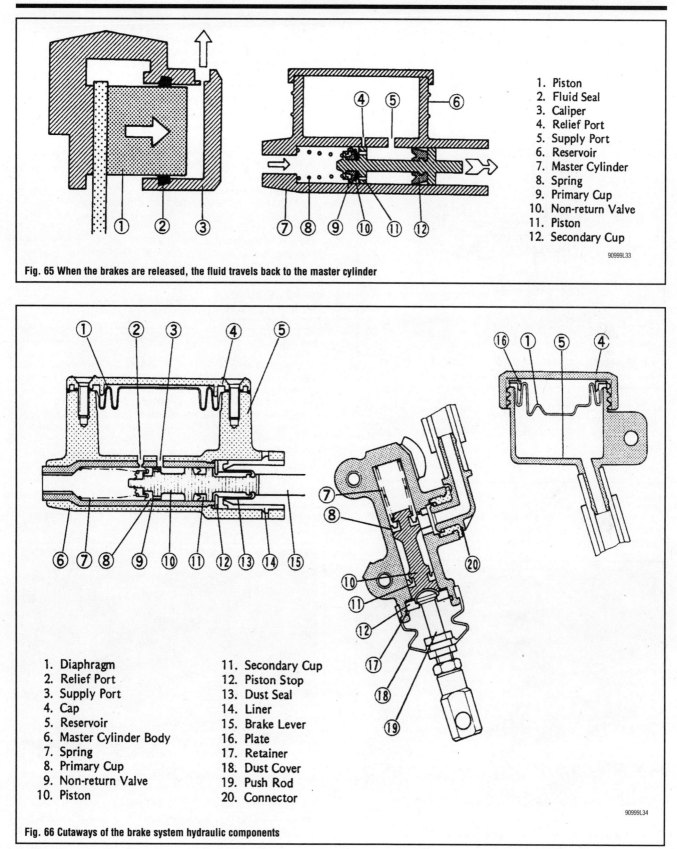

1. Piston
2. Fluid Seal
3. Caliper
4. Relief Port
5. Supply Port
6. Reservoir
7. Master Cylinder
8. Spring
9. Primary Cup
10. Non-return Valve
11. Piston
12. Secondary Cup

90999L33

Fig. 65 When the brakes are released, the fluid travels back to the master cylinder

1. Diaphragm
2. Relief Port
3. Supply Port
4. Cap
5. Reservoir
6. Master Cylinder Body
7. Spring
8. Primary Cup
9. Non-return Valve
10. Piston
11. Secondary Cup
12. Piston Stop
13. Dust Seal
14. Liner
15. Brake Lever
16. Plate
17. Retainer
18. Dust Cover
19. Push Rod
20. Connector

90999L34

Fig. 66 Cutaways of the brake system hydraulic components

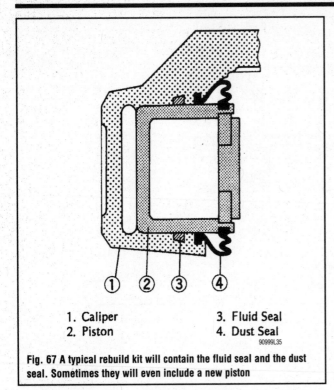

1. Caliper
2. Piston
3. Fluid Seal
4. Dust Seal

90999L35

Fig. 67 A typical rebuild kit will contain the fluid seal and the dust seal. Sometimes they will even include a new piston

applied to this piston, it presses its pad against the disc, and the caliper shifts slightly in the opposite direction bringing the opposing pad into contact as well. The "floating caliper type" is very similar to the "sliding" and can use the same description.

DRUM BRAKES

▶ See Figure 68

Drum brakes are usually found on smaller, lower priced ATVs, and on many utility type ATVs (which require heavy duty brakes, but do not need the racing

91235P13

Fig. 68 A typical drum brake assembly (drum removed)

advantages offered by rear discs). Because of the design of ATV drum brakes, hydraulic pressure is not usually required to provide adequate braking, so cables or other mechanical linkage can be used.

Drum brakes are either single leading shoe or double leading shoe types, with the single leading shoe being the most common.

A single leading shoe brake consists of two brake shoes mounted on a plate. On one side, the shoe rests on a stud or pivot, while the other end of the shoes hear against a cam. The shoes are held in place by coil springs. When the brake lever or pedal is activated, the cam is turned, pressing the brake lining against the drum. Since there is only one cam, only one end of the brake shoe is pressed against the drum. The other end is a fixed pivot. No matter how the brake plate is arranged on the ATV, the leading side of one shoe and the trailing side of the other will be resting on the cam.

Drum brakes are self-energizing. That is, once the leading shoe has been brought into contact with the drum, the drum's rotational movement tends to draw it against it. The trailing shoe, on the other hand, tends to be forced away from the drum.

Twin-leading shoe brakes are different in the following way. Instead of a single fixed pivot and single cam, each shoe is mounted on its own pivot and has its own cam. The shoes are mounted so that the leading end of both shoes are those activated by the cam. A link rod connects the two cams together so both shoes are operated in unison.

LINKED BRAKING SYSTEMS

▶ See Figure 69

The majority of all ATV braking systems use a hand actuated lever to operate the front brakes. A foot lever takes care of the rear brakes, or if the ATV has an automatic clutch, a lever opposite of the throttle is used to activate the rear brakes in addition to the brake pedal on the right side of the ATV.

Other ATVs use a system that actuates both front and rear brakes simultaneously by operating a lever on the handlebars. When the foot lever is actuated, only the rear brakes are applied.

Another form of linked braking can be the result of a four-wheel drive system. Of course, this depends on the configuration of the drive line, but in most cases, applying one set of brakes (front or rear) will cause all four wheels to be slowed down.

If you are unsure of the configuration of the braking system on your ATV, simply follow the cables to find what is being activated when you operate the

91239P58

Fig. 69 The rear brake assembly on this four-wheel drive ATV activates both the front and rear brakes when the front driveline connects with the rear

lever. Also, check your owner's manual for a specific operation description for your ATV.

The advantage of a linked system is that you can share the braking chores with both ends of the ATV without having to think about it too much. This is good for heavily loaded utility ATVs and others that have similar weight distributions. The bad side is that for riders who are used to standard braking systems, it can feel quite bizarre and you can't lock/slide the rear in the dirt . . . bummer.

Brake Troubleshooting

DISC BRAKES

Refer to the brake system troubleshooting chart for information on how to diagnose disc brake problems.

Common problems with disc brakes include bad fluid seals, damaged or corroded caliper pistons and seized caliper slides.

Using the wrong friction material can lead to improper braking. The brakes may react too strongly or require too much pressure to activate them. If the fluid seal on the caliper is leaking, the friction material can get soaked and lose effectiveness.

INEFFECTIVE DRUM BRAKES

▶ **See Figure 70**

1. If the brakes become ineffective even if adjustment is correct, check lining thickness first. If thickness is within acceptable limits, the loss of braking power may he caused by an excessive angle between the brake rod or cable and the brake lever.

2. A common cause of poor operation of cable operated drum brakes is caused by the build-up of dirt or corrosion between the inner brake cable and the cable sheath. Ensure proper cable lubrication by periodically disconnecting the brake cable from the hand lever and pouring motor oil or one of the molybdenum disulfide or graphite-based lubricants between the inner and outer cables. Apply sufficient amounts. The lubricant should appear at the lower end of the cable to show that the entire length is lubricated. A cable lubrication tool (available at ATV and motorcycle shops) is the best way to lubricate a cable. An alternate method involves removing the cable from the ATV completely and immersing it in a pan of light oil. Leave one end of the cable above the oil in the pan so the lubricant can seep through. Try to get some light grease into either end of the cable after lubrication to keep out dirt and moisture. You should note that cables which have gone without periodic lubrication for an extended length of time can usually not be repaired by lubrication. If the sticking or binding persists, the cable must he replaced.

3. Glazed linings can also cause poor braking. This can be fixed by removing the wheel and inspecting the surfaces of the brake linings and the brake

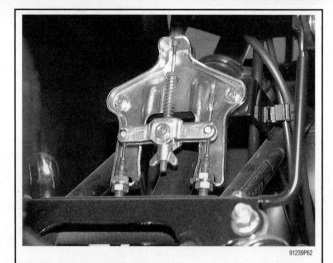

Fig. 70 This ATV uses a split setup for operating the front brakes; but because of the design (for safety), if one cable breaks, both brakes will be inoperative

drum. Use light sandpaper to rough up the linings. Sandpaper can also he used to clean up rust or corrosion on the brake drum. The drum should be shiny. Also, check the drum for wear. On some ATVs, brake drum maximum allowable diameter is stamped somewhere on the hub. If not, it is contained in the shop manual. Worn drums must be replaced.

4. Although not common, ineffective brakes can be the result of oil or grease on the linings. It is almost impossible to remove lubricant from the porous linings, surfaces and brake shoes in this condition should be replaced.

5. On twin leading shoe brakes, improper adjustment of the brake connecting rod will cause a lack of performance. Adjust this according to the manufacturers instructions. Another cause, often overlooked, is worn or damaged clevis pins. Once these pins wear a good deal of slop may develop in the brake linkage. The remedy is replacement of the pins.

6. Dragging brakes may be caused by an improperly lubricated cable as discussed above. Other causes include worn or damaged return springs. Most manufacturers give a maximum allowable length for brake springs, and those which exceed this limit should be replaced.

7. Binding of the brake cam(s) in the brake plate is another cause of dragging brakes. This may happen either because the cams have not been properly lubricated or because they are bent.

8. Squealing is most often caused by dirt on the brake linings. Clean linings and drum thoroughly.

BRAKE TROUBLESHOOTING

Problem	Possible Cause	Inspection/Remedy
Brakes do not hold (Drum)	Brake shoes glazed or worn	Repair or replace shoes
	Brake shoes oil or grease impregnated	Replace shoes
	Brake linings worn away	Replace linings
	Brake drum worn or damaged	Replace or have drum turned down
	Air in brake lines or insufficient hydraulic fluid	Drain system and refill with fresh fluid, then bleed system
	Brake linkage incorrectly adjusted	Adjust linkage as necessary
	Brake control cables insufficiently lubricated or binding	Lubricate or replace cable as necessary
Brakes drag (Drum)	Lack of play in the linkage	Adjust linkage as necessary
	Weak or damaged return springs	Replace springs as a set
	Rusted cam and lever shaft	Replace as necessary
Unadjustable Brakes (Drum)	Worn brake shoe linings	Replace shoes or rotate the actuating lever a few degrees on its splined shaft (if applicable)
	Worn brake shoe cam	Replace the cam as necessary
	Worn or damaged brake drum	Replace the drum or have it turned down
Scraping noise (Drum)	Linings worn down to the rivets	Replace the linings and have the drum turned or replaced as necessary
	Broken brake shoe	Replace the shoes and repair or replace the drum as necessary
	Dirt in the drum	Clean out the assembly and replace or repair the drum as necessary
	Scored or out of round brake drum	Repair or replace the drum as necessary
	Broken pivot	Replace the pivot
Brakes shudder (Drum)	Unevenly worn shoes	Replace shoes
	Out of round brake drum	Repair or replace drum
Excessive lever travel with loss of braking power (Disc)	Air in hydraulic system	Drain and replace fluid, then bleed system
	Master cylinder low on fluid	Refill the cylinder and bleed system
	Loose lever adjuster bolt	Secure and adjust lever and bolt
	Leak in hydraulic system as evidenced by fluid loss	Rebuild system as necessary
	Worn disc pads	Replace pads as necessary
Brake squeal (Disc)	Glazed pads	Clean up or replace pads
	Improperly adjusted caliper	Adjust caliper
	Extremely dusty brake assembly	Thoroughly clean out assembly
Brake shudder (Disc)	Distorted pads	Replace pads
	Oil or brake fluid impregnated pads	Replace pads
	Loose mounting bolts	Secure assembly
	Warped disc	Replace disc
Pads dragging on rotor (Disc)	Loose adjusting ring	Secure adjusting ring
	Piston binding in bore	Rebuild caliper assembly
	Relief port blocked by piston in master cylinder	Rebuild caliper assembly
	Caliper out of adjustment	Adjust
	Caliper pivot frozen	Clean and lubricate pivot

10

LONG-TERM STORAGE

STORING YOUR ATV

Not all of us are lucky enough to live in an area where you can ride your ATV twelve months out of the year. Depending on the severity of the winters where you live and depending upon your own desire to ride in cold weather, you should take steps to preserve your precious machine(s).

The use of proper riding gear (including electric apparel) and well selected winter days can allow for comfortable riding most of the year (barring long winter blizzards). But, extra care should be taken in the winter to assure that your ATV will be in top shape, preventing you from becoming stranded on a cold, lonely trail.

If you know (or even suspect) that you will not be using your ATV for a month or longer, you should follow these storage procedures to assure proper care and readiness of your ATV.

If you live in an area where this sort of scene is even remotely possible, then you should take steps to protect your ATV in the winter (NOTE: Geo Tracker under snow pile)

Cleaning your ATV

▶ See Figures 1 and 2

Hopefully, you already understand the benefits of washing your ATV. Besides giving you a chance to inspect all the various components of your ATV (while you clean them), you have the opportunity to protect these parts from moisture and corrosive agents in the atmosphere. Everything from painted parts to powdercoat to plastic should be cleaned and given a coating of some protectant to reduce the possibility of damage or corrosion during storage.

Refer to the Cleaning Your ATV section of this book for recommendations regarding the care and treatment of the different materials on your ATV. Obviously plastic is not protected in the same fashion as rubber or paint. The key is to completely clean the ATV (with a proper wash) and THEN protect the various surfaces of the ATV before placing it in storage.

➡Regular washing and cleaning of your ATV should be part of your routine whether or not you are planning on putting your ATV in storage.

While washing your ATV, you have a perfect opportunity to look out for potential problems. Keep your eyes open for loose or missing fasteners, cracked or damaged components and weeping or leaking seals. A loose or missing fastener may be a wake-up call to pay closer attention to basic maintenance and your pre-ride checks, or it could be a warning sign that some other problem is developing. A good cleaning, followed by observation after operation of the ATV will help determine if a seal is leaking badly (and should be replaced) or if a

Fig. 1 Your ATV should be thoroughly cleaned and lubricated before placing it into storage

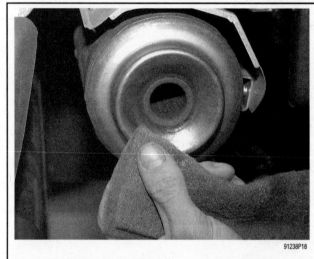

Fig. 2 Little things like polishing metal components will prevent corrosion from setting in during storage, and will keep your ATV looking new

slight amount of seepage is responsible for accumulated fluids, dirt or grime on a part of the ATV.

The longer you plan on keeping your ATV in storage, the more important your cleaning and protecting ritual will become. If an ATV is only going to be in storage for a few months, chances are that few components are going to wear out just because of time and exposure (unless of course they were just about gone to begin with, but your inspection should have revealed that). If however, the ATV may be stored for a longer period of time (measured in years instead of months) then your chance of items like seals drying, cracking or melting their way onto shafts becomes greater. One of the biggest advantages of cleaning your ATV before placing it into storage is if a seal were to fail during storage, you will more quickly identify it when removing the ATV from storage later, since you knew it wasn't leaking before.

➡Cleaning and protecting your ATV before storage is definitely a case of an ounce of prevention being worth a pound of cure. But if your ride requires a pound of cure when it is removed from storage, it will simply require that much LESS than it would if it hadn't been properly detailed.

There are a lot of products available to beautify rubber and plastic. Keep in mind, the truth is that rubber will eventually dry out and crack, no matter how much you use protective treatments. Exposure to ultraviolet radiation, the evaporation of component oils and oxidation will take their toll on everything from tires to seats. Most products on the market cannot prevent the natural aging of these components, but you should be able to at least lengthen their usable life while making them better looking in the process.

Preparing The Engine and Drivetrain For Storage

FUEL SYSTEM

◆ **See Figures 3, 4 and 5**

Over time the most volatile compounds found in a sample of gasoline will evaporate, leaving the remaining fluid less combustible. This will lead to difficult starting and rough running for your engine. BUT, this is the least of your worries when it comes to gasoline and any form of long term storage.

As gasoline evaporates it can leave behind a varnish which will coat and possibly clog critical fuel delivery systems. Needle jets, floats and valves in carburetors can be rendered useless by enough of this varnish. All of this adds up to a poor running ATV (if it runs at all) and lengthy or costly repairs as parts must be removed and cleaned, or in some cases, replaced.

You basically have two options when it comes to preventing fuel system damage during months when your ATV is being stored. Either you can completely drain the fuel system or you can add a fuel stabilizer to the system and make sure it is completely mixed with the gasoline.

Add Stabilizer Or Drain?

Your decision on whether to add fuel stabilizer or to completely drain the system should really depend on how long the ATV is going to be stored and how willing you are to go through the trouble. Frankly, adding stabilizer is the

Fig. 3 The water and sediment in the bowl of this carburetor has accumulated over winter storage—draining the carburetor before placing your ATV in storage will help prevent these kind of problems

Fig. 4 Without fuel in the carburetor, the chance of corrosion inside the carburetor may be increased—use a light spray oil to coat the inside of the carburetor to prevent corrosion from forming

Fig. 5 Its not a bad idea to replace the fuel filter with a fresh one before storage

easier of the 2 solutions, but for long term storage (again, speaking more in terms of years than months) draining is the better solution. If your ATV is a two-stroke, there is not much of a choice. Two-strokes which have to pre-mix the oil and fuel before it goes in the tank should be drained completely. The lubricating properties of the oil in the fuel will be long gone when spring comes around. In general, you should wait until your going to ride before mixing fuel and oil for a two-stroke engine.

ADDING FUEL STABILIZER

◆ **See Figure 6**

This is the solution most people prefer because it is a lot easier than draining the system. But, remember that, using fuel stabilizer is more suited to a storage time that is measured in months and NOT years. This makes it sufficient for most winter storage needs. If you decide to use this method, be sure to fol-

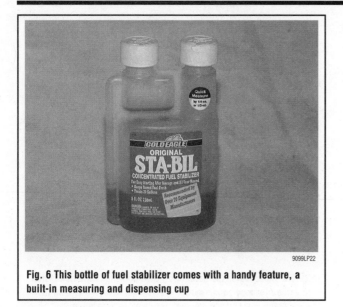

9099LP22

Fig. 6 This bottle of fuel stabilizer comes with a handy feature, a built-in measuring and dispensing cup

low the stabilizer manufacturer's instructions, but keep the following points in mind:

• It is best to add most stabilizers right before filling the tank, as this gives the stabilizer the best chance to fully mix with the gasoline as the tank is filled.

• After adding stabilizer, be sure to operate the engine for a few minutes to give the fuel/stabilizer mixture an opportunity to reach all parts of the system, like the internals of the carburetor.

• Gas from your last fuel fill-up will be in the system for a long time, so if possible, avoid oxygenated fuels which use alcohol, since alcohol absorbs water and may promote corrosion in the fuel system. If you can't avoid fuel with alcohol in it, then pay extra-close attention to the next point.

• Be sure to TOP-OFF the fuel tank to minimize the amount of air (and therefore moisture) that is present in the tank. If you store a metal fuel tank with air in it, the moisture will cause rusting on the inside of an uncoated tank and that rust can play havoc with your fuel system come spring. Most ATVs have plastic fuel tanks these days, so rust may not be a problem, but water in the fuel can still cause problems

DRAINING THE SYSTEM

If you are really serious about storing your ATV (and you should be if it is going to be stored for time periods measured in years instead of just months), then you should completely drain the fuel system. But remember that if you do remove all of the fuel (and therefore remove the danger of varnish build-up), you have another concern, in the form of corrosion. Remember that air contains a certain amount of moisture, so if you drain the fuel system completely, leaving only air behind, then there will be moisture to help corrode metal surfaces in the system.

To prevent your carburetor from becoming corroded, remove the carburetor float bowl, and apply a light spray oil to the bowl and float, and the venturi. After everything is oiled down, install the float bowl and install the carburetor to the ATV.

OIL & OTHER FLUIDS

It doesn't matter what the fluid's job is normally, when it comes to storage, ALL FLUIDS have one major job. During winter months when the ATV is idle, all of your fluids are there simply to fight corrosion. Once the ATV is removed from storage, those fluids will be called upon to lubricate, cool and/or transmit power, but for now, you want them to inhibit corrosion and nothing more.

There is a lot of debate between "experts" who will advise you to change all fluids before storage or only after storage. Some people advise that you only

change some fluids. Many will draw upon years of experience, saying that they never changed this or that fluid and have never had a problem (and they may be right). But it is hard to make generalizations. What works for one make or model (or in one part of the country) may not work for another.

With that said, we are going to make a generalization here. You never LOSE by changing all of your fluids before storage (except in some cases, you might spend a few dollars more on fluids that you didn't absolutely need). Add up all the fluids your ATV needs, and compare the dollar amount to the value of the ATV. If the value of the ATV is greater (and it should be significantly so in most cases), then your motivation is simple. Changing all fluids is CHEAP INSURANCE.

Engine Oil

▸ See Figures 7, 8 and 9

During engine operation, all sorts of nasty acids are formed, and some work their way into your engine oil. Acids and moisture are enemies of the bearings

91234P52

Fig. 7 Change your engine oil . . .

91234P73

Fig. 8 . . . and filter. . .

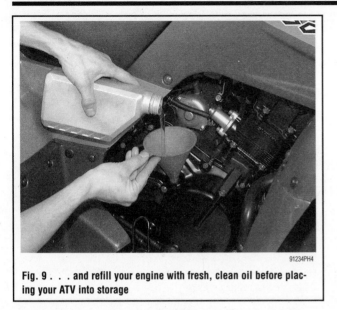

Fig. 9 . . . and refill your engine with fresh, clean oil before placing your ATV into storage

Fig. 11 . . . you should do it NOW, to prevent the engine from freezing, which could destroy the cylinder head

and metal surfaces found in your engine, and should be minimized to assure long life. Luckily, periodic engine oil changes remove most of the corrosives, and the normal operating temperatures of the engine should be sufficient to purge the crankcase of moisture. But, what about when your ATV is parked for the winter?

The last time the engine is run before storage, make sure it comes completely up to operating temperature. This will help to make sure that moisture is boiled-off from inside the muffler. Then, you should drain your engine oil. Change the oil and filter to make sure that you have removed the most corrosive agents and moisture from the engine prior to letting it sleep for the next few months. Your engine will thank you.

Engine Coolant

♦ See Figures 10 and 11

Engine coolant has 2 purposes. The primary purpose is temperature control of the engine (to cool it during operation). But it also contains rust inhibitors to prevent corrosion as well as lubricants for the water pump and

Fig. 10 If the coolant in your water cooled engine is due for a change . . .

seals. If your coolant is close to the replacement interval in your ATV's owners manual, then you should replace it now, before putting it in storage. Like engine oil, it is best to put nothing but fresh fluids in the system to sit all winter.

※ WARNING

Replacing the coolant before storage is especially important if the ATV is to be stored outside or in an unheated garage/shed where it may be subjected to sub-freezing temperatures. As coolant ages, it not only loses its ability to inhibit corrosion and cool the motor, but it also will lose its ability to resist freezing. As the freezing point of your coolant is raised by age, the possibility of severe engine damage caused by the coolant freezing and expanding increases. It would be a shame to loose an engine all because you wouldn't spring for a gallon of coolant.

Transmission and Gear Oil

♦ See Figure 12

Many transmissions, differentials and drive housings are vented to the atmosphere. They will acquire moisture through condensation as the ATV is used. Hopefully during use, the oil heats up sufficiently so that moisture will evaporate, but this becomes less likely as winter approaches and ambient temperatures drop. To be sure you have removed as much moisture as possible from your driveline, take this opportunity to change all drive fluids (if you have enough drain pans, do it as the engine oil drains).

Once again, by changing these fluids you will help to reduce the amount of corrosion which will take place during the time the ATV is left in storage.

Brake/Hydraulic Clutch Fluid

♦ See Figure 13

One of the most ignored parts of maintenance tends to be the replacement of hydraulic brake fluids. Remember that DOT 3 & 4 fluids are highly hydroscopic, meaning that they will readily absorb moisture from the atmosphere. Even if you never remove the master cylinder cover, it is likely that some moisture will get into the system over time and this can cause corrosion. If the reservoir is cloudy, or the fluid is more than 2 years old, its time for a brake fluid change.

Fig. 12 Changing gear oil will help remove any accumulated moisture, which can cause corrosion during storage

91234P80

Fig. 14 Adjusting the chain before storage means that you'll have less to do when spring arrives

91236P38

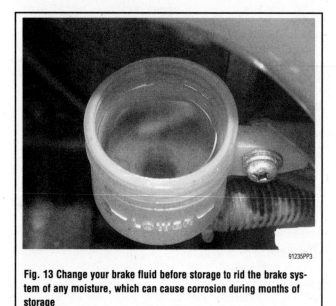

Fig. 13 Change your brake fluid before storage to rid the brake system of any moisture, which can cause corrosion during months of storage

91235PP3

Fig. 15 If you want to add oil to the cylinder for rust prevention, you'll have to remove the spark plug

91234P10

Drive Chain

♦ See Figure 14

If your ATV is equipped with a final drive chain, take the opportunity to clean, lube and adjust the chain now. A fresh coating of lubrication will help to assure that the chain and sprockets remain as corrosion-free as possible during the long winter months. By cleaning and adjusting it now, you will be sure the chain is ready when it is time to remove the ATV from storage.

SPARK PLUG & CYLINDER

♦ See Figure 15

If the engine was run (in order to change the oil) then the cylinder should not require any special attention for normal winter storage (consisting of a few months). But, if the storage is going to be any longer OR if you want the extra level of protection, you can coat the cylinder with some additional engine oil.

Remove and inspect the spark plug (if it needs to be replaced, you might as well do it since you're going through the trouble to remove it anyway). Next, pour 1–2 tablespoons of fresh, clean engine oil through the spark plug hole. Rotate the engine to spread the oil around the cylinder, then install the spark plug.

➡Rotating the engine should be done slowly to prevent the addition of gasoline to the cylinder.

To rotate the engine, you've got a few options. Keep the spark plug out to relieve engine compression, and use the back-up pull starter or kick starter. Remember, don't rotate the engine too fast, or gasoline might be sucked into the cylinder and wash away all of the oil. Another way that you can rotate the engine is to put the ATV in gear and push it a few yards up and down the driveway (with the spark plug removed of course). Or you can lift the rear axle (using a lift or a workstand), place the transmission in gear and turn the rear wheel.

Prepare The Battery For Storage

CHECKING THE FLUID

▶ **See Figure 16**

One of the most important parts of battery care is to maintain the fluid level. If the electrolyte level is allowed to drop beyond a certain point the plates will corrode and the battery will not be able to receive or hold a charge. Before placing the ATV into storage, be sure to remove the cell cap(s) and check the fluid level. If necessary, top-off any cells using DISTILLED water. Only fill the battery to the fill lines on the case or to the bottom of the cell opening in the top of the battery case if no fill line is present (or as directed by the battery manufacturer).

➡**After adding any water to the battery, be sure that it gets a chance to mix with the electrolyte. The best way to do this is to operate the ATV (but since you just went through a lot of trouble to NOT OPERATE IT, we recommend attaching a TRICKle charger for a few hours, this should do the trick. (Uh, pun intended.)**

If you are using a sealed dry cell or gel cell battery, you obviously won't be opening any cell caps to add distilled water, but there still may be a way to check the electrolyte. Automotive batteries use sight glasses in the top of the battery case, so check with the battery manufacturer to see if they have provided a similar method of checking your battery.

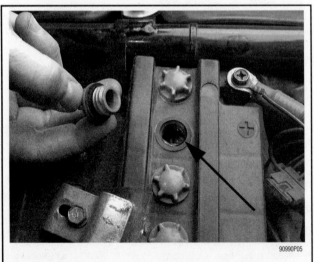

Fig. 16 Unless you have a sealed, maintenance-free battery, you should remove the caps and check the battery fluid level before storage

REMOVE IT OR TEND IT?

▶ **See Figures 17, 18 and 19**

The second most important part of battery maintenance is making sure that it is properly charged. If you have just checked the fluid level, then you are in the perfect position to check the charge using a hydrometer designed just for that purpose. Because the specific gravity of electrolyte will change with the amount of charge present, you will be able to check the exact condition of each battery cell by using a hydrometer (that is, unless it is a sealed battery).

Fig. 17 If your ATV is to be stored outside, it is best to disconnect the battery . . .

Fig. 18 . . . remove it from the ATV, and store it indoors

But even if the charge is fine now, there is no telling how it is going to be in a few months. Chances are, it is NOT going to be fully charged after a couple months, and may be dead. Batteries will self discharge over time (which will allow for changes to the chemical composition of the plates inside the battery). If allowed to discharge often enough or long enough, the battery will become permanently discharged and useless.

For this reason you are going to want to make sure that the battery is fully charged when you put the ATV into storage and then hook it up to an automatic charger (such as the Battery Tender®) which will maintain a proper charge, without overcharging it. Or, if you do not have an automatic battery charger, use a trickle charger for a few hours at least once every month.

If you are lucky enough to be storing the ATV in a heated or attached garage, then you will be fine leaving the battery in place. You will be fine, that is, as long as an extension cord or outlet is handy to make sure the battery can be kept fully charged. But, if the ATV is to be stored outside, in a detached garage or shed, you really should remove the battery and store it somewhere warmer. Remember that as a battery discharges, more of the electrolyte is converted to

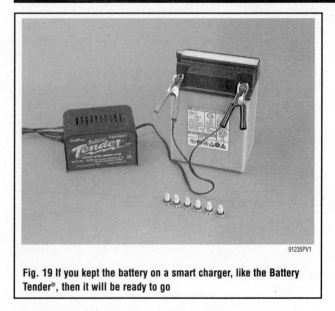

Fig. 19 If you kept the battery on a smart charger, like the Battery Tender®, then it will be ready to go

Fig. 20 Whether you choose to use a jackstand . . .

water, which could freeze. Should the electrolyte freeze, come spring, you will likely find a dead battery, with a cracked case that has spilled a weakened acid (but an acid nonetheless) all over your ATV.

Prepare The Chassis For Storage

You are just about ready to put your baby to sleep for a while, with only the chassis remaining to be given some attention.

LUBING THE CHASSIS

Now is a good time to lube and grease any pivot points, such as suspension bushings, steering gear, cables and levers. The depth to which you pursue lubing will have something to do with your normal maintenance routine.

If lubing items such as the steering shaft only involves a grease gun and a zerk fitting you will be much more likely to do that now (regardless of when it is next due), then you would be if it involved removing the steering shaft by hand.

CHECKING THE TIRES

▶ **See Figures 20, 21 and 22**

If your tires are approaching replacement time, NOW IS NOT THE TIME TO DO IT, wait for spring.

If you are really lucky, or if you time it just right, your tires will be worn, close to the end of their usable lives right before storage. This will allow you to pay little attention to them and not worry about what affect storage and time will have on them.

But since it is rare that we are that lucky or that methodical, let's tell you how to best get your tires through the winter. There are 3 things you can do to help assure the survival of your tires:

• **Make sure they are properly inflated**—The first and most important thing to do is to inflate your tires to the manufacturer's specification.

• **Cover the ATV or keep it out of direct sunlight**—Since ultraviolet radiation is probably the most significant cause of dry rotting and cracking, the next most important thing to do for your tires is to keep them out of direct sunlight.

• **Raise the tires off the ground**—The last thing you can do to preserve your tires is relatively easy if you have a workstand or lift and much less so if you don't. Support the ATV securely, under the frame, to keep the wheels off the ground.

Fig. 21 . . . or a workstand, keeping your ATV's tires lifted off the ground during storage will help prevent "flat spots" from forming on the tires

➡Remember that time is a tire's enemy just as much as is usage. If the ATV is going to be stored for a LONG time (measured in years and not months) then there may be nothing you can do to assure that the tires will be good when the time period ends. But, following our recommendations will give you the best shot.

COVERING & PROTECTING THE ATV

Ideally, you will want to place a high quality cover over the machine to keep it away from prying eyes, ultraviolet radiation, and whatever else might come its way. BUT, there are a few things to be careful of with covers. If you are going to buy one, make sure it has a soft inner lining to prevent scratching of the plastic. Also, make sure it is not made of a plastic material, but instead choose one that breathes. A non-breathable, plastic material will trap condensation, promoting

91235P64

Fig. 22 Make sure that the tires are inflated to the correct pressure before storage

corrosion and mold, while a breathing cover will allow moisture to evaporate, further protecting your ATV.

Unfortunately, ATVs have lots of neat, tight, little nooks and crannies (like Thomas' English Muffins®). This is not only a problem when it comes to cleaning, but when it comes to RODENTS. Many small, furry animals are attracted to these nooks and may think it is nest building time. They also have the unfortunate habit of shredding things like seats, wiring harnesses and air filters. If possible, set a rodent trap or two in order to protect your ATV. Or if you are THAT humane about it, check the ATV every week or so to discourage nesting. Hey, you can always get a cat and allow them access to the storage area (as long as they don't like to stretch their claws on your seat).

Leaving It In Storage

Once you have put your ATV into storage mode, LEAVE IT ALONE. You can drool on it (as long as you dry it afterwards). You can rub body parts against it (as long as you don't scratch it up). You can get dressed up in your gear, sit on it and go "Vroom . . .Vroom." while spitting on yourself. But don't start it just to listen or to "warm the motor." Idling it won't warm the motor very much, probably will not charge the battery, definitely won't do anything for the drivetrain and will most likely leave some condensation in the exhaust to help rust get started. LEAVE IT ALONE UNTIL IT IS PROPERLY REMOVED FROM STORAGE.

REMOVING YOUR ATV FROM STORAGE

If you followed our instructions last fall, then you should be in GREAT SHAPE and we will have you riding by the afternoon (barring any unexpected problems).

Also, if you come across an abandoned baby (the proverbial ATV that has been forgotten about in the shed or barn for the past decade or so) then you should follow these steps towards reawakening an ATV. Of course, the longer the ATV has been in storage, the more items you are going to need to check. If the ATV was stored for more than one winter you should start to suspect ANY RUBBER item (tires, hoses, seals) and any wear items (cables, fluids, lights). Don't assume that anything is in good shape until you have checked and proven it to be serviceable.

Check The Chassis After Storage

PERFORMING A MICKEY MOUSE CHECK

▶ See Figures 23, 24, 25 and 26

Before attempting to fire up your ATV, check for evidence of visiting or nesting rodents. Look for signs that your ATV has not wintered alone, such as small turds, gnawed wiring, shredded hide of the naugha (that strange, elusive animal with a fake leather skin), etc.

Make sure there are no rodents sleeping in the machine (and that no nesting rodents have left anything behind). The only way to be sure of this is to disassemble the air intake tract (air cleaner and any ducting) as well as any plastic which could hide a sleeping rodent. This is an excellent time to check the condition of the air filter and clean or replace it, as necessary and as applicable to your model. Use a flashlight to inspect the opening in the muffler to make sure no one is residing in there either. You WON'T BELIEVE the SMELL if you miss a nest in the muffler and start the ATV.

✳ WARNING

If any evidence of extra-rodential activity is found, be sure to check the ATV's electrical, air intake and exhaust systems VERY CAREFULLY to avoid causing unexpected damage when attempting to start the motor.

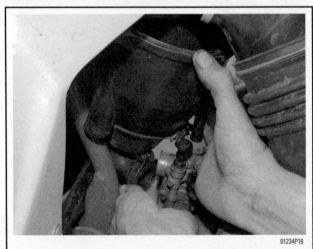

91234P16

Fig. 23 Before starting the engine, check for signs of rodent nesting around the airbox inlet . . .

CHECKING THE TIRES

▶ See Figure 27

Start by grabbing your trusty tire gauge and check that the tires are properly inflated. The longer the ATV has been in storage, the less likely this is to be true. Use a hand pump to inflate the tires back up to specification. Listen for any audible air leaks.

With the tires properly inflated, check for cracks or dry rotting. Look between the tread blocks and check the sidewalls for any evidence of weathering or cracking. Any tire which shows evidence of dry rotting should be replaced. Don't risk a possible tire failure.

CHECKING LUBE POINTS

Make sure that all levers, pivot points and cables move freely without binding or excessive resistance. Check the suspension for smooth, proper travel. If

Fig. 24 . . . and the air intake duct

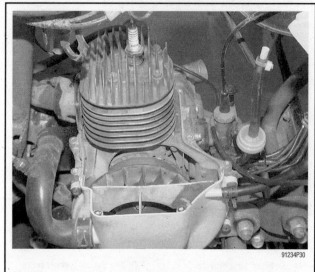

Fig. 26 . . . and look for any signs of rodent nesting

Fig. 25 On engines with forced-air cooling, remove the ductwork . . .

Fig. 27 Even the best valve stems will lose air over time, so ALWAYS check the air pressure in the tires after storage

you are replacing any tires it is also a good idea to check the wheel bearings. If the bearings are not sealed on your ATV, it is time to clean, inspect and repack the bearings too.

It is never a bad idea to lube all chassis points when you are removing the ATV from storage. If it has been more than one winter of storage for this machine, then you should lube all points to prevent sudden and troubling binding.

✳✳ CAUTION

Any source of binding or excessive resistance on levers or pivot points MUST be found and repaired before any attempt is made to ride the ATV. Chassis or control instability could easily lead to a very serious accident. Improperly operating components may be signs of an impending equipment failure.

Check The Battery After Storage

◆ See Figure 28

Once again, if you have had the battery on a Battery Tender® or other automatic charger, then you are probably in good shape, but, just to be sure, make an electrolyte level and charge check. Remove the vent caps (unless it is a sealed battery) or peer through the transparent casing and make sure the fluid is at the proper level. Use a hydrometer to check for proper charge.

➡**While you are checking the fluid level, use a flashlight to take a look at the tops of the battery plates. If there is a significant amount of white corrosion, then your battery is either toast, or almost toast and you really should replace it, even if it does seem to take a charge. You don't want it to strand you next week, do you? Having to use the manual pull starter on your 500cc four-stroke can be a real pain (in the back).**

Fig. 28 Before you put the battery back into your ATV, make sure that the level of electrolyte in each cell is correct

Fig. 29 Even if you choose not to change your oil after storage, at least check and top off the engine to assure a proper oil level

If the battery is not fully charged, place it on a charger to make sure it is ready to go when you are finished prepping the ATV.

If the battery is completely discharged, you are going to want to consider replacing it. Even though you may be able to get it to hold a charge, a battery which has sat discharged for any length of time will never hold a full charge again. And the longer it sat discharged, the worse off it will be. It may very well bail at an inconvenient time, making you get acquainted with that back up pull starter.

Check The Engine And Drivetrain After Storage

CHECKING ALL FLUIDS

Engine Oil

▶ See Figure 29

DO NOT CRANK OR ATTEMPT TO START THE MOTOR YET!

Whether or not you properly prepped the ATV, you should change the engine oil at this time. If the oil filter was replaced when the ATV was put into storage you can reuse it, but be sure to drain as much oil as possible from the filter or from the cartridge housing (as applicable).

OK, it is obvious why you would change the oil if the ATV was found in a barn. But, you are probably asking, "If I followed the proper storage preparations last fall, why should I trash that perfectly good oil now?" Well, the answer is simple. If the oil is worth more than the ATV, don't sweat it and don't bother changing it either. But if the ATV is worth more than the oil, then it is cheap insurance. Even if you kept the ATV in a heated garage, there is no guarantee that no condensation formed and that all of the nasty corrosives were removed by the last change, so we recommend that you don't risk it.

Engine Coolant

▶ See Figures 30 and 31

If the ATV was properly prepped and the coolant was changed before storage, just make a quick level check.

If the ATV is being resurrected or if you didn't change the coolant before storage, you should at least check the level and check the specific gravity. Specialized hydrometers (available in most auto parts stores) are available to give

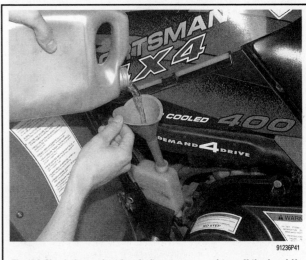

Fig. 30 Check the coolant level after storage, and top off the level if necessary

you an indication of the coolants ability to resist freezing and boiling. If the level is OK and the coolant is still giving adequate protection, then you are free to leave it in the system.

Of course, if you don't know how long the coolant has been in the system, you should change it. Remember that the other job coolant performs is to prevent corrosion while lubricating the water pump seal(s). Coolant usually looses its ability to do these jobs properly LONG BEFORE a hydrometer will tell you that it is bad. If the coolant is more than a year old, then you probably want to save yourself the hassle down the road and replace it now.

Transmission or Gear Oil

Check the fluid level. If the level has gone down, look for a leak. If the level has gone up, then you have a significant amount of condensation (water) mixed in with the oil and it should be replaced to prevent damage to the ATV's components.

Fig. 31 Check the coolant hoses for soft spots or for brittleness by giving them a light squeeze—they should be springy, but not hard

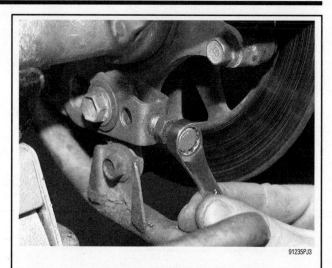

Fig. 32 If you haven't already adjusted the chain before you placed the ATV in storage, you'll have to do it now

→Keep in mind that although these fluids will not contain the corrosive byproducts of combustion, they are JUST as likely to contain condensation. If you want to be certain that your gears and shafts are protected from moisture, then you should replace the oil before running the ATV.

As usual, if you are resurrecting a beast which has been in storage for some years, then do yourself a favor, just drain and replace all gear oils now.

Brake/Hydraulic Clutch Fluid

Check the fluid level in the clutch and/or brake master cylinders, as applicable. If the ATV has mechanical brakes, double check that the linkage moves freely.

Recently, manufacturers have been recommending annual or bi-annual brake or clutch hydraulic fluid changing. Obviously this is an area that a lot of people ignore with seemingly little trouble (until their machines start to age and a caliper piston freezes or seals are torn by corrosion and begin to leak). If your fluid is due for a change, then well, there is really no better time than the present. But, even if it is not due for one, consider performing one now anyway. We aren't talking about a lot of fluid in most cases. The smartest course of action is to flush and refill these systems EVERY YEAR. It is the best way you can assure yourself that the system components will continue to operate properly and remain corrosion free for many years.

Of course, if you don't know when any of the hydraulic fluids were changed last, DO IT NOW!!!

CHECKING ADJUSTMENTS

Drive Chain

♦ See Figure 32

Refer to the drivetrain maintenance section of this manual and to your ATV owner's manual. Check the drive chain for proper adjustment and lubrication. . If the chain appears dry, it can be cleaned and pre-lubed; but since chains should usually be lubed when warm, you will have to redo this after your first ride.

Levers, Pedals or Linkage

♦ See Figures 33, 34 and 35

You should have checked the levers and pedals for freedom of movement while you were checking the chassis out, but now it is time to make sure they are all properly adjusted. Refer to the maintenance sections of this book and check your ATV owner's manual to make sure that all controls and linkage are properly adjusted within specification. Improperly adjusted controls can lead to VERY SHORT and VERY DANGEROUS rides.

Fig. 33 Before you even THINK about riding your ATV after you've taken it out of storage, make sure that the levers . . .

REMOVE & INSPECT THE SPARK PLUG

If you checked the spark plug (spark plugs, for those who own a Yamaha Banshee) and coated the cylinder with fresh oil before storing the ATV, then the plug will be in good shape, but you will still want to pull it out so you can recoat the cylinder wall with oil before attempting to start the engine.

But if you didn't properly prep the ATV or if you are resurrecting a beast after a lengthy storage, you are definitely going to want to check the plug and prime the cylinder with oil. This can be done easily enough:

1. Remove the spark plug and check the gap. Replace the plug and/or adjust the gap, as necessary.

→Remember that a sleeping ATV may be difficult enough to awaken without adding poor spark to the equation.

2. Pour 1–2 tablespoons of fresh, clean engine oil through the spark plug hole.

3. Rotate the engine to spread the oil around the cylinder. You have a few choices on how to rotate the engine. You can rotate it by hand, which is slower and more gentle (lowering the chance of gouging a cylinder wall if a ring is reluctant at first) or you can use the electric starter (if you are more sure that the

91235PQ6

Fig. 34 . . . throttle cables . . .

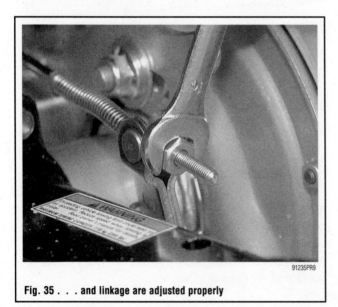

91235PR9

Fig. 35 . . . and linkage are adjusted properly

rings won't be reluctant) To rotate the engine by hand, keep the spark plug out to relieve engine compression.

➡**If, even after adding oil, the engine is difficult or impossible to turn, DO NOT FORCE IT. First, add a few tablespoons of kerosene to the cylinder through the spark plug threading and give it some time to work on the rust. Then after allowing it to sit (for as long as overnight if necessary) add some more oil to lubricate the surfaces (should be piston and rings break free). Just remember, that if rust has frozen the seized the motor, there is a good chance the rings are already ruined. But, if you force the motor and break the rings, chances are even better that the cylinder and piston could be further damaged by the pieces.**

4. Install the spark plug.

FILL THE FUEL TANK

If you drained the fuel system before storage then it is time to refill the gas tank and prime the system using fresh gasoline. As usual, be very careful when working around gasoline.

Gasoline is VERY DANGEROUS STUFF. It is HIGHLY flammable and it is very easy to get yourself killed. Don't work around open flames or things that might cause a spark.

If you used fuel stabilizer, than you've got another choice to make here. The longer the ATV has been in storage, the less volatile the fuel will be, even if you used stabilizer. If you just stored it for one winter, then you are likely to be in good shape.

If you didn't add stabilizer or if you are resurrecting a long forgotten beast, then chances are that your fuel system is clogged with varnish, and the carburetor bowl is corroded. Both of these potential nightmares must be remedied before the engine can come to life.

If your carburetor contains varnish, then it may require a rebuild before it will perform properly. To help determine if this is going to be a problem, remove the float bowl (assuming that you have drained any fuel that was left, or that it was in storage so long that no fuel is present). Once the float bowl has been removed from the carburetor, examine the float and chamber for varnish and corrosion. If either is evident, you are probably going to have to disassemble and clean or completely rebuild the carburetor.

Priming The System

Once you are ready to go you will want to prime the fuel system before attempting to start the engine (this helps to prevent unwanted excessive drain on your new or freshly charged battery). Usually, priming is as easy as turning on the petcock. BUT, you may have a vacuum actuated petcock which prevent fuel from flowing to the carburetor unless engine vacuum is applied to one side of a pressure valve. Most vacuum actuated petcocks have a prime setting which allows fuel to flow without vacuum, but if yours does not then you will either need a hand held vacuum pump, or you are simply going to have to crank for a little while.

Performing The Pre-Ride Check

Before attempting to start and ride the ATV, you should now take an opportunity to perform a COMPLETE pre-ride check as detailed in Section 6 of this manual. Obviously you have already addressed some of the items (like checking fluids and tires), but you don't want to leave anything out.

Starting And Riding The ATV

Once you are certain everything is working, hop on and give the starter a whirl. If the engine is tough to start, remember that a starter needs time to cool down between tries. DON'T hold the starter button for more than a few seconds, and try to wait a minute between tries. It can be frustrating, but there is no reason to burn out a perfectly good starter motor with excessive cranking, especially when your ATV is just waking up for the first time this season.

If the engine does not seem to catch after a few tries, double check the basics:

*   Is the FUEL on?
*   Is the IGNITION on?
*   Is the transmission in NEUTRAL?
*   Is the ENGINE kill switch in the ON position?
*   Is the CLUTCH lever pulled in?

If the engine will still not start, refer to the troubleshooting section to see what you've forgotten.

When the engine fires, give it a few seconds to warm up and for the oil to circulate before revving the motor. Follow your usual warm-up routine, which probably means riding slowly and moderately until the engine has fully warmed. During that first ride of the season, take special care to listen and feel for potential problems you may have missed.

Have fun !!!!

GLOSSARY

Understanding your mechanic (should you decide to use the services of one) is as important as understanding your ATV. Many riders have difficulty understanding mechanical terminology. Talking the language of ATVs and machines makes it easier to effectively communicate with professional technicians. It isn't necessary (or recommended) that you diagnose the problem for him/her, but it will save time, and you money, if you can accurately describe what is happening. It will also help you to know why your ATV does what it is doing, and what repairs were made.

ACCELERATOR PUMP: A small pump located in the carburetor that feeds fuel into the air/fuel mixture during acceleration.

ADVANCE: Setting the ignition timing so that spark occurs earlier before the piston reaches top dead center (TDC).

AFTER TOP DEAD CENTER (ATDC): Some point after the piston reaches the top of its travel on the compression stroke.

AIR CLEANER: An assembly consisting of a housing, filter and any connecting ductwork. The filter element is made up of a porous paper, foam, or cotton gauze, and is designed to prevent airborne particles from entering the engine through the carburetor or throttle body.

AIR/FUEL RATIO: The ratio of air-to-gasoline by weight in the fuel mixture drawn into the engine.

ALTERNATING CURRENT (AC): Electric current that flows first in one direction, then in the opposite direction, continually reversing flow.

ALTERNATOR: A device which produces AC (alternating current) which is converted to DC (direct current) to charge the ATV's battery and run the ATV's current consuming devices.

AMMETER: An instrument, calibrated in amperes, used to measure the flow of an electrical current in a circuit. Ammeters are always connected in series with the circuit being tested.

AMP/HR. RATING (BATTERY): Measurement of the ability of a battery to deliver a stated amount of current for a stated period of time. The higher the amp/hr. rating, the better the battery.

AMPERE: The rate of flow of electrical current present when one volt of electrical pressure is applied against one ohm of electrical resistance.

ANTIFREEZE: A substance (ethylene or propylene glycol) added to the coolant to prevent freezing in cold weather.

ARMATURE: A laminated, soft iron core wrapped by a wire that converts electrical energy to mechanical energy as in a motor or relay. When rotated in a magnetic field, it changes mechanical energy into electrical energy as in a generator.

ATDC: After Top Dead Center.

ATMOSPHERIC PRESSURE: The pressure on the Earth's surface caused by the weight of the air in the atmosphere. At sea level, this pressure is 14.7 psi at 32°F (101 kPa at 0°C).

ATOMIZATION: The breaking down of a liquid into a fine mist that can be suspended in air.

AXIAL PLAY: Movement parallel to a shaft or bearing bore.

AXLE: A shaft that is used to provide support across portions of the frame or swingarm.

AXLE CAPACITY: The maximum load-carrying capacity of the axle itself, as specified by the manufacturer. This is usually a higher number than the GAWR.

BACKFIRE: The sudden combustion of gases in the intake or exhaust system that results in a loud explosion.

BACKLASH: The clearance or play between two parts, such as meshed gears.

BACKPRESSURE: Restrictions in the exhaust system that slow the exit of exhaust gases from the combustion chamber.

BAKELITE®: A heat resistant, plastic insulator material commonly used in printed circuit boards and transistorized components.

BALL BEARING: A bearing made up of hardened inner and outer races between which hardened steel balls roll.

BALL JOINT: A ball and matching socket connecting suspension components. It permits rotating movement in any direction between the components that are joined.

BALLAST RESISTOR: A resistor in the primary ignition circuit that lowers voltage after the engine is started to reduce wear on ignition components.

BATTERY: A direct current electrical storage unit, consisting of the basic active materials of lead and sulfuric acid, which converts chemical energy into electrical energy. Used to provide current for the operation of the starter as well as other equipment, such as lighting, etc.

BEAD: The portion of a tire that holds it on the wheel.

BEARING: A friction reducing, supportive device usually located between a stationary part and a moving part.

BEFORE TOP DEAD CENTER (BTDC): The point just before the piston reaches the top of its travel on the compression stroke.

BEZEL: Piece of metal surrounding radio, headlights, gauges or similar fairing mounted components; sometimes used to hold the glass face of a gauge in the dash.

BI-METAL TEMPERATURE SENSOR: Any sensor or switch made of two dissimilar types of metal that bend when heated or cooled due to the different expansion rates of the alloys. These types of sensors usually function as an on/off switch.

BLOW-BY: Combustion gases, composed of water vapor and unburned fuel, that leak past the piston rings into the crankcase during normal engine operation. These gases are removed by the breather system to prevent the buildup of harmful acids in the crankcase.

BOOK VALUE: The average value of an ATV, widely used to determine trade-in and resale value.

BORE: Diameter of a cylinder.

BRAKE CALIPER: The housing that fits over the brake disc. The caliper holds the brake pads, which are pressed against the discs by the caliper pistons when the lever or brake pedal is depressed.

BRAKE FADE: Loss of braking power, usually caused by excessive heat after repeated brake applications.

BRAKE HORSEPOWER: Usable horsepower of an engine measured at the crankshaft.

BRAKE PAD: A brake backing plate and lining assembly used with disc brakes.

BRAKE SHOE: The backing for the brake lining. The term is, however, usually applied to the assembly of the brake backing and lining.

BREAKER POINTS: A set of points inside the distributor, operated by a cam, which make and break the ignition circuit.

BTDC: Before Top Dead Center.

BUSHING: A liner, usually removable, for a bearing; an anti-friction liner used in place of a bearing.

CALIFORNIA ENGINE: An engine certified by the EPA for use in California only; conforms to more stringent emission regulations than Federal engine.

CALIPER: A hydraulically activated device in a disc brake system, which is mounted straddling the brake rotor (disc). The caliper contains at least one piston and two brake pads. Hydraulic pressure on the piston(s) forces the pads against the rotor.

CAMSHAFT: A shaft in the engine on which are the lobes (cams) which operate the valves. The camshaft is driven by the crankshaft, via a belt, chain or gears, at one half the crankshaft speed.

CAPACITOR: A device which stores an electrical charge.

CARBON MONOXIDE (CO): A colorless, odorless gas given off as a normal byproduct of combustion. It is poisonous and extremely dangerous in confined areas, building up slowly to toxic levels without warning if adequate ventilation is not available.

CARBURETOR: A device, usually mounted to the intake manifold of an engine, which mixes the air and fuel in the proper proportion to allow even combustion.

CENTRIFUGAL ADVANCE: A mechanical method of advancing the spark timing by using flyweights in the distributor that react to centrifugal force generated by the distributor shaft rotation.

CHECK VALVE: Any one-way valve installed to permit the flow of air, fuel or vacuum in one direction only.

CHOKE: The valve/plate that restricts the amount of air entering an engine on the induction stroke, thereby enriching the air to fuel ratio.

CIRCLIP: A split steel snapring that fits into a groove to hold various parts in place.

CIRCUIT BREAKER: A switch which protects an electrical circuit from overload by opening the circuit when the current flow exceeds a predetermined level. Some circuit breakers must be reset manually, while most reset automatically.

CIRCUIT: Any unbroken path through which an electrical current can flow. Also used to describe fuel flow in some instances.

CLEARCOAT: A transparent layer which, when sprayed over a vehicle's paint job, adds gloss and depth as well as an additional protective coating to the finish.

CLUTCH: Part of the power train used to connect/disconnect power from the engine to the drive wheels.

COIL: Part of the ignition system that boosts the relatively low voltage supplied by the electrical system to the high voltage required to fire the spark plugs.

COMBUSTION CHAMBER: The part of the engine in the cylinder head where combustion takes place.

COMPRESSION CHECK: A test involving removing each spark plug and inserting a gauge. When the engine is cranked, the gauge will record a pressure reading in the individual cylinder. General operating condition can be determined from a compression check.

COMPRESSION RATIO: The ratio of the volume between the piston and cylinder head when the piston is at the bottom of its stroke (bottom dead center) and when the piston is at the top of its stroke (top dead center).

CONDENSER: An electrical device which acts to store an electrical charge, preventing voltage surges..

CONDUCTOR: Any material through which an electrical current can be transmitted easily.

CONNECTING ROD: The connecting link between the crankshaft and piston.

CONTINUITY: Continuous or complete circuit. Can be checked with an ohmmeter.

CONTROL ARM: A suspension component which is mounted on the frame and supports the ball joint.

CONVENTIONAL IGNITION: Ignition system which uses breaker points.

COOLANT: Mixture of water and anti-freeze circulated through the engine to carry off heat produced by the engine.

COUNTERSHAFT: An intermediate shaft which is rotated by a mainshaft and transmits, in turn, that rotation to a working part.

CRANKCASE: The lower part of an engine in which the crankshaft and related parts operate.

CRANKSHAFT: Engine component (connected to pistons by connecting rods) which converts the reciprocating (up and down) motion of pistons to rotary motion used to turn the driveshaft.

CURB WEIGHT: The weight of a vehicle without passengers or payload, but including all fluids (oil, gas, coolant, etc.) and other equipment specified as standard.

CYLINDER HEAD: The detachable portion of the engine, usually fastened to the top of the cylinder block and containing all or most of the combustion chambers. On overhead valve engines, it contains the valves and their operating parts. On overhead cam engines, it contains the camshaft as well.

CYLINDER: The bore in which a piston reciprocates; also known as a combustion chamber.

DEAD CENTER: The extreme top or bottom of the piston stroke.

DETERGENT: An additive in engine oil to improve its operating characteristics.

DETONATION: An unwanted explosion of the air/fuel mixture in the combustion chamber caused by excess heat and compression, advanced timing, or an overly lean mixture. Also referred to as "pinging" or "knocking."

DIAPHRAGM: A thin, flexible wall separating two cavities, such as in a CV carburetor.

DIESELING: The engine continues to run after the key is shut off; caused by fuel continuing to be burned in the combustion chamber.

DIGITAL VOLT OHMMETER: An electronic diagnostic tool used to measure voltage, ohms and amps as well as several other functions, with the readings displayed on a digital screen in tenths, hundredths and thousandths.

DIODE: An electrical device that will allow current to flow in one direction only.

DIRECT CURRENT (DC): Electrical current that flows in one direction only.

DISC BRAKE: A hydraulic braking assembly consisting of a brake disc, or rotor, usually mounted on a wheel, and a caliper assembly usually containing two brake pads which are activated by hydraulic pressure. The pads are forced against the sides of the disc, creating friction which slows the ATV.

DISPLACEMENT: The total volume of air that is displaced by all pistons as the engine turns through one complete revolution.

DOHC: Double overhead camshaft.

DOUBLE OVERHEAD CAMSHAFT: An engine type that utilizes two camshafts mounted in one cylinder head. One camshaft normally operates the exhaust valves, while the other operates the intake valves.

DOWEL PIN: A pin, inserted in mating holes in two different parts allowing those parts to maintain a fixed relationship.

DRIVE TRAIN: The components that transmit the flow of power from the engine to the rear wheel. The components can include the primary drive, clutch, transmission, driveshaft, chain or belt

DRUM BRAKE: A braking system which consists of two brake shoes mounted on a fixed backing plate, and a brake drum, mounted on an axle or wheel, which revolves around the assembly.

DRY CHARGED BATTERY: Battery to which electrolyte is added when the battery is placed in service.

DVOM: Digital volt ohmmeter.

DWELL: The rate, measured in degrees of shaft rotation, at which an electrical circuit cycles on and off.

ECU: Electronic control unit.

ELECTRODE: Conductor (positive or negative) of electric current.

ELECTROLYTE: A solution of water and sulfuric acid used to activate the battery. Electrolyte is extremely corrosive.

ELECTRONIC CONTROL UNIT: A digital computer that controls engine (and sometimes the Anti-Lock Brake system) functions based on data received from various sensors.

ELECTRONIC IGNITION: A system in which the timing and firing of the spark plugs is controlled by an electronic control unit, usually called a module. These systems have no points or condenser.

ENAMEL: Type of paint that dries to a smooth, glossy finish.

END-PLAY: The measured amount of axial movement in a shaft.

ENGINE: The primary motor or power apparatus of a vehicle, which converts liquid or gas fuel into mechanical energy.

ENGINE CASE: The basic engine casting containing the crankshaft main bearings, as well as machined surfaces for the mounting of other components such as the cylinder head. On many ATVs it may also hose the transmission shafts and gears.

EP LUBRICANT: EP (extreme pressure) lubricants are specially formulated for use with gears involving heavy loads (transmissions, rears, etc.).

ETHYL: A substance added to gasoline to improve its resistance to knock, by slowing down the rate of combustion.

ETHYLENE GLYCOL: The primary substance found in most most antifreeze/coolant.

EXHAUST MANIFOLD: A set of pipes which conduct exhaust gases from the engine.

FAST IDLE: The speed of the engine when the choke is on. Fast idle speeds engine warm-up.

FEDERAL ENGINE: An engine certified by the EPA for use in states other than those which adopt California standards.

FEELER GAUGE: A blade, usually metal, of precisely predetermined thickness, used to measure the clearance between two parts.

FILAMENT: The part of a bulb that glows; the filament creates high resistance to current flow and actually glows from the resulting heat.

FINAL DRIVE: Term used to describe the system used to transmit power from the engine to the transmission. Usually a chain or gear, but can be a belt or driveshaft as well.

FIRING ORDER: The order in which combustion occurs in the cylinders of an engine.

FLAME FRONT: The term used to describe certain aspects of the fuel explosion in the cylinders. The flame front should move in a controlled pattern across the cylinder, rather than simply exploding immediately.

FLAT RATE: A shop term referring to the amount of money paid to a technician for a repair or diagnostic service based on that particular service versus dealership's labor time (NOT based on the actual time the technician spent on the job).

FLAT SPOT: A point during acceleration when the engine seems to lose power for an instant.

FLOODING: The presence of too much fuel in the intake manifold and combustion chamber which prevents the air/fuel mixture from firing, thereby causing a no-start situation.

FLYWHEEL: A heavy disc of metal attached to the rear of the crankshaft. It smoothes the firing impulses of the engine and keeps the crankshaft turning during periods when no firing takes place. The starter also engages the flywheel to start the engine.

FOOT POUND (ft. lbs. or sometimes, ft. lb.): The amount of energy or work needed to raise an item weighing one pound, a distance of one foot.

FUEL FILTER: A component of the fuel system containing a porous paper element used to prevent any impurities from entering the engine through the fuel system.

FUEL INJECTION: A system replacing the carburetor that sprays fuel into the cylinder or intake through nozzles. The amount of fuel can be more precisely controlled with fuel injection.

FUSE: A protective device in a circuit which prevents circuit overload by breaking the circuit when a specific amperage is present. The device is constructed around a strip or wire of a lower amperage rating than the circuit it is designed to protect. When an amperage higher than that stamped on the fuse is present in the circuit, the strip or wire melts, opening the circuit.

FUSIBLE LINK: A piece of wire in a wiring harness that performs the same job as a fuse. If overloaded, the fusible link will melt and interrupt the circuit.

GAWR: (Gross axle weight rating) the total maximum weight an axle is designed to carry.

GCW: (Gross combined weight) total combined weight of a tow vehicle and trailer.

GEAR RATIO: A ratio expressing the number of turns a smaller gear will make to turn a larger gear through one revolution. The ratio is found by dividing the number of teeth on the smaller gear into the number of teeth on the larger gear.

GEARBOX: Transmission.

GEL COAT: A thin coat of plastic resin covering fiberglass body panels.

GENERATOR: A device which produces Direct Current (DC) necessary to charge the battery.

GVWR: (Gross vehicle weight rating) total maximum weight a vehicle is designed to carry including the weight of the ATV, passenger, equipment, gas, oil, etc.

HALOGEN: A special type of lamp known for its quality of brilliant white light. Originally used for fog lights and driving lights.

HEAT RANGE: A term used to describe the ability of a spark plug to carry away heat. Plugs with longer nosed insulators take longer to carry heat off effectively.

HEMI: A name given an engine using hemispherical combustion chambers.

HORSEPOWER: A measurement of the amount of work; one horsepower is the amount of work necessary to lift 33,000 lbs. one foot in one minute. Brake horsepower (bhp) is the horsepower delivered by an engine on a dynamometer. Net horsepower is the power remaining (measured at the flywheel of the engine) that can be used to turn the wheels after power is consumed through friction and running the engine accessories (water pump, alternator, etc.)

HUB: The center part of a wheel or gear.

HYDROCARBON (HC): Any chemical compound made up of hydrogen and carbon. A major pollutant formed by the engine as a by-product of combustion.

HYDROMETER: An instrument used to measure the specific gravity of a solution.

HYDROPLANING: A phenomenon of driving when water builds up under the tire tread, causing it to lose contact with the road. Slowing down will usually restore normal tire contact with the road.

IDLE MIXTURE: The mixture of air and fuel being fed to the cylinders when the engine is running at base speed (no throttle applied). The idle mixture screw(s) are sometimes adjusted as part of a tune-up.

INCH POUND (inch lbs.; sometimes in. lb. or in. lbs.): One twelfth of a foot pound.

INDUCTION: A means of transferring electrical energy in the form of a magnetic field. Principle used in the ignition coil to increase voltage.

INJECTOR: A device which receives metered fuel under pressure and is activated to inject the fuel into the engine at a predetermined time.

INPUT SHAFT: The shaft in a transmission to which torque is applied, usually carrying the driving gear or gears.

INTAKE MANIFOLD: A casting or passage used to conduct air or a fuel/air mixture to the cylinders.

JOURNAL: The bearing surface within which a shaft operates.

JUMPER CABLES: Two heavy duty wires with large clamps used to provide power from a charged battery to a discharged battery mounted in a vehicle.

JUMPSTART: Utilizing the sufficiently charged battery of one ATV to start the engine of another ATV with a discharged battery by the use of jumper cables.

KEY: A small block, usually fitted in a notch between a shaft and a hub to prevent slippage of the two parts.

KNOCK: Noise which results from the spontaneous ignition of a portion of the air-fuel mixture in the engine cylinder caused by overly advanced ignition timing or use of incorrectly low octane fuel for that engine.

LABOR TIME: A specific amount of time required to perform a certain repair or diagnostic service as defined by a vehicle or after-market manufacturer.

LITHIUM-BASE GREASE: Chassis and wheel bearing grease using lithium as a base. Not compatible with sodium-base grease.

LOCK RING: See Circlip or Snapring.

MANIFOLD VACUUM: Low pressure in an engine intake manifold formed just below the throttle plate. Manifold vacuum is highest at idle and drops under acceleration.

MANIFOLD: A casting of passages or set of pipes which connect the cylinders to an inlet or outlet source.

MASTER CYLINDER: The primary fluid pressurizing device in a hydraulic system. On ATVs, it is found in brake and hydraulic clutch systems and is lever or pedal activated.

MISFIRE: Condition occurring when the fuel mixture in a cylinder fails to ignite, causing the engine to run roughly.

MODULE: Electronic control unit, amplifier or igniter of solid state or integrated design which controls the current flow in the ignition primary circuit based on input from the pick-up coil. When the module opens the primary circuit, high secondary voltage is induced in the coil.

MULTI-WEIGHT: Type of oil that provides adequate lubrication at both high and low temperatures.

NEEDLE BEARING: A bearing which consists of a number (usually a large number) of long, thin rollers.

NITROGEN OXIDE (NOx): One of the three basic pollutants found in the exhaust emission of an internal combustion engine. The amount of NOx usually varies in an inverse proportion to the amount of HC and CO.

OCTANE RATING: A number, indicating the quality of gasoline based on its ability to resist knock. The higher the number, the better the quality. Higher compression engines require higher octane gas.

OEM: Original Equipment Manufactured. OEM equipment is that furnished standard by the manufacturer.

OHM: The unit used to measure the resistance of conductor-to-electrical flow. One ohm is the amount of resistance that limits current flow to one ampere in a circuit with one volt of pressure.

OHMMETER: An instrument used for measuring the resistance, in ohms, in an electrical circuit.

OSCILLOSCOPE: A piece of test equipment that shows electric impulses as a pattern on a screen. Engine performance can be analyzed by interpreting these patterns.

O2 SENSOR: See oxygen sensor.

OUTPUT SHAFT: The shaft which transmits torque from a device, such as a transmission.

OVERHEAD CAMSHAFT (OHC): An engine configuration in which the camshaft is mounted on top of the cylinder head and operates the valve either directly or by means of rocker arms.

OVERHEAD VALVE (OHV): An engine configuration in which all of the valves are located in the cylinder head and the camshaft is located in the engine case. The camshaft operates the valves via lifters and pushrods.

OXIDES OF NITROGEN: See nitrogen oxide (NOx).

OXYGEN SENSOR: Used with a feedback system to sense the presence of oxygen in the exhaust gas and signal the computer which can use the voltage signal to determine engine operating efficiency and adjust the air/fuel ratio.

PARTS WASHER: A basin or tub, usually with a built-in pump mechanism and hose used for circulating chemical solvent for the purpose of cleaning greasy, oily and dirty components.

PAYLOAD: The weight the vehicle is capable of carrying in addition to its own weight. Payload includes weight of the rider, passenger and cargo.

PERCOLATION: A condition in which the fuel actually "boils," due to excessive heat. Percolation prevents proper atomization of the fuel causing rough running.

PICK-UP COIL: The coil in which voltage is induced in an electronic ignition.

PING: A metallic rattling sound produced by the engine during acceleration. It is usually due to incorrect ignition timing or a poor grade of gasoline.

PINION: The smaller of two gears in a ring and pinion set. The pinion drives the ring gear which transmits motion to the axle shaft at a 90 degree angle.

PISTON RING: An open-ended ring which fits into a groove on the outer diameter of the piston. Its chief function is to form a seal between the piston and cylinder wall. Most four-stroke ATV pistons have three rings: two for compression sealing; one for oil sealing.

POLARITY: Indication (positive or negative, DC current) of the two poles of a battery.

POWER-TO-WEIGHT RATIO: Ratio of horsepower to weight of an ATV.

POWERTRAIN: See Drive train.

PCM: See Electronic Control Unit (ECU).

Ppm: Parts per million; unit used to measure exhaust emissions.

PREIGNITION: Early ignition of fuel in the cylinder, sometimes due to glowing carbon deposits in the combustion chamber. Preignition can be damaging since combustion takes place prematurely.

PRELOAD: A predetermined load placed on a bearing during assembly or by adjustment. Also used to describe the amount of weight a shock is adjusted for by pre-compressing the spring.

PRESS FIT: The mating of two parts under pressure, due to the inner diameter of one being smaller than the outer diameter of the other, or vice versa; an interference fit.

PRIMARY CIRCUIT: The low voltage side of the ignition system which consists of the ignition switch, ballast resistor or resistance wire, bypass, coil, electronic control unit and pick-up coil as well as the connecting wires and harnesses.

PROFILE: Term used for tire measurement (tire series), which is the ratio of tire height to tread width.

Psi: Pounds per square inch; a measurement of pressure.

PUSHROD: A steel rod between the valve lifter and the valve rocker arm in OverHead Valve (OHV) engines.

RACE: The surface on the inner or outer ring of a bearing on which the balls, needles or rollers move.

RADIATOR: Part of the cooling system for a water-cooled engine, usually mounted in the front of the vehicle and connected to the engine with rubber hoses. Through the radiator, excess combustion heat is dissipated into the atmosphere through forced convection using a water and glycol based mixture that circulates through, and cools, the engine.

RECTIFIER: A device (used primarily in alternators) that permits electrical current to flow in one direction only.

REGULATOR: A device which maintains the amperage and/or voltage levels of a circuit at predetermined values.

RELAY: A switch which automatically opens and/or closes a circuit.

RELUCTOR: A wheel that rotates inside a housing and triggers the release of voltage in an electronic ignition.

RESIN: A liquid plastic used in body work.

RESISTANCE: The opposition to the flow of current through a circuit or electrical device, and is measured in ohms. Resistance is equal to the voltage divided by the amperage.

RESISTOR SPARK PLUG: A spark plug using a resistor to shorten the spark duration. This suppresses radio interference and lengthens plug life.

RESISTOR: A device, sometimes made of wire, which offers a preset amount of resistance in an electrical circuit.

RETARD: Set the ignition timing so that spark occurs later (fewer degrees before TDC).

ROCKER ARM: A lever which rotates around a shaft pushing down (opening) the valve when the other end is pushed up by the pushrod. Spring pressure will later close the valve.

ROLLER BEARING: A bearing made up of hardened inner and outer races between which hardened steel rollers move.

ROTOR: The disc-shaped part of a disc brake assembly, upon which the brake pads bear; also called a brake disc.

RPM: Revolutions per minute (usually indicates engine speed).

RUN-ON: Condition when the engine continues to run, even when the key is turned off. See dieseling.

SEALED BEAM: A headlight or running light in which the lens, reflector and filament form a single unit.

SECONDARY CIRCUIT: The high voltage side of the ignition system, usually above 20,000 volts. The secondary includes the ignition coil, coil wire, distributor cap and rotor, spark plug wires and spark plugs.

SENDING UNIT: A mechanical, electrical, hydraulic or electromagnetic device which transmits information to a gauge.

SENSOR: Any device designed to measure engine operating conditions or ambient pressures and temperatures. Usually electronic in nature and designed to send a voltage signal to an on-board computer, some sensors may operate as a simple on/off switch or they may provide a variable voltage signal (like a potentiometer) as conditions or measured parameters change.

SHIM: Spacers of precise, predetermined thickness used between parts to establish a proper working relationship.

SHIMMY: Vibration (sometimes violent) in the steering, sometimes caused by misaligned components, out of balance tires or worn suspension components.

SHORT CIRCUIT: An electrical malfunction where current takes the path of least resistance to ground (usually through damaged insulation). Current flow is excessive from low resistance resulting in a blown fuse.

SINGLE OVERHEAD CAMSHAFT: See overhead camshaft.

SKIDPLATE: A metal plate attached to the underside of the body to protect the fuel tank, transfer case or other vulnerable parts from damage.

SLAVE CYLINDER: A device in the hydraulic clutch system which is activated by hydraulic force, disengaging the clutch.

SLUDGE: Thick, black deposits in engine formed from dirt, oil, water, etc. It is usually formed in engines when oil changes are neglected.

SNAPRING: A circular retaining clip used inside or outside a shaft or part to secure a shaft, such as a floating wrist pin.

SOHC: Single overhead camshaft.

SOLENOID: An electrically operated, magnetic switching device.

SPARK PLUG: A device screwed into the combustion chamber of a spark ignition engine. The basic construction is a conductive core inside of a ceramic insulator, mounted in an outer conductive base. An electrical charge from the spark plug wire travels along the conductive core and jumps a preset air gap to a grounding point or points at the end of the conductive base. The resultant spark ignites the fuel/air mixture in the combustion chamber.

SPECIFIC GRAVITY (BATTERY): The relative weight of liquid (battery electrolyte) as compared to the weight of an equal volume of water.

SPLINES: Ridges machined or cast onto the outer diameter of a shaft or inner diameter of a bore to enable parts to mate without rotation.

SPONGY LEVER (OR PEDAL): A soft or spongy feeling when the brake is applied. It is usually due to air in the brake lines.

SPRUNG WEIGHT: The weight of an ATV supported by the shock absorbers.

STARTER: A high-torque electric motor used for the purpose of starting the engine, typically through a high ratio geared drive connected to the flywheel ring gear.

STRAIGHT WEIGHT: Term designating motor oil as suitable for use within a narrow range of temperatures. Outside the narrow temperature range its flow characteristics will not adequately lubricate.

STROKE: The distance the piston travels from bottom dead center to top dead center.

SWING ARM: An assembly that attaches the axle to the frame, while allowing the wheel(s) to move up and down (suspension travel).

SYNTHETIC OIL: Non-petroleum based oil.

TACHOMETER: A device used to measure the rotary speed of an engine, shaft, gear, etc., usually in rotations per minute.

TDC: Top dead center. The exact top of the piston's stroke.

THERMOSTAT: A valve, located in the cooling system of an engine, which is closed when cold and opens gradually in response to engine heating, controlling the temperature of the coolant and rate of coolant flow.

TIMING BELT: A square-toothed, reinforced rubber belt that is driven by the crankshaft and operates the camshaft.

TIMING CHAIN: A roller chain that is driven by the crankshaft and operates the camshaft.

TOP DEAD CENTER (TDC): The point at which the piston reaches the top of it's travel on the compression stroke.

TORQUE: Measurement of turning or twisting force, expressed as foot-pounds or inch-pounds.

TRAIL: The distance between the imaginary point where the steering head axis strikes the ground and the center of the tire contact patch.

TRANSDUCER: A device used to change a force into an electrical signal.

TRANSISTOR: A semi-conductor component which can be actuated by a small voltage to perform an electrical switching function.

TREAD WEAR INDICATOR: Bars molded into the tire at right angles to the tread that appear as horizontal bars when only a small amount of tread remains.

TUNE-UP: A regular maintenance function, usually associated with the replacement and adjustment of parts and components in the electrical and fuel systems of a vehicle for the purpose of attaining optimum performance.

UNLEADED FUEL: Fuel which contains no lead (a once common gasoline additive). The presence of lead in fuel will destroy the functioning elements of a catalytic converter, making it useless.

UNSPRUNG WEIGHT: The weight of components not supported by the shock absorbers (wheels, tires, brakes, control arms, etc.).

VACUUM GAUGE: An instrument used to measure the presence of vacuum in a chamber.

VALVE CLEARANCE: The measured gap between the end of the valve stem and the rocker arm, cam lobe or follower that activates the valve.

VALVE GUIDES: The guide through which the stem of the valve passes. The guide is designed to keep the valve in proper alignment.

VALVE LASH (clearance): The operating clearance in the valve train.

VALVE TRAIN: The system that operates intake and exhaust valves, consisting of components like camshaft(s), valves, springs, lifters or shims, pushrods (sometimes) and rocker arms.

VALVE: A device which control the pressure, direction of flow or rate of flow of a liquid or gas.

VAPOR LOCK: Boiling of the fuel in the fuel lines due to excess heat. This will interfere with the flow of fuel in the lines and can completely stop the flow. Vapor lock normally only occurs in hot weather.

VARNISH: Term applied to the residue formed when gasoline when it becomes stale.

VISCOSITY: The ability of a fluid to flow. The lower the viscosity rating, the easier the fluid will flow. For example, a 10 weight motor oil will flow much easier than 40 weight motor oil.

VOLT: Unit used to measure the force or pressure of electricity. It is defined as the pressure

VOLTAGE REGULATOR: A device that controls the current output of the alternator or generator.

VOLTMETER: An instrument used for measuring electrical force in units called volts. Voltmeters are always connected parallel with the circuit being tested.

WATER PUMP: A belt, chain or gear driven component of the cooling system that mounts on the engine, circulating the coolant under pressure.

WHEEL WEIGHT: Small weights attached to the wheel to balance the wheel and tire assembly. Out-of-balance tires quickly wear out and also give erratic handling when installed on the front.

WHEELBASE: Distance between the center of front the wheels and the center of the rear wheels.

MASTER
INDEX